Advance Praise

"This intimate epic surveys, with novelistic flair, the lives of men and women, free and enslaved, famous and forgotten, who dared to stand up against slavery in the United States in the years leading up to the Civil War, often at the risk of their own lives.....The story-telling is inviting and detailed, brought to life with judicious quotes and an eye toward still-pressing themes: mob violence...the "revolutionary concept" that women "could change society"; the courage of abolitionist truth-tellers; the "monstrous moral wrong" of slavery; and a Southern-controlled Congress's anti-democratic efforts to silence abolitionists...."
—*Publishers Weekly BookLife Reviews*

"Rogers offers a scenic walk through a vivid, harrowing, and heartbreaking history of the abolitionist movement...exceptional research and fresh perspectives...A raw and emotional look at the sacrifices made by those who gave all to end slavery. Our verdict: √ GET IT"
— Kirkus Reviews

"...a wide-ranging, sophisticated, and detailed account."
—Stanley Harrold, author of *Lincoln and the Abolitionists*

"...a magisterial treatment of the anti-slavery movement in America....Highly-recommended."
—John Oller, author of *American Queen, The Rise and Fall of Kate Chase Sprague*

"Rogers' vivid writing features real people who, whatever their failings and foibles, had moral courage and used it."
—Nancy Koester, author of *Harriet Beecher Stowe: A Spiritual Life*

"Rogers shows how slavery and the debate over slavery functioned at the everyday, ground level in multiple locations across the country, North and South....Yet, she never loses sight of the dramatic big picture...."
—Tom Peebles, former U.S. Department of Justice attorney presently living in Paris.

"Revelatory, filled with inhumanity and humanity, this epic history reveals how precious and precarious freedom and democracy can be."
—Johnny D. Boggs, editor, Western Writers of America's *Roundup Magazine*

"…an engaging and highly informative account of a pivotal era in U.S. history."
—Dr. Brittany Jones, assistant professor of Social Studies at the University of Buffalo and 2024 National Council for the Social Studies FASSE Research Award Winner

"Whether you are a history buff or casual historian, there is something new for all in this book."
—Anthony Swierzbinski, 2024 Gilder-Lehrman Delaware State American History Teacher of the Year

"Rogers' storytelling brilliance lies in her ability to humanize historical figures as multi-dimensional individuals grappling with moral complexities, personal struggles, and the weight of their times….historical writing at its finest…"
—Emma Harris, 2024 Gilder Lehrman Maryland State American History Teacher of the Year

"As it has become increasingly difficult to engage young people with historical reading materials, this book's story-telling style, pictures, and quoted primary sources presents itself as a possible solution. The abolitionist movement is brought to life by Ms. Rogers in a way that both moves and inspires. Students of American history would benefit from more of these in-depth examinations."
—Stephanie Meek, 2024 Gilder Lehrman Alaska State American History Teacher of the Year

"Rogers does an outstanding job of providing insight into the complexities of the slavery issue as it existed nationally and regionally…."
—Michelle Nystel, Founding Forward Teacher Ambassador of Freedom, Iowa

"compelling…Rogers is a masterful storyteller, bringing these courageous activists to life with nuance and humanity….powerful read."
—Lexy Faist Largent, Book Reviewer

"…I was enraptured from the first chapter and could barely put it down….Highly recommended."
—Bruce Raterink, Book Reviewer and former Barnes & Noble Bookseller

"The disparate stories helped set the stage for the Civil War so well—placing you into the local mindsets and against the various forces on all sides, with particular attention paid to the female voices and their place….Highly recommended."
—William Largent, Book Reviewer

Harriet Beecher Stowe (1854-1860)

Abraham Lincoln (1809-1865)

WHEN PEOPLE WERE THINGS

Harriet Beecher Stowe, Abraham Lincoln, and The Emancipation Proclamation

Lisa Waller Rogers

BARREL
CACTUS
PRESS

3904 Berryhill Way
Austin, TX 78731
lisawallerrogers.com

PRINTED IN THE UNITED STATES OF AMERICA
Publisher's Cataloging-in-Publication Data

Names: Rogers, Lisa Waller, 1955-, author.
Title: *When People Were Things: Harriet Beecher Stowe, Abraham Lincoln, and the Emancipation Proclamation* / Lisa Waller Rogers.
Description: Austin, TX: Barrel Cactus Press, 2025.

Identifiers: LCCN: 2025930310
ISBN: 979-8-9994096-2-1 (hardcover) | 979-8-9994096-1-4 (paperback)
979-8-9994096-0-7 (ebook)

Subjects: LCSH Antislavery movements--United States--History--19th century. | Slavery--United States—History. | Abolitionists--History. | Stowe, Harriet Beecher, 1811-1896. | Lincoln, Abraham, 1809-1865. | United States. President (1861-1865: Lincoln). Emancipation Proclamation. | Enslaved persons--Emancipation--United States. | United States--Politics and government--1861-1865. | BISAC HISTORY / United States / Civil War Period (1850-1877) | HISTORY / United States / 19th Century

Classification: LCC E453.R64 2025 | DDC 973.7--dc23

Cover design by David Provolo
Cover photography ©North Wind Pictures Archives/Alamy Stock Photo

For Tom

A Note to Readers

In the course of writing this book, current events continually reminded me of the need to keep writing it. Writing about slavery and the abolition movement is a painful endeavor. American slavery is our collective stain, a brutal injustice. Many people are trying with all their might to deny slavery's horrible truths. The Florida Board of Education is doing its part in rewriting history. They want their students to believe that slavery was a work training program. Its social studies standards include this clarification:

"Instruction includes how slaves developed skills which, in some instances, could be applied for their personal benefit."

Asked to name the cause of the Civil War, a former South Carolina governor joked that it was not an easy question. She then offered up "how government was going to run," the need for "capitalism," and so forth. The next morning, when asked why she did not mention slavery, she said that "of course" the war was about slavery. She said she was trying to reframe it in modern terms.

The Civil War was about slavery, yet many Americans do not believe this. When people offer doubtful claims—"it was about states fighting with one another about money"—we can respond with facts. Chiefly, after the Republican Party candidate Abraham Lincoln won the 1860 Presidential election, eleven Southern states left the Union, so certain were they that Lincoln would interfere with slavery in their borders. These breakaway states formed the Confederacy, its vice president, Alexander H. Stephens, making it crystal clear what the cornerstone of that new nation stood for:

"[I]ts foundations are laid, its cornerstone rests, upon the great truth that the negro is not equal to the white man; that slavery—subordination to the superior race—is his natural and normal condition. This, our new government, is the first, in the history of the world, based upon this great physical, philosophical, and moral truth."

—Lisa Waller Rogers
Austin

Contents

Part I

WORDS

(1775-1831)

But words are things, and a small drop of ink,
Falling like dew, upon a thought, produces
That which makes thousands, perhaps millions, think....
—*Lord Byron*

CHAPTER 1

Lyman Finds His Family

Lyman Beecher wrote about the day in 1775 on which he was born:

> I am the son of father's third and best-loved wife, Esther Lyman...My mother was tall, well-proportioned, dignified in her movements, fair to look upon, intelligent in conversation, and in character lovely. I was her only child. She died of consumption two days after I was born. I was a seven months' child; and when the woman that attended to her saw what a puny thing I was, and that the mother could not live, she thought it useless to attempt to keep me alive. I was actually wrapped up and laid aside.
>
> But, after a while, one of the women thought she would look and see if I was living, and finding I was, concluded to dress me, saying, 'It's a pity he hadn't died with his mother.' So you see it was but by a hair's breadth I got a foothold in this world.

Lyman weighed three-and-a-half pounds. One of his mother's sisters found him a nurse and another, Aunt Catherine Benton, took him home to live with her and grow up on the farm she shared with her husband, Lot, in Guilford, Connecticut. In the fall and winter, there was wood to be cut. Crops had to be rotated, corn following grass, oats following corn, and then grass again. In the spring, the maple trees were tapped to make sugar. Uncle Lot kept cattle, two horses, and sheep, which had to be sheared in June. In this way,

Lyman grew strong on farmer's work and farmer's food. Having taken care of the physical, he went off to Yale College and then on to Yale Divinity School to build up the intellectual, where he would study to become a Presbyterian preacher.

In 1799, Lyman Beecher, 23, was ordained to the priesthood. Two weeks later, he married Roxana Foote, 24, and moved to a dilapidated parsonage in East Hampton, New York, where Lyman began his ministry. Rev. Beecher believed the Bible to be the exact Word of God. He implored his parishioners to come forward, confess their sins, and give their souls to God for salvation. Otherwise, he thundered, when you die, you will be cast into an eternal Hell of fire and brimstone. Brimstone is sulfur, which smells of rotten eggs. Lyman became known as "Brimstone Beecher."

Lyman's proselytizing extended into his marriage as well. Roxana, baptized and raised in the Episcopal Church, was a devout Christian, but Lyman did not consider her to be one. He insisted that a Christian must have a conversion experience. He tried to convince her of her sinful nature. But Roxana, of a gentle and balanced temperament, shrugged off this nonsense. But Lyman's persistent badgering caused Roxana to grow quiet and turn inward. Her family feared Lyman was crushing her spirit.

Lyman's whirlwind of activity brought a lot of company to their house. These public duties as a minister's wife bore down on Roxana. In the space of ten years, she ran the household, bore six children, ran a private school and, to make ends meet, took in student boarders. Lyman was paid only $300 a year for the first five years. Afterward, it was raised to $400.

As a girl, Roxana spent hours reading and spinning flax into cloth. She loved both activities so much that she rigged up a bookstand to her spindle so she could read as she spun. But with all her chores, babies, and houseguests now, and Lyman's pastoral calls keeping him away so much of the time, there was little time for reading or spinning.

In 1808, Roxana and Lyman's month-old baby, their sixth child, Harriet, came down with whooping cough. The baby coughed and gasped for breath. Night after night, Roxana stayed up with her. One night, Lyman told his wife to leave her vigil and get some sleep. When Roxana awoke, she found that little Harriet was dead. Lyman wrote that Roxana was so resigned that she seemed almost happy. I never saw such resignation to God." But Roxana was not happy.

After the baby was laid out, she looked so very beautiful that Roxana sketched her likeness on ivory, an item preserved as a precious relic.

In need of more income, in 1810, Rev. Beecher moved the family to the village of Litchfield, Connecticut, where he accepted a position at the First Congregational Church. His new annual pay was better—$800 supplemented by a load of wood donated by every local family. To make ends meet, the family planted the yard with fruit trees and vegetable gardens. They enlarged the parsonage to take in paying boarders. The household included indentured servants Rachel and Zillah Crooke, students and teachers from the law school and Female Academy, and relatives. Visiting ministers gathered in the front parlor, debating theology amid clouds of tobacco smoke.

Roxana's sister, Mary Ward Foote Hubbard, lived with them also. At age seventeen, Mary married a rich merchant and went to live with him on his island plantation in Jamaica. When she arrived there, she discovered that her husband was the father of the light-skinned slave children running around. Mary could not get off the island fast enough. As she waited for the ship to take her to live with Lyman and Roxana, she sat by her window, wishing the island might sink into the ocean with all its terribleness and that she might sink with it.

Roxana wrote Lyman's half-sister, Esther Beecher, of the problems she faced as a housewife:

January 13, 1811

Dear Esther,

Would now write you a long letter, if it were not for several vexing circumstances, such as the weather, extremely cold, storm violent and no wood cut: Mr. Beecher gone; and Sabbath day, with company, a clergyman, a stranger; Catharine sick, Rachel's finger cut off, and she crying and groaning with the pain. Mr. Beecher is gone to New Hartford to preach and did not provide us wood enough to last….

Roxana Beecher

Five months later, on June 14, Roxana gave birth to another daughter she also named Harriet. Two more children would follow, Henry Ward and Charles, before Roxana died in 1816, at forty-one, from tuberculosis. Lyman maintained that Roxana's dying wish was for her sons to become ministers and for her daughters to become godly wives and mothers.

The family went into mourning, covering the mirrors in the parsonage with white cloth. Henry Ward, 3, was too young to go to the funeral. A few days afterward, Catharine, 16, saw Henry digging a hole in the dirt beneath her window. "I'm going to heaven to find Mama," he said.

A year later, Rev. Beecher married again to Harriet Porter, 27, of Maine. She shared Lyman's intense religious zeal. She would never be intimately involved in the raising of her eight adopted children. Harriet Porter would bear four more Beecher children, three of whom lived.

CHAPTER 2

Harriet Worries about Lord Byron

Lyman's preoccupation with the religious state of his children's souls cast a dark shadow on their young lives. He was tortured that sudden death would sweep them away before he could bring them to God. He was rigid. He did not allow his family to celebrate Christmas. There was nothing written in the Scriptures, he said, that stated that Jesus was born on December 25.

Even so, Lyman Beecher could be playful. "To let down" after a long Sabbath of preaching, Lyman came home and played "Go to the Devil and Shake Yourself" on the violin. If his wife had gone out, he danced the "double shuffle" in his stocking feet to delight his children. Fall apple peeling time found everyone standing around with apple peelers and Lyman quizzing the boys about the events in *Ivanhoe* (which Harriet had read seven times one summer). They were a musical family with a piano in the house. Lyman treated the boys to fishing and hunting outings while Harriet was given sewing to do.

Harriet was constantly on the prowl in her father's upper study for something wonderful to read. Mostly, though, she just found stacks of grim sermons and essays. Then, one day, at her Aunt Esther's house, she found a volume of Lord Byron's poetry called "The Corsair." She had heard her father and stepmother talking about Lord Byron. (Harriet was always listening to others.) They said that he had separated from his wife. Harriet asked Aunt Esther about Lord

Byron, but it made Esther uneasy. Harriet found Byron's poems beautiful but mysterious. Harriet left Aunt Esther's wondering about the secret that was Lord Byron.

Then, one day, in spring of 1824, when Harriet was almost thirteen, her father said to her in deep anguish, "My dear, Byron is dead—*gone*." After a pause, he continued, "Oh, I'm so sorry that Byron is dead. I did hope he would live to do something for Christ." Harriet grabbed a basket to pick strawberries on Chestnut Hill but was too worried to do anything that merry. She lay down among the daisies and looked up into the blue sky, thinking of "that great eternity into which Byron had entered, and wondered how it might be with his soul."

―――――

Lyman Beecher had made a name for himself outside of Litchfield. His fiery sermons were printed as tracts and distributed locally, nationally, and globally. After fifteen years in Litchfield, he wanted a change. He expected all his six sons to go to college and that was going to cost money that Lyman did not have. Then, in 1826, Lyman got a job offer from Hanover Street Church in Boston. The salary was generous. The elders needed a dynamic leader to build up the Congregational Church. Their old-style religion was losing congregants to a new, rival religion—Unitarianism. Lyman had been itching for this fight. "It was a fire in my bones, my mind was all the time heating—heating—heating." He took the Boston job.

CHAPTER 3

Harriet Picks up Her Pen

B y the time Lyman Beecher moved to Boston, Harriet was fifteen. Several of her older siblings were already out on their own. Harriet followed sisters Catharine and Mary to Hartford, Connecticut, where Catharine had founded a new school, the Hartford Female Seminary. By 1827, Harriet completed her studies at the Seminary and became one of its teachers.

As director, Catharine created an ambitious educational system that offered young ladies the same studies found at boys' academies—*but with an emphasis on building character.* Catharine had a zeal for bringing about social change. Catharine and Harriet's first cause was the fate of the Cherokee Indians. In 1827, the Cherokees were ordered to vacate their lands in Georgia. The Cherokees owned rich, fertile land that white settlers wanted. Catharine believed that women had a moral duty to plead with the national government to honor their treaties. Anonymously, Catharine addressed the issue in a 1929 circular, "To the Benevolent Women of the United States," in which she urged:

> Have not then the females of this country some duties devolving upon them in relation to this helpless [Cherokee] race? They [women] have [no] right to dictate the decisions of those that rule over them....It may be, that female petitioners can lawfully be heard, even by the highest rulers of our land.

Catharine's circular was widely distributed. Her students and teachers got caught up in the movement, circulating petitions and writing letters of protest. Harriet recalled:

> Last night we teachers all sat up till eleven o-clock finishing our Cherokee letters. We sent some to the principal ladies of New Haven [Connecticut]….Margaret Brown says the circular is making a great excitement in New York….There is great wonderment as to who composed the circular.

But the petition went unheeded. Gold had been discovered on Cherokee lands, and the whites wanted the gold and the land for cotton production. In 1830, President Andrew Jackson signed the Indian Removal Act, forcing the Cherokees in Georgia off their homelands. The federal government ordered them to relocate to new lands across the Mississippi River. The Cherokees walked hundreds of miles; many died along the way.

At this time, writing was how people kept in touch and registered their opinions. Women—who were denied the right to vote, to hold political office, to serve on a jury, essentially, denied a voice in the political arena—found writing letters to be a satisfying outlet for airing opinions and feelings. Through letters, women and men maintained their friendships. Harriet confessed to her brother George that she sometimes could scarcely keep her letters from turning into sermons. In December 1829, she wrote, "You see my dear George that I was made for a preacher." She felt that God might be calling her to be a writer.

In 1827, Harriet's sister, Mary Beecher, was no longer teaching at Hartford Female Seminary. She had married a local Hartford lawyer, Thomas C. Perkins. In July of 1831, Mary received a letter from a woman named Angelina Grimké of Philadelphia, announcing that she and a friend would be arriving at Mary's house to stay for a week. Angelina wanted to visit Catharine Beecher's nationally prestigious school to see if she would like to pursue a career there as a schoolteacher.

At that time, there were twelve boarders—Catharine, Harriet, and Mary's family—living at Mary Beecher Perkins' house. Mary scurried to get the house ready for the visitors when she heard a knock at the door. Standing in her doorway were two oddly dressed women, Angelina and her companion, who had arrived at almost the same time as Angelina's letter. The women wore their hair severely parted down the middle, tucked flat under a tight, crimped cap. Their dresses were drab. The women were Quakers.

Angelina Grimké

Wherever Angelina Grimké appeared, heads turned. She refused to join in the Perkins' family prayers and, at the Seminary, remained seated during Scripture reading. She did not believe in forms of worship. Two years before, the Presbyterian Church in her hometown of Charleston, South Carolina, had expelled her for her demand that each church member openly condemn slavery. Angelina, therefore, had left home, following her older sister, Sarah, to Philadelphia to join her Quaker chapter. Angelina and Sarah were attracted to the Quaker's social justice beliefs. Quakers actively challenged slavery, denounced it as evil, and believed it their duty to call for its abolition. Back in South Carolina, Angelina and Sarah's parents were major slaveholders. The sisters had been raised on a plantation. They knew firsthand the horrors of slavery.

Angelina told Harriet that Quakers allowed women to speak in their meetinghouses. This was simply not done in Protestant churches. Society also did not allow women to speak in mixed groups of men and women. When Angelina returned to Philadelphia, she informed the Quakers of her desire to enroll at Hartford Female Seminary. The elders refused her petition.

In 1832, Lyman Beecher—now referred to as *Rev. Dr. Lyman Beecher*—was the most famous clergyman in America. After six years in Boston, he wanted to move on. Therefore, he accepted an offer to become the president of Lane Seminary, a Presbyterian school for educating ministers in Cincinnati, Ohio. He was solicited by Arthur Tappan, the wealthy New York silk merchant and philanthropist. Indeed, Arthur and Lewis Tappan's financial pledge to Lane Seminary altogether depended upon "the eminent Rev. Dr. Beecher" being appointed to the presidency. The Tappans belonged to a group of New York philanthropists who devoted their surplus gains to good works and supported the newspaper, *The New-York Evangelist*.

Dr. Beecher was ecstatic to go West. The population to the west of the Allegheny Mountains was exploding, and the Presbyterian Church suffered a monumental shortage of preachers. The Church leaders were terrified that the influx of Irish immigrants with their Roman Catholic beliefs would stamp out Protestantism. Lyman trembled at the thought, expressing to daughter Catharine that, "if we gain the West, all is safe; if we lose it, all is lost." Lyman was especially troubled by the appearance of Catholic convent schools on the Western frontier. Two years earlier, he had told Catharine to give her life to the education of female children of "the rising generation, in which Catholics and infidels have got the start of us."

Henry Ward fairly danced the first half hour after he read sister Harriet's letter with the news. The West! The adventure! After his graduation from Amherst College in two years, he would join the others. Their brother Edward was already out west as the president of Illinois College. Catharine, too, embraced the idea of moving to a pioneer city. She would do as her father wished and open a school in which to train teachers. Harriet would teach there.

In March of 1832, Catharine and her father went to Cincinnati to find a place to build a house. Catharine wrote Harriet that she had learned the names of all the cultured New England-type people in Cincinnati with whom she and Harriet could associate.

The summer before they departed, Harriet began writing a textbook called *Primary Geography for Children*. Cincinnati was the fastest-growing city in America, the commercial city of the West and a bustling river town. She would publish her book there. Once in Cincinnati, Harriet, 21, vowed to herself to mingle among others rather than hanging back and criticizing them from a corner chair. Her uncle, Samuel Foote, an old sea captain, lived in a mansion there and knew interesting people.

CHAPTER 4

Abraham Grows Up in a Slave State

In 1811, when Abe Lincoln was two, his family moved to land along Knob Creek in Hardin County, Kentucky, where his father farmed the green fields long held by Native American Indians. He would live there until he was almost eight years old. Abe ran errands, gathering wood, and carrying water. He fished in the creek and picked berries in the hills. He took corn to Hodgen's mill three miles away. He and his sister, Sarah, planted corn and pumpkin seeds in the fields. Once, while playing with his friend, Austin Gollaher, on Knob Creek after a heavy rain, the log Abe was standing on suddenly shifted, and Abe fell into the fast-moving creek. Austin thought quickly, grabbed a sycamore limb, and held it out to Abe, struggling in the water, thus saving his life.

Slavery was legal in Kentucky. As Abe freely moved about, he saw slaves working in the fields, being sold at auctions, and being walked along the road to be sold downriver. At that time, there were 1,007 slaves in their county, compared to 1,627 white males (ages sixteen or older). The Cumberland Trail ran through the valley, right beside the Lincoln homestead. The Trail was an overland route used by slave traders to transport slaves to markets. The 1808 Constitutional ban on the Atlantic slave trade had not put a dent in the slave trade nor, as many hoped, had it led to the abolition of slavery. Rather, the trade market had shifted to a domestic one. Slave states began selling slaves.

With the government's purchase of Louisiana (1803) and Florida (1822), countless acres of Southern virgin land opened up for agricultural production of tobacco, rice, sugar, and cotton. Plantations multiplied. Slave labor was in high demand.

Planters in states in the Upper South watched as their land values dropped and the price of slaves climbed. Unlike land, they noted, slaves were portable commodities—articles of commerce—that could be transported to market. Slaves were a form of wealth, used as collateral in business transactions or to pay off debt. To tap the lucrative slave market, some states in the Upper South, notably Virginia, became "breeding states." Slave girls, as young as twelve, became breeders, subject to uninvited and often violent sexual intimacies. These girls both toiled in the fields and gave birth there. White slave owners were often the fathers of slave children. They sold their slave children to the slave states in the Lower South.

The passage of the Missouri Compromise of 1820, designed by Kentucky Senator Henry Clay, had alarmed Northerners. Slavery was not confining itself to the South. Rather, it was expanding *westward*. That measure admitted two new states into the Union—Missouri, in the West, *as a slave state*, and Maine, in New England, *as a free state*. There were then twelve free and twelve slave states. The balance of power in the U.S. Senate remained unchanged. However, in the U.S. House of Representatives, the South gained more seats due to the Constitutional provision for the counting of three-fifths of the slave population for purposes of determining congressional representation. One-sixth of the American population were slaves. The Missouri Compromise also banned slavery from all remaining lands of the Louisiana Purchase north of the 36° 30' parallel (except for Missouri, which lay north of the line). The Mason-Dixon Line and the Ohio River created an imaginary line dividing the free Northern states from the Southern ones where slavery was permitted.

The slave trade created enormous wealth for human traffickers, such as the notorious Kentucky slave trader, Edward Stone. Stone built himself a grand Greek Revival brick mansion. With one-and-a-half floors, the house boasted five chimneys, gabled dormers with round-arched windows, a Doric portico, Palladian windows, and a long, narrow basement that ran beneath the front hallway. This basement served as a dungeon where Stone stored his slaves until he assembled a boatload to sell downriver at a Southern slave market.

Neighbor J. Winston Coleman, Jr. said Stone "[was] stowing them [slaves] in his…cellar in irons [shackles], then dressing them in good cloth, daubing grey hair with shoe black, rubbing oil on their dusky faces to give a 'sleek, healthy color.'"

Stone rubbed oil on the slaves' faces to enhance their marketability. Southern slave buyers considered greased and supple skin a mark that a slave had a robust immune system and was, thus, more seasoned for the long, hot, humid summers of the sugar country. Stone advertised:

> CASH FOR NEGROES! I wish to purchase TWENTY NEGROES, BOYS & GIRLS from 10 to 25 years of age. A liberal price will be given for those answering the description on early application to the subscriber.—EDWARD STONE, living on the Limestone Road, 4 miles from Paris [Kentucky] leading to Millersburg.

Once Stone had gathered his boatload of slaves, he marched them in chain gangs called "coffles" to the Ohio River landing at Maysville. Presbyterian minister Rev. James Dickey saw one of Stone's coffles on the march:

> In the summer of 1822…I witnessed a scene such as I never witnessed before, as such I hope never to witness again. Having passed through Paris, in Bourbon County, Kentucky, the sound of music, (beyond a little rising of ground) attracted my attention; I looked forward and saw the flag of my country waving.

Supposing I was about to meet a military parade, I drove hastily to the side of the road; and having gained the top of the ascent, I discovered, I suppose, about forty Black men, all chained together after the following manner: Each of them was handcuffed, and they were arranged in rank and file. A chain perhaps forty feet long, the size of a fifth-horse chain, was stretched between the two ranks, to which short chains were joined which connected with the handcuffs. Behind them were about thirty women, in double rank, the couples tied hand to hand. A solemn sadness sat on every countenance, and the dismal silence of the march of despair was interrupted only by the sound of two violins; yes, as if to add insult to injury, the foremost couple were furnished with a violin apiece, the second couple were ornamented with cockades [decorative badges], while near the center waved the Republican [United States] flag, carried by a hand, *literally in chains.*

EDWARD STONE'S COFFEE GANG

From an old print

Slave Coffle

I pursued my journey till evening, and put up for the night;

when I mentioned the scene I had witnessed, 'Ah!' cried my land-lady, 'that is my brother.' From her I learned that his name is [Edward] Stone, of Bourbon County, Kentucky, in partnership with one Kinningham of Paris [Kentucky].

Slaves feared being sold to the Deep South, to be forever parted from loved ones, and further away from the free North and escape. Furthermore, Louisiana sugar planters worked their slaves so hard that they expected many to die from overwork. William Johnson, a Virginia slave, recalled his master saying "…that if we didn't suit him he would put us in his pocket quick—meaning he would sell us." Although sugar cane cultivation required hard, year-round labor, the harvest season—from mid-October through December—was the most grueling. Racing against the possibility of a damaging early frost, slaves toiled in the fields for eighteen to twenty hours a day, cutting the cane and processing it into sugar, with Sundays off only on some plantations. Planters thought of their slaves in purely economic terms. They knew that slaves forced to keep up this punishing, relent-less tempo would be used up in seven or eight years when they would "expire" and simply be "replaced."

———

Four years later, Stone's name popped up in the Southern news-paper, the *Richmond* (Virginia) *Enquirer*. On Sunday, September 17, 1826, Stone, age 43, his nephew, and three other white men had been floating a cargo of seventy-odd slaves down the Ohio River, bound for sale in a distant market. About ninety miles below Louisville, the slaves rose up and, armed with hatchets, clubs, and knives, killed all five of their white captors. The mutineers weighed down their victims' bodies and threw them overboard. Then they sank the boat. They tried to escape into the free state of Indiana, but, apparently, the size and condition of their group drew unwanted attention. An Indiana posse recaptured about fifty-five of them and returned them to Kentucky justice. Five men were hanged, their names possibly being Jo, Duke, Resin, Stephen, and Wesley. Forty-seven were sold; the remainder were brought back to Bourbon County. Nineteen escaped in Indiana.

CHAPTER 5

Abraham Takes to the River

I t was March 1831. Abe Lincoln was twenty-two years old. Tragedy had marked his young life. His mother, sister, and infant brother were lying in their graves. His father had remarried. Abe was now a grown man, a big man, skinny, bony, and tall—six feet four— with long arms and legs that gave him a spidery look. He had rare strength in his muscles. He could take an axe by the handle and hold it out in a straight horizontal line, easy and steady. Watching Abe cut timber, a friend said, "You would say there was three men at work by the way the trees fell."

In the preceding twelve months, Abe had fulfilled his last obligation to his father. Abe helped the family move from Kentucky to Indiana and then to yet another plot of raw, untamed land his restless father had bought further west in Illinois. Abe cut more trees, built another log cabin, cleared ten acres, and planted corn. He stayed with the family through the fall of the malarial fever, then the Winter of the Deep Snow, but it was almost spring now, and Abe was leaving home—*forever*. He had nothing good to say about his father who had nothing good to say about his son. Abe did not know what he would do with his life once he left, but the tedious farming life of endless, hard physical labor was not for him. He was bitter about the way his life had turned out, but on this particular March day, Abe was a satisfied man. He had landed a job as a riverman. He had tried to get a job as a steamboat pilot before but had been turned down because he was not yet twenty-one. Well, he had turned twenty-two a month ago. Rivers fascinated Abe. At this time in the largely undeveloped West, there were few "roads"; the ones that existed were mostly animal paths—primitive—full of sinkholes, stumps, and deep ruts, easy for a wagon to get mired in, and ever-changing. Rivers were more reliable than roads. Rivers were Abe's escape.

The Lincoln homestead sat on a high bluff just a few steps above the Sangamon River. So, it was on that first day of March in the year 1831 that Abe and his cousin, John Hanks, walked away from the family cabin, slid their canoe into the little river, paddled downstream to Springfield and met up with Abe's stepbrother, John D. Johnston. They had a deal with a frontier hustler named Denton Offutt. Offutt hired them to run a flatboat loaded with farm produce down to New Orleans. Offutt promised he would have the fully loaded flatboat ready once Abe and John Hanks reached Springfield.

But Offutt neglected to buy them their boat. He then paid Abe and John to build the boat themselves, which they did. Six weeks passed before it was ready. Finally, on Tuesday, April 19, 1831, the men took the completed wooden flatboat—eighty feet long and eighteen feet wide—and shoved it into the Sangamon River. Then, they loaded sacks of corn, sides of bacon, and barrels of pork onto it. Corrals had been added to the boat to pen the live hogs they would pick up downriver. Offutt, Abe, John Hanks, John Johnston, and some hitchhikers set off from Sangamo Town, poling down the sometimes-turbulent early spring waters of the Sangamon. The first town on their long voyage was sixteen miles downriver, the small but growing commercial town of New Salem.

Abe steered the massive boat away from sandbars, stumps, low water, and overhanging branches. Because of their delay, the snow-melt was close to done; the water level was dropping. Things went smoothly until, rounding the curve at New Salem, the boat suddenly jolted to a stop. It was lodged on the New Salem milldam that had been erected over the river. In such shallow water, the flatboat was too heavy to float over it. It began filling with water at an alarming rate.

The villagers of New Salem came running down the steep bluff to see the calamity. Young Abe, a lanky, lean giant of a man with dark, fuzzy hair, drew special attention as he and his crew worked in the water, frantically trying to save both boat and cargo, aiming to dislodge the boat before the wooden dam gouged a fatal hole in the hull. But the boat would not budge. The day grew late.

Abe borrowed an empty flatboat and poled it alongside his stranded boat. The crew could then transfer the heavy cargo to the second boat. Abe's flatboat sprang upwards. He gathered volunteers from New Salem to stand on the front of the boat to shift the weight. Water sloshed to the front where Abe had bored a hole with an auger he borrowed from Onstot's cooper shop. The water drained out. Abe carved a plug from a tree limb to match the size of the hole and used it to plug the hole. With a little more effort, the flatboat finally tipped over the dam and slid into the river below. The craft with the cargo followed. Once anchored close to the riverbank, the crew reloaded the cargo onto their flatboat. The hitchhikers departed at New Salem.

The people of New Salem marveled at Abe's cleverness. Offutt saw the promise in Abe. He offered him a job. Complete the voyage to New Orleans, he said, then return to New Salem where I will make you the clerk in a new store. This gave Abe something to think about on the trip. At that point, Abe and the others were focused on getting the boat out of the shallow Sangamon, into the broader and straighter Illinois River and then into the Mississippi River. But first, they had to pick up some hogs. John Hanks got off at St. Louis. It was then 1,400 miles to New Orleans.

Traveling less than five miles per hour, the journey took weeks. In mid-May, John Johnston, Abe, and Offutt arrived safely at the bustling wharf of New Orleans. After Offutt sold his cargo, Offutt, John Johnston, and Abe Lincoln took a steamboat on their return journey north. At St. Louis, though, John Johnston and Abe departed, walking the rest of the way—three hundred miles—to the middle of Illinois. Abe had made up his mind to take up Offutt on his job offer.

He arrived in New Salem to find out that Offutt had not lived up to another of his promises. There was as yet no store. However, Offutt had ordered a stock of goods from St. Louis with which to stock it, once he and Abe built the log cabin store. Abe would be the manager. He would receive $15 a month and a back room to sleep in—among the crates and barrels.

In the meanwhile, Abe found odd jobs to tide him over. The residents of New Salem took an instant liking to this hardworking boatman. Many villagers commented on the persistent gap between the bottom of his pants and the top of his shoes; his blue jeans were four or five inches too short.

From July 1831 until April 1837, New Salem was Abe's home. In his job at the store and after hours, he got to know all his neighbors, exchanging news and gossip with farmers, swapping jokes and telling funny stories in his slow-talking, folksy way, maybe standing on a stump and mimicking a ranting preacher, flinging his arms wildly in the air. He competed in foot races and wood-chopping contests, though, in no time, he was asked to judge them, as he had proven to be both honest and fair. He drew people to him like a magnet. When he talked, people listened. He talked about politics a lot. He was opposed to slavery and said he thought it a curse to the land. Denton Offutt bragged of his protégée, saying that Abe was not merely the "smartest man in New Salem," but the strongest, too.

Abe always had a book with him. If just for five minutes, he read between the arrivals of customers at the store. A villager once saw him stretched out on top of a woodpile, reading a book on the law. He devoured newspapers when he could get his hands on them. He needed to understand everything, minutely, exactly. He felt he needed to make up for lost time; he was aggrieved that he had not had a proper education. Having only had, altogether, no more than one year of schooling—here a month, there a month—in his entire life, Abe took lessons from the local school teacher. He learned how to speak using excellent grammar. He studied a book of legal forms and, with the help of the justice of the peace, learned to write simple documents. He joined the New Salem Debating Society. He fished with a man who introduced him to the works of William Shakespeare.

When people heard Abe speak, they thought: this thinking man should go into politics. He could get things done. On March 9, 1832, eight months after his arrival in New Salem, Abraham Lincoln declared his candidacy for the legislature of Illinois as a member of the Whig Party, saying:

> My politics is short and sweet, like an old woman's dance. I am in favor of a national bank, a high and protective tariff, and the internal improvement system. If elected, I will be thankful. If beaten, I can do as I have been doing, work for a living.

The "internal improvements" naturally included making the Sangamon River more navigable.

Abe would lose this political race because, just a month later, in April, he was called up to fight in the Black Hawk War. Lincoln borrowed a horse and rode nine miles across the grassy prairie to Richland Creek to join a militia of local friends and neighbors. The men voted for Lincoln to be their captain. No other success in his life ever equaled his personal satisfaction of having been chosen the leader of his peers. Abe poked fun at his short time in the military, writing that instead of running up against "any live, fighting Indians," he had endured "many bloody struggles with the musquetoes [sic]."

Abe's six years in New Salem were transformative. When he arrived in town, he was homeless, jobless, ill-clothed, and direc-tionless—"a piece of floating driftwood," he said. When he left for Springfield, he was an Illinois congressman, the political floor leader of the Whig party, and a licensed lawyer.

CHAPTER 6

Willie Garrison Is on Fire

William Lloyd Garrison was born December 10, 1805, in Newburyport, Massachusetts. His father, an unemployed merchant sailor fond of strong drink, abandoned the family when Garrison was three. "Willie" was raised by his mother, Frances Maria (née Lloyd) Garrison, a devout Baptist and, for a time, was sent to live with a Baptist deacon. Willie was desperately poor and had little schooling. To help support his family, he sold homemade molasses candy and delivered firewood. At age thirteen, he began an apprenticeship at the *Newburyport Herald* as a compositor, learning to arrange movable type for printing. He began writing articles. After his seven-year apprenticeship ended, he became the owner, editor, and printer of the *Newburyport Free Press*.

In the 1820s, Garrison became involved in the anti-slavery movement. Massachusetts was a free state. Garrison credited the 1826 book, *Letters on American Slavery*, by the Presbyterian Reverend John Rankin of Ripley, Ohio, as having cemented his devotion to the cause. Garrison published articles in favor of colonization, the relocation of American freeborn Blacks and emancipated slaves to Africa. He spoke at the annual conference of the Massachusetts Colonization Society on July 4, 1828, in Boston.

In 1829, Garrison left New England for Baltimore, Maryland, to write for the anti-slavery paper, the *Genius of Universal Emancipation*. This was Garrison's first time living in a slave state. That fall, Garrison wrote about the transportation of seventy-five slaves from Baltimore to New Orleans on a ship owned by the New England merchant, Frances Todd. Garrison burned with moral indignation at Todd, who was from the free state of Massachusetts yet was selling human beings. In the November 20, 1829 issue of the *Genius*, Garrison took aim at Todd, declaring that:

> [T]he men who have the wickedness to participate therein [the slave trade], for the purpose of heaping up wealth, should be SENTENCED TO SOLITARY CONFINEMENT FOR LIFE; they are…highway robbers and murderers….

Although Garrison had not written anything untrue about Todd, Garrison was arrested, jailed, prosecuted for libel, found guilty, and fined. After seven weeks' imprisonment, the New York abolitionist and philanthropist, Arthur Tappan, who did not know Garrison, paid the fine. Garrison was released. Garrison then toured, lecturing on abolition. He now advocated the immediate and peaceful emancipation of slaves—an extreme view, disavowing colonization—and began lecturing.

In October of 1830, the only Unitarian minister in Connecticut, Rev. Samuel May (Louisa May Alcott's uncle), was on a visit to Boston. With his brother-in-law, Bronson Alcott (Louisa May Alcott's father), Rev. May attended a lecture by William Lloyd Garrison. Garrison spoke in graphic sketches of the suffering of the enslaved. Never before had Rev. May, a graduate of Harvard University and Harvard Divinity School, been so deeply moved by someone's words. He said to those around him:

> [Garrison] is a prophet; he will shake our nation to its center, but he will shake slavery out of it. We ought to know him, we ought to help him. Come, let us go and give him our hands.

Alcott and May went up and introduced themselves to Garrison. Alcott invited Garrison into his home. They sat and talked with him until midnight, both Alcott and May becoming disciples of Garrison.

On January 1, 1831, Garrison launched the first issue of his weekly anti-slavery newspaper, *The Liberator*, vowing to "strenuously contend for the immediate enfranchisement [historical meaning: 'liberation from slavery'] of our slave populations."

> I determined, at every hazard, to lift up the standard [flag] of emancipation in the eyes of the nation....That standard is now unfurled....Let Southern oppressors tremble——let their secret abettors tremble——let their Northern apologists tremble——let all the enemies of the persecuted blacks tremble.

Garrison predicted that the oppression of slavery would bring about resistance and doom:

> Wo if it come with storm, and blood, and fire,
> When midnight darkness veils the earth and sky!
> Wo to the innocent babe—the guilty sire—
> Mother and daughter—friends of kindred tie!
> Stranger and citizen alike shall die!

Upon reading this, Rev. Samuel May was worried. He visited Garrison, where he and his printing partner, Isaac Knapp, both lived and worked in the little upper chamber at No. 6 Merchants' Hall in Boston. "My friend," said May to Garrison, "do try to moderate your indignation, and keep more cool, why, you are all on fire."

Garrison laid his hand gently but firmly on May's shoulder and replied, slowly but with deep feeling, "Brother May, I have need to be all on fire, for I have mountains of ice about me to melt."

Masthead of the Liberator (1861)

Garrison set out to melt Northerners' indifference toward slavery, an institution most in the North considered a sin, an evil, but a problem brushed off as a regional one best left to the South to handle. Besides, many Northerners were just as intent as Southerners in maintaining their white supremacy. Once freed, the former slaves might move north, a prospect much of the North dreaded. Ending slavery would require a revolutionary and often unwelcome change in social structure.

CHAPTER 7

Nat Strikes Back

We have all seen the sun of a dusky red or copper color; but who, until Saturday, the 13th of this month [August], ever saw it clad in sky blue and pea green? On Saturday, and yesterday morning at its rising, it was of a light but lively green, and as it ascended above the horizon, changed first to cerulean [sky blue], then to silver white, and finally to pale yellow....A black spot near the centre, was discernible by the naked eye, apparently the size of a walnut....—*Washington* [D.C.] *National Intelligencer*, August 13-14, 1831

Our ebony friends [Black people]...had their religious devotion sensibly stimulated. [They were] considering the sun shining blue as undeniable proof that the end of time approached.— *Constitutional Whig* (Richmond, Virginia), August 22, 1831

The blue-green sun with its black dot was seen in the south of Europe and in America, causing wonder, astonishment, scientific speculation, and worry. The superstitious—not just "our ebony friends"—were terrified that a great calamity was impending. On Sunday, August 14, 1831, the second morning of the peculiar sun—the sun having been alternately hazy, white, brassy, and blue that day—it was reported that Nat Turner, an enslaved Black man, preached to a large gathering of Blacks at Barnes' Methodist Church near Hertford County, North Carolina, although Turner neither lived in that county nor resided in that state. Rather,

Nat lived on the Joseph Travis plantation in Southampton County, Virginia. Nevertheless, Nat knew the slaves for many miles around, as he had been granted more freedom of movement than was permitted the ordinary slave. He had no quarrel with his master, Joseph Travis, whom Nat said treated him with kindness. Travis was his fourth master. Turner was skilled as a carpenter, blacksmith, and field hand.

Nat read Revelation 6:2 to his congregation, a passage that carried insurrection implications:

> And I saw, and behold a white horse: and he that sat on him had a bow; and a crown was given unto him; and he went forth conquering and to conquer.

Slaves in Southampton County were free to conduct religious meetings. Despite Nat's fanatical preaching, the whites were not concerned. Religious education, it was asserted, made slaves docile and manageable, so it was allowed in some Southern areas.

For almost three years, Nat had been telling both the whites and the Blacks that "the great day of judgment was at hand" when "the last shall be first, and the first last" (Matthew 20:16). Because he could read and write (and almost no other slaves could) and spoke with tremendous authority, Nat had acquired great power over the minds and emotions of his fellow slaves. His devotees called him "The Prophet." He boasted that this influence over the slave community had begun in his youth:

> Yet such was the confidence of the negroes in the neighborhood… in my superior judgment, that they would carry me with them when they were going on any roguery, to plan for them….— Having soon discovered to be great, I must appear so…and wrapped myself in mystery….

Secretly, Nat had been conspiring with a handful of other enslaved men to revolt against their white enslavers. Many in the Barnes' Methodist Church congregation that day signaled their willingness to join him by tying red bandanna handkerchiefs around their necks.

A week later, on a breezy but warm Sunday, August 21, Nat and six other men gathered at Cabin Pond, a wooded hideaway not far from the Joseph Travis place, to feast on pig and get drunk on brandy. Nat, the "General," arrived late, saluting his team upon approach. They schemed. The plan was to comb the countryside and kill all the whites, expecting that their army would swell in number with slaves they would free as they went by. Their destination was the arsenal at Jerusalem, Virginia, twenty miles away.

At about 3 a.m. the next morning, the dangerous men arrived at the Travis plantation (the home of Nat's master). They located a plentiful amount of hard cider and drank deeply. One of the men, Hark, got a ladder and leaned it against the house chimney. Nat and Will, Nat's associate, ascended the ladder and entered the Travis house. Armed with a hatchet and an axe, they crept into the bedrooms of Mr. and Mrs. Travis, Mrs. Travis' son, Putnam Moore, and an apprentice, murdering them in their beds. A little infant sleeping in a cradle was overlooked, but Henry and Will were sent back to kill it. Nat searched for Miss Mariah Pope, who lived with the Travis family, but she was not at home. Nat detested her and hoped to make her his first victim.

Having just committed five heinous murders, there was no turning back. The seven began to think of themselves as a real army. From the spoils of their Travis raid, they devised uniforms, sticking feathers in their hats and tying long red sashes around their waists and over their shoulders. They stole guns and pressed Moses, a slave, into their ranks. Before leaving, Nat formed his men into a line of soldiers and marched them off on the business of slaughter. Drunk on liquor, high on armed power, and short on sleep, the insurgents would become as ferocious as their General instructed them to be. They had tasted of blood. They launched a campaign of total annihilation, going systematically from house to house and farm to farm, eventually decimating people at eleven different plantations, instilling terror and alarm throughout the vicinity, and killing every white person they sought and could corner. White witnesses to this wanton destruction who miraculously escaped detection spread the word that murderers were on the loose, helping some neighbors to hide in the swamps near Pate's Hill, where they stayed for two days, sleeping on beds of leaves and eating little.

Many slaves were protective of the white people. Old Red Nelson hid Mrs. Lavinia Francis, eight months pregnant, in a dark cubby space above the kitchen. When the insurgents came asking for her, Old Red pretended to sympathize with them and joined in on their frenzied search for her. Not finding Lavinia, Old Red sent the men out into the garden to look among the tall cabbages. At Levi and Martha Waller's neighborhood center—a school, distillery, a black-smith, and a wheelwright shop—the Wallers' enslaved blacksmith, Davy, provided a diversion for Levi to escape detection by running in the opposite direction of his master, yelling at the insurgents, "Here goes the old fox." Levi watched as his wife and ten others were killed, mostly children. During the attack, their daughter Martha was concealed under the large apron of her Black nanny. Little Martha, though, hearing all the terrible killing noise around her, cried out, was discovered, and dashed against the ground. Two of the Wallers' eighteen slaves, Albert and Yellow Davy, joined in the killings. Levi Waller hurried to Murfreesboro, North Carolina, the largest nearby town, to tell the story of his dead family and to sound the alarm.

On their bloody march, the band—some of whom were drinking apple brandy mixed with gunpowder—would grow to approximately seventy, some riding on horseback, brandishing clubs, swords, shotguns, and axes. Within the next twelve to fifteen hours, they murdered approximately sixty white people—mostly women and children—before they were stopped by a heavily armed white state militia before they reached Jerusalem. Upon confronting such a force, the insurgents disbanded, and many fled into the woods and swamps. They were all eventually captured or killed. Nat would get away, though, hiding in a cave-like hollow for over six weeks before a farmer found him on October 31. Although their illusion of safety had been permanently shattered by the slave uprising, a collective sigh was breathed across the traumatized South when Nat's arrest was announced. Nat Turner was tried, convicted, and then hanged in Jerusalem. His body was skinned.

For their role in the insurrection, fifty-four men and one woman, Lucy Barrow, were executed by the state. Fear of another uprising spread through the white population of the South. To terrorize the local Blacks, some of the militia decapitated about fifteen of the captured insurgents and put their heads on pikes on a road that came to be called "Blackhead Signpost Road." Many hundreds of innocent Blacks, enslaved and free, were brutally murdered by vigilante white mobs. Patrols rode at night. Blacks had no protection from white violence.

For a brief time afterward, some Virginians contemplated whether Garrison, writing in *The Liberator*, had been correct. He claimed that holding down a race of people in oppression endangered the welfare of the state. The Virginia State Legislature received petitions from concerned citizens. The Quakers pushed for gradual emancipation and the ultimate removal of Blacks from Virginia. The petitions were thoughtfully considered. But louder voices insisted that even talk of freeing the slaves might stir up another uprising. Ultimately, lawmakers ended up restricting Blacks' freedom even more. It became illegal for slaves to preach, to be "insolent" to white people, to carry a gun, to hunt in the woods, to live with a free Black or white person, or to own livestock—this on top of already being a slave. There was a demand for the removal of free Blacks from the slave country.

These newest Black Codes also imposed penalties on white people who taught an enslaved person to read. The logic was that if a slave could read, he or she might read the abolitionist pamphlets and newspapers, which the paranoid Southern planters believed to be in secret circulation in the slave quarters (but were not). That Nat Turner had received a lot of Bible learning, an education allowed because it was thought to make slaves more submissive, had, conversely, made Nat aggressive. The churches of the South squirmed as they delayed taking a stand for or against slavery.

Slaveholders made journalist Garrison the scapegoat for the Nat Turner revolt. Garrison was reviled; his name and paper were notorious in the South. Slaveholders and abolitionists flooded Garrison with letters that were printed in newspapers. On January 10, 1832, an Athens, Georgia, slaveholder wrote him:

> You impudent scoundrel! And I will blow you where the buzzards will never find you. Meet me, sir, in Washington City, on the 4th day of March, prepared to meet the fate which you so richly deserve. Write me whether or not you accept this challenge; if not, sir, expect to die in at least one month….

The state of Georgia made the circulation of anti-slavery publications a capital offense. Georgia offered a reward of $5000 for Garrison's arrest and conviction. Georgetown, in the District of Columbia (a slave district), passed a law prohibiting any free Black from taking *The Liberator* from the post office or risk a $20 fine or thirty days' imprisonment. State after Southern state passed ever-stricter laws to repress Blacks and to silence anti-slavery discussion.

In late 1831, Mayor Harrison Gray Otis of Boston received Southern appeals to silence Bostonian Garrison. Mayor Otis, bewildered, responded that honestly, until he had received those requests, he had not previously known of either a Boston newspaper called *The Liberator* or a resident named William Lloyd Garrison. Soon, though, white and free Black Northerners would know of Garrison and his anti-slavery positions—thanks to the South's obsession with him. Southern newspapers were thick with editorials denouncing what they considered incendiary writings in *The Liberator*, which Southern editors quoted, week by week in their exchanges. Naturally, these Southern screeds were picked up by Northern papers and commented upon. Soon, Garrison's name was on every tongue.

———

A month prior to the Nat Turner revolt, twenty-five miles off the coast of Sicily, a new volcanic island was born. An immense amount of molten lava, volcanic gases, and pumices were ejected from the crater and spewed fifteen miles high. Winds carried the sulfuric aerosol plume north to Europe and north and west to America, causing the sun to appear blue, green, and purple for several days and giving the sunsets the appearance of a forest fire. The scientists decided that the red twilights and the blue suns were caused by vapors thrown out by the eruptions and not by the dust because after every eruption, the sea rushed in and cooled the volcano before ash was shot out.

Once news of the island's birth spread, a four-way territorial dispute over its sovereignty was ignited. Britain visited and planted a flag there, naming it Graham Island. Ferdinand II, the King of Naples, sent ships to claim it for the Bourbon crown, naming it Ferdinandea. The French Navy made a landing, calling the island Julia, after its birth month. Spain declared its interest as well. The ownership of the island, which, at its peak height was a mere two hundred feet above sea level, was still unresolved when, in early 1832, the island sank twenty-five feet under the waves and disappeared. It remains submerged even to this day.

Part II

FREEDOM

(1830-1839)

So the traveler who lets the current carry him down the Ohio till it joins the Mississippi sails, so to say, between freedom and slavery; and he has only to glance around him to see instantly which is best for mankind.

—*Alexis de Tocqueville*

CHAPTER 8

Gamaliel Goes West

Gamaliel Bailey was once again without a job. He was unable to establish a medical practice in Philadelphia. He had moved to Baltimore to become an editor for a religious newspaper. Despite his best editorial efforts, the newspaper lost money, and by December 1831, Gamaliel, 24, was looking for a new venture.

A month earlier, Gamaliel read something in the newspaper that captured his fancy. An expedition was forming to set up a new colony in the far Northwest in Oregon Country in the spring of 1832. Of course, a single man of such a romantic, restless, and adventurous nature—he had sailed to China as a common sailor after completing medical school—would become enchanted by the idea of joining a wagon train of emigrants heading west of the Rocky Mountains. To join Hall J. Kelley's expedition required an advance of only twenty dollars. The starting point for the overland journey was St. Louis. Interested people were told to rendezvous there in January of 1832, just a month away.

The 1832 Kelley expedition was sure to be a journey full of great risk and danger because, to date, no wagon trains had yet to make the trip, the trail only having been traversed on horseback or foot by missionaries, Native Americans, fur traders, and trappers. It was doubtful the entire party would make it to the "delightful and fertile region" situated "eighty miles up the Columbia [River]," two thousand miles away, due to starvation, torrential rivers, storms, hostile Native Americans, wild animals, winter in the mountains, disease, snakebite, broken bones, broken wagon axles, and assorted accidents. Besides this, the ownership of Oregon was still in dispute; both the Americans and the British claimed the territory. Kelley's promise to award settlers with plots of land was just that—a promise. In time, the land deed might prove worthless.

Ever daring and a bit rash, Gamaliel signed up for the venture. He promptly left Baltimore, investing his scanty money in the fastest means of transportation to St. Louis. At that time, there were only 73 miles of railways in America, all but three of which were in Pennsylvania. The canal system totaled 1,277 miles, almost half of which were in New York. Gamaliel took a stagecoach east of the mountains to the Ohio River and then boarded a steamboat down the Ohio and up the Mississippi Rivers.

Gamaliel arrived in St. Louis to find that the whole expedition was a fraud. The promise of wagons and oxen, tents, provisions, an armed guard, and a thousand men to gather and organize an expedition did not materialize. Gamaliel had no desire to stay in St. Louis, which he called "a scattering little place, with scarcely a respectable private residence." Even if he did want to return East, he had no fare. He decided to start walking to Cincinnati, where his family had moved the year before.

In late January, the coldest winter in ages, so cold that the Ohio River froze and steamboats had to cut their way through the ice, Gamaliel walked in deep snow across southern Illinois and Indiana and arrived at the winding Ohio River, on its north side, the free side, just across from Louisville, Kentucky, where slaves could be seen laboring. He turned and walked upriver to Cincinnati. There he found a booming river town of 28,000 people blessed with fertile soil and woodlands, bustling with commerce, labor, and industry, a mixture of Black and white Americans, Irish and German immigrants. There was both street and river traffic, with people moving about in every sort of way, going here and there on horses, in buggies, carts, and coaches, and on foot. The landing was crammed with crates and barrels and passengers. Hundreds of boats—double and triple-decked steamboats, low-lying canalboats, canoes, and flat-bottomed riverboats weighed down with lumber, coal, and livestock—made their way down the Ohio or vied for a place to dock.

Farmers drove herds of swine through the streets to the slaughterhouse. Dock workers loaded barrels of pork, lard, and bacon onto moored flatboats, idling in the easy current of the Ohio. Some newly arrived flatboaters deposited cargo on the Public Landing paved with limestone, extending three hundred feet along the riverbank, then boarded the decks of the steamboats to gamble and drink. Passengers boarded and disembarked the steamboats. To pay for their passage on these "pleasure palaces," young men leapt ashore to buy and then carry wood back to the engine room.

This pleasing view was complemented by beautiful woods on high hills extending two miles beyond and above the city hubbub. Below, stretching along the banks of the river, the city was laid out in fine, wide, and paved streets lined with elegant wood-framed shops, trim brick houses surrounded by gardens, and thatched cottages. There were warehouses, green fields, houses under construction, rubble in the streets, twenty-five churches, benevolent societies, a theatre, schools, mills, four libraries, a medical college, museums, shipbuilding yards, fourteen newspapers, three ferries, foundries, factories, a hospital, nine hotels, banks, breweries, a button factory, a college, a lyceum, publishing houses, a court house, and a lunatic asylum. There was a fire department.

Every sort of occupation was represented in the thriving Western city known both as "The Queen City" and "Porkopolis." There were fifty-five attorneys, seventy-nine butchers, twenty-one barbers, one bell hanger, five hundred sixty-five carpenters, druggists, dentists, two French teachers, seven glass cutters, fifty-seven hatters, lumber merchants, seven mattress makers, and fifty-eight physicians.

With Gamaliel's arrival, that made fifty-nine physicians in Cincinnati. During the summer of 1832, he made contact with the medical community. His favorite professor from Jefferson Medical College, Dr. John Eberle, lived in the city. Dr. Eberle helped Gamaliel set up a private practice. He put his editorial skills to good use writing for *the Western Medical Gazette*. He lectured at a medical lyceum and at Lane Theological Seminary, where Dr. Lyman Beecher, just that year, had been hired as Lane's new president. Lyman Beecher was rumored to be arriving very soon in Cincinnati with his extended family.

In late September, Asiatic cholera broke out in the city. Apparently, the disease had arrived in May via an immigrant vessel landing in Quebec. From there, it spread in epidemic proportions down the St. Lawrence, through the Great Lakes, the canals, arriving with the steamboat passengers on the Ohio River.

Under the emergency leadership of the esteemed Dr. Daniel Drake, Gamaliel was appointed the physician in charge of the Hospital for Strangers during the cholera outbreak. He had no more capacity then for curing the cholera than he had possessed in Canton, China, when the epidemic swept through the city and into the harbor. However, he did observe that there was more disease in the unsanitary, crowded neighborhoods of poor Blacks and immigrants. Dr. Daniel Drake acknowledged this later, writing that, "[O]ur colored population suffered more severely than the white …. Of the 545 who died in Cincinnati, 45 were negroes; although our black population does not exceed 1500." This population of free Blacks, mostly former slaves, was largely concentrated in the neighborhood known as Bucktown or the Bottoms, described as a "wretched basin of tenements and shanties drained by an odiferous stream that carried the bloody run-off from slaughterhouses."

Some victims developed symptoms in the morning and were dead by nightfall. Others lived through it. But if death was your due, when it came, it was horrific: producing a voluminous discharge of rice-like white diarrhea. One doctor described the signs of cholera's victims as: "[face] quite shrunk, eyes sunk, lips dark blue, as well as the skin of the lower extremities; the nails ... livid [blue]."

———

Physicians still did not know that the *Vibrio cholerae* bacterium spread by consuming contaminated water. The flourishing canal and steamboat traffic along the Ohio River predisposed Cincinnati to cholera contamination in the waterways. Local disposal of human and animal sewage remained a lasting problem; Cincinnati was built without drains. Consequently, with the mode of transmission unclear, the Cincinnati Board of Health woefully failed to make the sanitary changes in living conditions that other cities, such as Pittsburgh and Charleston, implemented that would reduce the effect of future cholera epidemics.

CHAPTER 9

Harriet Comes Out of Her Shell

The Boston Beechers and the Hartford Beechers had not lived together since their Litchfield years. In October 1832, the two groups reunited in New York and prepared to set out together on their westward journey to Cincinnati, "the Gateway to the West," where, you will recall, Harriet's father, the Reverend Dr. Lyman Beecher, had accepted the vaunted position of President and Professor of Theology at the new Lane Seminary, a college for training Presbyterian ministers. Lyman considered himself a general going into a great conflict to save the West from Catholics and infidels.

Nine of the Beechers were making this trip: Harriet, her father, stepmother, Aunt Esther, and five of her ten siblings, Catharine, George, and her younger half-siblings, Isabella, Thomas, and James. Within the next three years, though, three more, Henry, Charles, and William, would relocate to Ohio. Edward was still president of Illinois College, two states west of Ohio. Mary, though, remained in Hartford.

The founders and patrons of Lane Seminary placed great confidence in Rev. Dr. Lyman Beecher's ability to lead an institution that could become the "great Andover or Princeton of the West," wrote Rev. Franklin Y. Vail, a member of Lane's Board of Trustees. To this end, New York philanthropist Arthur Tappan donated $20,000 to Lane and pledged even more to fund buildings and scholarships.

It was incumbent upon Lyman, as he and his tribe migrated west, to stop along the way in Eastern cities, preaching and raising funds for Lane. In New York, they tarried for a considerable time while Lyman solicited donations, particularly for the Biblical Literature professorship of Calvin Stowe. Lyman was less successful in opening purses in Philadelphia. From there, the entourage traveled west across the Appalachian Mountains by stagecoach to Wheeling, where they learned of the cholera outbreak in Cincinnati. Their travel westward came to a dead halt. They delayed at Wheeling eight days, eventually opting for chartering a stage for Cincinnati rather than risking infection among steamboat passengers. It was rough-going on a stagecoach, traveling over "corduroy roads," as George Beecher called them, "made of logs laid crosswise, for the benefit of dyspeptics." They arrived safely at their destination on November 14, happy to discover their furniture had arrived a day before.

Because Harriet's three half-siblings were all under the age of ten, they lived with their father, Harriet's stepmother, and Aunt Esther in a magnificent house specially built for them in Walnut Hills, the hillside village two miles above Cincinnati, on the sixty acres that made up the grounds of Lane Seminary. Catharine, 32, and Harriet, 21, rented rooms in town at Mrs. Wright's boardinghouse near their new school, the Misses Beechers' Western Female Institute, on the corner of Fourth and Sycamore Streets in Cincinnati itself. The school opened in May of 1833 with forty students. Harriet and Catharine were co-principals. They, along with two women from back east, Mary Dutton and Ann Tappan, shared the teaching responsibilities. Whereas the Beecher sons could go to college and become ministers, these avenues were not open to the Beecher daughters. They could be teachers—and writers. Harriet went along with Catharine's school plan on the condition that Catharine allowed her time to follow her true calling and passion—writing.

That same May, Harriet's first book, *Primary Geography for Children*, was published by Corey and Fairbank of Cincinnati. (Catharine added her name as coauthor because the textbook was used in her school, but the book was written by Harriet.) To engage her young readers, Harriet used a chatty tone in *Primary Geography*. The content touched on cultural matters:

> The countries of Asia are sometimes called oriental countries... Most of these countries are very warm indeed....For this reason, the people dress differently from what they do in cooler climates. Instead of hats, they wear great rolls of cloth around their heads, called turbans....They wear very loose dresses....
>
> In these countries there never are any parties where men and women all meet together, and talk, as they do in our country. The women are kept shut up in rooms which belong to themselves, and never go without veils over their faces....
>
> In all these countries where the bible is unknown, females are despised and cruelly treated. There is no such thing as a school for females in any of them....In these countries, the women, instead of marrying the man whom they love, are sold and given away to any man whom their father pleases; after that they are regarded as their husband's slaves. In many of these countries, a wife is not considered fit to eat at the same table with her husband. She eats by herself, after he has done.
>
> In Hindostan, a man does not mention his wife by her name, but calls her 'my slave,' or 'my dog.'

Primary Geography earned Harriet $187, about fifteen percent of Lyman Beecher's annual salary, and would continue to make her money through the years. After the publication of Harriet's book and the success of the sisters' school, Harriet and Catharine became something of a *cause célèbre*. They were invited to join the Semi-Colon Club, a literary society made up of learned people, doctors and lawyers, professors and clergy, educators, literary people and businessmen. The club admitted white women and men, single and married, and met Monday evenings at 7:30 p.m., often at Uncle Samuel and Aunt Elizabeth Foote's mansion, at Third and Vine

Streets, to discuss the issues of the day and to read each other's writing. Although the meeting was called to order with the ringing of a bell, it was not a stuffy crowd but one full of hijinks, silly compositions, and verse. Dr. Daniel Drake, now the Beecher family physician, was a member. Harriet met the very popular Eliza Tyler Stowe, 25, and her new husband, the bookish Calvin Stowe, the professor of biblical literature at Lane.

Lawyer Salmon Portland Chase was sometimes present. His first name tormented him. He ardently wished to change it, as well as the spelling of his last name, to something more regal like "Spencer de Cheyce" or "Spencer Payne Cheyce," he told Charles Cleveland. Chase was physically impressive—being six feet two inches tall, big-boned, muscular, clean-shaven, with a massive head. He was immaculately dressed. Although he appeared self-assured, he had some difficulty speaking, having a slight lisp and an occasional stammer, both drawbacks for a courtroom lawyer. Caroline Lee Hentz, who had just published her first novel, *Lovell's Folly*, was labeled a bluestocking by the group because she was a literary lady. Judge James Hall, the editor of the *Western Monthly Magazine*, was an active participant.

At every meeting, a man read aloud a submission by one of the club's members, but the author's name was often kept secret. The evening closed with square dancing, wine, sandwiches, and coffee.

When one of Harriet's pieces was read anonymously at a club meeting in November 1833, editor Judge James Hall chased down her identity, urging her to enter her story in a contest. "A New England Sketch," a character portrayal of Uncle Lot Benton, won her a fifty-dollar prize. The story was then published in the *Western Monthly Magazine* in April 1834. It was Harriet's first signed piece of fiction.

When Harriet was seven, Harriet's father realized that she was uniquely gifted. In January 1819, Lyman wrote a letter to George Foote: "Harriet is a great genius—I would give a hundred dollars if she was a boy & Henry a girl—She is as odd—as she is intelligent & studious."

CHAPTER 10

Lane is Open for Business

fter a year studying the classics in Rochester, reporting for the local *Monroe Telegraph*, and clerking at the county, Henry Brewster Stanton, 26, left New York in the spring of 1832 to enroll at Lane Theological Seminary in Cincinnati to become a Presbyterian minister. His two brothers traveled with him. Their father having abandoned the family, Henry was obliged to pay for his brothers' education as well as his own. Therefore, Henry sought cheap transportation to the West:

> I helped to load a raft at Olean, N.Y., and then aided to guide it
> down the whirling currents of the Alleghany River to Pittsburgh.
> There I took deck passage on a steamboat to Cincinnati. I believe
> I did my full share of the work of managing an oar on the raft, and
> preventing it from following the bad example of several other rafts
> which lost their heads and scattered their bones along the banks of
> the turbulent river.

Student dissatisfaction at a New York work-study institution of higher learning, Oneida, had led to a walkout; two dozen Oneida students, recruited by their classmate and *de facto* leader Theodore Weld, followed the Stanton brothers to Lane. The Oneidans, like Augustus Wattles, were attracted to Lane largely because it offered a manual labor curriculum by which poorer students could work three hours a day and defray their education costs. Students could work in the farming, mechanical, coopering, or cabinet-making departments, but the print shop with its six presses would become their favorite.

Theodore Weld was not just a student leader from Oneida. He had actually been commissioned by the Tappan brothers to scout for a suitable location for a school that would combine theology and manual labor education. After a year tour, Weld recommended Lane to the Tappans. Although Lewis Tappan preferred Rochester, Weld believed that the future of Christian missionary work lay in the West; thusly, the Tappans endorsed the Cincinnati site.

Weld's tour experiences and his conversations with Southern slaveholders and Northern intellectuals had converted him to the idea that the slaves must be freed immediately. Weld converted Arthur and then Lewis Tappan to Garrisonian immediatism. Weld exerted great influence on the Tappans. Lewis Tappan first met him at Oneida, where Lewis' young sons had been enrolled. Weld had converted the boys to Christianity. Since that time, Lewis and Arthur Tappan kept Weld close. They not only funded his tour, but offered him first a ministry and later a professorship at Lane, which he declined. Although Weld—an untidy man with unruly dark hair and disheveled clothes—was officially just a member of the Lane student body, the Tappans accorded him so much power that he and the "Oneida Boys" advised the Board of Trustees as to faculty appointments.

Lane Theological Seminary, situated in the secluded village of Walnut Hills above Cincinnati, was so new at the opening of the fall semester of 1833 that the campus was made up of only one main brick building and a few smaller, scattered structures not yet completed. The one hundred students were housed in raw log cabins in a clearing dotted by fresh stumps. President Beecher's two-story brick house stood in a grove of oak trees on the Seminary's vast acreage. Beecher's study was on the ground floor. From the study's outside door, a path led across the driveway to the gate in the Seminary fence, convenient for the president, the students, and the faculty to come and go with ease. Weld trod that path often to talk with Dr. Beecher; they sometimes chatted well into the early morning hours.

There was every reason that Lane Theological Seminary would become the premiere school in the West for training young Christian evangelists. It boasted both financial security and leadership. The reputation of the faculty, which included the Biblical scholars Professor Calvin E. Stowe of Massachusetts and John Morgan of New York, attracted a student body of pious and capable men—from the North and the South—eager to be educated, to go out and preach the Gospel.

These were not your average college students. Of the forty men in the theology department, thirty were over the age of twenty-six. Most were college graduates. Nine of these were in their thirties. One had practiced medicine for ten years. Six were married. Thus, being mature, independent, and intelligent, these students were not easily restricted by authoritarian figures. When they developed an intense dislike for Professor Thomas J. Biggs, the professor of ecclesiastical history, for example, the students boycotted his lectures. Dr. Beecher had to negotiate a settlement, persuading the students to attend Biggs' lectures once a week, with the understanding that he and Professor Stowe would teach the rest of Biggs' classes.

Dr. Beecher said that Weld, 29, "took the lead of the whole institution. The young men...thought he was a god." At her brother George's spring 1833 examination for the ministry, Harriet noted Weld's restlessness:

> Over in the pew opposite to us...is Theodore Weld, all awake, nodding from side to side and scarce keeping still a minute together.

Slavery—the most pressing social issue of the day—was of intense interest to the Lane students. While most Northerners accepted slavery as an unpleasant fact, those who actively opposed it generally joined the local Colonization Society. A large Colonization Society had been formed at Lane, of which almost all the students and the faculty, and all but one of the twenty-five members of the Board of Trustees were members. Dr. Beecher was a warm friend of the Colonization Society. Colonizationists wanted America to become a white nation.

CHAPTER 11

Lydia Maria Child Follows Her Heart

Lydia Maria Child" (ca. 1865)

I n August of 1833, before the first semester of Lane Seminary was underway, *The Boston Post* advertised the publication of a new book, *An Appeal in Favor of that Class of Americans Called Africans*, written by the famous author Lydia Maria Child of Boston. Child, who went by her middle name, Maria, yet pronounced it Ma-RYE-a, had thrown caution to the wind in aligning herself with the abolition movement. Her book's title alone was a shocker; few other whites thought of the "Africans" as "Americans." *An Appeal* was a real departure in subject matter for Child, as the reading public associated her with instruction manuals for mothers and her monthly periodical for children called *The Juvenile Miscellany*. Child, through her reading of Garrison's articles in *The Liberator*, had become a fierce advocate for the abolition of slavery. In *An Appeal*, Child echoed Garrison's call for immediate emancipation with no compensation for slaveholders. Child dedicated the book to Rev. Samuel J. May. Child's *Appeal* was the second anti-slavery work printed in book form, the first being *Letters on American Slavery* by Rev. John Rankin of Ripley, Ohio.

In Chapter V of the *Appeal*, Child took aim at the colonizationists:

> I object to the Colonization Society, because it tends to put public opinion asleep, on a subject where it needs to be wide awake.

The American Colonization Society was entrenched in church and state. Southern legislatures endorsed and sometimes funded it. It was the only emancipationist organization tolerated in the South. It was considered a "most glorious of Christian enterprises." Churches set aside one Sunday every year for a sermon and offering for the Society, which employed traveling agents and published *The African Repository* monthly. In *An Appeal*, Child presented a scathing critique of the impractical scheme:

> The [Colonization] Society has been in operation more than fifteen years, during which it has transported between two and three thousand *free* people of color. There are in the United States two million of slaves, and three hundred thousand free blacks; and their numbers are increasing at the rate of seventy thousand annually….While one hundred and fifty *free* blacks have been sent to Africa in a *year*, two hundred *slaves* have been born in a *day*. To keep the evil just where it is, seventy thousand a year must be transported. How many ships, and how many millions of money, would it require to do this?…And if such a great number could be

removed annually, how would the poor fellows subsist?...

And why should they be removed? Labor is greatly needed, and we are glad to give good wages for it. We encourage emigration from all parts of the world; why is it not good policy, as well as good feeling, to improve [educate] the colored people, and pay them for the use of their faculties?...

As for the removal of blacks from this country, the real fact is this; the slave States are very desirous to get rid of their troublesome surplus of colored population....Neither the planters nor the Colonization Society seem to ask what *right* we have to remove people from the places where they have been born and brought up....Africa is no more their native country than England is ours....

Up until this time, Child, age 31, had enjoyed unparalleled literary success. With *An Appeal*, she braced herself for some public censure, but the uproar was thunderous, not just in the South but in liberal Boston. Parents canceled subscriptions to *The Juvenile Miscellany*, which folded shortly, editors shunned her, and the Boston Athenaeum revoked her library privileges. Massachusetts politician James T. Austin hurled *An Appeal* out the window—not deigning to touch it—with a pair of tongs. Particularly galling to her fellow Bostonians was her indictment in the book of Northern racism. Clergymen denounced her from the pulpit. Her brother James, who had named one of his daughters Lydia Maria, turned hostile, as he detested either "n----rs" or n----r-lovers." Friends cut her dead on the street. Bookstores would not stock her books; her book sales plummeted. As she was the family breadwinner, this was exceedingly painful.

Abolitionists, though, praised *An Appeal* for the extensive research written in a style that was both simple and elegant and were confident that anyone who read the book could not help but be converted to immediatism. Child was propelled to the forefront of the abolitionist movement.

The same month of *An Appeal's* release, the United Kingdom passed an act making enslavement officially illegal in every province and freed the last remaining enslaved people in Canada. This news shook up the South. Americans recognized Great Britain as the leading power in the world. Mexico had abolished slavery in 1829. That left the United States as the only slaveholding country in North America.

Then, in December, sixty Americans met in Philadelphia at the Adelphi Building and formed the American Anti-Slavery Society. Arthur Tappan was elected president. The meeting was attended by Black and white men and four white women, including Quaker minister Lucretia Coffin Mott. The women were allowed to attend but not to sign the constitution nor to join the organization. This led to the formation of female societies. The Declaration of Sentiments, drafted by Garrison, was based on the spirit of the Declaration of Independence, whose doctrine was that all men are created in equality. The Society's stated purpose was the immediate, complete, and uncompensated emancipation of the slaves and its recognition of equal rights for Blacks. The Society sought "mighty agents who will electrify the mass wherever they move—and they must move on no small scale." The founders condemned slavery as a moral sin.

CHAPTER 12

The Lane Debates Unfold

B y January 1834, Weld, Stanton, and other Lane students felt they had recruited enough students to the abolition side for Weld to call for a student debate on slavery. Weld had no intention, however, of holding a true and open debate on the pros and cons of anti-slavery. He knew that in order for abolition to gain support, the colonization scheme had to be discredited. After consulting with the Lane faculty and trustees, Dr. Beecher advised postponement of such a debate while also assuring his benefactor Arthur Tappan and the students that the students would have the right to freely express their opinions. Weld ignored Beecher's suggestion, forging ahead with scheduling and publicizing a series of debates.

For eighteen nights beginning in early February, 1834, students, faculty, townspeople, and eminent special guests packed the Prayer Hall at Lane. Dr. Gamaliel Bailey, who lectured weekly on physiology at Lane, had been invited. Rev. John Rankin from nearby Ripley, the famous author of *Letters on American Slavery*, requested an invitation from Weld. Rev. James Dickey, another Ohio minister from the same presbytery as Rankin, the man who had witnessed Edward Stone's slave coffle on the Kentucky road, rode sixty-five miles on horseback to attend. Dr. Lyman Beecher, George, and Catharine Beecher attended some nights, as possibly did Harriet Beecher. The entire faculty showed up, except the unpopular Biggs, who refused to attend.

If the audience expected fireworks, they were to be disappointed. The event was courteous and peaceful, more like a revival meeting.

The debate questions posed to the students were:

1st: "Ought the people of the Slaveholding States to abolish Slavery immediately?

2nd: "Are the doctrines, tendencies, and measures of the American Colonization Society, and the influence of its principal supporters such as render it worthy of the patronage of the Christian public?

Weld and Stanton spoke of the sin of owning and enslaving another person and taking away his or her liberty. The only way to effectively end such a brute injustice, Stanton believed, was to persuade slaveholders to free their slaves "with the blessing of God, to be reached and influenced by facts and arguments." They presented authenticated facts gleaned from documents from the Colonization Society, Child's *An Appeal*, Rankin's *Letters on American Slavery*, and other sources. As theologians, they called for Christians to be true to Christ—to treat the poor and oppressed as one would treat oneself. They called for Americans to be true to the fundamentals of American liberty.

William T. Allan, son of a distinguished Presbyterian minister who had grown up in the midst of slavery in Alabama, explained why he supported immediate emancipation:

> At our house, it is so common to hear the screams from a neigh-boring plantation, that we think nothing of it. The overseer of this plantation told me one day that he laid a young woman over a log and beat her so severely that she was soon delivered of a dead child....

Allan said that on plantations where slavery is practiced, "cruelty is the rule, and kindness is the exception." (After his speech at Lane was publicized, Allan's former Alabama neighbor promised to slit Allan's throat if he returned there.)

Andrew Benton from Missouri recounted the story of "a young woman who was generally very badly treated," and who:

…after receiving a more severe whipping than usual, ran away. In a few days, she came back and was sent into the field to work. At this time, the garment next to her skin was stiff like a scab from the running sores made by the whipping. Towards night, she told her master that she was sick and wished to go to the house. She went; and as soon as she reached it, laid down on the floor exhausted. The mistress asked her what the matter was? She made no reply. She asked again; but received no answer. 'I'll see,' said she, 'if I can't make you speak.' So taking the tongs, she heated them red hot and put them upon the bottoms of her feet; then upon her legs and body; and finally in a rage took hold of her throat. This had the desired effect. The poor girl faintly whispered, 'Oh, missee, don't—I am most gone,' and then expired. The woman yet lives there and owns slaves.

Former slave James Bradley, the only Black student at Lane (having been recruited by Weld), spoke of being captured as a toddler in Guinea in 1810 (two years after the international slave trade was ruled illegal in America), taken on an overland journey, and put on a ship bound for America. He said, "The soul-destroyers tore me from my mother's arms." He brought his listeners to tears with his tale of how, after toiling in the nighttime for over eight years and saving money, he had purchased his freedom from bondage for $700 by pursuing many endeavors, one of which was the sale of horse collars he braided from corn husks and sold for fifty cents apiece. "I could weave one in about eight hours; and generally, I took time enough from my sleep to make two collars in the course of a week."

The Southern planters were fond of saying that they were kind to their slaves, that their slaves were happy. Bradley shook his head:

I do not believe that there ever was a slave, who did not long for liberty. I know very well that slave-owners take a great deal of pains to make the people in the free states believe that the slaves are happy; but, I know, likewise, that I was never acquainted with a slave, however well he was treated, who did not long to be free....

The students from New York and New England were profoundly distressed to hear reports of beatings, whippings, and tortures perpetrated upon slaves in a Christian land and felt deep guilt. No student spoke on behalf of slavery.

A vote was taken at the end of the ninth evening on the first question. With the exception of four or five students who were as yet undecided on the matter and abstained from voting, every student voted for the immediate emancipation of slaves in the slaveholding states.

Colonization was the topic for the next nine evenings. Before the discussion, it was commonly believed that the Colonization Society was in favor of the gradual emancipation of slaves, when, in fact, it had nothing at all to do with liberty. Its true intent was to deport the free Black population from the United States. Many of the students at the debates, and many right-feeling Northerners and some Southerners, thought of colonization as a humanitarian effort, one that offered free Blacks voluntary immigration to a place where they might enjoy racial equality and education since the chance of this happening in America seemed an impossibility. The crowd was surprised to learn the hollowness of the colonization plan. The conditions in Liberia were dire, illness was epidemic—close to half the arrivals in Liberia died from tropical diseases—education and religious instruction were nonexistent, and many of the free Blacks arriving there had been coerced into leaving America. The Colony was bankrupt. In truth, the Colonization ideology both supported and perpetuated slavery. It envisioned an America in which only the whites were free and all Blacks were slaves.

A vote was taken on the second question. Only one student voted in support of the American Colonization Society. He was the son of Robert Finley, an agent of the Colonization Society. Abolition won and colonization lost. Right away, the students formed their own anti-slavery society, the object of which was the:

> ...immediate emancipation of the whole colored race within the United States; the emancipation of the slave from the oppression of the master, the emancipation of the free colored man from the oppression of public sentiment, and the elevation of both to an intellectual, moral, and political equality with the whites.

Student Augustus Wattles sent his debate notes to anti-slavery newspapers in Boston and New York. As this was one of the first public discussions on slavery and one of the first anti-slavery societies established on a college campus, the report went speedily throughout the land.

CHAPTER 13

The Cincinnati Sisters Arrive

Following the debate, Lane student Augustus Wattles felt a strong anti-slavery impulse. He met with Dr. Beecher:

> Here in Cincinnati are three thousand colored people, most of them in great ignorance. Last night I could not sleep. My present duty is plain, which is to take a dismission [leave] from the seminary, throw myself among these…outcasts, establish schools, and work in all practicable ways for their elevation.

Wattles and Dr. Beecher wept together, Dr. Beecher saying, "Go, my son, and may God be with you."

The Black population of Cincinnati, most of whom were dirt poor and lived in ramshackle housing, were barred from attending its public schools and institutions of higher learning yet were required to pay city taxes that supported public schools for whites. Any education Blacks received was done discreetly in Black homes for fear of mob violence. Into this void stepped Wattles and his fellow student Marius R. Robinson, who also took a leave.

Wattles and Robinson moved out of the Seminary and went down to live and work in the city among the Black community. The Cincinnati papers published the students' declaration of principles, one article of which proclaimed their belief in "social intercourse according to character, irrespective of color." Dr. Beecher cautioned Weld about the danger of putting this principle into practice:

If you want to teach colored schools, I can fill your pockets with money; but if you will visit in colored families, and walk with them in the streets, you will be overwhelmed [defeated completely].

On March 1, 1834, Wattles opened a school in one of the Black churches. There were so many students that Wattles had to stagger class times. His Lane friends volunteered to help with the teaching load and raised hundreds of dollars among themselves to establish a library, a reading room, lyceum lectures, Bible classes, and day, night, and Sunday schools.

It was often said that, though Cincinnati stands in the North, it turns its face to the South, where across the river lay the hills of Kentucky, a slave state. Cincinnati was a regional market for Virginia planters, Kentucky farmers, and Louisiana merchants, serving as well as a fuel stop for steamboats hauling their shackled gangs of slaves to the New Orleans market. While there was a fear among the local merchants that those Southerner customers, angry to learn that anti-slavery activity was taking root in Cincinnati, might take their business to another river town, the truth is that the Cincinnati citizens were more upset that whites were mixing with Blacks on a basis of equality. Many hated living among free Blacks. Blacks were shunned unless they were needed to perform menial tasks. Ohio, though considered a free state, was only nominally free for Blacks and had passed Black Codes so restrictive that many Blacks went north to Canada to experience liberty.

Proslavery mobs began to gather outside the church school organized by Wattles and Robinson. The instructors were forced to move their classes to the house of a wealthy Black man, Baker Jones.

In a letter to Arthur Tappan, Theodore Weld boasted of the men and their charity work in the city. What was lacking, though, wrote Weld, was a female school. The Tappans enthusiastically placed an appeal in the *New-York Evangelist* for volunteer female teachers to move to Cincinnati to teach persons of color, a majority of whom had been slaves and purchased their freedom. When Susan E. Lowe, 22, of Clinton, New York, read the appeal, her heart was stirred to action. She left her studies at the Young Ladies' Domestic Seminary and, with three companions, traveled eight hundred miles to Cincinnati at the Tappans' expense. Challenging the social norms of women at the time, they traveled without male escort and not to meet a husband or fiancé, or attend a family meeting. Independent movement of women was deemed unacceptable. Women were to be under the control of a man or performing domestic duties. Women and men were supposed to inhabit separate spheres.

Emily Rakestraw, a Quaker, joined them from New Garden, Ohio, going against her parents' wishes. These female teachers became known as the "Cincinnati Sisters." In exchange for their teaching, the Cincinnati Sisters had their room, board, and clothing funded by the Tappans.

Separated from their families, arriving in a strange city, the Sisters looked for lodgings. Many boardinghouse keepers refused to have them under their roofs, saying they had no accommodation for "'N----r' Teachers." To their good fortune, the Sisters met Mrs. Cleaveland, who welcomed them into her boardinghouse. Three of the resident boarders tried to oust the Sisters, but Mrs. Cleaveland backed the Sisters, and the complainers moved out. The Sisters moved freely among the Black population, teaching their girls, visiting in their homes, eating with them and, ultimately, when Mrs. Cleaveland moved away, *sleeping* under their roofs. This suggestion of *physical intimacy* caused many ears to tingle. A friend recalled that "Mr. Wattles and the lady teachers were daily hissed and cursed, oaths and threats; filth and offal [animal parts] were often thrown at them…."

In June, Augustus Wattles was seen walking a Black lady to a church meeting. Articles in the newspaper criticized the students for self-righteousness, advising them to attend to "their business," which is study, and to leave social reform to those more qualified. Another writer to the *Cincinnati Journal* stated that God had ordained the separation of the races.

Wattles and the Sisters were not deterred by proslavery opposition as they found their work so rewarding; Emeline Bishop wrote Weld that her students were "leaving off bad habits, forming good ones, and are twisting themselves most closely around my heart." In the same letter, Susan Lowe added that, "[w]e make many visits and very frequent calls and are treated with great cordiality and kindness by all our coloured friends." To her great dismay, Sister Phebe Mathews discovered that some of the abolitionists working with her in the Black schools were visibly prejudiced against their Black students. These "half-hearted abolitionists" were willing to elevate Black people through education and religion, but they could not be made to love them and treat them as their social equals. Mathews wrote Weld:

> I said to Br[other] Wattles the other evening I shall be glad when Mr[s?]. Mahan, Mrs. Gridley, Misses Dewey, Fletcher, etc., etc., are gone, for none of them are more than half-hearted abolitionists and I cannot endure to be shackled as they wish me to be....I love these dear sisters but they do wish us to stoop so often to prejudice, to shake hands and say how do you do to it. And they feel so bad if perchance we lay our hands on a curly head, or kiss a coloured face.

The schools were a great success. By July, Augustus Wattles was supervising four schools with five teachers and a total of two hundred students. The enterprise was supported by funds from Arthur Tappan, Black community leaders, Lane students, and Elnathan Kemper.

CHAPTER 14

Harriet Goes East

Harriet was in high spirits. Catharine Beecher had closed the Western Female Institute for the summer. Harriet, traveling with Mary Dutton, was going back east for the first time in close to two years. She would visit her grandmother Foote in Connecticut and, in late August, see her brother Henry graduate from Amherst in Massachusetts. They would take a stagecoach from Cincinnati to Toledo, Ohio, board a Lake Erie steamer to Buffalo, New York, see Niagara Falls, then, via Albany, New York, ride a stage into New England.

Harriet needed a life change. She had turned twenty-three in June. Her brothers were already calling her an "old maid," as she, like her sister Catharine, was unmarried. At her age in that period, it was expected of her to find a husband or settle for a career—in teaching, which was the only real profession offered to a respectable and educated young white woman. Harriet, who mostly kept to herself and was not famed for her brilliant conversation, did not have any romantic prospects. Unlike Catharine, Harriet wanted to marry. Harriet had set her sights on more than one eligible young man in the Semi-Colon Club. Yet she had stood by *in silent but excruciating pain* as, one by one, these prospects evaporated; she had listened bravely as the bachelors announced their engagements to other young ladies.

Given the separation of the women's and men's spheres at the time, there was little opportunity for sophisticated women and men to mingle outside of Sunday church, Monday night Semi-Colon meetings, prim tea parties, and the occasional house party where the women congregated in one part of the room and the men in the other, and sometimes were forced to mix awkwardly in cheery singsongs around the pianoforte. Even the men did the marketing. Cincinnati had no public parks. Society frowned upon women moving about outside the interior of their homes, which was their prescribed sphere. Although Harriet and Mary were going East unaccompanied by a man, society would not frown upon such a journey, as an exception was made if the woman in question was traveling on family business, as Harriet was.

Harriet continued to write little sketches and letters and longed to make a living as a "literary woman," a profession open to only a talented few. Still, Catharine's neglect of the school in favor of her incessant travel to raise school funds, her socializing among the Cincinnati elite, and her writing (and some say, plagiarizing) spelling textbooks and articles on education left too many of the school responsibilities to Harriet. The Western Female Institute was small and struggling.

Relieved to be departing Cincinnati ahead of the July summer heat and the certainty of the return of the summer cholera, Harriet and Mary Dutton were delighted to be on their way east in a stagecoach bound for Toledo. As was her nature, Harriet eavesdropped upon her fellow passengers. One was a chivalrous Irishman who was always popping up to give his seat to a lady. She and Mary watched as this quiet gentleman was, unfortunately, drawn into an unpleasant conversation with a blowhard. Scarcely anything happened to Harriet that didn't find its way into her writing. In a letter to her cousin Elizabeth Lyman, Harriet described this second, disagreeable passenger as a man:

> …whose mode of reasoning consists in repeating the same sentence at regular intervals as long as you choose to answer it. This man, who was finally convinced that negroes were black, used it as an

irrefragible [*sic*] [undisputed] argument…that they might just as well be slaves as anything else, and so he proceeded till all the philanthrophy [goodwill] of our friend [the Irish gentleman] was roused, and he sprung up all lively and oratorical and gesticulatory and indignant to my heart's content. I like to see a quiet man than can be roused.

The abolition controversy was not confined to Cincinnati. In the first week of July, anti-abolitionist rioters had gone on a rampage throughout New York City, destroying churches, homes, and businesses and attacking Blacks. One such attack occurred on Lewis Tappan's Rose Street home. Spurred on by "well-dressed merchants," the ruffians smashed windows and doors, demolished the interior, dragged prized artwork and furniture into the street, piled it high, and set it on fire. Throngs stoned Arthur Tappan's store but were driven off by his employees, armed with muskets and guarded by a hundred watchmen. The crowds had been spurred, in part, by rumors spread by colonizationist leader James Webster Webb in his *Courier and Enquirer* that Arthur Tappan had divorced his wife and married a Black woman. The truth was that Arthur Tappan, a member of the Rev. Samuel Cox's Laight Street Church, had invited Samuel Cornish, a Black man, to sit with him in his pew at Sunday services. There was a tremendous row among the congregation; Rev. Cox, in his attempt to settle things down, actually made matters worse, arguing that Jesus was probably dark-skinned like Samuel Cornish—"of a dark Syrian hue."

Dr. Beecher assured Harriet that the abolitionist controversy—at least in Cincinnati—would soon blow over once Lane was dismissed for the twelve-week summer vacation on July 19. The trustees were also ready for the spring semester to end; they had been bombarded with hate mail from citizens opposing the students' missionary work among the city's Blacks. The trustees worried that the Seminary would be burned to the ground. The trustees held a meeting with the student body, making crystal clear to them that social intercourse with Black people was going against the public sentiment. The students were instructed not to move too fast in their experiment. Their words fell on deaf ears. Soon after, the trustees reported that:

> The next excitement was caused by a visit paid to the seminary by several female colored persons, in a carriage, and the marked atten- tion said to have been paid to them by the students....Sometime after this, a new excitement was created by the walking of the instructor, who boarded in a colored family, with a colored female to the seminary or its vicinity, and returning in like manner.

Finally, the summer break arrived. All but twenty of the students departed the campus. The entire faculty—except Professor Biggs— left. Harriet and Mary were on their way east, as were Dr. Beecher and Catharine, to raise school funds. Certain the storm had calmed, Dr. Beecher turned over running the Seminary to the trustees and left Walnut Hills.

CHAPTER 15

Biggs Gets His Revenge

In the first week of August, a vengeful eye observed Weld and some other students in the third hall, with their sleeves rolled up, surrounded by paper, paste and ink, preparing for the mail some thousands of copies of a "Letter on Colonization." This groundbreaking letter, which electrified abolitionists nationwide, was written by James G. Birney, Esq., a former slaveholder, in which he renounced colonizationism and declared his conversion to abolition. Someone reported the students' activity to the Board of Trustees.

Professor Biggs then published a letter in the *Cincinnati Journal* favoring colonization and opposing the discussion of the slavery question at theological schools. Weld's response to a similar editorial had been that, "He who would preach in the nineteenth century, must know the nineteenth century."

Meanwhile, Lyman Beecher, now in Boston, delivered a caustic sermon on August 10, 1834, decrying Irish immigration and the influx of Catholics. He offended Westerners, too, preaching the need to save the West through Eastern influence. The next day, a rabble sacked and burned the (Catholic) Ursuline Convent in Charlestown, Massachusetts. Although the arsonists had not heard Beecher's speech, he and others had been, for some time, actively stirring up anti-Catholic, anti-immigrant sentiment, leading to the charge of Beecher's having incited the mob to attack the convent.

Back in Cincinnati, in late August, things with Lane were heating up again. A carriage of Black women visited the Seminary, purportedly for a picnic. Cincinnati was never so convulsed. Weld and two Board members wrote to Dr. Beecher imploring him to hurry home as the Board was planning to take drastic actions against the students.

The Board did not wait for Beecher's return before they took steps. In its view, the crime committed by the students was their offense against public sentiment. Lane Seminary depended upon funds from people on both sides of the slavery issue. Any association of the Seminary with anti-slavery might discourage Southern planters from sending their sons to Lane. The Board drafted recommended rules to abolish the students' anti-slavery society, outlaw all discussions of slavery, even in private, and reserving the right to expel any student without giving a reason. They fired Professor Morgan, an abolitionist, and made plans to expel Weld. Professor Stowe, whose wife Eliza had died in early August, abandoned his support of the students and sided with the Board.

Although the resolutions had not yet been adopted, the Board ordered copies to be made and distributed as a warning to the students and then leaked the resolutions to the local press. They appeared in the *Cincinnati Gazette* on August 30 and in the *Cincinnati Journal* on September 5. The story was then picked up first in reform and religious newspapers and then by the mainstream press. The local dispute now became a national spectacle. On September 10, the Board turned the students out of their dorm rooms and locked up the Seminary until the next term began in October.

Fully apprised of this situation, Beecher, instead of hurrying home, stayed away. Trustee Asa Mahan, who sided with the student body, wrote Beecher to return immediately "to save the school from dismantlement." Beecher did start west, but when he reached Columbus, Ohio, he lingered there for several days, then turned north instead of south, visited Granville, Ohio, and returned to the East to continue his fund-raising campaign for a new chapel, a library, and an endowment for a professorship at Lane.

On October 6, at the beginning of the fall term, Beecher had still not returned and the Board adopted their resolutions. The students asked the Board if they could discuss the new rules imposed upon them, which was denied.

By the time Beecher returned in mid-October, the matter was settled. Disingenuously, he wrote, "When I got back, I found all in a flurry. If I had arrived a little sooner, I should have saved them [the students]; but it was too late." He neither opposed the Board nor did he stand up for the students. The students would not compromise their principles in order to stay at the school, and on October 21, most of them walked out. About a dozen of them established a short-term informal school in Cumminsville, with Dr. Gamaliel Bailey serving as an advisor and instructor. Many of the Lane Rebels enrolled at one of the nearby Ohio colleges, Oberlin and Western Reserve; some went to Yale Divinity School. Weld became a full-time agent of the American Anti-Slavery Society.

When Harriet returned to Cincinnati that fall, her brothers, Henry Ward and Charles, followed, enrolling at Lane. The student body had dispersed. Of the one hundred-eight students from the previous year, only five—plus the two new Beecher men—remained.

The Tappans were furious. They cut off funding to Lane and transferred their support to Oberlin, which agreed to accept students regardless of race. Lane could not win. In anti-slavery circles, the Seminary earned the reputation of suppressing free speech. Proslavery advocates, on the other hand, regarded the Seminary as "a cauldron of radicalism and race mixing."

Rev. John Rankin sided with the students:

The history of the world shows that public sentiment has been oftener wrong than right. Many of the greatest enormities ever witnessed on earth have been sanctioned by public sentiment.... The object of the students in their society was to...change what they deemed wrong in public sentiment. This they and all others had a right to do. Without such right there could be no public reform....Better far for the Seminary and the honest religion, the mob had torn the building to the ground.

Henry liked the relaxed atmosphere of the West and the pretty girls he met at church. Buoyant and flirtatious, Henry liked a good time; his fiancée Eunice Bullard was still back east, where she would remain for almost three more years. As he was just settling in at the Seminary, Henry dearly wanted the Lane Debate matter to die down, but Catharine kept it alive. She rushed to her father's defense, particularly targeting Judge James Hall who ridiculed Beecher's Boston snobbish anti-Western remarks in the December issue of the *Western Monthly Magazine*. Catharine began a vicious campaign to exclude Hall from elite society. She thought her New England background made her morally and intellectually superior in Western society, declaring to Edward King's niece that she, Catharine, "set the fashion in Cincinnati." Her attempt to assert control over polite society failed miserably; she succeeded in alienating many, including local families who might have sent their daughters and their money to the Misses Beecher's Western Female Institute.

In April 1835, Weld and other Lane Rebels and members of local anti-slavery societies established the Ohio State Anti-Slavery Society. In May, Dr. Bailey, Marius Robinson, and others established the Cincinnati Anti-Slavery Society. The Lane Rebels fanned out across Ohio, lecturing on abolition and energizing Ohio men and women to found local anti-slavery societies.

Lyman Beecher had not seen the last of his troubles. Before 1834 drew to a close, his archrival in Cincinnati, the Rev. Joshua Wilson, an Old School Presbyterian, would charge him with heresy. This new kerfuffle proved the downfall of the family's social standing in Cincinnati. Cincinnati was tired of being continually at the center of a national controversy. It seemed to Cincinnati that the "fabulous Beechers," who had been met by a delegation of citizens when they first arrived, had turned out to be nothing but Eastern troublemakers.

CHAPTER 16

Harriet Goes to Ripley

Before the student exodus at Lane, when Harriet Beecher had still been in the East, she received a letter from her stepmother informing her that Professor Calvin Stowe's wife, Eliza, had died from cholera on August 6, 1834.

After the funeral, Mrs. Beecher took Calvin to their house where, she reported, "we have all administered to his comfort as we could." When Harriet returned to Walnut Hills, she joined this benevolent effort. Harriet's Christianity was soft, not harsh like her father's. She did not judge Calvin's reaction of pain, confusion, and anger as evidence that he was not submitting to God's will and was, therefore, a poor Christian. Rather, Harriet believed that "[w]hen the heart-strings are all suddenly cut, it is...a physical impossibility to feel faith or resignation....and though we may submit to God it is rather by a constant painful effort than by a sweet attraction."

Harriet's gentle acceptance allowed Calvin to openly express his feelings to her. They grew close. They began appearing at Semi-Colon meetings as a couple. In October, during the Lane crisis, Harriet and Calvin—with the black band of mourning around his hat—accompanied Lyman Beecher to a meeting of the Presbyterian clergy in Ripley, Ohio, a river town sixty miles east of Cincinnati, where they were received as houseguests of Rev. John Rankin and his wife, Jean. The whole Rankin family was actively abolitionist. Their real-life adventures made a lasting impression on Harriet.

In addition to John's abolitionist preaching and writing, the Rankins were conductors on the Underground Railroad, and their house was a station in the network. They lived on sixty-five acres of thick, forested land in a house on a hill that stood five hundred forty feet above the Ohio River.

The family home was a modest story-and-a-half brick dwelling with a narrow porch running along the side facing the river. From this perch, they could see nearly five miles of the winding river that separated Ohio from the land of slavery. Importantly, they could see horsemen, slave catchers, coming up the hill to the house in time to prepare for trouble. Behind the house was a log barn with a hidden cellar beneath the hay to hide runaways. Signaling to runaway slaves that their house was a safe haven, the Rankins placed a lantern in the front window every night. A slave from Mason County, Kentucky, imagined the Rankins' "Liberty Hill" beacon to have been a "big lighthouse in [the] yard, about thirty feet high....It always meant freedom for a slave if he could get to this light." The Rankins might shelter as many as twelve fugitives at a time, split between the house and the barn. Jean Rankin fed them and sewed their clothes.

In the Ripley area, fighting slavery was part of daily life. The anti-slavery crusade was often a "family business," having involved some-times two to three generations in a family. Abolitionists married other abolitionists. Families were large and children were raised to know which families had a concealed room beneath the hearth, a cellar in the barn, a hay wagon with a secret compartment, a fast horse, a safe attic, or a proslavery neighbor. Thomas Collins and his wife hid runaways in the coffins Thomas made in his workshop. Free Blacks strengthened the Ripley line, notably wagoneer John D. Hudson of the Gist Settlement, who blew on a conch shell to alert neighbors to slave catchers, and "Aunt Polly" Jackson of Africa, Ohio, who tricked slave catchers into thinking she was a harmless, weak, old lady while concealing a butcher knife under a cloth draped over her shoulder and carrying pots of boiling water she hurled at the men stealers who lurked at night.

Fugitives arriving at the Rankins' house would then go by wagon or on horseback to Red Oak where the Gillilands or other families would shelter them and pass them along the chain to one of the nearby free Black settlements or even further north. Plans changed according to the specific circumstances of the night. Sometimes conductors sent coded notes in advance to give opinions as to the safest route for their human freight.

Helping fugitive slaves was a risky business. It was against the law and it made slave owners vengeful. Kentucky slave owner Pete Driscoll used to boast that he made his slaves so very happy that they would never run away. "Not even 'Uncle Johnny' [Rankin] whom all n----rs like, could persuade my n----s to leave me," he once said. He grew so bold in this fantasy that, after his slaves had done their work, he allowed them to move about at will. He even sent them to Ripley on errands. In Ripley, Driscoll's slaves made contact with the underground and helped slaves escape from nearby Kentucky plantations. This, of course, infuriated the Kentucky slave owners who had lost slaves, especially when they learned that it had been Driscoll's slaves who helped their slaves get away. These irate planters pressured Driscoll to sell his slaves downriver. Before he could do so, his slaves got word and fled across the river to Ripley and, with the help of their Underground Railroad contacts, disappeared into Ohio. Driscoll chased them all the way to Sandusky, where he watched helplessly from the dock as they boarded a boat and sailed across Lake Erie to freedom in Canada.

CHAPTER 17

Lowry Rankin Boards the Uncle Sam

A month after Calvin, Harriet, and Lyman Beecher visited Ripley, Theodore Weld preached at Rankin's Presbyterian Church there, speaking for eleven consecutive nights, hoping to stimulate and organize anti-slavery activity. He was now a paid agent of the American Anti-Slavery Society, launching his yearlong mission to abolitionize Ohio. He asked his white crowd to imagine being enslaved:

> Every man knows that slavery is a curse. Whoever denies this, his lips libel his heart. Try him; clank the chains in his ears; and tell them they are for him; give him an hour to prepare his wife and children for a life of slavery; bid him make haste and get ready their necks for the yoke, and their wrists for the coffle chains, then look at his pale lips and trembling knees, and you have Nature's testimony against slavery.

Weld was up against Southerners preaching that slavery was ordained by God and that the Bible supported slavery. They quoted Leviticus 25:44:

> Thy bondmen [slaves] and thy bondmaids which thou shalt have, shall be of the heathen [unChristian] that are round about you;

of them shall ye buy….And they shall be your possession. And ye shall take them as an inheritance for your children after you, to inherit them for a possession they shall be your bondmen forever.

The Rankins' oldest child, Adam "Lowry," 18, was impressed by Weld's conviction of purpose and eloquence. Lowry, too, had strong anti-slavery sentiments, but, to his parents' dismay, Lowry had no interest in following Weld or his father into the ministry. He had dropped out of school to learn carpentry. He had already spent eighteen months as an apprentice to a Scottish architect and carpenter, William McNish, who was Lowry's uncle through marriage. One year remained in Lowry's apprenticeship. Lowry spent most nights studying architectural drafting. During the day he built steamboat cabins.

Lowry was jubilant when he learned that the largest steamboat in the country, the *Uncle Sam*, had docked at the Ripley wharf in December 1834. The steamer was loading five hundred barrels of pork for transport to New Orleans. Carpenter McNish knew his staff was eager to walk *Uncle Sam's* decks and tour her cabins, so one day, he let them stop work at 4 p.m. to visit the big steamer.

Thrilled, Lowry Rankin inspected the ship's cabin, marveling at the fine workmanship of its floors, windows, and walls and letting his fingers run along the exquisite brass and woodwork. Then, he ventured below deck, ogling the engine room and venturing into the end of the boat, called "the aft." Lowry recalled:

[O]n going aft of the engine room an unexpected scene came to view. Two groups of slaves, about twenty-five in each, were chained to the sides of the deck, the men on my left and the women on my right. No seat or bed was provided; they were compelled to use the deck floor….

Farther from me at my right at the extreme end of the long chain was a woman, young, not more than twenty. She had a pretty face; it might with propriety be called beautiful. She had long, fine, wavy shiny black hair put up with care and taste, and she was as white as any woman of my acquaintance, requiring the closest scrutiny to detect the least touch of African blood. I said to myself, 'Can it be possible that she is a slave, bound for a Southern slave mart to stand on the auction block and be knocked down by some brutal auctioneer to the highest bidder?'

…As I leaned against a stanchion for support, I asked myself why let all my sympathies be expended upon that one woman. Were the women, her companions in slavery, though they be of a darker hue than she, any less the daughters of the Lord Almighty?…

I caught a fragment of a conversation between two men who were approaching. The words I heard were, 'Ain't she a beauty!' The men passed by me, scarcely noting my presence, and stopped in front of the woman I have just described. One of the men was coarse and hard-featured. He carried in his hand a small rawhide cane.…He was the owner of the slave and had the usual characteristics of the 'negro trader,' fond of whiskey, rough, profane and unchaste in conversation, brutal, and passionate in disposition. They were a class of men that were a product of slavery, dreaded by the slaves and despised by the slaveholders.…

The other was a tall, well-dressed young man.…Under proper influence he might be an honorable, moral man who would command the respect of the good. I gathered from the conversation that he was a single man, engaged in some business in New Orleans, and the son of a Southern planter. His conversation was free of profanity and obscenity.…I inferred from the first part of the conversation that he had some conscience about the propriety of the business in hand, the purchase of the woman.

I decided not to leave my post but to watch the transaction. The trader used the vilest language, proposing the woman as a mistress for the young man and insisting she was worth more than he asked, $2500, and swearing he could get $3000 for her in New Orleans….

All the time she had her face covered with her hands and was crying as if her heart would break. The other women were crying also, and more than one man muttered curses, and I saw clenched fists and angry eyes, all showing how helpless they felt to protect the woman. As the trader, with an oath, said, 'No more of that, you black sons of ---,' he struck the woman on the shoulder and ordered her to take her hands from her face and stop her crying or he would half kill her. She obeyed, and after a little more talk the young man offered $2000. This was rejected at this stage of the proceedings, and the trader played what might be called the last card in his game of debauchery. He asked the young man if he was the only occupant of his stateroom, receiving an affirmative reply. He then said, 'How fortunate. You have to go to your room by the door that opens on the deck, and no one will be the wiser, and you can have a splendid time. It will cost you nothing. I have paid her passage and bond.' The young man was evidently tempted but shook his head.

The trader then ordered the woman to unfasten the front of her dress. She declined, but a stroke on the shoulder brought a reluctant obedience; a second expedited the work. When done, her hands lingered, but pushing them away he exposed her bosom to view and induced the young man to feel of her breast, then of her thighs. By this time the young man was carried to the point of yielding, and, the money paid, the woman relieved of her chain, followed her new master to his room.

As I left the boat my indignation reached the boiling point over the wicked transaction and, lifting my right hand toward the heavens, I said aloud, 'My God helping me, there shall be a perpetual war between me and human slavery in this nation of which I am a member and I pray God I may never be persuaded to give up the fight until slavery is dead or the Lord calls me home.'

When the sun came up the next morning, Lowry knew he would no longer be content just to voice his abhorrence of slavery; he had to do something about it. Slavery had become real to him. Once he finished his carpentry apprenticeship, he would return to Ripley College, graduate, and then enter the ministry and, like Weld and his father, fight slavery with the determination to obliterate it.

CHAPTER 18

_____

The Birneys Cross the River

In October of 1835, native Southerners James and Agatha McDowell Birney, along with their five sons and baby, Florence, left their home in Danville, Kentucky, and crossed the Ohio River—the dividing line between the land of slavery and the land of liberty—to make their new home in Cincinnati. They had sold their farm and said their farewells. Birney accompanied on horseback the carriage in which his family traveled. Since May, when James announced his intention to begin the publication of an anti-slavery paper in Danville, the South had become a dangerous place for them. His denunciation of the Colonization Society and his embrace of immediate emancipation for the slaves caused such a social upheaval that local ladies berated him in the street. Birney's sons had been taunted by playmates. Birney could not find a single Kentucky legislator who believed that a slave was entitled to freedom. The Danville postmaster withheld Birney's mail and burned any correspondence he deemed inflammatory. Birney could not think of very many respectable men in Kentucky who would stand between him and a mob.

Birney, a former slaveholder who had freed his slaves, given up his lucrative law practice, and earned the animosity of friends, his sister, and his slaveholding father, was undaunted in his crusade to put an end to slavery, which he called "a monstrous moral wrong." He had been converted to the cause of immediate emancipation by the Lane Debates. Once it was plain he could not bring out his paper in Kentucky, Theodore Weld convinced Birney that Cincinnati was a safer place to start his abolition newspaper.

Once in Cincinnati, Birney, 43, plunged into furnishing the family home on the west side of Race Street, two doors above Eighth Street (buildings were still unnumbered), went about meeting people in the streets, and presented the family's letters of membership at the Sixth Street Presbyterian Church. He wrote and published a pamphlet in defense of abolitionists.

In the free state of Ohio, Birney expected to enjoy the rights accorded to him under the Constitution. Birney wanted to bring up his children away from the contaminating influence of the slave system that made white people lazy and act like aristocrats. Birney sent his sons James and William to Oberlin, where they accepted people of all races. Dion and David, of elementary school age, were sent to boarding school. George, at three-and-a-half, and Florence, less than a year old, stayed at home with Agatha, who was largely an invalid. She did not support her husband's abolitionist views and, in his opinion, failed in her support of him in the challenges it presented him. Such a home was "dreary and cheerless" for Birney.

Once settled, he called on Cincinnati friends, among them Salmon P. Chase, whose wife Kitty had just died two weeks after giving birth to their first child, Kate. Chase was guilt-ridden. Kitty had been deliriously ill and incoherent following Kate's birth but recovered sufficiently after a week to convince Salmon to travel to Philadelphia on business. Therefore, he was not at her bedside when she died. He blamed the doctors (one was Dr. Isaac Colby, Chase's brother-in-law) for her death. Suffering from fever, the doctors diagnosed Kitty with peritonitis. At Dr. Drake's urging, the doctors had drained fifty ounces of Kitty's blood in the belief that bleeding new mothers relieved the buildup of harmful body fluids. They had bled her to death.

Chase was deeply troubled for his dead wife's soul and where it had ended up, as he was not sure she had accepted Christ as her savior. This was a time when many Christians would sooner save a soul than a life. Although Kitty and Salmon had attended services at Beecher's Second Presbyterian Church, Kitty had been more of a socialite than a devotee, and she and her husband of less than two years had conversed so little on religion. Salmon, raised by his uncle, a distinguished Episcopal bishop, wrote in his diary his regrets for not having continually lectured Kitty and turned her into a true Christian. "But I procrastinated, and now she is gone."

The Birney family did not have to wait long before Cincinnati leaders made known the "public sentiment" in regard to an abolition newspaper being established in their Southern-facing city. On the evening of November 1, Mayor Davies, the city marshal, and Charles Hammond, the editor of the city's leading newspaper, the *Gazette*, called at Birney's home to advise him that a mob was forming to destroy his home that very night, on account of a rumor that Birney had published an incendiary handbill on behalf of the Cincinnati Anti-Slavery Society. The mayor informed Birney that, should he persist in his plans for abolitionist publications, the police would be powerless to protect his home and family against the fury of a mob. Adopting a friendly manner, Birney thanked the delegation for its concern for his welfare and assured them that it was the Society, and not he, that had legally printed its constitution. Walking the visitors to the door, he told Mayor Davies that he had every faith that, as mayor, he could suppress any such madness that might arise in the Queen City.

Once the guests were gone, Birney and his boys set about securing the house against possible attack. They gathered forty muskets and double-barreled shotguns, placing them strategically around the house, on the landing of the front staircase, and at other places that looked out upon approaches. The Birneys were vigilant that night but no mob appeared. However, the visit from the sinister mayor had convinced Birney of the wisdom of publishing *The Philanthropist* outside Davies' jurisdiction. He selected the village of New Richmond, twenty miles out of town.

Southern goodwill always meant a great deal to Cincinnati businessmen, particularly then. With the recent construction of the new canals and railroads connecting the West with the East Coast, Western merchants who had formerly bought their stock from Cincinnati were finding it easier to do business more directly with the East. Cincinnati felt the pinch. To remain competitive with these new rival cities who were cutting into their business, Cincinnati leaders proposed the establishment of a vast new transportation system, the chief link being the Charleston-Cincinnati railroad, to open up new markets for Cincinnati. The project was under negotiation. Cincinnati could not afford to ruffle Southern feathers.

The *Cincinnati Whig* kept a running fire of denunciations against Birney. Birney's enemies had him in their sights. Nevertheless, *The Philanthropist* launched its first issue on January 1, 1836. Editor Birney explained his Christian motives for starting the paper and his peaceful intent. He invited discussion on both sides of the slavery issue. He felt that the North, as well as the South, was implicated in slavery and should share in its solution. An extract from a proslavery speech by South Carolina Governor George McDuffie was featured. McDuffie likened abolitionists to the serpent in the Biblical Garden of Eden, tempting Black people to aspire above their station. McDuffie called upon communities to punish "this species of interference [abolitionists] by death without benefit of clergy."

To the dismay of Birney's enemies, no inflammatory anti-slavery article or editorial could be found in Birney's first issue of *The Philanthropist*. Nevertheless, this did not prevent the Cincinnati daily papers, with the exception of the more moderate *Gazette*, from renewing their attempts to arouse a mob against him. On January 22, what came to be known as the Great Mob Meeting was held at the courthouse to protest the publication of Birney's newspaper.

Birney appeared at the meeting and showed that he was a peaceful man. The moderate *Gazette* gave a faithful account of the proceedings, calling Birney a man whose "conduct had disarmed the madness of the multitude." Violence was averted. Birney continued to publish.

In the February 8, 1836 issue of *The Philanthropist,* Birney compared the differing values of the advocates of slavery and its opponents:

> You have *ARISTOCRACY*—we, the *PEOPLE;*—you have *INDO-LENCE* [laziness]—we, *ACTIVITY*: you have *WEALTH*—we, PRINCIPLE;—you have *PASSION*—we *CONSTANCY*; you have the spirit of *OPPRESSION*—we, of *LIBERTY*; you have *VIOLENCE* and *CURSES*—we, *PATIENCE* and *PRAYERS*; —you have the *DISPLEASURE* of God—we, his *BLESSING.* Which side do you think will triumph?

CHAPTER 19

Birney Misreads the Tea Leaves

From February to April, no more threats of violence were made against Birney's press. Subscriptions to *The Philanthropist* increased. The heat applied by the *Whig* and the *Republican* had cooled off. Birney felt safe enough to move his press and types from New Richmond to Cincinnati, where he contracted with the Quaker printer, Achilles Pugh. Boldly, Birney hung an eighteen-foot-long sign on the Main Street front of the printing shop declaring, "Anti-Slavery Office." There, customers could buy abolition pamphlets, books, among them Lydia Maria Child's new and revised edition of her *Appeal* (37½ cents), her new book, *The Oasis* ($1.00), *The Memoirs of Phillis Wheatley* (25 cents), newspaper subscriptions, anti-slavery handkerchiefs, letter paper, cards, and medals.

Trying to print the paper in New Richmond had been arduous for James Birney. For months, he had ridden the twenty miles in all sorts of weather, often on horseback, carrying papers in his saddlebags to his subscribers in the city. The mail service was unreliable. More and more, he returned nights exhausted, only to sit up all night with Agatha, now mostly confined to the house and bedridden. Dr. Isaac Colby diagnosed Agatha's chronic cough and recurrent fever as unmistakable symptoms of an incurable case of tuberculosis. She was also pregnant; the baby was expected in May. This was her tenth pregnancy. Weak, with a new baby on the way, small children to care for at home without the help of Kentucky slaves, and James often away overnight on his abolitionist lecture tours and meetings throughout Ohio, Agatha was desperately in need of more household help.

The last week in April, Birney left town to attend the Ohio State Anti-Slavery Society convention at Granville. Cincinnati Sisters Susan Lowe, Phebe Mathews, and Emeline Bishop were among the thirty or forty female delegates. The OSASS voted to make Birney's *Philanthropist* their official organ, putting Birney on their payroll. *The Philanthropist* reported only seven hundred subscribers, but Gamaliel Bailey, appointed its assistant editor, was determined to raise that number. Over the next several months, Birney would find himself relying more and more on Dr. Bailey in writing editorials for the newspaper. Dr. Bailey could not sustain his medical practice, stigmatized now as a dangerous zealot due to his association with the Cincinnati Anti-Slavery Society, whose goal was to convince the most influential people in Cincinnati to break off commercial relations with Southern planters. Bailey was glad to return to his real love, professional journalism. Augustus Wattles, as secretary of the newspaper, would handle incoming communications. Marius Robinson, who was in New York being ordained to the ministry, would return to Cincinnati to throw himself into the publication of *The Philanthropist*.

As Granville, Ohio, had hardly rolled out the red carpet to the abolitionists, the Ohio State Anti-Slavery Society moved the seat of operations to Cincinnati. Continuing to face hostility in Xenia and Columbus, Birney wrote to Lewis Tappan on April 29, 1836, that "we were dreadfully mobbed by a drunken rabble. We lectured in the neighborhood…[and] some of these meetings were broken up by the mob. The mob collected on Wednesday afternoon in Granville—on Thursday they were beastly drunk. Some half a dozen horses were disfigured by having their manes and tails (the hair) cut off. Mine… was among them. As I left G., the mob raised a shout, and made several discharges of Eggs at me….[N]ot one hit me."

James Birney was still on his lecture tour when, on May 2, his wife, Agatha, gave birth to a daughter she named Georgiana.

CHAPTER 20

Harriet Begins Her New Life

T hat same May, when Agatha Birney delivered a baby girl, Harriet Beecher, living up the road in Walnut Hills, was still pregnant. She and Calvin Stowe had married five months earlier in January, the month of the Great Mob Meeting. The couple had only been able to enjoy a brief honeymoon as Calvin departed for New York in late spring to set sail for England in June. Calvin had two commissions to carry out in Europe. Firstly, he was to buy books for the library at Lane Seminary and, secondly, to study the Prussian education system as a model for Ohio public schools.

Upon Calvin's departure, Harriet, 24, moved out of the house Calvin shared with Eliza and moved in with her father, Aunt Esther, and her youngest three siblings in the President's House at Lane. Harriet's stepmother, a most unpleasant woman, had died the previous summer, and as a result, the family home was much cheerier. Harriet had resigned her teaching job to marry; married women did not work. Even while employed as a teacher, she kept up her writing, having published four more stories in the *Western Monthly Magazine*. Catharine virtually deserted the school following the Lane Rebellion, leaving its running in the hands of Harriet and Mary Dutton, preferring to travel the country, lecturing on her educational theories and plans and making herself quite unwelcome as she flitted from town to town, stopping for weeks at a time at the homes of family and friends, scolding her hosts' children for interrupting, monopolizing mealtime conversations, and becoming more and more opinionated and dictatorial.

Busy, important Catharine had not been present for Harriet's wedding; Mary Dutton, faithful friend and colleague, served as Harriet's maid of honor. Catharine's domineering nature had made such a mark on Harriet's personality—Catharine, eleven years older, had been telling Harriet what to do, "shaping her," since she was five years old—that Harriet felt it was "Sister Katy" who, despite her absence, was giving her away in marriage rather than her father. In a letter Harriet dashed off thirty minutes before the wedding ceremony, Harriet wrote friend Georgiana May that in the week preceding the wedding, she had lost sleep, dreading the "overwhelming crisis," wondering how she should live through it, when she would "cease to be Hatty Beecher and change to nobody knows who." Calvin had no such qualms, having said to Harriet that, "I [feel] as though my blood somehow circulated through your veins, and if you were to be torn from me, I should bleed to death."

The details of the wedding, its date and particulars, had been changed so often due to the uncertainty of Calvin's impending travel plans that one of the newspapers scrambled the facts, reporting that, on January 6, 1836, Calvin married *Catharine* Beecher! Of course, other papers reprinted the article and spread the error. The Beecher siblings, scattered as they were across the continent, were understandably befuddled as to which sister had made the match to the distinguished clergyman/professor/scholar nine years Harriet's senior. Some of her brothers knew nothing of the union. The confusion caused much family merriment.

Former New Englander Calvin Stowe—who had begun life as Calvin Stow and acquired the "e" in Stowe at some point during his college years—was more than a bit peculiar. At one of the Semi-Colon meetings, one of his papers was read aloud, revealing that, from the age of four, he had received visitations from ghostly visitors ranging from spooky, sky-blue goblins to tiny, dancing fairies who acted out elaborate dramas in front of his eyes yet took no notice of him. The apparitions, he had explained, while preferring darkness to daylight, would sometimes appear in the daytime, even when Calvin was having tea with friends. Balding and sporting bushy sideburns, Calvin looked every bit of the eccentric mystic. He owned nothing but thousands of dull, scholarly books. Calvin spoke German as well as French, Spanish, Hebrew, Greek, and Arabic. Harriet said he was rich in languages but nothing else. Harriet was used to scraping by on little money. Marrying a preacher was as close as Harriet could get to becoming one herself.

Calvin and Harriet's baby was due in the fall. That May of 1836, she, like Agatha Birney, was mostly confined to the house, living under her father's roof for the first time since she was twelve. In May, her father left for the Presbyterian Assembly in Pittsburgh (where his final heresy trial would take place), accompanied by Rev. Thomas Brainerd, the editor of *The Cincinnati Journal & Luminary*, who also was Lyman's assistant at the Second Presbyterian Church where Lyman preached. Brothers Henry and Charles were studying at Lane. With Aunt Esther and the servants managing the housework, Harriet caught up on her writing.

As instructed by Calvin, Harriet made daily visits to the grave of his first wife, Eliza, buried next to Harriet's stepmother in the Lane cemetery directly behind the Beecher home. Harriet was told to visit at precise hours, which were synchronized with Calvin's London and German watches. Because Harriet had entered Calvin's world as his helpmate in coping with his grief, their relationship would retain this lopsided dynamic, with his expectation that she would devote her energies to propping up his often-sagging spirits. He was anxious about traveling without her, sleeping without her. He suffered from nervous headaches and depression, which he called the "hypo." During his transatlantic crossing, he wrote Harriet:

> I have half a mind to relinquish my aquatic journey and return with you to Cincinnati; I think all the time of you and Eliza, and hardly know which I want to see the most.

Calvin expected Harriet to type up his travel letters and "embellish them," sending them to be published in *The Journal* as "notes from a correspondent." Harriet continued in the subservient secretarial mode, a pattern she had allowed to form during the courtship. Calvin wrote to his mother how pleased he was with his new wife, as Harriet was as well adapted to his character and needs as Eliza had been.

CHAPTER 21

The South Stops the U.S. Mail

H arriet Beecher Stowe was cheered that her brother Henry, still enrolled at Lane, was around those days, especially with Calvin away. Henry was ecstatic at having just been chosen by Rev. Brainerd to be his substitute as editor *pro-tem* at *The Cincinnati Journal and Luminary*, a Presbyterian weekly with a circulation of 3,600.

To become a newspaperman had been Henry's wildest dream. Newspapers gave him a voice and an audience. Newspapers were abundant and popular; they were the media of the day. A newspaper writer could shape public opinion by putting a particular slant on a situation, especially if his articles were picked up and reprinted in other newspapers. Newspapers were cheap and common; newspaper readers could be found everywhere. Even those who could not read had the papers read to them daily. In 1836, Cincinnati had twelve newspapers, a type foundry, and the Graham paper manufacturing company. Newspapers were highly partisan. Editors and publishers were often powerful political figures representing commercial and political interests, and the Cincinnati papers were a case in point.

Editor Brainerd felt Henry demonstrated his competence for the job as Brainerd had earlier published some of Henry's anti-Catholic editorials in *The Journal*. Although Harriet was a many-times published author—her *Primary Geography* was used in classrooms widely, boasting sales of over 100,000 copies to date—Brainerd had hired second-year Lane divinity student Henry Beecher instead, to take charge of the newspaper from the end of May until October. His first *Journal* issue debuted on May 26, featuring conservative diatribes that promoted temperance and condemned theatre-going. Henry wrote frequently on slavery, taking great care to present both sides of the issues, assailing Garrison while supporting anti-slavery action, keeping a balance so the postman would deliver his newspapers, as the anti-abolitionist Jackson Administration had tacitly supported allowing local postmen the discretion not to deliver abolitionist publications they deemed "incendiary" or "seditious." On May 19, the postmaster at Pontotoc, Mississippi, William D. Lusher, told *the Journal* to no longer send their paper to his office, stating his view that the "sentiments expressed in that paper on a *certain subject*, are not congenial to 'Southern feeling.'"

For the past ten months, the American Anti-Slavery Society had deluged the mail with over a million pieces of anti-slavery literature to make slavery an issue no one could ignore. Funded largely by Arthur and Lewis Tappan, a list of influential Southerners was created to receive anti-slavery mailings in the hope they would do something about the issue. This pamphlet campaign sent the abolitionist gospel into places American Anti-Slavery lecturers could not safely travel. The mail campaign irked slaveholders, provoking them to reveal how they really cherished slavery, as expressed by this Southern writer:

'We of the South have been hitherto much to blame, in allowing such notions to gain ground at the North as that we regard slavery as an evil, and are anxious to get rid of it. It is but lately that we have begun to make the Northern people to understand, that we hold slavery to be neither *a sin nor a curse*, but an ordinance of Providence [God], and a *practical blessing.*'

The backlash from this anti-slavery propaganda campaign was tremendous. On the night of July 19, 1835, a mob pried open the windows of the Charleston, South Carolina, post office and got inside. The men grabbed a sack of abolitionist journals and newspapers. The next night, these Southern fire-eaters publicly burned the mail along with effigies of Arthur Tappan and William Lloyd Garrison in a large bonfire on the parade grounds adjacent to the Citadel, Charleston's military academy, before a crowd of thousands. Anti-abolition meetings were held throughout the South. In many places, abolitionist documents were suppressed. Abolitionists and suspected abolitionists were attacked by mobs, like Lane Rebel Amos Dresser, who was publicly flogged in Nashville for the possession of abolitionist material. Others were hounded and murdered.

Race riots occurred in major Northern cities. Abolitionist Lydia Maria Child wrote from Brooklyn, New York, on May 15, 1835, of the excitement:

> I have not ventured into the city, nor does one of us dare go to church to-day….'Tis like the times of the French Revolution, when no man dared trust his neighbors. Private assassins from New Orleans are lurking at the corners of the streets to stab Arthur Tappan….Mr. [Elizur] Wright [secretary of the American Anti-Slavery Society] was yesterday barricading his doors and windows with strong bars and planks an inch thick.

Someone erected a gallows on Garrison's Boston doorstep with two nooses; a note was affixed, announcing that the gallows were compliments of "Judge Lynch." A month later, Garrison was dragged through the streets of Boston with a rope around his body.

While the abolitionist pamphlet campaign may not have succeeded in swaying slaveholders to see the error of depriving another human being of his or her God-given liberty, it did inform Southerners of the opposition that existed to their half-slave, half-free society. Additionally, the ill-chosen defense tactics of the Slave Power that were taken to preserve and spread slavery—the burning and banning of abolitionist tracts and newspapers, the efforts by their

Northern friends to silence anti-slavery speakers and the breaking up of their meetings, the violence toward abolitionists—reflected the same tyrannical spirit that sustained the institution of slavery. In attacking slavery, abolitionists had maneuvered the South into taking ever more extreme action in its defense, threatening the civil liberties of white Americans, and exposing the danger that slavery posed to free institutions throughout the country.

The number of anti-slavery societies grew from two hundred in May 1835 to five hundred twenty-seven a year later. In retaliation, however, Northern free states suffered a backlash. Southerners manipulated their Northern friends to push their state governments to suppress anti-slavery societies. In debating whether or not to permit these groups to exist, these legislatures, in free states, sent a loud message to their citizens that anti-slavery societies were not to be tolerated. Such a move gave mobs the green light to attack abolitionists. Thus, the Slave Power succeeded in diverting Northern energy away from attacking slavery as an evil to attacking the abolitionists as the real evil.

CHAPTER 22

Birney and Bailey Step on Powerful Toes

A
s was traditional, in June, Southern planters with their slave retinues arrived in Cincinnati for vacation, filling up the hotels and boardinghouses and spreading their money around. *The Philanthropist* now boasted seventeen hundred subscribers. In *The Philanthropist*, Birney counseled his readers to treat the Southern vacationers differently this summer:

> Hitherto, when our Southern brethren have come to the North, they have met with about as little sense of the wickedness of slavery as they left behind them. Henceforth let it be different. Let them witness our strong abhorrence of it, and let there be nothing from our lips or in our practices to soothe their consciences. Especially let them see us treating the colored man, as a man.

News of the Texas revolt from Mexico filled hopes among proslavery advocates that, following Arkansas' admission to the Union in June as a slave state (and Michigan's entry as a free state early the next year), Texas would be the next slave state to be admitted. American slaveholders had aided in the wresting of Texas from Mexico with a plan to bring the enormous region into the Union for the purpose of both increasing slave territory and maintaining a majority of Southern influence in the U.S. Congress. Under the guise of patriotism, a group of Cincinnati men called the "Texas Aid Association," led by Dr. Daniel Drake, was formed to send money to the Texians and to agitate for the annexation of Texas to the Union. Opposed to the interference of the United States in a war with Mexico, *Philanthropist* editor Birney ran a series of articles by David Lee Child (husband of Lydia Maria) that exposed the desire for the "acquisition of Texas for a slave market" and in the interest of land speculators in the big cities.

The railroad excitement begun by Dr. Drake was at fever pitch with anticipation that tracks, cutting through the heart of the South, would link Cincinnati to Charleston, South Carolina, a city whose very prosperity relied upon slave labor. Any whiff of anti-Southern sentiment might sour the deal. The Southwestern Railroad Convention was meeting in Tennessee in July to decide on the new railroad links.

Despite this, on June 10, Bailey and Birney wrote an editorial in *The Philanthropist* disparaging the South Carolina legislature. In yet another article, *The Philanthropist* skewered South Carolina again, where fifty-five percent of its citizens were Black, for its hostility to any people of color:

A citizen of Connecticut, visiting South Carolina, is in danger, on the bare suspicion of his having African blood in his veins, of losing his liberty forever.

Birney considered abolitionism to have a religious basis, and he, along with most everyone in the movement, fervently expected that the churches would rally to their cause and denounce as a sin the enslavement, from cradle to grave, of two million Black Americans. The Methodist Church, though, holding their general conference in Cincinnati that May, wanted Birney excluded from reporting on their discussions on slavery, as they feared he would publish an unfavorable report in *The Philanthropist*. Birney realized the churches were not going to disturb the Southern slaveholders' argument that the unique relationship between master and slave was Bible-ordained. Birney wrote that the Methodist Church was "staggering more and more under the life-destroying influence of the pestilent atmosphere with which it [slavery] has enveloped her."

CHAPTER 23

Matilda Arrives in Cincinnati

This is the story of Matilda Lawrence, as best understood. On the night of Sunday, June 18, 1836, the steamboat *Eagle* anchored at the Cincinnati wharf. Matilda, an enslaved woman in her late teens or early twenties, was aboard with her younger sister, four more slaves, their owner, Larkin Lawrence, 42, and Lawrence's teenage nephew. On May 25, they departed Anne Arundel County, Maryland, coming through Virginia to the Ohio River, with the purpose of settling in Missouri to farm. Matilda's mother, Polly, did not make the trip. Lawrence had sold her (or, according to his nephew, set her free) before they left Maryland.

The *Eagle*, bound for St. Louis the next evening, was detained in Cincinnati for twenty-four hours, just long enough to unload and take on new freight. This was the first stop in a free state since Matilda's journey had begun.

Free Blacks who found work on the Ohio River steamboats were often part of the Underground Railroad that assisted slaves in escaping their masters. Through this network, Matilda learned of a Black barber living in Cincinnati who would hide her and her sister until her owner left for St. Louis. Under cover of night, the sisters fled the *Eagle* and took shelter in the Black neighborhood of Church Alley.

On Monday, after dinner, Lawrence and his nephew noticed the absence of Matilda and her sister. They made a search and came across the little sister, capturing her, and putting her on board the *Eagle* to take with them to Pike County, Missouri. But by the time the *Eagle* was set to depart, they had still not found Matilda. The boat sailed without her. Matilda had only the clothes on her back but she was free of Larkin Lawrence, who was not only her master but also her father.

Through her new friends, Matilda was given the address of a kind family in need of a housemaid to help care for an invalid mother (whose husband was often absent), her two young ones, and a sickly newborn. The house was on the west side of Race Street, two doors above Eighth Street; it was the Birney house. She knocked at the door.

Agatha Birney hired Matilda on the spot. One look at the girl's calloused hands and Agatha knew Matilda was no housemaid. She knew nothing of housework; she had worked in the fields. She had a small scar in the center of her forehead. Matilda's complexion was so light as to be almost considered white. The law would classify her as a mulatto, a person of mixed Black and white ancestry.

When James Birney returned from his lecture trip and found Matilda so gainfully employed in running the household, he committed to paying her above-average wages, even though he was in great debt, with the cost of educating his four sons, mounting medical expenses for Agatha's treatment, and with only a small salary. James Birney's father, a wealthy Kentucky slaveholder, was so disgusted by his son's reformist work that Birney had little chance of receiving an inheritance from his estate.

Matilda was willing to learn. "Cheerful, and good-hearted among the children," noted James Birney. Agatha used an easy spelling book to teach Matilda to read and she made good progress. The family was aware of her status as a runaway slave. Although Ohio was a free state, any Black or mulatto person who entered Ohio had to prove he or she was free. The Birneys, in harboring a fugitive slave, were committing a criminal offense. No matter: Matilda was a welcome addition to their family.

Matilda's attentive care of the sick baby, Georgiana—as well as her mother's love—could not stave off the inevitable. The first week of July, James Birney returned home from a college lecture to find his two-month-old daughter's tiny and inert body "laid out in its shroud and coffin," he wrote Lewis Tappan. They buried her on July 3.

CHAPTER 24

Flame Jets Burst Forth

At five o'clock in the afternoon of Tuesday, July 12, 1836, two men were seen snooping around the back of a large building at the northeast corner of Main and Seventh Streets in Cincinnati. On the second floor of that building was Pugh's printing business, where *The Philanthropist* was printed, and the Ohio State Anti-Slavery Society had its office and depository. A lady reported that the prowlers entered the backyard adjacent to Pugh's premises and had taken reconnaissance of the place. One man was "elderly and gray-haired, wearing a palmetto hat, and a brown Holland coat." The other man was young and wearing summer clothes.

That night, at midnight, a gang of fifteen or twenty men assembled at Pugh's. Using a ladder and a plank, six or eight of them scaled the outer walls. Through a window on the roof, they descended into Pugh's printing room. A boy was lying asleep in the office. The intruders pulled his bedclothes over his head so that he could not see the faces of the raiders. They demanded to know where the type was kept. The vandals then began to destroy the press, carrying away the smaller parts. They found the blank paper intended for the journal and took it to an adjoining lot, tearing it up and pouring a keg of ink on it.

The next night, some of these same hooligans snuck through the dark city, carrying stacks of paper, buckets of glue, and big, wide brushes. The next morning, citizens were confronted with handbills plastered on the corners of city streets with this warning:

Abolitionists Beware

The citizens of Cincinnati, embracing every class, interested in the prosperity of the City, satisfied that the business of the place is receiving a vital stab from the wicked and misguided operations of the abolitionists, are resolved to arrest their course. The destruction of their Press on the night of the 12ᵗʰ instant, may be taken as a warning. As there are some worthy citizens engaged in the unruly cause of annoying our southern neighbors, they are appealed to, to pause before they bring things to a crisis. If an attempt is made to reestablish the Press, it will be viewed as an act of defiance to an already outraged community, and on their heads be the results which will follow.

Merchants opened their shops to find, slipped under their doors, a menacing note:

Sir, It is said that you profess friendship to the cause of abolition. We wish you immediately upon the reception of this to put your answer in your window so that one of many may see it, and report the same. The simple word *Yes*, or *No*, will suffice. Be sure you comply immediately. ANTI-ABOLITION

James Birney swiftly moved his family and Matilda to safety. Agatha went to visit her friends and family in Kentucky, taking George, 4, while William, 17, stayed behind in Cincinnati, moving with his father to the Franklin House, a boardinghouse, until it was once again safe to live at their residence. Florence, at eighteen months, sick due to teething, was sent to stay with friends three miles from town, perhaps with Matilda.

Upon discovering the damage to the press, Printer Pugh and several members of the Anti-Slavery Society appealed to Mayor Davies to track down the perpetrators, contributing $100 to the effort, but the mayor was more in sympathy with the wreckers than with the injured party.

In his proclamation, he blamed the abolitionists for having brought the trouble upon themselves. In the same breath, he requested that order be maintained and then admonished the abolitionists to "abstain from further persecution of such measures as may have a tendency to inflame the public mind, and lead to acts of violence and disorder."

The display of force and the lack of support from the mayor did not deter Birney from publishing, but Pugh was harder to persuade. To get him to continue printing the paper, the Anti-Slavery Society had to guarantee Pugh's property for two thousand dollars. They patched up the press and brought out the regularly scheduled edition of *The Philanthropist*. In that issue, Birney did not hold back his outrage at the attack on the press. He stated:

> That any of our citizens, who belong to what we choose to call the respectable class, that any such are engaged in a midnight conspiracy to overthrow the most solemn safeguards of their own and their offspring's liberty, in order that our slaveholding neighbors may pat them on the back, and commend their servility, we do not, for one moment, believe.

That day, fifty boarders at the Franklin House convened after tea. A petition was drawn up and signed by seventeen men demanding that the proprietor, Colonel William Johnson, expel Birney and his son from the place. Johnson refused; a dozen of the disgruntled boarders moved out.

Two days later, a second handbill appeared on the streets:

"A Fugitive from Justice!
"$100 REWARD.
The above sum will be paid for the delivery of the body of one *James G. Birney*, a fugitive from justice, now abiding in the city of Cincinnati. Said *Birney* in all his associations and feelings is *black*; although his external appearance is white. The reward will be paid, and no questions asked by OLD KENTUCKY.

CHAPTER 25

Harriet's Blood Boils and Her Pen Flows

H enry Beecher asked Harriet to compose an anonymous letter to the editor for *The Journal*. To mask her identity and lead her readers to believe she was a man (political discourse was a male sphere), Harriet adopted a male pseudonym, "Franklin," with which to sign her piece.

Her "Franklin" letter appeared in the *Cincinnati Journal* of July 21, 1836:

MR. EDITOR:—a few days ago at the dinner table of a friend [Mr. L, the host], a man of sense and intelligence, the following conversation took place:

'So,' said Mr. L., flourishing his carver, 'I hear Birney's press is broken open at last. I knew it must be so. Well, I can't say that I'm sorry. It will teach him better than to be setting these ultra measures on foot in our city.'

'You are glad of it!' said I. 'You, a Christian man and a lover of good order, not sorry that the laws of the city have been violated and the rights of private property invaded? My good sir, I am astonished at you!'

'Why, no,' said my friend, looking somewhat puzzled, 'I disapprove of mobs and unlawful proceedings of every kind—no man more—but then Birney and these fellows are so ultra and

immoderate, and their measures are so calculated into a ferment....
But you must allow that it is undesirable to have that Birney here
sending out these inflammatory things.'

'Why? What harm do they do?'

'Why? They inflame community.'

'Well, and what harm is there in inflaming community?'

'Why it makes men furious, gives rise to popular commotions
and disturbances, and *mobs*, and so forth,' he said, hastily, beginning to see where his own logic was taking him.

'...Now, my friend, do you think the liberty of the press is a
good thing?'

'Certainly—to be sure.'

'And you think it a good article in our Constitution that allows
every man to speak, write, and publish his own opinions, without
any other responsibility than that of the laws of his country?'

'Certainly, I do.'

'Well, then, as Mr. Birney is a man, I suppose you think it's
right to allow *him* to do it in particular?'

'But Mr. Birney's opinions are so dangerous!'

'That is to say, so *you* think them. There are a large class
of people in the nation who are just as sure that they are not.
Now, how is the Constitution to be worded: Every man in the
State may speak, write, print, and publish his own sentiments on
any subject, provided that nobody in the nation thinks they are
dangerous?'

'Pshaw!' said my friend. 'Of course, no law could run that
way: but there is a point, you know, where all men of sense are
pretty much agreed.'

'Then,' said I, 'perhaps you would recommend that the
Constitution should provide that every man may print and
publish his sentiments, except in cases where all men of sense are
pretty much agreed that they are dangerous?'

'Why,' said my friend, after an uneasy silence of a few

moments, 'really you are getting to be quite a warm Abolitionist. I had no idea that you were so much inclined to favor Birney.'

Franklin denies this and preaches this sermon:

Just suppose that there was a train of gunpowder extending under every house in the city and the incendiaries had begun to explode it under some unsightly old buildings which specially disfigure the place. You stand on a hilltop and look down with great complacency—'That's right—can't say I'm sorry—glad to see those ugly old things blown sky-high.' 'You fool,' says a man, running up out of breath, 'don't you know that the same train of powder runs under your house and mine and every house in the city? Let it go twenty minutes longer, and they will all go together!' Now, this is precisely the case with these mobs. Every man is glad of a mob that happens to fall in with his views, without considering that if the mob system gets thoroughly running, it may go *against* as well as *for* them.

In a letter to Calvin, Harriet played down the publication of her witty Franklin letter, referring to it in her letter as "scribbling for Henry's newspaper." So as not to be perceived as having strayed outside her socially prescribed womanly sphere of domesticity, she wrote, "I thought…that I was, like a good wife, defending one of your principles in your absence, and wanted you to see how manfully I talked about it."

CHAPTER 26

Judge Burnet Throws His Weight Around

B irney had been wrong in thinking that the "respectable class" of the community was not supportive of the mob action against his paper. Joseph Graham, who owned a paper mill, had been the leader of the July 12 break-in at Pugh's and was an active leader of the Texas Aid Committee. He had been one of the authors of the anti-abolition handbills. Morgan Neville, the man who reported a summer sighting of Black ladies on the Lane campus to the trustees, thus provoking the Lane Exodus, and super-rich land speculator Nicholas Longworth were busily manipulating the daily presses, the *Whig* and the *Republican*, to paint Birney as a danger to the public. The July 21 edition of the *Republican* addressed this warning to the members of the executive committee of the Ohio State Anti-Slavery Society:

> …Publish no more cards or addresses about midnight invasions. Eschew the society of James G. Birney. Avoid him as you would a viper….

Despite the ongoing threats, on July 22, Birney came out with his regular Friday edition of the paper. Furious at being unable to silence Birney, the same men who had organized the Great Mob Meeting called for a town meeting for the next day at the Lower

Market House. Longworth and Neville, both friends of Salmon Chase, declared the paper would be put down "peaceably if it could, forcibly if it must." A committee was formed and headed by former Ohio Supreme Court Judge Jacob Burnet, a not disinterested party, as his half-brother, David G. Burnet, was serving as the first president of the new Republic of Texas. Judge Burnet, who had accrued great wealth through profitable land speculation, presented the Market House resolution to Birney and his associates that they desist from publishing their paper. He said the committee would not be responsible for the consequences if they persisted.

Harriet wrote in her journal:

> For my part, I can easily see how such proceedings may make converts to abolitionism, for already my sympathies are strongly enlisted for Mr. Birney, and I hope that he will stand his ground and assert his rights. The office is fire-proof, and enclosed by high walls. I wish he would man it with armed men and see what can be done. If I were a man I would go, and take good care of at least one window.

At a subsequent meeting, Burnet warned Birney that "two-thirds of the property holders of the city" would join a mob should he continue to publish. He said that small armies of indignant and violent men from Columbia, Covington, and Newport were forming to suppress the paper, to be joined by local gangs of workmen from the foundries and boat yards.

Birney did not change course. On Friday, July 29, he released issue number 41 of *The Philanthropist*.

The next day, Saturday, July 30, at six o'clock, the crowd began to gather in front of the Exchange Hotel on Front Street. Joseph Graham presided over a meeting at which it was resolved that the crowd would destroy the abolition press and tar and feather Birney. Some men were appointed to find out the addresses of the abolitionists. A few hours later, after a meeting of the Texas Aid Committee, a group of citizens assembled at the corner of Main and Seventh Streets and proceeded to break and enter the printing office of Achilles Pugh. Editor Birney was away speaking in Hillsboro, but Lane Rebel Marius Robinson was working inside. Upon seeing the approaching mob, he grabbed the printing plates and forced them through some loose masonry into a carpenter shop next door. The two carpenters, the Bushnell brothers, grabbed them and carried them to the attic for safekeeping.

Robinson disguised himself, left by the rear of the building, and blended in with the crowd out front. The mob looked into the office for Birney and Robinson, whom they called "the little brown devil," but saw the place was empty. The intruders then began its destruction, tossing Robinson's books into two barrels and breaking an oil lamp over them. They dismantled the press, hurtling pieces of type, books, and assorted office equipment out the windows and into the street. Then, with a great heave and push, the press itself was shoved out the window. The crowd roared its approval. Then, strong men hitched a rope to it, hauled it to the river, and pitched it in. Not a policeman intervened, yet the mayor stood by silently, approvingly. As the press sank into the water, the crowd chanted, "Birney! Birney!"

Amply supplied with tar and feathers, the crowd, whipped into a murderous frenzy, went hunting for abolitionists.

On the way to Birney's, they stopped at Pugh's house, looking for more print materials, but found none. They then rushed to Birney's house, where his son answered the door. Joseph Graham questioned the young man:

"Who are you?"

"My name is William Birney."

"Where is your father?"

"In Warren County."

"Is anyone else in the house?"

"No."

William stepped hurriedly back inside and latched the door, grabbing a rifle and bounding up the stairs, ready to fire upon any intruder. The crowd, satisfied that Birney was not there, left the home undisturbed, and William relaxed his grip on the gun. When William was questioned by Graham at the door, Marius Robinson had been hiding in the crowd. When a shout was raised to race to Dr. Colby's house at Broadway between Fourth and Fifth Streets, Robinson took the opportunity to flee, go to the attic above the carpentry shop, rescue the printing forms, and take them to Wilmington, Ohio, on horseback. He returned the next day to Cincinnati with the printed edition. Due to his quick thinking, the next edition of the paper was printed on time the following Friday.

Not finding anyone at home, the mob ransacked Dr. Colby's office, piling up its contents in the street to make a bonfire. Joseph Graham, standing atop the pile, advised against the bonfire, lest it set off a fire among the neighboring houses. Their next stop was the home of William and Christian Donaldson, where they found only ladies at home. Frustrated that they could not ferret out a single abolitionist to harm, the crowd turned their wrath on the innocent Black community of Church Alley, smashing windows, ripping doors off hinges, breaking into houses, destroying the interiors, chopping up furniture, and chasing the residents out of their beds at midnight. The mob thought, *That will teach them to remember their place in the racial order.* Around midnight, Mayor Davies, who had allowed the violence to continue uninterrupted for four hours, announced to the rioters, "We have done enough for one night….The abolitionists themselves must be convinced by this time what public sentiment is."

The next night, a Sunday evening, a large group of people collected on Main Street opposite the Franklin House. They were under the impression that James Birney, who was still out of town, was hiding inside the boardinghouse and demanded a search be made. As Salmon Chase recalled:

I stood in the doorway, and told them, calmly but resolutely, no one could pass. They paused. One of them asked who I was. I gave my name. One, who seemed a ringleader, said I should answer for this. I told him I could be found at any time. The mob did not choose to attack me in my position, and after a while, to my great relief, the Mayor, who had been in the House, came out and declared to the mob that Mr. Birney was not there, upon which they drew off.

At another mass meeting, the city government agreed to cooperate to restore order. The mayor established a volunteer vigilante posse to keep the peace. Henry Ward Beecher was among those deputized to patrol the streets, armed with orders to shoot to kill. Harriet saw Henry in the kitchen, pouring melting lead into a mold—making bullets for his pistols.

Harriet was relieved when law and order was restored, as there had been talk that the mob was moving toward Walnut Hills. Northern newspapers picked up the story of the riots and excoriated Cincinnati for its disgraceful conduct. Northern white people were waking up to the danger the slave power posed to all people's rights—freedom of speech and a free press. Many began to view the abolition movement more favorably.

It was not until Tuesday, August 2, when Birney, fourteen miles away outside the city and returning, was informed of the demolition of the press. For a few days, friends sheltered him in the country until it was safe to return to the city. Once back in Cincinnati, though, to avoid being murdered, Birney did not show his face in the business district near the riverfront; for many weeks, he did not sleep regularly in the same place. By the end of September, his wife Agatha and other household members had returned to their house on Race Street. Birney continued to receive threats on his life.

On August 10, Birney wrote to Lewis Tappan for a change in assignment. He proposed the eventual transfer of the editorship of

The Philanthropist to Dr. Bailey. Birney planned to relocate to New York as an agent for the American Anti-Slavery Society. Birney began training Bailey for the editorship.

In addition to Birney joining the national lecture circuit, Theodore Weld was recruiting and training a first-rate team of agents for the AASS in the North called "The Seventy," which would include Rev. John Rankin, Henry B. Stanton, and three Lane Rebels who would be married to Cincinnati Sisters before the end of 1836—Augustus Wattles (Susan Lowe), Marius Robinson (Emily Rakestraw), and Edward Weed (Phebe Mathews).

Birney praised the writers at the *Journal* (Harriet and Henry) as they had "condemned, in the most fearless and spirited language, the proceedings of the mob from its first onset on the 12th of July, up to the consummation of the Vandal outrage." Gamaliel Bailey never forgot the courageous actions of Harriet and Henry.

After publishing the August 5 issue of *The Philanthropist* on the borrowed press, the executive committee of the Ohio Anti-Slavery Society was forced to suspend the paper due to a lack of funds. Dr. Bailey appealed to abolitionists throughout the country for aid, asking for additional subscriptions and extra donations to purchase a new press. By the end of September, the new press was humming, the paper was revived and published unmolested.

Salmon Chase represented Pugh and the leaders of the Ohio Anti-Slavery Society in lawsuits against prominent members of the mobs. Chase was willing to risk losing some of his very important clients by associating with the abolitionists because, he said, "a man must perform his duty and leave consequences to Him [God], who requires the duty." In both cases, Chase would win verdicts for his abolitionist clients.

CHAPTER 27

Lyman and Harriet Surprise Everyone

In August of 1836, Lyman Beecher returned to Cincinnati with a new bride on his arm. She was the former Mrs. Lydia Jackson, a forty-seven-year-old widow with six children, two of whom they brought to live with them in Walnut Hills. Lyman, 61, found his wife very beautiful. Lyman looked like a new man, spiffy, his shoes shined, his coat brushed, and "his cravat tied so genteelly," Catharine wrote her friends. Lydia had run a boardinghouse for ministers in Boston and was very active in benevolent societies. Competent and organized, she was well-suited to be the wife of a busy yet scatter-brained clergyman.

On September 29, 1836, with Calvin still abroad, now in Stuttgart, Harriet went into early labor. As luck would have it, Dr. Drake was in the house tending to Aunt Esther, severely ill with cholera. This was a time when no one understood the importance of sterile hands, not even the eminent Dr. Drake. Miraculously, as he assisted Harriet in childbirth, Dr. Drake did not infect Harriet with cholera. At ten o'clock, she gave birth to a baby girl. She then proceeded to give birth to another. On his journey to Europe in June, Calvin had written Harriet with strict instructions for the naming of their girl child, saying, "Remember, if female, the name is Eliza E. Tyler without hesitation, curtailment, or addition. This is indispensable."

Henry reported that one twin looked like Harriet and the other was the perfect image of Calvin. Harriet named the first baby, "Isabella," and the second baby, who looked like Calvin, "Eliza." Calvin would not learn of the twins until his return four months later. He was pleased that Harriet had named one "Eliza" but insisted that they rename the second one "Harriet," which they did, thereby naming their daughters after Calvin's two wives.

Back in Walnut Hills, Calvin discovered that he, Harriet, and the twins were sharing their small brick cottage with Anna Smith, 19, a newly arrived English immigrant who had become Harriet's loyal helpmate. As the years rolled by and the babies piled up in their cramped quarters, Harriet would hire additional servants—a stout German girl, a wet nurse, and many Black women—to help her with the cooking, cleaning, and childcare. She refused to be a household drudge; she would write to pay for the cost of the domestic help and she would have domestic help to allow her to write.

The fact that Harriet had produced twins delighted the Beechers. Brother William's wife, Katherine Beecher, wrote to her from Putnam, Ohio, that Harriet had served them "such a trick that made them all jump & laugh & shout & cry & feel glad & sorry…only because you are such a genius, and therefore cannot be expected to walk in a beaten track."

CHAPTER 28

Salmon Chase Does His Level Best

On March 10, 1837, only one of the Birney children, Florence, 2, was home with her ailing mother. James Birney was away on one of his frequent lecture trips. The five boys were in school. Agatha Birney had sent the housemaid, Matilda, up the street with an empty pitcher to get some milk. Shortly afterward, Agatha heard the door slam. Matilda ran into the room, trembling, tears running down her face. She told Agatha that a rough man had accosted her in the street and accused her of being a runaway slave.

While they were trying to figure out what to do next, a constable knocked on the Birneys' door. He presented a warrant for Matilda's arrest and imprisonment, an affidavit having been filed with the court by a notorious Missouri slave hunter, John Riley, who was acting as an agent for Matilda's former master, Larkin Lawrence. Matilda was taken into custody and locked up in the county jail.

Once James Birney was back in town and apprised of Matilda's arrest, he rushed to Salmon Chase's office and begged him to take the case. Chase agreed at once. Chase obtained a writ of *habeas corpus* from Judge D. K. Este, hoping to be granted some time to prepare a case on the poor woman's behalf, but the judge gave him less than twenty-four hours. Judge Este directed the sheriff to bring Matilda and her accusers to court the next morning. The next day, Matilda was put on trial. The *Cincinnati Republican* of March 16, 1837, reported its version of the proceedings. Richard D. Lawrence, the nephew of the claimant, was sworn in. He identified Matilda as the property of his uncle. He was not mistaken; he referred to the scar on her forehead as evidence that he knew her. He claimed the scar was from a wound Matilda had gotten years before from falling off a hominy mortar.

The next witness for the claimant was the constable E. D. Brooks. According to the *Republican*, when he arrested Matilda, he informed her that he was going to send her back to her master. He claimed that she replied that:

> [S]he wanted to go back to her master's, and would have went long ago if she had known where he lived. She said she had been as much a slave to Mr. Birney as she had ever been to master Larkin; that Mr. Birney had never paid her anything….She said she had some good clothes, and did not want to leave them; he told her she should have them.

William Birney was sworn in next, his father being out of the city. He said his father's character had been impeached but "the source from whence it came was hardly worth minding." He described how Matilda had appeared at his house and had worked there. The *Republican* stated that William "knew after she had been at his father's a short time, she was a slave; and that she had went out to Mrs. Cumner's to avoid detection. [Birney] had been absent part of the time from home, and did not know particularly about the matter…."

Matilda did not testify on her own behalf because, by state law, she was forbidden. The 1807 Ohio Black Laws stated that "no black or mulatto person or persons, shall hereafter be permitted to be sworn or give evidence in any court or record, or elsewhere in this state…where either party to the same is a white person." This Ohio law applied to Blacks and mulattos, free or slave. Matilda, being a slave, had no identity in the eyes of the law other than being the property of another human. In 1837, the Constitution of the United

States of America did not legally regard Matilda as a person. She was considered a thing.

Riley's lawyers argued that Larkin Lawrence was legally allowed to recover Matilda, as she was his property, under the provisions of the Fugitive Slave Act. Chase argued that Matilda became legally free when she set foot on the Ohio (free) side of the river. Chase also fruitlessly argued against the constitutionality of the federal Fugitive Slave Act. A better point to stress would have been that the Fugitive Slave Clause of the Constitution defined a fugitive as "a person held to service or labor in one state…escaping into another." Matilda had not escaped from any state; Lawrence had brought her to the free state of Ohio on a steamboat, thus freeing her.

Judge Este extended to Chase the courtesy of listening to his long and able discourse, but his mind was already made up. Este, satisfied that Matilda had been proved to be the property of Larkin Lawrence, ruled that she should be returned to him. Riley and his burly men hustled her away. Birney was convicted and fined for harboring a fugitive slave, but later, Chase made a more skillful argument in front of the Ohio Supreme Court and got that decision reversed.

Upon their return to their masters, fugitive slaves often faced a violent reckoning for their escape. They might be stripped naked, male and female, and subjected to tens and hundreds of lashings, each stroke drawing blood, with strong brine or urine applied to their lacerated wounds or "have some of their front teeth torn out or broken off, that they may be easily detected when then run away." Whipping on plantations was an everyday occurrence, as "chastisement must be inflicted until subordination was produced." Whipping came under the head of general treatment and slaves had no legal redress for the cruelties inflicted upon them. If Matilda did indeed tell the constable that she wanted to return to her master, she would have done so to save her skin. The fact that she had nice clothes at the Birneys speaks of their kind treatment of her, despite the words attributed to her in the *Republican*.

CHAPTER 29

Marius Robinson Takes it on the Chin

little over a month after they had married, Marius and Emily Robinson were separated. After the Christmas holidays of 1836, Marius and fellow Lane Rebel Edward Weed were dispatched across central and eastern Ohio as itinerant abolition lecturers. For the next two months, Emily stayed behind in Cincinnati, teaching in the Black schools. Robinson and Weed's trip was extensive, taking them through more than twenty towns in two months. Their travel, especially in winter, was arduous. The rides were cold and difficult, as they went by horseback, wagon, or sleigh through snow, ice, and perhaps blizzards on slushy, muddy, and primitive roads.

When Robinson entered a new town, he sought a school, public hall, or church where citizens could gather to hear his lecture. Ministers, town leaders, and school trustees were less and less agreeable to offering these places. Being an abolitionist was a lot like being at war, although Weld's agents were nonviolent activists. Every day, Robinson psychologically prepared himself for encountering proslavery opposition. His letters to Emily were full of reports of mobs trying to crush his freedom of speech with "curses, cries of drag him out, kill him, etc., accompanied with brandishing of clubs." In some counties, where there were sprinklings of Quaker communities, he found a warmer reception.

By the end of February, the speechifying and rigors of travel had taken a toll on Robinson's health. His voice was weak and he had a cold. He returned to Emily in Cincinnati. For the month of March and much of April, he rested. At the end of April, the Robinsons went to Mount Pleasant, Ohio, where they served as delegates at the annual meeting of the Ohio Anti-Slavery Society. After the convention ended, the Robinsons and Edward and Phebe Mathews Weed moved to Putnam in Muskingum County. Emily and Phebe were to remain there while Marius and Edward went out on their second agency tour—Marius traveling to the northeastern section of Ohio.

On Thursday, June 1, Robinson arrived in Berlin in Trumbull County and asked for the use of the schoolhouse. He was refused. A Quaker merchant and his wife, Mr. and Mrs. Jesse Garretson, opened their home to the meeting, which was held there the next day. Robinson asked his audience of listeners to think independently, not like some people, who, like young robins, "sat in their nests with their mouths open, and swallowed whatever the old ones dropped in." Although a mob had been forecast, Robinson's lecture came off without incident. Robinson announced that he would speak again on Sunday to refute the slaveholders' charge that the Bible supported slavery.

On Saturday, there were buzzings of unrest in Berlin. About ten o'clock that night, Robinson was sitting in Garretson's store chatting with the Garretsons and J. F. Powers. Suddenly, Mordecai B. Hughes burst into the room, grabbed Robinson by the arm, and dragged him to the door, insisting, "You have got to leave town tonight. You have disturbed the peace of our citizens long enough."

Mrs. Garretson rose and crossed the room, telling Hughes, "If you take him, you must take me, too."

A second man entered the store, seizing Robinson by his other arm. Even more men were trying to get inside. Mrs. Garretson tried to shut the door against them. Hughes demanded that Jesse Garretson throw Robinson out of his place. Garretson refused. In the scuffle, the men had dragged Robinson's leg over a scythe and sliced it open. All the while, Mrs. Garretson was struggling to block the men outside. Hughes ordered her to let go, but she would not yield. Hughes then pushed her violently and struck her twice, spraining her wrist and bruising her chest.

Once free of Mrs. Garretson, the ruffians dragged their prey into the street, hurrying him along with violence for a mile, cursing, taunting, and threatening him. One man held each of his wrists and another, a more savage man, had hold of his collar. The third man, Robinson said, "...frequently jerked me with violence towards him and would then thrust his fists violently against my breast; and once he struck me on the head...."

They poured hot tar on his body and covered him with feathers. Then, they loaded him into a wagon, drove him ten miles to the center of Canfield and dumped him in a field. Robinson, wracked with pain, semi-conscious, with a frightful appearance, went from door to door until he came to the house of a good Samaritan who gave him clothes and first aid.

Robinson's health was broken. He went to stay with his in-laws for a month in Guilford to recuperate. In August, he resumed his duties for the American Anti-Slavery Society.

Part III

CONSCIENCE

(1835-1850)

Have English women then done so much for the negro, and shall American women do nothing? Oh no! Already are there sixty female Anti-Slavery Societies in operation. These are doing just what the English women did, telling the story of the colored man's wrongs, praying for his deliverance, and presenting his kneeling image constantly before the public eye on bags and needle-books, card-racks, pen-wipers, pin-cushions, &c. Even the children of the north are inscribing on their handy work, "May the points of our needles prick the slaveholder's conscience."

—*Angelina Grimké*

CHAPTER 30

The Grimkés Break Out

In 1829, whereas Angelina Grimké had followed in the footsteps of her sister, Sarah, leaving her family's South Carolina plantation, moving to Philadelphia and joining the Society of Friends, she had never loved the Quakers as Sarah did. The Quakers instructed Angelina to sit still with her hands folded in her lap. They assigned her endless rounds of boring charitable work. Angelina was restless for a field of action all her own. Since 1831, when the elders discouraged her from enrolling at Hartford Female Seminary (those dangerous Presbyterians!) and made her feel she was abandoning her charities, she had begun to doubt herself and the Quakers.

Angelina, too, was disappointed in the Quakers' anti-slavery work. Granted, the Society had been the first religious body in North America to condemn slavery. They continued to educate Blacks and to help runaway slaves. But they did not treat Black people as equals. Quaker churches had segregated seating for them. The "negro seat" in the Grimkés' Fourth and Arch Street Meeting was placed in the back. Angelina and Sarah were not allowed to sit in church with their Quaker friends, free Blacks, Grace Bustill Douglass and her daughter, Sarah Mapps Douglass. Sarah and Grace, both educators, were members of the biracial Philadelphia Female Anti-Slavery Society, of which Angelina and Sarah Grimké were members.

Reading about the mob action of 1835 and William Lloyd Garrison's rousing editorials in *The Liberator* compelled Angelina to speak out. She could think of nothing else but helping the slave, asking herself continually, "What can I do?" Overcoming agonizing self-doubt, she wrote a letter to William Lloyd Garrison, expressing sympathy with the abolitionists and expressing her belief that fighting slavery was worth dying for. Much to her surprise, Garrison printed her letter in the August 30, 1835 issue of *The Liberator*. The letter was reprinted in other abolition papers. Whereas other women had spoken out against slavery, none of them were Southern women who had owned slaves. This made her an exceptional asset for the anti-slavery movement. The Quakers pressured Angelina to recant her letter. Angelina held firm.

Since the publication of her letter in *The Liberator*, Angelina had become somewhat of a celebrity. Abolitionists wrote to her. She received many invitations to present lectures in New York and New England. She felt that God had been preparing her for a mission, but she could not yet discern it. She undertook a serious study of slavery. She read the abolition newspapers. She started and stopped multiple writing projects until, one day, she found her subject. She spent two weeks at the end of July 1836 writing this manuscript, after which she mailed it to the American Anti-Slavery Society, in the hopes of publication. In October, her *Appeal to Christian Women of the South* was released in pamphlet form and was advertised in the anti-slavery press. In her *Appeal*, Angelina strove to arouse Southern women to do something about slavery:

> But perhaps you will be ready to query, why appeal to women on this subject? We do not make the laws which perpetuate slavery. No legislative power is vested in us; we can do nothing to overthrow the system, even if we wished to do so. To this I reply, I know you do not make the laws, but I also know that you are the wives and mothers, the sisters and daughters of those who do, and if you really suppose you can do nothing to overthrow slavery, you are greatly mistaken. You can do much in every way: four things I will name:

1st. You can read on this subject.

2d. You can pray over this subject.

3d. You can speak on this subject....Speak then to your relatives, your friends, your acquaintances on the subject of slavery; be not afraid if you are conscientiously convinced it is sinful, to say so openly, but calmly, and to let your sentiments be known....

4th. You can act on this subject. Some of you own slaves yourselves. If you believe slavery is sinful, set them at liberty....If they wish to remain with you, pay them wages....Should they remain teach them.

The idea that women could change society was a revolutionary concept. Southerners were incensed by the controversial *Appeal*. Besides calling for the abolition of their economic base and aristocratic lifestyle, Angelina further endangered the Southern status quo by inviting women to step outside the parlor, the kitchen, and the nursery to participate in a political matter. The mayor of Charleston barred Angelina and her letters from entering the city.

Although few Southern women ever saw her *Appeal*, as abolitionist literature was banned, it was remarked upon in Southern papers. It was read in New York, Ohio, and New England. It made a deep impression on Theodore Weld. Consequently, Angelina, 30, accepted a commission to become one of his lecturing agents and the only woman for the American Anti-Slavery Society to talk to groups of women. Sister Sarah, 44, would accompany her and speak some. The women attended the New York City Agents' Convention in November of 1836. The Grimkés, who had been raised in privilege on a South Carolina slaveholding plantation, the daughters of a judge of the South Carolina Supreme Court, had a unique history to share with audiences of Northern women, having seen firsthand cruelties of the slave system. Here, Sarah Grimké shares her motivation for daring to speak the truth about slavery:

As I left my native state on account of slavery, and deserted the home of my fathers to escape the sound of the lash and the shrieks of tortured victims....I feel impelled...to give my testimony respecting the system of American slavery,—to detail a few facts, most of which came under my personal observation. And here I may premise, that the actors in these tragedies were all men and women of the highest respectability, and of the first families in South Carolina; and, with one exception, citizens of Charleston; and that their cruelties did not in the slightest degree affect their standing in society.

A handsome mulatto woman, about 18 or 20 years of age, whose independent spirit could not brook the degradation of slavery, was in the habit of running away: for this offence she had been repeatedly sent by her master and mistress to be whipped by the keeper of the Charleston work-house. This has been done with such inhuman severity, as to lacerate her back in a most shocking manner; a finger could not be laid between the cuts. But the love of liberty was too strong to be annihilated by torture; and, as a last resort, she was whipped at several different times, and kept a close prisoner. A heavy iron collar, with three long prongs projecting from it, was placed round her neck, and a strong and sound front tooth was extracted, to serve as a mark to describe her, in case of escape. Her sufferings at this time were agonizing. She could lie in no position but on her back, which was sore from scourging, as I can testify, from personal inspection, and her only place of rest was the floor, on a blanket. These outrages were committed in a family where the mistress daily read the scriptures, and assembled her children for family worship. She was accounted, and was really, so far as alms-giving was concerned, a charitable woman, and tender hearted to the poor; and yet this suffering slave, who was the seamstress of the family, was continually in her presence, sitting in her chamber to sew, or engaged in other household work, with her lacerated and bleeding back, her mutilated mouth, and heavy iron collar, without, so far as appeared, exciting any feelings of compassion.

The Grimkés' first "parlor talk" to a small crowd of women was scheduled for December. So many ladies wanted to attend the lecture, however, that the meeting had to be moved to a larger space, in the session room at the Baptist Church. The idea of women lecturing in a public place shocked some in the community. Angelina grew anxious and considered canceling the meeting. But Weld encouraged the sisters to go on. "His visit was really a strength to us," Angelina said. "I felt no more fear."

At three o'clock on the appointed day, Rev. Henry Ludlow opened the meeting with prayer. Rev. Dunbar welcomed the three hundred women attendees. Then, both clergymen scurried out as it was not proper for women to speak in gatherings where men were present. Such a mixture of men and women was referred to as "promiscuous." Angelina spoke for forty minutes, followed by Sarah. Afterward, the sisters went to tea at Lewis and Julia Tappan's home, where Weld was waiting. Julia Tappan spoke of its success and mentioned, laughingly, that a man had tried to get into the meeting and had to be put out by Rev. Ludlow. Weld exclaimed, "How ridiculous to think of a man being shouldered out of a meeting for fear he should hear a woman speak." Angelina and Weld spent the evening engrossed in conversation.

By the middle of January 1837, the Grimké meetings enjoyed such a great turnout that the gatherings had to be held in the church sanctuary. Their tour continued throughout New York, with no opposition except in the press. Clad in simple gray dresses with matching bonnets, the sisters were described as plain, soft-spoken, well-mannered, deferential, and modest. They advocated "Immediate emancipation, gradually accomplished," a more palatable pitch that drew hundreds of converts to the AAAS. The agents' task was the conciliation of communities made hostile by Garrison's anti-government/anti-church form of immediate emancipation.

Meanwhile, the right of petition dominated deliberations in Washington, D.C. Since 1835, the petitions had included the request for Congress to immediately abolish slavery in the District of Columbia, home to over six thousand slaves. The Constitution protected Southern states' rights in regard to slavery, so the federal government had no say in those matters. However, the federal government did have jurisdiction over the federal District of Columbia. Led by the U.S. representative from South Carolina, Henry Pinckney, a committee was appointed to study the matter, as the proslavery congressmen were infuriated by the mountains of anti-slavery petitions arriving daily for their consideration. A gag rule against all petitions relating to slavery was adopted by the Southern-dominated Congress.

With a gag rule in place, the hundreds of thousands of petitions that were sent to the Legislature were tabled, unread, a violation of the First Amendment of the Constitution that guaranteed that "Congress shall make no law...abridging the freedom of speech, or of the press; or the right of the people peaceably to assemble, and *to petition the Government for a redress of grievances.*"

Despite the gag rule, the former president and congressman from Massachusetts, John Quincy Adams, persisted in his efforts to have the petitions heard. Women's signatures outnumbered men's on the petitions, as women had built a national system of female societies to support a petition campaign. Petitioning was their only way of being heard by the Congress, and they longed to be involved in reform that got results. Unlike many of his colleagues, Adams defended the right of women to be heard by petition on the floor of Congress. Southerner Pinckney's viewpoint was that a woman, in petitioning, had unsexed herself by "meddling in man's affairs," which he deemed unscriptural. These activist women were called "devils" and "old maids" by others to get them to withdraw in shame from agitation in the field. But the women, more disturbed by suffering humanity than by chauvinist name-calling, kept the petitions flowing to Congress. As the women went door-to-door seeking signatures, they met with some refusals from women who were as yet unconverted. However, they brought a neighborhood influence that no pamphlet or lecturer could provide; they did the movement good by conversing along the way with those who did not share their principles. Importantly, they drew more women into their networks, which would prove invaluable for future reform activity.

John C. Calhoun, the senator from South Carolina, followed the House's example and instituted a gag rule in that chamber. Discussion of slavery was now forbidden in both houses of Congress, reducing the chance of defeating slavery in the District of Columbia to almost zero. Calhoun said abolitionism was a danger that was infecting the North. Unless abolitionists were silenced, he threatened secession. He asserted, "We of the South will not, cannot, surrender our institutions." Slavery was not an evil, he said, but "a good–a positive good…."

———

On May 9-12, the Female Anti-Slavery Convention met in New York. Seventy-one women, both Black and white, from eight different states, were delegates. Lydia M. Child, Lucretia Mott, Grace Douglass, and Ann "Nancy" Fitzhugh Smith were chosen as vice presidents. Many resolutions were offered.

Lydia M. Child urged abolitionists to do business with Blacks and to sit with them in the churches. Angelina Grimké resolved that "it is the duty of woman, and the province of woman, to plead the cause of the oppressed in our land, and do all that she can by her voice, and her pen, and her purse, and the influence of her example, to overthrow the horrible system of American slavery."

The *New York Spectator* published a derisive commentary. The attendees arrived in:

…'clouds of petticoats'…for a GRAND FEMALE ABOLITION CONVENTION….'our female brethren'…have been lifting up their voices like the sound of an octave flute….The spinster has thrown aside her distaff—the blooming beauty her guitar—the matron her darning-needle—the sweet novelist her crow-quill;—the young mother has left her baby to nestle alone in the cradle—and the kitchen maid her pots and frying-pans—to discuss the weighty matters of state….

From New York, the Grimkés traveled to Boston, where they received a cordial welcome. In Boston, a minister and two or three other men slipped into the lecture room and took a back seat. As reported in the July 29 issue of the *Boston Courier*, Angelina spoke of the cruel color prejudice of the white Northerners:

The white excluded the negro from the railroad car, the stage-coach, and the steamboat. How could the negro rise, while the foot of the white man was upon his neck? Physician, heal thyself. The North could not ask the South to free the chains of the slave, while the black man at the North was bowed down by the iron bonds of prejudice.

The sisters visited John Quincy Adams. They addressed the ladies of Dorchester. They attended meetings of reform societies and were entertained in private homes. They spoke in Lynn, Salem, Newburyport, and other Massachusetts towns. In Lowell, an audience of one hundred fifty men and women crowded into the City Hall to hear the Grimkés speak. By the end of June, men were attending the gatherings regularly. News of these promiscuous gatherings traveled fast. Therefore, some ministers in small towns closed their church doors to them, refusing to publish their meeting notices.

Even though so many voices were raised against the Grimkés, people still poured in to hear them. During July alone, they had covered New England, speaking to audiences totaling twelve thousand people at nineteen appearances in fourteen separate towns. While there had been much glory for the cause, there were a few sour notes. There had been the usual negative press about the propriety of women speaking in public and with men present, some just curious to hear what "Devil-ina" had to say.

Two of the reproaches were the hardest hitting. On July 28, a group of Northern churchmen issued a series of "Pastoral Letters," which appeared in the press, in which they denounced women "who so far forget themselves as to itinerate in the character of public lecturers and teachers." The ministers threatened that, if women continued to interfere in the political arena, then God would render their wombs barren. Though their names were not mentioned, the clergy was clearly referring to the Grimké sisters. Angelina and Sarah had not set out to challenge the male rule of society, but that condescending letter got their dander up. Soon, the sisters would argue that women were just as oppressed as slaves.

For Angelina, the most painful attack came in a book written by someone she had once considered a friend. Catharine Beecher, 36, published *An Essay on Slavery and Abolitionism, with Reference to the Duty of American Females*, and addressed it, scoldingly, to Angelina Grimké. Among other criticisms, she lambasted women abolitionists for straying from their moral and domestic sphere to establish abolition societies. She asserted that "Heaven has appointed to one sex the superior, and to the other the subordinate station….[W]oman holds a subordinate relation in society to the other sex."

James Birney did not think much of Catharine Beecher's *Essay*, saying that a book reviewer just needed a brush to clear away "Miss B's cobwebs." Many Southern papers praised Beecher, assured that she had the power to stop Angelina in her "unfeminine course."

Catharine Beecher was a contradiction. She was a professional woman, lecturing, teaching, and writing to make a living. She did not occupy the domestic sphere. She operated in the public sphere.

She had neither home, nor husband, nor children, yet she saw fit to dictate to other women how they should conduct themselves.

Angelina struck back at Catharine in thirteen letters printed in *The Liberator*, skillfully presenting her abolitionist views. She pointed out that Beecher's insistence that Angelina display "proper behavior" was a method to keep women in their place, just as "the colored people are to be taught to be 'very humble' and 'unassuming,' 'gentle,' and 'meek.'"

By the end of the summer, all the Grimkés' frank talk about the rights of women and their speaking to mixed audiences caused great quarreling in the male-run American Anti-Slavery Society. The Tappans distanced themselves from the Grimkés. Theodore Weld became alarmed that the Grimkés' feminist views overshadowed their original mission. Angelina asserted herself with Weld, saying, "We cannot push Abolitionism forward with all our might *until* we take up the stumbling block [opposition to women speaking] out of the road." She believed that human liberation required a universal application.

By August, the AASS disclaimed all connection with Angelina and Sarah as agents. The Society could exercise no control over them as the Grimkés drew no salary and covered their own expenses. Weld even denied to them that they had ever actually been agents, asserting that the sisters, who had barnstormed the country from New York to Boston for almost a year, had never been more than "helpers."

CHAPTER 31

The Beechers Make Some Changes

On June 5, three days after Marius Robinson was attacked by the Berlin mob, and while Angelina and Sarah Grimké were lecturing in Massachusetts, Henry Ward Beecher was graduating from Lane Seminary in Walnut Hills outside Cincinnati. "It was hot as mustard," that day, wrote Mary Wright to Henry's little sister, Isabella Beecher, who was out of town. Despite the heat, the Lane chapel was crowded with young people. Because of his sunny, funny personality, Henry made lots of friends. Dr. Lyman Beecher opened the ceremony with a prayer. Hymns were sung. Some dull speeches followed. Then, Dr. Beecher summoned Henry to the pulpit to speak.

Mary Wright recalled, "As he opened his mouth, every one seemed to wake up, his manner is so impressive, and his voice so deep and commanding....Isabel, Isabel, what shall I do, he is going to be married. Oh dear me." Mary was one of Henry's female admirers in Cincinnati—Henry craved female attention—even though, for five and a half years, he had been engaged to Eunice Bullard, who bided her time in West Sutton, Massachusetts, until he was ordained as a minister. He proposed to her one winter evening in 1832 when paying her a call at her aunt's house. Henry, in his role as her Latin tutor, asked Eunice to translate the Latin "amo" to English—which means "I love"—and then slipped a note to her which read, "Will you go with me as missionary to the West?" While his proposal was romantic, his idea was pragmatic. A minister had to have a wife. While Eunice's brothers were given advanced education, Eunice stayed home, sewing and cooking for her seven teasing brothers and a critical father, who was strict to the point of violence. Once, when Eunice and her sister appeared at the dinner table in relatively low-cut gowns, Dr. Bullard hurled a bowl of hot soup at them, saying that he supposed they must have been cold and needed warming up. Eunice jumped to accept Henry's proposal of marriage.

Henry's relationship with Mary Wright, the writer of the letter to Isabella Beecher, had caused a rift to develop between Henry and his younger brother, Charles, with whom he had previously been close. Charles was hopelessly in love with Mary Wright, who was in love with Henry. Furthermore, Charles doubted his faith in God and dropped out of Lane Seminary, infuriating Henry, and began teaching music lessons in Cincinnati. Father Lyman was disappointed in Charles. He expected all his sons to become ministers. To date, William, Edward, George, and now Henry had done so, Lyman sometimes having to pull strings to get them positions. A month after his graduation, Henry, 24, had begun preaching at his new church in Lawrenceburg, Indiana. In August, he would go East, marry Eunice, 25, and bring her to that destitute village of five hundred, where, after arriving by steamboat, Eunice said they would pick "their way from the wharf to the house through mud and over pigs."

The Beecher Family (1850) Photograph includes, standing from left to right, Thomas, William, Edward, Charles, Henry Ward, and seated from left to right, Isabella, Catherine, Lyman, Mary, and Harriet. Not pictured: George and James.

Isabella Beecher received Mary Wright's letter in Hartford, Connecticut, where, by August, she was living with sister Mary Perkins, her husband, their four children, and Aunt Esther. Isabella had been forced to leave Cincinnati after Catharine's Western Female Institute failed and left her without a school. Later, she recalled that:

> At fifteen my dear good father (instigated of course by his new wife) came to me and suggested that I should begin to teach school now and support myself. I, who had never been to school in earnest, for two years together in my whole life.

That summer, Harriet and brother George arranged for Isabella to live in Hartford. Mary and Aunt Esther could watch over Isabella, and she could attend the girls' school Catharine had founded there.

Mary's husband, Thomas Perkins, a lawyer, had failed financially several times in his life through speculation and, at that moment, was experiencing a financial crisis. The creditors were confiscating his land and other assets, including the family's parlor furniture and Mary's beautiful piano. Aunt Esther reported that Thomas had no salary; the household staff was reduced from two girls and a man to one girl and no man. Mary and Esther needed Isabella's help.

For Isabella, it was hard to be separated from Harriet; she always felt that Harriet was the most truly religious person she had ever known. What Isabella was not going to miss was the badgering interrogations her father had subjected his children to over the state of their souls.

The Perkins were among the many Americans who were hit hard by the Panic of 1837 when the economy crashed. A bubble had been growing for years as land speculators used paper notes to buy land and to finance turnpikes, canals, and railroads. This paper money was not sufficiently backed by gold or silver. There was a bank run; when too many people tried to redeem the paper notes for coins, banks turned them away. Six hundred banks failed, food and rent prices rose, and unemployment spread. The price of cotton dropped dramatically. The ill effects were felt for seven years.

In Cincinnati, Uncle Samuel Foote went bankrupt and sold his mansion, leading to the demise of the Semi-Colon Club. A few days after July 4, a bank messenger arrived at Dr. Beecher's house in Walnut Hills with appalling news. The New York bank refused to honor the draft for Dr. Beecher's salary. Arthur Tappan's silk-importing business failed and there was no more endowment for Dr. Beecher's professorial chair. Dr. Beecher was left with his small salary from the Second Presbyterian Church, which graciously agreed to raise the stipend $200 a year. George and Sarah sent him $200, and several sympathetic Cincinnatians made donations. The Panic almost finished off Lane Seminary; in the fall, only fifteen boys would enroll for the beginners' class.

Harriet and Mary Dutton both lost money when The Western Female Institute closed. Catharine kept all the proceeds from the sale of the school furniture for herself. Harriet had lost $200 and Mary, $500. Catharine felt that everyone but herself was to blame for the failure of the WFI. The previous year, Catharine had traveled throughout New York and New England, from April to October, peddling a nonexistent agency to bring teachers to Cincinnati to train and collecting the names of interested "missionary teachers" and possible donors. Mary Dutton had written countless letters to Catharine alerting her to the school's problems. Catharine replied to Mary not to trouble her with the school's problems as she was engaged in more important matters. Mary Lyons, the founder of Mount Holyoke Female Seminary in Massachusetts and a respected educator, pointed out that while Catharine promised a great deal, she guaranteed nothing. With the demise of her school, she had no institutional base for carrying out her educational scheme. This made Catharine even more quarrelsome than usual.

Fortunately, Calvin Stowe's salary was unaffected by the Panic of 1837. Conversely, the Lane trustees increased it to $1100 that year. Blessedly, he and Harriet would not feel the pinch right away as others would. They were out of debt and free of worry. Nevertheless, he continued to complain to the Lane trustees. They had not yet awarded him the full-sized house they initially promised. In a July 22, 1837 letter Calvin wrote from Marietta, Ohio, where he was staying on business, to Harriet, back at home in Cincinnati after her short stay in Putnam, he gave vent to his dissatisfaction. Calvin pledged to:

> throw Lane Seminary to the dogs if they do not do justice to me in this respect, and you may tell them so. Our miserable accommodation, the covenant-breaking conduct of the board, and the degrading contrast between me and the other professors has been the cause of three-fourths of my unhappiness since I returned from Europe.

Eventually, the trustees allowed a $250 supplement in lieu of the house. Since their marriage eighteen months earlier, Harriet and Calvin had spent half of it apart, yet Calvin was already grumbling about being unhappy—while on a trip away from home with no one to manage but himself. Meanwhile, back at their cottage in Walnut Hills, Harriet shared space with the twins, the nanny, the wet nurse, and Calvin's widowed mother, Hepzibah Stowe, who had come from Massachusetts for an extended stay. Harriet's mother-in-law disapproved of the expense of paying for domestic help, accusing Harriet of being extravagant with Calvin's salary, of Harriet needing much waiting upon, and of Harriet of being inclined to hire too much help. Calvin echoed his mother's sentiments. Together, Calvin and his mother dwelt on Harriet's faults and criticized her often. This changed the power balance in the household, factoring into Harriet's decision to take a short summer break to stay with her brother William and wife Katherine in Putnam, Ohio.

After the birth of her twins, Harriet told Catharine that she had not planned on having any more babies for a while, but here she was, pregnant again, only months away from the twins' one-year birthday.

───────

By the end of that summer of 1837, all the adult Beecher siblings and spouses, except Mary and Thomas Perkins, were living in the West. Harriet, Calvin, Charles, and Catharine lived in Cincinnati. William and wife Katherine lived in Putnam, Ohio. George and wife Sarah lived in Batavia, Ohio. Henry and wife Eunice lived in Lawrenceburg, Indiana. Edward and wife Isabella lived in Jacksonville, Illinois, where Edward, though an ordained minister, was the president of Illinois College.

During Harriet's June/July visit to brother William's family, Harriet found the subject of slavery was out in the open before the people of Putnam, Ohio. The county's Female Anti-Slavery Society was busily distributing petition forms throughout Ohio that called for the abolition of slavery in the District of Columbia. One of these ladies stopped by William and Katherine's house to present Catharine Beecher (who was also visiting) with a copy of the proceedings of the female anti-slavery convention. The article made a strong impression on Harriet. She thought the measures the delegates had proposed for dealing with slavery were extreme, but she credited the proceedings for having been conducted in a better spirit than was usually present at such gatherings.

Harriet found herself reading *The Philanthropist* because, as she explained to Calvin, abolitionism was the fashion in Putnam, so it was natural to look at abolition papers. On July 4, the Beechers celebrated Independence Day at an event in Putnam. *The Liberator* of August 11, 1837, included this mention:

> Dr. Beecher's Sons.
>
> The last number of the Philanthropist contains an account of an Anti-Slavery meeting which was holden at Putnam, Ohio, on the 4th of July. It is said that George Beecher was present by invitation, and gave an address, which for clearness, force, and correctness of sentiment, was considered excellent. He has been requested to write it out for publication. At the close of the exercises, Wm. H. Beecher, Pastor of the Presbyterian church in Putnam, came forward and enrolled his name among the advocates of universal and immediate emancipation. We hope the father will follow the example of his sons.

Harriet found herself wondering where she fit in. She wished an intermediate anti-slavery society existed, one she could reasonably associate with that would not invite social ostracism, compromise Calvin's professorship at Lane, and incur disapproval from her colonizationist father and sister Catharine. Proclaiming yourself an abolitionist in Putnam was one thing, but in the border city of Cincinnati, it was akin to painting a target on one's back. Harriet wrote Calvin:

Pray [I ask you] what is there in Cincinnati to satisfy one whose mind is awakened on this subject? No one can have the system of slavery brought before him without an irrepressible desire to do something, and what is there to be done?

CHAPTER 32

Edward Beecher Considers Lovejoy's Request

At about this same time, over in Jacksonville, Illinois, another of Harriet's brothers, Edward Beecher, was, like Harriet, contemplating doing something more about slavery. Aware that as president of Illinois College, his actions would reflect on the school, he had judiciously and continually resisted the persistent entreaties of his great friend, Elijah P. Lovejoy, to lend his name to the formation of an Illinois anti-slavery society. Lovejoy, the editor of the *Observer*, lived sixty miles to the south in the Mississippi River town of Alton, Illinois (situated across from Missouri, a slave state). Edward had recently decided to give Lovejoy's proposal a fresh look. Two events since the beginning of 1837 pushed Edward to do more than just talk to his peers about abolitionism.

Firstly, in January, the Illinois General Assembly, bowing to Southern pressure, passed a resolution disapproving of the formation of abolition societies. Seventy-seven members of the House voted "Yay," but six congressmen, led by Abraham Lincoln of Sangamon County, refused to sign. Lincoln, though not a fan of abolitionist tactics, lodged a written protest against slavery, saying the system was founded on both "injustice and bad policy."

Secondly, in early summer, Lovejoy and Edward attended the Presbyterian General Assembly in Philadelphia. The Southern and Northern churches had split into two distinct groups along regional lines, as the Southern churches refused to take a stand against slavery.

By nature, Edward Beecher deliberated cautiously before taking action, while Lovejoy raced ahead of public sentiment and acted impetuously, as he did on July 4 in Alton when he called for the formation of a statewide anti-slavery group with headquarters in Alton. As had done their counterparts in Cincinnati just a year before, the commercial class of Alton vehemently opposed this. They were dealing with an economic panic and were dependent upon Southern trade. Immediately, handbills appeared calling for a meeting at the Alton Market House for all citizens who disapproved of the course of the *Observer*. Lovejoy was informed that should he continue to publish his anti-slavery views, he would be met with mob violence. Incensed, Lovejoy wrote more reckless and extreme editorials. Calls to seize his press intensified.

On August 22, the mob destroyed Lovejoy's second press. From then on, the Lovejoy family, Elijah, wife Celia (French), and toddler Edward, were stalked and harassed. Whether in their own home or at friends', prowlers spied upon them through the windows, hurling bricks and stones at them. Celia, who was pregnant, began sleeping in the windowless attic. Because the police did nothing, the mob grew more confident.

Even though his abolitionist friends did supply funds for a third press, Lovejoy's support dwindled. In late September, Lovejoy traveled to Jacksonville to meet with Edward Beecher and other anti-slavery men to discuss holding an anti-slavery convention on October 26 in Alton. Edward agreed to attend only if the event was not dubbed an anti-slavery gathering but rather, addressed "to the friends of free discussion." Optimistic Edward was certain that unity between the two warring factions could be achieved if the "wise and the good" were to meet and talk.

On September 21, the third press arrived, was installed in a warehouse, yet was destroyed before sunup the next day. Shortly afterward, Lovejoy and his family were subject to a home invasion. Two men tried to drag Elijah out into the yard to face a drunken mob. One of the men beat him with his fists. Celia came into the room. One of the men pushed her back and drew his dirk upon her. She struck him in the face with her hand, and then, as Lovejoy recounted:

> ...[Celia] rushing past him, she flew to where I was, and throwing her arms around me, boldly faced the mobites....While they were attempting with oaths and curses to drag me from the room, she was smiting them in the face...or clinging to me to aid in resisting their efforts....Her energetic measures, seconded by those of her mother and sister, induced the assailants to let me go and leave the room.

Fortunately, a friend appeared and got the thugs out of the house, but they would not leave the yard, camping out, drinking, shouting curses, and shooting off pistols. From then on, Elijah slept with a loaded musket by his side, discarding the Garrison ideal that violence should be met with passive resistance. He ordered a fourth press.

As the date of the convention for a "free inquiry on the subject of slavery" approached, the proslavery backlash in Alton intensified. A whisper campaign against Lovejoy infected the town. It was rumored that should Celia die, he would marry a Black woman within a week.

On October 26, despite a frigid town welcome, eighty-five abolitionists (men) from sixteen Illinois counties and two from Ohio arrived in Alton for the meeting. To Edward Beecher's great disappointment, no "wise and good men" of Alton joined them. The fourteen locals who did appear came to disrupt, the chief disrupter being Attorney General Usher F. Linder. Beecher was forced to disband the meeting.

The abolitionists then reconvened at a private home. As they were praying for the success of their mission, a mob tried to break down the door. Mayor Krum swore in some temporary constables to clear away the mob in the street and to guard the house. The meeting continued and Edward drew up the "Declaration of Sentiments," which expressed his view that slavery was a national sin, as all Americans benefitted from it. The Declaration was adopted, and after several days of stormy excitement, a society was formed.

The limits of the citizens' tolerance for abolitionists fast approached its zenith. Town meetings were held in which one faction wanted Lovejoy to be stopped from writing his abolitionist newspaper while the other side defended his right to publish. Attorney General Linder denounced Lovejoy as "a very wicked fellow" and as "a fanatic who…ought to be taken care of."

Undaunted, Lovejoy stood up at this final meeting, faced the crowd in Hogan's store, and spoke:

> I am but one and you are many. You can crush me if you will, but I shall die at my post, for I cannot and will not forsake it. Why should I flee from Alton? Is this not a free state?…You may burn me at the stake, as they did [Francis] McIntosh at St. Louis…but you cannot disgrace me.

The committee approved a resolution stating that the *Observer* was not to be reestablished in Alton.

A tense waiting game followed as Lovejoy's fourth press was expected to arrive daily from Cincinnati. Enemy spies, armed with pistols and clubs, rushed to the dock to check incoming steamboats for the cargo, intending to destroy it before it was even unloaded. Although a horn was sounded, vandals were nowhere in sight when, on Tuesday, November 7, at three a.m., the fourth press made its much-anticipated appearance at the Alton wharf aboard the *Missouri Fulton*. Mayor Krum was there to oversee its unloading. Under cover of darkness, twenty to thirty good men under the leadership of Winthrop Gilman—who had agreed to store the press at his riverside warehouse—unloaded the massive press. Beecher and Lovejoy were on hand to help the other men heave the box to the third floor of the warehouse of Godfrey, Gilman, & Co. This press would be heavily guarded by squads of armed men, drilling and marching in the manner of militia, permitted by the mayor to protect Gilman's warehouse by force if necessary.

When the sun rose the next morning, Edward and Lovejoy left the warehouse for Lovejoy's house. They united in prayer. Celia Lovejoy was weak and had not risen, so they said their prayers in her chamber. Confident that the danger had passed, Edward left on the stagecoach for Jacksonville. Lovejoy and his associates breathed a sigh of relief that the press had been delivered so bloodlessly. After dark, though, a mob of armed and drunk men assembled at Gilman's warehouse and tried to break in. Shots were exchanged and a rioter was killed. The enraged crowd spliced together ladders to reach the top of the three-story warehouse and set it on fire. Lovejoy ran out the south door and shot at the man firing the roof. A sniper fired five bullets into Lovejoy's body and killed him. The guards inside fled the warehouse, and the mob destroyed the press.

Lovejoy at 1837 Alton Riot

When the nation learned of Lovejoy's murder, it was, as statesman John Quincy Adams wrote, "a shock as of an earthquake throughout this continent, which will be felt in the most distant regions of the earth." Lovejoy's death as a martyr in defense of the freedom of the press formed an era in the history of the Union. Northern newspapers lamented his death and spoke of his legacy, as in this excerpt from the Portland, Maine *Transcript*:

> They desired to silence him, and he is dead — and the press they
> feared is destroyed. And yet, though Lovejoy has earned the crown
> of martyrdom, and been taken from among us, he speaketh, and
> in a voice of thunder that shall penetrate where his living voice
> would never have been heard — and move thousands of hearts
> which his arguments never could have moved.

The press in the slave states behaved in predictable fashion. The *Missouri Republican* disparaged Lovejoy and planted a lie claiming, with no evidence, that Lovejoy was the man who shot and killed the rioter, Bishop.

Throughout the North, meetings were held protesting Lovejoy's murder. At a prayer meeting in Hudson, Ohio, a failed land speculator named John Brown proclaimed, "Here, before God, in the presence of these witnesses, from this time, I consecrate my life to the destruction of slavery."

The American Anti-Slavery Society declared Lovejoy a martyr and issued an AAAS writing paper inscribed with a new logo and motto: "LOVEJOY the first MARTYR to American LIBERTY. MURDERED for asserting FREEDOM of the Press. Alton Nov. 7, 1837."

Citizens across the nation, angered that a journalist was killed in a free state, staged demonstrations to condemn the mob action. On December 8, 1837, five thousand people packed into Boston's Faneuil Hall. If the Alton mob intended to silence abolitionist speech, their actions had quite the opposite effect. One hundred prominent citizens under the leadership of Unitarian minister William Ellery Channing spoke to the crowd. A cross-section of political opinion was represented in the noisy Hall; present were abolitionists, free speech advocates and their opponents, and swing voters. Channing sponsored resolutions in favor of citizens airing unpopular opinions and decrying vigilante justice.

The mood in the Hall was harmonious until Massachusetts Attorney General James T. Austin rose to declare that "Lovejoy died as a fool dieth." He called Lovejoy "a clergyman with a gun" and commended the Alton mob for their virtuous action. He denounced abolitionists for frightening the public with their wild schemes of emancipating hordes of Blacks, saying:

> We have a menagerie in our city with lions, tigers, hyenas, an elephant, a jackass or two, and monkeys in plenty. Suppose, now, some new cosmopolite...who believes that all are entitled to freedom...should engage in the humane task of giving liberty to these wild beasts...?
>
> The people of Missouri had as much reason to be afraid of their slaves as we should have to be afraid of the wild beasts of the menagerie. They had the same dread of Lovejoy that we should have of this supposed instigator, if...the caravan let loose to prowl about our streets.

William Lloyd Garrison was noticeably absent at Faneuil; he had been shocked to learn that Lovejoy had resorted to the armed defense of free speech. He pronounced Lovejoy a martyr but not a Christian martyr. Henry B. Stanton and other abolitionists were furious that Garrison would condemn Lovejoy. Garrisonian ideals of passive resistance were inadequate for the current climate. Garrison's grip on power was loosening.

When news of Lovejoy's murder reached the Beecher family,

with it came a rumor that Edward Beecher had been killed fighting alongside him. Tension remained high until they learned that Edward was safe in Jacksonville, where he was hastily preparing for distribution of the pamphlet, *Narrative of Riots at Alton: In Connection with the Death of Rev. Elijah P. Lovejoy.* In this full-throated defense of his and Lovejoy's actions in the recent tragedy, Edward wrote that the citizens of Alton hated mobs but they hated abolitionists more. Edward's wife, Isabella, was outspoken about her anti-slavery views, albeit in a less public way than Edward. On January 22, 1838, she wrote in a Beecher family circulating letter a message for her sister-in-law, Catharine:

> Do not be alarmed, I am not coming out in print like Miss Grimké....Stir up your stumps, you are quite behind the spirit of the age; you must become an Abolitionist, or you will be left in the background. The Alton murder has brought us all over to the faith.

Upon learning of Lovejoy's murder, Angelina Grimké, ill with typhoid fever and confined to bed in the home of Boston friends, mustered enough strength to write a stinging rebuke of Elijah Lovejoy for his use of force in self-defense. She then turned her wrath on his pregnant widow Celia, criticizing her for her use of force in protecting her husband during the home invasion:

> Instead, then, of smiting the mobocrats in their faces, let her either surrender herself to them, to suffer with her husband...or let her follow him afar off, as did the mother of our Lord...[L]et us look at Mary standing by the cross of her beloved son, in perfect silence, in holy resignation.

On January 20, 1838, an Alton jury exonerated leaders of the mob who had killed Lovejoy. A week later, in Springfield, Illinois, Congressman

Abraham Lincoln made an address before the Young Men's Lyceum in which he condemned the mob violence, "now abroad in our land." He was the only state legislator in Illinois or Missouri to denounce the spirit of the mob. He recalled one of the effects of mob law, scenes rapidly becoming so common in a land "famed for love of law and order." He spoke of the mob murder in St. Louis of a free Black man:

> Turn, then, to that horror-striking scene at St. Louis. A single victim was only sacrificed there. His story is very short; and is, perhaps, the most highly tragic, if anything of its length, that has ever been witnessed in real life. A mulatto man, by the name of McIntosh, was seized in the street, dragged to the suburbs of the city, chained to a tree, and actually burned to death; and all within a single hour from the time he had been a freeman, attending to his own business, and at peace with the world.

The danger of the mobocratic spirit, he explained, was that it broke down the people's attachment to the government:

> Whenever this effect shall be produced among us; whenever the vicious portion of population shall be permitted to gather in bands of hundreds and thousands, and burn churches, ravage and rob provision-stores, throw printing presses into rivers, shoot editors, and hang and burn obnoxious persons at pleasure, and with impunity; depend on it, this government cannot last.

He answered the question, "How shall we fortify against it?"

> Let every American...swear by the blood of the Revolution, never to violate...the laws of the country; and never to tolerate their violation by others.

CHAPTER 33

Charles Sumner Brushes Up His French

On December 8, 1837, the same day as the Faneuil Hall meeting, Charles Sumner was sailing out of New York harbor, bound for Paris. No steamers had yet crossed the Atlantic Ocean. Sumner traveled on the *Albany*, a wooden sailing ship and a swift one, Sumner wrote his friend, borne out to sea that day by a "smacking breeze" and a "bellying wave."

Sumner, 26, had shocked everyone when he announced that he was taking a sabbatical from his fledgling Boston law practice to visit Europe. Friends, colleagues, and his father were disapproving. But Sumner loved to travel; he yearned to know more about everything. With loans from three friends, he went abroad with the purpose of self-improvement: to learn languages and observe foreign manners, customs, and institutions, with a focus on the study of law. He carried with him letters of introduction provided by friends, which would allow him to socialize with European writers, lawyers, and judges. In order to converse with such notables, Sumner had brushed up on his French, which he had studied at Harvard.

Upon his arrival in France, Sumner discovered that his "French was no more fit for use than a rusty gun barrel." He decided he would make no attempts to enter French society until he had mastered French. He hired two tutors. To develop his listening skills, he went to the theater or opera at night and tried to follow along with a copy of the play in hand.

In the mornings, he sampled lectures in French at the Sorbonne, where things were done much differently than in American schools of higher learning. For instance, the professors sat when they taught and seldom taught from notes. They did not wear a badge or distinctive dress; they were identified by a piece of red ribbon on the left lapel of their coats. The students often did not remove their hats in the classrooms. To applaud the close of the lecture, the students stamped their feet. Students were older than the average. One of the lecturers attracted a considerable number of women in the student seats.

On January 22, 1838, Sumner went to a lecture at the École de Droit, where he found Professor Ducaurroy in the midst of pontificating on the Institutes of Justinian. In his diary, Sumner described Ducaurroy as an old, mild-mannered gentlemen of graying hair and slow speech. Of Ducaurroy's eloquent mastery of subject, he did not record because what struck Sumner particularly was the racial composition of Ducaurroy's class:

> He had quite a large audience, among whom I noticed two or three blacks, or rather mulattoes,—two-thirds black, perhaps,— dressed quite *à la mode*, and having the easy, jaunty air of young men of fashion, who were well received by their fellow-students. They were standing in the midst of a knot of young men; and their color seemed to be no objection to them. I was glad to see this; though, with American impressions, it seemed very strange. It must be, then, that the distance between free blacks and the whites among us is derived from education, and does not exist in the nature of things.

Never before had Sumner given much thought to the topic of slavery or racial prejudice. Living in cosmopolitan and free Boston had sheltered him from contact with slavery's evils. Matter of fact, he had not even seen a slave until four years earlier, when he traveled by rail through Maryland to Washington, D.C., and passed a group of slaves working in a field. He wrote to his family about his impressions of them:

> They appear to be nothing more than moving masses of flesh, unendowed with anything of intelligence above the brutes.

Sumner's spirit underwent a transformation in Ducaurroy's lecture room. The scene he witnessed, Black and white students learning together harmoniously, made an indelible impression on him. When he returned to Boston, he would carry back with him the radical idea of racial equality.

CHAPTER 34

Angelina Makes a Command Decision

A lthough they had declared their passionate love for each other in February 1838, the turtle doves had managed, for a good while, to keep their affair in perfect secrecy. But when their abolitionist friends got wind of their March engagement and plans for a May wedding, word leaked out. The *New York Daily Herald* wrote:

> A great excitement prevails in the city, about the intended wedding between the he-male and she-male abolition orators, Angelina Grimké and Theodore Weld. They have a 'moving' to be welded together.

If New York was excited, Philadelphia was electrified. The date of the Grimké-Weld wedding ceremony was the evening of Monday, May 14, an auspicious day in Philadelphia; one that would begin with the triumphant dedication of Pennsylvania Hall, a brand-new, three-story building, measuring one hundred feet long and sixty-two feet wide, lighted by gas, ventilated through the roof for fresh air, with luxurious interior appointments. The ground floor contained four offices. One was for an abolitionist reading room and bookstore; another held the office of the *Pennsylvania Freeman*, the abolitionist newspaper edited by poet John Greenleaf Whittier. The newspaper's press and the type had yet to be moved to the Hall.

The other two first-floor offices were for the state anti-slavery society and a store selling items produced by non-slave labor. Also, on the first floor was a lecture room with seating for two to three hundred persons, committee rooms, and three large entries and stairways seven feet wide leading to the second floor. The second floor comprised a large auditorium with, on the third floor, three galleries surrounding it, with, altogether, seating for three thousand. This two-story lecture hall had a ceiling hung with a mirrored chandelier lit by gas. Above the stage was a banner with Pennsylvania's motto, "Virtue, Liberty, and Independence." Angelina, Lucretia Mott, Maria Chapman, and Abby Kelley would speak in this resplendent Hall on the night of Wednesday, May 16.

Monday's inauguration event heralded a week of celebratory meetings. Raising over forty thousand dollars, the structure had been financed by the sale of twenty-dollar shares to two thousand supporters, many of whom were women, as well as with donations of money and labor. The Hall was dedicated to free inquiry on all subjects. Pennsylvania Hall was a dream come true for the abolitionists; no longer would they have to scrounge for a meeting hall to rent for their lectures. The Hall's event calendar for the week was fully booked.

Theodore and Angelina were aware that their impending marriage was controversial. Theodore had once made himself a pledge never to marry until the last slave was free, but his love for Angelina was all-consuming. Lewis Tappan had to admit a grudging admiration for Theodore in marrying a feminist, the most notorious woman in America. Some of his abolitionist friends pitied him. The AASS leadership worried that marriage would further weaken Weld's ambition. He had been mobbed at Troy, New York, a year before and had not spoken in public since then. His health was poor and his voice was so impaired from months of lecturing that he could barely speak above a whisper.

Angelina heard rumors that her Boston friends were offended that she was getting married, some saying that she and Theodore were public property and had no right to enter into such an agreement. William Lloyd Garrison took her aside and told her he was worried Theodore would drag her into his theology; Garrison was pulling away from established churches and influencing Angelina and others to do so, too. Angelina asked Theodore, "Are thy friends mourning over thee as mine are over me?" Soon enough, Angelina would drop all the Quaker "thees" and "thous"; in marrying Theodore, a Presbyterian, a man outside her Quaker faith, Angelina would be committing an excommunicable offense and be disowned by the Society of Friends. Sister Sarah and any other Quakers who attended the ceremony faced a similar fate. Angelina accepted this penalty. She was fed up with the Quakers' unrelenting shunning and criticism of her actions. Just as she had broken with her Charleston past and moved to Philadelphia to join the Quakers, she would now break with the Quakers and make a new life with Theodore. She felt they were "two halves of one whole."

In the eight weeks preceding their wedding, Theodore and Angelina stayed busy. Theodore was in New York working at his desk job at the AASS office, which he preferred to lecturing, while Angelina was delivering a series of weekly lectures on slavery at Boston's Odeon. Out of necessity, they did their wedding and family planning through personal letters, which is how they had handled their long-distance courtship. Theodore endeavored to find the three of them a house; yes, Sarah Grimké would live with them. He was eager to please Angelina, who wrote him on March 28, "If you procure [a house] soon, can you not go and plant some vegetables in the garden? If so, I will send you some beans, potatoes and squash seed." By April 17, he wrote that he rented a small farm with a cottage and a fruit orchard in Fort Lee, New Jersey, and was going up there that very afternoon to plow up the ground for the garden. He needed Angelina's advice on furniture. What kind of parlor tables did she prefer, one with four legs, or six, or with a pedestal sort of post in the middle? Did she and Sarah prefer the cane or the flag (rush) bottom chairs? What kind of knobs should go on the bureau? Angelina told Theodore not to have a mattress made for them in New York, where she felt it would be impossible to find free ticking, a mattress cover made from cotton grown by free labor. Theodore, too, had his own design frustrations:

> [I]t is [hard] to find *plain* furniture. Everything is so tricked out and covered with carved work or bedizened and *gew gawed* and gilded and tipt off with variagated [*sic*] colors....

After much difficulty, Theodore settled upon his wedding clothes. He had a coat made of cloth to match Angelina's brown Quaker dress, to be worn with a white vest and light drab pantaloons. For a man who felt duty-bound to save the world, focusing on domestic arrangements and wedding planning proved a welcome distraction for Theodore, who had energy for a thousand people, and he undertook the tasks with gusto.

Although both James Birney, now living with wife Agatha and their children in New York, and Lewis Tappan had offered up their homes as wedding sites, it was decided to hold the ceremony in the Philadelphia parlor of another of Angelina's sisters, Anna Frost. Angelina composed the invitations and handwrote them on stationery emblazoned on top with a black-and-white engraving of a young Black male slave kneeling in chains:

> Dear Friend,
>
> Wilt thou grant us thy presence, sympathy & prayers on the occasion of our marriage which (the Lord permitting) will take place at 8 o'clock on the evening of the 14th inst[ant] at Anna H. Frost's No 3 Bellmont Place. Pray for us that our dear Master may be present with us, and spread before us all who meet on that solemn occasion a spiritual feast.

Angelina E. Grimké
Theodore D. Weld
May 1ˢᵗ

When on Monday, May 14, 1838, the doors of Pennsylvania Hall were thrown open for the dedication ceremony, the building was so new that the painters were still at work. The second-floor auditorium soon filled with one of the largest audiences in Philadelphia history. At ten a.m., President Neall of the Pennsylvania Hall Association took the chair and the meeting began. The Secretary read a short statement about the Hall's financing and purposes. Letters from leading lights in the abolitionist movement were read aloud, including one by Theodore Weld, who sent his regrets, on account of his throat ailment. Weld exulted that a "Temple of Freedom" had been erected in the city of Benjamin Franklin. *The Augusta* (Georgia) *Chronicle and Sentinel*, however, published a letter that referred to Pennsylvania Hall as a "tabernacle of mischief and fanaticism." Before the 10 a.m. meeting, protestors gathered around the outside of the Hall and harassed conventioneers—Blacks and whites, men and women—as they filed into the building and sat side by side. Heterogenous audiences had never existed in Philadelphia before. This commingling of the races and the sexes, as well as abolitionists convening in their city, gave rise to intense public hostility. For many, this was a threat to the social status quo. Throughout the "City of Brotherly Love," proslavery advocates were distributing racist pamphlets. A New Orleans paper wrote that "Men were seen gallanting black women to and from the Hall."

At eight o'clock that night, about forty of Angelina and Theodore's friends gathered in Anna Frost's Spruce Street home, a few blocks from Pennsylvania Hall, to witness the most untraditional wedding they would see in their lifetimes. Although two clergymen were present, a Black one and a white one, they would not preside over the ceremony. Instead, the bride and the groom conducted their wedding, each speaking vows from the heart. Angelina promised to love and honor her husband but omitted the word "obey." Further defying convention, Theodore renounced his legal right to be entitled to full control of Angelina's property. Theodore was penniless, and Angelina had a comfortable inheritance of five thousand dollars.

The guests included Lane Rebel Henry B. Stanton, New York's Gerrit Smith, Lewis and Julia Tappan, and Philadelphia friends, Sarah and Grace Douglass. Twelve signed as witnesses to make the marriage contract legally binding. Philadelphia's most famous abolitionist, a Hicksite Quaker minister, Lucretia Mott, did not attend for fear of excommunication. Newspaper journalist and poet John Greenleaf Whittier, also a Quaker, was there but slipped outdoors during the actual ceremony to avoid expulsion.

Everyone knelt for prayers and blessings. The contract was signed then read aloud by William Lloyd Garrison. Two former slaves of Angelina's father, Betsy Dawson and her daughter, delivered a short address to the group, testifying "against the horrible prejudice which prevails against colored persons." The wedding cake, baked by a Black confectioner with sugar produced from non-slave labor, was served, at which time John Greenleaf Whittier felt comfortable to rejoin the party.

Finally, Wednesday night arrived for the debut of the star attraction of the convention, Angelina Grimké Weld, at Pennsylvania Hall. All were welcome: men, women, Blacks and whites. The event was well-publicized, appearing on placards on city walls. Unfortunately, the day before, another type of placard began to appear around town, each one handwritten, that called upon citizens to interfere, "forcibly, if they must," with the abolition meetings at the Hall. The Convention of Anti-Slavery Women was aware of these calls to mob action against them. News that Black people had been at the Grimké-Weld wedding party further fueled the public hostility. Throughout the day, scores of people gathered ominously outside the entrance to the Hall, subjecting meeting attendees to jeers and abusive language as they arrived. The building managers hired two watchmen to stand guard.

The auditorium was overflowing when an ailing William Lloyd Garrison rose to give a short address to the three thousand gathered. His thunderous voice drowned out the occasional heckling, hissing, and groaning that interrupted his speaking. Southern slaveholders and proslavery advocates tried to end the meeting. Maria Chapman, next in the speakers' lineup, was pushed and shoved as she tried to make her way up the aisle to the platform. Someone looking out the window into the street shouted that an angry mob had formed in front of the Hall. The mob was hurling projectiles and stones at the windows. The yelling of the mob and the sound of shattered glass made it hard for Chapman to bring the room to order with her words. The shutters protected the people from the stone-throwing.

Angelina, the bride of three days, rushed up the center aisle to help the besieged Chapman and called the convention to order. The crowd inside settled down. Speaking above the noisy mob rabble and stones clattering at the windows, she said:

What is a mob? What would the breaking of every window be? Any evidence that we are wrong, or that slavery is a good and wholesome institution? What if the mob should burst in upon us, break up our meeting and commit violence upon our persons— would this be anything compared to what the slaves endure?

Although the great noise and danger continued, Angelina spoke for an hour and managed to keep the majority of the audience inside. She reminded women to keep flooding Congress with anti-slavery petitions, as that was the only political voice they had been accorded by law. Abby Kelley then said a few words. Lucretia Mott gave closing remarks. As the crowd left their seats, Garrison spied Theodore Weld in the back of the room where he had been somewhat hidden. This was the first time that Weld had heard Angelina speak and witnessed her remarkable power.

The mob outside had grown to several thousand. The white women linked arms in solidarity with their Black sisters and walked out the front doors. Unexpectedly, the angry men in the mob grew silent upon seeing this display of courage and parted to let the women pass safely.

The next evening, the mob assembled in great numbers. Wearing a borrowed wig and coat, John Greenleaf Whittier disguised himself as part of the mob in order to enter the building and retrieve his newspaper materials. Although the mob was seemingly composed of ordinary working men—many angered to have to compete with free Blacks for jobs in a depressed economy—in truth, these masses represented the moneyed, "respectable" classes—the Northern merchants who made their fortunes out of Southern cotton, the politicians who wanted votes, the preachers who wanted peace in their churches. These "respectable" citizens were as much against the anti-slavery agitation as the Southern slaveholders.

Dockworkers armed with beams and axes smashed open the front doors. They broke into the various rooms, jerked blinds down, piled up gorgeous silk plush chairs and abolition books, and set the piles on fire. Although firefighters did arrive, they concentrated their water hoses on spraying the adjacent buildings and did not try to save Pennsylvania Hall. The one firefighting team that did turn their hoses on Pennsylvania Hall was threatened by the mob if they should continue to do so. By midnight, only the charred outer walls remained, the inside of the structure gutted by fire. Four days after its glorious opening, Pennsylvania Hall was a total loss.

Destruction by Fire of Pennsylvania Hall

CHAPTER 35

Gerrit Talks the Talk and Walks the Walk

The murder of Elijah Lovejoy and the destruction of Pennsylvania Hall led to a watershed moment for the abolitionists. Clearly, they needed a fresh approach with new tactics. Nothing they tried accomplished what they had hoped. Angelina Grimké Weld urged women to exercise their petition rights, but what good was that with a congressional gag rule? Why bombard the South with propaganda if it was banned from distribution? Sending lecturers from town to town invited hostility, painted the abolitionists as disturbers of the peace, and united the advocates of slavery. As for drawing recruits by moral suasion, the churches had been no help, as they refused to call slavery a sin and oppose it.

Then there was the problem with Garrison, the AASS' original leader, who had become a lightning rod for criticism with his radical condemnation of the churches, his call to abolish the government, his insistence on woman's rights to speak, vote, and hold office in meetings, and his impractical doctrine of immediate emancipation. He still adhered to his belief that abolition would come about through the personal spiritual awakening of slaveholders. Garrison was driving people away from joining the cause with his extreme and repellent views; he wanted to overturn the social order on a thousand fronts. Furthermore, the two American political parties, the Whigs and the Democrats, would not include anti-slavery principles in their platforms.

James G. Birney and Henry B. Stanton, in their roles as corresponding secretaries for the AASS, and Gerrit Smith, the prominent New York philanthropist and abolitionist, were among the anti-Garrisonian faction that believed that treating slavery as a moral and religious matter had failed. They determined it was a political matter. What was needed for their movement to be successful was to form a third political party, a distinct group, one that was exclusively devoted to anti-slavery. Although Gerrit Smith supported woman's rights, Birney, Stanton, and others in this new faction did not, feeling that attaching that white-hot controversy to slavery alienated many who might otherwise embrace abolitionism. The Garrisonians cried hypocrisy. They felt strongly that denying women—half the population—full participation in public life was a denial of the abolitionists' basic belief that all human beings were equal.

James G. Birney had cultivated a relationship with Gerrit Smith from early days, when both were colonizationists. After handing over the editorship of the *Philanthropist* to Gamaliel Bailey in the fall of 1837 and moving his family from Cincinnati to Brooklyn, Birney found himself traveling more and more to the home of Gerrit and Ann "Nancy" Smith in the quaint town of Peterboro, New York, twenty-five miles southeast of Syracuse. The Smith home was a haven for abolitionists, where they carried on stimulating debates and refreshed their "spirit of reform."

The summer after the May Pennsylvania Hall fire, Birney took Agatha, 40, and their children for a vacation there, hoping that relaxing on the Smith estate's lush grounds would invigorate Agatha's health, although it was fruitless to hope for recovery from her tuberculosis infection. Since 1833, she had been enduring the cycles of remission and illness common to the disease, and, in Brooklyn, she had been completely confined to her bed, dispirited. Compounding her chronic disease and diminished strength, she had given birth to yet another baby, Ellen, her eleventh, in January of 1838.

The Birney's baby died that August. Three months later, Agatha was dead. With so much travel involved in his job, James Birney was at a loss as to how to care for his little ones, George, and Florence. The four older boys were able to take care of themselves. Gerrit and Nancy Smith offered to take care of the youngest two. Being so close to Brooklyn, Birney was able to make frequent visits to Peterboro to see the children, to lay plans for the new political party, dubbed the Liberty Party by Gerrit Smith, and later, after a respectable period of mourning had passed, to court Nancy Smith's sister, Elizabeth Fitzhugh, with the aim of marrying her and providing his children with a mother and a new home.

Gerrit Smith was one of the richest men in America and among the most generous. He owned land in all but six New York counties as well as property in several other states. Like the Tappan brothers, there was almost no facet of abolitionist work he had not funded from his deep pockets. Although he did donate enormous sums to anti-slavery and other reform organizations, he much preferred giving assistance to individuals who were in distress. He purchased slaves directly from slaveholders and gave land to fugitive slaves for farming, but chiefly, he was interested in liberating individual slaves.

In October 1839, Gerrit's cousin, Elizabeth Cady, 24, from Johnstown, New York, was on an extended visit to Gerrit's Peterboro mansion. One day, when she, her friend Laura, and Gerrit's daughter Libby, were singing in the parlor, Gerrit entered the room. He told them, "I have a most important secret to tell you, which you must keep to yourselves religiously for twenty-four hours." After securing such a pledge from each of them, he beckoned them to follow him up the stairs to the third story, which they did.

He opened the door to the garret, revealing a large room. There in the center sat a beautiful woman of mixed race, the same age as Elizabeth Cady. Gerrit addressed the stranger, "Harriet, I have brought all my cousins to see you. I want you to make good abolitionists of them by telling them the history of your life—what you have seen and suffered in slavery."

Gerrit went downstairs. Harriet Powell told how, at age fourteen, she had been separated from her family and sold for her beauty in a New Orleans slave market. The young women wept as she told what that sorry fate looked like for her. When, two hours later, Gerrit returned and summoned the women away, all were sworn abolitionists.

Just three weeks earlier, Harriet Powell had escaped from her master, John Davenport of Mississippi, who was vacationing with his wife and baby in Syracuse, New York. Once the Davenports learned that Harriet was missing, search parties were sent out in every direction in pursuit; hot on her trail were police, citizens, as well as bounty hunters, eager to claim the two-hundred-dollar reward Davenport had posted. Harriet managed to stay just one step ahead of her pursuers, who were able to track her movements. The Smith home was her fourth and last stop before Gerrit was to spirit her away to Canada.

At twilight, Harriet dressed as a Quaker and departed with one of Gerrit's clerks in a carriage for Cape Vincent. Meanwhile, John Davenport and some Syracuse marshals had traced Harriet's last whereabouts to Smith's property. This posse appeared there the next day with their questions. Gerrit, ever the genial host, received them into his home. He assured them that he harbored no fugitive slave and invited them to conduct a thorough search of the premises. Davenport took him at his word and did not order a search. Gerrit invited the men to stay for dinner. Gerrit kept them talking as long as he could, as every minute he detained them meant Harriet was that much further from their reach.

The guests departed. Soon, the clerk returned with the report that Harriet was safe in Kingston, Canada, stating, "I saw her pass the ferry this morning into Canada." With this knowledge, Gerrit then wrote a letter to John Davenport, which was published in the *New-York Tribune*, saying "he would no doubt rejoice to know that his slave Harriet, in whose fate he felt so deep an interest, was now a free woman, safe under the shadow of the British throne. I had the honor of entertaining her under my roof, sending her in my carriage to Lake Ontario, just eighteen hours before your arrival, hence my willingness to have you search my premises."

CHAPTER 36

Elizabeth Cady Goes Rogue

D espite Dr. Gamaliel Bailey's vehement opposition to the formation of a third political party, the Liberty Party made its debut in the spring of 1840. It was a party of protest against slavery. Its leaders entertained no illusions that its presidential nominee, James G. Birney, would win the fall election, especially in view of the fact that he was to be in London at the World's Anti-Slavery Convention from May until the November election.

The stated purpose of the World's Convention was to coordinate anti-slavery actions between nations. Departing with Birney from New York on the sailing ship the *Montreal* on May 12, 1840, was Henry B. Stanton, 34, accompanied by his bride of twelve days, Elizabeth Cady, 25, of Johnstown, New York. Both men were traveling as delegates for the newly formed American and Foreign Anti-Slavery Society, the anti-Garrisonian wing. The national society had finally split in two over the "woman question."

During Elizabeth's six-week stay with Cousin Gerrit the previous October, Henry B. Stanton had been at the center of the circle of reformers who had warmed themselves at the Smith fireside. Elizabeth had been impressed with Henry's power of oratory at anti-slavery conventions she attended in Madison County; Henry could make an audience both laugh and cry. Plus, he was ten years older and handsome. After a month of courtship often conducted on twilight horseback rides on the Smith estate, Henry and Elizabeth became engaged. When notified of this development occurring on his watch,

Cousin Gerrit suggested caution; though he loved both Henry and Elizabeth, he had his reservations about the suddenness of it all. Elizabeth's father, the wealthy and conservative lawyer, Judge Daniel Cady, did not allow for abolition talk in their home; it was a stifling atmosphere. Gerrit knew Daniel Cady would not abide his daughter, well-educated and brought up in privilege, to marry a radical abolitionist with no career. Gerrit suggested that she break the news to her family in a letter while she was safely ensconced with him, her chief ally, in the safe harbor of Peterboro. When she got home, though, Elizabeth's happiness was shattered as her father, having read her letter, lectured her on the impossibility of executing such a plan. He threatened to disinherit her. Elizabeth, her dreams dashed, broke her engagement.

But then, upon learning that Henry was soon to depart for London and that the Atlantic Ocean would roll between them for eight months, she frantically reinstated her engagement so she could go with him. On May 1, Elizabeth, wearing a simple white evening dress, was quietly married in Johnstown to Henry with a few friends invited. Although the Presbyterian minister objected, they omitted the word "obey" from their vows.

Henry was owed two years' back salary from the AASS. In April, he borrowed from friends to pay debts, buy two ocean passages at $120 each, and pay their living expenses while abroad.

Before they boarded the ship for England, the newlyweds took a stage to Belleville, New Jersey, to visit Henry's best friends, Theodore Weld, Angelina Grimké Weld, and Sarah Grimké. Elizabeth Stanton found their house "was severely destitute of all tasteful, womanly touches." Adherents of the Graham diet, the Grimké Welds served their guests a cold meal of rice, molasses, bread, milk, hominy, vegetables, pie made without shortening, and no caffeinated warm drinks. Elizabeth Stanton had hoped for "a hot beefsteak and a teapot." The next month, Angelina wrote Gerrit and Nancy Smith of the visit:

We are very much pleased with Elizabeth Stanton who spent several days with us, and I could not help wishing that Henry was better calculated to mold such a mind.

Although James G. Birney, 48, disagreed with Angelina Grimké on the "woman question," he agreed with her that Elizabeth needed molding. During their Atlantic crossing, Birney, a Southern gentleman of the "Old School," took it upon himself to improve her manners and to tone down her high spirits. Elizabeth playfully confronted Birney, asking, "Well, what have I said or done to-day open to criticism?

He replied graciously, "I heard you call your husband 'Henry' in the presence of strangers, which is not permissible in polite society. You should always say 'Mr. Stanton.'"

Elizabeth found Birney slightly annoying, somewhat amusing and was delighted when she could beat him at chess. Elizabeth read widely, particularly her father's law books, but she was new to the anti-slavery movement. Both Henry and Birney threw themselves into bringing her anti-slavery education up to speed. They supplied her amply with books and made slavery their chief conversational topic as they strolled the deck on their eighteen-day voyage.

As previously touched upon, while the Stantons and Birney had been crossing the Atlantic, the Garrisonian wing of the American Anti-Slavery Society won a victory at their May convention. Garrison arrived at the New York meeting with hundreds of his devoted women followers and aimed to take control of the Society by tipping the scale of power, which he did, by putting the "woman question" to the test. He nominated Abby Kelley to the business committee. Those opposed to including women in the society, Lewis Tappan and other men, refused to serve on a committee with a woman, saying it was unconstitutional. A vote was taken overwhelmingly in favor of her nomination. Tappan's group decided on a complete separation from the national society.

Poet John Greenleaf Whittier, who had skipped this convention, allied as he was with the opposition, did not want to be subject again to Garrison's caustic criticism. On June 30, 1840, Whittier wrote his sister that the "anti-Slavery society has as thee are doubtless aware blown up....Our friend Abby...was...the bomb-shell that exploded the society."

This opposition group, which Birney and Henry Stanton were representatives of in London, formed the American and Foreign Anti-Slavery (known as the "new organization"), taking with them over three hundred delegates from eleven states. The new organization departed from the Garrisonian belief in immediate emancipation; instead, they held that emancipation was a process that could be begun immediately but transacted gradually.

Emboldened by their ability to grant American women full participation in AASS proceedings, the Garrisonian wing ("the old organization") ventured to send a nine-woman delegation from Philadelphia and Boston to attend the June 1840 World's Anti-Slavery Convention in London, despite the invitations plainly stating that only gentlemen were invited. The women's leader for the old organization was Lucretia Mott, 47, who had credentials from the American Anti-Slavery Society, the Pennsylvania Anti-Slavery Society, the Philadelphia Female Anti-Slavery Society, and the Association of Friends for Promoting the Abolition of Slavery.

Lucretia Mott (1842)

After a rough passage across the North Atlantic on the *Roscoe*, Mott's group of men and women landed in Liverpool on May 27. They slowly made their way to London, stopping for sightseeing at Oxford and Warwick Castle with Lucretia riding the twenty miles from Windsor to London on top of a stagecoach and seeing gypsies and their wagons on the wayside. They finally arrived at their lodgings at Mark Moore's at No. 6 Queen Street Place on June 5, one day after the Stantons and Birney had checked in there. It was an awkward arrangement as under the same roof were housed delegates from both branches of the American anti-slavery ranks, with differing views as to the "woman question."

In England, women were excluded from equal participation in reform organizations. Scriptural texts were offered as justification for this prejudice. St. Paul's first letter to Timothy (2:11-12) was often cited:

> Let a woman learn in silence with full submission. I permit no woman to teach or to have authority over a man; she is to keep silent.

William Lloyd Garrison, his sailing ship delayed from New York due to the lack of wind, wrote to his wife that it was probable "we shall be foiled in our purpose" of letting the American women participate in the London convention. Referring to Queen Victoria, he asked rhetorically, "With a young woman placed on the throne of Great Britain, will the philanthropists of that country presume to object to the female delegates from the United States, as members of the Convention, on the grounds of their sex?"

The day before the Convention began at the Freemasons' Hall, Lucretia Mott recorded in her diary that "Several [men] were sent to us to persuade us not to offer ourselves to the Convention—[Rev. Nathaniel] Colver [was] rather bold in his suggestions—[I] answered & of course offended him….Prescod of Jamaica [*sic* Barbados] (colored) thought it would lower the dignity of the Convention and bring ridicule on the whole thing if ladies were admitted—he was told [I told him] that similar reasons were urged in Pennsylvania for the exclusion of colored people from our meetings—but had we yielded on such flimsy arguments, we might as well have abandoned our enterprise. Colver thought Women *constitutionally* [physically and mentally] unfit for public or business meetings—he was told [I told him] that the colored man too was said to be *constitutionally* unfit to mingle with the white man. He left the room angry."

On June 12, the meeting opened. Birney was named one of the vice-chairmen, and he presided at most meetings. Henry Stanton was named one of the six secretaries, as was Wendell Phillips, a Garrison ally. Birney was all nerves to see what would happen with the Garrison delegation as to the seating of the women delegates. Samuel Prescod of Barbados made a speech in which he reported that he had firsthand knowledge that the "Goddess Delegates" had come to the convention with full knowledge that they might not be seated due to English custom. He threw the meeting into confusion and was ruled "out of order" for having repeated mere private conversations.

Wendell Phillips introduced a motion that all persons bearing credentials from any anti-slavery body be added to a list of convention members. Birney and Rev. Colver spoke in opposition. There was booing, hissing, and cheering.

Nearly all the Quakers present were opposed to the women's admission to the meeting. Being Orthodox Quakers, they believed Lucretia Mott, a Hicksite Quaker, to be a heretic. With one half of the delegates being either ministers or Quakers, there was a definite religious cast to the debates. Predictably, the clergymen argued that the Bible decreed woman's subjection to man. One of the women's champions, the Unitarian minister from Nantucket, George Bradburn, said to these men of the cloth, "Prove to me, gentlemen, that your Bible sanctions the slavery of woman—the complete subjugation of one-half the race to the other—and I should feel that the best work I could do for humanity would be to make a grand bonfire of every Bible in the Universe."

For hours, these remarkable women—speakers, writers, and leaders—were forced to sit and listen to these men lecture them as to women's proper sphere of influence. The "woman question" was debated hotly for the entire day. Finally, when it was clear that Phillip's motion would be overwhelmingly defeated, it was reported that Henry Stanton then stood and made a very eloquent speech in support of seating the women. Elizabeth Cady Stanton believed that Stanton had voted yes on the motion but others recalled that he had voted against seating the women. The tally was unrecorded, but the outcome was clear: the women delegates were to be excluded.

Denied participation in the convention, the women were demoted from delegates to observers and politely conducted to their seats in a low-curtained gallery in the back. The refusal to allow the women to speak would plague the proceedings for the remaining nine days. Then, Garrison showed up. Having been apprised of the women's exclusion, he refused to participate as a delegate and, making a grand gesture, took his seat with the women in the segregated visitors' gallery. The ill-treatment of the female delegates remained a festering wound. At their lodgings on Queen Street, the delegates from both factions continued the bitter debate. At times, the discussions became quite heated, even during mealtimes. Birney packed his suitcase and sought quieter quarters.

Elizabeth had a high regard for Lucretia and Lucretia found Elizabeth much to her liking. They found time to talk over breakfast or on excursions around London to visit a school for poor children, the British Museum (where Lucretia fell asleep), and a prison. They discussed the equality of the sexes and the trouble with Orthodox religion. This new friendship opened up a new world of thought for Elizabeth. Upon her return to America, Elizabeth would correspond regularly with Mott and the other free-thinking women she had met in London.

CHAPTER 37

Angelina, Sarah, and Theodore Collaborate

N ow that she was a married lady, Angelina Grimké Weld felt she had to prove a lot of people wrong. Before her marriage, her critics had made much of her unmarried state. The prevailing opinion of the age was that if a woman stepped too far outside her assigned sphere, as Angelina had with her speeches and writings, she was spoiled for marriage. True, after her marriage to Theodore, she had indeed struggled to handle her new responsibilities on the home front. Although their wedding had been far from conventional, their home life fell into traditional male/female patterns. Theodore left for the office, and Angelina and Sarah were consigned to the domestic sphere. Angelina did not know how to handle domestic chores. For the first twenty-five years of her life, she had been waited on by slaves. In the eight years after she had moved to Philadelphia and then gone on tour, she had lived in other people's homes.

But Angelina threw herself into her new role, determined to make herself a good wife to Theodore. She took pride in little accomplishments like being complimented by Sarah for "cooking potatoes to admiration." She wrote her friends that little successes showed her and them that her public career had not ruined her for domesticity. She was determined to practice good housekeeping. She followed the strict efficiency system prescribed in the book the *Young*

Housekeeper by William Andrus Alcott, for limiting the time taken up by the endless tasks of cooking, washing, and cleaning so that the extra moments could be spent on something more useful. Mr. Alcott advised that the young housekeeper should dispense with all help, except for her children and her husband, and do all the housework herself. Fortunately, Angelina ignored this piece of advice. When her baby was due to be born in December 1839, Betsy Dawson moved into their cabin as a live-in helper.

Prior to the birth of Charles Stuart Weld, Angelina and Theodore devoured many books on the proper care of an infant—too many books, as it turned out. Due to mastitis, Angelina was unable to nurse her baby and had to resort to bottle feeding, which, according to the expert she was reading, should be done five times a day, one spoonful of milk per feeding, as it was believed that was all a newborn's stomach could hold. For the first month of his life, the baby dwindled, day by day, until he looked like a shrunken little old man who fretted round the clock. One day, when Angelina and Theodore were out of the house, Sister Sarah ran an experiment to see just how much liquid that baby's tummy really could hold. "To her surprise, the baby took a pint bottle full of milk, and had the sweetest sleep thereon he had known in his earthly career," wrote Elizabeth Cady Stanton. From then on, the baby was allowed to take as much milk as he wanted, and in no time, grew into a healthy, bouncing boy. Angelina advised Elizabeth against trusting the popular theories of the day. Angelina had almost starved her baby to death.

When Henry and Elizabeth Cady Stanton visited the Grimké-Welds before their London trip, Elizabeth had found their Belleville home "destitute of all tasteful, womanly touches, and though neat and orderly, had a cheerless atmosphere." Although Angelina loved flowers, she did not cultivate them, as that time might be better employed, she thought. Although the Quakers had disowned Angelina, she could not shake off the Quaker asceticism the Friends had drilled into her.

Just inside the entrance to their parlor, the trio had hung a picture of a kneeling, supplicant slave. Angelina wrote to a friend:

It is just such a monument of suffering as we want in our parlor. We want those who come into our house to see at a glance that we are on the side of the oppressed and the poor.

Theodore, Angelina, and Sarah were content with their smaller lives. Nevertheless, abolitionists still needled Angelina and Sarah to return to the public sphere. In Elizabeth Cady Stanton's 1840 letter to Angelina from London, she included a nudge to the sisters from Lucretia Mott:

[S]he thinks you have both been in a state of [reticence] long enough, and that it is not right for you to be still, longer; that you should either write for the public or speak out for *oppressed* women.

In April 1839, Angelina and Sarah received a letter from Lydia Maria Child chiding them for leading more private lives. Child wrote:

I began to think it was with you as with a [servant], who being met by a person with whom she had formerly lived at service, was asked,
'Where do you live now, Nancy?'
'Please ma'am, I don't live anywhere now; I'm married.'

In August of 1839, abolitionist Deborah Weston told a friend, "The Grimkés, I think, are extinct." The agitators had evidently judged that the only worthy reform work was such that was done in full view. Some people winked and suggested that the relationship between the three of them tucked away in New Jersey was far from wholesome.

Theodore was infuriated at the whispers and criticisms, especially knowing that Sarah and Angelina had, in fact, been hard at work at home for the anti-slavery cause. From late 1838, Theodore and the sisters had been engaged in conducting a massive study to expose the horrors of slavery through the testimony of slaves, slave owners, and overseers and through the use of public records. They composed questionnaires that they mailed to abolitionists, newspaper editors, freed slaves, public and religious officials, and members of Congress. Using newspaper files purchased from the New York Commercial Reading Room, Sarah and Angelina worked six hours a day for six solid months sorting articles. While Theodore conducted his AASS business in New York, the women catalogued anything pertaining to slavery from Southern newspapers—runaway slave notices, slave sales, punishments, court proceedings, and more. After the work was finished, the trio were curious as to how many newspapers had been examined. They went up into the attic and began to count. They stopped counting when they had reached twenty thousand. Sarah found the work absorbing, writing in January 1839:

> I do not think we ever labored more assiduously for the slave than we have done this fall and winter....We have been almost too busy to look out on the beautiful winter landscape...although our work is of the kind that may be privately performed, yet we find the same holy peace in doing it which we found in the public advocacy of the cause.

Published in the summer of 1839, *American Slavery As It Is* consisted of a collection of facts relating to the actual condition and treatment of slaves. Weld was listed as its author; unfortunately, there is no credit given in the book to the sisters. *American Slavery As It Is* sold one hundred thousand copies in its first year. Weld stated the book's purpose in its introduction:

> We will prove that the slaves in the United States are treated with barbarous inhumanity; that they are overworked, underfed,

wretchedly clad and lodged, and have insufficient sleep; that they are often made to wear round their necks iron collars armed with prongs, to drag heavy chains and weights at their feet while working in the field, and to wear yokes, and bells, and iron horns; [They are] bruised and mangled by scores and hundreds of blows…and terribly torn by the claws of cats, drawn over them by their tormentors…that their ears are often cut off, their eyes knocked out….

We shall show, not merely that such deeds are committed, but that they are frequent; not done in corners, but before the sun….

Over in Cincinnati, Harriet Beecher Stowe received a copy of *American Slavery As It Is*. The atrocities described on the pages overwhelmed her. The depictions of the sufferings stayed with her forever. She placed that slim but powerful volume in her sewing basket so she would always know where it was.

CHAPTER 38

Lincoln Escapes Twice

braham Lincoln wanted to be the DeWitt Clinton of Illinois. New York Governor Clinton had been the pioneering visionary who made the Erie Canal happen. The Erie Canal was the first waterway to link the Atlantic Ocean to the Great Lakes. Its opening in 1825 spurred the great westward movement of American settlers and reduced the cost of moving goods to market, transforming New York City into the leading commercial city in the United States.

As an Illinois state legislator, a Whig, Lincoln hoped to make a similar imprint by promoting internal improvements for his frontier state and opening opportunities for Illinoisians. Having piloted a flatboat bringing meat and grain to New Orleans from Illinois, Lincoln knew firsthand the difficulty of navigating rivers clogged by debris. Without dependable roads, farmers could not reliably get produce to market. Better roads and waterways and railroads crisscrossing north to south and east to west would enable thousands of farm families to rise from the kind of poverty experienced by the Lincolns. To this project, Lincoln brought passionate dedication. In 1836, the governor authorized close to $11 million financed by state bonds to complete it. The law was wildly popular with the citizens. The *Sangamo Journal*, the organ of the Whig Party, reported on March 4, 1837:

> The huzzas and acclamation of the people were unprecedented. All Vandalia was illuminated. Bonfires were built, and fire balls were

thrown in every direction....The names of those who have been conspicuous in bringing forward and sustaining this law will go down in the future as great benefactors.

But when the Panic of 1837 struck, people lined up at banks, trying to get their paper money exchanged for actual silver or gold, only to be turned away when they discovered that the vaults were empty because the banks had issued too much paper money without coins (specie) to back it up. Banks closed. The Illinois state debt exploded, evidence of corruption among private builders was discovered, and the internal projects were shut down. Scattered here and there were half-built bridges, partially dug canals, and roads with no meaningful beginning or end. By the end of 1840, bank-issued paper notes were worthless and the state was a wreck. Understandably, public sentiment turned against the disastrous internal improvements project, but to the detriment of his political career, Lincoln stubbornly hugged it tighter. In 1840, Lincoln was reelected for a fourth term, but narrowly. With the collapse of the internal improvements project, gone were his dreams of being the DeWitt Clinton of Illinois.

Lincoln and his fellow Whigs supported the charter of the Illinois State Bank, which was near collapse. The Democrats wanted to kill the state bank. The General Assembly had kept the state bank alive by granting it a reprieve—a suspension of specie payments—until the end of the next legislative session, which was assumed to take place at some time in 1841. Two weeks prior to that regular legislative session, the Assembly called a special two-week session that convened on November 23, 1840, to address the debt crisis. The meeting was in the Second Presbyterian Church in the new capital of Springfield, as the new Capitol building was still under construction.

Saturday, December 5, was to be the last day of the special session, the regular session to begin the following Monday. The Whigs assumed, wrongly, it turned out, that the business of the Assembly would just carry over into Monday, and there would be no need for the body to vote for a formal adjournment of the session. Such a vote would throw the state bank into immediate dissolution. This was exactly what the Democrats set out to do, to force the issue and damage the Whigs.

The only recourse for the Whigs to prevent a vote for adjournment was to prevent there being a sufficient number of people in the room to qualify for a vote, known as a quorum. Most of the Whigs left the building, but the rules required that two Whigs be in the House to call for a roll call. Lincoln and Joseph Gillespie were selected to remain and the other Whigs kept out of the way. The motion for adjournment was made; the ayes and the noes were called out—Lincoln's and Gillespie's were counted—and there was no quorum voting.

But the Democrats were not to be foiled. They sent out the Sergeant-at-Arms William Murphy, who had police powers, to round up some Whigs. One Whig threatened Murphy with a cane but another was more cooperative. The two additional Whigs hustled into the House provided a quorum.

Lincoln and Gillespie asked the two new Whigs to take over the responsibility of calling for the roll call to determine if a quorum was present. Meanwhile, Lincoln scouted for an escape. The doors were blocked by assistants to the sergeant-at-arms, so Lincoln and Gillespie, and perhaps a third man, took the only possible course. They jumped out of the window. Their effort was in vain. Despite their absence from the House, Lincoln and Gillespie were included in the new count, a quorum was reached, and the bank was forced to resume its payments. Lincoln both failed to save the state bank and made a laughing stock of himself. The *Illinois State Register* of December 12, 1840, referred to Lincoln's "gymnastic performance" and that of "his flying brethren," wondering if any were hurt in their adventure, yet doubting that Lincoln was wounded as "his legs reached nearly from the window to the ground." The article speculated that it might be expedient for the builders of the new State House to raise it one story higher to prevent members from jumping out of windows. "If such a resolution passes," went the paper, "Mr. Lincoln in the future will have to climb down the spout."

Following Abraham Lincoln's humiliating "jumping scrape," the Christmas season went into full swing. Springfield was blanketed with snow. The holiday spirit was everywhere, but Lincoln was not feeling it. His political career was sunk. His best friend, with whom he lodged, was moving to Kentucky. And, most crucially, he was stuck in a worse predicament than a locked room; he was engaged to a woman he did not love—the petite, blue-eyed Southern belle, Mary Ann Todd, with her chestnut-colored hair and hoop skirts, of Lexington, Kentucky.

It all happened so fast he could not pin down when they actually had become engaged. He must have given her encouragement through the letters he wrote to her in the summer and fall of 1840, when he was on the road, campaigning for the Whig candidate for the presidency, William Henry Harrison—making speeches across Illinois and Missouri, organizing grassroots "get out the vote" measures, and fundraising. Before leaving town, Lincoln had become enchanted with Mary, an outrageous flirt yet a well-educated one. He was particularly intrigued by her family's Kentucky connection with the venerable Henry Clay, who was Lincoln's hero. Usually, when they sat on the horsehair sofa in Mary's sister's parlor, it was Mary who did the talking and Lincoln who listened, caught up in her spell. They both loved to discuss politics—her sisters described Mary as a "violent little Whig"—current events, and the poetry of Robert Burns. Although poorly matched in background, social standing, and size, they found they had many shared interests. Whenever Lincoln came calling, Mary turned on the full force of her seductive charms and sparkled. Then suddenly, he was no longer in Springfield, and she could no longer slip her dainty, white hand into his big, rough one and usher him toward the altar.

At 21, Mary was fast approaching spinsterhood. If she did not find a husband in Springfield, she would be forced to return to Kentucky and support herself as a teacher. Mary had to step up her game. She bombarded Lincoln with letters. Although he lacked social polish—those Conestoga boots!—she saw the political promise in him. She fancied intelligent politicians. Lincoln had ambitions for high political office and Mary wanted to be married to a president. Both desired advancement. She wanted prominence and the grandest social position. Lincoln had great prospects for both. For the next several months, while he was out of her reach, she stalked him through letters.

He replied and she kept the letters coming. In the late fall, after Harrison was elected and Lincoln returned to Springfield, Lincoln discovered, to his surprise, that many of the two thousand residents of Springfield believed that he and Mary had an understanding that they were engaged to be married. Evidently, Mary had talked of her affair with Mr. Lincoln freely with others, though it had been months since they had seen one another.

Upon his return, Lincoln discovered a hard truth; he no longer felt the strength of his love for Mary. He had made a mistake. They were very different. He was a man given to quiet, solitary thought. He loved to read books late into the night. The fun-loving Mary needed constant attention and excitement and was prone to swift and extreme changes of mood. Although he had a prosperous law practice, he may have doubted his ability to provide for a woman brought up in luxury and wealth and waited on by slaves. Although she claimed to be engaged to Lincoln, admiring beaux still fluttered around her, like Lincoln's archrival, the most popular Democrat in the state, Stephen Douglas. She seemed to wickedly delight in attracting men only to spurn them. Lincoln wanted to break up with Mary. He had too many misgivings to marry this complex woman and—it was said—that he was attracted to someone else. But the law was on Mary's side. To save his honor and to avoid a breach of promise lawsuit, it would be up to Mary to release him from whatever bond she felt they had forged. Lincoln did not know how to get out.

He wrote a letter, took it to his best friend, Joshua Speed, and told him to deliver it to Mary. Speed confiscated the letter and refused to give it back to Lincoln, saying that words put in writing stand "as a living and eternal monument against you." He told Lincoln to break up with Mary in person. This is how Lincoln handled it, according to Speed:

> Went to see 'Mary'—told her that he did not love her—She rose—and Said 'The deceiver [*sic*] shall be deceived [*sic*] wo is me.'; alluding to a young man She fooled—Lincoln drew her down on his Knee—Kissed her & parted—He going one way & She an other.

Now, things were more mixed up than ever. Mary wrote Lincoln a letter stating she would release him from his engagement, yet she "would hold the question an open one," allowing him to renew the vow. She left the matter in limbo, troubling Lincoln's conscience to the degree that he fell apart. In January, he stopped showing up regularly at the Assembly, missing six days. He took to his bed. He called in the doctor. He wrote Dr. Daniel Drake in Cincinnati to treat him for his melancholia. He wrote his former law partner, "I am now the most miserable man living. If what I feel were equally distributed to the whole human family, there would not be one cheerful face on the earth." When he did return to the legislature, he could barely speak above a whisper. He had lost weight. Everyone in Springfield and a lady in Jacksonville were worried about his decline. Speed said that, "Lincoln went crazy. I had to remove razors from his room—take away all knives and other such dangerous things—&c—it was terrible."

By February, he had begun to improve, but months would elapse before Mary would see him out in society again. He dealt with his depression and anxiety by staying busy and getting together with friends, activities he found that gave his mind rest from "that intensity of thought that will sometimes wear the sweetest idea threadbare." The matter of the breakup continued to bedevil him for months, weighing on him, and he could not banish Mary from his thoughts. A year later, he wrote to Speed:

> There is one still unhappy that I have contributed to make it so. That still kills my soul, I can not but reproach myself, for even wishing to be happy while she is otherwise.

After he learned of Speed's happiness in his new marriage, his own doubts of marriage began to fade. He realized that he had entertained unrealistic expectations of what love was supposed to be like. He wanted to restore his honor. All his life, he had prided himself in his ability to keep his promises. This honor, Lincoln wrote, was the "chief gem of my character." After eighteen months of no contact, it was arranged by a mutual friend for Lincoln and Mary to meet. Both desired to renew their relationship. Mary had waited him out. On November 4, 1842, they were married in the parlor of Mary's sister's house in Springfield.

Abraham Lincoln (1846-47)   *Mary Todd Lincoln (1846-47)*

Lincoln had been willing to die and had been engulfed by crippling sadness when his dreams fell to earth, shattered. When he realized, however, that he had done nothing yet to make a human being remember that he had lived, he began to recover and grow. He would suffer spells of sadness all his life, spells he called an affliction rather than a failing. He would live to make his mark.

CHAPTER 39

Harriet Knows Something About Slavery

I n the late spring of 1841, the Ohio Supreme Court announced a shockingly progressive ruling, declaring that a slave "became free when brought to this State [Ohio] by his master...." Slave transit was no longer permitted in Ohio. This was great news for abolitionists but distressing news for Kentucky slaveholders doing business in Cincinnati and slave traders who regularly stopped in the city on their way down the Ohio River to markets in Missouri and the Southwest. In the late summer of 1841, Cincinnati was, once more, the scene of several days of extreme white violence against Black residents. After the mob wrecked the office of the *Philanthropist* and destroyed its press, a cry was raised to set fire to Lane Seminary. The mob assembled to march up to Walnut Hills, where it was believed that slave runaways found assistance from the students and professors. Calvin and Harriet Beecher Stowe, now living in their new brick house on the other side of the Lane Seminary campus, braced for the assault, as did the Beechers. Harriet's younger brother, Charles, newly returned from having spent a few years in New Orleans (and having finally given up his fantasy of marrying Mary Wright), was living with his new wife, Sarah Coffin Beecher, his father, the third Mrs. Lyman Beecher, and Aunt Esther in the President's House, and studying for the ministry. Frightened by the lawlessness in the city, Aunt Esther had not slept for days.

From the brow of the hill, the Beechers and Stowes looked down upon Cincinnati and saw the flames of the conflagration and the smoke from the buildings burned by the anarchists. They could hear the cries of the victims, the shouts of the marauders, and the sounds of cannon shots and gunfire. The Stowes sheltered some of the Black citizens fleeing the terrors of death and comforted them. The Stowe family slept with guns in the house and a large bell they would ring to call the Lane students in case the mob should come up to the house and try to search it for the fugitives they were hiding. Although a mob had formed to "ferret them out," those plans changed when it was learned that a company of fifty armed and mounted citizens guarded the Seminary. The two-mile hike up to Walnut Hills was another strong deterrent. Lane was spared.

After nine years of living in a frontier border state, Harriet Beecher Stowe continually confronted the presence of slavery. When she first arrived in Cincinnati, she traveled with Mary Dutton to visit Mary's friends in Kentucky. There she saw slaves and masters at home and in church. In addition, as a married lady, she learned more about slavery from the Black women she employed in her home, one of whom, in the fall of 1839, Calvin and one of Harriet's brothers, Henry or Charles, had to rush to sanctuary, as the young woman's previous master had been seen in Cincinnati looking for her, suggesting that she was not yet free. In the darkness of night, Calvin and Beecher, armed, traveled by carriage twelve miles by back roads to transport the woman to John Van Zandt's cabin, a station on the Underground Railroad. Van Zandt harbored slaves in his basement and arranged for their safe passage north.

Furthermore, Harriet's river travel gave her exposure to the brutalities of the slave trade. Once, on an Ohio River steamboat, Harriet had witnessed a fraud perpetrated by a Kentucky slave master, who sold a woman to a trader by tricking her into thinking she was being taken down the river to work at the same hotel with her husband. The separation of families caused by the slave trade cut Harriet to the quick. Family meant everything to a Beecher, especially to Harriet, who had been without her own mother since she was five.

Harriet's brother Charles, whose years as a bill collector for a large New Orleans mercantile house had required him to travel to plantations across Louisiana, told her about slavery in the deep South. On one of these tours, Charles met a slave owner so cruel that:

> He actually made me feel of his fist, which was like a blacksmith's hammer, or a nodule of iron, telling me that it was 'calloused with knocking down n------s.' When I left the plantation, I drew a long breath, and felt as if I had escaped from an ogre's den.

Harriet had established herself as a literary woman. A gifted storyteller, by 1842, she had published three dozen articles in prestigious national magazines such as *Godey's Lady's Book* and the *New-York Evangelist*. Editors at other periodicals petitioned her writing. She earned $200-300 a year by her pen. Harper and Brothers of New York had just reached out to her to publish a collection of her short stories. She had cultivated an audience for her Christian writings and stories, both for children and adults, that often contained a moral lesson or an urge for reform. Although filled with deep pity for the suffering slaves, she did not use her writing platform to write about abolition, the most important reform movement of the day. The subject of slavery, she felt, was so dark and painful, so utterly hopeless to discuss, that a person could go insane to read, think, or distress one's self about it. It had not escaped her notice either that to agitate on slavery was dangerous. She remembered the murder of Lovejoy. Then, to further illustrate the danger, in April of 1842, the same month she was traveling to New York to negotiate that book deal, the Ohio Underground Railroad Conductor "Honest John" Van Zandt was arrested for loaning his wagon to eight fugitives in their escape from Kentucky slavery.

Harriet would stick to writing what she believed people wanted to read. She now had four small children to consider. She was dependent upon childcare by the ever-faithful Anna and meals prepared by a succession of cooks. She would continue writing for periodicals, carving out bits of time here and there amid the daily chaos of her home, with its thousands of cares that included frequent sickness, her closely spaced pregnancies (live births and miscarriages), Calvin's long trips away, and little money to grind out articles, essays, and stories about young lovers, alcoholic husbands, charming New England villagers, funny canal boat passengers, and privileged women bent on errands of mercy.

CHAPTER 40

Charles Dickens Visits America

On January 22, 1842, when English novelist Charles Dickens, his wife, Catherine, and her maid arrived in Boston aboard the *RMS Britannia*, Dickens was met by adoring crowds. This was his first trip to America and Canada, and he was at the height of his popularity on both sides of the Atlantic. Taking his seat in a train, men and boys, he wrote, came:

> …round the carriage in which I sat; let down all the windows; thrust in their heads and shoulders; hooked themselves on conveniently, by their elbows; and fell to comparing notes on the subject of my personal appearance, with as much indifference as if I were a stuffed figure.

Dickens loved the adulation, but he had professional business to conduct. His work—to date, *The Pickwick Papers*, *Oliver Twist*, *Nicholas Nickleby*—was being pirated in America, as there were no international copyright laws to prevent the theft of his intellectual property. He also had an ambitious travel itinerary.

After stops in Massachusetts and Connecticut cities, Dickens visited New York and then Philadelphia. From there, he traveled to Washington, D.C. Arriving late in the day, he saw only a beautiful view of the Capitol, with which he was impressed. The next day, he got a better view of the town and found it wanting. He was particularly appalled by the filthy and omnipresent custom of the chewing and spitting of tobacco. He crowned Washington, D.C., "the head-quarters of tobacco-tinctured saliva." In courtrooms, steamboats, hospitals, and in all public places, men and boys took out their tobacco boxes, tore off a plug or carved it out with a penknife, and stuck that ball in a cheek and chewed. In a short time, they would squirt out a large amount of yellow rain into nearby spittoons, fireplaces, the floor, or a base of a marble column. When the plug was spent, a man would shoot "the old one from his mouth." Not even steady old chewers, noted Dickens, were expert marksmen.

Dickens visited President Tyler and, with Mrs. Dickens, afterward attended a reception at the White House. Dickens toured the Capitol building. Although both houses were carpeted handsomely, he advised all strangers who entered to not look down, as the rugs were squirted upon by tobacco expectorators and the carpet's design was disfigured by brown dabbles. He suggested that if someone were to drop a purse on the ground, not to pick it up with an ungloved hand. The honorable members of the chambers had swelled faces caused by the volume of tobacco stowed in the hollow of their cheeks. Woe to the women trekking across that germ-ridden carpet with their long, trailing skirts brushing across that spit and sweeping it up, as it was probably contaminated with deadly tuberculosis bacteria, which would then be spread into their homes through their hemlines. Sixty or more years would pass before science would show that the bacteria could survive an entire day in this manner.

The heat of Washington had been very trying, so Dickens scrapped his plan of undertaking the long journey to Charleston, South Carolina, to see something of slavery, settling for visiting Richmond, Virginia, instead, before turning to the West. On the night steamboat, Dickens discovered the floors to be as disgustingly unclean as in the Capitol and for the same reason. At Potomac Creek, he and his party disembarked, took a rollicking, muddy ride on a stagecoach to Fredericksburg, and then took the train to Richmond, which passed through former tobacco fields where the soil was depleted. Dickens wrote that "it is now little better than a sandy desert overgrown with trees." Continuing, he wrote:

> In this district, as in all others where slavery sits brooding…there is an air of ruin and decay abroad, which is inseparable from the system. The barns and outhouses are mouldering away; the sheds are patched and half roofless; the log cabins are squalid….There is no look of decent comfort anywhere….
>
> In the negro car belonging to the train in which we made this journey, were a mother and her children who had just been purchased; the husband and father being left behind with their old owner. The children cried the whole way, and the mother was misery's picture.

Dickens visited a tobacco farm where he supposed there was enough tobacco in one storehouse to fill every jaw in America. At another plantation, he visited the slaves' quarters but was not allowed to enter their "crazy, wretched cabins, near to which groups of half-naked children basked in the sun, or wallowed on the dusty ground." The planter's house was airy and cool, protected from the hot sun by blinds on the windows, which looked out onto a piazza with hammocks slung, where the family and guests refreshed themselves from the heat by drinking iced tumblers of Mint-Juleps and Sherry Cobblers.

Then, a few stops later, Dickens arrived in Cincinnati in April of 1842. Although weary from so much travel, Dickens enjoyed more personal freedom out West and more anonymity. He found much to admire in Cincinnati, calling it a "beautiful city; cheerful, thriving, and animated." He then traveled as far west as St. Louis and as far north as Quebec.

Upon his return to England, he described his impressions of his American journey in the travelogue *American Notes for General Circulation*. While finding much to admire in Americans he met, and in their lifestyles, he saw major flaws in the society of the United States, the first and most serious being slavery and its attendant violence. He devoted an entire chapter to his observations. Below is an excerpt from this chapter in which he condemns the slave owners themselves for the lies that they promulgate: that their slaves are happy, how seldom they run away, and that they treat their slaves with kindness. In the widely circulated public newspapers, slave owners submitted these advertisements:

Ran away, Negress Caroline. Had on a collar with one prong turned down.

Ran away, a black woman, Betsy. Had an iron bar on her right leg.

Ran away, a negro boy about twelve years old. Had round his neck a chain dog-collar with 'De Lampert' engraved on it.

Ran away, a negro woman and two children. A few days before she went off, I burnt her with a hot iron, and much scarred with the whip.

Ran away, a negro woman named Rachel. Has lost all her toes except the large one.

Ran away, a negro girl called Mary. Has a small scar over her eye, a good many teeth missing, the letter A is branded on her cheek and forehead.

Ran away, my Mulatto woman, Judy. She has had her right arm broke.

Ran away, a negro man, named Ivory. Has a small piece cut out of the top of each ear.

Dickens was back in London when, on July 13, 1843, the *New-York Evangelist* ran an essay criticizing his literature. The author, a woman, thought his work lacked a strong Christian foundation. This critic found it incomprehensible that Dickens' young character, Oliver Twist, having grown up among such despicable ne'er-do-wells as thieves and prostitutes, could develop such a sterling character; he seemed unchurched. She found Dickens inconsistent, as he opposed slavery yet apparently approved of strong drink, in portraying drunkenness as normal. The author thought of intemperance as being a form of bondage. In closing, she classified Dickens' popularity as a "literary epidemic," a fad that would not last long.

The author was our very own Harriet Beecher Stowe. Poor Harriet, brought up by temperance activist Lyman Beecher, whose power over his own children was real, lasting, and damaging! Henry recalled his father saying to him at age seven: "Henry, do you know that every breath you breathe is sin?" Lyman's unrelenting preoccupation with his children's conversions and Godly pursuits manifested itself in different harmful ways with each of his children. For Harriet, it meant wrestling continually with an impulse to be more perfect and pious and be doomed to morbid self-introspection about the Final Judgment. For her brother, George, now preaching in Chillicothe, Ohio, it meant becoming a minister to please your father, ridding the country of slavery, and trying to become perfect in this world.

For George, the pressure to become perfect became crippling, and ten days before Harriet's Dickens critique came out in print, he killed himself with a gun in his garden while his sister Catharine was visiting. Harriet wrote her brother Thomas, "The sudden death of George shook my whole soul like an earthquake." Three weeks later, Harriet gave birth to her fifth child, a daughter whom she named Georgiana, after her sensitive brother. Georgiana was a sickly, fussy child and Harriet, also poorly, was unable to nurse her.

For the next several years, Harriet's writing output would be considerably less, her health being undermined by depression, a series of miscarriages, some unexplained, weird neurological symptoms, the management of a houseful of five small children, Calvin's diminishing salary, and their poverty, which forced them to turn their lovely home into a boardinghouse. Trying to meet the demands of the day, to be a perfect wife and mother and Christian, she fell into an emotional and physical slump. Oftentimes, she was unable to use her arms, at other times, unable to use her eyes. She had trouble concentrating and was exhausted. "Dr. Drake gave me blue pill[s] enough to last one lifetime," she told her brother Henry, "in consequence whereof I have been four or five times saturated." "Blue pills," also known as "blue mass," or "calomel" referred to a mercury-based medicine commonly prescribed for a variety of ailments from tuberculosis, constipation, toothache, syphilis, to the pains of childbirth. Mercury, in the form of a blue pill, has the potential as a neurotoxin. Ingesting mercury leads to mercury poisoning, a form of heavy-metal poisoning. Calomel had harmful effects causing gangrene, loss of teeth, deterioration of the gums, facial deformities, and behavioral irregularities. Harriet's symptoms suggest that she suffered from chronic mercury poisoning. If she had taken calomel pills when pregnant, her babies would also have suffered toxic metal poisoning.

CHAPTER 41

Mr. Lincoln Goes to Washington

I n December 1847, when Abraham Lincoln arrived in Washington, D.C. with Mary and their two sons, the Mexican-American War was almost over. Texas had joined the Union. The war was extremely controversial. Democratic President Polk's critics, the Whigs, blamed him for deliberately provoking Mexico into open warfare by putting American soldiers in disputed territory. Lincoln had been elected a U.S. congressman from the Seventh District of Illinois for one term, the only Whig in the Illinois delegation, a testimony to his persuasive politicking. By the time Lincoln took his oath of office, the fighting was over. The Americans had won substantial victories and occupied Mexico City. Like many leading Whigs, Lincoln questioned the constitutionality of the war and the justice of it. Lincoln was also keenly aware that the following year was a presidential election year, and the opposition party, the Democrats, were vulnerable on their President's role in originating the Mexican conflict. That month, Polk asked Congress for more money to end the conflict that he said Mexico had started.

Freshman Congressman Lincoln led the Whig charge against Polk, determined to show that the American army and Polk had started the war with an unprovoked attack on a Mexican settlement. On December 22, Lincoln introduced resolutions asking Polk to provide the U.S. House of Representatives with "all the facts which go to establish whether the particular spot of soil on which the blood of our *citizens* was so shed," belonged to Mexico or to the United States. Polk ignored Lincoln's "Spot Resolutions."

Lincoln believed that the U.S. Army had provoked the war. General Zachary Taylor had even informed the War Department that there had been no necessity for U.S. troops in Texas for its defense or its protection. The Whigs' attack on the President continued, with George Ashmun of Massachusetts introducing a resolution declaring that the war had been "unnecessarily and unconstitutionally begun by the President of the United States." Lincoln signed it, as did eighty-five Whig representatives. Lincoln accused the President of seeking "military glory—that attractive rainbow, that rises in showers of blood."

If Lincoln hoped to achieve any distinction through his actions, his hopes were quickly dashed. Nobody paid much attention to his resolutions except to subject them to ridicule. The Democratically controlled newspapers criticized his attack on the President. The *Peoria Press* denounced Lincoln as a traitor for his anti-war stance, reminding readers of his desire to know where the "spot of soil" was where American blood was shed, dubbing him the "miserable man of spots." An Illinois newspaper called him "spotty Lincoln."

With American victory in the Mexican war, the terms for the surrender and reparations were dictated by the Americans. On February 2, 1848, the Treaty of Guadalupe Hidalgo was signed, which authorized the U.S. payment of $15 million to Mexico for the purchase of California and New Mexico and named the Rio Grande as the Texas border. The Mexican Cession, the nation's largest land acquisition since the Louisiana Purchase, included territory that would later become the states of California, Nevada, Arizona, New Mexico, Colorado, and Utah. In June 1848, the British and the Americans divided up the Oregon Country, setting the Forty-Ninth Parallel as the border between British Canada and the United States. Together, these acquisitions meant that America's territory extended across the continent from the Atlantic to the Pacific Coast.

The war victory brought the issue of slavery extension to the fore-front of American politics. The "Wilmot Proviso," introduced in the

House but repeatedly blocked in the Southern-dominated Senate, proposed that "neither slavery nor involuntary servitude shall ever exist in any part of said territory" acquired from Mexico. Congressman Abraham Lincoln voted for the proviso. He had long stood against the expansion of slavery into the territories, in his staunch belief that while the Constitution protected slavery in the states where it already existed:

> [W]e should never knowingly lend ourselves directly or indirectly, to prevent that slavery from dying a natural death—to provide new places for it to live in, when it can no longer exist in the old.

Slavery in the territories would become the most important issue in the following years. The idea that slavery would be shut out of the new territories provoked cries of outrage and injustice and threats of secession from Southern leaders who felt entitled to take their slaves with them there. For the internal slave trade to stay lucrative, the slave-breeding border states were always in need of more slave-consuming states. The admission of Texas had already opened a new market for the slave trade. For the slave trade to increase, the demand for slave labor had to increase. Greedy eyes looked toward the opening of the territories for slave labor.

While the Mexicans and Americans had been signing over California to America and the politicians were arguing over slavery extension in the territories, over at Sutter's Fort in Coloma, California, James W. Marshall was building a sawmill. On the morning of January 24, he was examining the channel below the mill when he noticed some shiny flecks in the river bed. Marshall recalled:

"I picked up one or two pieces and examined them attentively; and having some general knowledge of minerals, I could not call to mind more than two which in any way resembled this, iron, very bright and brittle; and gold, bright, yet malleable. I then tried it between two rocks, and found that it could be beaten into a different shape, but not broken. I then collected four or five pieces and went up to Mr. Scott (who was working at the carpenter's bench making the mill wheel) with the pieces in my hand and said, 'I have found it.'

"'What is it?' inquired Scott.

"'Gold,' I answered.

"'Oh! no,' replied Scott, 'That can't be.'

"I said, 'I know it to be nothing else.'"

CHAPTER 42

Harriet Goes to a Spa

Harriet Beecher Stowe recovered her health somewhat following her brother's death and Georgiana's birth and was able to write. In January 1845, "Immediate Emancipation," her first anti-slavery story, appeared in the *New-York Evangelist*. The story was inspired by an actual event that occurred in Cincinnati. A Southern gentleman is persuaded to free his slave through moral arguments. By year's end, though, Harriet's health and spirits had plummeted so low that it was apparent she needed more than a local doctor's care. With money raised from friends and family, in March 1846, Harriet checked into an upscale "water-cure" sanitarium at Brattleboro, Vermont, that offered an unconventional therapy for sick people. Harriet would remain there a year, eating healthfully, getting fresh air and exercise, drinking a dozen tumblers of water daily, and subjecting herself to the ice-cold baths, soaks, and compresses that promised recovery. She was free from chores and enjoyed the new community she found among her fellow patients. When Harriet returned to her family in Ohio, she was healthy and strong. She became pregnant right away. In January 1848, she gave birth to her sixth child, Samuel Charles, known as Charley (sometimes spelled "Charlie"). She had no trouble nursing this beautiful, healthy, little baby boy. He was her joy.

During Harriet's long absence from March 1846 to March 1847, Calvin had gained weight and become depressed, so off he went to Brattleboro in June 1848, Lane Seminary generously paying him his full salary for his first real vacation in fifteen years. He would remain at the spa for fifteen months.

Harriet, at home with six children, was grateful that recently Lane Seminary had made the bold move to divide the campus into small lots, which they rented cheaply to poor families, including free Blacks, who built houses in the neighborhood and provided Harriet with a pool of hired domestic help. It is from this female network of free Black cooks, servants, and washerwomen passing through Harriet's parlor that she heard the real stories of what it meant to have been born a slave.

Her cook, Eliza Buck, for example, although raised as a nurse and a seamstress in Virginia, told of having been suddenly sold as a cook to a plantation owner in Louisiana to settle a family debt. Eliza told of sneaking out in the night to nurse poor slaves who had been horrifically beaten, mangled by the overseer's whip. Then, Eliza was sold to a Kentucky man who fathered all her children. Eliza referred to her white former master as her "husband." Eliza and other slave women had no protection from any white man's sexual advances. To not submit was to invite terrible whippings and worse.

On behalf of another free (but illiterate) Black woman, Harriet wrote letters to this woman's slave husband in Kentucky. This slave husband had unlimited liberty to come and go on errands between Kentucky and Ohio and yet refused to break his loyalty to his master and run away, although that master had, year after year, broken his own promise of freedom to his slave.

To cope financially, Harriet took in boarders and opened a school for her children. The neighborhood Black children were invited to attend, including those of Eliza Buck. One day, one of her smartest Black pupils did not show up for class. The mother informed Harriet that the child was not yet emancipated and had been snatched up and carried off to be sold at auction by the sheriff. Harriet and her neighbors gathered a collection and secured the child's ransom.

Harriet said, "Time would fail me to tell you that I learnt incidentally of the working of the slave system, in the history of various slaves, who came into my family, and of the *underground railroad,* which I may say ran through our barn."

While Harriet was at the Vermont spa, on October 1, 1847, the Reverend Henry Ward Beecher boarded the first train ever to leave Indianapolis, where he had lived and preached for eight years. His wife, Eunice, and their three young children had gone on ahead of him. He had accepted a job offer to be the pastor of Plymouth Church, a new Congregationalist church in Brooklyn, New York, wooed by the wealthy merchant Henry Bowen and his wife, Lucy Tappan Bowen. Henry Beecher was glad to be shaking the dust of Indianapolis off his boots. The members of the Second Presbyterian Church owed Henry $940 in back salary. Consequently, Henry left behind tremendous debt. As was his custom, he also left behind sobbing, heartbroken female admirers. His temperance crusades—editorial attacks on drunks, grogshop owners, and distillers—had made him powerful enemies who waged arguments with him in the newspapers. Henry's refusal to take a stand against slavery angered the Indianapolis Presbytery, which required its ministers to preach adamantly against the sin of slaveholding. In more liberal settings, Henry did speak against slavery, but on his home turf, where racial hatred bred brutal mob violence, he steered clear and with good reason.

Indeed, on Independence Day 1845, John Tucker, a former slave from Kentucky, was just walking in the Indianapolis street when a white man blocked his path. He was chased by a mob and, with clubs and bricks, beaten to death by white men as a crowd watched. Less than a hundred yards away, the congregation in Henry's church heard the shouts and curses of the crowd shouting, "Kill the damned n-----r, kill him." Henry rushed into the street to find a mob looking for other victims. Henry said:

It grew on me that [slavery] was a subject that ought to be preached upon; but I knew that just as sure as I preached an abolition sermon they would blow me up sky high. It seemed to me that my church would be shut up, and that I should be deprived of the means on which I depended for the support of my family.

The trials of malarial fevers, the death of a son, poverty, Western roughness, and Henry's declining popularity had taken a dreadful toll on the health of Eunice *and her appearance*. Nine months earlier, Eunice, 35, had written to Harriet Beecher Stowe, "If you were to step in, I think you would have some trouble to recognize your sister [in-law] in the thin faced, grey haired, toothless old woman you would find here."

There was hope that moving to the New York seashore would put some healthy color back in Eunice's ashen and sunken cheeks. Additionally, Lucy Bowen hoped to put some teeth back in her mouth. Along with the handsome salary extended to Henry—$1,500 the first year, $1,750 the second, and $2,000 after that—Lucy offered to give Eunice "a present of a full set of teeth." Henry Bowen raised money to pay off Beecher's debts. When the Beechers arrived in Brooklyn Heights wearing old, raggedy, darned, and torn clothing, the Bowens bought them all new clothes and housed them in the Bowens' grand four-story townhouse until they could get settled in their own home. Plymouth Church was ecstatic that the dynamic and theatrical Reverend Henry Beecher, who had made a name for himself as a Western revival preacher, would be their new pastor.

Henry Ward Beecher (1850)

At Plymouth Church, Henry could forge his own identity as a preacher, discarding the social constraints under which he had labored for a decade in Indiana. From the beginning, he let his new Plymouth Church parishioners know that he planned to "wear no fetters" and that he would speak out on the pressing issues of the day, applying the Gospel as he understood it, "sharply and strongly to the overthrow of every evil, and the upbuilding of all that is good." He was now his own man. He would not dress like a city slicker. He would continue to sport the look of a hard-working Westerner, with his broad-brimmed hat, his thick brown hair worn at shoulder length, brushed back behind his ears, and a rough, gray shawl thrown over his shoulders to ward off the cold wind.

CHAPTER 43

Absence Often—
but not Always—Makes the
Heart Grow Fonder

U.S. Congressman Abraham Lincoln was a moderate anti-slavery man but was, by no means, an abolitionist, yet there he was, living in a Washington boardinghouse dubbed the "Abolition House." Mrs. Ann G. Thornton Sprigg's was the preferred stopping place for anti-slavery folk. The congressional leader of the anti-slavery campaign, Joshua R. Giddings of Ohio, boarded there. Mary Todd Lincoln did not find life at this boardinghouse as congenial as Abe, where he was wildly popular, his storytelling and joke-cracking gently breaking up the many heated arguments that regularly erupted there among his fellow Whig congressmen.

Mrs. Sprigg was a Virginian but she did not keep slaves, although slavery was legal in Washington. She employed Black servants, some who waited upon the table and others who cooked and minded children. Mrs. Sprigg's boardinghouse was directly in front of the Capitol, its iron railing coming to within fifty feet of her door.

When Abraham and Mary arrived in D.C. before the start of the congressional session, they found the cosmopolitan atmosphere of Washington exhilarating. They visited the Adelphi Theatre to see "Romeo and Juliet," heard the Marine Band on Saturday nights on the Capitol lawn and, at Carusi's saloon, had twice seen the famous minstrel show of the Ethiopian Serenaders, with its sweet tunes and rubbery juba dancing. Washington, according to the 1850 Census, with its 43,000 inhabitants, including 3,600 slaves and 10,000 free Blacks, was the largest and most sophisticated city the Lincolns had ever seen. From their single large room at the boardinghouse, they had a view of the unfinished yet imposing Capitol building, with its temporary, old, blue-painted wooden dome, sitting ninety feet above the Potomac and surrounded by a thirty-five-acre wooded park. Looking down from the dome was the vacant mall traversed by a canal that emptied into the Potomac. South of the White House, preparations were underway to lay the cornerstone of the Washington Monument. The bell towers and spires of some thirty-seven churches added to the skyline. Public buildings like the Patent Office and the Treasury Building, designed in the Greek style, were under construction.

The Federal City had both mansions and slums, grandeur and squalor. Paths and streets were swampy. The cobblestones on the broad tree-lined Pennsylvania Avenue were so few and far between that carriages risked loosening their wheels. To accommodate congressmen living far from home, there were hotels and boarding-houses aplenty. Taverns outnumbered churches; there were brothels and gambling dens. Pigs, chickens, geese, dogs, and cows roamed the unpaved streets and alleys. There was no adequate sanitation or sewage system to manage waste or animal carcasses. Viewed from the windows of the Capitol, Lincoln recalled "a sort of negro-livery stable, where droves of negroes were collected, temporarily kept, and finally taken to Southern markets, precisely like droves of horses." At least a dozen slave traders operated in Washington, D.C., the capital city of a nation founded on personal freedom, and a major port and distribution center for the domestic slave trade. The heavy slave traffic—the visible presence of slavery in the city—kept the political combat among abolitionists, moderates, and proslavery advocates at a semi-boil. Washington was a Southern city surrounded by slave states. The majority of the permanent population was proslavery.

Slaveholders and proslavery advocates were newly agitated when, in 1847, Gamaliel Bailey moved from Cincinnati to D.C. and established, with the support of Lewis Tappan, the national abolition newspaper, the *National Era*. Gamaliel, his wife Margaret, their six children, and Gamaliel's aging parents settled into one of the finer neighborhoods; their next-door neighbor was Mayor William Seaton, the editor of the *National Intelligencer*. Gamaliel arranged for his press to be housed adjacent to the *National Intelligencer* and near the imposing U.S. Patent Office. It took tremendous courage for Gamaliel Bailey to take an abolition paper into a Southern city. By situating his office and his family in prominent locations, he signaled his intent to assume an important place in the life of the city.

Because Gamaliel was an avowed abolitionist and a member of the Liberty Party—although moderate in his views—Margaret was initially snubbed by local ladies, having received only one caller in the first six months of living in Washington. Besides being denied Southern hospitality, the Bailey children contended with taunts of "damned abolitionist."

After sixteen months of living inoffensively in Washington, though, the chilly reception began to thaw. The *National Era*, although an abolition paper, had not promoted radical measures for addressing the slavery question in its editorial content, nor did Bailey use harsh language to address slaveholders. His editorials and those of other writers did not immediately call for abolition in the District of Columbia. Although not departing from his anti-slavery stance, Bailey, unlike Garrison, did not encourage slaves to run away or to rebel. Bailey, ever conciliatory in his dealings, forged friendships with other newspapermen in the city and with members of Congress. Bailey wanted a voice in the capital; he wanted to avoid violence, having seen friends almost beaten to death for their anti-slavery views and having twice experienced the destruction of the *Philanthropist* press. The *Era* was wildly successful, heralded for its original and high-toned literary content. Gamaliel encouraged women and Southern writers to submit their writings for publication, and well-known writers such as Lydia Maria Child, Grace Greenwood, and John Greenleaf Whittier were featured. The *Era* was noted for its reliable and candid Congressional news. It became a paper of broad general interest. In time, the *Era* would exchange with sixty papers in slave states and be second only to the *New-York Tribune* in circulation. The Baileys hosted a weekly salon in their home for political (particularly anti-slavery) and literary luminaries to gather for brilliant evenings of dinner, discussion, and parlor games. With the help of a governess to tend to the children, Margaret had resumed her literary career. Gamaliel said that he and Margaret shared a marriage of perfect equality.

Abraham and Mary Lincoln's marriage had a much different dynamic. As the winter wore on, Abraham Lincoln, very busy with meetings in the House of Representatives, began to regret having brought Mary and the children with him to the city. Mary required amusements and Lincoln wanted to work, as he had soaring ambition, which his law partner, Billy Herndon, described as "a little engine that knew no rest." With Lincoln thus occupied, Mary was mostly confined to her rooms with the restless Bobbie and the coughing and nursing Eddie. Occasionally, she and her husband took part in Washington's brilliant and vibrant social scene. They attended some social affairs, including a visit to Polk's White House, but Mary failed to make the social splash she had expected, as she had counted on her Southern roots and her marriage to an up-and-coming politician to zip her up the social ladder. Yet no matter how beautiful her gown, how refined her breeding, how elegant her manners, or how popular her husband, she was the wife of a freshman senator from the West, and many balls, dinners, and receptions were closed off to her due to her low ranking in the social pecking order. Abraham discovered— to his dismay—that while he was serving in the House, Mary had vanquished boredom and soothed her injured ego by shopping in the small stores along Pennsylvania Avenue, creating charge accounts and running up huge debts at the clothiers P.H. Hood and Co. and

Walter Harper and Co., buying the silks and dress goods she coveted and which they could definitely not afford.

Lincoln, who longed to become a statesman, had not yet made a single speech in the House of Representatives on the burning issue of the day—slavery—and in particular, slavery in the capital city. Unable to pass the Wilmot Proviso, the anti-slavery congressmen thus turned their attention toward ending or restricting slavery in the District of Columbia. Lincoln rarely participated in these angry debates conducted on the House floor, concentrating his energies on getting a Whig elected to the presidency that fall, which meant working closely with Southern Whigs. He did not want to stir up sectional division that would imperil his goal and so he kept a low profile.

After three months at Sprigg's, Mary bolted with Bobbie and Eddie, retreating to Kentucky to split her time between her father's Lexington brick mansion and summerhouse. At both places, Mammy Sally and a household of slaves would look after Mary's sons—particularly Eddie, with his persistent cough—and provide her with the many comforts so lacking in that D.C. drafty boardinghouse where she was often the only woman at the dinner table, as most congressmen wisely left their wives and children back home.

At first, after Mary's departure, Abraham did not miss her. But, as they say, absence makes the heart grow fonder. On Sunday, April 16, 1848, he was missing Mary, and so he wrote her a letter:

Dear Mary:

In this troublesome world, we are never quite satisfied. When you were here, I thought you hindered me some in attending to business; but now, having nothing but business---no variety---it has grown exceedingly tasteless to me. I hate to sit down and direct documents, and I hate to stay in this old room by myself. You know I told you in last [S]unday's letter, I was going to make a little speech during the week; but the week has passed away without my getting a chance to do so; and now my interest in the subject has passed away too....

I went yesterday to hunt the little plaid stockings, as you wished; but found that McKnight has quit business, and Allen had not a single pair of the description you give, and only one plaid pair of any sort that I thought would fit Eddy's dear little feet....

All the [boarding] house—or rather, all with whom you were on decided good terms—send their love to you– The others say nothing–

...And you are entirely free from head-ache? That is good--good---considering it is the first spring you have been free from it since we were acquainted. I am afraid you will get so well, and fat, and young, as to be wanting to marry again. Tell Louisa I want her to watch you a little for me. Get weighed, and write me how much you weigh.

What did he [Robert] and Eddy think of the little letters father sent them?

Dont let the blessed fellows forget father....

Most affectionately

A. LINCOLN

———

On that same Sunday morning that Abraham Lincoln was missing Mary, Francis Dodge Jr., the owner of a prosperous local shipping company, was missing three of his slaves. Forty other Washington area slave owners and employers woke up to find their servants missing, their fireplaces cold, and no breakfast on the table. Seventy-seven local slaves had disappeared. Church bells sounded the alarm.

Among the missing were two enslaved hired house servants, the Edmonson sisters, Mary, 15, and Emily, 13, of Montgomery County, Maryland, who had fled with four of their older brothers on the 54-ton schooner, the *Pearl*, the night before.

Mary and Emily Edmonson (1848)

The escape plan, arranged by Washington-area free Blacks and white abolitionists and funded by Gerrit Smith, had been long in the works. Near midnight, in a drizzly rain, the *Pearl*, operated by two white captains, Daniel Drayton and the drunk Edward Sayres, had quietly set sail from the Seventh Street Wharf down the Potomac River with the seventy-seven slave escapees crowded into the ship's hold. The destination was Frenchtown, New Jersey, where members of the Underground Railroad were scheduled to transport the slaves overland to safety and freedom.

But the wind and the tide did not speed them down the Potomac to the Chesapeake; they were becalmed overnight after drifting only a half mile from the city, forced to drop anchor just to prevent being pulled back upstream. When the sun rose, a slight breeze finally filled the slack sails of the vessel and pushed it down below Alexandria, where, thankfully, it being the Sabbath (Sunday), the wharves were quiet, and the *Pearl* passed by undetected.

By now, search parties on horseback were underway, first investigating the obvious escape routes, the roads out of the city. There were guesses and conjecture as to which way the slaves had gone until it was discovered that a schooner that discharged a cargo of firewood had recently departed without a word. Captain Drayton, being a Northerner and a stranger in those waters, was suspected. The tip came from a disgruntled hack driver, a free man of color named Judson Diggs. Diggs had carried two of the fugitives' belongings to the wharf on his dray. Anticipating a huge reward, the next day, he turned informer to the slaveholders and described the *Pearl* as the getaway vessel.

Telegraphic dispatches were sent off forthwith to Baltimore; several steamboats set off from there to proceed down the Bay one hundred miles to intercept the *Pearl* as it emerged from the Potomac. At the same time, Francis Dodge Jr. gathered a posse of thirty-five angry men—armed to the teeth with guns, pistols, Bowie knives and well-lubricated with brandy and other liquors— who clambered aboard Dodge's small steamboat, the *Salem*, powered by a potent engine and took off in hot pursuit down the Potomac from Georgetown, a Washington suburb. The posse reached the mouth of the river but could not find the *Pearl*. The steamer could not proceed into the Bay as it was not insured there. Before turning back, the posse took a last look into Cornfield Harbor, where it found the *Pearl* tucked into a cove. There it found safe harbor, as it had been cut off from its chance to sail north up the Bay by a fierce storm. This was at two o'clock Monday morning. About noon, the *Salem* began towing the *Pearl* to Washington.

There was great excitement in Washington when it was learned that the posse arrived with the captured slaves. The captives were marched in shame down Pennsylvania Avenue, the men bound with ropes. All were greeted with ugly taunts and jeers. Armed ruffians brandished knives and pistols and crowded around Drayton and Sayres, threatening violence. One of them cut Drayton's ear, which

Emily Edmonson saw was bleeding. Also in the crowd were relatives of the poor captive slaves. A brother-in-law of Emily and Mary was so overcome when he saw those beautiful and fine young women marched as prisoners to jail that he fainted away. He fell down in the street and was carried home.

Drayton, his crew, and the fugitives were swiftly bundled off to jail and safety. Washingtonians wanted Drayton alive. They were on tenterhooks to hear his testimony on the witness stand. Who had paid for the *Pearl* and its crew? The supplies? They wanted to penetrate the Underground Railroad cell operating in their city. In July, Sayres would be fined for transporting escaped slaves and Drayton convicted of larceny and sentenced to twenty years in prison. Numerous unsuccessful appeals followed and both men would remain in prison for some time.

When Emily and Mary's mother, Milly, heard the terrible news, she knew her daughters were doomed. Before the next morning, the guardian of the Edmonsons, acting for the real owner, sold all six children of Paul and Milly Edmonson to Bruin and Hill, the keepers of the large slave warehouse in Alexandria. Bruin paid the guardian $4,500 and would listen to no other terms that any of Edmondsons' friends proposed. Mary's employer in the city offered a thousand dollars for her, but Bruin laughed, saying he would get double that sum in the New Orleans slave market. Bruin had had his eye on purchasing that family for twelve years, the guardian being unwilling to sell them until that moment. Mary and Emily were beautiful, light-skinned young women and Bruin planned to sell these Christian girls as "fancy girls"—a term for prostitutes, sex slaves, or mistresses.

With Drayton and Sayres locked up, the angry mob turned its wrath against Gamaliel Bailey and his paper, the *National Era*. Abolitionists must be to blame, reasoned the slaveholders. For the next three days, anti-abolitionist mobs focused their anger on the *National Era* and Gamaliel Bailey, concluding wrongly that the mere presence of an abolitionist paper in the city had encouraged the slaves to escape. Mobs attacked the *Era* office, breaking windows, smashing doors, and damaging a sign. A committee appeared on the front steps of Bailey's home and demanded that he remove his press by the next morning or face uncontrollable violence. His aged father appeared at the door and gave them "what-for." With the mob shouting in the distance, Gamaliel stepped out and told those assembled that as the representative of a free press, he would rather die than have his constitutional rights degraded. Shortly thereafter, the *Era* office was again assaulted. Friends rushed to Bailey's house and, taking his children from their beds, escorted them next door to the house of Mayor Seaton, who was ill, to protect them. The next day, Marylanders and Virginians appeared at the *Era* office but dispersed when met by government troops. President James K. Polk had learned the details of the *Pearl* incident and the threats against the *National Era* and began working with the police to maintain peace in the city. The crisis ended—for the white people.

CHAPTER 44

The Women Hold Their Own Convention

Earlier, in July 1848, at Seneca Falls, New York, the very first woman's rights convention was held, organized by Elizabeth Cady Stanton, Lucretia Mott, and other progressive Quaker women. Both men and women attended but the only Black attendee was the former slave, Frederick Douglass, the editor of the *North Star*. Elizabeth's husband, the nationally prominent abolitionist, Henry B. Stanton, was noticeably absent.

In the days leading up to the convention, Henry Stanton helped his wife, Elizabeth, draw up her Declaration of Sentiments and resolutions. However, he backed off when he saw that Elizabeth had included in her list of grievances a line about men depriving women of the vote. A political aspirant, Henry did not want to be associated with such an unpopular cause, so he left town. On the other hand, Elizabeth's cousin, Gerrit Smith, made a major address at the Liberty Party's convention in which he demanded "females as well as males being entitled to vote."

At that groundbreaking woman's rights convention in Seneca Falls, eleven resolutions were read and each one voted on individually. A heated debate arose regarding women's right to vote. Lucretia Mott wanted the resolution to be struck off, saying to her friend, Elizabeth Cady Stanton, "Why, Lizzie, thee will make us ridiculous." Frederick Douglass stood and argued in favor of the measure. Douglass' words had power. The resolution passed by a large majority.

CHAPTER 45

Lincoln Meets Seward

During the fall congressional recess of 1848, Abraham Lincoln traveled to speak at Whig rallies. Lincoln, former New York Governor William Henry Seward, and Southern Whig Alexander Stephens were in the vanguard of Whigs who saw war hero General Zachary Taylor as the one candidate to win the presidential election for the Whigs. Seward was reluctant to back Southerner Taylor, who owned over two hundred slaves, a man who had no political party and had never voted in a presidential election. Even though Taylor, 64, stood for nothing, he had broad appeal as a military leader, and Lincoln and Seward supported him in the hope that his popularity would help them widen the Whig voter base. Importantly, Taylor had promised, as President, not to veto the Wilmot Proviso should it pass Congress. Lincoln promoted the Whig Party as the true anti-slavery party.

The nominee for the Democratic Party was General Lewis Cass of Michigan, another slave owner. Cass opposed the Wilmot Proviso. Cass had good odds of succeeding President Polk, as Polk had presided over a highly successful war and brought both California and New Mexico into the Union.

Salmon Chase and Charles Sumner formed the Free Soil Party, one that united thousands of disaffected Whigs, Democrats, and Liberty men. The Free Soilers nominated former president Martin Van Buren for president. The Free Soilers pledged to abolish D.C. slavery and to exclude slavery from the federal territories.

The election between two slaveholders and former president Van Buren, who had, in 1836, referred to slaveholders as "sincere friends to the happiness of mankind" would be decided by the votes of American white men, landed or not, and a sprinkling of free Black, land-owning New York men.

―――

In his fall 1848 campaign swing through Massachusetts, Lincoln devoted most of his speeches to deriding Cass and Van Buren and defending Taylor. The Boston Whig papers praised Lincoln's speeches, whereas the *Norfolk Democrat* found his remarks "nauseous," and the Free Soil editors were dismissive altogether. Lincoln's appearance and mannerisms drew much attention. His spectacular height—six feet four inches—startled his audiences. Oddly but effectively, he began his speeches by:

> leaning himself up against the wall,…and talking in the plainest manner, and in the most indifferent tone, yet gradually fixing his footing, and getting command of his limbs, loosening his tongue, and firing up his thoughts, until he had got entire possession of himself and of his audience.

William Henry Seward" (1844)

On October 15, at a great Whig rally at the Tremont Temple in Boston, Lincoln, 39, shared the same platform with William Henry Seward, 47. It was their first meeting. Seward was the star attraction for his anti-slavery record. As governor of New York, he had refused to extradite accused fugitive slaves. Seward believed that the Whig party would bring about a gradual end of slavery through a coalition of anti-slavery Northerners and progressive Southerners. Lincoln, while morally opposed to slavery, saw that, politically, it had to be handled gingerly to maintain both national and North/South Whig Party unity.

Seward spoke for a long time mostly about slavery. Lincoln spoke next and, according to Seward, put the audience in good humor, though he noted that Lincoln had largely avoided talking about slavery. The next night, Seward and Lincoln shared the same room in a Worcester hotel, where they spent much of the night talking. Lincoln told Seward he had been thinking about Seward's speech. Lincoln was forced to examine his views on slavery. He told Seward,

"I reckon you are right. We have got to deal with this slavery question, and got to give much more attention to it hereafter."

———

Taylor handily won the presidency, but Free Soiler Van Buren received ten percent of the vote, proving that anti-slavery had become a force in national politics. Taylor would be inaugurated in March 1849, at which time Lincoln would return to Springfield to practice law, as Lincoln had agreed with his party members that he would only serve one term.

Both William "Henry" Seward and Salmon Chase would become U.S. senators in March. Chase had stood up for anti-slavery himself, having (unsuccessfully) defended the Underground Railroad conductor John Van Zandt when he was sued in Ohio federal court by the Kentucky slave owner, Wharton Jones, for aiding his escaping slaves in 1842. As Chase left the courtroom, a judge said of Chase, "There goes a young man who has ruined himself today."

Van Zandt appealed to the Supreme Court and Seward assisted Chase in his defense. Nevertheless, Van Zandt lost and was forced to compensate Jones.

———

A month following the presidential election, the Thirteenth Congress returned on December 7 for a rump session. Despite Zachary Taylor's victory, Lincoln found the congressional Whigs in disarray. The issue of slavery was tearing the Whig Party apart, and Lincoln sought a compromise to end the debate before President-elect Taylor took office. Influenced by Seward, the events in Washington, and Joshua Giddings, Lincoln set out to craft a bill to address the matter of slavery in the District of Columbia. He believed that the U.S. government did have the right to abolish slavery in the District of Columbia with its (white male) citizens' approval.

Lincoln met with dozens of his fellow Whigs, particularly those with whom he boarded at Mrs. Sprigg's, listened patiently to their concerns, drafted a proposal, and secured their approval, although many parts of the plan were distasteful to them. He visited with the mayor and felt he had the backing of leading citizens for a gradual, compensated emancipation. Radical abolitionist Joshua Giddings noted in his diary, "I believed it as good a bill as we could get at this time."

On January 10, 1849, Lincoln prepared to introduce his bill, only to discover that its support among the fifteen leading Washingtonians had evaporated once the plan had gone public. Southern slaveholders visited those leading citizens and persuaded them to withdraw their support. Southerners believed the abolition of slavery in the District was the first step to abolishing it in the nation. Lincoln also doubted his fellow Whigs would have united to pass his plan. Consequently, he never introduced his bill.

CHAPTER 46

Milly and Paul Fight for Family

Paul Edmonson was a former slave who, in his lifetime, would own forty acres in Montgomery County, Maryland, less than fifteen miles from Washington, D.C. Paul had been set free when his mistress died, but his wife Amelia "Milly" remained a slave. The guardian of her mistress, Rebecca Culver, allowed Milly to live with Paul on his farm while taking home her sewing tasks. In truth, Milly's real task was to give birth and bring up children to be sold in the slave market, enriching her mistress' purse. Both Paul and Milly were light-skinned people of mixed white and Black blood, regarded by the federal census takers as "mulattos," and highly prized in the slave market to become house servants or, sometimes, when a woman, be sold into prostitution.

Before Milly married Paul, she had harbored grave doubts about their union. Although Milly loved Paul very much, she had become terribly distressed once they became engaged, as it preyed upon her mind that, as a future mother, she would be bringing children into the world, knowing they would be ripped from her breast and forced into perpetual bondage. The laws in Maryland, a slave state, declared that any child born to a slave mother was born a slave. After prayerful reflection, Milly told her folks that she had decided never to marry and was breaking her engagement to Paul. Her folks said she would be turned out of the church. Therefore, she married Paul. Being thought a good Christian was central to Milly's life. Paul and Milly were members in good standing in the Methodist Episcopal Church, as were their children.

Once they were married, Paul and Milly were happy enough, but Milly could not shake off the sadness she felt. Then, in 1815, their first child, Hamilton, was born. Milly said to her husband, "There 'tis, now, Paul, our troubles is begun; this child isn't ours."

With every child they had, and they had fourteen together, Milly's woe increased.

"Oh, Paul, what a thing it is to have children that isn't ours!"

Paul did not empathize:

"Milly, my dear, if they be God's children, it ain't so much matter whether they be ours or no; they may be heirs of the kingdom, Milly, for all that."

Milly had much to do with raising all those babies and doing the housework, cooking, cleaning, washing, and keeping up with her mistress' sewing, patching sheets and sewing shirts. Milly took pride in being a good mother, making sure her children were taught "the very best ways" and that they always looked "sweet and clean." All the while, she was eagle-eyed, on the lookout for white men passing by who might be coming to look at her fine children and buy them. When she saw a white man skulking near, she called in her brood and hid them from his eyes. Yes, Milly suffered, but after talking to the Lord a bit, she would feel lighter and that she could live a little longer.

In this way, the Edmonsons passed their years together in their humble cottage, a large, loving, and close-knit family, praying in the morning and at night, knowing that one day, each child would mature to the age for sale and leave the nest. With the exception of Hamilton, who ran away from the Culvers and then, as a runaway, was sold south to Louisiana, Paul and Milly were blessed that their children were hired by families in the Washington, D.C. area and not thrown into the vile trader's pen to be sold to the dreaded Southern market! Several of the older Edmonson daughters, with the help of their fiancés, had purchased their freedom from the Culvers and thus, when married, had children they could call their own.

Milly and Paul's safety evaporated when six of the remaining Edmonson children, four sons, Mary, and Emily, were among the captured escapees from the *Pearl* that were marched down Pennsylvania Avenue, thrown in the city jail, and then by morning, sold to slave traders for sale in the Deep South.

When this news reached the Maryland cottage of Paul and Milly Edmonson, their hearts were torn asunder. Milly said, "Never a morsel of anything could I put into my mouth. Paul and me, we fasted and prayed before the Lord, night and day, for our poor children!"

Rebecca Culver was the owner of Milly Edmonson and six of her children. Rebecca Culver was a mentally incapacitated person whose Maryland estate was managed by her brother-in-law, Frances Valdenar. Although Valdenar had, in the past, allowed the five oldest Edmonson daughters to raise the money to buy their freedom, prior to the *Pearl* incident, he had changed course; he told the Edmonsons that he would not manumit any more of the Edmonson children. While Josiah and Louisa were too young to work and remained at home, Valdenar had hired out six of the children—Samuel, Richard, John, Ephraim, Emily, and Mary—to work in elite private homes in Washington, D.C., with all their wages going to Rebecca Culver. Unable to buy their freedom, on April 15, 1848, these six Edmonson siblings made a command decision. They had cast their lot with the other passengers on the *Pearl* who dreamed of reaching Northern shores and freedom.

Imagine how impotent Paul Edmonson must have felt. He could buy acres of land, a farm, and yet not buy his own wife and children. The only consolation for Milly and Paul was that, because they were all living in the same area, they could regularly gather for church and meals at the older girls' Washington homes on Sundays. Life as they had known it changed in a flash. Valdenar, at a huge profit, sold Mary and Emily to Joseph Bruin, who boasted publicly of the price the two virginal Christian sisters would fetch in New Orleans as sex slaves.

Paul tirelessly knocked on doors of Washington area abolitionists and Methodist ministers, intent upon raising the funds to buy his children back. He had only a dribble of success. He wrote letters to New York. Meanwhile, for weeks, Emily and Mary were held, first, in an Alexandria, Virginia, slave pen before being transported to one in Baltimore, where they were to be shipped to New Orleans. The sisters were issued a blanket and slept on the bare floor in damp, dark cells, locked up. They had to wash clothes for the incarcerated men and dispose of their "night soil"—buckets of urine and excrement. The disgusting Baltimore slave trader looked the girls up and down and made lewd comments; he forbade them to pray.

A month after the *Pearl* was captured, Mary, Emily, and their brothers were put in the cramped cargo hold of the packet ship, the *Union*, with other slaves to be transported to New Orleans. On June 14, after a twenty-day sea voyage, almost suffocating below deck, over rough seas, with a shortage of food and water and bouts of severe seasickness, the captives on the *Union* finally approached New Orleans. While the brig was towed upriver, the Edmonson sisters stood on deck to take in some fresh sea air. Their first sightings of Louisiana were of mud flats and swamps. Soon, they saw fields of sugar cane and cotton dotted with silhouettes of plantation slaves stooped over as they worked the crops. The heavy, hot, and humid air buzzed with swarms of vicious mosquitoes.

Early the next morning, Emily, Mary, their brothers, and the thirty-four other passengers disembarked onto the city wharf in New Orleans. They were marched from the busy riverfront six blocks east to Jonathan Wilson's slave pen on Esplanade Avenue on the eastern border of the French Quarter. This slave pen looked much like the other two they had experienced, with its large, wall-enclosed yard with small, indoor sleeping quarters. In addition, Wilson's pen had a showroom for buyers. Mary, Emily, and the other newcomers were turned over to the custody of Jonathan Wilson and placed in the yard, where they found men, women, and children standing about miserably, in small groups or alone. They awaited their turn to be displayed for sale to potential buyers in the showroom. The sisters watched as slaves left with new owners.

Suddenly, on that first day, Emily was called into the showroom. An ostentatiously dressed young man was shopping for a "house-keeper" and willing to pay $1,500. He had seen Emily and wanted to check her over. Emily began to cry. When the dandy saw Emily's tear-stained face up close, he refused to buy her and told Wilson he had "no room for the snuffles in my house." When the man left, Wilson slapped Emily's face. She had cost him a $1,500 sale. Then, pointing in the distance, he said to her: "[T]here was the calaboose, where they whipped those who did not behave themselves."

Day in, day out, Mary, Emily, and the others had to stand on an open porch facing the street to advertise themselves to passersby. If buyers were interested, the slaves were paraded in an auction room in rows and exposed to vulgar jokes and taunts. If a man took a liking to a female slave, he summoned her for an inspection, opening her mouth, looking at her teeth, and touching her as familiarly as he desired, often making obscene remarks. Prospective buyers could take her into a back room for an intimate inspection, demanding that she strip to the waist. Buyers might say they were looking for scars or signs of beatings that would indicate a slave's defiant nature, but it was a transparent opportunity to molest a defenseless woman.

While at this prison, Mary and Emily learned of more horrible cruelties of the slave system. Before the sisters arrived in New Orleans, a young woman whose name is lost to us, of no more than fifteen years of age—Mary Edmonson's age—small of build, who had arrived in New Orleans with beautiful long and straight hair, had been sold by Wilson. A few days after her sale, she was returned to the slave pen. Bought for the worst of purposes, she did not suit her master. Therefore, Wilson had to refund the buyer's money. When the sisters first arrived in New Orleans, they saw and talked with her. She was then just beginning to sit up, having been so cruelly flogged, so much that some of her flesh was mortified and her life hung in the balance. Her brutal tormentors had cut her hair short. It was not unheard of for a "disappointing" slave to be condemned to a week of flogging, about two hundred lashes by an overseer, and for the male slaves in the prison to be required to apply lashes on their fellow slaves. The penalty for a slave not obeying this order was to be flogged himself.

Mary and Emily saw gangs of women cleaning the streets, chained together, some dragging a heavy iron ball. This was a common punishment for house slaves who had displeased their mistresses.

While in New Orleans, Richard Edmonson had done some sleuthing; he was determined to find his runaway brother, Hamilton, after fifteen years of separation. Richard found him working as a cooper and going by the name Hamilton Taylor. He was a free man. Hamilton learned of the terrible conditions Emily and Mary endured at the slave pen. They shared sleeping quarters with twenty or thirty other women sleeping on the floor. The girls woke up every morning with itchy feet and swollen with bug bites. Hamilton negotiated with Wilson to allow his sisters to sleep at Hamilton's house at night and return to the showroom each morning. Wilson agreed; he wanted his merchandise to be healthy-looking and free of disease.

Back home, Paul Edmonson had managed to raise enough money to pay for the freedom of his son, Richard. In New Orleans, Samuel had found work as a butler for a wealthy cotton merchant and the other Edmonson brothers, Ephraim and John, were soon sold. While Emily and Mary awaited their sale, an epidemic of yellow fever swept through the city in July. The slave trading season had been over since May, when wealthy citizens regularly fled the heat and the season's tropical diseases. At the slave pen, Mary and Emily noticed that a lot of their fellow inmates had turned a deathly shade of yellow, a sign of liver failure and approaching death. Death was all around, and no buyers were interested in putting down money for a slave who might die and spread "yellow jack" to their household.

Bruin and Hill wanted to protect their investment, so Emily, Mary, and Richard were ordered back to Virginia. The slave trader told Emily and Mary that their family had not just bought Richard's freedom but had raised a considerable amount of money on their behalf. The sisters hoped that they could return as free people. They arrived in Baltimore after a voyage of sixteen days. Mr. Bigelow of Washington came for Richard, who would return to his wife and children, but the girls remained in the slave prison. By September, their fate had still not been determined. They were returned to the same room in the Alexandria, Virginia, pen. Bruin and Hill set their combined price at $2250 and would not lower it. Bruin and Hill were also disappointed that money had not been raised to buy the sisters and were planning on sending them south a second time. As the day of departure drew near, Bruin bought calico fabric for the girls to make up into "show dresses," in which they would be displayed in South Carolina for sale. They felt as if they were sewing their own burial shrouds. Emily and Mary would be part of a slave coffle, marched overland.

The night before the coffle was to depart, Emily and Mary wept and prayed. In the morning, they woke up and gathered their things. From their quarters, they could see the slaves gather in the yard. The fiddle and the banjo began to play. The poor, unfortunate slaves were shackled together. They all would be required to sing as they marched. The sisters watched in astonishment as the gates to the slave pen opened and the coffle departed without them! Mary and Emily had been spared.

The night before, Joseph Bruin had met with William Chaplin, one of the Edmonsons' supporters, and worked out a last-minute reprieve. Chaplin had given Bruin a $600 deposit. A new deadline was established for the full payment of $2250.

There was a groundswell of interest in ransoming the Edmonson girls from slavery. In New York, a committee of Methodist Episcopal Church leaders had booked the Broadway Tabernacle "for the purpose of laying the matter of the Edmondson [*sic*] girls before the public." They had published "The Case of the Edmondson [*sic*] Sisters," a pamphlet that included letters attesting to the family's Methodist faith and exemplary reputations. Methodist ministers had been reaching out to ministers of other denominations to join them at the October 23 rally. The organizers from the Anti-Slavery Society circulated the pamphlets and promoted rally attendance.

The morning of the rally arrived. The Reverend Henry Ward Beecher, a Congregationalist minister, arrived at his Brooklyn home to find Paul Edmonson sitting on his front steps. The Black pastor of the Shilo Presbyterian Church in New York City had recommended that Edmonson take the Fulton ferry from Manhattan to ask the influential Beecher for help. Several months earlier, Beecher had spoken at a fundraiser to redeem a boy from slavery. Beecher invited the weary man into his library. Edmonson told his story. Beecher was dumbfounded to hear that the slave trader Bruin had spoken brazenly in public of selling Edmonson's two young daughters for sex. Beecher could envision what this life would look like for Emily and Mary. He could see and feel the suffering. He would make others see it. He decided to speak at the rally.

The evening of October 23, the two-thousand-seat Broadway Tabernacle was filled to capacity; many were members of Beecher's Plymouth Church. The gaslights flickered when it was Beecher's turn to step onto the platform. He was a man of universal curiosity and the crowd wondered what he would say. He spoke directly to the people in the seats, asking in essence:

"How would you feel if your daughter were kidnapped and sold to a man who would rape her, sell her children for a profit, and whip her if she put up resistance?"

He assumed the role of a slave auctioneer, shouting, in effect:

"Gentlemen, they say she is one of those praying Methodist n-------s; who bids? A thousand—fifteen hundred—two thousand—twenty-five hundred! Going, going! Last call! Gone!"

The audience was electrified and this lit up Beecher. He had roused them from apathy to action. The people in the crowd were no longer thinking of slavery in the abstract. They were focused on the plight of two real slaves. Slavery had faces, those of Emily and Mary. Beecher lay the responsibility for them at the feet of those present and made a direct, emotional appeal—only they could save the girls' purity—and the clock was running.

After the speeches were over, a collection basket was passed for donations to the cause. The tally was a disappointing $600, far short of the $2250 needed. Someone shouted, "Take up another!" The basket was passed again, but still, hundreds were lacking. Beecher whipped up the crowd some more. He was determined that the full sum would be raised before the crowd departed. Beecher popped around the stage, exhorting the people to dig deep into their pockets and give more. People started shouting pledges. Women deposited rings and bracelets in the collection basket. People called out, "How much is wanting now?" When the sum was raised, the room erupted in cheers; shouts, hats and handkerchiefs were waved, people smiled, and tears flowed.

Later, when the celebrants dispersed, it was determined that there was some confusion as to what was pledged and what was received. Depending upon what newspaper you read, the organizers were short somewhere between $300 and $850. Church collections and a corporate donation made up the difference.

On November 7, Mary and Emily were sewing near a window in Joseph Bruin's home when they saw "that white man we have seen from the North." It was William Chaplin, one of the organizers of the ill-fated *Pearl* debacle. Paul Edmondson was with him. After Bruin received the money, he wrote out the bill of sale:

Received of W. L. Chaplin twenty-two hundred and fifty dollars, being payment in full for the purchase of two negroes, named Mary and Emily Edmondson [*sic*]. The right and title of said negroes we warrant and defend against the claims of all persons whatsoever; and likewise warrant them sound and healthy in body and mind, and slaves for life.

Given under our hand and seal, this seventh day of November, 1848. $2,250

BRUIN & HILL. (Seal.)

Bruin pressed a $5 gold piece into each girl's hand. Paul Edmonson had splurged on a carriage. In it, the four of them set off jubilantly across the Potomac to join family and friends awaiting in Washington. Later in the day, Chaplin sent off a telegram to New York City that read, "Thank God! Mary and Emily Edmonson are free!"

CHAPTER 47

Water is Life and Water is Death

Californian James Marshall had tried to keep his January 1848 gold strike a secret. Nevertheless, the word got out. When it reached the streets of San Francisco, then an isolated village of five houses, American sailors deserted their ships to seek their fortune in the Sierra foothills. One hundred thousand people from all over the globe followed on their heels, bewitched by sensational newspaper reports such as this one from England:

> A person lately returned from the 'diggings' states that…he has read no account that at all exaggerates either the quantity or quality of the gold….[G]old is found in dry ravines….A party of some 20 or 30 …came suddenly upon a spot which glittered with gold dust and ore….

Cincinnati wrote:

> But the riches of California do not consist in gold alone….Two mines of silver have lately been discovered…Platinum. A rough diamond nearly the size of a hen's egg…Emeralds of large size are frequently met with…quicksilver mines have been discovered….

The Gold Rush was on! Everyone wanted to get there before the others, but California was so far away! While some American gold hunters splurged on the simpler but long sea voyage around Cape

Horn to California, others plotted a cheaper but more circuitous route, as did shoemaker Samuel McNeil of Lancaster, Ohio, who said goodbye to his wife with promises to return with great wealth and headed for the Pacific Coast. Departing February 7, 1849, McNeil, with a dozen others in his company, took the stagecoach from Lancaster to Cincinnati, where, McNeil wrote, they:

> obtained the necessary outfit, consisting of two years' provisions and the appropriate weapons of defence [*sic*]. The articles were sea biscuit, side pork, packed in kegs; six tents, knives, forks, and plates; each man a good rifle, a pair of revolvers, a bowie knife, two blankets, and crucibles....

The Independent Gold Hunter on His Way to California

After a week in the Queen City, McNeil's company boarded the steamer *South America* for a trip down the Mississippi to New Orleans.

From New Orleans, they booked passage for Chagres, Panama, but after passing Belize in the Gulf of Mexico, the ship sprang a leak, and they had to return to New Orleans. Travel continued by steamer, wagon, and horseback across Texas with wagonloads of cargo pulled by mules and horses. As they waited to cross the Rio Grande to Reynosa, Mexico, cholera appeared, sickening two of the men. On March 30, the adventurers crossed to Reynosa in canoes, taking the wagons apart and carrying them in pieces, swimming over the mules, which took three days. On April 10, 1849, the Ohio company arrived at Monterrey, where the cholera was raging. They would travel across Mexico to Mazatlán to catch a Pacific ship to San Francisco. McNeil recalled, "That night, about 6 o'clock, Course (a colleague) and myself were attacked by cholera. At 6 o'clock the next morning, Course died...."

Back in February, when McNeil and his company stopped in Cincinnati for a week, the cholera had already arrived there. The Cincinnati media, in protecting the business community, was aware and downplayed it. The Cincinnati *Daily Gazette* included a mention that, on Christmas Day 1848, a dying man was carried from a New Orleans steamboat moored at the public landing into the city. However, the editor did not urge caution; rather, it urged citizens "to go quietly about their ordinary occupations."

Cholera was bad for business. Cincinnati was a prosperous trading town on the Ohio River, its very livelihood dependent upon steady riverboat traffic and a reputation as a city of 110,000 residents in good health. The number of steamboat arrivals in Cincinnati was more than ten per day. The gold hunters needed outfitting. They stayed in hotels. They dined out. They frequented bars. They spent money. They kept the economy pumping. With no quarantine in place, thousands of immigrants and gold hunters from infected ports traveling by sea and rivers unwittingly spread the cholera contagion inland and westward.

By spring, the cholera had gained momentum, taking down first the poor people of Cincinnati, a much-maligned group that included working-class Blacks and unskilled Irish immigrants, who lived by the dirty docks with their filthy puddles and stinky slaughterhouses, where they found work. These unfortunates had the least access to clean water and safe food and lived in crowded and unsanitary slums. Cincinnati newspapers blamed the cholera on the Irish immigrants and their ways, stoking anti-Irish, anti-Catholic hatred and painting immigrants as undesirables. In portraying cholera as a disease of the Germans, Irish, and Blacks, the newspapers did the remaining fifty percent of the population a grave injustice. They were wholly unprepared for the catastrophe to come.

Although Cincinnatians were ignorant of the source of the cholera, they could see and smell gutters in the principal city streets that carried dung from semi-feral and unfettered swine, horses, and dogs and the discharge from slaughterhouses. Since the cholera epidemic of 1832, improvements in Cincinnati's water infrastructure were focused more on its quantity than quality. By the end of the decade, the Cincinnati Water Company pumped Ohio River water to one-third of the city's population, thus recycling the riverine filth where pig waste was shoveled. The rest of the citizens got their water from rainwater cisterns (safe) or artesian wells (unsafe due to groundwater pollution from upstream privies and sewage runoff).

The cholera was spreading. Finally, on May 16, four and a half months after cholera had entered the city, Dr. Daniel Drake announced in the *Gazette* that the Board of Health would make daily reports on the disease's spread. The Board did this in response to the numerous "exaggerated reports of the ravages of that dreaded disease, Cholera, in Cincinnati." Dr. Drake, the most influential physician in the American West, blamed the cholera on tiny gnat-like organisms that were activated by bad air. He endorsed the burning of coal bonfires laced with lime and sulfur on the corners of every city street and in courtyards, which he believed would combat the bad air. The smudge pots did nothing to stop the disease but did spread foul-smelling smoke and soot indoors as well as outdoors. Drake also endorsed that calomel (mercurous chloride) be given to the afflicted in large doses, which had no efficacy and had unpleasant side effects such as heavy salivation, mercury poisoning, and death. Dr. Drake further recommended that cholera victims be laid out for long periods in case they were not really dead but merely in "suspended animation."

Calvin Stowe was still enjoying the Brattleboro health spa in faraway Vermont. He had been there for a year. He and Harriet exchanged letters about the cholera. Calvin wrote Harriet that the doctors at the water cure establishment advised him to stay at the spa and not travel to Cincinnati. Harriet was disappointed, but she supported his decision, writing him that he should stay away because his system was "rendered sensitive by water cure treatment." On June 29, Harriet wrote to Calvin that 116 people had been reported dead in one day. In haste to remove the dead from their houses, Harriet wrote that, "Hearse drivers have scarce been allowed to unharness their horses, while furniture carts and common vehicles are often employed for the removal of the dead." This made Calvin worry that, in such haste, "many a poor creature has probably been buried alive."

The Cincinnati mayor designated June 30 as a day of community fasting and prayer. Riverboats passed Cincinnati without stopping. Coffins were stacked in the road, awaiting transport. It was rumored that hearse drivers, in haste to get to the graveyards, sometimes pitched a coffin and its contents onto the street.

By July 6, the cholera had made its way into Walnut Hills, no longer the exclusive domain of Lane Seminary but surrounded by inexpensive homes inhabited by a number of poor people, many of whom Harriet employed from time to time. The Stowes got their water from wells that were subject to groundwater contamination. Harriet wrote a letter to Calvin describing a mechanical problem with both of their water pumps, which she had a man from town come and repair. More worrisome, the water had a suspicious odor:

> [T]he water smells like despair just as it did last summer. We have to send to Miss Parkhursts for all our water.

On July 10, Harriet and Calvin's eighteen-month-old son, Charley, was taken ill. Harriet rushed him to the doctor, who mentioned "dropsy of the brain." Then, at one o'clock in the morning of July 12, Miss Stewart, one of Harriet's many boarders, awakened Harriet with a shout that Henry, 11, was vomiting. For several days, Harriet nursed Henry. Charley seemed to be improving. Henry recovered completely.

On July 16, Daisy, the family dog, ran out into the yard and died in a spasm. Then, news arrived that Aunt Frankie, a Black washerwoman who had done Harriet's washing the day before, died of cholera that morning. The twins, Hattie and Eliza, helped Harriet and Anna make a shroud for her. Harriet sewed a burial cap for good-natured Frankie. They attended her funeral.

The next day, the baby Charley fell ill with what was unmistakably cholera. For seven terrible days, Harriet sat by the infant's bed and watched as the cholera ravaged his once robust yet tiny body. Then, twin Eliza fell dangerously ill with the cholera and was carried to Mrs. Blackwell's. After great suffering, Charley breathed his last on July 24. Harriet wrote her sister-in-law, George's widow, Sarah Beecher, of her six children, only twin Hattie and Frederick had been spared from the plague:

> July 29
>
> Dear Sarah
>
> The day after Charlie was buried Georgie was taken violently ill and after coming down to the very gates of death was mercifully restored to us—She and Eliza are both now recovered—(nanny)

Anna was seized with billious [*sic*]dysentery in a most violent manner the day or two after Charlie was taken—I am too much worn out and exhausted to write much but your sympathy would be a comfort and I trust you will write me—I can say that God gives me strength to resign my will to his—and to offer up my flower— my darling—my best beloved to Him without a struggle….Every thing has seemed for the last fortnight like a troubled dream….

I am too tired to write much farewell.

Yours affectionately

H Stowe

CHAPTER 48

Harriet Tubman Chooses Liberty

Harriet Tubman (undated)

The death of the master sent a tremble of fear throughout the slave quarters, especially when the master was deeply in debt, as was Edward Brodess, the legal owner of Harriet Tubman. On March 7, 1849, Brodess died at Bucktown, Maryland. Prior to his death, he had begun selling off his slaves, including three of Harriet's sisters, putting Harriet next in line for sale, as she was then the eldest daughter of Ben and Rit Ross. In Edward Brodess' will, though, he permitted his widow, Eliza, only "the use and hire" of his slaves and not their ownership. Nevertheless, within three months of her husband's death, Eliza filed petitions in a Dorchester County court to sell several of the estate's slaves. Strapped for cash, she borrowed $1,000 from a neighbor, who expected to be paid back.

Throughout the summer, Eliza posted newspaper ads to sell Harriet's enslaved nieces, but the sales did not materialize because, suddenly, there was a new tangle. Edward Brodess' uncle filed a lawsuit against Eliza for the ownership of Harriet's mother. Until the matter was legally resolved, the court blocked the sales of any of Rit's offspring. Eliza did not wait for the court's ultimate judgment, however. On September 17, 1849, she returned to court to petition it to allow her to sell Harriet's niece, Kessiah, and her two young children.

It was on that same September day that Harriet and her brothers, Ben and Henry, while working on Anthony C. Thompson's plantation at Poplar Neck in Caroline County, Maryland, made a wild dash for freedom. After hiding for some time in the woods, though, the siblings lost their courage and turned back. Shortly thereafter, however, Harriet struck out alone, the fear of being sold South being more frightening to her than death. She prayed unceasingly for God to guide her steps to the North. She did not tell her husband she was leaving, certain he would betray her.

In October, Eliza Brodess posted a runaway slave ad in which she offered a one-hundred-dollar reward if "Minty [Harriet], aged about 27 years, [who] is of a chestnut color, fine looking, and about 5 feet high" was captured and returned to her.

Runaway Ad for Harriet ("Minty") Tubman

Hiding by day and traveling by night, her eyes on the North Star, Harriet traveled the ninety miles on foot that stood between Poplar Neck on the Eastern Shore of Maryland and Philadelphia. There she found a multi-racial community where over 20,000 Black people were living large and free and keeping the wages they earned. She blended in, finding jobs as a domestic and a cook. Lucretia Mott would become one of Harriet's benefactors, as well as a devoted friend. Mott's home was a stop on the Underground Railroad.

Before Harriet married John Tubman in 1844, she went by her birth name of "Araminta," called "Minty" for short. Minty Ross was born into slavery in Dorchester County, Maryland, in 1822. At age seven, Minty was hired out as a nursemaid to a woman known simply as "Miss Susan." Minty was told to watch over Miss Susan's rather large baby from before breakfast until late at night. Harriet had that baby on her lap the whole time unless the mother was feeding the child.

One night, the baby was sick and fretful. Minty was ordered to sit on the floor, close to her mistress' bed beside the child's cradle and rock it all night. Minty dropped off to sleep. The cradle went still. The baby, used to the rocking motion, woke up and cried. Minty woke up, realized what had happened and quickly reached out to begin rocking the cradle, but Miss Susan was that much quicker. She had already reached below her pillow and gotten out her whip. She lashed Minty on her face, head, and neck, raising welts and knots that caused scars Minty would carry to her grave.

Miss Susan liked finding fault with Minty. One morning after breakfast, Miss Susan was holding the baby while haranguing her husband. Minty had her hands free. With the grown-ups embroiled in a domestic dispute, Minty's eye wandered over to the sugar bowl on the breakfast table. A lump of white sugar was just within her reach.

Minty recalled later:

> Now you know, I never had nothing good; no sweet, no sugar, and that sugar, right by me, did look so nice….

Temptation overrode good sense. Minty reached for the sugar cube. Miss Susan sensed her movement, paused yelling at her husband, turned, and caught Minty in the act. Before Miss Susan could grab her trusty rawhide lash, hanging conveniently nearby, Minty dashed out the door. "I just flew," said Minty. She scrambled to the top board of a pigpen fence and fell into the muck. There she hid with the sow and eight or nine piglets, the excrement, mud, and detritus coating her skin and filling her nose and eyes. Dodging the sow, her powerful snout, and appetite, Minty carefully managed to pilfer some food scraps to stay safe and hidden. After four days, hunger drove her back to the house.

Later, when still a little girl, Minty was hired out to a planter named James Cook. Her job was to check the muskrat traps in the neighboring marshes, even after she came down with measles. After being nursed back to health, she was sent to work in the fields and forests, driving oxen, plowing, and hauling logs. She expertly knew how to use the hoe and shovel, pitchfork, and felling pick. She could lift, dig, haul, chop, and do the roughest fieldwork. Her muscles were hard, her legs were powerful, and her strength so prodigious that she would demonstrate to a crowd how many pounds she could lift, being only a small girl. At her tallest, she would only attain five feet.

It was October of 1835 and Minty was thirteen years old. She had been hired out again, this time to work a flax patch. Flax was grown for its fiber, to weave into rope and become tow sacks—fabric for rough slave clothing. Minty had to wade through the scratchy, knee-high stalks, pulling up each stalk separately. After the flax had been retted, it could be broken into small bits.

While breaking flax in a field outside Bucktown, her new master, Thomas Barnett, ordered his cook to pick up supplies at the dry goods store. As the sun set, signaling the end of the workday, Harriet tagged along. Before departing for the store with the cook, Harriet put a shoulder shawl of her mistress' over her hair, which had never been combed. It "stood out like a bushel basket," she said, "and when I'd get through eating I'd wipe the grease off my fingers on my hair."

At the store, Minty remained at the doorway while the cook did her shopping. There was a commotion going on. Apparently, one of Barnett's slaves was in the store without permission. An overseer had cornered him and wanted to haul him back to the farm for a flogging. There was a lot of yelling. The Black man started to flee toward Minty. Irate, the overseer grabbed a two-pound iron scale weight from the counter, hurling it at the man, but it fell short and hit Minty instead. She recalled how the weight "broke my skull and cut a piece of that shawl clean off and drove it into my head." She was knocked out cold, but her wild mass of hair had saved her life.

They carried her back to the master's house, bleeding and fainted. When she woke up, she was still in a daze. "I had no bed, no place to lie down on at all, and they lay me on the seat of the [mistress'] loom, and I stayed there all that day and next." On the third day, she was sent back to the fields, "and there I worked with the blood and sweat rolling down my face till I couldn't see."

From then on, Minty would suffer cruelly from what that blow did to her brain. She had headaches, dizziness, and seizures. She would fall asleep mid-sentence. While working, she would grow unexpectedly tired and struggle to keep up. Her left eye drooped. The iron weight had hit her about an inch above the bridge of her nose, on her forehead. The scar was a wide V, like a bird with its wings spread, and you can see it in photographs. The trouble in her head blocked her from learning to read and write. She began having what she called "visions," hearing music and conferring with God as to His plans for her. She never saw a doctor.

Harriet had heard that there were kind masters and mistresses out there, but she "didn't come across them."

———

Besides Harriet Tubman, an unprecedented number of slaves ran away from the Eastern Shore of Maryland in 1849. Washington, D.C., papers were flooded with ads that posted rewards for the return of runaway slaves. The *Easton Star* of Talbot County, Maryland, reported in August 1849:

RUNAWAYS

On Saturday night [a week ago], three slaves belonging to H. L. Edmondson, Esq., made their escape, and last Saturday night, one of Jas. L. Martin's Esq., and one belonging to Mr. George Hale, also absconded, and nothing has been heard of any of them since. Almost every week we hear of one or more slaves making their escape and if something is not speedily done to put a stop to it, that kind of property will hardly be worth owning. There seems to be some system about this business, and we strongly suspect they are assisted in their escape by an organized band of abolitionists....

Southerners imagined a vast conspiracy intent upon enticing their slaves to run away. Southern politicians found it advantageous to exaggerate the number of slaves escaping. Northern interference in Southern matters was considered by them as an insult. "Although the loss of property is felt," said Virginia Senator James Mason, "the loss of honor is felt still more."

When slaveholders perceived that the North wanted to take something away from them, what they called their "rights," they threatened to leave the United States and form a separate nation. Georgia Senator Robert Toombs warned, "I am for disunion." Which is what they did, threaten disunion when they learned that California—whose own citizens had formed a government and elected a government—had applied to be admitted to the Union as a free state and that President Taylor, a Southerner, backed this move. Taylor was opposed to the extension of slavery into the remainder of the lands acquired from Mexico. Southerners considered Taylor a traitor to his class. Even worse, they felt, was that Taylor had drawn New York Senator William H. Seward into his inner sanctum.

Seward further irritated the South by declaring, in his maiden speech as a senator, that the Constitution did sanction the power of Congress to exclude slavery from the territories. Speaking for three hours in a low, husky voice, twirling his glasses in one hand and gesturing with the other, Seward said that the Constitution does not recognize property in man. Southerners were incensed when Seward, in a key part of his argument to admit California as a free state, acknowledged that the Constitution's framers had recognized the existence of slavery and protected it where it existed, but the new territory was governed by a "higher law than the Constitution" a moral law established by "the Creator of the universe."

Seward's "Higher Law" speech made a great impact outside the walls of Congress. More than 100,000 pamphlets were distributed and an equal number reprinted in the nation's newspapers. Southerners considered it "monstrous and diabolical." The Fredericksburg *Recorder* called Seward "that most odious of all human creatures." Once again, the discussion of the extension of slavery in the territories strained relations between the North and the South, heading to a possible rupture, a pending split within Seward's Whig Party and war.

The Slave Power was outraged by Seward's speech. The institution of slavery—which permeated every aspect of Southern society, economically, politically, and socially—was under assault and Southern honor required an aggressive stance. An Alabama congressman claimed that, as a result of these policies, the South's liberty was at stake, for, "...it is clear that the power to dictate what sort of property the State may allow a citizen to own and work— whether oxen, horse, or negroes...is alike despotic and tyrannical."

Mississippi Congressman Albert Gallatin Brown warned of the danger these actions would bring upon the nation, saying, "We ask you to give us our rights...if you refuse, I am for taking them by armed occupation."

South Carolina Senator John C. Calhoun wrote that the Union was in danger and the South was discontent. This Southern discontent:

> commenced with the agitation of the slavery question...if the agitation goes on, the same force...will finally snap every cord, when nothing will be left to hold the States together except by force.

Southerners kept slaves enslaved by force through cruelty, violence, and threats of worse treatment. Southern lawmakers created this same climate of fear in the halls of Congress, threatening the violence of bloody war. They also frightened the nation as a whole, unsettling everyone as speeches by important legislators were transmitted to the people in tens of thousands of pamphlets and carried as newspaper editorials. Almost everyone read the speeches or had them read to them. William Lloyd Garrison, writing in *The Liberator*, remarked on the Southerners' use of aggression:

> Satisfy them that you do not intend to question their right to plunder, starve, lacerate, imbrute and murder their victims *ad libitum* [as often as necessary]—and they will be liberal in their hospitality...and courteous; but let them know or suspect that you regard the slave as a 'man and a brother,' that you hold his right to unconditional and immediate emancipation to be absolute, and their anger instantly 'burns to the lowest hell,' and they become transformed into demons. You had better trust yourselves among wolves and panthers than in their company....
>
> [T]hey employ threats, curses, lies, slanders, mobs and tumults, backed up by the bowie knife, the lash, and the noose, and all the other infernal accompaniments of the Lynch code.

Not surprisingly, the 31ˢᵗ Congress of 1849-1850 was marked by rancorous discord, paralysis, and personal violence. Fistfights flared in both Houses, Mississippi Senator Jefferson Davis challenged an Illinois congressman to a duel, and Senator Henry S. Foote, also of Mississippi, produced a loaded revolver during a heated debate. Over the course of three weeks and sixty-two ballots, the House in the 31st Congress failed to elect a speaker. It was only by the adoption of a special rule that allowed a speaker to be elected by a plurality on the sixty-third ballot.

It certainly seemed that the Union was in serious danger, and something had to be done about it. During this Congress, the hot-headed and deeply aggrieved Southerners demanded concessions to counterbalance the admission of California as a free state and assuage their wounded pride. Over the spring and early summer of 1850, the political leaders debated several resolutions in the form of an omnibus bill (including a strengthened fugitive slave law managed by the federal government), a cluster of resolutions proposed by Senator Henry Clay that would placate both the South and the North as a compromise. But months of debate and newspaper commentary yielded no solution. Clay's Compromise was, by summer, all but dead in the water.

In June, eight thousand soldiers and civilians convened in Santa Fe and wrote a free-state constitution for New Mexico. Taylor then urged the admission of both a free New Mexico and California, further disrupting the power balance in the Senate and insulting Southern honor yet a second time. A clash between the U.S. Army and Texas forces seemed imminent, as Texas still claimed New Mexico as within its borders.

On the Fourth of July, Taylor prepared orders for the Santa Fe garrison to stand their ground against the Texans. Afterward, Taylor spent a hot day outside, listening to Independence Day speeches at the yet-unfinished Washington Monument. He ate large amounts of raw vegetables and cherries, which he washed down with glasses of iced milk. The next day, he fell ill with violent gastric distress, dying on July 9 from cholera from Washington's contaminated water supply.

The new president was Millard Fillmore, a New York Whig who was opposed to the Seward faction. Politically, President Fillmore was the polar opposite of President Taylor. He shelved New Mexico's application for free statehood. He dismissed Taylor's Cabinet and pushed for Congress to revive and pass Clay's Southern-leaning Compromise.

CHAPTER 49

Harriet Beecher Stowe is Invigorated by the Sea Air

Three months before the office of the presidency passed from Taylor to Fillmore, in April 1850, when the new Fugitive Slave Law was still making its way through Congress, Harriet Beecher Stowe and her family were saying goodbye to Cincinnati and moving to Brunswick, Maine, where Calvin had accepted a teaching job at Bowdoin College. Calvin was ecstatic to receive such an offer, although the pay was no better than at Lane—$1,000 a year. Anyway, it was the honor of the thing, as Bowdoin was his *alma mater* and he, of the Class of 1824, had been the college genius. Desperate to keep him, Lane made him a counteroffer of $1500. Calvin informed Bowdoin who then sweetened their original offer by adding $500. Calvin accepted it. In moving to an East Coast college, he felt he was moving out of academic obscurity at age 49, having wasted years unappreciated in an obscure and somewhat disgraced Western Seminary.

The plan was for the family to travel east in waves. Harriet, Aunt Esther, and the three oldest children, would go on ahead to prepare the rental house. After Calvin completed teaching the spring term at Lane, he, Anna Smith, and the two youngest children would follow.

For eighteen years, Harriet had lived in the border town of Cincinnati with its race riots, immigrant problems, fugitive slave hunts, cholera summers, and rising crime and murder rates. While she had beautiful memories of life with her Beecher clan in Walnut Hills, all Harriet's siblings were now living elsewhere. With the exception of brother Charles and her father, both of whom would shortly leave the West, everyone now lived in the East (except the peripatetic Catharine). Harriet longed to return to New England, to be closer to her sisters and brothers, but it hurt her heart to abandon the grave of her Little Charley, now nine months gone, in the Lane Cemetery.

Harriet, 38, was interested in getting settled in her new home sooner rather than later, as she was six months pregnant. Not counting the miscarried babies, this would be her seventh child. So, that April, Harriet, Aunt Esther, thirteen-year-olds Eliza and Hattie, and Henry, 12, set out on an Ohio steamer bound east for Pittsburgh. From there, they took a canal boat pulled by horses or mules, traversed the Appalachians, then went by train and boat to Philadelphia and then to New York. Harriet had telegraphed ahead to Henry that they were coming. Exhausted, they stopped over in Brooklyn with Henry and Eunice. After a good night's sleep, Henry showed them his new beautiful horse and carriage, worth $600, a gift from his parishioners. He was paid $3,300 a year.

From there, they went on to Hartford, spending a week with the families of Harriet's sisters, Mary Beecher Perkins and Isabella Beecher Hooker. On May 13, Harriet and company arrived in Boston to see Edward and Isabella Beecher, who had left Illinois. Ardent abolitionists Isabella and Edward, loyal friends of abolitionist martyr Elijah Lovejoy, told Harriet of the tense and dangerous mood in Boston. Edward and Isabella and their anti-slavery circle were horrified that their once-distinguished Senator Daniel Webster was now endorsing the harsh new Fugitive Slave Bill. Webster chastised the North for not having fulfilled "their constitutional duties in regard to the return of persons bound to service, who have escaped into the free states." This was the same Daniel Webster who had purchased the freedom of several slaves. He had stood at Plymouth Rock and decried the American slave trade.

Edward and Isabella had become quite militant in their denunciation of the hated Fugitive Slave Bill and the traitor Webster, now Fillmore's Secretary of State. While Webster did enjoy support from moderates and the Cotton Whigs—Boston textile merchants with a warm association with Southern planters—the majority of Massachusetts citizens were united in disapproval of his course, his fellow Whigs calling it "madness." Webster's presidential aspirations and, therefore, his hunger for Southern votes made him an "archangel ruined," agreed Free Soiler Charles Sumner.

In Boston, Harriet spent $150 on bedsteads and mattresses, tables and chairs, and arranged to ship them to Brunswick. (At some point, Aunt Esther peeled away from Harriet's group because we don't hear of her in Brunswick for a year or so.) Having spent $76 on travel, Harriet was running short of cash. She had to earn money with her pen. In Brunswick, she made contact with several newspaper editors, notably Dr. Gamaliel Bailey of the *National Era*, a veteran, like Harriet and Henry, of the 1836 and 1841 mob attacks on *The Philanthropist* in Cincinnati. She arranged to write some pieces for publication in his anti-slavery paper and for other journals, often Christian periodicals, like the *New-York Evangelist*. The trickle of little checks from her writing sales would make a difference this lean year. It became even more critical that she write for pay when she discovered that their rental house would cost $125 a year as opposed to the $75 that Bowdoin had allotted Calvin.

Brunswick was a seaside town with lovely, brisk, dry Northern air. The two-and-a-half-story frame house they rented at 63 Federal Street needed some repair but was light, airy, and spacious. It was close to the campus. The famous poet Henry Wadsworth Longfellow, also a Bowdoin alum, had once lived there with his brother. Harriet plunged into unpacking, storing, lifting boxes, painting rooms, sewing bedspreads and pillows and upholstery, and organizing teams of workers. Walls needed papering and floors needed refinishing. Plumbing was the chief problem. Unlike Cincinnati, there was no municipal water system. For weeks, Harriet had to run the household with neither a sink nor water access.

In the midst of single-handedly managing all this hubbub, Harriet received a self-pitying letter from Calvin, Harriet paraphrasing its contents in a letter to her sister-in-law, Sarah Beecher. Calvin was:

> saying he is sick a bed—& all but dead [and] don't ever expect to see his family again wants to know how I shall manage in case I am left a widow—knows we shall get in debt and never get out—wonders at my courage—thinks I am very sanguine—warns me to be prudent as there won't be much to live on in case of his death, &c &c.
>
> I read the letter and poke it into the stove, and proceed.

Calvin, Freddie, and Georgie were there when the new baby arrived on July 8. They named him Charles Edward after the baby Charley, who had died. For two glorious weeks, Harriet and the baby enjoyed the care of a nurse. For a time, Harriet suffered painful nipples and a fever and had to hire a wet nurse. She hired a cook.

Harriet longed to write letters but found there was little time for that, writing Sarah Beecher,

> Since I began this note, I have been called off at least a dozen times; once for the fish man to buy a codfish; once to see a man who had brought me some barrels of apples; once to see a book man…then to nurse the baby; then into the kitchen to make a chowder for dinner; and now I am at it again, for nothing but deadly determination enables me ever to write. It is rowing against wind and tide.

But write she did—for pay and publication. On August 1, her first article for Dr. Bailey appeared, titled "The Freeman's Dream: A

Parable." In it, she registered her wrath against the pending Fugitive Slave Law. It is the story of a white farmer who turns away a fugitive slave family and then, on Judgment Day, is eternally damned. Following the story's conclusion, Harriet wrote directly to her readers:

> Of late, there have seemed to be many in this nation, who seem to think that there is no standard of right and wrong higher than an act of Congress, or an interpretation of the United States Constitution....Are not the hungry, the thirsty, the stranger, the naked, the prisoner, and every form of bleeding, suffering humanity, as much under the protection of Christ in the person of the black as the white—of the bond [slave] as the free? Has [H]e [Jesus] not solemnly told us, and once for all, that every needy human being is His brother, and that neglect of his wants is neglect of Himself?

The Bowdoin professors and their wives had been kindness itself to the Stowes. When the Stowes arrived at the wharf in a lashing rain, Phebe Upham was there to welcome them. For a whole rainy week, Phebe had taken the family and their baggage into her home. Phebe Upham also arranged for a woman to stay with Harriet until her baby was born. Harriet was happy in her new home, her newfound zest manifesting in her drawing and cooking and exuberant trips to the Atlantic shore, fishing for pollock with the children. So it was with great umbrage and terrific social humiliation that Harriet greeted Calvin's strange news.

When Calvin arrived in Brunswick that summer, he had solicited another $100 from Bowdoin, which they generously gave him. Then, he informed the Bowdoin Board of Trustees that Lane Seminary could not find a replacement for him. Calvin, therefore, agreed to return to Cincinnati to teach at Lane's winter term from November 1850 through March 1851 (with pay). He asked Bowdoin to grant him a leave of absence for that time period so he could fulfill this promise to Lane. He made this request before even taking his professorial seat at Bowdoin. He pleaded his poverty. Amazingly, Bowdoin agreed.

If it was not ungrateful enough to ask Bowdoin for a leave on top of all these additional money requests, Calvin revealed to Harriet a new development. He had been offered yet a third professorship, this time at the Theological Seminary of Andover, Massachusetts. Calvin accepted that third offer, and Andover announced it in the paper.

Meanwhile, Calvin's induction at Bowdoin was set for October 16, 1850. The invitations were out. Calvin wanted to resign from Bowdoin at once, but the trustees held him to his contract. Harriet, always the very soul of discretion, was mortified.

In an announcement of Calvin's induction at Bowdoin, a correspondent of the *New York Independent*, added this opinion:

> How far Dr. Stowe approximates to the faculty of omnipresence, we are not informed; but if, as the paper have stated, he is to have an actual and effectual connection with one college and two theological seminaries at the same time, he must stand in need of something like it.

Part IV

COMPASSION

(1850-1852)

I had two little curly headed twin daughters to begin with, & my stock in this line has gradually increased till I have been the mother of 7 children, the most beautiful of which, & the most loved, lies buried near my Cincinnati residence. It was at *his* dying bed, & at *his* grave, that I learnt what a poor slave mother may feel when her child is torn away from her.

—*Harriet Beecher Stowe*

CHAPTER 50

Citizens Protest the Bloodhound Law

The Fugitive Slave Law of 1850, which would go into effect on September 18 when President Fillmore signed it into law, gave unbridled Federal power to arrest fugitive slaves in the North and return them to Southern slavery. How did this new law differ from the original? Federal marshals were now authorized to require Northern citizens to assist in their slave catching. A citizen who failed to assist the slave catchers or who provided aid to a fugitive could be fined up to $1000 and jailed for up to six months. The new law, in essence, extended slavery into the free North, thus obliterating the line between the two sections.

Federal marshals would take the captive to a federal commissioner, who earned $10 if he ruled in favor of the slave catcher and only $5 if he ruled in favor of the captured person. Abolitionists, powerless to stop the passage of the Fugitive Slave Law of 1850, nonetheless held numerous protest conventions in anticipation of it. The most memorable of these protest conventions, the Fugitive Slave Law Convention, was held in Cazenovia, New York. It met on August 21-22, 1850, and was organized by New York abolitionist firebrand Gerrit Smith. Nearly fifty fugitive slaves attended. Four hundred other participants met inside the Free Congregational Church of Cazenovia. Hundreds of supporters gathered outside the building as there was no more space in the pews. The crowd swelled to two thousand strong, so the meeting was moved outdoors into Grace Wilson's apple orchard.

Frederick Douglass (1855)

Frederick Douglass, editor of the *North Star,* chaired the convention. Sessions began with prayer. Emily and Mary Edmonson arrived from Macedon, New York, and sang occasional songs. Frederick Douglass wrote up the proceedings in his paper and included this "Letter to the American Slaves from those who have fled from American Slavery":

AFFLICTED AND BELOVED BROTHERS: —The meeting, which sends you this letter, is a meeting of runaway slaves....

The chief object of this meeting is, to tell you what circumstances we find ourselves in—that, so you may be able to judge for yourselves, whether the prize we have obtained is worth the peril of the attempt to obtain it.

The heartless pirates, who compelled us to call them "master," sought to persuade us, as such pirates seek to persuade you, that the condition of those, who escape from their clutches, is thereby made worse, instead of better....When they told us, that the abolitionists, could they lay hands upon us, would buy and sell us, we could not certainly know, that they spoke falsely; and when they told us, that abolitionists are in the habit of skinning the black man for leather, and of [regaling] their cannibalism on his, flesh, even such enormities seemed to us to be possible....

[W]e are not as ignorant and credulous now....[W]e know it now, that slaveholders are as great liars, as they are great tyrants.

The abolitionists act the part of friends and brothers to us; and our only complaint against them is, that there are so few of them....

Numerous as are the escapes from slavery, they would be far more so, were you not embarrassed [hampered] by your misinterpretation of the rights of property. You hesitate to take even the dullest of your master's horses—whereas it is your duty to take the fleetest....Your consciences suggest doubts, whether...you are at liberty to put in your packs what you need of food and clothing. But were you better informed, you would not scruple to break your master's locks, and take all their money. You are taught to respect the rights of property. But no such rights belong to the slaveholder. His right to property is but the robber-right....For you are prisoners of war, in an enemy's country....—and therefore, by all the rules of war, you have the fullest liberty to plunder, burn, and kill, as you may have occasion to do to promote your escape.

Theodosia Gilbert, 31, a nurse and one of the proprietors of the Glen Haven Water-Cure Institute, although herself an abolitionist, also served on this occasion as a proxy for her fiancé, William L. Chaplin. Chaplin, who had been the organizer of the ill-fated *Pearl* flight and had arranged the ransom of the Edmonson sisters, was scheduled to make a triumphant appearance with some fugitive slaves he had rescued from Washington, Allen and Garland H. White, but was unfortunately imprisoned for this act.

Following the convention, Emily and Mary Edmonson spent much of September 1850 making appearances in small towns across New York out of gratitude to raise money for Chaplin's bail. They sang and begged for funds on Chaplin's behalf, even on Sundays, a holy day, because it was for a worthy cause. They felt Chaplin did the Lord's work so they did not consider their Sabbath-breaking to be sinful.

Finally, in January 1851, the entire $19,000 was raised, and Chaplin was released from Maryland. He then fled and forfeited $25,000 in bail money. Had he returned to Maryland for trial, he feared being hung or lynched. Chaplin made little to no effort to raise funds to reimburse his supporters. Gerrit Smith alone had donated thousands of dollars. Some charitable farmers were left penniless after having mortgaged their farms to come up with the money and then lost their farms altogether.

Chaplin suffered physical, emotional, and mental trauma from his imprisonment and as an agent on the Underground Railroad. He abandoned abolition activism. A year later, he married Theodosia Gilbert and joined her in operating the Glen Haven, New York, Water-Cure Institute. Despite his jumping bail, Chaplin was still held in high regard by his anti-slavery fellows. At his wedding, he was presented with a silver pitcher to acknowledge his contribution to the slaves' cause.

CHAPTER 51

Stephen Douglas Finds the Votes

By September, Senator Stephen A. Douglas, the ambitious Democrat from Illinois, had stepped into the Congressional leadership vacuum and, acting as Fillmore's toady, rescued the Compromise and mustered support for each of its parts, amounting to a series of trade-offs. These matters were settled by the end of September. Northern Democrats, Whigs and border-state Whigs voted for a free California, prohibition of the slave trade in the District of Columbia, and a $10 million payment to Texas to settle its dispute with New Mexico. Many Northern Democrats joined Southerners in enacting a stronger fugitive slave law and in organizing Utah, Nevada, Arizona, and New Mexico as territories *with no restrictions on slavery* for the time being.

Sarah Grimké was not surprised to see Northern men cooperate with Southern slaveholders. Having toured through New York and New Jersey and living in Philadelphia, the Grimkés had observed that Northern businessmen worked hard against abolition. Sarah said that Philadelphia was tough to labor in for the slaves' cause as "...ten thousand cords of interest are linked to the Southern slaveholder." In Newark, she saw that "Southern interest is powerful, shoes and carriages, etc. made in Newark are bartered for the gold of the South, which is gotten by the unrequited toil of the slave."

Seventy percent of Southern cotton was exported abroad and to Northern textile mills. The North's appetite for raw cotton spurred Southern cotton production. Reciprocally, the South imported two-thirds of its clothing from the North or abroad. Most of the ships carrying cotton from Southern ports were built and owned by Northern or foreign companies. Southern ships returning from Europe put in at Northern ports to trade and transport goods over-land. Free Soiler Charles Sumner charged that a conspiracy between Southern planters and the Northern textile magnates— an "…unholy union…between the lords of the lash and the lords of the loom"— had brought about Taylor's presidential nomination.

Slaves worked Southern crops with Northern hoes and ploughs. Slaveholders rode on Northern saddles, read Northern books, wrote on Northern-made paper with Northern pens and ink.

If the Compromise of 1850 passed, many believed the Union would be saved, or at least the crisis would be averted. But the effect of the Fugitive Slave Act among Northerners would come as "a sheet of lightning at midnight," wrote Ralph Waldo Emerson. Many Northerners believed that slaves had the right to flee from their masters and that good citizens everywhere were obliged to offer them aid and hospitality.

The new fugitive slave law was designed to be more heinous than the original 1793 law. Free Blacks were vulnerable to capture as the new law wiped out any legal devices that could protect the accused from false arrest, such as the right to call witnesses, trial by jury, and writs of *habeas corpus*.

At her home in Auburn, New York, William "Henry" Seward's wife, Frances Miller Seward, opposed the new law. New York had abolished slavery in 1827. What did it mean now to be a good citizen? Did one report a neighbor who had been formerly enslaved because the new federal statute said to do so? Every Northerner faced this quandary.

Frances Seward (1844)

Henry donated money to Frederick Douglass' anti-slavery news-paper, The *North Star*. Frances Seward joined the Underground Railroad. She and her husband employed a couple, Harriet and Nicholas Bogart, who had once been enslaved and who were now agents on the Underground Railroad. Frances fitted out the old base-ment kitchen and dining room as a shelter for fugitive slaves. On cold nights, when Harriet Bogart told her that travelers were expected, Frances kindled a warm fire on the hearth. She set out bedding and had a hot meal ready. In the spring and summer, she designated the woodshed behind the house as a sanctuary for any weary wanderer that might come her way. Henry and Frances Seward were faithful to the command to "extend a cordial welcome to the fugitive who lays his weary limbs at your door."

CHAPTER 52

The Crafts Energize Boston

On Saturday, September 21, 1850, cannons boomed on Boston Common, one hundred shots, to signal the passage of the Compromise of 1850 and the enactment of the Fugitive Slave Act. For free white citizens such as Fillmore and Webster, the sound of the guns was celebratory. Others trembled at its implications for citizens living in the American "cradle of liberty" and in the country altogether. Every Black person, formerly enslaved or freeborn, was in danger. In short order, a full third of the parishioners at Twelfth Baptist Church, the fugitive slave church of Boston, disappeared. In the last three months of 1850 alone, an estimated three thousand Black people left the country for Canada. Others hid in garrets and cellars.

The new Fugitive Slave Act became a rallying point for abolitionists of all stripes. The differences that had driven them into separate camps—over woman's rights, gradual vs. immediate emancipation, Black suffrage, integrated schools—dissolved overnight. Anti-slavery advocates agreed on the villainy of the law and the necessity to oppose it with every ounce of their beings.

In October, distressed by the law's passage and rumors of "men-stealers" moving about, a small group of Black and white abolitionists met in Boston's African meeting house and resolved to form a powerful vigilance force in the city, one that was dedicated to not letting even one Black person be returned to bondage. While many Blacks fled, others resolved to stay, such as the Georgian fugitives,

Ellen and her husband William Craft, who, for two years, had made a life for themselves in Boston and had many friends.

———

Ellen Craft's father was Major James Smith of Clinton, Georgia—a cotton planter and her white master. Her mother, Maria, was Smith's light-skinned Black house slave, who at 18, had become pregnant with Ellen after Master Smith raped her. Georgia law offered no protections to Maria regarding this assault, although it would have been a capital crime if a Black man had raped a white woman. In an accounting of Smith's estate, Maria's name would be listed on the same page as his chickens and pigs.

Little Ellen's skin was so very nearly white, and her resemblance to her father, James Smith, so strong, she was often mistaken as part of his white family. Consequently, Ellen's presence on the plantation was an irritant to his wife, and she made Ellen suffer. But fortune smiled upon Ellen when Mrs. Smith sent Ellen, 11, to Macon as a wedding present for her daughter, Eliza, now Mrs. Robert Collins. Painful as it was for Ellen to be separated from her mother, her new mistress was kinder to her. Ellen became a housemaid and Eliza Collins' favorite slave. Ellen and Eliza were both daughters of James Smith. They were half-sisters, yet one answered to calls of "n----r" and the other to the title of Mistress. Smith transferred ownership of Ellen and her future children to Eliza.

William Craft, who also lived in Macon, was owned by a different master and was hired out as a skilled cabinetmaker. He was allowed to keep some of his wages. In 1846, Ellen and William were married in a ritual among the enslaved where they "jumped the broomstick." Marriage between slaves was not legally recognized.

Two years later, creditors were hounding Eliza's husband, Robert Collins. He had been selling off his slaves to raise money. William and Ellen had to escape before Ellen was placed on the auction block. In the cold, predawn hours of December 20 or 21, 1848, Ellen and

William purchased two tickets from Macon to Savannah. William took his place in the "negro car," but Ellen rode with the whites.

Ellen posed as a sickly, white cotton planter traveling with her Black slave (William) to seek medical attention in the North. Because it was not customary for white women to travel with male servants, Ellen masqueraded as a man. To carry out such a daring deception, William had cut Ellen's hair to neck length. To hide her smooth facial skin, she wore a bandage around her chin, which also provided her with an excuse to not talk with strangers (in a woman's voice). An extra-tall silk hat gave her some height. To prevent her from being required to sign a hotel registry or other papers, as she could not write, Ellen propped her right arm in a sling. To further disguise her face, she wore green-tinted glasses. Her suit of clothes was elegant—she had made the slim-fit trousers herself—and the final touch of a black cravat at the neck showed she was indeed a very wealthy white gentleman of the South. She wore men's boots.

Ellen Craft in Disguise

Over a thousand miles, on steamer rides and train trips, they traveled toward Philadelphia, maintaining the charade of the loyal slave tending to his kind but ailing master. They slept little. They endured several close calls. A military man had noted Ellen's overfamiliarity with her slave (William) and approached her, saying, "[Y]ou are very likely to spoil your boy by saying 'Thank you' to him. The only way to make a n----r toe the mark and to keep him in his place is to storm at him like thunder and keep him trembling like a leaf."

Ellen had to make excuses for not partaking of brandy and cigars with the other traveling men. At a Virginia railway station, a woman mistook William for her runaway slave and demanded he go with her. Abolitionists approached William and told him to "leave that cripple and have your liberty." They arrived in Philadelphia on Christmas Day 1848. The Underground Railroad gave them aid and lodging yet recommended they move on to Boston, which was safer, or Canada. Three weeks later, they were welcomed and offered lodging at the brick home of Lewis and Harriet Hayden in Boston. The Haydens had escaped bondage in Kentucky six years earlier, their faces powdered with flour to make them appear fair-skinned from a distance. Their Boston boardinghouse was an activist headquarters with hidden entrances, exits, and hiding places for dozens of fugitives.

William, 24, and Ellen, 22, settled in Boston. Ellen worked as a seamstress and studied upholstery-making. William was a cabinetmaker. The story of their escape from slavery was heralded and broadcast all over the nation. The Crafts—or rather, William, as it was considered unseemly for Ellen to speak in public—told their story at anti-slavery meetings in Boston and throughout New England. Such visibility made them easy targets for slave catchers.

On Saturday, October 19, 1850, two men from Macon, Georgia, arrived by train at a Boston depot and registered at the United States Hotel. The leader was Willis H. Hughes, who had been hired to kidnap Ellen and William Craft by Ellen's debt-ridden slave owner, Robert Collins. Hughes, a jailer from Macon, Georgia, was also a "public Negro whipper," and had once nearly beaten Ellen's uncle to death. Hughes had short, black teeth from excess tobacco use and was a "short, rowdyish-looking fellow, five feet two, thirty or forty years of age," with "sandy hair, red whiskers."

Conversely, Hughes' partner, John Knight, was tall and dark-haired. He had worked alongside William Craft in a Macon carpenter's shop and could identify both William and Ellen. To carry out their plan, they first needed a warrant. They carried letters of introduction.

On Monday, Hughes's plan to get the warrant hit several snags. The lawyer that was recommended was out of town. At the court-house, Hughes was passed from judge to district attorney to commis-sioner, each official refusing to become involved in the "unpleasant business."

Hughes decided to try another approach. The next day, he dispatched John Knight to visit William at his shop. William was at his workbench, pistol beside him. Knight said he was in town on business and wanted William to show him around. Knight said he had come alone. William told Knight he was too busy for that, so Knight suggested that William could come to his hotel later with Ellen, when they could discuss Ellen writing a letter to her mother, Maria, which Knight offered to deliver to her upon his return to Macon. William Craft sniffed about town and discovered that Knight was the accomplice of the cruel Macon jailer, Hughes. He realized he and Ellen were in real danger of abduction.

That night, the Vigilance Committee, now eighty members strong and growing, met. A legal committee was formed to watch for warrants, create legal obstacles to fugitives being returned to bondage, and to alarm the citizens of kidnappers on the prowl.

Although slave catcher Hughes did find a lawyer—at Daniel Webster's law firm—it did him no good. Reappearing at the court-house, he discovered at every turn that the Vigilance Committee lawyers, Ellis Gray Loring and Samuel E. Sewell, had gotten there ahead of them to warn the officials against issuing warrants for the Crafts' arrest.

So it went—one infuriating delay after another—until, finally, on Friday, most of the officials whom Hughes had already met held a secret meeting and agreed to do their part in returning the Crafts to Georgia. The warrant for the Crafts was then issued in open court. The warrant was signed by the judge riding the circuit at that time, U.S. Supreme Court Chief Justice Roger B. Taney.

Warrant in hand, the Georgians scurried to the office of the U.S. Marshal, Charles Devens, one floor down. Earlier, however, the lawyers from the Vigilance Committee had also paid Devens a call, advising him that it would be illegal if his deputies were to make any arrest by knocking down any doors, as he, Devens, would be personally sued for any damages incurred. Devens left Hughes with the impression that the Crafts' arrest was imminent. Devens left the courthouse to arrange for a jail for them. A buoyed Hughes and Knight exited the courthouse to find a hostile crowd of Black and white protesters awaiting them. At the street corner, a well-dressed white man stood high atop a box, urging the "Negroes and their friends" to arm themselves with pistols, Bowie knives, and daggers. "Resist unto death!! Shoot down all slave catchers from the South!" he shouted. Hughes and Knight were shaken up.

By noon, handbills were posted on Boston's streets:

TO THE RESCUE!
Three fugitives about to be Arrested!!
WILLIAM CRAFTS SUPPOSED
TO BE ONE!
BE ON THE ALERT!
NO TIME TO BE LOST!

Friends hid Ellen outside the city. William, who had barricaded himself in his shop, was persuaded by Friday afternoon to move back into the Haydens' house. Lewis Hayden let it be known around town that he had placed kegs of gunpowder under his house with a fuse attached, ready to light if someone came to arrest Craft or any of the freedom seekers he and his wife sheltered. As a result, the police force told the marshal they would not serve the warrant as the process would mean bloodshed and armed conflict.

On Saturday, Hughes returned to the marshal's office. Hughes volunteered to serve the warrant with a posse. The marshal told him that William had left town. Hughes set out to prove this was a lie but was prevented from doing this because, to his astonishment, that afternoon, he and Knight were arrested and charged with slandering William Craft by calling him a slave and thus damaging his business and character. The writs were written by two justices of the peace, the unseen hand of the Vigilance Committee clearly at work. Bail was set at the extraordinary amount of $10,000, which was met by undisclosed parties. The slave catchers exited the courthouse through the back doors to avoid the protesters. The purpose of the arrest was not only to keep Hughes and Knight so occupied that they could not arrest the Crafts but also to confirm their identities.

New handbills were posted shortly, including unflattering physical descriptions of the "SLAVE HUNTERS IN BOSTON!" chocked full of information about their size and color as is usually found on public notices offering monetary rewards for escaped slaves. The hunters were now the prey. When the Georgians stepped out of their hotel, gangs of street boys pelted them with rotten eggs and old food. They were spat upon and cursed.

Monday dawned no better for the slave catchers. The Boston *Evening Transcript* reported the story of their notoriety, including a poem about Hughes:

That Macon Hews was surely daft

In coming here to capture Craft;
Instead of fixing slaves in collars,
He's fixed in jail—ten thousand dollars!

A notice was included:

☞ *MEN OF BOSTON!* ☜
SHALL THESE VILLAINS REMAIN HERE?
☞ *IT IS THE PRINCIPLE OF THE THING.* ☜

All was quiet Monday morning for Hughes and Knight until shortly after noon when Deputy Sheriff Coburn showed up at their hotel and placed them under a second arrest. "Macon Hews" and Knight were charged with conspiracy to kidnap, citing Knight's visit to William's shop, trying to lure them to the hotel. The writ had been issued by Justice List, at the request of Craft, whose damages were assessed at $10,000. Bail was met. The two slave catchers emerged from the courthouse to a crowd of two thousand people awaiting their exit, Knight reporting later that Blacks outnumbered whites, three to one. The crowd was united in protest, chanting, "Slave hunters!" Some called for tar and feathers.

Knight managed to return to the hotel undetected, but Hughes' cab was violently attacked, a window broken, a gun aimed at Hughes' face, with rioters hanging off the doors, chasing after the cab on foot, screaming, trying to poke sticks in the wheels to stop the cab. The cab raced at breakneck speed to escape while a man straddled the roof.

Upon Hughes' return to the hotel, the sheriff met him to place the slave catchers under arrest for the third time for trying to kidnap Ellen. An army of Black protesters milled menacingly outside the hotel while white men paced the interior halls. The slave catchers refused to return to the courthouse. The bailers were summoned to the hotel. Hughes and Knight hid out in a room reserved for ladies.

All the next day, Tuesday, October 29, Hughes and Knight received calls from an assortment of visitors. First came one hundred or so white men who told them to leave town. A committee of sixteen followed, warning them that a mob was poised to strike. Finally, a troupe of ladies made a call, but Hughes and Knight were unable to receive them as they were paying their own call on the marshal.

The elaborate scheme of harassment designed by the Vigilance Committee continued to unspool. The Georgians were slapped with new charges:

- Smoking in the streets
- Profane swearing and cursing
- Accusations of toll jumping and fast driving
- Carrying concealed weapons

Wednesday, Rev. Theodore Parker, who was hiding Ellen Craft at his home, called upon the Georgians to tell them they were no longer safe for even one more night. Somehow evading tight surveillance, the slavecatchers left the hotel and fled to New York on the two o'clock train. Had they fled in disguise, like the Crafts? In New York, they awaited further instruction from the slaveholder Robert Collins, who, infuriated, dashed off a letter to President Fillmore. A rumor spread that Fillmore was dispatching troops to Boston.

At the suggestion of Rev. Samuel May, Ellen and William arranged to leave Boston. On the morning of November 7, William and Ellen appeared at the City Registrar's Office and obtained a marriage certificate. At noon, they were married by Rev. Theodore Parker at the Haydens' house. May then accompanied the newlyweds to Portland, Maine, where the Crafts were outside the jurisdiction of the marshal's office, and the couple caught the night ship, the *SS Commodore*, to Canada and then sailed from there to England.

Willis H. Hughes and John Knight returned to Macon, Georgia empty-handed. Six weeks later, Hughes was socializing with the brother of his former partner in slave catching, Thomas Knight. Hughes was depressed. He had run in a city election and lost and Thomas Knight "made some insinuations about the defeat of Hughes." Harsh words were exchanged. Hughes struck Thomas Knight and grabbed him by the throat. Thomas Knight then pulled out a gun and shot Hughes dead.

CHAPTER 53

Harriet Hears the Knock and Opens the Door

Although Calvin Stowe was now officially on the Bowdoin faculty, he was not in Brunswick that fall or winter of 1850-1851 as Bowdoin had released him to teach at Lane until March. As Calvin and Harriet had become good friends with Phebe Lord Upham and her husband, Professor Thomas C. Upham, even with Calvin gone, Harriet often found herself in their company, at church or around the tea table. Harriet had become more vocal in her condemnation of the Fugitive Slave Law. Thomas Upham, the Bowdoin College professor of mental and moral philosophy, was also the vice president of the Colonization Society. He was a confirmed pacifist. Although he disagreed with the Fugitive Slave Law, he believed that following the law and maintaining peace were more important than helping the anti-slavery movement.

Harriet fumed when Thomas Upham said slaves should be educated, bought, and then sent back to Africa. Harriet and Thomas Upham argued back and forth. Harriet could not change his mind with words or clever arguments. She wrote sister Catharine, "[B]ut when I asked him flatly if he would obey the law supposing a fugitive came to him, Mrs. Upham laughed & he hemmed & hawed & little Mary Upham broke out 'I wouldn't I know.'"

As fate would have it, the following day, a runaway slave appeared in Brunswick and knocked at the door of the Bowdoin mathematics

Professor Smyth. Smyth sent him to Professor Upham, wrote Harriet, "who takes him into his study & hears his story, gives him a dollar & Mrs. Upham puts [him] in bountifully in the provision line."

The Uphams sent the fugitive on to Harriet and she took him in. Harriet wrote Catharine:

> Now our beds are all full & before this law passed I might have tried to send him somewhere else. As it was all hands in the house united in making him up a bed in our waste room & Henry & Freddy & Georgy seemed to think they could not do too much for him. There hasn't any body in our house got waited on so abundantly & willingly for ever so long—these negroes [possess] some mysterious power of pleasing children for they hung around him & seemed never tired of hearing him talk & sing.

This fugitive was John Andrew Jackson, who had escaped from slavery in South Carolina as a stowaway on a Boston-bound ship. In Boston, though, he soon heard that his old slave trader, Neddy Anderson, a brute animal, was looking for him. Jackson wrote:

> Just as I was beginning to be settled at Salem [Massachusetts], that most atrocious of all laws, the Fugitive Slave Law, was passed, and I was compelled to flee in disguise from a comfortable home, a comfortable situation, and good wages, to take refuge in Canada. I met with a very sincere friend and helper, who gave me a refuge during the night, and set me on my way. Her name was Mrs. Beecher Stowe. She took me in and fed me, and gave me some clothes and five dollars, She also inspected my back, which is covered with scars which I shall carry with me to the grave. She listened with great interest to my story, and sympathized with me when I told her how long I had been parted from my wife Louisa and my daughter, Jenny, perhaps for ever.

Since November first, 1850, snow had been on the ground in Brunswick, Maine. At Harriet Beecher Stowe's home, her five grown children were happily sledding, sleigh riding, and snowballing. Calvin was still gone and would not return until March. There was plenty to entertain the children, even when they became locked in a world of ice. Their Newfoundland puppy, Rover, liked to play fetch, even on an iced-over pond. Their cat had just had kittens. When the snow was too deep for wagons to travel, sleighs passed back and forth in the streets with their merry jingle-jingle-jingle. At Christmas, they would have friends over to play games and see their tree. Mrs. Upham invited them to spend New Year's with her family. Harriet's handyman, Mr. Titcomb, arranged for someone to make the children new sleds at a good price. The twins, 14, planned to name their sleds after characters in Sir Walter Scott's *The Talisman*, the book Harriet was currently reading to all her children, as she read to them every night for two hours. While she read, the girls sewed, Henry improved his handwriting, and Fred liked to peel apples.

The twins were independently reading *David Copperfield*, as was their mother. They were reading it in installments in magazines. Although this was a novel, Dickens made a practice of releasing the tale a segment at a time, in a series. After the serialized version finished its run, a book would be published.

As Christmas approached, Harriet rushed to finish writing two pieces for the *National Era* and the *New-York Evangelist*. She also wrote Dr. Bailey at the *National Era* to see if he was interested in receiving more material from her. He responded with enthusiasm, enclosing an advance of $100, telling her that, "she might write as much as she pleased, what she pleased, and when she pleased."

Harriet had a "shocking cold" and the baby kept her up at night. She dismissed the wet nurse as Harriet's own milk had increased. Twin Eliza broke her arm coming out of a [church] meeting, and now she was sleeping with her mother, too. Twin Hatty took charge of decorating the Christmas tree, a fine spruce. Her mother dressed a little doll like a fairy in white gauze with gilt spangles and a gilt band around her head with a star on the end. She had white gauze wings spangled with gold. The fairy angel who held a wand was placed at the top of the tree. Mr. Titcomb brought apples to hang on the tree, which they painted gold and placed them with nuts on the fragrant tree branches.

Three days before Christmas, a terrible storm hit Brunswick. Hatty wrote her father:

> It snowed & the wind blew & the windows rattled & the old house shook all over & there was not a room in the house that it did not snow in to….[I]t is so cold that I have to take a hot flatiron to keep me warm in bed.

In the front room where Anna, Georgy, and Harriet's niece, Nelly, Charles' three-year-old daughter, slept, the wind blew out a pane of glass. The drifts were so deep the train cars could not move on the snow-covered tracks. Harriet made up six new comforters for the beds, adding four pounds of cotton to each one, but still more were needed. Biscuit dough froze to the cutting board before the cook, Joanna, could roll it out. Water sitting in pails froze solid. The frigid nights in what Harriet called "the rattletrap house" were almost fifteen hours long. The cat and her kittens stayed warm and happy, crawling into the stove and nestling among the warm embers at the day's end.

Writing from Boston, Isabella and Edward Beecher deluged Harriet with letters telling of Black people ripped from their homes and families forced back into slavery. Harriet read these cruel tales in the newspapers as well. Harriet longed for someone to do something to stop the inhumanity. Sister-in-law Isabella thought Harriet was a genius. She wrote Harriet, "Now, Hattie, if I could use a pen as you can, I would write something that would make this whole nation feel what an accursed thing slavery is."

Harriet was deeply moved by Isabella's faith in her. She read this letter aloud to her children. When she came to the part where Isabella urged her to write something about slavery, her children remember that their mother rose up from her chair and, holding the letter in her hand, crushed it, promising to write something. "I will if I live," she declared.

Harriet knew what it meant if she, as a woman, was to write something political. She thought a man better suited to challenge slavery. Seated at her gateleg table in the parlor, where the largest fireplace was, she wrote to Calvin, "I wish Father would come to Boston and preach on the Fugitive Slave Law....I wish some Martin Luther would arise to set this community right."

By February, the number of kidnappings was growing daily, and not just in Boston. Henry Long, a waiter at the Pacific Hotel in New York, was violently captured at his job and taken to the office of the U.S. Clerk. John T. Smith of Richmond, Virginia, claimed him as his property despite evidence that Henry was in New York months before the date he was accused of having fled his master. Henry Long was returned to John T. Smith, who promptly sold him South. Whereas many people reading these stories of abduction and return to bondage became conditioned to them and were no longer affected by them in their souls, Harriet had the opposite reaction. Each new outrage intensified her pain. How could she make the sleeping people of the North see and feel what was happening to their Black brothers and sisters?

Henry Beecher preached disobedience against the Fugitive Slave Law from his Brooklyn pulpit. He was famous and lecturing at the time before record crowds in New York and New England. His sermons were reprinted in the newspapers. Henry was powerful and people were listening to him. Harriet loved Henry but he was very selfish and did not take the time to reply to her letters. She was so close to Henry emotionally that she described him as "he who is to me another self." She wanted to exchange ideas with him on the Fugitive Slave Law. Could he come to see her in March when he was in Maine to speak? She would defer to Henry and let him be the one to wake up the North. She wrote to him of her frustration and her faith in him:

> Must we forever keep calm and smile and smile when every sentiment of manliness and humanity is kicked and rolled in the dust and lies trampled and bleeding....I feel as if my heart would burn itself out in grief and shame that such things are—I wish I had your chance—but next best to that it is to have you have it—so fire away—give them no rest day or night.

CHAPTER 54

Harriet is Called into Greater Being

On Saturday morning, February 15, 1851, two officers posing as customers arrested Frederick "Shadrach" Minkins at the Cornhill Coffee House and Tavern in Boston. Shadrach, "a stout, copper-colored man," had worked there as a waiter for almost a year. He was taken away, with his apron on, and carried to the federal courthouse for a swift hearing.

An angry crowd soon gathered and gained strength outside the courthouse. The judge refused to consider the defense lawyer's *habeas corpus* petition to release the prisoner on bail. About one-hundred-fifty Black and white abolitionists appeared like a flash in the courtroom, having overpowered the armed guards at the door. A chaotic struggle ensued. Meanwhile, twenty Black men grabbed Shadrach by the collar, lifted him up, and ran with him out the door, down the stairs and into the crowded street. The leader, Lewis Hayden, arranged for Shadrach's safe travel to Canada.

Harriet Beecher Stowe (1852)

Harriet's heart was bursting with anguish for the suffering slaves and the families being torn apart by slavery. She continually prayed to God that He let her do something, to let her cry for them to be heard. One cold Sunday morning that same February, Harriet attended a Sunday communion service at the First Parish Church in Brunswick. As she was seated in her pew, suddenly, like the "unrolling of a picture," she had a vision. She saw a vivid scene of a bedraggled, old Black man lying on the ground, being savagely beaten by two Black men who were urged on by a white master. The old man on the ground did not beg for mercy and kept taking the beating. He refused to tell the white man something he wanted to know. So strongly was she affected, she had trouble suppressing her sobs. The vision had been blown into her mind like the rushing of a mighty wind.

With the memory of the scene still fresh in her mind, Harriet hurried her family from the church to their house. She sat down at her writing table to write down in pencil what she had seen. She used up all the foolscap in the house and then scrounged for something more to write upon. She found "some brown paper in which groceries had been delivered" and continued to write feverishly until she wrote the end of the scene. Then, she got up and mechanically prepared the children's dinner, still thinking about what she had experienced at church. After the dishes were cleared, she gathered her children in the sitting room, took out the story, and read it aloud to them. She and the children were all in tears by the time she finished reading. One of the boys sobbed, "Oh, mamma, slavery is the most cruel thing in the world."

The next day, she experienced a change of heart regarding the sketch. She was shocked at how violent and bloody it was. So much of this story still eluded her. Why was the old man whipped? What did he refuse to divulge? And why did he not call for mercy? Much remained to puzzle out, but Harriet knew one thing for sure: the name of the old Black man. Back then, male slaves were called boy until they were too old for that, and then they were called "uncle." The old man would be named "Uncle Tom."

She refolded the written sheets and stuffed them into a bedroom drawer for careful reconsideration later.

In early March, in Philadelphia, a "colored woman HELEN or HANNAH, and her son," were seized and taken into custody as fugitives from service. Hannah or Helen had friends in the courtroom "of various shades of color," said one newspaper, and one of them was Lucretia Mott. Hannah or Helen's husband, another son, and a daughter were still at liberty. The woman was so near giving birth that there was real concern she would give birth in the courtroom. The judge decided that the woman was the property of John Perdu of Baltimore and sent her, her son, and her unborn child back into slavery.

On March 9, 1851, Harriet sat down and wrote a long overdue response to Dr. Gamaliel Bailey of the *National Era* in Washington, D.C.:

Mr. Bailey,

Dear Sir:

I am at present occupied upon a story which will be a much longer one than any I have ever written, embracing a series of sketches which give the lights and shadows of the "patriarchal institution" [slavery], written either from observation, incidents which have occurred in the sphere of my personal knowledge, or in the knowledge of my friends. I shall show the <u>best side</u> of the thing, and something <u>faintly approaching the worst</u>.

Up to this year I have always felt that I had no particular call to meddle with this subject, and I dreaded to expose my mind to the full force of its exciting power. But I feel now that the time is come when even a woman or a child who can speak a word for freedom and humanity is bound to speak….I hope every woman who can write will not be silent.

My vocation is simply that of <u>painter</u>, and my object will be to hold up in the most lifelike and graphic manner possible slavery, its reverses, changes, and the negro character, which I have had ample opportunities for studying. There is no arguing with <u>pictures</u>, and everybody is impressed by them, whether they mean to be or not.

I wrote beforehand because I know that you have much matter to arrange, and thought it might not be amiss to give you a hint. The thing may extend through three or four numbers. It will be ready in two or three weeks….

Yours with (sincere) esteem,

H. Stowe

On May 8, 1851, the *National Era* ran this:

A New Story by Mrs. Stowe

Week after next we propose to commence in the *Era*, the publication of a new story by Mrs. H.B. Stowe, the title of which will be, 'UNCLE TOM'S CABIN, OR THE MAN THAT WAS A THING'....

This same spring, "Uncle Tom's Cabin" was taking shape in Harriet's mind; a minister from nearby Harpswell happened to be walking along the Brunswick wharf one afternoon and saw Harriet and her children gathered there, seated on casks. Harriet looked "tired and worn, unkempt and even dilapidated, with holes as large as silver dollars showing at the heels of her low shoes."

CHAPTER 55

Sojourner Goes West

Following the 1837 vicious tarring and feathering of Lane Rebel Marius Robinson, Marius and his wife, Cincinnati Sister Emily Rakestraw Robinson, gradually withdrew from abolition activity. For a decade, they lived quietly on a farm in Putnam. Marius had toyed with the idea of planting a mulberry orchard, raising silkworms, and producing silk but, he wrote in his journal, he refrained, fearing he would be "…making myself a sort of laughing stock for those who are ignorant of the business or who do not like it because it is new or unfashionable."

Through the 1840s, Marius corresponded with abolitionist leaders. James G. Birney visited him several times. Birney had invested in *multicaulis* mulberry trees, a project that was a complete failure and mired Birney in debt.

Farm life was great for raising a family and staying safe, but Marius and Emily soon found that their spirits were flagging. Consequently, Emily Robinson joined the woman's (singular was the term then) rights movement. In early 1850, she opened the first Ohio woman's rights convention. It was at the first national woman's rights convention in Worcester, Massachusetts, that October where former slave Sojourner Truth had made her debut on the platform as a woman's rights speaker. Lucretia Mott, in her closing remarks, acknowledged Sojourner's rising star by repeating words from Sojourner's convention speech:

Goodness never had any beginning; it was from everlasting, and could never die. But Evil had a beginning, and must have an end.

Influenced by Frederick Douglass and Sojourner Truth, the convention included the resolution that among women, those in bondage were "the most grossly wronged of all."

Seal of the Female Philadelphia Anti-Slavery Society

Marius, like Emily, soon reentered reform activity. After the passage of the September 1850 Fugitive Slave Law, Marius was elected president of the Western Anti-Slavery Society. Marius and his multi-state organization were circulating radical Garrisonian petitions to be submitted to the U.S. Senate and Congress in which they called for a dissolution of the Union "so that those states which wish to sustain the system [slavery] can do so."

May 1851 was a big month for Marius and Emily. They moved to Salem, Ohio, for Marius to start his new job as editor of the *Anti-Slavery Bugle*. Emily would act as the *Bugle*'s publishing agent. The *Bugle* had become one of the most powerful abolitionist papers in the nation. At the end of the month, Marius and Emily were heavily involved in the production of the Ohio woman's convention to be held in the Stone Church in Akron, Ohio. Emily was presenting a report on female education, and Marius would serve as one of the three secretaries. All interested in woman's rights were welcome to attend the event, including men.

Marius Robinson reported in the *Bugle* that Sojourner Truth was spending the summer of 1851 in Ohio. William Lloyd Garrison signed up Sojourner to be among his traveling abolition lecturers. Sojourner, though free now, had been a slave for thirty years. Sojourner drew crowds who wanted to hear the inside story of slavery. Sojourner embodied the twin disabilities of the time, being both Black and a woman. To raise her profile, Garrison had underwritten the publication of her life story, the *Narrative of Sojourner Truth*. Sojourner kept the price low, at 25 cents apiece, to make it sell better. Book sales were her chief source of income, although Garrison was paying some of her traveling expenses.

Sojourner Truth (1863)

Prior to departing for her summer Ohio tour, Sojourner stayed with her friends, Isaac and Amy Kirby Post, in Rochester, New York.

Their home was a busy station on the Underground Railroad. It was also a gathering spot for spiritualists. Sojourner and Amy were conducting séances. They were trying to contact the spirit of Amy's daughter, Matilda, who died young. Amy had fallen under the influence of the notorious Fox sisters, Maggie and Kate, the young spirit mediums associated with the mysterious Rochester Rappings.

Sojourner was sad to leave the Posts but adventure awaited her in Ohio. Arriving in Cleveland, Sojourner wrote Amy that she had "stopped among colored friends and was treated with great kindness. Attended a meeting and sold three dollars' worth of books." She then headed south to Akron, where she heard there was to be a woman's rights convention.

She arrived at the hotel where the convention guests were staying. Looking for a friendly or familiar face, she paced the lobby. Two white Ohio women, the president of the convention, Frances D. Gage, and a secretary, Hannah Conant Tracy, saw Sojourner loitering. Just who was "the tall colored woman" with the basket of books on her arm? they wondered.

Heads turned when Sojourner entered a room. A thin woman, she stood almost six feet tall, straight as a pine tree, and her skin color was described as "black as the ace of spades" and "hideously black," the latter phrase amusing her. She towered over women and men, made even taller by the white turban wrapped exotically on the top of her head. Her dress was simple; a shawl was draped over her shoulders. A pair of wire-rimmed glasses perched on the bridge of her nose. She smoked a clay Dutch pipe and had done so since childhood.

Sojourner's peculiar way of talking defied description. Her English diction was inflected with a hint of Dutch, her first language. When speaking to a crowd, she often lapsed into a folksy Black *patois*, giving herself a voice her listeners expected of a stereotypical slave. Although Sojourner had a mind of rare power, she was unable to read or write a single word or even recognize the alphabet, which appeared "jumbled" to her. She had dictated her *Narrative* to Olive Gilbert and, sadly, could not read it for herself. Her friends wrote letters for her. Marius Robinson tried to teach Sojourner to read, but she told him it was no good because, at age 54, "My brain is too stiff now."

Convention vice president and Cincinnati lawyer Lucius Hine, passing through the hotel lobby, noticed Sojourner, too and picked up on the discomfort of the women, Gage and Tracy. Hine watched as Gage and Tracy gingerly ducked into a side parlor to avoid Sojourner. Both Gage and Tracy were abolitionists. Tracy was a widow. Her husband had died when a mob attacked him while he assisted a fugitive slave escape. They both wrote popular columns for the *Ohio Cultivator*. They were political activists, having helped to elect Salmon Chase to the U.S. Senate on the anti-slavery Free Soil ticket. Yet these confident women, so committed to improving the lot of Black people and women, were uncomfortable in the presence of a Black lady.

Hine, equally ignorant of Sojourner's identity and her national reputation as a speaker on reform movements, followed Gage and Tracy into the parlor and quipped, "This I suppose is one of the delegates to your convention."

The two women confessed to him that they did not know who Sojourner was. Hine plopped down in an armchair, spreading wide his newspaper to cover his grinning face. Meanwhile, Sojourner spotted Gage and Tracy in the parlor. She strolled over and introduced herself, informing them that she was in Ohio for her summer abolition lecture tour yet first would attend the woman's convention. Gage and Tracy bought copies of her *Narrative*. Later, Tracy keenly regretted that she and Gage did not "give [Sojourner] as royal a welcome as her merits deserved."

The first day of the meeting dawned on Wednesday, May 18, 1851. The conventioneers began to drift in as the hour approached nine o'clock. Soon, the church was packed and loud with convivial talk. Then, some of the people were suddenly:

...thrown into a panic...by seeing a tall, gaunt black woman in a gray dress and white turban, surmounted by an uncouth sun-bonnet, march deliberately into the church, walk with the air of a queen up the aisle, and take her seat upon the pulpit steps.

A buzzing disapproval was heard all over the church. Words were whispered and called out. "An Abolition Affair!" Trembling people said to Gage that should he allow the Black woman to speak, "It will ruin us. Every newspaper in the land will have our cause mixed with abolition and n_____rs, and we shall be utterly denounced."

Editor Jane Swisshelm of the *Pittsburgh Saturday Visiter* [*sic*] enjoyed perverse satisfaction in observing the uproar. Hadn't she warned these women that abolition and woman's rights were matters to be treated separately?

President Gage, somewhat ruffled by the shaky start, took the chair and called the meeting to order. A prayer was given. Gage gave an able opening address. On both days, letters were read from luminaries who could not attend, such as Gerrit Smith, Elizabeth Cady Stanton, and Amelia Bloomer. Business was conducted. The Hutchinsons sang songs. At the intermissions—there were three sessions each day—Sojourner sold books.

Resolutions were made and discussed. The first read:

Resolved, That the inequalities which manifestly exist in the privileges of the sexes, as bestowed or allowed by institutions or customs, demonstrate in their practice, criminal injustice and gross tyranny on the part of man, and in her unresisting toleration of them a reprehensible submissiveness on the part of Woman.

Jane Swisshelm objected to the harsh wording of the resolution, accusing man of "gross tyranny." Marius Robinson and two other men flew to the defense of the resolution, but the term was stricken. Swisshelm maintained that men never oppressed women who respected themselves. And, on the chance that the woman had married a tyrant, then she got what she deserved.

Swisshelm did not believe in the equality of the sexes. She thought women should be placed on a pedestal and treated like a princess by men. She insisted that woman, being of the weaker sex, should claim her right to be helped over bad roads by chivalrous men.

This was too much for Sojourner, who said that she had never found any man ready to carry her over mud puddles, yet, "Aren't (or Arn't or Ain't) I a woman? Look at me!" she thundered. "Look at my arm!" She rolled up her right sleeve to the shoulder and showed the tremendous muscle power of her black arm. Gage remembered Sojourner saying, "I have plowed and planted and hoed and gathered into barns, and no man could head me—and aren't I a woman?" The cheering was loud and long.

On the second day, a Thursday, more reports were read and business conducted. A convocation of male preachers from Christian faiths had come into the meeting to hear and discuss the resolutions being put forth. One minister claimed that men had a superior intellect to women—everyone knew that women's brains were smaller than men's and, therefore, could not hold much knowledge. Yet another preacher said that women were cursed because, in the Garden of Eden, Eve had disobeyed God and tasted forbidden fruit. Another one pointed out that Jesus was a man. God had not deigned to come to earth in the form of a woman. Yet another one decided that because Jesus' twelve apostles were men, Jesus had not given any "token of his will" in his life for the equality of women. He admonished the women present to "Go home to your husbands and to your children!"

The rowdy boys in the galleries and the scoffers in the pews enjoyed the obvious unease of the polite feminists, who squirmed and fumed in their seats, offering little interruption to the male bombast.

Sojourner Truth had hardly raised her head throughout the meeting. She rose slowly from her seat in the corner, making eye contact with President Gage for permission to speak. She set her sunbonnet at her feet. A gasp and a hiss could be heard. Gage announced to the crowd, "Sojourner Truth."

A hush passed through the room. Sojourner began to speak. She did not raise her voice to be heard, as she was blessed with a deep voice, and her words could be heard by everyone in the room. She divided her speech into sections, responding with rebuttals to each of the preposterous statements made by the clergymen, saying, in essence, what was reported in the *New-York Tribune*:

> She said she was a woman, and had done as much work as any man there. She had heard much about the equality of the sexes, but would not argue that question. All she could say was, if she had a pint of intellect and man a quart, what reason was there why [she] should not have her pint full.

The audience was convulsed with laughter.

> She had heard the Bible read, and was told that Eve caused the fall of man. Well, if woman upset the world, do give her a chance to set it right side up again. She learned also from the new Gospel that man had nothing to do with bringing Jesus into the world, for God was his father, but woman was his mother.
>
> Jesus respected woman and never turned her away. By woman's influence the dead was raised, for when Lazarus died, Mary and Martha, full of faith and love, came to Jesus and besought him to raise their brother to life. He did not turn them away, but 'Jesus wept,' and Lazarus came forth.
>
> But the women are coming up, blessed be God, and a few of the men are coming up with them, but they have a heavy burthen to bear, for the slaves and the women look to them for redemption.

The crowd responded with rounds of applause and Sojourner returned to her corner. The boys in the galleries and the scoffers in the pews were silenced.

The local paper noted that:

...an old colored lady from Massachusetts [*sic*], nearly six feet high, once a slave in New York, who boasts the somewhat singular name Sojourner Truth, won upon all by her quaint utterance of good hard sense.

At the end of the second night's meeting, the convention-goers pushed past one another to shake Sojourner's hand. She was flooded with so many invitations that she hardly knew which to accept first. Soon enough, Sojourner set off to begin her summer Ohio campaign. One of her friends loaned her a pony and buggy. Whereas the other abolitionist lecturers traveled in pairs, she traveled alone. Whenever she came to a fork in the road, she would lay down the reins and say, "God, you drive." He always took her to a good place. She would go around to religious camp meetings and hang up a white banner with an anti-slavery motto on it. She would begin to sing, often singing songs she had composed. People would be curious and gather round, and she would commence preaching and have a good meeting.

CHAPTER 56

Women Put on the Pants

I n late 1850, Gerrit and Ann "Nancy" Fitzhugh Smith gave their daughter, Libby, 28, and her husband, Charles Dudley Miller, a gift of a house across the green just south of the Smiths' Peterboro estate. Libby set about to make a nice home for her husband and their three sons, Gerrit, 6, Charles, 3 ½, and their newborn, William. Libby also loved to entertain guests. She attached great importance to mealtimes around the dining table, writing that "its influences for good and ill form no mean part of the warp and woof of our lives." As a gracious hostess, she believed in not just providing wholesome and tasty food for family and guests but in bringing the table to perfection. If the tablecloth was soiled, the silver was tarnished, cruets dingy, and most repugnant of all, the salt in the salt-cellars was lumpy with spatters of gravy, then even rolls of ambrosia and coffee of nectar could not tempt the appetite, she wrote. True elegance was displayed in the final touches to the table from the garden. Libby wrote that, "A fern leaf, a branch of roses, or spray of ivy by your child's plate may prove in later years to have been its first incentive to the study of art."

That first spring in her new house, Libby spent many hours in her garden, cultivating flowers and greenery for her table and perhaps some carrots and potatoes, too. However, she could not move freely, prevented by her long skirts, which clung to her legs and ankles, especially in the heat. The long, draggling skirts collected manure, dirt, and filth, which Libby carried into her clean home. She had been thinking of chopping off her long skirts and wearing a short dress with pants underneath, which, though not a new idea, was radical. Society dictated that men wore pants and women wore long skirts and layers of them.

Libby's thought of freeing herself from the bondage of the cumbersome skirts "ripened into the decision that this shackle should no longer be endured." Libby adopted this new form of dress and began wearing it full-time. Now she could hold little William in one arm and an oil lamp in the other and walk up the stairs with less danger of tripping on the hems of the exasperating garments.

Libby wrote later:

> Soon after making this change, I went to Seneca Falls to visit my cousin Mrs. [Elizabeth Cady] Stanton. She had so long deplored with me our common misery in the toils of this crippling fashion, that this means of escape was hailed with joy and she at once joined me in wearing the new costume. Mrs. Bloomer, a friend and neighbor of Mrs. Stanton, then adopted the dress, and as she was editing a paper [*The Lily*] in which she advocated it, the dress was christened with her name. Mrs. Stanton and I often exchanged visits and sometimes travelled together. We endured, in various places, much gaping curiosity and the harmless jeering of street boys.

Wearing the trousers and short skirt, cousin Elizabeth Cady Stanton wrote that she felt like:

> a captive set free from his ball and chain, I was always ready for a brisk walk through sleet and snow and rain, to climb a mountain, jump over a fence, work in the garden, and, in fact, for any necessary locomotion.

The fad took off. Newspapers breathlessly reported sightings of women wearing the Bloomers. By June 12, Bloomers had appeared in Belknap, New Hampshire:

We…announce the appearance in our streets, this afternoon, of a young lady clad in the Turkish costume.

It was rumored that some of the ladies in Erie, Pennsylvania, were contemplating the adoption of "short dresses." In Wisconsin, the mania for the short dresses was "fast gaining ground." The *Ohio State Journal* was in favor of the new style of female dress. "We may laugh at it…and yet it will come! And why? Because every physician, every man who is acquainted with anatomy…is aware that the present mode of female dress is very injurious to the human frame…."

On June 12 at two o'clock in the afternoon, Theodosia Gilbert (who had attended the Cazenovia Convention) and Dr. J. C. Jackson held a dinner prepared on hydropathic principles. To launch their Glen Haven Water-Cure establishment, one hundred sixteen well-known abolitionists, feminists, newspaper editors, and friends flocked to the resort located picturesquely on the forested shore of a clear New York lake. Mrs. Jackson prepared the "hygienic dinner" in which there was no salt, no spices, no tea, coffee, or wine, and no butter or lard. Flavor was provided in the piles of fruits and custards, rice, asparagus, potatoes, and fruit and pumpkin pies. Fresh trout and plainly prepared meat were provided for the carnivores.

The event was described in the papers:

At Glen Haven, a pleasant little town on Skaneateles Lake, the Hydropathists held a cold water festival, a few days ago, whereat the veritable Mrs. Bloomer…our old acquaintance, Mrs. Stanton, Mrs. Burleigh…Miss Burleigh, Miss Beebe, Mrs. Fuller, and Miss Bennett, came out in full Bloomer [figures].

The hostess, Theodosia Gilbert, was also wearing the Bloomer outfit and had worn it since 1849. She had written about its virtues in the May 1851 issue of the *Water Cure Journal*. The *Frederick Douglass' Paper*, in its extensive coverage of the banquet, mentioned that one of the toasts given was by J.C. Hathaway in thanks to Theodosia Gilbert for being, "...the first American woman to advocate and adopt woman's apparel in accordance with comfort, convenience, and the laws of life and health...."

Speeches were made. Ossian E. Dodge broke out in song:

I am asked for a ditty, but what shall I sing?
For to get a subject is no easy thing;
And I hope that my actions will not be thought wrong,

If I make out improvement the theme of my song....
There's reform in our eating as well as the rest,
And the Glen-Haven table is surely the best;
For Miss Gilbert, Mrs. Jackson, have furnished all food
That the friends of cold water pronounce to be good....

And the ladies—God bless 'em—we all understand,
Are reforming their dresses all over the land;
And the 'Lords of Creation' are laid on the shelves,
For the women are learning to think for themselves.

But the new dress was not popular with everyone. Many men perceived a threat. If women wanted to wear their pants, next, they would take away men's rights. (No man was wearing harem pants.) Opponents of the movement spread rumors that if women dressed like men, showing that they had legs, they would become hybrid creatures, becoming unsexed, morphing then into beings that were classed as neither women nor men. These unholy creatures would then begin to act like men, smoke cigars, propose marriage, and ignore their children. Men were the rightful owners of pants, it was argued.

"Bloomerism – an American custom", cartoon from Punch, 1851

The doomsayers howled in the press. The radical dress became linked in the public's mind with radical feminists and the idea that they were out to dismantle the social structure. It was feared that if women's dress allowed them to move about with ease, it would naturally follow that they would have a larger sense of their freedom. If they no longer wore clothes that made it hard to move about—stepping into a cab or crossing a puddle without assistance—then it would be much harder to keep women indoors and sedentary and content to be at home. Women might leave the domestic sphere and move about the public sphere at will, expanding their boundaries, testing all limits placed upon them—perchance to travel without male escort. In wearing trousers, more professions would open up to women. In a society grounded on female passivity, the dress reform movement evinced not just a shudder but a tremor. This was earth-shaking change.

The objections to the Bloomer outfit got louder and more frequent. Feminists soon realized that the reform dress was causing more harm than good to their campaign for woman's rights. Newspaper coverage of women's dress reform had eclipsed discussion of more important reform movements. People were more concerned with what feminists were wearing and not what they were saying. Additionally, women began to feel that the dress was unbecoming. Being attractively, correctly, and fashionably dressed in that period, was very important to a woman's self-esteem. Dressing for occasions was what affluent, unemployed white women spent their time doing. There were outfits for walking, for dinners, for traveling, for horseback riding.

Elizabeth Cady Stanton agreed that the Bloomer did not accentuate the positive in many women's figures, remarking that "to tall, gaunt women with large feet and to those who were short and stout, it was equally trying."

Libby Miller's father, Gerrit Smith, loved her Bloomer costume. Elizabeth Cady Stanton's father did not. He had barred her from visiting him in the outfit. Her sons did not want to be seen with her. Her older sister wept. Her husband Henry, a New York state senator, told her that "some good Democrats said they would not vote for a man whose wife wore the Bloomers."

Elizabeth began to regret having even tried the experiment. After wearing the trousers and short skirt for two years, she abandoned them and reverted to the long skirts. Now she could appear in public and move about anonymously. Other feminists—tired of the ridicule and the street stares—followed suit. For the time being, the woman's movement separated itself from matters such as corsets, tight stays, and weighty skirts and returned to the long skirts.

Gerrit Smith criticized his cousin, Elizabeth Cady Stanton, for abandoning the new costume. Pressured by her father, Gerrit, Libby continued wearing the Bloomer costume for much longer than she desired—in sitting, the short skirt had an uncouth effect. To Gerrit Smith, it seemed that the whole revolution in woman's rights hinged on her clothing, long skirts symbolizing her degradation.

At long last, after seven years of wearing the Bloomers, Libby Smith Miller lengthened her skirts and cast aside the trousers. The outfit was just not artistic. And artistic was everything to Libby. She had a perpetual love of the beautiful, as evidenced in the artistry she employed in the precise design of her dining table. Libby found herself once again the slave of fashion, wearing the "old, swaddling clothes." However, she added, defensively, "I do not wear a heavy, trailing skirt, nor have I ever worn a corset...my shoulders are not turreted, nor has fashion clasped my neck with her choking collar."

CHAPTER 57

Harriet Beecher Stowe
Churns Out the Chapters

H arriet Beecher Stowe had never written any fiction longer than a short story. Now she was learning *on the job* how to write like the Great Charles Dickens, churning out a chapter or so each week, getting it to the post office in time to be shipped, copyedited, and published on Thursdays. Harriet had never worked under such deadlines. What guarantee did she have that she would be able to create something clever each week?

But Harriet need not have worried. From the onset, she was on fire. She prayed for guidance and she received it. The story was coming at her, unbidden, taking shape in her active mind; the characters were presenting themselves to her. Now, the distant memories of all she knew of slavery dislodged themselves from the depths of her active mind, floated to the surface, and informed her storytelling.

She wanted to give slavery a death blow, but there was still much she needed to know about slavery. She always read widely, but now she began to devour everything in her own house. She gathered research materials. Besides the abundance and availability of newspapers everywhere, she and Calvin, although desperately stretched for money, kept up their subscriptions to the *Era* and *A Friend of Youth*, a children's anti-slavery periodical edited by Dr. Bailey's wife, Margaret. She kept her well-thumbed edition of the Grimkés/Weld book, *Slavery As It Is*, next to her in her sewing basket during the day and, at night, she had told Angelina, tucked under her pillow. On her writing table was a copy of the notorious *Code Noir of Louisiana*. She consulted a legal pamphlet by Judge George Stroud of Philadelphia. *The Life of Frederick Douglass*, travel writing by Northerners who had traveled South, the writings of the lawyer Richard H. Dana, Jr, and more were studied.

When the first installment of "Uncle Tom's Cabin, or, Life Among the Lowly" appeared in the June 5, 1851, issue of the *Era*, the subject of the Fugitive Slave Law and its terrors was still on everyone's tongue. In June, Boston abolitionist Lewis Hayden was tried for aiding in the rescue of Shadrach Minkins. The proceedings were reported in the newspapers. The jury was deadlocked and the case was set aside. The next case taken up was of Robert Morris, a Black lawyer. During these "Rescue Trials," Richard H. Dana, Jr., a lawyer for the defense, was able to cross-examine witness John Caphart, one of the agents sent from the South to assist in the capture of Shadrach. Caphart referred to himself as a policeman of Norfolk, Virginia:

Question. Is it a part of your duty, as a policeman, to take up coloured persons who are out after hours in the streets?

Answer. Yes, sir.

Q. What is done with them?

A. We put them in the lock-up, and in the morning they are brought into court and ordered to be punished....

Q. What punishment do they get?

A. Not exceeding thirty-nine lashes.

Q. Who gives them these lashes?

A. Any of the officers. I do sometimes.

Q. Are you paid extra for this? How much?

A. Fifty cents a head. It used to be sixty-two cents. Now it is fifty. Fifty cents for each one we arrest, and fifty more for each one we flog.

Q. Are these persons you flog men and boys only, or are they women and girls also?

A. Men, women, boys, and girls, just as it happens.

Q. Is your flogging confined to these cases? Do you not flog slaves at the request of their masters?

A. Sometimes I do. Certainly, when I am called upon.

Q. In these cases, too, I suppose you flog women and girls, as well as men?

A. Women and men.

Q. Mr. Caphart, how long have you been engaged in this business?

A. Ever since 1836.

Q. How many negroes do you suppose you have flogged, in all, women and children included?

A. [Looking calmly round the room.] I don't know how many n----rs you have got here in Massachusetts, but I should think I had flogged as many as you've got in the State.

———

How was this legal? Did the people of the North not see the hell that these slaves were escaping? Harriet felt the weight of time on her, and not just from deadlines, but from the urgency of stopping this dread law before it could shatter any more lives. Every day, newspapers carried reports of new slave abductions and returns to bondage. Slavery was the great homewrecker. Charles Sumner had been elected to the Senate from Massachusetts. The senators could move to repeal the law if the public protested it enough. Harriet wrote in a frenzy. Harriet could not enact a statute, but she could try to change public sentiment in such a way that people could have sympathy for the suffering slave. Henry Long, Shadrach Minkins, Hannah or Helen, Thomas Sims—their names and their stories brought humanity to the abstract concept of slavery.

Harriet strove to create characters in "Uncle Tom's Cabin" as memorable as the ones created by Dickens, characters her readers would remember, have a stake in, worry about, laugh at, weep for, think about, remember, talk about. Anti-slavery sermons, speeches, and pamphlets had failed to erode the influence of the Slave Power. She would make her readers feel what slavery was like. She would pour her heart into the work so that her readers were imbued with her sense of righteous indignation. Her saga would be sprawling and gripping, filled with humor and pathos. She would draw out the story to keep her readers thinking long and hard about slavery for a sustained period of time. This was no three to four installments story. All told, Harriet would submit the story to Bailey in forty-one installments, missing only three deadlines. Her main characters were a Black man, Uncle Tom, and a Black woman, Eliza Harris. Harriet would tell their stories of bondage, escape, and freedom in dialogue using speech with an approximated Black dialect. From her youth, Harriet had demonstrated a knack for mimicking different speech patterns and she delighted in them.

The readers' response to the publication of "Uncle Tom's Cabin" was both "immediate and electric." The story's instant popularity prompted Dr. Bailey, consequently, to pay Harriet an additional $200. It had been his wife, Margaret, and Senator Salmon Chase, who encouraged him to do this. Regarding "Uncle Tom's Cabin" in the *Era*, Chase remarked that he "always read it before anything else." At the end of the serialization, Bailey would pay Harriet another $100. Bailey also placed Harriet's story prominently on page one of the *Era*. The serial edition of "Uncle Tom's Cabin" would run in the *Era* from June 1851 until April 1852. Thanks to the rousing success of Harriet's serial, the circulation of the *Era*—a relatively obscure paper—would leap from 17,000 in 1851 to 28,000 in 1853. A great many people were following "Uncle Tom's Cabin," not all of whom were *Era* subscribers. As more people heard about this great tale, copies of the *Era* were passed from house to house until the newspaper was quite worn out.

During the composition of her masterpiece, Harriet had countless distractions, day and night, to impede her thoughts and her writing. She still had a nursing infant. Although Calvin had returned to Brunswick in the spring and would be home for many months, he was never a help with the household, and he became quite difficult when things were out of kilter. Then, in June, the first month of the *Era* installments, Harriet's father, Lyman Beecher, appeared in Brunswick, suitcase in tow, bringing with him his stepdaughter, who would act as his secretary and become another of Harriet's house guests. Lyman, retired now from Lane Seminary, had brought with him fifty years' worth of his journals, letters, and sermons, stacks of which he unceremoniously deposited on Harriet's writing table. He and his stepdaughter were writing his memoirs, using Harriet's breezy seaside home as their base. Neighbors reported seeing Harriet sitting outside on the back steps, head down, her writing portfolio balanced on her petticoated knees, writing away.

Two months later, in August, sister Catharine arrived, promising to help Harriet for a year while she wrote her story. Catharine, being Catharine, brought with her many tales of woe, of injustice done to her, of her failing Milwaukee school, her disagreements with Henry Ward, etc. She proceeded to manipulate Harriet—who was vulnerable to her oldest sister's entreaties while also recognizing that Catharine was unstable—in setting up a school with boarders in Harriet's home and in mediating between Catharine and Henry.

Catharine wrote Mary Beecher Perkins about how she, the heroine, was running Harriet's household so Harriet could write her book:

> I am trying to get Uncle Tom out of the way. At 8 o clock we are thro' with breakfast & prayers & then we send off Mr. Stowe & Harriet both to his room [study] at the college. There was no other way to keep her out of family cares & quietly at work & since this plan is adopted she goes ahead finely.

A Brunswick neighbor witnessed Harriet one morning in route to Bowdoin:

As soon as she had swallowed her breakfast she would hurry down to the village and write, write, write, till the dinner bell sounded. Then [she would] hurry home, eat, and [go] right back and write till tea time.

This neighbor judged that Harriet was a bad mother, neglecting her children as she was too absorbed by her writing. She described Harriet's appearance as "her frizzy hair tossing in an unkempt disheveled mass upon her neck and shoulders, and her clothes hanging loosely about her form, as if they got there by accident."

"Uncle Tom's Cabin" was causing quite a stir in the nation. In the October 2, 1851 issue of the *Era*, there was a letter from Grace Greenwood, who was considered one of the top writing talents at the *Era*. She had just returned from a visit to Ohio, to the Western Reserve. She wrote that, "Wherever I went among the friends of the 'Era,' I found 'Uncle Tom's Cabin' a theme for admiring remark—everywhere I saw it read with pleasant smiles and gushes of irrepressible tears. Mrs. Stowe is winning, not alone 'golden opinions,' but love and gratitude, and a hearty reverence, by this incomparable story. Its style, its spirit, its construction, scope, and purpose, are alike admirable."

Catharine hoped that Harriet would be done with Uncle Tom before the opening of their school on October 15, but Harriet was only halfway done with the tale.

The plan for the school meant that Harriet, in agreeing to this scheme, had to put out money she did not have to purchase furnishings. After four months, the school failed as Catharine could not find enough paying boarders. Harriet landed in debt, both with the school expenses and the cost of Catharine's room and board.

Toward the end of 1851, Harriet traveled to Boston for research at the Anti-Slavery Society office. She had written some installments in brother Edward Beecher's study and read the drafts to the family. She complained of a stiff neck and extreme fatigue. In February 1852, Harriet went to Andover—Calvin's third post. There she would finish the story. Catharine stayed behind in the Brunswick house to watch Harriet's children and two of their nieces. One of these nieces was Mary's child, Catherine Perkins, who described what life was like at the Stowe's house when "Aunt Kate" was in charge, saying, "Aunt Kate's head is in a very precarious state so she can't bear any noise."

Catharine stayed mostly upstairs, though she appeared "once in a while like a comet." She never missed meals, sitting "with a very martyrized air," piling prodigious amounts of food upon her plate, until the noise got to her, and she dashed off to hide upstairs again.

By March 1852, Harriet had a book contract with publisher John P. Jewett, who had been prodded by his wife, a huge fan of "Uncle Tom's Cabin," to solicit the story for publication. Harriet did not expect the book to sell, nor did Jewett. The topic was so controversial and the nation was so deeply divided. She only hoped to earn enough money to buy herself a silk dress. Her contract stated that she was to receive ten percent of the sales. Jewett had hoped to release the book in a slim volume, but the story had ballooned to two volumes. Jewett ran off a first edition of a mere five thousand copies. The book was available in three styles of bindings: paper for $1, cloth $1.50, cloth full gilt $2.

March 20 was the day the book version of *Uncle Tom's Cabin* appeared for sale. Jewett did not expect the rumble that was coming, but he had noticed some strange behavior in the book trade. Atypically, bookshops were announcing, in advance, the amount of stock they would have on hand of *Uncle Tom's Cabin*. In Boston, Bookseller Light advertised that it would send a copy of *Uncle Tom's Cabin* by mail five hundred miles, free of postage with a discount for anyone buying copies in bulk.

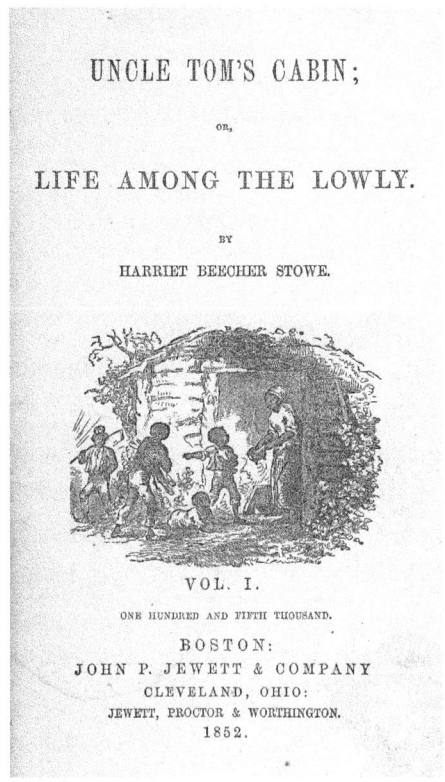

Title Page of Uncle Tom's Cabin, 1ˢᵗ Edition (1852)

By the end of the first week, in America, the book sold 10,000 copies and 300,000 by the end of 1852. In England, where Harriet had no copyright protection, the book sold 1.5 million copies in a year. The Boston *Traveller* detailed the massive effort to keep *Uncle Tom's Cabin* in print, reporting that Jewett's publishing house had three power presses running twenty-four hours a day, with "Sundays only excepted." One hundred bookbinders were at work, with three mills running to supply the paper. Harriet's book was a publishing phenomenon. *Uncle Tom's Cabin* was billed as "The Story of the Age." In many homes in New England and the Midwest, *Uncle Tom's Cabin* was the first novel to be added to the family bookshelf. In a nod to the book's sweeping popularity, The Portland, Maine *Inquirer*, printed this tongue-in-cheek apology:

> Our readers will please excuse any omissions this week, for we are reading *Uncle Tom*.

At the end of June, Harriet received her first royalty check for the first three months of her book sales. The check was for $10,000. For perspective, Jane Austen earned a lifetime total of £668 or $850 on all her books. Nathaniel Hawthorne earned the lifetime sum of $1500 for *The Scarlet Letter*, written in 1850.

Harriet would have her silk dress. Harriet rewarded herself, first, in May, with a trip to Brooklyn to see Henry. At Henry's house, Mary and Emily Edmonson, after a four-year separation, were reunited with their mother, Milly. With Harriet and Henry's help, money was raised to purchase the freedom of Milly's youngest two children. Harriet supported Mary and Emily's studies at Oberlin College in Ohio, arranging their lodging, buying them clothes, and supplying some education funds. While the young women were at Oberlin, Harriet stayed in touch with their landlady, Mrs. Cowles, and emphasized the girls' need for a pious environment. Harriet was unhappy with how William Chaplin treated Mary and Emily. She believed they had fallen under the control of an "unprincipled man who on pretense of raising money for their education made a show of them in public exhibitions." Harriet and the Edmonson sisters wrote letters to one another.

In March 1853, after only nine months of study at Oberlin, Mary passed away from tuberculosis. Emily returned to her parents' home. Soon, though, Harriet found Emily an assistant position at Myrtilla Miner's Normal School for Colored Girls in Washington, D.C. Founded in 1851, the school's goal was to train young Black women to become teachers. Henry Ward Beecher had promised to send money for furniture for the school. Harriet shared some of her

"Uncle Tom" royalties with Miner to buy a three-acre farm on which to build a school. The Sewards and the Motts gave money and moral support. Frederick Douglass, however, said that Miner's venture "would bring only persecution and death." Washington was a thoroughly Southern town. Soon enough, written threats were sent to Miner, giving her a deadline for the getting the "young n____rs" out of the house or it would be set on fire. Miner wrote a friend: "Emily and I live here alone, unprotected, except by God. The rowdies occasionally stone our house in the evening."

They built a picket fence around the property, installed locks on the house, and learned to shoot a gun. From then on, if any menacing group came near the school, Miner stood at the window and brandished her revolver. In time, Paul and Milly Edmonson would move into one of the cottages on the new campus, bringing their dog as an extra measure of security.

CHAPTER 58

Harriet Beecher Stowe Gets Feedback

After her spring 1852 New York stay and her meeting with the Edmonsons at Henry's, Harriet turned to the grueling task of packing up her family to move to Andover, Massachusetts, where Calvin had recently been installed as professor of Sacred Literature at an annual salary of $2,000. Starting in July, Harriet devoted a few months of her life to a whimsical project. Finding the house supplied by Andover unacceptable, she began a renovation of a plain, stone gymnasium into a home.

Every day, the mailman brought her an avalanche of fan letters. People from all over the world wrote such nice things about her book and how deeply it had affected them. Gushing commentaries also appeared in newspapers and periodicals. After reading intensely emotional scenes in the book, others privately recorded their feelings in their diaries, which Harriet would not see. Now, when Harriet appeared in public or society, people who previously had not given her a moment's notice were crowding in for a closer look. She was a phenomenon as a superior woman. Her book was making a lasting impact, and overnight, Harriet became famous and celebrated.

In August, Senator Charles Sumner made a motion in the Senate to repeal the Fugitive Slave Law. In an emotionally charged speech, he said:

Who could sing for Slavery?...And now, sir, behold a new and heavenly ally. A woman, inspired by Christian genius, enters the lists, like another Joan of Arc, and with marvellous power, sweeps the cords of the popular heart....In a brief period, nearly 100,000 copies of Uncle Tom's Cabin have been already circulated. But this extraordinary and sudden success...cannot be regarded merely as the triumph of genius...[I]t is the testimony of the people... against the Fugitive Slave Bill.

Frederick Douglass praised *Uncle Tom's Cabin* "as a flash to light a million camp fires in front of the embattled hosts of slavery." Frances Seward's daughter, Fanny, 9, was reading Uncle Tom and, in a letter to her mother, sketched two of the novel's characters. At Christmas of 1853, Frances gave Fanny a gift of a puzzle called "Uncle Tom's Cabin Dissected." It was one of the many tie-ins to the novel that were on the market and were referred to as "Tom-itudes." The jigsaw puzzle pieces were housed in a pasteboard box shaped like a cabin.

Poet Henry Wadsworth Longfellow, Sumner's best friend, wrote Harriet a congratulatory note, calling the success of *Uncle Tom's Cabin* "one of the greatest triumphs in literary history, to say nothing of the higher triumph of its moral effect." On February 24, 1853, Longfellow had the Stowes over to dinner at his Boston mansion, afterward writing in his diary:

How she is shaking the world with her Uncle Tom's Cabin! At one step she has reached the top of the stair-case up which the rest of us climb on our knees year after year. Never was there such a literary coup-de-main as this. A million of copies of a book within its first year of publication.

Elizabeth Cady Stanton wrote her cousin, Libby Smith Miller, that she had read *Uncle Tom's Cabin* in the fall, before her daughter, Margaret, was born. "It is the most affecting book I ever read....

That book will tell against slavery; of that you may be sure." Senator Salmon Chase wrote in his diary, "I cannot read [Uncle Tom's Cabin] without tears."

For Harriet, though, with fame came scrutiny and friction. Predictably, the book aroused intense yet hostile feelings in some people. Harriet was thrust into the harsh glare of the spotlight and was vulnerable to biting criticism, even from those close to her. Edward Beecher worried her celebrity would make her vain. Henry was jealous and did not read *Uncle Tom's Cabin* until it had been out for a year. Harriet's younger sister, Isabella Hooker, was bitter that Harriet, who had come to abolitionist thinking a long time after she, Isabella, had, should be getting so much credit for being anti-slavery, when Harriet knew so little of politics.

Abolitionist Harriet Tubman said that "Mrs. Stowe's pen hasn't begun to paint what slavery is as I have seen it at the far South." She was opposed to the theatrical adaptations of *Uncle Tom's Cabin* that were springing up all over the country and were immensely popular. "I've seen the real thing," she continued, "and I don't want to see it on no stage or in no theater."

Another Philadelphia abolitionist, Robert Purvis, of mixed-race heritage, voiced his objection to what he believed was Harriet Beecher Stowe's endorsement of the colonization movement. In *Uncle Tom's Cabin*, some slaves flee to Liberia of their own free will. They were not deported, as the Colonization Society proposed. Harriet did not endorse colonization.

Southern newspapers hit Harriet way below the belt, as did this critique from South Carolina:

Mrs. Harriet Beecher Stowe...has lately published an Abolition Novel....A very convenient substitute for talent and genius is a miserable conformity to a bad popular passion. And mediocre writers can...pocket some money by pandering to the public taste.

Harriet's name, spoken so admiringly by crowds in New York, had become anathema in the South. The *Alabama Planter* accused Harriet of assaulting "the best institutions in the world [slavery]" and, in doing so, proved to be a "wicked," "very bad," and "very fanatical person." She was shamed for having breached decorum in writing about rape and prostitution, true occurrences though they were, as they were taboo subjects, off limits for comment. Finally, the Southerners attacked *Uncle Tom's Cabin* for containing factual errors, being utterly false in its representation of Southern life, or, at the very least, an exaggeration. This riled Harriet the worst.

Claiming the depiction of slavery in *Uncle Tom's Cabin* was fiction was the "most unwise thing…ever done by slaveholders, said Frederick Douglass." In response, Harriet answered this kind of attack with her next book, *The Key to Uncle Tom's Cabin: Presenting the Original Facts and Documents Upon Which the Story is Founded, Together with Corroborative Statements Verifying the Truth of the Work* (1853). The Southerners were made to regret what they wished for. The *Key* was a best seller and added more facts about slavery to the body of knowledge and showed slavery to be much worse than portrayed in *Uncle Tom's Cabin*.

Uncle Tom's Cabin, a masterpiece of persuasion, was converting many readers to abolitionists. Dozens of Southern proslavery writers, consequently, rushed to publish anti-Tom novels as foils to Harriet's powerful novel, to portray slavery as benign. One writer of particular curiosity was Caroline Lee Hentz (the bluestocking of the Semi-Colon Club), whose novel, *Marcus Warland; or, The Long Moss Spring*, was released the same year as Harriet's. Here is an excerpt:

> On each side of the mansion house a long row of neat, white cabins, individualized by some favourite tree, or vine, or plant, showed that the master, who had so amply provided for his own comfort, had not forgotten the accommodation of his slaves. Behind each of these cabins was a small garden, belonging to the

negro who occupied it, which was as much his exclusive property as the fields he assisted to cultivate were his master's....It is true, they were *slaves*, but their chains never clanked. Each separate link was kept moist and bright with the oil of kindness, applied with a downy touch.

Part V

JUSTICE

(1854-1859)

Gentlemen…The only way to make the Fugitive Slave Law a dead letter is to make half a dozen or more dead kidnappers. [Laughter and applause] A half dozen more dead kidnappers carried down South would cool the ardor of Southern gentlemen and keep their rapacity in check.

—*Frederick Douglass*

CHAPTER 59

Stephen Douglas Explodes
a Bomb

The Mississippi River provided a natural highway for North-South traffic, but there was no such waterway or easy path to carry people, mail, and goods to the Western lands. A transcontinental railroad to link the Eastern states to the Pacific would be a dream come true, especially with the discovery of gold in California—San Francisco was, by the 1850s, a global port—but what could not be agreed upon was what route the railroad would take. In the early 1850s, multiple government surveys were conducted and various routes mapped.

Illinois Democratic Senator Stephen A. Douglas favored a Northern route, with Chicago as the Northern terminus. Southern slaveholders and their allies preferred a Southern route that ran through the already-organized territory of New Mexico with its Eastern terminus at New Orleans. The Northern (Chicago) route would have to pass through the unorganized Nebraska Territory, the remaining land from the Louisiana Purchase, and land occupied by Native American tribes. To use that land required the government to extract land cessions from the Indians and to organize the area as a territory. Until then, the land could not be surveyed and opened to farmers. Douglas' biggest obstacle to his plan, however, was the fact that the Nebraska Territory lay north of the 36° 30' parallel, above which slavery had been forbidden by the Missouri

Compromise of 1820 (excepting Missouri). Americans considered the Missouri Compromise to be fixed law as it had been for thirty-four years.

The Northern fallout from the passage of the 1850 Compromise with its notorious Fugitive Slave Law had, by 1854, largely dissipated in the North. People thought that perhaps the compromise had settled the sectional dispute. Abraham Lincoln thought so. Then, along came Senator Stephen A. Douglas, a Northern man with Southern principles, to upset this peace. Utilizing his position as chairman of the Senate Committee on Territories, in January 1854, Douglas introduced a scheme to promote his Northern railway plan. To pass it, he needed six Southern votes in the Senate. Southerners wanted land *in the West* on which they could farm with slave labor. One of these senators, David R. Atchison of Missouri, pledged to "extend the institutions [slavery] of Missouri over the territory at whatever sacrifice of blood or treasure."

With the backing of President Franklin Pierce, Douglas' bill organized two territories—Nebraska west of Iowa and Kansas west of Missouri. Douglas made it look as if he was reserving Nebraska for freedom and Kansas for slavery. To open up the Kansas Territory to slavery, he repealed the Missouri Compromise's ban on slavery north of the line of 36° 30'. Douglas said to let the residents of the territories decide in their elections, and not the Congress, if they wanted to be a free state or a slave state, thus reviving the doctrine termed "popular sovereignty," or self-government. This was unheard of policy for addressing slavery in the territories.

Northern Democrats and Whigs were astonished by this bill, but Free Soil Senators Salmon Chase and Charles Sumner were not. Chase and Sumner, along with others, wrote an anti-Nebraska manifesto that denounced the Nebraska bill as "a gross violation of a sacred pledge" to convert the territory "into a dreary region of despotism, inhabited by masters and slaves." They urged the American people to oppose it as if they were repelling an invading army.

The *Appeal* had a great effect in rallying anti-slavery advocates around the single issue of an anti-Nebraska movement. On February 3, 1854, Salmon Chase and Douglas engaged in a heated debate on the Senate floor. Chase accused Douglas of sponsoring a bill to raise his profile for his next bid for the presidency. Sumner watched appreciatively as Chase verbally shredded Douglas' claim that "popular sovereignty" would settle the matter of territorial concerns. Chase asked Douglas:

> What kind of popular sovereignty is that which allows one portion of the people to enslave another portion? Is that the doctrine of equal rights?...No, sir, no! There can be no real democracy which does not fully maintain the rights of man, as man.

Douglas began his concluding speech at midnight and spoke for four hours. Senator William Henry Seward interrupted him to ask for an explanation. Douglas replied, "Ah, you can't crawl behind that free n----r dodge."

Seward said: "Douglas, no man will ever be President of the United States who spells 'negro' with two gs."

The debate over the Kansas-Nebraska Bill further inflamed the Northern anti-slavery impulse already agitated by the Fugitive Slave Law and the publication of the bestseller *Uncle Tom's Cabin*. In Congress and in the North, angry sermons and speeches were made and distributed and newspaper editorials of an increasingly militant nature were written. Reverend Henry Ward Beecher was infuriated. Writing for the *Independent* and signing his pieces with a *, Beecher had this to say to those optimists who, four years earlier, had believed that the 1850 Compromise would bring peace:

> This whole nation lies spread out like a gambler's table, before the Washington politicians. They are casting their dice upon it, and watching for strokes of luck, with as little consideration or fight or

wrong as if they were professional gamblers in a secreted chamber of mischief....

Is this the peace?...Is not this the very sequence which we told you would come? That compromise was a ball of frozen rattle-snakes....You persisted in bringing them into the dwelling. You laid them down before the fire. Now where are they? They are crawling all around. Their fangs are striking death into every precious interest of Liberty! It is your work!...

There has been no division among the abettors of slavery. They have seen eye to eye. They have walked with undivided ranks.... They have marched and conquered. Only among the advocates of liberty have there been divisions....

But now, is there not at length, a ground upon which the whole North can gather?

...If civil wars are to be prevented, now is the time; courage to-day, or carnage to-morrow. Firmness will give peace; trembling will bring war.

Henry begged the public to express its anger in letters, protests, and petitions to lawmakers. After reading Beecher's call to arms in the *Independent*, a father wrote the newspaper to say that his son was so inspired that he collected one hundred forty anti-Nebraska signatures in a day. Hundreds of anti-Nebraska meetings were held. Petitions were drawn up and sent to Congress.

Harriet Beecher Stowe, with encouragement from Sumner, contributed money to finance a campaign to gather signatures of 3,050 New York and New England clergymen who opposed the bill. The clergy intended to read the petition in the Senate but permission was denied. It was of no matter to the Southerners. They had their own clergy to support their heresy.

The Kansas-Nebraska Act was signed into law on May 30, 1854, by President Pierce. Now slavery could take root wherever the people voted for it. Simultaneously, in a heartless move, Southern senators killed a bill that would have provided settlers with a 160-acre home-stead grant on public lands. There was to be no encouragement for free farms in the territories.

Northern Whigs had all voted against the bill. Twenty-five out of thirty-four Southern Whigs, however, voted or were paired for it. This disagreement led to a final North/South split in the Whig party. That summer, the anti-Nebraska movement spawned multiple political parties, and coalitions of parties, traveling under a variety of names, but the one party that would arise and stick would be estab-lished in Wisconsin as the new Republican Party, organized as the one true anti-slavery party.

Five days after the passage of the Kansas-Nebraska Act, William Henry Seward addressed the Senate:

> Come on, then, gentlemen of the slave states, since there is no escaping your challenge, we accept it in the name of freedom. We will engage in competition for the virgin soil of Kansas, and God give the victory to the side which is stronger in numbers, as it is in right.

In Boston, there was a man who would do just this—send settlers to Kansas to establish it as a free state. His name was Amos A. Lawrence. He had just lived through a brutal two weeks in Boston. While President Pierce was signing the Kansas-Nebraska Act in Washington, Pierce placed Boston under martial law. A slave catcher from Virginia had arrived there and arrested the young fugitive, Anthony Burns. Word of Burns' capture had spread through Boston's abolitionist community. After a nine-day trial that transfixed the city, the Vigilance Committee put a plan in action to rescue Burns from the courthouse, which was surrounded by chains, where Burns was under armed guard on the top floor.

On Friday evening, May 26, at 9 p.m., the men of the committee and others, all heavily armed, gathered at the courthouse. The crowd swelled to about two thousand. A small group of men, led by Reverend Thomas Wentworth Higginson, began their assault on the courthouse. They used a beam as a battering ram to break down the doors. Abolitionists and marshals engaged in hand-to-hand fighting. A pistol went off, and one of the federal marshals was killed. Burns remained in secure custody. President Pierce authorized the stationing of federal troops to guard the courthouse and prevent another rescue attempt.

On June 2, hundreds of soldiers marched Burns down State Street to the Long Wharf to be returned to slavery. Over 50,000 protesters lined the streets. Abolitionists had strung up a coffin over the street with the word "liberty" engraved on it. Buildings were draped in black crepe bunting.

The event was nationally publicized. The South's barefaced aggression into the North, its inhumanity to man, and President Pierce's alliance with the Slave Power had brought about a tremendous change in Boston textile magnate Amos A. Lawrence. The return of Burns to slavery moved Lawrence from the sidelines into the anti-slavery struggle. On June 1, 1854, he wrote his uncle about the transformative effect these events had on him and others in his circle:

> We went to bed one night, old-fashioned, conservative, compromise Union Whigs, and we woke up stark mad Abolitionists.

Lawrence was a rich and influential textile merchant. He contacted Eli Thayer, a member of the Massachusetts Legislature and founder of the New England Emigrant Aid Company. The purpose of the NEEAC was to provide sponsorship and funds for the settlement of Kansas by New England anti-slavery proponents before slavery was introduced there. To this aim, Lawrence promised to give large sums, his time, and energy.

———

Abraham Lincoln, now 45, was thunderstruck to hear that the extension of slavery in the territories was now legalized. Lincoln, who had not held political office since 1849, was riding the Eighth Circuit as a lawyer in the backcountry of Illinois when he learned of the passage of the Kansas-Nebraska Act. He was roused as if "by the sound of a fire-bell at night." Lincoln, who was sharing a room with fellow lawyer, T. Lyle Dickey, "sat on the edge of his bed and discussed the political situation far into the night." At dawn, when Dickey woke up, Lincoln was still sitting up in bed and lost in thought. Lincoln said, "I tell you, Dickey, this nation cannot exist half-slave and half-free." No longer could Lincoln fool himself into thinking that slavery would die out on its own. Rather, it was multiplying. He said that slave owners were like hungry cows. Take down the fences from the free soil meadows and "they would rush in" and lay waste to them. Of his abhorrence that one man had power over another man without his consent, Lincoln wrote:

> Although volume upon volume is written to prove slavery a good thing, we never hear of the man who wishes to take the good of it, *by being a slave himself.*

Lincoln did not speak out immediately against the Act. Over the summer, he neglected his flourishing law practice and was seen with his nose buried in books in the State Library in Springfield, reading past and present congressional debate records. He would not express his opinion on any subject, said his law partner, William Herndon, until he knew it "inside and outside, upside and downside."

Lincoln admitted this to be true:

> I could not sleep, although I tried to, when I got on such a hunt after an idea, until I had caught it; and when I thought I had got

it, I was not satisfied until I had repeated it over and over; until I had put it in language plain enough....This was a kind of passion with me, and it has stuck by me; for I am never easy now, when I am handling a thought, till I have bounded it north and bounded it south, and bounded it East and bounded it West....

Lincoln told his good friend Joshua Speed:"I am slow to learn and slow to forget that which I have learned. My mind is like a piece of steel, very hard to scratch any thing on it and almost impossible after you get it there to rub it out."

Shortly after Congress adjourned in August 1854, Stephen Douglas hurried home to Illinois. He was stunned to learn of the storm of protest he had raised in the North. He had torn up the Missouri Compromise which had kept slavery in place! Douglas' friends urged him to stay away. He laughed it off, saying that, on his train trip home, he could have made his way by the light of the burning effigies of himself. In the early evening of September 1 in Chicago, more than eight thousand people gathered in Market Square to hear what Douglas had to say for himself. The bells of local churches rang out a funeral dirge in disapproval. As he began to speak, he was met with silence, not cheers. Silence soon gave way to catcalls, hisses, taunts, and boos. Douglas put up with it for two hours before storming off the platform, beet-red in the face, shaking his fist at the crowd.

Douglas was alarmed that his fellow Democratic Party candidates in Iowa and Maine had suffered election losses. Determined to put across his case, staunch the wound to the Democratic Party, and reclaim his reputation, Douglas, trailed by newspaper reporters, embarked on a nonstop lecture tour. At each stop, he claimed the same thing—that it was his duty, as chairman of the Senate Committee on Territories, to provide for a government in the Nebraska Territory.

Frederick Douglass and other anti-Nebraska men followed close on Douglas' heels, speaking in rebuttal. On October 3, 1854, Douglas arrived to speak on what he hoped to be friendlier turf, at Springfield, at the opening of the Illinois State Fair.

Douglas was nicknamed "the Little Giant." He stood five feet four and had a deep and booming voice. He had blue eyes and an expressive face. His head was large. He wore his abundant black hair in a flamboyant pompadour, swept back in waves. While in the midst of speaking, he would throw off his cravat, unbutton his coat, and look like a boxer entering the ring, half-naked. Given his theatrical bravado and such an astounding mass of hair, one reporter said it gave Douglas "the appearance of a lion prepared to roar or crush his prey."

Douglas began speaking outside on the fairgrounds, but heavy rains forced him and his audience to move into the hall of the House of Representatives. He felt he was in his element; he was frequently interrupted by affirming cheers and applause. He spoke freely, his lips trembling with emotion:

> I tell you the time has not yet come when a handful of traitors in our camp can turn the great State of Illinois, with all her glorious history and traditions, into a negro-worshiping, negro-equality community.

Lincoln was listening in the lobby, pacing. When Douglas finished speaking, the crowd filed past Lincoln, standing on the stairway, who announced that he would respond to Douglas the next day. Although Lincoln had a moral opposition to slavery and the bedrock belief that all men are created equal, he had no idea what to do about slavery in Southern states where it was protected by the Constitution. As to its extension elsewhere, he would oppose it with all his might. He believed the federal government was responsible for excluding it from the territories.

The next afternoon, Douglas was present to hear Lincoln speak. Douglas sat in a chair directly in front of Lincoln. Lincoln, at this point, was a political nobody. He had served in the Illinois Assembly and one unremarkable term in the U.S. House. He had not held political office in five years. Lincoln was a private citizen who would occasionally stump for fellow Whig candidates in Illinois. Douglas, on the other hand, had been in politics, at the state level and the national level, since 1840. The former bigwigs of the Senate, Calhoun, Clay, and Webster, were all dead, and Douglas' star was rising. He was born Stephen Arnold Doug*lass*, but, in 1846, at the age of 33, he suddenly changed the spelling of his last name from "-ass" to "-as," possibly as a reaction to the 1845 publication of former slave, Frederick Douglass' first autobiography, or more likely because it looked better, especially being saddled with the dreadful middle name of (Benedict) *Arnold*.

Lincoln had been trying to debate Douglas for weeks, to appear on the same platform with him, but Douglas had refused. Lincoln was fully prepared to rebut Douglas' claims. Horace White, reporting for the *Chicago Tribune*, said Lincoln spoke:

> with a tin, high-pitched falsetto voice of much carrying power, that could be heard a long distance in spite of the hustle and bustle of the crowd…[with] the accent and pronunciation peculiar to his native state, Kentucky.

Lincoln, dressed in only his shirtsleeves, without collar or tie, began by assuring the crowd that he was only addressing the matter of the extension of slavery and was giving an answer to "Judge Douglas." He gave a little history lesson on the treatment of slavery by the Founding Fathers. He spoke of Thomas Jefferson, a slaveholder, the author of the Declaration of Independence, who used his influence to prevent the future extension of slavery in the territories, as established in the Northwest Ordinance of 1787. He elaborated on the origins of the 1820 Missouri Compromise, which established the Ohio River as the understood Northern boundary of slavery. He said that this Compromise:

> had been canonized in the hearts of the American people, as a sacred thing which no ruthless hand would ever be reckless enough to disturb.

He then assailed Douglas' introduction of the Kansas-Nebraska Bill in which Douglas repealed the Missouri Compromise, "letting slavery into Kansas and Nebraska…allowing it to spread to every other part of the wide world, where men can be found inclined to take it." He disbelieved Douglas' claim that he was indifferent to slavery. Lincoln saw that Douglas was lying. He thought Douglas had:

> real zeal for the spread of slavery…[which] I can not but hate. I hate it because of the monstrous injustice of slavery itself. I hate it because it deprives our republican example of its just influence in the world—enables the enemies of free institutions, with plausibility, to taunt us as hypocrites….

Lincoln did not pace back and forth on the platform or lean on the podium. He stood square on his feet. He held his hands behind his back when he began, clasped, not gesturing much with his hands but using his body and head for emphasis. He did not use high-flown language but spoke plainly, using humor and stories to make his point. The more he spoke, the more the words took hold of him emotionally. His conviction in what he said was conveyed to his listeners.

Lincoln reminded his listeners that Douglas had flip-flopped on the issue of the extension of slavery. In 1849, Douglas had not only backed the Missouri Compromise but had introduced a bill in the Senate to extend the 36° 30' parallel west to the Pacific! From his seat in the front row, Douglas cried out: "And you voted against it!"

To which Lincoln snapped: "Precisely so...I was in favor of running the line a great deal further south."

Lincoln addressed Douglas' claim that "popular sovereignty" was the just use of democracy—let the people decide if they want to allow slavery in the territory:

> The doctrine of self-government is right...but it has no just application, as here attempted....When the white man governs himself that is self-government; but when he governs himself, and also governs another man, that is more than self-government—that is despotism. If the negro is a man, why then my ancient faith teaches me that 'all men are created equal': and that there can be no moral right in connection with one man's making a slave of another.
>
> [N]o man is good enough to govern another man, without that other's consent.

As for the reason that the Founding Fathers had allowed the existence of slavery in the founding of the Republic, Lincoln referred to it as having been a necessity:

> ...[having] found the institution existing among us...and they cast blame upon the British King for having permitted its introduction.... At the framing of the constitution, they forbore to so much as mention the word 'slave' or slavery'....[T]he slave is spoken of as a 'PERSON HELD TO SERVICE OF LABOR'....
>
> Thus, the thing is hidden away...just as an afflicted man hides away a wen [a boil] or a cancer, which he dares not cut out at once, lest he bleed to death; with the promise, nevertheless, that the cutting may begin at the end of a given time....

Thus, Lincoln refuted Douglas' claim that Douglas was acting in the Spirit of 1776. After speaking for three long hours, Lincoln wound to a close, urging the crowd to re-adopt the Declaration of Independence, and "return [slavery] to the position our fathers gave it; and there let it rest in peace."

The crowd shouted, "Hurrah! Hurrah! Hurrah!" Women waved white handkerchiefs. Afterward, Douglas stepped up and offered a rebuttal of two hours, but the day belonged to Lincoln. Immediately after Lincoln finished speaking, two anti-slavery men, Ichabod Codding and Owen Lovejoy, brother of the martyr Elijah Lovejoy, held a meeting. They organized a Republican Party in Illinois to oppose further ingresses of the Slave Power. Although Lincoln would call himself a Whig for a little while longer, his eloquent speech, which he repeated two weeks later at Peoria by torchlight, contained the principles that would form the foundation of the new Republican Party. Without asking his permission, Lovejoy and Codding named Lincoln to their state central committee.

That fall, Lincoln was elected to the Illinois State Legislature, but shortly afterward, he resigned his post in order to qualify to run for a U.S. Senate seat to open in 1855. The nominating vote for the U.S. Senate was conducted in the state legislature in February 1855. Lincoln did not win. Dejected from this stinging defeat, Lincoln told his old friend, Joseph Gillespie, that he was never going to run for office again.

CHAPTER 60

Kansas or Bust

March 30, 1855 was the day established for Kansas citizens to elect a territorial legislature. That morning, about one thousand proslavery men from Missouri arrived in Lawrence, Kansas. Lawrence had been founded nine months earlier by pioneer emigrants subsidized by Amos A. Lawrence of the New England Emigrant Aid Company. These Free Soil settlers aimed to create a free state by lawful means. But the Missouri men, who had flooded across the border, were determined that Kansas would be a slave state. These "Border Ruffians," as they were called—hard-drinking, dirty, unshaven men—arrived in over a hundred wagons and on horseback, playing music and with banners flying, set up a tent city outside Lawrence in a ravine. They were well-armed with guns, pistols, rifles, and Bowie knives. They brought two cannons loaded with musket balls. They voted as Kansans, although they were residents of Missouri. Throughout the territory, they would overrun the polls, stuff the ballot boxes, and disrupt the peaceful voting process. After all, had Senator Douglas not said that the decision as to whether Kansas would be free or slave would be decided by the ballot box?

One of the election judges, N.B. Blanton, notified this rowdy band that they would have to swear an oath as residents in the territory before being allowed to vote. They threatened him with hanging and he did not appear on election day. A new judge was appointed in his place who declared that any man had a right to vote if he had been

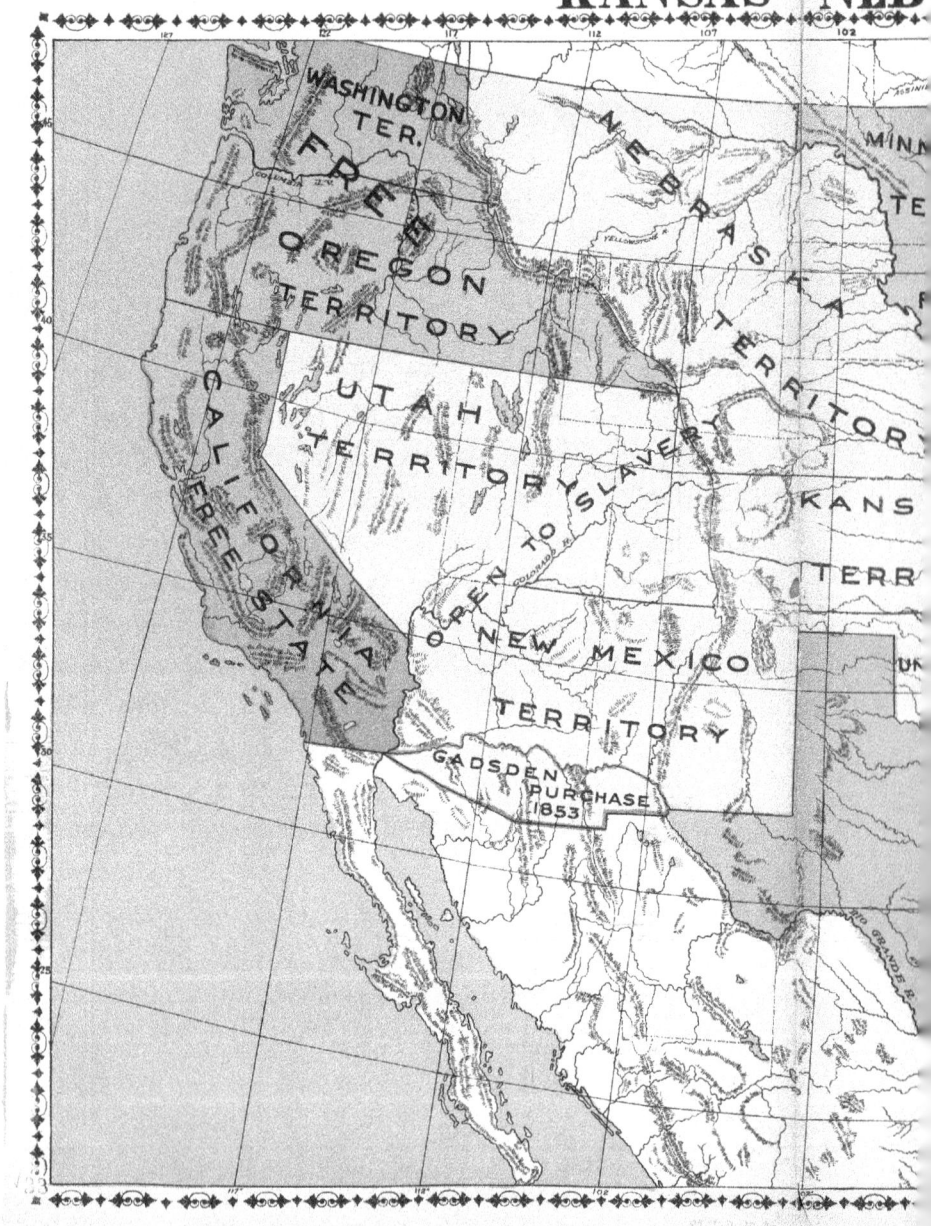

McConnell's Political Map of the United States (1854)

KA ACT, 1854.

The Kansas-Nebraska Bill, introduced by Douglas in 1854 provided that the territory north of the 37th parallel between the Missouri River and the Rocky Mountains be divided into two Territories, Kansas and Nebraska, and that the people residing in these territories should decide the slavery question for themselves.

Settlers rushed in from the North and the South, rival governments were established and war followed. In 1861 Kansas was admitted as a free state.

In 1853 Gen. Gadsden conducted negotiations with Mexico for a tract of territory lying south of the Gila River. For this territory, known as the Gadsden Purchase, the United States paid $10,000,000.

33

Copyright by JAMES McCONNEL

in the territory for but one hour. Another judge named Mr. Abbott became indignant at these practices and resigned.

The voting took place in a log cabin. The Missouri men voted first. When it came time for the citizens of Lawrence to cast their votes, they were made to walk through a narrow passageway inside the log cabin between a double file of these stinky and foul-mouthed rowdies, who wore white or blue ribbons in their buttonholes as identification with certain fiendish secret societies. The menacing behavior of the marauders kept many of the actual settlers away from the polls. After voting, many of the Missourians left for home, while others hung around Lawrence a bit longer to further intimidate, freely entering the houses of the citizens and taking meals there without invitation.

When President Pierce appointed Andrew Horatio Reeder as governor of the Kansas Territory, Reeder had fully sympathized with the South and supported the Kansas-Nebraska Bill. After observing the March election fraud, though, Governor Reeder was converted to the side of the Free Soilers, especially after the Missourians threatened to kill him if he interfered with their activities. Reeder ordered new elections to be held in one-third of the districts.

In the new elections, Free Soil candidates won most of the seats but were not recognized on July 2, 1855, when the legislature met at Pawnee City. Instead, the original proslavery victors were seated. Reeder went to Washington to plead with Pierce to stop the "burlesque."

Senators Atchison of Missouri and Douglas of Illinois persuaded President Pierce that the unrest in Kansas was the fault of the Emigrant Aid Company and that Reeder needed to be replaced. Reeder was fired and replaced with the pliable Wilson Shannon. The bogus legislature had enacted a draconian slave code that, among other things, imposed a fine and prison sentence for expressing opinions against slavery, made it a capital crime to help a slave escape, required all voters to vow to obey these laws, and required no Kansas residence as a qualification to vote. Yet the Kansas-Nebraska Act had specified that "every free white male inhabitant above the age of twenty-one years, who shall be an actual resident of said Territory" could vote. The Bogus Legislature was serving illegally, but it held the power.

The Free Soilers were enraged. They had no intention of obeying these "Bogus Laws" or regarding the legislature as the legitimate government.

Even Free Soil settlers not previously aligned politically with abolitionists joined them in forming the new Free State party in October 1855 in Topeka. They drew up a rival constitution prohibiting slavery in the territory and called elections for a new legislature and governor. On the question of whether or not to allow free Blacks to live in Kansas, the people voted it down. All of these actions by the Free Staters were considered extralegal and their government illegitimate. In response, the proslavery advocates created their own party, calling it "the Law and Order" party.

By January 1856, Kansas had two territorial governments, two governors, and two capitals, the official one of the "Bogus Legislature" at Lecompton, twelve miles from Lawrence, and an unofficial one at Topeka that represented a majority of actual residents.

The nation was closely following the developments in Kansas. This was a presidential election year. The South was alarmed when Republicans in Congress introduced bills for the admission of Kansas as a free state. The Democrats moved to admit Kansas as a slave state under the (Bogus) Lecompton territorial government. The pressure was on the Missourians to push out the Free Staters. Passions were running hot. In March 1856, Congressman Preston Brooks of South Carolina declared: "The admission of Kansas in to the Union as a slave state is now a point of honor. The fate of the South is to be decided with the Kansas issue."

Attitudes among abolitionists were shifting, too, becoming more radical, more militant, more heated; nonviolent tactics lost ground with each new drip, drip, drip of reports of atrocities, murder, and mayhem committed against the Free Staters. Both sides of the conflict were walking arsenals, although, in January, the *Independent* predicted a massacre of Free Staters by the spring should they not be sent more men, money, ammunition, and guns. Though sporadic outbreaks of violence had occurred, the severe winter of 1855-1856, with its icy winds and deep snowdrifts, had kept people huddled inside their cabins and kept things quiet for a time, but with the winter thaw came the annual migration of settlers from the North and the Midwest, swelling the free state majority and further rankling the South.

Many Christians began to see the need to fight back against the lawlessness. Rev. Henry Ward Beecher, in February 1856, said that he:

> believed that the Sharps Rifle was a truly moral agency, and that there was more moral power in one of those instruments, so far as the slaveholders of Kansas were concerned, than in a hundred Bibles. You might just as well...read the Bible to Buffaloes as those fellows who follow Atchison; ...but they have a supreme respect for the logic that is embodied in [the] Sharps rifle.

In March, a fundraiser was held in New Haven to raise rifles for the Connecticut-Kansas Company. Beecher attended and pledged to find money to buy twenty-five rifles if those in the audience would match that number. By the end of the evening, they'd raised enough money to buy twenty-seven rifles for twenty-five dollars each. Beecher's Plymouth Church sent the rifles and also twenty-five Bibles. The Sharps rifles were nicknamed "Beecher's Bibles." Lucretia Mott and William Lloyd Garrison opposed armed retaliation.

Frances Seward followed the events in Kansas closely and read Beecher's speeches in the *Times*, the *Tribune*, and *Frederick Douglass' Paper*. Unlike her friend Lucretia, Frances supported the arming of the Kansas Free Staters. In April, William Henry Seward made a speech in which he blamed President Pierce for not protecting the Kansas settlers from the Ruffians in the fall Wakarusa War. The *Times* praised Henry's speech. Frances and Henry Seward were in Washington when Henry received a letter from Frances' sister, Lazette Miller Worden, back in Auburn, New York, who could not bear to write her sister about a sad matter. She wrote Henry that the Sewards' adored bulldog, Watch, had died from having been poisoned by one of Henry's enemies.

In April, three U.S. congressmen arrived in Kansas, sent by the House Speaker to investigate the Kansas conflict. They held a series of dramatic hearings at Leavenworth and Lawrence. Witnesses, some trembling, came forward to give evidence of violence and fraud in elections, about Missourian secret societies, and the murders and intimidations of Free Soil settlers with cries of "Cut his throat!" and "Tear his heart out!" Representatives from both sides in the conflict were present. Edward Bourne of Atchison County testified:

> I have been beaten and bruised because of my political opinions and had to show my pistol to defend my life; and I think I am in danger now, when I tell what I do here. My wife has scarcely changed her clothes for the last six weeks, and a mob has threatened to come about my house and hang me if I did not leave in ten days, and called me an abolitionist, which I am not.

As the Southern press publicized these testimonies, the hateful feeling grew among the Southerners, the *Kansas Pioneer* calling upon "Southerners to come with rifle, knife and revolver to annihilate the abolitionists." The Atchison, Kansas *Squatter Sovereign* of May 8 demanded, "Blood for Blood!"

The proslavery faction, facing full disclosure of their doings, took drastic measures to contain the damage. Then, in the midst of these congressional hearings, Judge Lecompte instructed a grand jury to indict all members of the rival Free State Topeka government and charge them with high treason. Dr. Charles Robinson, the Free State governor, was seized on a steamboat and taken to prison at Lecompton. A warrant was issued for several others, including ex-Governor Reeder.

On May 11, a federal marshal and proslavery advocate, J.B. Donaldson, issued a proclamation stating that an attempt by one of his deputies to serve warrants in Lawrence was thwarted by a disorderly and violent mob of men. This was a lie. Donaldson's deputy had walked into a room of thirty men in Lawrence and tried to arrest former governor Andrew Reeder. Reeder told him to get lost, which the deputy did. Donaldson called upon a law-and-order force to assemble to support him.

A grand jury then issued indictments against two Lawrence newspapers, the *Herald of Freedom* and *Free Press*, for treasonous language and against the Free State Hotel, accused of being a fortress. Because there was no way to arrest the newspapers or the hotel, the proslavery rowdies considered the indictments as licenses to enter Lawrence and destroy them. Douglas County Sheriff Samuel J. Jones, a Missouri resident, would lead the invasion, as he had a bone to pick with the people of Lawrence. On April 23, in his attempt to arrest some Free State men in Lawrence, Jones was shot in the back. Now recovered, he sought revenge.

On May 21, 1856, dragging along five cannons, eight hundred Missourians, deputized as a posse, descended upon Lawrence, the bastion of abolitionists. They sealed off any escape routes. The Free State leaders, though, had decided against offering any resistance to the invasion. The Ruffians poured into the town, demolished the two newspaper offices, smashing the presses, and throwing the type in the river. They raised a banner above the office of the *Herald of Freedom* with "Southern Rights" inscribed on one side and "South Carolina" on the other. They tried to blow up the stone Free State Hotel, but that only made a big noise and big smoke. At each failure of the cannonballs, the free state crowd in the street sent up a huge shout. Jones was mortified at his inadequacy and resorted to burning the hotel to the ground. After having used (the imprisoned) Free State Governor Robinson's home for a headquarters, Jones ordered Robinson's hilltop home burned to the ground. The marauders smashed and looted shops and houses. Only one person died in the violence, and it was one of Jones' men, killed when rubble from the Free State Hotel fell on his head.

The invaders had come expecting a siege and a surrender, but the townspeople denied them such satisfaction. When the press reported "the Sack of Lawrence," it became a national disgrace for the proslavery faction. A territorial grand jury, a county sheriff, and a U.S. marshal had collaborated to start a mini-civil war in Kansas, thus confirming the Republicans' fears of a violent Slave Power conspiracy.

CHAPTER 61

Sumner Vents His Wrath

On May 15, 1856, six days before the Sack of Lawrence, Senator Charles Sumner of Massachusetts, 45, wrote his friend, Salmon Chase, now governor of Ohio: "I shall make the most thorough and complete speech of my life. My soul is wrung by this [Kansas] outrage, & I shall pour it forth."

Sumner met with the Sewards in Washington, during which he read aloud his speech titled "The Crime Against Kansas." Frances advised Sumner to remove passages in which he used "cutting personal sarcasm" against his Senate colleagues. Sumner, though, did not heed her advice.

Sumner memorized all 112 pages of his five-hour oration. On May 19 and 20, 1856, as Border Ruffians were preparing to sack Lawrence, Sumner delivered his speech in the Senate chamber. The "crime," he claimed, was the conspiracy to make Kansas, at any price, a slave state. He pointed out two Democratic senators as principally responsible for this crime—Stephen Douglas of Illinois and Andrew Butler of South Carolina. Douglas was present in the Senate chamber to hear Sumner's speech but Butler was not, as he was recuperating from a stroke. Sumner mocked the absent Senator Butler as a Don Quixote of slavery, who has chosen "the harlot Slavery," as his mistress.

Sumner's speech was lauded by the *New-York Tribune*, remarking that "Mr. Sumner has added a cubit [eighteen inches] to his stature." Sumner received an outpouring of praise in letters for his lofty, moral tone. But many of Sumner's Republican cronies whispered among themselves their regret at what they viewed as his intemperate remarks, which did not become a man of character. Southerners and most Democrats were openly hostile toward his speech. Proslavery advocates demanded that redress should be taken for the insults to the South.

Congressman Preston S. Brooks of South Carolina had gone over to the Senate chamber on May 19 and stayed long enough to hear Sumner call Butler, who was Brooks' distant cousin, the Don Quixote of slavery. Brooks was enraged. Brooks set his mind upon defending the honor of his state and of Butler. He waited until he had read the printed version of Sumner's speech before deciding how to proceed. He consulted fellow South Carolina Representative Laurence M. Keitt on dueling etiquette. Brooks had already fought two duels, but in this case, a duel was out of the question. A duel could be fought only between equals, two gentlemen, said Keitt. Brooks did not consider Sumner a gentleman. Anyway, Brooks concluded, Sumner would not accept the challenge anyway, as his having become a "Black Republican would make him incapable of courage."

Brooks settled upon a punishment that the Southern code ruled was appropriate for a social inferior, like a slave. He decided he would administer a blow to Sumner, but not with a horsewhip, which Sumner might wrest from his hands and then use on Brooks, but rather, a cane. He chose a thick, gutta-percha walking stick with a gold head. It was a light cane he might use to strike an unruly dog. Brooks also took into his confidence Representative Henry A. Edmundson of Virginia and asked him to accompany him, saying: "Sumner may have friends with him, and I want a friend of mine to be with me to do me justice...."

After the noon hour on Thursday, May 22, when the Senate chamber had almost emptied, Brooks, accompanied by Keitt and Edmundson, entered. Sumner was hunched over his Senate desk, franking copies of "The Crime Against Kansas," his armchair pulled up close, and his long legs fully under the desk.

Brooks walked over and addressed him: "Mr. Sumner."

Sumner raised his head to identify his visitor. Sumner was near-sighted but too vain to wear glasses, so he could not clearly see the man who now approached his desk. Even so, he did not know Brooks by sight.

"I have read your speech twice over carefully," Brooks said in a low voice. "It is a libel on South Carolina, and Mr. Butler, who is a relative of mine—"

Sumner moved to stand. But before he could get on his feet, Brooks lifted his thick, gold-headed cane in the air and, with the smaller end of it, beat Sumner severely on the head. The force of the blow so stunned Sumner that he lost his sight immediately: "I no longer saw my assailant, nor any other person or object in the room."

Sumner threw out his arms to cover his head, and Brooks struck him harder and harder. Brooks rained down the blows in quick succession on a trapped and defenseless man. Sumner was pinned in his chair under his heavy desk, which was bolted to the floor. Sumner's chair was on rollers and he would have to push it back on its track to get out from under the desk. He did not think to do so. Brooks landed about a dozen blows before Sumner managed to rise and, with the pressure of his thighs, rip the desk from the floor to escape his attacker. Blinded now by his own blood, Sumner staggered up the aisle to escape, but he now became an even easier target for his assailant, out in the open, whose cane was now snapping and breaking to bits. Still, Brooks continued his frenzied attack.

Sumner lost consciousness, knocking over another desk, but Brooks would not stop hitting him. Once his cane was in complete splinters on the floor, Brooks stuck the gold head in his pocket, and then he grabbed Sumner by the lapel of his coat with one hand while he hit him with his other hand.

Although the attack had taken place in less than a minute, the sound made by the strikes of Brooks' cane—thirty, by Brooks' count—got everyone's attention who remained in the chamber.

People rushed forward. No one, though, tried to stop the assault. When Senator John J. Crittenden tried to intercede, Keitt lifted a cane over his head and threatened to hit anyone who stepped up to interfere with Brooks. Sitting out in the anteroom, Stephen Douglas was advised of the attack, yet neither interceded nor called in a guard or a medic before, during, or after the incident.

Sumner remained as "senseless as a corpse for several minutes, his head bleeding copiously from the frightful wounds, and the blood saturating his clothes," said Congressman Edwin B. Morgan, who had rushed into the chamber from the vestibule, alerted by the sounds of the cane blows. Senator Henry Wilson of Massachusetts, upon learning of the attack on his friend and colleague, rushed back to the Capitol, helped Sumner into a carriage, took him to his lodgings, and put him to bed. Brooks walked away, a free man.

About an hour later, a doctor went to Sumner's rooms and examined him. The doctor said it was mandatory for his patient to have absolute quiet. It was too early to tell the extent of his injuries, he said. Before Sumner fell into a dazed sleep, he said he could not believe such "a thing like this was possible."

SOUTHERN CHIVALRY — ARGUMENT versus CLUB'S.

Caricature of the Caning of Charles Sumner

CHAPTER 62

Hell Hath no Fury Like John Brown Scorned

John Brown (1846-47)

I n the spring of 1855, a year before the Sack of Lawrence, John Brown, his second wife, Mary Day Brown, 39, and their four youngest children were living in North Elba, New York. Gerrit Smith had started the North Elba colony in the Adirondacks to help three thousand Blacks become citizens. John Brown bought 244 acres here, paying Gerrit Smith only $1 an acre. He picked up part-time work helping colonists survey and till their land while farming his own patch.

Meanwhile, five of his grown sons—John Jr., Jason, Owen, Frederick, and Salmon Brown—emigrated with their families from Ohio to Kansas to farm and make Kansas a free state. These sons of

John Brown settled forty miles south of Lawrence in Osawatomie. John Brown's oldest son, John Jr., wrote to his father of the Kansas conditions. He reported that he and his brothers were "threatened by hundreds and thousands of the meanest and most desperate of men, armed to the teeth with Revolvers, Bowie Knives, Rifles & Cannon," provided to them by slaveholders. The brothers realized that, together, they had only two small squirrel rifles and a revolver to defend their colony they named "Brown's Station." John Jr. wrote to his father to send arms and ammunition if he could.

In June, John Brown Sr. attended the founding convention of the Radical Political Abolitionist Party in Syracuse, led by Frederick Douglass and Gerrit Smith. He brought with him two of John Jr.'s letters and circulated them among the conventioneers. John Sr. wrote Mary that:

> John's two letters were...read with such effect by Gerrit Smith as to draw tears.... I received today donations amounting to a little over sixty dollars—twenty from Gerrit Smith, five from an old British officer; others giving smaller sums...

John Brown planned to deliver the arms himself. His sons were living in the most primitive of conditions, living together in tents and wagons. They had not brought their stoves. Using the money from Gerrit Smith and the other abolitionists, Brown bought a case of rifles and some provisions. He sold several cows and gave the money to Mary. Then, he and his son, Oliver, bade the North Elba family goodbye and took off for Kansas. They made stops in Massachusetts and Ohio to solicit further appeals for arms and money. Sons Jason, John Jr., and Owen, glad that their father was coming, wrote letters to him advising him to travel in a covered lumber buggy drawn by one horse or mule on the road from St. Louis to Kansas, as the Missouri River was generally in a low state of water, and unreliable as a water route.

John and Owen Brown arrived in Kansas on October 7, 1855. Once reunited, John Brown and his sons threw themselves into the fight to make Kansas free. John Brown joined the militia, the Pottawatomie Rifles, commanded by son John Jr. Nine months later, on the afternoon of Wednesday, May 21, 1856, while John Jr. was planting corn, news arrived of the attack on Lawrence (described earlier). John Brown Jr. mustered his militia to give relief to the defenders of the town. They set off on horses and wagons loaded with supplies and weapons. They camped that night and were joined by three other companies. John Jr. was chosen as the commander of these combined forces. But, early the next day, as the Pottawatomie Rifles were crossing the Marais des Cygnes, they received word that the crisis was over, the United States troops were in charge in Lawrence, and their Lawrence expedition was asked to turn back. The men also heard rumors that their families, left unprotected along the Pottawatomie Creek, had been threatened with an attack and were going to be driven from their homes by slavery men.

Upon learning the Lawrence men had not fought back against the proslavery raiders, John Brown Sr. became enraged. Brown went crazy, said witnesses, when informed of the caning of Sumner. He conceived of a "radical, retaliatory measure" against "the slave hounds" in the vicinity of Pottawatomie Creek. The next day, May 23, John Brown Sr. organized a small party of eight men and, in the afternoon, set out on the backtrail with them toward Pottawatomie Creek. With him were sons Owen, Frederick, Salmon, and Oliver, a son-in-law, Henry Thompson, Theodore Wiener, and James Townsley. Wiener rode a pony and Townsley carried the others in his horse-drawn wagon. Before splitting from John Jr. and his Rifles, the elder Brown very publicly declared that he and the others were embarking on a secret mission.

John Brown heard that Judge Sterling Cato had issued warrants for the arrest of him and some of his sons. The charge was unclear. John Brown Sr. had observed the recent arrival of proslavery men living along Pottawatomie Creek. He assumed these were the men who would serve the warrants. John Brown carried with him a list of Judge Cato's cohorts. Calculating like an Old Testament warrior, he figured that about five Free Staters had been killed, to date, by Border Ruffians. He believed in "a tooth for a tooth, an eye for an eye." None of the men he would visit next had anything to do with those murders of Free Staters.

The party set out on their trek, armed with short swords and guns. They passed several riders coming the other way. One rider remembered that John Brown was railing against the outrages of the slavery men. "His manner was wild and frenzied," said this rider. He noted that Brown's followers were enthralled by their leader, watching with "excited eagerness every word or motion" he made. The night of the 23rd, the seven men camped at the edge of a wood about a mile from the Pottawatomie settlement. The next day was a Saturday. The men rested and waited for the dark to come. By ten o'clock, the group was on the move, and the first stop was at the cabin of a proslavery man, James Doyle. The dogs started barking. Mahala Doyle, James Doyle's wife, recounted the events that followed in an affidavit prepared for the U.S. House Special Committee to investigate the troubles in Kansas.

In her testimony, Mahala said that, on the night of May 24, everyone in the Doyle family was in bed. At about eleven o'clock, there was a knock at the door. Her husband got up to answer it. He did not open the door but asked what was wanted. One of John Brown's men said they were looking for someone named Wilkinson. Doyle opened the door and several of Brown's men entered, identified themselves as from the "Army of the North," and asked them to surrender. They had pistols and large knives. Mahala Doyle recalled:

They first took my husband out of the house, then they took two of my sons—the two eldest, William [22] and Drury [20] … my son John, 16, was spared because I asked them, in tears, to spare him. In a short time…I heard the report of pistols—after which I heard moaning, as if a person was dying; then I heard a wild whoop.

Young John Doyle said:

I found my father and one brother (William) lying dead in the road, about two hundred yards from the house. I saw my other brother [Drury] lying dead on the ground…in the grass…. His fingers were cut off; his head was cut open; there was a hole in his breast. William's head was cut open, and a hole was in his jaw, as though it was made by a knife, and a hole was also in his side. My father was shot in the forehead and stabbed in the breast. An old man commanded the party; he was of dark complexion, and his face was slim.

The death squad moved on to the house of Allen Wilkinson, a known proslavery man. His wife Louisa was sick with the measles. Brown wanted to take Wilkinson with them. Louisa begged the invaders to let her husband stay with her as she had two young children. She recalled: "The old man, who seemed to be in command, looked at me and then around at the children and replied, 'You have neighbors.' Brown would not let Allen Wilkinson put on his boots before they took him away and murdered him. They took away the only horse the Wilkinsons had.

William Sherman was staying overnight as one of three guests at the house of James Harris. About two o'clock in the morning on the 25th, John Brown and his party, again calling themselves the "Northern Army," entered Harris' house, some of them with sabres and revolvers drawn, and approached the bedside where Harris, his wife, and child were sleeping. There was but one room in the house. Brown told Harris and the others to surrender as they were now prisoners. The intruders ransacked the house and took all the weapons and ammunition they could find. One by one, they took the four inhabitants of the cabin outside and interrogated them. James Harris recalled:

> They asked me if I had ever taken any hand in aiding proslavery men in coming to the Territory of Kansas, or had ever taken any hand in the last troubles at Lawrence....[T]hey asked me what made me live at such a place. I then answered that I could get higher wages there than anywhere else.

> They made Harris saddle a horse and then let Harris go back inside.

> [O]ld man Brown asked Mr. Sherman to go out with him...Two of the Northern army...stayed in with us until we heard a cap burst, and then these two men left. That morning, about ten o'clock, I found William Sherman dead in the creek near my house....I... examined him. Mr. Whiteman was with me. Sherman's skull was split open in two places, and some of his brains was washed out by the water. A large hole was cut in his breast, and his left hand was cut off.

There was no doubt in the region that John Brown, Sr. had given the orders for and participated in the five Pottawatomie killings, and his name was mentioned many times as the ringleader in testimony by witnesses in the U.S. House report on Kansas. Some Free-Staters excused the bloodletting as a just reprisal for the Sacking of Lawrence (where only one person died, and that was an accident), but the citizens of Lawrence "denounced the deed." Brown's actions at Pottawatomie triggered a summer of Kansas guerrilla warfare, characterized by hit-and-run raids, in which more people died and no slaves were freed. As news of the Pottawatomie murders reached the East Coast, anti-slavery advocates wove tales of fragile fiction that Brown acted in self-defense or was not even involved in the murders. "News from Kansas" press coverage of Brown's supposedly daring exploits in battle at Black Jack and Osawatomie soon obscured discussion of the shadowy Pottawatomie massacre. In no time, "Captain Brown" was recast as an anti-slavery hero.

———

Brown and his family left Kansas that September and headed East. Brown could not live safely in Kansas. The St. Louis *Daily Missouri Republican* reported his movements, labeling Brown "the most blood-thirsty murderer, perhaps, in the whole world" and wondered if "his Black Republican friends make a hero of him?" By January 1857, Brown was in Boston, with the *Boston Evening Transcript* heralding his arrival with this article: "A Kanzas [*sic*] Hero. Captain John Brown, himself the hero of the Osawatomie fight...is now in this city."

Brown carried with him glowing letters of introduction: two from Kansas Governor Charles Robinson (now freed), one from Ohio Governor Salmon Chase, and another from George Walker, who had known Brown when Brown was a wool merchant in Springfield, Massachusetts. Walker provided the introduction to Franklin Sanborn, the secretary of the Massachusetts State Committee. Brown knew that anti-slavery activists in New England, upset by the Border Ruffian atrocities as reported in the Northern papers, had collected guns, money, and supplies for Free Staters in Kansas. Brown wanted a piece of that action. He had a plan for the defense of the territory; would Sanborn help him get two hundred Sharps rifles and $30,000 to carry out his plan? Would he help him line up support among committee members and other friends of Kansas? Yes, indeed, Sanborn would. Sanborn was infatuated with this real-life hero, whose fame and noto-riety preceded him, and assumed that he had military genius. Brown explained that he was in the process of recruiting a volunteer army of vigilance patrol units and home guard outfits to protect Free State communities. Brown's role in the Pottawatomie Massacre was not known in Boston or had been written off as self-defense.

On January 5, Sanborn wrote his friend, the Unitarian Rev. Thomas Wentworth Higginson of Worcester and invited him to meet with Brown in Boston. Higginson had been in the small group that tried to free the fugitive Anthony Burns from the federal courthouse in Boston using battering rams and axes. In that melee, Higginson received a deep sabre slash on his chin, a scar he wore proudly. After meeting John Brown, *The Liberator* reported Higginson's impression:

> And if I wanted a genuine warrior of the Revolution, where could I find him better than in the old Vermonter, Capt. John Brown, the defender of Osawattomie [*sic*], the defender of a little log fort, with twenty-seven men, against two hundred, sending away eighty-two…killed and wounded, with only the loss of one man… who swallow a Missourian whole, and says grace after the meat.

Once in the East, Brown was no longer fighting off gunfire in a ravine but was welcomed with open arms into polite and dignified public and private settings. He appeared before the Massachusetts legislature, appealing for funds for his Kansas cause. He visited Charles Sumner in his home. He asked to see the blood-stained coat the senator had worn when he was attacked by Brooks. Sumner, limping, retrieved the relic from his closet, still stiff with blood. He handed it to Brown. Brown said nothing but "his lips compressed and his eyes shown like polished steel." From there, Brown departed Boston, riding trains all over New England and New York to speak to anti-slavery audiences, pleading for guns and money for the defense of Kansas. He visited Gerrit Smith at Peterboro who opened his purse wide and repeatedly to his old friend. In February, Brown was at Concord, lunching with the famous Transcendentalists Henry David Thoreau and Ralph Waldo Emerson, who listened with rapt attention to his grandiose and thrilling (embellished) recitations of his war days in Kansas.

When Brown returned to Kansas on October 30, 1857, it was as the agent of the Massachusetts Committee. In addition to the funds he had received from generous individuals, the committee gave him money. They also voted to supply him with two hundred Sharps rifles and ammunition, taking him at his word that they were only to be used defensively in Kansas. Out of his own pocket, George L. Stearns, a member of the committee, paid $1,300 for two hundred revolvers for Brown. These new weapons, along with the old muskets, rifles, sabres, a field piece, and other weapons used in the Kansas struggle, were stored in Jonas Jones' cellar in Tabor, Iowa. As requested by Brown, Amos A. Lawrence of the New England Emigrant Aid Company and Stearns had raised $1000 to complete the purchase of Brown's and his daughter's North Elba farms to provide for his wife and younger children. Sanborn gave the money to Gerrit Smith, the owner of the land. John Brown, already well-supplied with arms, privately contracted with a Connecticut toolmaker to make him a thousand custom "pikes"— Bowie knives fastened to poles six feet long.

In November, Brown organized a Kansas company of about a dozen men. One of these recruits, John E. Cook, met up with Brown in Lawrence where Brown told him that the purpose of the company would be "putting a stop to the aggression of the proslavery men." The group departed Kansas. They stopped at Tabor where they were informed that they were transporting the weapons and supplies to Springdale, Iowa, where they would be attending a military school. Their drillmaster, a specialist in guerrilla warfare, was the Englishman Hugh Forbes. Brown was to pay him $100 a month. He had already been paid an advance and, on his way to Iowa, Forbes had begged money from Gerrit Smith, who gave him $150. At Tabor, the men got a shock. Cook recalled:

Here we found that Captain Brown's ultimate destination was the state of Virginia. Some warm words passed between him and myself in regard to the plan, which I had supposed was to be confined entirely to Kansas and Missouri. [Richard] Realf and [Luke] Parsons were of the same opinion with me. After a good deal of wrangling, we consented to go on, as the rest of the party were so anxious that we should go with them.

Brown told his band that "God had created him to be the deliverer of the slaves the same as Moses."

Like Cook, Realf, and Parsons, Brown's Eastern benefactors had signed onto Brown's campaign because they believed it was to be waged for defense in Kansas. Brown would let the Easterners continue to think this. He needed their money for his private war against slavery. With more funds and men, Brown's team would be ready to strike—but it would be without drillmaster Forbes, who had challenged Brown's plans, quarreled with him, left camp, and headed East.

CHAPTER 63

The Republican Party Rises

In the aftermath of the May 1856 caning of Charles Sumner, both he and his assailant, Preston Brooks, became heroes in their own regions. Approving Southerners sent Brooks dozens of replacement canes. The *Richmond Enquirer* of June 9 called Brooks' actions good:

> The vulgar Abolitionists...have grown saucy....They must be lashed into submission.

Brooks boasted that "every Southern man sustains me. The fragments of the stick are begged for as sacred relicts [*sic*]." The House took steps to expel him, but Brooks resigned anyway in order to return home and seek validation by reelection. Upon his return to South Carolina, he was entertained as a conquering hero and returned to the Legislature in Washington with unanimous backing. Charles Sumner, however, was saddled with a traumatic brain injury. Frances Seward was distressed to see her good friend in such agony. Aside from recovering from bruises, cuts, and two serious wounds on his head that had to be stitched, Sumner struggled to think clearly, was reliant on morphine to manage pain, and had to learn how to walk all over again. Previously, Frances had professed opposition to the death penalty. Now though, when a friend asked if she thought Brooks should be hanged if Sumner died, Frances said Brooks should be hanged either way and that "none are punished but the poor slaves who rebel against their masters."

Lydia Maria Child wrote a friend that "the outrage on Charles Sumner made me literally ill for several days….Such a man as Charles Sumner will not bleed and suffer in vain! Those noble martyrs of liberty in Kansas will prove missionary ghosts, walking through the land, rousing the nation from its guilty slumbers. Our hopes, like yours, rest on Fremont. I would almost lay down my life to have him elected. If the Slave Power is checked now, it will never regain its strength. If it is not checked, civil war is inevitable, and, with all my horror of bloodshed, I could be better resigned to that great calamity, than to endure the tyranny that has so long trampled upon us."

Child was expressing her support for John Charles Frémont, the man the Republican Party chose in June 1856 as their presidential candidate. Although Seward and Chase were the most likely candidates, both had created enemies among groups of voters this relatively new party desperately needed to attract. Chase was bitterly disappointed that he was not selected. He had an all-consuming desire to be the president, yet he did not even appoint a manager. Seward, a more astute politician, did have a manager, Thurlow Weed, who advised Seward to wait four years for better odds of being elected.

While the (new!) Republican party platform was important—centrally, its opposition to the extension of slavery—a charismatic candidate could do much to shape the party image. Whereas Governor Chase was stiff and awkward, Frémont was dashing. He was called the "Pathfinder" of the West for his role in the California conquest during the Mexican-American War. Frémont had almost no political experience and, beneficially, had no record to defend. He was married to Jessie Benton, the daughter of Thomas Hart Benton, who had a long history of serving in the U.S. Senate and a brief time in the U.S. House. Frémont won the nomination on the first ballot.

In the balloting for Vice President, Abraham Lincoln, the

recognized leader of the new Republican Party in Illinois, came in second place. Lincoln had not expected this and did not take it seriously at first, remarking that "there's another great man in Massachusetts named Lincoln, and I reckon it's him."

At 43, Frémont was the youngest presidential candidate yet. He was married to a beautiful woman. The Democratic candidate, bachelor James Buchanan, 65, was among the oldest candidates. In his lifetime, Buchanan had held so many offices that he was nicknamed "Old Public Functionary." At the Democratic convention, Buchanan would receive mostly Northern votes. Not tainted with the Kansas conflict, Buchanan wrested the nomination from the incumbent Pierce and the hopeful Douglas. A third party, the anti-immigrant, anti-Catholic American Party, also known as the "Know-Nothing" party, nominated former president Millard Fillmore, who had signed the Fugitive Slave Act.

Buchanan and the Democrats charged the Republican party as a sectional Yankee party, which was true, and that, if they won the election, the Union would fall apart. Southerners, in turn, threatened secession should Frémont win. Governor Henry Wise of Virginia put his militia on alert for a revolution he thought was in the offing. Even Thomas Hart Benton, Frémont's father-in-law, backed Buchanan. Frémont had no Southern support and thus would have to carry all Northern states to win. An Ohio Democratic-controlled newspaper told voters that: "Black Republicans" intended to "turn loose… millions of negroes, to elbow you in the workshops, and compete with you in the fields of honest labor."

Democrats in Pittsburgh said the Republicans wanted to give complete equality to the African race. In Indiana, Democrats paraded young white girls wearing white dresses who carried banners that said, "Fathers, save us from n----r husbands."

With such wild accusations hurled at them, Republicans denied that they sought racial equality. In doing so, they stirred up abolitionists like Lewis Tappan and William Lloyd Garrison, who, from a second flank, attacked the Republican Party, denouncing it and saying it was a party for white men, and not for all men. After denials failed, Republicans went on the offensive. They distributed a million copies of "The Crime Against Kansas." Their campaign slogan was "Bleeding Kansas" and "Bleeding Sumner." They reminded voters of the aim of the Slave Power, to nationalize slavery. They held huge torchlight parades and chanted, "Free Soil, Free Speech, Free Men, Frémont!"

On Tuesday, November 4, 1856, Democrat James Buchanan won the presidential election. The Democrats had gotten across their argument that they, and only they, could protect the Union from crumbling and could preserve the racial status quo. Buchanan won because he appeared to be safe.

———

Preston Brooks never apologized for his attack on Sumner. In announcing his June 1856 resignation from the House of Representatives, he admitted not having challenged Sumner to a duel, prohibited in the United States, because it would have presented him with legal penalties more severe than would be imposed for "a simple assault and battery." Brooks' only punishment for his vicious attack on an unarmed and trapped man was a $300 fine imposed by a district court. He was not jailed.

As mentioned, after his resignation from the House, Brooks returned South, where he was reelected as a member of the House from South Carolina's Fourth District. On January 27, 1857, Brooks died suddenly from a violent attack of croup. The official telegram announcing his death stated: "He died a horrid death, and suffered intensely. He endeavored to tear his own throat open to get breath."

His cousin, Senator Andrew Butler, died four months later. Sumner still was not well enough to return to the Senate, which kept his seat for him. In a March 9, 1857 letter to her son Augustus, Frances Seward mentioned that her great friend Sumner:

sailed in the Fulton for Paris last Saturday...was here a week previous—I went twice to see him—he dined with us—looks much as he did formerly in the face—rises with great difficulty—and cannot walk erect—Most persons think he is incurably disabled— He is sanguine in the expectation of great benefits or perfect restoration from his voyages and travels....

CHAPTER 64

Taney Rules on Dred Scott

At noon on March 4, 1857, President-Elect James Buchanan stepped into an open barouche outside the Willard Hotel. Buchanan, recovering from ptomaine poisoning, feared he might collapse at his inauguration. Riding with him that day down Pennsylvania Avenue toward the Capitol were President Pierce, the outgoing president, Vice President Elect John Breckenridge, and two senators. The bright sky and mild temperatures were a welcome relief after two days of disagreeable weather that had threatened to detract from the enjoyment of the pomp and ceremony of the Buchanan inauguration, heralded throughout the preceding night with movements of ball-goers, fireworks, the march of military companies, and "the weary tramp on the sidewalks of thousands of visitors unable to obtain lodgings."

The inaugural procession was long. Sidewalks and house fronts were deluged with spectators. Pretty ladies stood at the windows and balconies, waving at the presidential car as it passed. Following the car was a high platform drawn by six horses. On this float stood a lady who represented the Goddess of Liberty. After this came a miniature ship-of-war. A tremendous crowd greeted Buchanan and his party when he mounted the steps to the Capitol at one o'clock, at which time he addressed the people from the raised platform. Afterward, the ceremony was concluded in the Senate chamber when Chief Justice Roger B. Taney administered the oath of office to Buchanan. Taney, you will recall, was the signatory of the warrant issued in 1850 for the arrest of William Craft in Boston.

Senator Seward, the leading Republican in the country, was present for the inauguration. At Buchanan's swearing-in ceremony, Seward noted excessive chumminess between Buchanan and Chief Justice Taney, 78. There was much secretive whispering. Added to that were the curious remarks Buchanan made in his inaugural address to the nation, regarding the judiciary.

Buchanan said that a "difference of opinion" existed regarding the extension of slavery into the territories. Upon that, all could agree. The question of the extension of slavery had given birth to the new and rising Republican Party. Then, Buchanan suggested that Congress, which *was* constitutionally empowered to legislate "all needful rules and regulations" in the territories, actually *did not* have this power. Buchanan claimed that:

> A different opinion (popular sovereignty) has arisen in regard to the time when the people of a territory shall decide this question for themselves….This is a judicial question which, legitimately, belongs to the Supreme Court of the United States, before whom it is now pending and will, it is understood, be speedily and finally settled.

For those scratching their heads about Buchanan's allusion to the judiciary being in charge of the slavery extension question rather than the Congress, the answer was revealed two days later when, on the ground floor of the Capitol, in the Supreme Court, Judge Taney read his decision in the case of *Dred Scott v. Sandford*, a case he had sat on until Buchanan's election victory was secured.

For eleven years, the *Dred Scott v. Sandford* case had wound its way through the legal system. In 1846, Dred Scott, a slave living at the time in Missouri, had sued for the freedom of his wife, their children, and himself, on the grounds that his slave master, an army doctor, had taken him for several years to military bases in the free state of Illinois and the Wisconsin Territory. Taney ruled against Dred

Scott, denying that he was a free man, as Blacks "are not included…
under the word 'citizens' in the Constitution," and therefore, he had
no standing in federal court and, therefore, no right to sue. According
to Taney, being a Black man in America gave him no rights at all. This
decided the case.

But Taney went further. He wanted to settle the matter of slavery's
extension permanently. Because of the repeal of the 1820 Missouri
Compromise, which had drawn a line between slave states and free
states, Taney asserted that the Wisconsin Territory, where Dred Scott
lived, had never indeed been free. Taney then asserted that the Fifth
Amendment protected persons from being deprived of "life, liberty,
or property"—and slaves were property. Therefore, a ban on taking
slaves into the territories represented an unconstitutional deprivation
of property. Taney was determined to affirm that Congress had no
power to rule on the question of slavery and, thus, put the matter to
bed by judicial fiat.

Taney's bombshell ruling by a divided court, 7-2, inflamed
rather than calmed the controversy, invigorating and strengthening
the Republicans and dividing the Democrats along sectional lines.
The Taney ruling had voided Stephen Douglas' pet doctrine, popular
sovereignty, as there was no need for a citizen vote as the Dred Scott
ruling effectively legalized slavery in all the territories. A storm of
anger broke out in the North. Further suspicion fell on Buchanan;
rumors spread that he had applied pressure on Supreme Court
Judge Robert C. Grier, writing him letters to persuade him to join
the majority voters. Obviously, Buchanan knew of the ruling well
in advance of the nation and had influenced the Court. Seward was
disgusted with Buchanan and the judges' violations of ethics and the
confidentiality of the Court. Two days after the Buchanan inauguration, Seward said:

the judges, without even exchanging their silken robes for courtiers' gowns, paid their salutations to the President, in the Executive

palace. Doubtlessly the President received them as graciously as Charles I did the judges who had, at his instance, subverted the statutes of English liberty.

———

Seward's charges of conspiracy between Buchanan and Taney in the Dred Scott decision caused an uproar in the South. Buchanan banned Seward from the White House. Taney was even angrier, proclaiming his refusal to administer the oath of office to Seward should he be elected to the presidency in 1860. Opposition papers such as the Albany (New York) *Atlas and Argus* falsely claimed that Seward was threatening to end slavery in South Carolina and Georgia. The *New York Herald* branded him a "more repulsive abolitionist, because a more dangerous one, than Beecher, Garrison, or Rev. [Theodore] Parker."

Yet Seward was not an abolitionist. He, like Lincoln, believed that Southern slavery was beyond the control of the national government. Yet he abhorred slavery. He was an optimist. He envisioned an America that would become free, affluent, and less dependent on foreign industry for the production of its manufactured goods. His unfortunate use of the radical phrase "a higher law" had harmed him politically, branding him as an extremist when, in truth, he was a moderate anti-slavery crusader.

Seward, by temperament, was a unifier. He fancied himself as gentle as a lion. He refused to give in to anger when people said abusive things about him or to him. Northerners and Southerners broke bread at his Washington home, with Frances often his hostess. He maintained polite relations with everyone, often to Frances' dismay. Charming and generous, he put his guests at ease with his funny stories that made him hoarse with laughter. He made intelligent conversation on many topics—he particularly loved the theatre—and gave lavish feasts that became legendary.

At one of these banquets, seventeen courses were served, beginning with turtle soup. Plates were changed between each serving of fish, meat, asparagus, sweetbreads, quail, duck, terrapin, and ice cream. Extravagant pyramids of iced fruits, oranges, and "French kisses" adorned the table. Five different wines were offered, each poured into a fresh glass. After dinner, women adjourned to the parlor for coffee. Men gathered in the study to bond over Cuban cigars and liqueurs. Seward wanted to give his guests good cheer to strengthen the bonds of the people of his country, from the North and the South.

People were drawn to Seward. He was small in stature and stooped after years of sitting at a desk. He was no dandy. His clothes were disheveled, out-of-style, and perpetually smudged with cigar ashes. Yet he moved quickly like a young man, with elasticity, although, in 1857, he was fast approaching sixty. His voice was husky. He had gigantic and protruding ears. His nose was large and beaked, and his eyes, peeking out from under his gray, grizzly, bushy eyebrows, gave him the look of an inquisitive bird. Young Henry Adams longed to dye Seward's hair a bright crimson, paint his face an absurd green and his nose yellow, and then exhibit him as a parrot.

Having been away for most of July and August in Canada, Seward found, upon his return, that Kansas was still in turmoil. Although the majority of the Kansas settlers were opposed to slavery and in favor of joining the Union as a free state, that fall, (as previously mentioned) a group of proslavery forces (a bogus legislature) met in Lecompton, Kansas, and rigged a proslavery constitution, and applied to Congress for statehood. In December 1857, when Congress opened, President Buchanan, along with many other Democrats, backed the Lecompton Constitution and recommended the speedy admission of Kansas as a slave state. Lincoln called it "the most exquisite farce ever enacted."

Then, in a surprise move, Senator Stephen A. Douglas decided to oppose the Lecompton Constitution. He broke with President Buchanan, who had made a mockery of Douglas' doctrine of popular sovereignty. Douglas was upset that a small minority in Kansas had cheated and defrauded the majority by trickery. Douglas knew if he supported the Lecompton Constitution, he would be betraying his own doctrine, an action that would harm his 1858 reelection chances to the Senate. Douglas led the fight in the Senate against the Lecompton Constitution. Republicans were ecstatic, believing Douglas was getting ready to join their party. Lincoln, though, was wary. He thought Douglas was playing a trick to deceive Republicans. He said Douglas and his cronies were "like boys who have set a bird trap" and were now "watching to see if the birds are picking at the bait and likely to go under."

Frances Seward shared Lincoln's opinion. Henry had written to her that Douglas' break with Buchanan signaled that "the Administration and slave-power are broken." Frances knew that when she was not with her husband, his judgment was often skewed by his impulsive goodwill. On December 12, she wrote her husband:

> My dear Henry,
> I have many kind letters from you….
> I wish I could with your hopeful disposition see as much good in prospect from the change of course in Stephen A. Douglas as you do, or that I could as generously forget all that he had done heretofore—but I cannot—I have no faith now, in his adherence to any right principle any longer than he shall find it in his own interest to do so….I believe he would support slavery again tomorrow, if he thought that, the readiest way to attain the goal of his ambition….
> Your own
> Frances

Horace Greeley, the influential editor of the *New-York Tribune*, began collaborating with Douglas on ways to defeat the Kansas application for admission as a slave state. The *Tribune* had between 5,000 and 10,000 readers in Illinois. In the spring, Eastern Republicans praised Douglas for his heroism in opposing the Lecompton measure. Lincoln's law partner, Billy Herndon, made a trip to Washington and the Northeast and reported back to Lincoln that Eastern Republicans supported Douglas' reelection and that Greeley thought any Illinois Republicans who did not do so were fools. Lincoln had been favored as the Republican to oppose Douglas in the Senate race, but rumors surfaced that Lincoln was losing support. Herndon wrote Greeley:

> Douglas' abuse of us as Whigs—as Republicans—as men in society, and as individuals, has been so slanderous—dirty—low— long, and *continuous*, that we cannot soon forgive and *can never forget*.

Lincoln's friends, of which he had many, began to carefully plan for only the second time in American history to have a party's state convention, not the legislature, nominate a senatorial candidate. It signaled to Greeley and the other Eastern Republicans that they would never back the Democrat Stephen Arnold Douglas.

CHAPTER 65

John Brown Meets a Genuine Moses

I n late January and early February 1858, while Congress was battling over the admission of Kansas as a slave state under the bogus Lecompton Constitution, John Brown was hiding out at Frederick Douglass' house in Rochester. Having left his small army at Iowa, Brown spent the three weeks at Rochester perfecting his Virginia plan, pleading with Douglass to join him in an invasion to free the slaves and crush the Slave Power. He was also writing his own version of the U.S. Constitution to be used when all were free. Brown imagined that he could recruit 100,000 Black men to join him. Douglass tried to impress upon Brown the madness of his plans, the sureness of its failure, but Brown was not listening. He was manic and could talk of nothing but his plans, from sunup to sundown, and Douglass had his fill of it. Brown's contempt and hatred for the Slave Power had grown more intense, as he now blamed them for the death of one son and the insanity of another.

Brown acted like a desperado. For his correspondence, he used the alias "Nelson Hawkins." He wrote appeals to his benefactors for money. By now, this core group was composed of five Massachusetts men and one New Yorker. Subsidizing Brown's "great experiment" were Rev. Thomas Higginson, Dr. Samuel Howe, Rev. Theodore Parker, Franklin Sanborn, George Stearns, and Gerrit Smith, a group that came to be known as the "Secret Six." These outspoken and radical abolitionists, though largely pacifists, had given up hope of opposing slavery through Northern politicians. They saw Northern politicians blatantly conspiring with the Slave Power, which would go to any lengths to keep slavery in place and spread it all over the continent. The Secret Six were looking for a revolutionary and felt they had found him in John Brown. He had their individual and coordinated support. Higginson had grown impatient, though, interminably waiting for Brown to light a fire in Kansas and blow the sections apart. Sanborn found the combination of danger and heroism in Brown irresistible. Parker was taken with the famous Kansas chieftain. Whereas George Stearns was entranced with Captain Brown, his wife, Mary, was positively enchanted by him, on the edge of her chair as he regaled her and her son with a blow-by-blow account of his victory at Black Jack. Gerrit Smith and Samuel Howe were on board. Brown hypnotically kept them in his fold, manipulating them to fund—what amounted to—his private war against slavery, but what they believed was for the defense of Kansas. Brown always had his hand out for money.

After leaving Rochester, John Brown traveled to Peterboro to reveal his Virginia plan to Gerrit Smith and Franklin Sanborn and enlist their continued support. Keeping it vague, he explained his scheme to invade the South, gather hundreds of slaves, and establish for them a new state in the Blue Ridge Mountains. Such a project, he told them, might involve a raid on the Federal Arsenal at Harper's Ferry and a bloody battle with the government soldiers. Sanborn, the young idealist schoolteacher, predicted that the day was coming when, "[t]reason would not be treason much longer, but patriotism." Gerrit Smith, who had increasingly come to accept that bloodshed might be required to end slavery, requested that Brown spare him from the details of his approach.

Brown showed up in Boston, met with Parker, Howe, Stearns, and Higginson, and shared his plans. Arriving later at Syracuse, he teamed up with Black activist Jermaine Loguen and boarded a train for Canada. Gerrit Smith had paid their fare and had also sent with them twenty-five dollars in gold to give to Harriet Tubman, who lived at St. Catherines in Canada. They arrived there on April 7, 1858. Loguen found where Tubman lived and arranged for her to meet with John Brown. Tubman, after her 1849 escape from bondage in Maryland, had been compelled to move to Canada because, after the enactment of the 1850 Fugitive Slave Law, Philadelphia was no longer a safe haven for a runaway. From St. Catherines, she had arranged and carried out plans to get her family and loved ones to safety. To date, she had made eight forays into the South and, with the help of the Underground Railroad, had brought, at the risk of her own life, sixty slaves north to freedom.

Tubman did not feel safe visiting Brown in his hotel, so he came to her house on North Street, where she lived with her parents and other freedom seekers, some of whom were present when Brown pitched his plan to Tubman. Brown was the only white person in the room. All others were Black and had been slaves. Brown hoped to persuade Tubman to join his effort and to help him recruit some soldiers in Canada. Thirty to forty thousand Blacks lived in colonies and towns in Canada, many former fugitives from America.

Brown fixed his powerful and steely gaze on Tubman—some said he had "flashing eyes"—shaking her strong hand and saying, "The first I see is General Tubman." He repeated this ritual two more times. He wanted her to be his commander, appealing to her vanity by calling her "General." He told her of his plan for the guerrilla uprising. He guaranteed the success of his mission, saying that, after his first incursion South, the slaves would immediately rise up, abandon their bondage, and rally to his cause. He told the roomful of people about a convention he was holding in May in Chatham, Canada, where he was to present a new constitution to his followers. All should attend. When he left Tubman's home, he was convinced Harriet was on board with his plans. Referring to Harriet Tubman as a man, he wrote to John Jr. on April 8: "I am succeeding, to all appearance, beyond my expectations. Harriet Tubman hooked on his whole team at once."

Although seven of Tubman's acquaintances were among the thirty-four Black Canadians who joined the Iowa army of 12 at the Chatham convention, neither Tubman, Douglass, nor any of Brown's East Coast supporters attended. Harriet had her own missions—and due to Brown's visits—she had learned of a network of wealthy and generous abolitionists who might help fund her future slave rescues. Gerrit Smith sent her a letter of introduction to Franklin Sanborn, who seemed to know every reformer worth knowing in Boston and Concord. Harriet was planning another trip into the South and that required money. She had to get the last of her family out.

———

After gathering recruits at Chatham, Brown was ready to implement his plan. Hugh Forbes, his former drillmaster, however, forced a delay. In April, the disgruntled Forbes was in Washington, D.C., stirring up a hornet's nest. He paid a call to Dr. Gamaliel Bailey, editor of the *National Era*. Forbes told Bailey of Brown's scheme to free Southern slaves using guns supplied by the Massachusetts Kansas Aid Committee. Forbes was already sending angry letters to the Secret Six, threatening to expose Brown's illegal plan and their complicity should they not give him money. Having failed to wring money from the Secret Six, Forbes decided to take his story to a Washington journalist.

Bailey, a Republican and an anti-slavery proponent, wanted nothing to come about that would hinder the chances to elect an anti-slavery president in 1860. If Forbes publicly told this story—that Massachusetts leaders were funding slave insurrection plots—it could sink the rising Republican Party. Bailey immediately sent Forbes to Senator Seward. Forbes told Seward that John Brown was a "very bad man." Seward did not take the matter seriously.

A week later, Bailey contacted Republican Senator Henry Wilson from Massachusetts. Bailey told Wilson to write to Samuel Howe and others on the Massachusetts Aid Committee and tell them "to get those arms out of Brown's hands." Brown had a well-known reputation for violence. Wilson wrote Howe:

If they [the guns] should be used for other purposes [than Kansas defense], as rumor says they may be, it might be of disadvantage to the men who were induced to contribute to that very foolish movement.

Senator Wilson's letter to Dr. Howe panicked the Brown conspirators. On May 7, Smith wrote Sanborn:

I never was convinced of the wisdom of [Brown's] scheme….[I]t seems to me it would be madness to attempt to execute it…I write Brown this evening.

On May 18, Sanborn wrote Thomas Higginson:

Wilson as well as [Senator] Hale and Seward, and God knows how many more have heard about the plot from [Forbes]. To go on in the face of this is mere madness.

Right away, Dr. Howe wrote Senator Wilson that the matter had been handled properly, leading Wilson to assume that Brown no longer had control of the weapons, but this was not true. While the two hundred rifles had originally belonged to the state Kansas Committee, their ownership had been transferred to George Stearns in consideration of a debt. On his own responsibility, George Stearns then gave them to John Brown and verbally notified his fellow conspirators of this transaction. Remember also that Stearns had personally paid for the two hundred revolvers, also in Brown's possession. Senator Wilson was deceived.

The Secret Six, meeting in the Revere House in Boston, informed Brown by letter that he was to postpone any action until the danger from the Forbes disclosures had passed. Higginson and Howe had argued against this delay. Nevertheless, Brown was told to return to Kansas and reassociate himself with that conflict so as to discredit Forbes' story. To sweeten the deal, the Six agreed to raise $2,000 in the spring so Brown could resume his project. Furthermore, they requested that Brown no longer share details of his plan with the committee.

Brown was discouraged and cast blame on his sponsors, who had favored postponement, deriding them. In confidence, he told Higginson that they "were not men of action." He belittled Gerrit Smith, calling him a "timid man."

That same May, when Forbes was nosing about and the Secret Six were in a tight spot, conflict broke out anew in the southeastern part of the Kansas Territory. A proslavery band led by three Hamilton brothers from Georgia had taken eleven Free State men prisoners and fired upon them. Five of them fell dead, five were badly wounded, and one was unharmed. But they all fell and seemed to be dead, thinking this was the only way to escape more savage treatment.

This happened in Linn County and became known as the Marais des Cygnes Massacre. Northerners were horrified. John Greenleaf Whittier was inspired to write a poem on the murders, "Le Marais du Cygne." Verse one speaks of the blood-stained killing ground where the massacre occurred:

A blush as of roses
Where rose never grew!
Great drops on the bun-grass,
But not of the dew!
A taint in the sweet air

For wild bees to shun!
A stain that shall never
Bleach out in the sun!

Lane Rebel Augustus Wattles, who had settled in Moneka in Linn County with his wife, Cincinnati Sister, Susan Lowe Wattles, and their children, remembered that after the massacre, Capt. Hamilton and his men:

> gave out word that they were going to take all the settlers in Linn County and shoot them in the same way. We all assembled; some 200 men…on the [Missouri] line and detailed a company to stand guard all the time….
>
> [John] Brown came in at this time and wanted to know if he could be of any service in guarding the line. I told him that he could, and we should be very glad to have him. At my suggestion, a paper was drawn up, which Brown signed, and all the men who went into [Brown's] company to guard the line signed, stipulating that he should not go into Missouri….

Brown, going by the name of Shubel Morgan now and cultivating a long, white, shovel-shaped beard, had the fifteen volunteers of his military corps sign a contract in which they were bound to give obedience to the commander. Wattles continued:

> Brown went on to the claim where these murders had been committed…bought the claim, and fortified it, and gave out word that he was Old Brown; and that they could make as good a neighbor of him as they wanted, or as bad a one. He remained there a month or two…and these men passed out of the State of Missouri….All danger from them disappeared….Brown…was taken sick and came to my house and stayed, perhaps, two weeks.

John Brown wrote wife Mary that, while Augustus, Susan, and their four children had been "Angels of mercy," nursing him through yet another bout of advanced malaria, he remembered most fondly their eldest daughter, Sarah Grimké Wattles, 21. Meanwhile, on August 2, 1858, as Brown lay ill, Kansas voters, guarded by federal troops, defeated the bogus Lecompton Constitution by 11,300 to 1,788. This settled the matter of extending slavery into the territories for now; in time, Kansas would be a free state.

CHAPTER 66

Lincoln Throws His Hat
in the Ring

A t eight o'clock on the night of June 16, 1858, when John Brown was reestablishing himself in Bleeding Kansas, Abraham Lincoln was going to give a speech in Springfield, Illinois, to accept his party's nomination to run against Stephen A. Douglas in the fall Senate election. Douglas was his great rival. Lincoln had known "Dug" for two decades. Lincoln won Mary Todd from Douglas when he was Mary's suitor, and Lincoln wanted to beat him again.

Earlier that month, Lincoln sat in the audience, bristling, to hear Douglas distort the words of the preamble to the Declaration of Independence which read:

> We hold these truths to be self-evident, that all men are created equal, that they are endowed by their Creator with certain unalienable Rights, that among these are Life, Liberty and the pursuit of Happiness.

Douglas claimed the Founding Fathers had never intended for Black people to have these rights. Lincoln, deeply hostile to slavery, felt passionately that no majority—white people—should have the power to limit these fundamental rights of a minority. Rather, Douglas, the advocate of majority rule, said that when the founders spoke of equality, they meant equality among whites. Appealing to negrophobia, Douglas claimed that Blacks were not included in the Declaration, thus supporting the Dred Scott decision.

Even with the Marais des Cygnes fresh on people's minds, Douglas insisted that popular sovereignty—let the Kansas settlers decide to be a free or slave state—could still work. Lincoln said Douglas' popular sovereignty doctrine was "as thin as the homeopathic soup that was made by boiling the shadow of a pigeon that had starved to death."

Lincoln did not trust Douglas to preserve the Union. In Lincoln's opinion, Douglas was an utterly unprincipled person and had to be defeated. Lincoln would use his nomination acceptance speech to drive home that point, as some Republicans thought Douglas was a hero for going up against Buchanan, his own party leader, in opposing the Lecompton Compromise. Lincoln thought about his acceptance speech for two weeks, writing it in fits and starts, on scraps of paper and backs of envelopes, and then stuffing these bits inside his tall hat. In time, all those thoughts would float into place and find their way into an organized draft. Lincoln would then deliberate over it carefully, editing and rewriting passages, until it was just what he wanted to say. He would, of course, read it aloud to Billy Herndon and a few others. By the time he was to give the speech, though, he no longer needed to look at the manuscript. The words were fixed indelibly in his mind.

The night of his speech arrived. Following a summer downpour, the Republicans gathered in the statehouse. It was hot and muggy. Lincoln's audience, some twelve hundred sweating men, had rolled up their shirt sleeves to listen to their candidate. Lincoln opened with:

Mr. President and Gentlemen of the Convention.

If we could first know *where* we are, and *whither* (to what place) we are tending, we could then better judge *what* to do, and *how* to do it.

We are now far into the fifth year, since a policy [Kansas-Nebraska Act] was initiated, with the *avowed* object, and *confident* promise, of putting an end to slavery agitation.

Under the operation of that policy, that agitation has not only, *not ceased*, but has *constantly augmented*.

In *my* opinion, it *will* not cease, until a *crisis* shall have been reached, and passed.

'A house divided against itself cannot stand.'

I believe this government cannot endure, permanently half *slave* and half *free*.

I do not expect the Union to be *dissolved*—I do not expect the house to *fall*—but I do expect it will cease to be divided.

It will become *all* one thing or *all* the other.

Either the *opponents* of slavery, will arrest the further spread of it, and place it where the public mind shall rest in the belief that it is in the course of ultimate extinction; or its *advocates* will push it forward, till it shall become alike lawful in *all* the States, old as well as new—*North* as well as *South*.

Whereas the Republican party was strictly made up of Northerners, united by their determination to stop the extension of slavery, the Democratic Party was still a national party, boasting membership in both the North and the South. Northern Democrats were beholden to the Southern Democrats to garner enough votes to win national elections. Lincoln believed, as did Seward, that the Democrats conspired with the Slave Power in a dangerous plot to nationalize slavery. Their plot's First Act unfolded in 1854. That was when Democrats Stephen A. Douglas and President Franklin Pierce obliterated the 36° 30' line that had long separated the free North from the slave South and, thus, opened up the territories to slavery (Kansas-Nebraska Act). The Second Act occurred just months before the convention, when the Roger B. Taney Court, with the complicity of President James Buchanan, ruled that a ban on taking slave property into the territories was illegal (Dred Scott decision).

Lincoln believed these four men, Stephen Douglas and Franklin Pierce, James Buchanan and Roger Taney, were working in tandem, using a common blueprint. These four "carpenters," he believed, were building the United States into a slave house.

Lincoln posed a question. If a territory cannot exclude slavery, what about a state? Was a state allowed to exclude it? The Dred Scott decision left this an open question. The case of *Lemmon v. The People*, involving the right of a Virginia slaveholder to bring his slaves into the free state of New York while in transit to Texas, was working its way to the U.S. Supreme Court. While Lincoln was a well-informed lawyer, it took no genius to see which way the courts would rule on that. What was the Third Act of the carpenters? Lincoln saw it. Peering into the imaginary slave house, he spied an empty niche just aching to be filled:

> Put that and that together, and we have another little niche, which we may, ere long, see filled with another Supreme Court decision, declaring that the Constitution of the United States does not permit a state to exclude slavery from its limits.
>
> Such a decision is all that slavery now lacks of being alike lawful in all the States.
>
> Welcome, or unwelcome, such decision is probably coming, and will soon be upon us, unless the power of the present political dynasty shall be met and overthrown.
>
> We shall lie down pleasantly dreaming that the people of Missouri are on the verge of making their State free; and we shall awake to the reality, instead, that the Supreme Court has made Illinois a slave State.
>
> To meet and overthrow the power of that dynasty is the work now before all those who would prevent that consummation....

According to Herndon, the Republicans at the convention were ecstatic over Lincoln's speech, but some Republicans and Republican newspaper editors thought it too radical. The "house divided" statement was controversial, interpreted by some to indicate a threat by the Republicans to declare war upon the slave states. Lincoln denied such a thing but feared public disapproval would destroy his senatorial chances. In July, Douglas spoke before a huge outdoor audience in Chicago and, referring to Lincoln, who sat behind him, said he had advocated "boldly and clearly a war of sections." For the next six weeks, Lincoln trailed Douglas across the state, Douglas stumping for himself, which was not the custom. After Douglas spoke, Lincoln stood up and spoke. The *Illinois State Register* lampooned Lincoln for not attracting his own crowds. The Democratic *Chicago Times* suggested that Lincoln, a "poor, desperate creature," join one of the circuses touring through the state as they always drew big audiences.

Lincoln changed tactics, challenging Douglas to a series of debates. Douglas was the incumbent; he had nothing to gain by debating Lincoln. However, in refusing, Douglas might seem to be afraid of Lincoln. Douglas unhappily agreed to participate in seven debates, which started in the north-central part of Illinois at Ottawa on August 21 and ended in the south at Alton on October 15. The election was to be held on November 2, with neither the name of Lincoln nor Douglas, oddly enough, appearing on the ballot, as the state legislature majority would determine the winner.

Douglas told a newspaperman that he was aware that Lincoln was a formidable opponent: "I shall have my hands full. He is as honest as he is shrewd; and if I beat him, my victory will be hardly won."

In the early debates, Douglas, while hammering his policies, complimented Lincoln on his intelligence and abilities. Lincoln did not return the compliment. Lincoln could not manage to tell even a white lie. But seeing the opportunity to use humor with his audiences, Lincoln confessed that he was not used to such flattery.

Lincoln said: "I was rather like the Hoosier [a citizen of Indiana], with the gingerbread, when he said he reckoned he loved it better than any other man, and got less of it."

CHAPTER 67

Lincoln Explains His View on Equality

D ouglas, 45, missed no opportunity to paint Lincoln as a radical abolitionist hellbent on obliterating all distinctions between the races. The belief in white supremacy was deeply embedded in the country, even among the leaders in the anti-slavery movement. No politician who professed a belief in social or political equality of Blacks and whites could win in Illinois, where Black Laws prevented Blacks from voting, holding political office, testifying against whites, and serving as jurors.

At the first Douglas-Lincoln debate, Lincoln arrived in Ottawa on a special train seventeen cars long that carried his supporters. The debates were social occasions, with bands, floats, and marching militias. Douglas told the crowd that Lincoln's policies would "cover your prairies with black settlements...turn this beautiful state into a free negro colony." Douglas insisted that "this government of ours is founded on the white basis. It was made by the white man, for the benefit of the white man, and to be administered by white men."

Lincoln denied Douglas' charge that he intended to be a race-leveler:

> I will say here, while upon this subject, that I have no purpose, directly or indirectly, to interfere with the institution of slavery in the States where it exists. I believe I have no lawful right to

do so, and I have no inclination to do so. I have no purpose to introduce political and social equality between the white and the black races. There is a physical difference between the two, which, in my judgment, will probably forever forbid their living together upon the footing of perfect equality, and in as much as it becomes a necessity that there must be a difference, I, as well as Judge Douglas, am in favor of the race to which I belong having the superior position. I have never said anything to the contrary, but I hold that, notwithstanding all this, there is no reason in the world why the negro is not entitled to all the natural rights enumerated in the Declaration of Independence, the right to life, liberty, and the pursuit of happiness. [Loud cheers.] I hold that he is as much entitled to these as the white man. I agree with Judge Douglas he is not my equal in many respects-certainly not in color, perhaps not in moral or intellectual endowment. But in the right to eat the bread, without the leave of anybody else, which his own hand earns, he is my equal and the equal of Judge Douglas, and the equal of every living man. [Great applause]

At the fourth debate in Charleston, Illinois, on September 18, 1858, 12,000 people arrived to boost their candidates. Lincoln numbered many friends in this county, and some of his supporters spread a gigantic banner, eighty feet long, across the main street, with a painting of a Kentucky wagon pulled by oxen, with a caption that read, "Old Abe Thirty Years Ago." Charleston, though, was in the Southern part of Illinois where anti-Black feeling was strong. The Democrats had brought and hung their own banner. It showed a white man standing with a Black woman and a mulatto boy in the background. Its caption was "Negro Equality." Republicans found the Democrats' banner repugnant and tore it down before allowing the debate to begin.

Lincoln was the first to speak. Taking in the size of the enormous crowd, he began by requesting that the audience maintain silence while he was speaking so that all present could hear his remarks. Douglas had continued to accuse Lincoln of favoring race mixing and "Negro citizenship." Lincoln further explained his views on race:

> I will say then that I am not, nor ever have been, in favor of bringing about in any way the social and political equality of the white and black races, [applause]-that I am not nor ever have been in favor of making voters or jurors of negroes, nor of qualifying them to hold office, nor to intermarry with white people....I do not understand that because I do not want a negro woman for a slave I must necessarily want her for a wife. [Cheers and laughter.] My understanding is that I can just let her alone....
>
> I will add one further word, which is this: that I do not understand that there is any place where an alteration of the social and political relations of the negro and the white man can be made except in the State Legislature...and as Judge Douglas seems to be in constant horror that some such danger is rapidly approaching, I propose as the best means to prevent it that the Judge be kept at home and placed in the State Legislature to fight the measure. [Uproarious laughter and applause]

Even if voters could not attend the debates in person, the speeches were reported almost *verbatim* in newspapers across the country. In the last few debates, Douglas' energy began to flag and his voice was hoarse. His propensity for heavy drinking was taking its toll. On the contrary, Lincoln, four years older at 49, a teetotaler, thrived on the frenetic pace and stimulation of the campaign. Douglas relied heavily on repetitions of his previous speeches, while Lincoln gained fluency, speaking more freely and appearing fresh. In the hundred days before the election, Lincoln traveled more than 4,300 miles around Illinois—600 by carriage, 350 by boat, and 3,400 by train—and made sixty speeches. In contrast, Douglas usually moved from place to place in a private railroad car bedecked with flags. In the same period, Douglas covered 5,227 miles. Douglas was accompanied by a secretary, a reporter, a traveling band, and his beautiful second wife, Adèle Cutts, 22, a leading social doyenne of Washington, D.C.

Mary Lincoln, 39, was only able to attend one debate as she had charge of three sons in Springfield. Lincoln had no secretarial staff, no full-time assistants, and no grassroots organization but had attracted a solid core of deeply devoted foot soldiers and advisers. He was his own political manager. He planned strategy. He raised money. He influenced newspaper editors to run pro-Republican articles in newspapers large and small, in both German and English. He tried to further the divisions between Douglas and the National Democrats aligned with Buchanan.

Douglas came across as a polished and commanding statesman. He bowed gracefully when applauded. Lincoln did not know what to do with his long arms and legs and looked to some like a jackknife folding up when he bowed. However, attendance at rallies and picnics gave him endless opportunities to talk with voters about their concerns. He established an image of an honest and incorruptible man, wearing his everyday clothes when campaigning. Oftentimes, after Lincoln finished speaking, the crowd, so swept up by their candidate and all he stood for, surged forward, swept him up and lifted him on the shoulders of Republican men, who bore him through the street, preceded by a band, with Lincoln's long "legs dangling," and "his pantaloons pulled up so as to expose his underwear almost to his knees."

Although election day, November 2, was cold, wet, and raw, Illinois voters (all male and white) turned out in larger numbers than in the 1856 presidential election. Lincoln and some friends in the telegraph office awaited the election returns. Although the Republicans had won the popular vote, the Democrats retained control of the state legislature, thus ensuring Douglas' return to the U.S. Senate. When asked how he felt about the election, Lincoln told a client that he felt like "the boy who stumped his toe. I am too big to cry and too badly hurt to laugh."

Nevertheless, Lincoln was cheered that he had won the vote of the people and that the debates had given him "a hearing on the great and durable question of the age, which I could have had in no other way; and though I now sink out of view, and shall be forgotten, I believe I have made some marks which will tell for the cause of civil liberty long after I am gone."

Lincoln returned to his law practice, yet soon discovered he was not only in great demand on the circuit but as a political speaker across the nation. As the *New York Times* observed, Illinois in 1858 was "the most interesting political battle-ground in the Union," and people throughout the land had read the speeches made by Lincoln and Douglas. Lincoln achieved a national platform. He forged alliances with prominent Republicans. His courtship of the National Democrats kept Douglas from winning a clear majority. Although Eastern Republicans stayed out of his campaign, Ohio Governor Chase was not beguiled by Douglas and had gone to Illinois to stump for Lincoln and spoke to thousands on his behalf. Lincoln valued Chase's sacrifice.

A few Illinois newspapers began mentioning Lincoln as a possible presidential nominee in 1860. On April 16, 1859, he replied to the editor of the *Rock Island Register*, who wanted to call on other editors to make a simultaneous announcement of Lincoln's name for the presidency:

> I certainly am flattered, and gratified, that some partial friends think of me in that connection; but…I must, in candor, say I do not think myself fit for the Presidency.

While Lincoln did not have the usual qualifications for high office—he had served only one two-year term in the U.S. Congress—Lincoln had the ability, just not the experience of a career politician in administrative matters. Presidents Buchanan and Pierce were both career politicians, and look at the turmoil they brought to the people—Pierce gave them the never-ending saga of Bleeding Kansas, and Buchanan was allowing slavery to plant itself anywhere. Lincoln was ambitious and wife Mary even more so, having told many people in her youth that she expected to marry someone who would one day be president. Although Lincoln wanted to be president, he was canny. The Republican coalition formed by the union of Whigs and Know-Nothings and Liberty Party men was fragile and needed careful tending. Whatever moves he made to boost his national reach, he had to do so quietly. No use showing his cards now and letting the opposition form against him. He contacted newspapers to send him the clippings from the 1858 Senate debate speeches. He made a scrapbook.

As a result of his 1858 reelection to the Senate, Stephen Douglas was the favorite for the Democratic nomination in the 1860 presidential election. However, his power was solely concentrated in the North; he had alienated even more Southerners who learned of a harebrained proposal he concocted for his Freeport debate in which he outlined how citizens could keep slavery from a territory. Douglas would regret this refutation of the Dred Scott decision. At the start of the 36th Congress, Buchanan and his allies retaliated by removing Douglas as chairman of the Committee on Territories.

CHAPTER 68

Frances Seward Expands Her Mission

I n Auburn, New York, Frances Seward was one of many agents ferrying fugitives north along the Underground Railroad. Another agent was her great friend, Martha Coffin Wright, the sister of Lucretia Coffin Mott. Frances and Martha had met through their husbands, who were once law partners in Auburn. Martha's abolitionist activities were well-known locally and marked her, socially, as a dangerous woman. In 1854, it became known that Frederick Douglass, also a conductor on the UGGR in Rochester, New York, had been an overnight guest in Martha's home. Shortly after his departure, Martha attended a local bridal party, where she was asked "with the slightest possible sneer after our recent guests." Her interrogator asked if she had given Douglass the best room, to which Martha replied, "Certainly, in conversing with a man of superior intellect one forgot whether he was black or white."

Frances Seward, though, could not be as brazen as Martha in her associations with the UGGR and in her efforts to undermine slavery. Disobeying the Fugitive Slave Act was disobeying the Constitution. It was 1859 and William Henry Seward had high hopes that he would be chosen as the Republican Party's 1860 presidential nominee. Frances found the job as Henry's Washington hostess—writing and dropping off invitations, designing menus, planning flower arrangements, managing the servants, and chitchatting with Southerners like Senator Jefferson and Varina Davis of Mississippi, slaveholders, whose views she did not share—onerous, exhausting, meaningless, and demeaning. Frances estimated that dressing and socializing ate up two-thirds of upper-class white women's time, reducing them to a shallowness. After thirty-five years of marriage, Frances, 53, wanted out from under Henry's thumb. She longed to make her voice heard. In 1857, when hostile neighbors in Washington, D.C. had tried to force Myrtilla Miner to relocate her School for Colored Girls, Reverend Samuel May asked Frances to write a public tribute to Myrtilla Miner and to sign her name, signaling her support. Henry had forbidden her to do this. Henry thought it enough that she quietly supported Miner with supplies and funds. Henry feared that if Frances was known as a supporter of Black education, he would be labeled a "Black Republican," a label that could damage his political future. Because he was a public figure, Frances, by extension, was one, too.

By February 1859, though, Frances was ready to come out from under Henry's control. She watched as her friend, Martha Wright, came out of the shadows and joined the woman's movement. Frances wanted to be more daring, though she would never join the woman's movement. Frances informed Henry that she would no longer be serving as his Washington hostess. He balked at this but she stood her ground. Son Fred's wife, Anna, graciously stepped in and took over. Frances felt no regret for her actions, just relief. Besides being unfulfilled, Frances suffered from depression. It seemed Henry was often away or had more important things to do than spend time with her.

When Frances' father died in 1851, he bequeathed Frances their Miller family Auburn home and much of the property he had bought up around town, leaving the rest of the inheritance to her sister, Lazette Worden, also an abolitionist. The Miller House became the Seward House. Thanks to the New York Married Women's Property Act of 1848, the first U.S. law that allowed women to hold property separate from their husbands, Frances, not Henry, retained ownership of the estate. Through her tireless lobbying of the state legislature, Elizabeth Cady Stanton was largely responsible for this state reform.

Since Judge Miller's death, Frances and Henry had been building frame houses on the lots she owned and selling them cheaply to immigrant and Black families. If a Black man wanted to vote in New York, he was required to own at least $250 worth of property, and this measure by the Sewards moved more Black men toward full citizenship. Frances formed allegiances in the Black community of Auburn, helping people who needed jobs, education, and money.

Through Gerrit Smith and Lucretia Mott, Frances and Martha befriended Harriet Tubman. Harriet's parents were finding Canada's bleak, frigid winters unbearable and Harriet was looking for another home for them. Seeing that Auburn was midway on Harriet Tubman's UGGR route through New York from Philadelphia to St. Catherines, Harriet desired to buy a home from Frances. Among the properties Frances had inherited was a plot of land perfect for Harriet's needs. It was about a mile from the Seward House on South Street, bordering the line with Fleming, New York. On the property were seven acres of farmland, a new frame house, a barn, and some outbuildings. Frances would have liked to make this all a gift, but Harriet insisted on paying for it. Frances' son Will drew up the contract. On May 25, the house was sold to Harriet for $1200. By the time Will wrote his father of the arrangement, Harriet had already made a payment of $225 and would pay off the balance in installments.

Between her trips to the Eastern Shore, Harriet took odd jobs and appeared in ladies' parlors to tell her story in order to raise money for her rescue operations. Harriet's family expected a great deal of her. She suffered greatly from debilitating spells from her head injury. On her journeys, she faced danger and was exposed to the elements for days, sometimes weeks, at a time. The lives she was rescuing were her responsibility. In this year, she planned to expand her connections in Massachusetts with the help of Franklin Sanborn and his network. Frances felt good that she could ease Harriet's burden by selling her a real home where her family and friends could live and could plant a vegetable garden, a fruit orchard, keep a milk cow, maybe raise some pigs, and keep chickens who would supply them with eggs. Frances felt she was making a big contribution to the abolition of slavery as Harriet was moving dozens from slavery to freedom in Canada. In doing so, Frances risked imprisonment and fines, as she was assisting not just a fugitive slave but a thief who "stole human property"—slaves. Harriet also risked discovery, as did the people in her home, who risked recapture.

When Harriet Tubman moved her brother John and her parents to Auburn, Senator Seward was not on hand to welcome them. On May 7, he left for an eight-month tour of Europe, Palestine, and Egypt. His closest political allies and manager, Thurlow Weed, thought it would be best for Seward to be away during the presidential campaign for fear he would say or do something that might jinx his nomination. At a recent state political rally, Seward had rashly delivered a speech in which he opined that a war between the South and the North was "irrepressible." When his words reached the newspapers, they inflamed the South. Alarm bells rang. Henry did not need Frances to endanger his reputation; he was quite capable of doing so on his own.

So, with good reason, in May 1859, a year before the nominating convention, Seward's cronies dispatched him from New York Harbor on the *Ariel* bound for Southampton, England. In Europe, he was fêted by Queen Victoria, King Victor Emmanuel of Italy, King Leopold I of Belgium, and Pope Pius IX, who all treated Seward as the heir apparent to the presidency. In France, he met up with Senator Charles Sumner, who, though still recuperating, planned on returning to the Senate by the start of the next session.

Back home in Auburn, Seward's daughter, fourteen-year-old Fanny, was dreadfully missing her father. While Fanny was close to her mother and modeled herself after Frances, it was her father she idolized. Fanny thought William Henry Seward was the greatest man alive.

CHAPTER 69

Gamaliel Bailey Sails Away

A week after Seward's departure, Dr. Gamaliel Bailey posted the following notice in the May 26, 1859 issue of the *National Era*:

To my readers.

It is my purpose to leave this week for Europe. I go from necessity, not choice, in quest of health....

The *Era* will be well cared for during my absence. It will continue to be what it has been, the stanch [sic] supporter of the Republican movement....

Unfortunately, Bailey left on bad terms with his old friend from Cincinnati, Governor Salmon Chase. Bailey had decided to back Seward for the 1860 Republican nomination election and not his old Cincinnati friend Chase. He informed Chase of his preference. With Chase back in Ohio and Senator Seward still in the capital city and a frequent guest in the Bailey home, Bailey clearly saw the contrast between the two favorites for the nomination. Seward was strong and Chase was weak. In mid-January 1859, Bailey wrote Chase and asked him to step aside from the presidential contest. Bailey acted in the best interest of the Republican Party's chance of capturing the White House in 1860.

Chase was furious. His head was turned by flattery and reports of his popularity. He felt entitled to the nomination. He rejected Bailey's reasoning, and the two had a major falling-out. Bailey was not a well man and was traveling on the advice of his wife and his physician. Earlier in the year, Bailey had pleaded with Chase for understanding, writing:

> When I tell you that I have not been to Congress once this winter—that I have not walked out of my house since the middle of December—that I avoid company & social intercourse as much as possible—and shall probably leave the country in April and to be gone till November—you will understand that my influence one way or another is of little account.

The prospects for the survival of the *Era*—and Dr. Bailey—were in doubt. Bailey hoped that an ocean voyage might restore him to health. His friends cobbled together the money to buy his passage and supplement his finances. He was looking forward to meeting up with Charles Sumner in Paris on June 12 and then proceeding with some friends to Italy. On the morning of May 26, 1859, Bailey and his son, Marcellus, boarded a train for New York City. Bailey had barely walked for months and this leg of the trip proved challenging. Bailey and son had to wire Washington for the passports they accidentally left behind. Two days later, they boarded the *Arago*. Also taking passage on the ship was Henry Raymond of the *New York Times*, who was shocked at Bailey's thin, pale, and feeble appearance. Bailey's personality, though, did not betray his suffering. He was cheerful and talked of politics. Dr. Bailey conveyed the idea that he was not seriously ill, his lungs were healthy, and that he had long suffered from dyspepsia and the nervousness brought about through his work. For the first two or three days, he was up on deck, where the weather was fresh and the sea air not too cold. The motion of the boat, though, soon drove him indoors to his cabin.

Although the sea soon became smooth, Bailey had no relief. His appetite and strength began to fade. He came down with a cold and had trouble breathing. The ship's doctor was sent for and others appeared. They tried to give Bailey a stimulant, but he could not swallow it. His breathing gradually slowed and then stopped. Raymond said that "[n]ot a movement of a muscle…betrayed the moment when his spirit took its departure."

Bailey's body was placed on ice and taken to Le Havre, France, to be then shipped back to New York. His obituary appeared in many newspapers. Here is a passage from Garrison's *Liberator*:

> The sad intelligence is received of the death of Dr. Gamaliel Bailey…so long identified with the Anti-Slavery struggle in this country—having been associated with the late James G. Birney, Esq., more than twenty years ago, in editing *The Philanthropist*, at Cincinnati, in the midst of fiery trial and at the imminent hazard of life. He afterwards became sole editor of that paper. Twice was his press thrown in to the Ohio river by a mob. He was a man of great kindness of heart, of true courage….

The June 23, 1859 issue of the *Baltimore Sun* wrote about Dr. Bailey's medical career, one he later swapped for journalism, a most providential career move, resulting in what was considered by many to have been Bailey's crowning achievement. As editor of the *National Era*, it was Bailey who had first given Harriet Beecher Stowe's story of "Uncle Tom's Cabin" to the world.

CHAPTER 70

John Brown Surfaces in the East

In May of 1859, John Brown was back in Boston, staying at the U.S. Hotel, needing more money, seeing friends, and finalizing his plans for his Virginia expedition. A year had elapsed since the Secret Six asked him to postpone the launch of his plan and return to Kansas. This was done to deflect any stories Hugh Forbes might have told the government about John Brown's Virginia plot.

During Brown's year-long stint in Kansas, he made it a point to publicly reassociate himself with the territory by engaging in the defense of the Free Staters on the border, all the while continuing to secretly plan and recruit for his covert raid in Virginia. In December 1858, Brown and his band went into Missouri and brought away eleven slaves, killing a slaveholder in the process. Brown's raiders seized livestock, food, bedding, clothing, boots, a wagon, and a shotgun, which Brown considered their "lawfully-acquired earnings." Pursued by a Missouri rabble, Brown traveled with his fugitives to Linn County, temporarily lodging this large group in the home of the Wattles family and then traveling with them to Canada.

It was common knowledge in Kansas that Brown had hidden out in the home of the Wattles. Settlers, even some Free Staters, petitioned Augustus Wattles to turn Brown over to the authorities. But Wattles refused—Brown was his friend. He did not agree with Brown's violent and lawless tactics; he urged Brown to see that his actions were imperiling the fragile peace. Wattles, nevertheless, was viewed as Brown's accomplice, and his name appeared on a list of settlers targeted for murder or expulsion by a vigilante group. A terrified Wattles—who was genuinely living in Kansas as a settler, not an agitator, went and saw Governor Samuel Medary, who put an end to the threat.

Because of his newest Missouri crime, Brown now traveled under the assumed name of Isaac Smith, as Governor Medary offered a $3,000 reward for his capture and President Buchanan offered $250.

Amos Lawrence saw Brown on May 28, recording in his journal that Brown "has been stealing negroes….He has a monomania on that subject, I think, and would be hanged if he were taken in a slave State….He and his companion both have the fever and the ague, somewhat, probably a righteous visitation for their fanaticism."

Three years earlier, Lawrence had hero-worshipped Brown as the pious "Miles Standish of Kansas," raising money among his gentlemen friends by personally vouching for Brown's good character. Since then, Lawrence had met with Brown a few more times and recognized the violence and volatility in him. Now he was a wanted man. Lawrence's support of him was waning. But the rest of Brown's supporters remained solid. Bronson Alcott of Concord heard Brown speak in May, writing later that Brown's newly acquired flowing, white beard, gave him a "soldierly air and the port of an apostle" and that "[o]ur people heard him with favor." While in the East, Brown met with five of the Secret Six frequently (Theodore Parker was out of the country, dying). Higginson had lost confidence in the committee and could not raise any more money among his Worcester friends, but he had not lost confidence in Brown.

Sanborn, Brown's faithful lackey from Concord, obtained $2,000 more from the Secret Six for Brown's plan to lead a servile insurrection in Virginia. Sanborn's school would not let him go to Canada, as per John Brown's request, to drum up some recruits from among the Black fugitives there. Given the year delay, the Canadian recruits had lost interest. Brown again met with Harriet Tubman, this time in Boston, in an effort to convince her to go to Canada for him, but

Tubman had just moved her parents from there to Auburn. Besides, she had her own plans to work out in Massachusetts. On June 3, John Brown unexpectedly appeared at the door of Connecticut toolmaker Charles Blair to put through the purchase of the thousand pikes. Blair was not interested in going on with the job, asking Brown, "What good can they be…; Kansas matters are all settled, and of what earthly use can they be to you now?"

Brown convinced Blair that he would dispose of them in some way and Blair agreed, for $450, to finish the weapons. Brown made more trips; on July 3, he rented the Kennedy Farmhouse, four miles north of Harper's Ferry, Virginia. At this base, Brown trained his twenty-one-man army and planned their capture of the Federal Arsenal at Harper's Ferry. He still wanted a Black person to go with him on his expedition and, in August, tried once more to interest Frederick Douglass in taking on this role. Douglass was convinced that Brown's plan was lunacy. He predicted the attack would be fatal to Brown's troops and fail in its prospects of freeing any slaves. Brown was proposing to attack the federal government which would arouse the whole nation against him. Brown did not heed Douglass' warnings. Brown believed capturing the Arsenal would serve as a trumpet call to rally the slaves to leave their bondage and come to his side. Douglass told Brown he was going into a "perfect steel trap, and that once in, he would never get out alive; that he would be surrounded at once, and escape would be impossible." But Brown would not listen to reason.

CHAPTER 71

Harriet Tubman Takes Curtain Calls

Whereas Frederick Douglass and Harriet Tubman were both formerly enslaved, Douglass' friends had purchased his freedom for him. Harriet, although self-emancipated, was still a fugitive and was, thus, illegally living in New York and in danger. There was a price on her head. She was also in the serious business of removing others from slavery on the UGGR, making her not just a runaway, in Southern eyes, but a thief. Traveling out of her comfort zone in Canada to now raise money in Massachusetts left her wide open to exposure, subject to arrest and a return to slavery. Therefore, she had to be cautious in all her dealings. One never knew who to trust, especially when money was involved. Besides, who would pay her Auburn mortgage and provide for her parents if she was abducted?

When Harriet arrived in Boston in May 1859, she bore letters of introduction from her friends in New York. She took a room at a boardinghouse at 168 Cambridge Street. Trusting that these letters would be delivered to the correct people, she handed them to messengers for delivery. Frank Sanborn, 27, received a letter addressed to him from Gerrit Smith and called upon Harriet at her boardinghouse. Sanborn wrote:

> It was curious to see the caution with which she received her
> visitor until she felt assured that there was no mistake. One of her

means of security was to carry with her the daguerreotypes of her friends and show them to each new person. If they recognized the likeness, then all was well.

With Sanborn's help, Harriet was introduced to many influential and helpful people in the Boston area. She found a lifelong benefactor in Boston reformer, Ednah May Cheney, who arranged receptions for Harriet in private and semi-public gatherings, where Harriet told her story and raised money. Harriet, humbly dressed in her homespun dress and kerchief, entranced the white audiences as she acted out scenes from her life. She was quite the entertainer. Cheney wrote that Harriet played all the parts, her voice and language changing with her different characters. She sang spirituals and quoted scripture. The audience thrilled to her first-person accounts of slavery and escape.

As word of Harriet's fame as a heroine spread, she became much in demand as a speaker and spoke boldly to larger and more public crowds. At the July 4, 1859 meeting of the Massachusetts Anti-Slavery Society, Unitarian minister Rev. Thomas Wentworth Higginson, one of the Secret Six, introduced her as a conductor on the Underground Railroad. During the months in Boston, she was able to raise $200 to pay toward her mortgage.

On August 1-2 in Boston, Harriet attended the New England Colored Citizen Convention. Many resolutions were made, as reported in *The Liberator*, among them this one regarding the deportation of freed slaves to Africa:

Whereas, from the year 1817, when the American Colonization Society was organized by slaveholders to get rid of the free people of color and superannuated slaves, the colored people of the United States have never ceased to denounce and protest against it, repelling the idea…that colored Americans are under any more obligations to emigrate to Africa than white Americans to return to the lands of their ancestors.

They spoke out against the colorphobia running rampant in the United States:

> Whereas, we are fully convinced that the prejudice against us is not on account of our condition alone, but that a deep-settled hostility exists against our complexion, and those who would be willing to extend the hand of sociality are intimidated by a corrupt public sentiment, that stigmatizes them as amalgamationists, therefore,
>
> Resolved, That, in our opinion, this prejudice pervades every grade and contaminates every portion of society….It is the barrier to our elevation…

To protect her identity, *Liberator* editor Garrison gave Harriet a pseudonym when he wrote a summary of her speech at the convention:

> Miss Harriet Garrison was introduced as one of the most successful conductors on the Underground Railroad. She denounced the colonization movement, and told the story of a man who sowed onions and garlic on his land to increase his dairy productions; but he soon found the butter was strong, and would not sell, and so he concluded to sow clover instead. But he soon found the wind had blown the onions and garlic all over his field.
>
> Just so, she said, the white people had got the 'n-----rs' here to do their drudgery, and now they were trying to root 'em out and send 'em to Africa. But, said she, they can't do it; we're rooted here, and they can't pull us up.
>
> She was much applauded.

CHAPTER 72

The Alarm is Sounded

A t 7:05 a.m. on Monday, October 17, 1859, a train conductor sent an urgent telegram to Baltimore from Monocacy, Maryland, to the Master of Transportation of the Baltimore & Ohio Railroad, W. Prescott Smith:

Express train bound east, under my charge, was stopped this morning at Harper's Ferry by armed abolitionists. They have possession of the bridge and the arms and armory of the United States. Myself and Baggage Master have been fired at, and Hayward [Shepherd], the colored porter, is wounded very severely….[The abolitionists] say they have come to free the slaves…

The leader of these men requested me to say to you that this is the last train that shall pass the bridge….if it is attempted, it will be at the peril of the lives of those having them in charge….[W]e were detained from half-past one o'clock to half-past six. It has been suggested you had better notify the Secretary of War at once. The telegraph wires are cut East and West of Harper's Ferry.

Two hours later, Smith finally replied to the conductor:

Your despatch [*sic*] is evidently exaggerated and written under excitement. Why should our trains be stopped by Abolitionists…. What is their object? Let me know at once before we proceed to extremities.

Smith was then notified by B. & O. Supervisor Alexander Diffey that a "body of armed men" had seized the armory and planted guns on the railway bridge. From Wheeling, a group of armed men were being sent to clear the bridge so the trains could pass. There was great excitement in Harper's Ferry. At 11:30 a.m., W.P. Smith reluctantly telegraphed his agent at Wheeling:

> Rioters have possession of Harper's Ferry Armory, and threaten our bridge and trains…. Matter is probably much exaggerated and we fear it may injure us if prematurely published…. Don't let our trains be interrupted, as troops have already gone to subdue it.

By then, the president of the B. & O. R.R. had received a communication that an insurrection was in progress at Harper's Ferry, "in which free negroes and whites are engaged." At 10:30 a.m., he notified Virginia Governor Henry A. Wise, President James Buchanan, and the Secretary of War, J.B. Floyd, of the dangerous events unfolding on the ground. He petitioned the Secretary of War to authorize government officers and military men from Washington to board an outbound express train that afternoon and hasten to the scene. Virginia Governor Wise called upon Virginia militia to report to him immediately at Harper's Ferry.

By 3:50 p.m., the B. & O. president believed the Black and white insurgents numbered seven hundred fifty and that they were taking slaves from their owners. They were engaged in fortifying their positions using weapons from the Arsenal, which was also in their possession. He informed Governor Wise of this new intelligence and that a detachment of marines was starting from Washington to be commanded by Colonel Robert E. Lee, assisted by cavalry officer J.E.B. Stuart of the U.S. Army.

The nation was startled when a telegraphic bulletin announced news of the riot. Rumors circulated that Captain John Brown of Kansas fame was the insurgents' leader.

Colonel Lee reported to Colonel S. Cooper, Adjutant-General U.S. Army, Washington City, D.C., the events of Tuesday, October 18:

As soon after daylight as the arrangements were made, Lieutenant J.E.B. Stewart…was dispatched, under a flag, with a written summon….Knowing the character of the leader of the insurgents, I did not expect it would be accepted. I had therefore directed that the volunteer troops, under their respective commanders, should be paraded on the lines assigned them outside the armory, and had prepared a storming party of twelve marines, under their commander, Lieutenant Green, and had placed them close to the engine-house and secure from its fire. Three marines were furnished with sledge-hammers to break in the doors, and the men were instructed how to distinguish our citizens from the insurgents; to attack with bayonets and not to injure the blacks detained in custody unless they resisted.

Lieutenant Stewart was also directed not to receive from the insurgents any counter propositions. If they accepted the terms offered, they must immediately deliver up their arms and release their prisoners. If they did not, he must, on leaving the engine-house, give me the signal….The summons, as I had anticipated, was rejected.

At the concerted signal, the storming party moved quickly to the door and commenced the attack. The fire-engines within the house had been placed by the besieged close to the doors. The doors were fastened by ropes, the spring of which prevented their being broken by the blows of the hammers. The men were, therefore, ordered to drop the hammers and, with a portion of the reserve, to use as a battering-ram a heavy ladder, with which they dashed in a part of the door and gave admittance to the storming party. The [gun]fire of the insurgents up to this time had been harmless. At the threshold one marine fell mortally wounded. The rest, led by Lieutenant Green and Major Russell, quickly ended the contest. The insurgents that resisted were bayoneted. Their leader, John Brown, was cut down by the sword of Lieutenant Green, and our citizens were protected by both officers and men. The whole was over in a few minutes.

The U.S. Marines storm the engine house at Harper's Ferry, from Frank Leslie's Illustrated Newspaper

After our citizens were liberated and the wounded cared for, Lieutenant-Colonel S.S. Mills, of the 53rd Maryland regiment, with the Baltimore Independent Greys, Lieutenant B.F. Simpson commanding, was sent on the Maryland side of the river to search for [insurgent] John G. Cook, and to bring in the arms, &c, belonging to the insurgent party, which were said to be deposited in a school-house....Subsequently, Lieutenant J.E.B. Stewart, with a party of marines, was dispatched to the Kennedy farm....
Colonel Mills saw nothing of Cook, but found the boxes of arms (Sharp's carbines and belt revolvers)....Lieutenant Stewart found also....a number of sword pikes, blankets, shoes, tents, and all the necessaries for a campaign....

[I]t appears that the party consisted of nineteen men—fourteen white and five black. That they were headed by John Brown, of some notoriety in Kansas...[who] avows that his object was the liberation of the slaves of Virginia, and of the whole South; and acknowledges that he has been disappointed in his expectations of aid from the black as well as white population, both in the Southern and Northern States. The blacks whom he forced from their homes in this neighborhood, as far as I could learn, gave him no voluntary assistance....

The result proves that the plan was the attempt of a fanatic or madman, which could only end in failure....I append a list of the insurgents....Cook is the only man known to have escaped. The other survivors of the expedition...I have delivered into the hands of the marshal of the western district of Virginia and the sheriff of Jefferson county. They were escorted to Charlestown by a detachment of marines....

The single great act of John Brown's life had been a catastrophe. Two more of his sons were dead, and he was lying wounded with sabre cuts around the head and in his breast, in a Southern jail, charged with treason and murder, facing a trial in a Virginia state court and hanging. No slaves had joined him as he launched a move to free them without ever notifying them that he was coming. After capturing the Armory and seizing the weapons, he had not scouted his escape route, and his men were, within thirty hours, trapped. He had not thought to bring food for his men or his hostages. In making their initial approach to the town on the railway bridge above the Potomac, one of his men had fired his gun, (fatally) wounding a free Black porter and making such a noise as to wake up Dr. Starry, who ran to the scene, discovered the dying porter, and spread the word of murderers in the vicinity. Surprised by the express train, Brown himself had stopped it, spoken with the conductor, then allowed it to proceed after a delay of several hours, which, of course, spread the alarm through the B. & O. telegraph. Was Brown purposely inviting a military confrontation? With four men back at the Kennedy farm, Brown and his ragtag army of eighteen had formed a pitiful force to fend off scores of militiamen who would quickly muster to the location from both Maryland and Virginia, much less a detachment of Marines. A whiff of fatalism can be detected in the lack of leadership on Brown's part to secure his objective or to protect his men.

Even stranger, around midnight on that first day, while the main body of Brown's group secured the Armory in the sleeping town of Harper's Ferry, Brown had sent out a six-man patrol four miles into the countryside on a weird errand. They went in the dark to the home of Lewis W. Washington, the great-grandnephew of President George Washington. Colonel Lewis Washington had a sword believed to have been given to General Washington by Frederick the Great of Prussia. The patrol captured Lewis Washington, his sword, and his human enslaved property.

Washington handed the sword to one of the raiders, Osborne P. Anderson, a free Black man who had learned of Brown's revolution at the Chatham meeting. Anderson recalled the events of Monday, October 17 as:

> a time of stirring and exciting events. In consequence of the movements of the night before, we were prepared for commotion and tumult, but certainly not for more than we beheld around us. …[D]aylight revealed great confusion, and as the sun arose, the panic spread like wild-fire. Men, women and children could be seen leaving their homes in every direction; some seeking refuge among residents, and in quarters further away, others climbing up the hill-sides, and hurrying off in various directions, evidently impelled by a sudden fear, which was plainly visible in their countenances or in their movements.

During the raid, Anderson gathered up some of the slaves they had captured, stationed them around the engine-house to guard the white prisoners, and armed them with pikes. He gave Brown the sword. During the day, Anderson remembered: "Capt. Brown was all activity, though I could not help thinking that at times he appeared somewhat puzzled."

Anderson recalled the arrival of the first militia:

It was about twelve o'clock in the day when we were first attacked by the troops. Prior to that, Capt. Brown, in anticipation of further trouble, had girded to his side the famous sword taken from Col. Lewis Washington the night before, and with that memorable weapon, he commanded his men against General Washington's own State.

When the Captain received the news that the troops had entered the bridge from the Maryland side, he, with some of his men, went into the street, and sent a message to the Arsenal for us to come forth also. We hastened to the street as ordered, when he said: 'The troops are on the bridge, coming into town; we will give them a warm reception.' He then walked around amongst us, giving us words of encouragement, in this wise:--'Men! be cool! Don't waste your powder and shot! Take aim, and make every shot count!' 'The troops will look for us to retreat on their first appearance; be careful to shoot first.' Our men were well supplied with firearms, but Capt. Brown had no rifle at that time; his only weapon was the sword before mentioned.

By late afternoon, another militia group and a band of citizens forced Brown and his group into the engine house. But Osborne and Albert Hazlett were opposite the engine house in the Arsenal. The morning Brown was taken by Lee's troops, Osborne and Hazlett went out the back of the Arsenal, climbed over the wall, went up the railway, and made for the Kennedy Farm, which they found ransacked and deserted.

CHAPTER 73

The Secret Six React to the News

W hen the Secret Six learned of Brown's complete inability to strike a significant blow against slavery, what was their reaction? Were they sore to learn he had misrepresented his military leadership? If so, disappointment and anger were quickly replaced by fear. At the Kennedy Farm, Brown left volumes of letters implicating the Secret Six as coconspirators. That correspondence was now in the government's hands.

By October 19, Frederick Douglas left Rochester for England. On October 20, George Stearns, Samuel Howe, and Frank Sanborn went to Canada. Theodore Parker was dying of tuberculosis in Italy. Harriet Tubman vanished into St. Catherine's for a time. Gerrit Smith's family had him committed to the State Lunatic Asylum in Utica, New York. The director of the asylum felt that Smith's deteriorating mental condition was life-threatening to such a degree that Smith was heavily medicated. Higginson did not take refuge.

Upon learning that Brown, wounded, was in a Virginia jail, Lydia Maria Child's heart went out to him. Maria happened to be in Medford, Massachusetts, visiting her friend, Lucy Osgood. Child's niece was Mary Prescott Stearns, the wife of George Stearns of the Secret Six. Maria Child felt impelled to go nurse John Brown and asked her niece to accompany her. But Mary Stearns declined; she was overcome with worry. Her husband, who had given rifles, revolvers, and money to Brown, was on the run to Canada.

Lydia Maria Child wrote Governor Wise of Virginia:

I and all my large circle of abolition acquaintances were taken with surprise when news came of Capt. Brown's recent attempt nor do I know a single person who would have approved of it....But I and thousands of others feel a natural impulse of sympathy for a brave and suffering man....He needs a mother or a sister to dress his wounds and speak soothingly to him. Will you allow me to perform that mission of humanity?...

She also enclosed a personal note to Brown asking his permission to see him. Governor Wise replied that she was allowed to visit Brown, referring to Brown as someone who "whetted knives of butchery."

Maria was now more determined to go than ever. She scraped lint to bandage Brown's wounds, collected donations, and packed supplies. Additionally, she shot off a sixteen-page rebuttal to the governor's charge that abolition-prodding, as Wise implicated, had not driven Brown to Harper's Ferry. John Brown, however, refused to see Maria. His lawyer believed that a visit by a woman "would unman [Brown's] heroic determination."

Maria accepted Brown's decision, but the matter was far from over. Governor Wise gave the Child-Wise letters to Horace Greeley's hands who printed them in his *Tribune*. This gave rise to a political hullaballoo. Child was praised by some and condemned by others, most memorably in a letter from Maria J. C. Mason of Virginia. Mrs. Mason questioned Child's Christianity:

Do you read your Bible, Mrs. Child? If you do, read there, 'Woe unto you, hypocrites,' and take to yourself with two-fold damnation that terrible sentence; for rest assured, in the day of judgment it shall be more tolerable for those thus scathed by the awful denunciation of the Son of God, than for you. *You* would soothe with sisterly and motherly care the hoary-headed murderer of Harper's Ferry!

On she went flinging insults and scripture at Child, asking her if her sympathy would extend to a dying old negro, to alleviate his sufferings. Would she help [an enslaved] woman in labor?:

> Do you soften the pangs of maternity in those around you by all the care and comfort you can give? Did you ever sit up until 'wee hours' to complete a dress for a motherless child....? We do these and more for our [enslaved] servants....

To this and more, Child replied:

> To all the personal questions you ask me....It would be extremely difficult to find any woman in our villages who does not sew for the poor and watch with the sick whenever the occasion requires. We pay our domestics generous wages...a process better for their characters, as well as our own, than to receive their clothing for charity after being deprived of just payment for their labor. I have never known an instance where the 'pangs of maternity' did not meet with requisite assistance and here at the North, after we have helped the mothers, *we do not sell the babies.*

Maria then released the Mason-Child letters to Greeley. She had three hundred thousand hardbound copies of the Child-Wise-Mason letters printed up. They sold overnight.

Brown was hanged on December 2. The South uttered a sigh of relief, as no slave uprisings had occurred, buttressing their contention that their slaves were happy. In the North, bells tolled in memorial, prayer meetings were held, and black bunting was hung on buildings. Brown's eulogists admitted he was guilty of errors of judgment while also acknowledging the nobleness of his aims.

Southerners were outraged that so many Northerners considered Brown a martyr. This really rankled them and deepened the chasm between the two sections. This paroxysm of anger brought about a complete revolution in the South; even the steadiest of the conservatives spoke of dissolving the Union. Democrats and Southerners seized the opportunity to pin the Harper's Ferry riot on the Republicans, singling out Seward for particular condemnation, as they assumed he would be the 1860 presidential party's nominee. Two days after Brown's arrest, the Democratic newspaper, the *New York Daily Herald*, went so far as to accuse Seward, who was still in Europe, of supplying Brown's men with guns "thus beginning the 'irrepressible conflict' in which Mr. Seward alluded in his brutal and bloody Rochester manifesto...."

That so many millions of Yankees seemed to approve of John Brown was hard to understand. The Northerners were desperate for a solution. The section was tired of being pushed around by the Slave Power in its blatant attempts to make the United States a slave nation. Whatever had been Brown's folly, his death crystallized Northern unity. Garrison, a pacifist, did not approve of Brown's use of violence but acknowledged that John Brown had signaled a clear and decisive moment for abolitionists: "In firing his gun he has merely told us what time of the day it is. It is high noon, *thank God*."

Part VI

DEMOCRACY

(1859-1861)

As I would not be a slave, so I would not be a master. This expresses my idea of democracy. Whatever differs from this, to the extent of the difference, is no democracy.
—*Abraham Lincoln*

CHAPTER 74

Lincoln Does the Work

On the day John Brown was hanged, Senator Seward was writing his daughter Fanny a letter. He was in the Hague, Holland. He wrote that he had just come from a ride to Scheveningen. It was on that beach, he wrote, that in 1660, Charles II set sail to return to his native England. When Oliver Cromwell assumed power as Lord Protector of the Commonwealth of England, Scotland, and Ireland, Charles II had been exiled to Europe for nine years. But with the death of Cromwell and the resulting power vacuum, Charles II was invited to return and restore the monarchy. This story had special meaning for Seward. Like Charles II, he had been semi-exiled to Europe by Thurlow Weed. He was slated to return to his native heath by Christmas and, as head of the Republican Party, receive its nomination for the presidency, a post he believed he so richly deserved. He let his manager, Thurlow Weed, do all the dirty work of backroom dealing and fundraising to secure his victory.

While Seward visited beaches and strolled leisurely through Dutch museums, admiring oil paintings by Rembrandt, Abraham Lincoln was busily introducing himself to tens of thousands of Westerners in the States. From August to December 1859, he made nearly two dozen speeches in Iowa, Ohio, Wisconsin, Indiana, and Kansas. He did not speak as a presidential candidate but, ostensibly, as a spokesperson for the Republican cause. On the day of Brown's execution, Lincoln, accompanied by a local politician, left Elwood, Kansas, in a buggy and set out for Troy, Kansas, to give another lecture in the small town's courthouse. Overnight, the weather changed dramatically. A blizzard was raging across the open prairie.

On this frigid journey, Lincoln and his friend met up with a man driving a heavy, two-horse wagon also heading to Troy. He was bundled up in buffalo robes. Icicles hung from the stranger's heavy beard. Lincoln almost did not recognize him, his appearance was so changed. It was Henry Villard, the famous newspaper reporter. He had driven his wagon all the way from Denver, having been to the Colorado goldfields for the *Cincinnati Commercial*. Villard recalled the moment he saw Lincoln approaching:

> About thirty miles from St. Joseph an extraordinary incident occurred. A buggy with two occupants was coming toward us over the open prairie. As it approached, I thought I recognized one of them, and, sure enough, it turned out to be no less a person than Abraham Lincoln! I stopped the wagon, called him by name, and jumped off to shake hands....
>
> It was a cold morning, and the wind blew cuttingly from the northwest. [Lincoln] was shivering in the open buggy, without even a roof over it, in a short overcoat, and without any covering for his legs. I offered him one of my buffalo robes, which he gracefully accepted....After ten minutes' chat, we separated.

Villard and his traveling companion, A. Carter Wilder, joined the Lincoln party at the Troy courthouse, where forty people had assembled for the lecture. Another journalist, Albert D. Richardson, was part of the crowd. When Lincoln began to speak, Richardson was unimpressed and wondered why the people of Illinois thought Lincoln was such a great man. After ten or fifteen minutes of listening to Lincoln speak, however, Richardson admitted to having become "irresistibly drawn by the clearness and closeness of his argument."

At Troy and Leavenworth the following day, Lincoln gave his opinion of John Brown and the Harper's Ferry incident. He said:

"Old John Brown has just been executed for treason against a state. We cannot object, even though he agreed with us in thinking slavery wrong. That cannot excuse violence, bloodshed, and treason."

He spoke directly to the Southern secessionists, who threatened disunion should a Republican be elected to the presidency in the fall:

> So, if constitutionally we elect a President, and therefore you undertake to destroy the Union, *it will be our duty to deal with you as old John Brown has been dealt with*. We shall try to do our duty. We hope and believe that in no section with a majority so act as to render such extreme measures necessary.

In a second speech at Leavenworth, Lincoln said the attempt by Democrats to identify the Republican party with the John Brown business was an electioneering dodge. Lincoln believed John Brown was insane and did not know of any Republican who endorsed John Brown's plan.

By mid-December, Abraham Lincoln was back home in Springfield with Mary and the boys. Although Lincoln had been well-received in Kansas, he was under no illusions—the Republicans there were solidly behind Seward and had floated Lincoln's name solely as Seward's vice president. Nevertheless, Lincoln had seen some encouraging signs that his presidential candidacy was not the long shot it had once been. Some Ohio Republicans had become aware of Lincoln's scrapbook collection of the Lincoln-Douglas debate speeches and desired to have them published in book form to encourage wider circulation of Lincoln's ideas. Lincoln gratefully consented. Responding to a request from the *Chester County* (Pennsylvania) *Times*, Lincoln prepared an autobiographical sketch to be used in an article about him. Enclosing the sketch in a letter to Pennsylvanian Jesse Fell, Lincoln remarked, "There is not much of it, for the reason, I suppose, that there is not much of me."

Lincoln wrote that he had grown up in the Indiana woods, a wild region with many bears. The little bit of formal education he received had taught him only to "read, write, and cipher to the Rule of Three." He did farm work until the age of twenty-two. He wrote of his proud time as captain of the volunteers in the Black Hawk War, his stints in the Illinois and the U.S. legislatures, his law practice, and his long affinity with the Whig Party—Lincoln was a party man. He closed with a reminder that it was the 1854 repeal of the Missouri Compromise that revived his interest in politics. He ended the four-paragraph essay with a physical description of himself:

> I am, in height, six feet, four inches, nearly; lean in flesh, weighing on an average one hundred and eighty pounds; dark complexion, with coarse black hair, and grey eyes—no other marks or brands recollected.

That December 1859, Norman Judd, a railway lawyer, was traveling to New York for a meeting of the Republican National Committee. The men were gathering in order to select the site for the 1860 Republican convention. Illinois loyalists wanted Chicago, the fastest-growing city in the country, to be selected. Lincoln nudged Judd to promote Chicago for the May convention. Lincoln had not announced his interest in the presidency and Judd would not reveal it at the meeting. As expected, loyalists for the leading contenders for the nomination lobbied for a city favorable to their candidate. Seward's men argued for the selection of Buffalo. In Ohio, three men, including Salmon Chase, aspired to the presidency; their Ohio representatives lobbied for Cleveland or Columbus as the convention site. Simon Cameron's advisors made a case for Harrisburg, Pennsylvania. Edward Bates' partisans from Missouri put forth St. Louis as the best choice. No agreement could be reached. It was then that Norman Judd put forward Chicago as "good neutral ground where everyone would have an even chance." The choice came down to selecting St.

Louis or Chicago. Judd promised that Chicago would be able to accommodate the needs of a large crowd and would provide a meeting place for deliberation free of charge. A vote was taken: Chicago beat St. Louis by one vote.

Having landed the deal, Judd used his contacts to arrange for the railroad companies to provide "a cheap excursion rate from all parts of the state" so Illinoisians short on funds could attend the Chicago convention in force to rally for Lincoln. Additionally, Judd would arrange the seating at the May convention to favor his man. He would put the New York delegation at one end of the massive hall and the Pennsylvania group at the other end. With Lincoln supporters in the middle, the New Yorkers and Pennsylvanians would be physically hard-pressed to wheel and deal with one another during the intense balloting sure to come.

While Lincoln had become a household name in the Midwest, he was still relatively unknown in the East. He would work to change that. On Saturday, February 25, 1860, he arrived in New York City. He had been invited to speak as part of a lecture series in Brooklyn. The organizers of this event were looking for an alternative to Seward for the Republican nomination. Chase, too, had been invited but had strangely declined. Lincoln's long journey—from Springfield to New York, four trains, a three-day journey—had worn him out; his clothes were travel-stained, and he looked exhausted when he arrived at the office of Henry Bowen, editor of the *New York Independent*, who had arranged the event. Lincoln stretched out his long legs on Bowen's couch as Bowen detailed Monday's itinerary. After checking in at the Astor House, he received some visitors. The next day was a Sunday. He took the two-cent ferry to Brooklyn to attend Beecher's Plymouth Church with Bowen.

On Monday afternoon, February 27, 1860, before Lincoln was to give his Cooper Union speech that evening, Lincoln showed up at Mathew Brady's photographic studio on Broadway to have his picture made. This three-quarter-length portrait of Lincoln, 51, clean-shaven, wearing his brand-new $100 black suit, standing straight and tall before a faux pillar, the fingers of his left hand spread over a small stack of books, would be reproduced in engravings and lithographs in the Northeast and would be the first image many would see of "Honest Old Abe, the Giant Killer." This portrait of a dignified and strong Lincoln would not only grace the cover of the printed copies of Lincoln's Cooper Union speech but be printed on little photographic cards for sale called *cartes de visite* to be placed in family albums, collected, placed on the mantelpiece, given as gifts, and exchanged with friends.

Abraham Lincoln photographed by Mathew Brady, New York (1860)

The wind was mounting and snow was falling when Lincoln arrived at the redbrick Cooper Union on Seventh Street in New York

City. Shortly before eight o'clock, the 1,800 seats in the basement auditorium began to fill, ultimately filling three-quarters of the hall with an audience of elite Easterners, ladies and gentlemen. Sharing the stage with Lincoln were many prominent and distinguished New York Republicans: a lawyer, three newspaper editors, a publisher, and a former governor. These men and others opposed Seward's candidacy, many because they resented his past scheme to form an alliance of the Republicans with Stephen Douglas. Horace Greeley of the *Tribune*, the most important Republican newspaper in the country, was seated on the platform that night and wanted to hear what this "Westerner" had to say. Greeley was bitter enemies with Thurlow Weed and Seward.

The *New York Evening Post* editor, William Cullen Bryant, introduced Lincoln as "a gallant soldier of the political campaign of 1858." Lincoln rose to speak, asking:

> Who were our fathers that framed the Constitution? I suppose the 'thirty-nine' who signed the original instrument may be fairly called our fathers who framed that part of the present Government.

Lincoln began hesitantly, losing his place at first but then getting his bearings and speaking in his high-pitched Indiana twang. He posed the question that had steered his months of meticulous research:

> Does the proper division of local from federal authority, or anything in the Constitution, forbid our Federal Government to control as to slavery in our Federal Territories?

Lincoln then methodically recited the voting records of these thirty-nine founding fathers to ascertain their opinions on the federal government's role in controlling slavery in the federal territories. He demonstrated that twenty-one of these men had consistently acted under the belief of the federal government's right to exercise power over slavery in the territories.

Lincoln then cleverly pivoted to the second part of his speech with the transitional, "But enough!" Now he stopped speaking to the North and imagined Southerners were listening to him—"if they would listen—as I suppose they will not." The audience, by now, was frequently bursting into applause, laughter, and cheers.

He answered the Southerners' repeated accusations that Republicans stir up insurrections among their slaves.

> We deny it; and what is your proof? Harper's Ferry? John Brown!! John Brown was no Republican; and you have failed to implicate a single Republican in his Harper's Ferry enterprise.
>
> John Brown's effort was peculiar. It was not a slave insurrection. It was an attempt by white men to get up a revolt among slaves, in which the slaves refused to participate. In fact, it was so absurd that the slaves, with all their ignorance, saw plainly enough it could not succeed.

Still speaking as if to Southerners, he took them to task for their loose talk of secession should a Republican be elected to the presidency.

> But you will not abide the election of a Republican president! In that supposed event, you say you will destroy the Union; and then, you say the great crime of having destroyed it will be upon us. That is cool.

Lincoln said that was like a highway robber holding a pistol to his ear, muttering: "Stand and deliver, or I shall kill you, and then you will be the murderer!" This was followed by continued laughter. He said this is how the South manipulated the North by threatening to break up the Union and thus keep the North voting their way.

In the third and final part of his speech, Lincoln addressed fellow Republicans, asking them to keep their tempers despite the provocations of the Southern people. He asked what would satisfy the Slave Power:

> Will they be satisfied if the Territories be unconditionally surrendered to them? We know they will not. In all their present complaints against us, the Territories are scarcely mentioned. Invasions and insurrections are the rage now….[W]e never had anything to do with invasions and insurrections; and yet this total abstaining does not exempt us from the charge….
>
> The question recurs, what will satisfy them? Simply this: We must not only let them alone [not touch slavery in Southern states], but we must somehow, convince them that we do let them alone. This, we know by experience, is no easy task. We have been so trying to convince them from the very beginning of our organization, but with no success….
>
> [W]hat will convince them? This, and this only: cease to call slavery wrong, and join them in calling it right….
>
> [T]hey have not, as yet, in terms, demanded the overthrow of our Free-State Constitutions. Yet those Constitutions declare the wrong of slavery…and when all these other sayings shall have been silenced, the overthrow of these Constitutions will be demanded….Holding, as they do, that slavery is morally right, and socially elevating, they cannot cease to demand a full national recognition of it…

He called upon all Republicans to stand by his or her duty fearlessly and effectively.

> Neither let us be slandered from our duty by false accusations against us, not frightened from it by menaces of destruction to the Government nor of dungeons to ourselves."

Great applause erupted. He closed with a flourish:

Let us have faith that right makes might, and in that faith, let us, to the end, dare to do our duty as we understand it.

Lincoln bowed and then retired to his seat amid "the loud and uproarious applause of his hearers—nearly every man rising spontaneously, and cheering with the full power of their lungs," reported the *New York Daily Herald*. Women waved handkerchiefs and men their hats, cheering. Greeley came forward to the podium and spoke of Lincoln as "my eloquent Western friend," which brought more applause. Noah Brooks, writing for the *New-York Tribune*, heard an audience member exclaim, "He's the greatest man since St. Paul."

The next day, the *Herald* and three other New York papers printed Lincoln's speech in full. Lincoln had spoken in Seward's home state. He had been invited to speak by a man partial to Chase. He had made a sound argument that the Republican Party was moderate and in keeping with the thinking of the majority of the Founding Fathers. For an unannounced presidential hopeful who had not yet established any network among the Republican bigwigs in the East, Lincoln had shown himself to be surprisingly statesmanlike and, perhaps more importantly, possibly electable. His Cooper Union speech was immediately printed and distributed in newspapers and pamphlets.

Lincoln was invited to make a speaking tour through New England. He eagerly accepted, and it also gave him an opportunity to visit his son, "Bob," who was spending a preparatory year at Phillips Exeter Academy in New Hampshire. Bob, 16, had been painfully humiliated by being denied admission to Harvard, having failed fifteen out of sixteen of his entrance exams.

Two days after Lincoln made his landmark speech in New York, a new and improved Seward was back from Europe, making a rival speech on the Senate floor. Gone now was the inflammatory phrase of an "irrepressible conflict." Seward now referred softly to the slave states as "capital states" and the free states as "labor states." Positioning himself as a president who could keep the Union intact, he spoke of North and South being bonded together as "the millions of fibers of millions of contented, happy human hearts," linked by their love for democratic government. It was a remarkable fantasy. The South was in a state of hysteria. Militias were being rapidly formed in both sections.

When Seward finished speaking, deafening applause rocked the galleries. Praise was widespread in the press, but many of his supporters were shocked at Seward's new, conciliatory tone. It was quite a political swerve. As governor of New York, he had extended Black suffrage—a radical move. He personally disobeyed the Fugitive Slave Law. His friend, Charles Sumner, back at his Senate desk once again, wrote to a friend that while Seward's speech was eminent, there was one passage he regretted, perhaps the one in which Seward disclaimed his intention to support equality for Black people. Frances Seward, too, was disappointed. The abolitionist Cassius Clay said that this speech "killed Seward with me forever." Frederick Douglass, however, wrote in his monthly paper that the speech was "a masterly and triumphant effort. It will reassure the timid wing of the party, which has rendered a little nervous by recent clamors against him." Douglass considered Seward "the ablest man of his party" and "as a matter of party justice," entitled to the nomination.

Seward, so confident that he had the Republican presidential nomination sewed up, had Henry B. Stanton write up the speech for the *New-York Tribune* and the scene in the Senate when it was delivered, telling his friend that with his speech, the both of them would "go down to posterity together."

———

When the Thirty-Sixth Congress met in December 1859, the first step taken in the Senate was the appointment of a committee to investigate and report upon the events at Harper's Ferry. The chairman was James Mason of Virginia. Witnesses were summoned, and daily interviews were conducted. After John Brown's hanging, the Canadian exiles—Stearns, Howe, and Sanborn—returned to Massachusetts. Howe and Stearns did go to Washington to testify. Higginson was never summoned nor was Gerrit Smith, out of regard for his infirm health. Theodore Parker was dying. Sanborn refused the January 16, 1860, hand-delivered summons to appear in Washington on January 24.

CHAPTER 75

The Parties Choose
Their Presidential Candidates

The Democratic Party was in disarray. Meeting in Charleston the last week of April 1860, they could neither agree on a platform nor a candidate. Ten days and fifty-seven ballots later, they reached a stalemate, disbanded on May 3, and agreed to come back together in six weeks in Baltimore.

When the Republicans arrived for their presidential convention in Chicago on May 16-18, Abraham Lincoln had the full backing of the Illinois delegation. Lincoln's advisors, chiefly Judge David Davis, lawyer Leonard Swett, and State Senator Norman Judd, would promote Lincoln's candidacy from the Fremont Hotel, five blocks from the new Chicago convention center dubbed the "Wigwam," a new, two-story wooden, barnlike structure built to accommodate over ten thousand Republican conventioneers. Abraham and Mary Lincoln remained in Springfield; it was unseemly for a politician to campaign for his own office.

Drawing of the Republicans in their Chicago Wigwam

Coming from the critical state of Illinois, Lincoln was a serious contender, though Chase of Ohio, Seward of New York, Edward Bates of Missouri, and Simon Cameron of Pennsylvania were better known in the party and the nation. Just the previous week, *Harper's Weekly* published a two-page spread illustrating the faces of the eleven most promising candidates. Front and center was the parrot-like face of Seward. In the bottom row, to the left, was the Mathew Brady headshot of Lincoln. Among the biographies that followed, Lincoln's figured last. However, in the critical state of Illinois, he received better treatment. Lincoln's operatives saw that the *Chicago Press and Tribune* kept up a blitz of pro-Lincoln editorials, starting on the day before the convention was called to order with an editorial titled "The Winning Man-Abraham Lincoln" listing eight reasons why he should be named and why he would win. Reason number V was that Lincoln, who had labored in the field, in the saw-mill, as a river boatman, soldier, student in a law office, overcoming "the defects of early training," made him "a man of the people," and would gain the vote from the men who toil.

While Lincoln was not widely known except in the West and did not have such a visible career as the others, he had not collected enemies, a distinct advantage. He was a moderate and did not challenge the Constitution, as Chase did in Ohio, trying to overturn the Fugitive Slave Law. Furthermore, Chase had alienated many influential people in Ohio when he compromised his anti-slavery values to work with the Democrats to gain his Senate seat. He did not go into the convention with the full support of the Ohio delegation. Seward, the acknowledged leader of the party, stood for Black suffrage when a governor and was considered, by the South, to be a rabid radical. Both Chase and Seward's names had come up in the Senate investigation of the Harper's Ferry incident, linking them, falsely, with the insurrectionist John Brown. Edward Bates, backed by Greeley, was not even a Republican and had an anti-immigrant record. Cameron was rumored to be corrupt and had no following outside Pennsylvania.

In the two days of wheeling and dealing, it became clear the Republicans needed a candidate who, in the November general election, could not only carry all the Northern states that had gone for Frémont in 1856 but win in Pennsylvania, Indiana, and Illinois. A rumor began to circulate that Republican gubernatorial candidates in those swing states would be fatally damaged should Seward be nominated and that they would resign. The Sewardites clung tightly, though, to "Old Irrepressible." In other quarters, though, Lincoln's star began to rise. He seemed electable. He was a moderate. He had managed to oppose the Know-Nothing party without rancor and actively courted the German-American vote. He was unequivocally against the extension of slavery.

Illinois had twenty-two delegates. Lincoln's manager, David Davis, sent out members of his team to talk with other state delegations, where he could secure at least one hundred votes on the first ballot for Lincoln, thus accruing more than any other candidate except Seward. He would get pledges of more than one hundred votes, holding off using the surplus in reserve for use in the second ballot, so it would appear that Lincoln was gaining strength. Additionally, Lincoln's men fanned out to pick off individual delegates so Seward would not sweep the field on the first ballot. One of Lincoln's surrogates, Leonard Swett, said, "I did not, the whole week I was there, sleep two hours a night." While some of Lincoln's men had their own political aspirations, most of them, it was observed, worked *con amore*—for love of Lincoln. While there was talk at this convention of horse trading between candidates and promises of future patronage, or even exchanges of cash for votes, Lincoln wanted no part of dirty dealing and sent a terse message to his team: "Make no contracts that will bind me."

Thurlow Weed's plan for a Seward victory was to bring more supporters to Chicago than any other candidate and, thus, carry the convention. He arrived in Chicago on a thirteen-car train filled with these Sewardites. Aware of Weed's plan to pack the Wigwam with Seward men the day of the voting, Lincoln partisans printed out duplicate tickets and gave them to Lincoln supporters who came early to occupy the seats and were primed to cheer for Lincoln. When the Seward faction arrived at the Wigwam on May 18, they were upset to find that many could not get into the crowded hall, as Lincoln troops had swarmed in ahead of them.

On the morning of the third day, after an intense and sleepless night of electioneering between the factions, the voting began. The first ballot showed Seward's weakness and Lincoln's strength. A candidate needed 233 votes for nomination. Seward polled 173 ½ and Lincoln earned 102. On the second ballot, Vermont, Pennsylvania, and scattered votes from other states, including Ohio, switched to Lincoln, giving him a total of 181 votes, with Seward still painfully short of the goal, at 184½.

During all this time, the Wigwam was teeming with excitement. Men and women jammed the first- and second-floor galleries, the women's bell-shaped hoopskirts taking up considerable space. Some sat, but others stood singly or in little knots, craning for a view past the top hats and bonnets of the platform where the speakers and the delegates sat. Lincoln's unexpected momentum created so much chatter, such commotion, that a reporter described the noise to be as if "all the hogs ever slaughtered in Cincinnati were giving their death squeals all at once."

The chairman announced that the convention would proceed to a third ballot. As the contest narrowed down, the crowd grew silent. Before the result was announced, David K. Cartter, the Ohio chairman, climbed onto his chair and announced with his characteristic stutter: "I arise, Mr. Chairman, to announce the change of four votes of Ohio from Mr. Chase to Abraham Lincoln."

This gave Lincoln the majority. This was an unforgettable moment for the forty thousand gathered in and around the Wigwam. The crowd broke out in enthusiastic and thunderous applause. Everyone in the hall rose to his or her feet, clapping madly, ladies waving their handkerchiefs, men waving and throwing up their hats by the thousands, cheering loudly and repeatedly; people were weeping. A cannon boomed from the roof and cheers erupted in the streets. When partial silence was restored, delegates from Massachusetts, Maine, Pennsylvania, etc., stood up to switch all their votes for Abraham Lincoln. A large photograph of Lincoln was carried onto the platform, greeted wildly by another outbreak of cheering and loud, rapturous applause by the audience. The president of the convention announced: "Abraham Lincoln, of Illinois, is selected as your candidate for President of the United States."

Hannibal Hamlin of Maine was nominated for Vice President. A man standing on the roof of the Wigwam shouted the news of Lincoln's nomination out into the crowd of thousands waiting in the street. Cannons were fired.

———

Seward was sitting in his Auburn garden, which overflowed with his admirers, when a rider on a fast horse approached bearing a telegram for him. It carried news of the first ballot. The guests and crowds gathered on his lawn sent up resounding cheers at this good omen. When Seward received news of his almost-tie on the second ballot, Seward announced to the multitude, "I shall be nominated on the next ballot." His optimism faded as the minutes, then hours, ticked by and no further news arrived. When he read the telegram announcing Lincoln's nomination, his face turned "as pale as ashes." The loaded cannon at the gate was rolled away, the flags were furled, and the sad throng departed. Daughter Fanny Seward wrote in her diary: "Father told Mother and I in three words, Abraham Lincoln nominated."

The editor of the local evening paper could find no one in the sad town of Auburn willing to write up the shocking news. Although angry, hurt, and humiliated, Seward took up his own pen, writing graciously of Lincoln and Hamlin:

> No truer or firmer defenders of the Republican faith could have been found in the Union than the distinguished and esteemed citizens on whom the honors of the nomination have fallen.

Seward's verdict on Lincoln's nomination was that the convention aimed to defeat him rather than elevate the relatively unknown Lincoln. While this could be true, it does not take into account the brilliant political strategy and acumen of Lincoln and his lieutenants, nor the popular appeal of Lincoln's impeccable character and consistent political stand on the issue of the day.

Chase was furious Ohio had not remained loyal to him. In a congratulatory letter to Lincoln, he could not refrain, even then, from licking his own wounds, confessing that the perceived disloyalty of the Ohio delegation brought him unbearable pain. He pleaded with Lincoln to condemn these Ohio delegates. Lincoln did not.

Where was Lincoln when cheers were heard from the telegraph office in Springfield, followed by a boy rushing through the crowds of people, shouting, "Mr. Lincoln, Mr. Lincoln, you are nominated"? There are many versions. Was he playing "fives" handball? Buying some items for Mary in a shop? Or was he at the *Illinois State Journal*, chewing the fat with friends when he received the scrap of paper announcing his victory? We do know that, upon learning the news, the first thing he did was rush home to tell Mary. The journalist John Hay reported that the townspeople of Springfield broke out into many expressions of joyful exultation. A hundred-gun salute was fired off. Lincoln banners fluttered from buildings. Church bells tolled. There were victory speeches at the Capitol. Happy crowds descended on the Lincoln's home, where all were received as guests.

By June, three more presidential candidates surfaced. The deadlocked Democratic party splintered. The Southern Democratic seceders nominated John C. Breckinridge of Kentucky on a proslavery platform. Stephen A. Douglas was chosen as the Democratic nominee from the Northern wing. Former Whigs and Know-Nothings, who did not expect to win, formed the spoiler Constitutional Union Party, putting forward John Bell as their candidate. Lincoln believed he would be elected, though he knew Douglas would still be a formidable opponent in the North.

CHAPTER 76

Lincoln Gets Ready

I t was soon apparent that Lincoln's white, two-story frame house in Springfield was wholly inadequate for all the tasks that beset him following his nomination. At home, his young sons, Tad, 7, and Willie, 10, were constantly underfoot. He hired a secretary, young German-American John Nicolay, to help him deal with the mass of correspondence besieging him. He gladly took up the offer to use the governor's room in the state house to receive the multitudes of job seekers, foreign diplomats, journalists, and others. Lincoln saw that his first task must be to secure party unity, and that particularly meant securing the cooperation of his rivals for the nomination: Chase, Seward, and Bates. Chase would stump for Lincoln in three states, but Bates declined, agreeing to pen a public letter of support. Seward, though, went all out for Lincoln, embarking on a grand tour of nine states with his fifteen-year-old daughter, Fanny, and her friend.

Meanwhile, Republicans mounted a fierce campaign to win the presidency. From June to November, party leaders delivered an estimated 50,000 speeches, while Lincoln remained silent, certain that any speech he gave at this point would be twisted by a hostile press, North and South, creating confusion and furor.

Lincoln had repeatedly stated that neither he nor his party had plans to dismantle slavery in the Southern states. They did not advocate racial parity. Nevertheless, immediately after Lincoln's nomination, the Southern press went on a rampage, stirring up Southern hysteria that a Republican presidency meant slaves poisoning their masters, Black men marrying white girls, and that Lincoln was pledged to the ultimate extinction of slavery. Lincoln was infuriated at the distortion of his views and record but held his tongue. As the election drew nearer, and Lincoln's victory seemed all but certain, Southern newspapers warned that:

The election of Abraham Lincoln means war upon the South.

On election day, Billy Herndon went to Lincoln's office to get his partner to go vote. Lincoln did not want to vote for himself but realized his votes in the state elections might help fellow Republicans, so he went with Herndon to the polls. He cut off the top portion of his ballot that listed the presidential electors and tossed it aside, casting his ballot only for those running for state posts. At the polls, he was cheered by the male voting crowds, Democrats and Republicans alike, raising their hats to see their favorite son moving among them.

After the polls closed, Lincoln joined with fellow Republicans who crowded the Capitol to hear the returns relayed from the telegraph office. In time, increasingly impatient to learn how the Eastern states had voted, Lincoln and a handful of friends migrated over to the telegraph office, where Lincoln reclined on a sofa. Early returns showed that the Lincoln/Hamlin ticket carried Illinois, Indiana, and other Western states, but it was not until ten o'clock that they learned of Republican victories in Pennsylvania. Awaiting news from New York, Lincoln and his cronies went over to Watson's Saloon, where Republican women were serving a meal. When Lincoln entered, the ladies greeted him with, "How do you do, Mr. President!" He remained at the telegraph office until he was sure his party had carried New York, making his election certain. Church bells were rung. Lincoln ran home to Mary with the final dispatch in his pocket, crying out,

"Mary, Mary, we are elected!" He did not crawl into bed until about two o'clock in the morning, exhausted but too excited to sleep.

The next night, the citizens of Charleston, South Carolina, held a torchlight parade at which two slaves lifted an effigy of Lincoln to a scaffold and, to the cheers of the whipped-up multitude, set the figure on fire.

In the final tally, the Republican ticket received 1,866,452 votes to 1,376,957 for Douglas, 849,781 for Breckenridge, and 588,879 for Bell. Lincoln and Hamlin won forty percent of the popular vote and 180 votes in the electoral college. Lincoln/Hamlin carried all but one of the free states, Douglas and Lincoln dividing the New Jersey votes. Lincoln/Hamlin received no votes in ten of the Southern states.

Four days later, the South Carolina legislature commissioned a December 6 convention to consider secession. Within a month, every state in the lower South followed South Carolina's lead.

Lincoln decided to grow a beard. He stayed up nights jotting down lists of names of men he might appoint to a cabinet position. He wanted Seward for secretary of state, Chase for treasury secretary, and Edward Bates for attorney general, and they accepted. Billy Herndon kept Lincoln abreast of secession talk in the Southern papers, but Lincoln did not believe Southern states would actually cut themselves off from the North.

On December 20, 1860, South Carolina seceded, followed six weeks later by Mississippi, Louisiana, Florida, Alabama, Georgia, and Texas. Lame Duck President Buchanan was taken aback. He blamed the North for the crisis and did nothing to quash the Southern rebellion. The garrison of three Union forts in Charleston Harbor was combined into one, Fort Sumter. Lincoln feared that the feckless Buchanan might surrender Sumter to keep the South in the Union. Frances Seward felt that her husband, William Henry Seward, had discredited himself in the Senate and the nation, perhaps permanently, when he pitched a plan to appease the South by admitting New Mexico as a slave state. She wrote him: "Compromises based on the idea that the preservation of the Union is more important than the liberty of nearly 4,000,000 human beings cannot be right."

Seward and other Northerners, worried about tumbling markets as Southern trade fell off, were scrambling to come up with stratagems to thwart Southern secession, mostly by offering the extension of slavery, a reversal of the Republican policy. Pressed to say something conciliatory, Lincoln refused to say anything that might seem like an apology to the South. He had been elected by the voters on the platform of the non-extension of slavery in the territories and he was not going to retreat from his firm belief that this was what the Constitution decreed. As for secession, it was anarchy. He told Nicolay that the states did not have the right to secede and that, as President, it would be his duty to maintain the existing government. He wrote Thurlow Weed:

> No state can, in any way, lawfully, get out of the Union, without the consent of the others.

Washington, D.C., a Southern city, was in turmoil. Thousands of Southern sympathizers and spies abounded. Varina Davis wrote to a friend that a pall had settled over Washington on New Year's Day 1861. There were no more jolly parties. The city she loved, she wrote, had become a "great mausoleum." Her husband, Senator Jefferson Davis, would soon resign from office, as had other Southern senators who departed, and they would return to Mississippi. Varina tried to persuade her Black seamstress, Elizabeth Keckley, a former slave, to go with her, but Keckley decided against going South. The Washington mansions of the old Southern aristocracy were closed up, their clothes, personal belongings, fine china, rugs, and furniture having been packed up in heavy trunks and crates and shipped by steamers to their Southern plantations.

On January 29, Kansas was admitted to the Union as a free state. It was the thirty-fourth state to join the Union.

Mounting dark clouds of foreboding threatened Lincoln's inauguration on March 4. As Mary Lincoln was preparing to leave Springfield for D.C., she received a painting from someone in South Carolina. It showed Lincoln tarred, feathered, chained, and his neck roped. Washington was rife with rumors that Lincoln was to be shot by a horseman riding by as he made his inaugural address. Yet Lincoln was not disturbed about the safety of his inauguration. He was worried about February 13, when the House would certify the electoral college votes. It was to be overseen by Vice President Breckenridge, his recent opponent and a Southern Democrat. Seward urged Lincoln to arrive in Washington before the certification of the vote, but Lincoln thought it best not to appear there until the "result of that ceremony is known."

Having leased out his house, sold some of the furnishings, put other items in storage, personally crated and then shipped his belongings to the White House, Abraham Lincoln, with moist eyes, bid goodbye to Springfield on February 11. Gathered at the Western Railroad Depot in the damp and biting air were more than a thousand people to see him off. After shaking hands with many, his face pale and quivering with emotion, he was escorted to the platform of his luxurious private railway car, festooned with American flags. He took off his hat, asked for silence, and spoke:

> To this place and the kindness of these people, I owe every thing....I now leave, not knowing when, or whether ever, I may return, with a task before me greater than that which rested upon Washington....I hope in your prayers you will commend me, I bid you an affectionate farewell.

Lincoln set off on a twelve-day train trip to Washington that would put him in contact with tens of thousands of his fellow citizens. That same morning, former Senator Jefferson Davis set out on his own journey, leaving his Brierfield plantation located on a stretch of the Mississippi River. He bid farewell to Varina, their children, and their slaves, and traveled to Montgomery, Alabama, the new capital of the Southern Confederacy, where he was to be inaugurated president. Varina did not like her husband being made president. He was no politician. She felt he did not know how to compromise, was hot-tempered, and better suited to a military role.

On the third day of Lincoln's journey, Lincoln was being entertained in the state capitol at Columbus, Ohio, when he was handed a telegram with the jubilant tidings that the Washington electors had met and his election was official. Back in Washington, Frederick Seward, like Lincoln, breathed a heavy sigh of relief. Frederick, the son of Frances and Henry Seward, would serve as the assistant to the Secretary of State, his father, in the new Lincoln administration. Fred Seward wrote his wife, Anna, of the February 13 certification in the House:

> The votes have been counted, and the Capital [*sic*] is not attacked. Gen. Scott had his troops all under arms…[b]ut there was no enemy.

CHAPTER 77

The Lincoln Train Draws Nearer to Washington

On Thursday, February 21, 1861, Lincoln was in Philadelphia, having spent the day speaking to the jubilant crowds who met his special train. Late that night, after speaking from his hotel balcony to the crowds in the street and as he prepared for bed, he was called to Norman Judd's room. There, he met privately with Allan Pinkerton, the Chicago-based detective, and Samuel Felton, the president of the Philadelphia, Wilmington, and Baltimore Railroad. Mental health reformer Dorothea Dix had alerted Felton of a secessionist plot to murder Lincoln as he changed trains in Baltimore on his way to Washington. Gen. Winfield Scott had also heard rumors and relayed them to Seward, who dispatched his son Frederick to Philadelphia to also inform Lincoln. Upon receipt of these two pieces of intelligence, Lincoln was not agitated but expressed regret that Southerners felt it necessary to kill him to advance their cause. He agreed to follow Pinkerton's advice for safe travel.

The next day, Lincoln went ahead with his previously scheduled engagements, only revealing the alteration in his tour schedule to his closest associates. Meanwhile, Kate Warne, the superintendent of the Female Detective Bureau in Pinkerton's agency, was buying tickets for four people to travel in the rear half of a sleeping car in a regularly scheduled midnight express train from Philadelphia to Baltimore. That night, Lincoln, accompanied by Pinkerton and bodyguard

Ward Hill Lamon, arrived at the Philadelphia station cleverly made up as a sick man, wearing a short, bob-tailed overcoat with a soft, felt hat pulled down low over his eyes and a shawl draped around his shoulders. He disguised his height by stooping over. Kate Warne was waiting for him, approaching him tenderly, taking his arm as if he was her invalid brother, helping him into the railway car and into his sleeping berth.

Pinkerton stationed men at all the rail bridges between Philadelphia and Baltimore, as some of the Baltimore plots involved blowing up the tracks. These undercover agents flashed lights at every crossing, signaling to Pinkerton that all was well. The train crossed through Delaware, the first slave state Lincoln entered since beginning his two-thousand-mile inaugural journey, arriving in Baltimore at 3:30 a.m. In Baltimore, Lincoln's sleeping car was "dragged without hazard" from one station to another; there was a two-hour delay, but the transfer went safely, their having arrived and departed without detection.

At six a.m. on Saturday, February 23, Lincoln arrived in Washington. The depot appeared to be empty. Then, a shadowy male figure stepped out from behind a pillar, looked at Lincoln, and said, "Abe, you can't play that on me." Pinkerton punched him. Lincoln grabbed Pinkerton before he could land any more blows on Representative Elihu Washburne, the only man besides Seward who had been apprised of Lincoln's secret arrival. Much to his embarrassment, Seward had overslept and missed Lincoln's arrival, though he would write Frances that he had been there at the station. Lincoln got into Washburne's carriage and rode with him to the Willard Hotel, where an out-of-breath Seward met him.

Caricature of Lincoln Sneaking through Baltimore in a Cattle Car

Later that afternoon, the special Lincoln train with Mary, her boys, and the rest of the entourage arrived in Washington. Mary was met by Washburne and Seward, who escorted her to the Willard Hotel, where the Lincoln family would reside until they moved into the White House on March 4, the day of Abraham Lincoln's inauguration.

Until that day arrived, Abraham, having his own parlor and bedroom, polished his inaugural speech and discussed it with Seward and others, completed his cabinet selections, and dealt with the crush of official business and office seekers. The crisis between the North and the South was worsening daily. Mary, meanwhile, made visits to important women. She held afternoon and evening receptions in her parlor at the Willard, inviting the local ladies to take tea with her, but many did not appear. Southerners who had remained in the city had no intention of mingling with the Republicans. Local women gossiped about Mary, saying she was common.

Mary interviewed half a dozen dressmakers before selecting Varina Davis' former seamstress, Elizabeth Keckley, who had once been enslaved and was now a much-sought-after Washington dress-maker. Lizzie Keckley would know how to dress Mary for a Southern audience; Varina Davis was known for her impeccable style.

Elizabeth Keckley (1861)

On Monday, March 4, 1861, General Winfield Scott stationed his troops along Pennsylvania Avenue and around the Capitol. Due to so many assassination and kidnapping threats against Lincoln, a wooden barricade shielded the immense crowd from the people on the inaugural platform. Contrary to Gen. Scott's assertion that his troops had been posted discreetly for the ceremony's security, Fred Seward saw that:

> there were squads of riflemen on housetops, along the avenue and at the windows of the wings of the Capitol, and under the steps

leading to the platform, while batteries of light artillery were ready for immediate service to quell any street riot. Groups of soldiers on horseback and on foot seemed to be everywhere.

Lincoln arrived in the inaugural parade seated in an open carriage with outgoing President Buchanan. Senators, representatives, diplomats, and the Supreme Court justices in their robes were seated on the platform on the East Portico. The day was chilly, and the high wind blew up dust from the avenue. Occasionally, the sun peeked out. Lincoln stepped to the low table that served as a podium and addressed an audience that numbered from twenty-five to fifty thousand people. Regal in his new black cashmere suit and black silk top hat, he was uncharacteristically carrying a black walking stick with a gold tip. Before he began to speak, Lincoln experienced an awkward moment. He secured his scrolling manuscript on the little table with his cane, but where could he lay his hat? Senator Stephen A. Douglas smiled, reached out, and took the hat to hold for him. Lincoln's old friend, Edward Baker, introduced him.

Putting on his steel-rimmed glasses, Lincoln spoke directly of the tension in the country, once again assuring the Southern states that a Republican administration would not endanger their property, their peace, or their personal security:

We are not enemies, but friends. We must not be enemies. Though passion may have strained, it must not break our bonds of affection.

He was firm, emphasizing the indivisibility of the Union, stating that "secession is the essence of anarchy." He declared his intention, as the nation's chief executive, "to hold, occupy, and possess the property and places belonging to the Government...but beyond what may be necessary for these objects, there will be no invasion, no using of force against or among the people anywhere."

The audience listened quietly, the peace broken only momentarily by the noise of a spectator crashing down from a tree where he had perched. It alarmed many who thought it might be a rifle shot. At the conclusion of Lincoln's speech, after all the cheering stopped, Mary Lincoln watched as her husband placed his left hand on the Bible, raised his right hand, and repeated the oath of office given to him by Chief Justice Roger B. Taney. Guns fired salute after salute to the sixteenth president.

For the inaugural ball, Mary wore a watered blue silk gown, accessorized with pearls, gold bracelets, and a few new diamonds. The celebration was held in the rear of the City Hall, in a room lit by five enormous chandeliers designed to hold two thousand people, but the women's hooped crinolines took up considerable space and made movement difficult. Rules of etiquette required that Mary promenade with someone other than her husband. Once again, Stephen Douglas stepped forward to help and she danced a quadrille with her former suitor. Abraham was exhausted and fidgeted with his new white kid gloves. He left the ball at midnight to attend to an urgent matter. Earlier that day, he had received a letter from Major Robert Anderson. He and his troops were boxed in at Fort Sumter, a U.S. sea fort on an island in Charleston Harbor, surrounded by armed Southern militiamen, the shore ringed with artillery batteries aimed at them, and running desperately low on food and supplies. Lincoln had to make a decision. Would he send a relief ship or tell Anderson to abandon the fort to rebel forces?

As Mary danced and Lincoln worried about Major Anderson and his men, Lincoln's inaugural address was carried across the nation by telegraph and printed in dozens of evening newspapers. West of St. Joseph, Missouri, where the telegraph lines stopped, pony express riders, traveling in relays, delivered the text to the Pacific Coast, which took a little over seven days to reach Sacramento, California. Reactions to his speech ranged widely. Democratic papers were predictably negative, calling it rambling, disjointed. While the *New-York Tribune* and the *New York Times* gave it rave reviews, radicals and abolitionists thought the President's words were too conciliatory to the South. Southern newspapers did not feel this way. Rather, the *Richmond Enquirer* blasted Lincoln's words as the "language of the fanatic" and asserted that his aim was to lead the country into a civil war. *The New York Times* doubted whether newspapers in the South had even taken time to read the address before denouncing it from every corner of the South as a declaration of war. Lincoln's stated intention to hold onto government property, i.e., the forts, did carry the hint of a battle cry, as George Templeton Strong of New York noted in his diary, writing, "I think there is a clank of metal in it."

CHAPTER 78

Mary Gets What Mary Wants

Mary Lincoln with sons, Willie (l.) and Tad (c. 1860)

At one of her first receptions in March, Mary Lincoln made the acquaintance of Mary Cook Taft, who revealed that she had two sons, Bud, 12, and Holly, 8. This was music to Mary Lincoln's ears. She was looking for playmates for her sons, Willie, 10, and Tad, almost 8. Mary Lincoln promptly invited the Taft boys to the White House the very next day. Accompanying them, at her mother's request, was their ringlet-headed sister, Julia, 16. The day was windy when Julia, Tad, and Holly walked the few blocks that separated their home near Franklin Square and "the President's House."

Contrary to their mother's wishes to go to the front door and ask for Mrs. Lincoln, Julia and the boys entered through the office of Mr. Watt, the head gardener, their good friend. He called up the stairs for Willie and Tad to come down. As there was no response, the Taft children went up into the conservatory and found Willie and Tad watching the goldfish in the water lily tank. The boys became rapid friends and had rollicking fun together. The next day, escorted by one of the gardeners, Willie and Tad visited the Taft home. From then on, the boys were inseparable and got into all kinds of mischief. Mary Lincoln often requested that Julia accompany her brothers when visiting the White House as an unpaid sitter. Julia said that Willie Lincoln "was the most lovable boy I ever knew" and that "Tad had a quick fiery temper."

Around that same time, Julia's mother ordered a new bonnet of delicate straw to be made for her by Willian, the fashionable milliner on Pennsylvania Avenue. Trimmed with purple ribbon, it had long strings which she tied with a bow under her chin. It was this bonnet that Mary Taft wore to the Marine Band concert held on the White House lawn on a Wednesday afternoon that spring. Mary Taft wore a purple and white silk dress over a moderate crinoline. Daughter Julia accompanied her, wearing a white Swiss dress but without hoop skirt or crinoline, which miffed Julia. The mother and daughter mingled with the other guests and enjoyed the music until the close of the concert was signaled by the playing of the national anthem. Everyone stood. Gentlemen removed their hats. As the guests dispersed, Julia and her mother walked over to where the presidential party was sitting. Mary Lincoln greeted Mary Taft, staring fixedly at her bonnet and took her aside. Julia could not hear what they were saying, but her mother's face bore a look of amazement.

Upon the Taft women's return home, they found Julia's father, Horatio Taft, an examiner at the Patent Office, reading the *Star* in the parlor. Julia's mother told him that Mary Lincoln had coveted her bonnet's purple ribbons and wanted them for herself. What could

Mary Taft do? Julia's father was a government employee who had been hired under a Democratic administration. Many of them were being dismissed, suspected of Southern sympathies. His job was insecure. Mary Lincoln was already known to arrange positions for people who could be advantageous to her. The Tafts were cornered.

As directed by the First Lady, Willian sent for Mary Taft's bonnet and replaced her purple strings with lavender ones. Shortly thereafter, on one of her visits to the White House, Julia spied Mary Lincoln wearing a purple dress topped off by a bonnet bedecked with what had originally been her mother's purple ribbons.

Part VII

PATIENCE

(1861-1862)

Not by one word or look can we detect any change in the demeanor of the Negro servants....You could not tell that they even hear the awful noise that is going on in the [Charleston] bay. And people talk before them as if they were tables and chairs, and they make no sign. Are they stolidly stupid, or wiser than we are, silent and strong, biding their time.

—*Mary Boykin Chesnut*

CHAPTER 79

The South Strikes

Lincoln's usual method of dealing with crises was to spend months researching, thinking, and formulating a response. But the letter from Major Anderson left Lincoln with only weeks to make a decision. Should he send a relief ship or tell Anderson to abandon the fort? Would surrendering the fort keep the four states in the upper South and four border states from joining the secession, or would resupplying the fort start a civil war?

General Winfield Scott favored abandoning Ft. Sumter, claiming the government had neither the large fleet nor the manpower. Seward agreed. Three rebel commissioners were sent to Washington to negotiate the question of the forts; Lincoln did not allow any dealings with them as doing so would legitimize the Confederacy. But Seward found a channel to them and sent word that Sumter would be evacuated. However, Lincoln was headed in a different direction, and Seward, who helped Lincoln draft his inaugural address, knew Lincoln's clearly-enunciated policy to protect federal forts. On March 15, Lincoln held a cabinet meeting with his seven new secretaries. Five concurred with Seward and Scott, recommending evacuation. Reading Northern newspaper editorials put Lincoln in touch with the public sentiment in favor of keeping the fort. This steadied Lincoln's resolve. Lincoln met again with his cabinet. The vote had changed. Four of the six present now favored resupplying Sumter. Seward was certain strong pro-Union sentiment still existed in South Carolina and that giving up the fort would avert war. Lincoln tested

Seward's theory. Lincoln received intelligence that the American flag could not be seen flying anywhere in that state. On March 29, Lincoln made his decision to resupply Sumter. Seward was irate. He still thought he was the man in charge. He had mistakenly thought Lincoln would follow his advice and surrender the fort, rather than stick to his own policy. On April 6, Lincoln directed Secretary of War Simon Cameron to send a message by courier to South Carolina Governor Andrew Pickens:

> An attempt will be made to supply Fort-Sumter with provisions only; and that, if such attempt be not resisted, no effort to throw in men, arms, or ammunition will be made.

Jefferson Davis interpreted this directive from Lincoln as a direct threat. Seward's meddling had caused great confusion. Davis had been deceived. He ordered Confederate General P.G.T. Beauregard to level Fort Sumter before the relief ships arrived. On April 9, a small relief fleet left New York with plans to rendezvous off Charleston Harbor. At noon on April 11, the Confederate Cabinet sent a message to Major Anderson demanding surrender. He refused, preferring to be starved out in a few days if help did not arrive.

The Union relief ships were delayed by a powerful Atlantic storm and three tugboats went missing. On April 12, the Union resupply ships, scattered and prevented from launching the supply boats as it was too treacherous to navigate their ships around the sandbar at the mouth of the Charleston Harbor, sat outside it, helpless to enter and intercede. Food ran out in the fort at noon.

Southerner Mary Boykin Chesnut was in Charleston at that moment and had not slept much after midnight on April 12. After four a.m., she wrote in her diary:

> There was a sound of stir all over the house, a pattering of feet in the corridor. All seemed hurrying one way. I put on my

double-gown and a shawl and went to the house top. The shells were bursting....

At 4:30 a.m., the rebels had unleashed a volley of shells upon the surrounded fort. Mary Chesnut's husband was acting as Beauregard's liaison with Major Anderson:

I knew my husband was rowing about in a boat somewhere in that dark bay, and that the shells were roofing it over, bursting toward the Fort....

The women were wild, there on the house top. Prayers from the women and imprecations from the men; and then a shell would light up the scene....

[T]his morning, truly—up on the house top, I was so weak and weary I sat down on something that looked like a black stool. 'Get up, you foolish woman! Your dress is on fire,' cried a man; and he put me out. It was a chimney, and the sparks caught my clothes....

––––––

Union Major Anderson and his men held out for thirty-four hours before surrendering to the Confederate forces, which allowed the garrison to board a Union ship bound for New York. On April 20, the largest group of Americans ever assembled held a patriotic event around Union Square in New York City in support of the Union Cause. Anderson brought with him the battered thirty-three-star American flag that had flown above the battered fort.

––––––

The country was now in a state of war, the South having fired the first shot. Seven states had seceded from the Union. To preserve the Union, Lincoln had to put down the rebellion. So, on April 15, President Lincoln called for 750,000 state militiamen to serve for three months. The governors of the free states promised they would cooperate. Old party lines seemed to vanish as Northerners united in support of the Union. Seward believed the conflict would be over in sixty days. Bloody and short, thought Lincoln's secretary, John Hay.

Then, on May 23, the citizens of Virginia voted to secede, offering Richmond to be the new capital of the Confederacy, a nod to Virginia's strategic importance. Three more states—Arkansas, North Carolina, and Tennessee—would follow Virginia's lead. Lincoln had to keep the border states of Kentucky, Missouri, Delaware, and Maryland, all four being slave states, in the Union if he was to win the war. Maryland enclosed Washington on three sides. To have Kentucky meant to move armies and supplies down the Ohio River. Lincoln had to have Kentucky. If he freed the slaves, the border states might secede. The North had to conquer the eleven rebel states and then hold them.

Lincoln needed good generals with strength and courage. At the recommendation of Gen. Scott, who thought fellow Virginian Robert E. Lee was the "very best soldier I ever saw in the field," Lincoln offered Lee the command of the Union Army. Lee was torn but ended up choosing state over country, resigning from the U.S. Army. On April 19, Lincoln issued a proclamation instituting a blockade of Southern ports.

Meanwhile, Washington, D.C. was a wide-open city and vulnerable to invasion, sharing the Potomac waterway with the slave states, Virginia and the belligerent Maryland. The defense of Washington had never been studied by Army engineers. A neglected fort was located twelve miles downriver. Washington relied on manpower.

Massachusetts was sending the Sixth and the Eighth Regiments, under the command of Major-General Benjamin F. Butler, to Washington. Every day, citizens of Washington gathered at the depot, anticipating the arrival of these soldiers. Then, on the day the

President issued the blockade proclamation, Washington received bad news from Maryland, telling of a street clash in Baltimore between Southern sympathizers and the soldiers of the Sixth Massachusetts Regiment. By five o'clock on April 19, the Washington depot was thronged with nervous people. The regular afternoon train arrived, followed by a special. Soldiers in uniform descended to be cheered by the crowd as the first armed volunteers came to the defense of the capital. They had battled their way through Baltimore, transferring from station to station, as an angry mob hurled stones and fired guns at them. Four men were dead and thirty-one wounded. The injured men were taken by stretcher to the E Street Infirmary, where volunteer ladies, under the leadership of Patent Office clerk Clara Barton, dressed their wounds with handkerchiefs. The regiment made do with makeshift quarters in the Senate Chamber.

The President met with a Baltimore delegation that asked that troops not be routed through their city. Lincoln was faced with a precarious balancing act, with Washington sandwiched between Virginia, a seceded state, and Maryland, a state seething with Southern passion agitating to secede at any given moment. After Sumter, Confederate flags appeared on many Maryland homes and buildings. Lincoln agreed for the time being that reinforcements would be marched around Baltimore. But this did not satisfy Maryland Governor Hicks. Days later, he demanded that no Union soldiers be allowed to pass through and thus "pollute" any part of Maryland. Lincoln had to have troops to defend the capital and they had to come through Maryland. Lincoln responded:

> Our men are not moles, and can't dig under the earth; they are not birds, and can't fly through the air. There is no way but to march across, and that they must do....Keep your rowdies in Baltimore, and there will be no bloodshed....[T]ell your people that if they will not attack us, we will not attack them; but if they do attack us, we will return it, and that severely.

CHAPTER 80

Washington is Transformed Overnight

Salmon Chase's daughters, Kate, 20, and Nettie, 13, were in New York City when Major Robert Anderson arrived. This was the same day of the Baltimore Riot. Confederate saboteurs had cut all the telegraph wires in Baltimore and demolished all the railroad bridges surrounding the city. Therefore, Washington was completely isolated from the nation for a week, as the only news the capital received came through Baltimore and Alexandria, Virginia. Washington, D.C. braced itself for a Confederate assault from Virginia, assisted by the thousands of secessionist sympathizers who remained in the capital.

Kate Chase (1861)

With no news, Kate Chase was worried the rebels were already attacking Washington, and she wanted to get home. Major Anderson, needing to report to the President, offered to take the Chase girls with him to Washington. It was a dangerous and circuitous journey. Departing by train to Philadelphia, they traveled to Perryville, Maryland, where they boarded a steamer for Annapolis. A hostile ship fired two cannon shots at the steamer's wake. From Annapolis, they took another train over a hastily repaired set of tracks and arrived in Washington.

The capital now resembled a vast military camp; white tents in neat rows dotted the city. The streets swarmed with soldiers. By the end of April, wrote Horatio Taft, there were about eighteen thousand men under arms in the city, with troops continuing to arrive daily by the thousands. The Rhode Island troops camped inside the U.S. Patent Office, bunking on shelves where patent prototypes were displayed. On May 9, 1861, Taft wrote:

> But little seems to be attended to except military matters. Soldiers marching, Drums beating and Bugles sounding, all the time, and

now and [then] one hears the deep booming of a heavy Cannon from Fort Washington or from the Navy Yard, or perhaps from some vessel on the River.

The enemy was just across the Potomac. From the roof of the White House, Lincoln and his cabinet observed through a spyglass an enormous Confederate flag fluttering defiantly from the roof of the Marshall House, a tavern in Alexandria, Virginia. By nightfall, campfires flickered from rebel forces camped along the shore.

———

Fortress Monroe, a sixty-three-acre stone and brick citadel located in Hampton Roads, Virginia, was the only Union-controlled military installation in the Upper South. The massive fort was situated at the mouth of the Chesapeake Bay and at the entrance to the James and York Rivers, a strategic route to Richmond. It would help enforce the Union naval blockade. On May 22, Major-General Benjamin Butler, in command of the Department of Virginia, was welcomed with a military salute at Fortress Monroe. The following day, Butler ordered that a detachment of men make a reconnaissance of the village of Hampton, where they found that the white inhabitants had generally disappeared in terror but that the "negroes gathered around our men, and their evident exhilaration was particularly noted," wrote Private Edward L. Pierce.

That night, three young enslaved men who had been field hands on a nearby farm—Frank Baker, James Townsend, and Shepherd Mallory—rowed across the James River to Fortress Monroe and turned themselves in to the Union pickets. This was the night of Virginia's referendum on secession, which passed. With picks and shovels, the men had been laboring, on the orders of their master, to construct trenches and gun platforms at Port Sewell to attack Fort Monroe. The men had recently learned that their master, Colonel Charles K. Mallory, was planning on sending them to North Carolina or Florida to build Confederate fortifications. They did not want to go.

The fugitives did not know how they would be received at the Union fort. President Lincoln was emphatic about not interfering with slavery in the states where it already existed. At Fort Sumter and Fort Pickens, enslaved fugitives were being "delivered up" to their masters as specified in Article Four of the Constitution, which was enforced by the Fugitive Slave Act of 1850.

On the morning of May 24th, the three men were presented to General Butler, who was particularly interested in gaining information about the Confederate battery at Port Sewell. He interrogated them before setting them to work to aid the masons in building a new bakehouse.

The next day, Major John Baytop Cary, a rebel officer, rode up to the picket line at Fortress Monroe carrying a flag of truce on behalf of Colonel Mallory, who requested the return of the three fugitives. Cary asked to be admitted to the fort to see Butler. Butler was not about to allow a rebel to enter the fort and see where sandbags were piled up to protect the weak points, so he rode out to the picket line to meet Cary. He informed Cary that he meant to keep the fugitives, as he was under no obligations to a foreign country, as Virginia now claimed to be. Butler stated that:

> I shall hold these negroes as contraband of war, since they are engaged in the construction of your [artillery] battery and are claimed as your property. The question is simply whether they shall be used for or against the Government of the United States. Yet, though I greatly need the labor which had providentially come to my hands, if Colonel Mallory will come into the fort and take the oath of allegiance to the United States, he shall have his negroes, and I will endeavor to hire them from him.

Butler was a lawyer. Using the South's own definition of its enslaved people as property, Butler recognized the military necessity of confiscating "property" that might be used against the United States.

"Contraband" took on a new meaning, designating formerly enslaved people now adopted under the protection of the federal government. General Butler reported his conversation with Major Cary to the Secretary of War and his purpose for employing the refugees. For the moment, the Secretary and Lincoln cautiously approved Butler's "Contraband Decision." Meanwhile, over the summer, hundreds of fugitives from bondage, sometimes whole families, applied for asylum at Fort Monroe, which came to be called Fortress Freedom. Private Pierce was put in charge of their supervision and only gave them work equal to that of the soldiers and paid them for their labor.

CHAPTER 81

The Conflict Deepens

By the end of June, Washington, D.C., ringed with camps, was very martial-looking, with the expiration of the contracts with the ninety-day soldiers looming. Upon hearing that the Confederate Congress was meeting in Richmond on July 20, the pressure of an immediate advance on Richmond reached fever pitch. Newspaper editors sounded the "Forward to Richmond" war cry. General Irwin McDowell, commander of the 35,000 Washington troops, knew these different regiments from different states wearing different uniforms were not ready for battle. Lincoln believed it was time for an attack on the enemy in the field. Gen. McDowell pleaded for postponement. Nevertheless, Lincoln urged action: "You are green, it is true, but they are green also…."

The two armies met along the banks of a stream called Bull Run in Virginia, near the important railroad depot of Manassas Junction. The Southern commander at Manassas was P.G.T. Beauregard, who headed up twenty thousand men; Joseph E. Johnston oversaw the rebel forces in the Shenandoah Valley. The North had more weapons than the South, but this battle would be fought on terrain unfamiliar to the Army of the North, giving the South a distinct advantage. Southerners, too, clamored for a military engagement and a march on their enemy's capital.

On Sunday, July 21, twelve days behind schedule, McDowell began his march with thirty thousand recruits. Washington citizens, newspaper reporters, photographers, and politicians had loaded up their carriages with picnic lunches and followed the Northern army to the battlefield as if it were a sporting event. Initially, the Union troops forced the Confederates into retreat up Henry House Hill. Dispatches of these early Union successes were relayed to the War Department in Washington from Fairfax, ten miles from the scene of battle. Gen. Scott reported to Lincoln that things were going well. Lincoln went to church.

After lunch, Lincoln walked over to the War Department's telegraph office to read some of the dispatches. At 4:30 p.m., the news was that "the Union Army had achieved a glorious victory." Lincoln took a carriage ride with his sons and Secretary Bates. During this time, the arrival of Confederate reinforcements at Bull Run bolstered Beauregard's forces. He unleashed a vicious charge made by men making a bloodcurdling scream—"the Rebel yell." The stunned Union forces retreated in panic to Washington. The day was lost.

After ten hours of fighting, about 400 Confederates were killed, 1,600 wounded, and 225 more would die of their wounds. On the Union side, 625 were killed and mortally wounded, 950 were non-mortally wounded, and more than 1,200 were captured as prisoners of war. The hope for a quick and bloodless war was dashed. For the North, the Battle of Bull Run was a wake-up call. Southerners erupted in wild triumph that gave them the sense that just one of them could whip any number of Yankees. Lincoln searched for a new general.

Shortly after the rout at Bull Run, Detective Allan Pinkerton knocked at the door of the Taft family home. He was making inquiries about a local woman, Rose O'Neal Greenhow, a widow and Washington socialite. Julia Taft confirmed that "Mrs. Greenhow" had asked her and her brothers about their visits to the White House and what Mr. Lincoln had said. Greenhow had quizzed Julia's father about the number of regiments that had arrived.

On August 23, Tad and Willie Lincoln arrived at the Taft house with the news that Mrs. Greenhow had been arrested as a rebel spy. She was confined, under guard, to her house with some others suspected of being spies. Rose Greenhow made no secret that she was a Confederate spy. She had cultivated a relationship with Senator Henry Wilson, a chairman on the Senate Military Affairs Committee. It was from Wilson that Greenhow heard that the Union Army was planning to advance on Manassas. To alert the Confederate troops at Bull Run of the Union movements, she had drafted Bettie Duvall as her messenger. Greenhow wrote a cipher and hid the note in Duvall's hair. Duvall, masquerading as a lowly farm woman, snuck out of Washington and made her way to Fairfax Courthouse, Virginia. Once the Confederate commanders granted her an audience, they watched in amazement as Bettie unraveled her hair to reveal the secret message. A search of Rose Greenhow's house turned up a map of Union fortifications and other incriminating materials.

CHAPTER 82

Lincoln Shakes it Up

On July 26, 1861, General George B. McClellan, 34, arrived in Washington on a train from Pittsburgh as a hero. His military conquests in western Virginia, pushing out Confederate loyalists in the state's northwestern counties, had motivated Unionists there to form their own state of West Virginia. McClellan was received warmly at the White House by President Lincoln, who had tapped him to replace McDowell as the Commander of the Army of the Potomac, the largest branch of the Union Army. Immediately following Bull Run, the President signed bills authorizing the enlistment of one million three-year volunteer soldiers. Upon their arrival in the city, these new recruits would find themselves in the capable hands of McClellan, a West Point graduate.

Lincoln had high expectations of not just McClellan, but another new commander he appointed that same month, General John C. Frémont of the Western Department. From his headquarters in St. Louis, Frémont aimed to stamp out the fighting between secessionists and Unionists in Missouri before it erupted into a full civil war.

On August 6, 1861, Lincoln signed the Confiscation Act, passed by Congress, authorizing Union forces to seize property, including slave property, being used to support the Southern rebellion. The act did not spell out the future status of these slaves.

Meanwhile, in Missouri, Frémont, faced with a rapidly deteriorating situation, on August 30, took over the administrative powers of the state, declared martial law, announced that guerrillas behind Union lines would be shot, confiscated property, and freed the slaves of all Confederate rebels in Missouri. He had not consulted President Lincoln about this last matter. Lincoln learned of Frémont's radical action along with the rest of the country, reading it in the newspaper. With his emancipation proclamation, Frémont had single-handedly recast the war to preserve the Union as a war for freedom for the slaves. Lincoln worried that such a perceived policy shift would lead Kentucky and the border states to join the rebellion. Lincoln's oldest and best friend, Joshua Speed, a Kentucky slave owner and a Unionist, was so distressed that he had been unable to eat or sleep. He wrote Lincoln: "Do not allow us by the foolish action of a military popinjay to be driven from our [Kentucky's] present active loyalty." If Frémont's emancipation order had been allowed to stand, Kentucky would have seceded, Lincoln wrote Orville Browning. With "Kentucky gone, we can not hold Missouri, nor, as I think Maryland."

Lincoln wrote Frémont, asking but not ordering him, to change the wording in his proclamation to reflect that of the Confiscation Act of Congress. Lincoln's private secretary, John Hay, personally delivered the President's kindly letter to Frémont. Frémont drafted his reply. He then dispatched his wife, Jessie, to deliver his reply to the President in person.

Jessie Frémont and her maid left Missouri on September 8 for their three-day train trip to Washington. Arriving on September 10, she wrote a note to the President at 8 p.m. asking him to name a convenient time for an audience with him. He responded, "A. Lincoln. Now." Without changing out of her wrinkled, sweaty, and dusty traveling dress, Jessie, escorted by Judge Edward Cowles, left her room at the Willard and went straightaway to the White House. It was approaching midnight when she was ushered into the Red Room. The President entered, bowed, but did not sit down, nor did he pull out a chair for his caller. She produced her husband's letter and Lincoln read it, still standing. Frémont had refused his commander-in-chief's private request to modify the proclamation, writing that the President must order him publicly to do so.

Jessie informed the President that he, Lincoln, was not aware of the complex situation her husband faced in Missouri. She said that her husband believed England was on the brink of recognizing the South, on account of its cotton interests, but that he, Frémont, could turn that around. Avowing the English feeling for emancipation, General Frémont thought England might be more inclined to support the Union if he freed the slaves. When Jessie was finished enlightening him, the President replied, "You are quite a female politician."

The next morning, Lincoln issued an open order to Frémont to revise his proclamation in line with the provisions of the Confiscation Act. He did not send it with Jessie—although she was waiting for it at the Willard—but mailed it and released it publicly. Turning General Frémont's earlier tactic against him, Frémont would discover the President's response at the same time as the rest of the country.

Lincoln later remarked to John Hay that Jessie Frémont had "taxed me so violently…that I had to exercise all the awkward tact I have to avoid quarelling [sic] with her….She more than once intimated that if Gen Frémont should conclude to try conclusions with me he could set up for himself."

———

Whereas, Lincoln's public invalidation of Frémont's proclamation had eased worry in the border states, it disappointed radical Republicans and abolitionists and stirred up disapproval of Lincoln. Frances Seward had been jubilant to learn of Frémont's action, writing her sister on September 4, "Were you not pleased with Fremont's proclamation?" Frances told husband Henry that she was sorry Lincoln had interfered with Frémont's proclamation, as it "was a measure so universally approved at the North." Frances felt the Union generals were better poised to assess the army's needs than the President and his cabinet.

When such criticism reached his ears, Lincoln was stung, but he was not having generals in the field set policy. Declaring slaves to be free was to be "settled according to laws made by lawmakers," he wrote Senator Orville Browning.

CHAPTER 83

Mary Pursues a Separate Agenda

With her husband busy with pressing national affairs, Mary Lincoln increasingly found herself lonely and shut out from his circle of confidants. He had forged a great friendship with Secretary of State Seward, took afternoon carriage rides with him, and after dinner, walked the short distance to his house on Lafayette Square to sit and talk politics, literature, and theatre and to tell jokes and stories and laugh. Jealous, Mary despised Seward and forbade her coachmen to even drive by the Seward House. Feeling deprived of her husband's focus, Mary sought comfort in shopping, travel, and the company of a retinue of mostly male admirers, from whom she sought advice and who became her intimates. This group of callers, some of dubious character, visited Mary Lincoln nightly in the Blue Room, one of the three parlors of the White House. Mary called this group "my beau monde friends of the Blue Room." The courtiers had only to flatter the First Lady to gain almost unlimited access to her and, thus, gain access to the goings-on at the Great White Palace, as did the oily Chevalier Henry Wikoff, a social spy planted by the *New York Herald*, a paper that regularly devoted columns of gushing praise of Mary Lincoln.

The reporters reported this new celebrity's every movement or lack thereof. Two weeks after Bull Run, she hinted at a pleasure trip to the New Jersey seashore, reported in the *Herald*:

At Long Branch (New Jersey), however, an event is anticipated which will set the hotels ablaze with excitement….Mrs. President Lincoln has selected Long Branch for her Vichy or Isle of Wight this summer, and is expected to arrive there in the course of a few days….Her state dinner to the Prince Napoleon, on Saturday last, was a model of completeness, taste and geniality; …this repub- lican queen…entirely eclipses the first ladies of Europe….

Mary took a side trip to New York to shop. She was renovating and refurnishing the White House. To truly triumph socially, she needed to reign from a magnificent setting, not a shabby, run-down house. The White House looked to some people like an old hotel. However, Mary Lincoln's extravagance, greed for beautiful things, impulsivity, and overwhelming desire to outshine others blinded her to respecting spending limits. Although Congress allotted the President a generous $20,000 for household expenses, in just six months, Mary's purchases exceeded that amount by close to $7,000. No money had been placed in reserve for any future pipe leaks or other repairs or to pay the painter to strip off the old wallpaper and apply the new French one. In addition, New York merchants extended Mary credit for her clothing purchases. Mary assumed the clothes were really donations to her so that the merchants had access to her husband. She was taken aback when, months later, those bills arrived in the mail.

In addition to the wallpaper, Mary bought sets of china and glass- ware, a carriage, gold-fringed drapery with tassels and lace curtains, a mahogany bed with rosewood carving and a Victorian canopy, and new carpets. These purchases in wartime prompted tongues to wag, as soldiers slept without blankets in the fields and the bread- winners of most families were away in the army. President Lincoln, preoccupied with reports of Frémont's incompetence in the West and discouraged with General McClellan's reluctance to take his well-trained troops out of Washington camps and into battle, had let

Mary handle the remodeling. Eventually, he learned of her over-expenditures. Infuriated, he told her that it was her "flub-a-dub" and that she had to take responsibility." She begged others to intercede in the matter of the White House bills. She looked for ways to raise money so her husband did not use his salary to pay for the overrun. She sold secondhand White House furniture, which brought in little. She then ordered John Watt, the gardener, to sell manure from the stables at the inflated price of ten cents a wagonload, which caused a stink, made people laugh, and produced few sales. She fired some of the staff, and those who remained gossiped that Mary pocketed the fired steward's salary to pay her bills. Gardener John Watt, who controlled the payroll for the groundskeepers, showed Mary how he would pad his expense accounts and give her a kickback. He signed vouchers for fictitious purchases of flowers and trees. In time, the Commissioner of Public Buildings found a way to pay the bills.

In late summer 1861, Henry Seward suggested to Frances that she might bring Fanny and daughter-in-law, Jenny, Will's wife, to Washington in September for a two-week visit. Frances and Henry's son, Augustus, was serving at Fort Defiance, and Will had just enlisted. Fred worked in the State Department. On a tour of the military camps on the hillsides around the capital, Frances met the President. She found him "amusing and friendly, with a manner like an unassuming farmer's." At another time, the President showed Fanny, 16, the two kittens her father had given Willie and Tad. Lincoln let the kittens crawl all over him.

After dinner on the evening of September 9, three days before Frances and her family were to return to Auburn, the Sewards attempted to pay the First Lady a pre-arranged courtesy call. The White House was in the midst of its extensive remodel when the President's secretary, John Nicolay, escorted the Sewards inside. Edward, the Irish doorman, showed them into the blue and gold room, and they were given chairs. Edward pulled up a chair for Mary Lincoln. Fanny's father asked the doorman to tell Tad and Willie they wanted to see the kittens.

Fanny Seward (c. 1860)

"Well," wrote Fanny in her diary, "there we sat."

They could hear the sounds of Tad and Willie laughing in the halls, but neither boys nor kittens greeted the Sewards. After a considerable lapse of time, an usher appeared to report that "Mrs. Lincoln begged to be excused," for she was "*very* much engaged."

Fanny went away thinking Mary Lincoln was snubbing her mother, but she misjudged. Lizzie Keckley, Mary Lincoln's dressmaker, said that Mrs. Lincoln despised Henry Seward and did not trust him. Mary Lincoln became enraged when she thought of him, believing he twisted the President around his finger. Lizzie Keckley recorded the President's response to his wife's complaint: "Mother, you are mistaken….Seward is an able man, and the country as well as myself can trust him…."

As October 1861 was drawing to a close, and General McClellan had still made no advance with his Army of the Potomac, the patience of Northerners wore thin. McClellan told his wife he would not move until he was certain he was completely ready to take on the enemy, however long it took. Senator Lyman Trumbull opined that if McClellan's army went into winter quarters without fighting a battle against the rebels camped in Virginia, he feared the recognition of the Confederacy by foreign governments. McClellan fell further from favor when radical Republicans learned he had issued a "slave-catching order" requiring commanders to return fugitive slaves to their enslavers.

Forty miles upriver from Washington, the rebels held the town of Leesburg, Virginia. McClellan ordered General Charles P. Stone to conduct "a slight demonstration on your part" on the Maryland side of the Potomac in order to rouse the enemy. After Stone's movement of troops failed to get the attention of the Confederates and to convince them that Federals were about to cross in force, Stone sent a scouting party to cross the Potomac at Ball's Bluff to determine the rebels' positions. An overzealous scout and about twenty men sent on this nighttime mission believed they had encountered a deserted enemy camp. Based on this bad intelligence, Stone ordered a three-hundred-man raiding party to attack the camp. At dawn, this group discovered that what had been described by the scouts as a row of army tents was nothing but a line of trees. The Union troops encountered rebel forces and a skirmish began.

Colonel Edward Baker, a sitting U.S. senator and an old friend of Lincoln who had named his second son after him, was assigned to General Stone's division. On the morning of October 21, Baker learned of the raiding party into the supposed camp and went to Stone to be briefed. Neither Stone nor Baker knew yet of the ambush of the Union troops. Stone ordered Baker to Ball's Bluff to evaluate the situation. Colonel Baker was killed in action as were forty-nine of his men. Baker's embalming proved challenging because his body had been torn to pieces by the passage of at least eight bullets. McClellan received notice of Baker's death when he had been meeting with Lincoln at the White House, yet did not choose to gently break the news to the President, departing after he received the telegram. Later, at the telegraph office, Lincoln discovered the dispatch with the information that Baker had been killed. A correspondent observed the President as he walked away "with bowed head, and tears rolling down his furrowed cheeks, his face pale and wan, his heart heaving with emotion." Stumbling, he almost fell as he stepped out into the street.

Just the day before, Lincoln and Baker had been together, leisurely talking on the White House grounds. An officer recalled that: "Mr. Lincoln sat on the ground leaning against a tree; Colonel Baker was lying prone on the ground his head supported by his clasped hands."

Nearby, ten-year-old Willie Lincoln, handsome and blue-eyed, was tossing and kicking the fallen leaves in the yard—purple, scarlet, and crimson—with happy and guileless abandon. When Baker said his farewells, he shook hands with Lincoln and lifted up Willie to kiss him.

Willie composed a small poem for his fallen hero, "On the Death of Colonel Edward Baker," which found publication in the *National Republican*:

There was no patriot like Baker,
So noble and so True;
He fell as a soldier on the field,
His face to the sky of blue.

The Lincolns would have liked to have had Baker's funeral service in the East Room, but the White House was in the midst of Mary's grand remodel, with gas piping lying about, unboxed furniture stacked in the passages, and the smell of paint and varnish suffocatingly strong. Instead, Baker's heavy bronze casket lay in the back room of his friend, Colonel James Webb. To the viewing, Mary Lincoln, indulging her manic desire for display, wore a lilac silk dress with matching gloves and bonnet, tossing aside the propriety of wearing black in mourning, furthering criticism of herself, her husband, and his administration.

CHAPTER 84

Lincoln Deals with McClellan

G eneral George McClellan cut a sharp figure sitting in his saddle, which bore his name, as he posted through the streets of the capital astride his favorite horse, Dan Webster. Everyone in the city recognized his stocky, high-booted figure, trailed by his staff and escort of dragoons. On the cool autumn days, sightseers flocked to Washington to see the grand reviews of the Army of the Potomac, staged week after week by the General. It was an imposing sight, miles and miles of divisions extending over the Virginia plain, with enemy cannonade booming in the distance.

McClellan, obsessed with his elaborate battle plans and perfecting his army, delayed and delayed, allowing the rebels to withdraw from the city front and deeper into Virginia, frittering away the opportunity of crushing the rebels in one campaign. The Confederates had blockaded the lower Potomac, impeding shipments to the Washington wharves, raising prices on the few goods that did arrive, like wood for winter heating, yet McClellan did not move to destroy the enemy batteries. Allan Pinkerton, the head of McClellan's secret service bureau, convinced McClellan that the rebel army was far superior in numbers, a wholly inaccurate report, as McClellan's forces tripled that of the enemy's and he had more than three times the weight of artillery than those at the front. As Lincoln and the Congress insisted that McClellan advance his army against the enemy, McClellan kept asking for more men. The public and the government grew impatient with "Little Mac," as his soldiers affectionately called him. The whispers turned into a great clamor for Lincoln to remove him, especially when the horrifying details of the military blundering at Ball's Bluff reached the country. In early November, corpses of Union soldiers floated down the Potomac from the battle scene on floodwaters to Washington, some clothed in blue uniforms, others naked, snagged and caught up in the Long Bridge, landing on driftwood, and washing up against the wharves.

McClellan was the darling of the Democrats, so Lincoln was reluctant to replace him and further alienate that party. Lincoln had no training in military maneuvers. He respected McClellan and deferred to his judgment. McClellan, though, despised Lincoln for his ignorance and deference. McClellan did not feel he should have to take orders from a civilian. Lincoln, who had known McClellan when the general was a railroad executive in Illinois, felt at ease with his old acquaintance and frequently called upon him, most often at night, to learn the latest news before he went to bed.

On the evening of November 13, 1861, Lincoln, Seward, and John Hay paid McClellan a visit at his private rooms at the corner of H and 16th Streets. McClellan's rooms were not really "private" in that they were always crowded with soldiers. On this particular occasion, a porter told the President's group that the general had gone to an officer's wedding. The three men sat down in the parlor to wait.

An hour passed. McClellan returned home. The porter announced that the President was waiting for him in his parlor. McClellan, passing the room where his guests were seated, went upstairs. The guests waited for him to come downstairs for another half hour, after which they sent up a message that they were still waiting for him. The reply from above was that the general had gone to bed.

Once Lincoln and Hay returned home (as both secretaries Hay and John Nicolay bunked at the White House), Hay spoke to the President about McClellan's "unparalleled impudence." Lincoln responded that it was far better, at this moment, "not to be making points of etiquette and personal dignity." Nevertheless, from thenceforth, when Lincoln wanted to talk over military matters with McClellan, the President summoned the general to the White House.

Just three days earlier, Mary Lincoln had taken the train with the White House gardener, John Watt, to New York to buy more items for the White House. Aside from aiding Mary Lincoln in "the making of false bills so as to get pay for private expenses out of the public treasury, Major Watt was her partner in influence peddling. For instance, with gardener John Watt's assistance, Mary found a new job for Julia Taft's father, Horatio Nelson Taft, after he had been dismissed from his position at the Patent Office in July 1861. It had been a wise move for Julia's mother to surrender her purple bonnet ribbons to Mary Lincoln. Without Mary Lincoln's influence with the Interior Department secretary, Horatio and Mary Taft would have been forced to move out of the city, taking with them Bud, Holly, and Julia—Mary's babysitter.

Rumors of collusion in the White House between Mary Lincoln and her gardener were now compounded with suspicion of treason. Major John Watt had long been suspected of rebel sympathies, and Mary's allegiances were now under review. She was rumored to be a Confederate spy passing White House secrets to rebels. Mary Lincoln had no friends in Washington but Elizabeth Keckley. Newspaper editors kept the rumor mill churning:

> It is said that Mrs. President Lincoln has three brothers who are in the army of the South, and three sisters among the Rebels who married to secessionists, one of them at the head of several thousand men.

Mary Todd Lincoln's brother, David Todd, was briefly in charge of the Richmond prison for Yankee prisoners of war, where Union soldiers captured at Ball's Bluff and Bull Run were kept. An Illinois paper claimed that:

> The most brutal man in the Southern Confederacy is said to be Capt. Todd, brother of Mrs. President Lincoln. Returned prisoners from Richmond assert that he kicked the dead bodies of Federal troops, calling them d—d abolitionists.

———

The same day McClellan snubbed the President, Mary returned to Washington following her four-day Eastern jaunt with her gardener. John Hay, who called the First Lady "the Hell-cat," noted with satisfaction that the President had finally begun to suspect Watt (and Mary) of having done something improper and yet probably no worse than foolish. Lincoln sought to remove Watt from Mary's orbit and thus wrote to his military superior to reassign him to another place.

The President was so involved with prosecuting the war—the progress of which all else depended, including the fate of slavery—that he failed to follow up on the Watt matter. He and his cabinet had just days to compose and submit their annual messages to Congress, which would be read there on December 3. Imagine Lincoln's shock when he discovered that, despite precautions for security, the *New York Herald* published excerpts of his message before Congress had even heard it. The *Herald's* source was Chevalier Henry Wikoff, Mary Lincoln's shady friend. Even worse, the *Herald's* rival paper, the *New-York Tribune*, implicated the President's wife as the source of the leak. The House Judiciary Committee investigated this matter, its revelations dragging on for weeks, reported in the papers. Wikoff would eventually testify that it was John Watt who had given him access to the message, Watt saying he had memorized it after having seen it on Lincoln's desk. No one swallowed that lie. Nevertheless, the committee eventually dropped the investigation, but Watt was not dismissed from the White House.

CHAPTER 85

Lincoln Commands

While the Union Army and Navy were engaged in important military campaigns in other parts of the country, the administration's principal focus in January 1862 was in the Eastern Theater: capturing the Confederate capital of Richmond, Virginia. That task fell to the Army of the Potomac led by General McClellan, who was now also the General of the Army. Richmond and Washington were separated by only one hundred miles. The rebels were likewise interested in capturing Washington. The federal army both needed to advance into Virginia to take Richmond yet also leave behind a sufficient military force to protect Washington.

Lincoln was frustrated by the delay of the generals both in the field and in Washington. McClellan was ill with typhoid fever. On January 10, the President dropped into Quartermaster General Montgomery Meigs' office, asking, "General, what shall I do? The people are impatient; Chase has no money and he tells me he can raise no more; the General of the Army has typhoid fever. The bottom is out of the tub. What shall I do?"

Without some forward progress by McClellan, Chase had no hope of raising funds from a disgruntled public to sustain the astronomical expense of feeding, sheltering, and clothing hundreds of thousands of soldiers immobilized in camps. Meigs advised Lincoln to create his own war council. Attorney General Edward Bates echoed Meigs' advice, reminding Lincoln that he was, by law, "commander in chief" and must command and discontinue his "injurious deference to subordinates." Radical Republicans in Congress pressed Lincoln to prod the army into action.

The President summoned several cabinet members, General Irvin McDowell and William B. Franklin, for an emergency strategy session at the White House. Learning at this time that there had been further delays in the campaign against New Orleans, Lincoln grew more irritated and thusly further committed to taking the army matters into his own hands. In their meeting, Lincoln remarked that General McClellan did not want to use the army, "he would like to borrow it." The group came up with two plans.

Once McClellan learned of this meeting, he was out of his sick bed, meeting with the same men on January 13. McClellan refused to reveal his plans, whispering to Meigs that the President "can't keep a secret, he will tell them to Tadd [sic]." McClellan assured the group that he did have both a plan and a timetable. Lincoln placed more faith in McClellan and adjourned the meeting.

———

Two days after the meeting with McClellan, the Senate confirmed Lincoln's nomination of former Democrat Edwin M. Stanton to replace Simon Cameron as Secretary of War. Lincoln had never wanted the unscrupulous Cameron in his cabinet, but he felt bound by the unfortunate pledges of his campaign managers at the 1860 Chicago Republican Convention in exchange for Cameron's release of his Pennsylvania delegates to Lincoln on the second ballot.

Cameron gave Lincoln a good reason for replacing him. In his December 1861 annual message to Congress, Cameron had slipped in a recommendation that the "Government" should "arm slaves." He did not have the President's approval for this. The President ordered him to remove this paragraph, but the wily Cameron had already submitted his message to the newspapers, which published it.

In dismissing the insubordinate Cameron, Lincoln had to move cautiously to avoid alienating Cameron's Pennsylvania base. Lincoln heard Cameron express a desire to be appointed to a less stressful yet desirable post. A post had opened in St Petersburg. Lincoln wrote Cameron that he knew that Cameron sought "a change of position, I can now gratify you, consistently with my view of the public interest by nominating you to the Senate, next Monday, as minister to Russia."

Cameron was shocked. He did not want to lose his cabinet position. Lincoln made it seem as if the whole matter had been Cameron's idea. Lincoln asked Cameron to recommend his successor. Cameron recommended Edwin Stanton. Cameron left believing he had picked his successor, but Lincoln had already settled on Stanton. The public thought Cameron had retired voluntarily, so Cameron left office with his reputation untarnished. All went well for Cameron until the House Committee on Contracts published its 1,100-page report in February 1862 exposing Cameron's awarding of War Department contracts that led to the purchase of malfunctioning weapons, blind horses, knapsacks that disintegrated in the rain, uniforms that ripped after a few weeks of wear, shoes that fell apart, and rotten food. Cameron was devastated by this scandal. Lincoln rallied around one of his own, writing a long public letter to Congress explaining that these unfortunate contracts were drafted in the aftermath of Fort Sumter and thus were a product of an emergency situation. Lincoln wrote that he and his cabinet "were at least equally responsible" for whatever wrong had been committed. Cameron never forgot the President's magnanimous action on his behalf at a time when Lincoln had been deserted by many in his party.

Although for months, Edwin Stanton had been McClellan's bosom friend, in his new position as War Secretary, he quickly grew disenchanted with the general's behavior. McClellan kept Stanton waiting on a number of occasions. Stanton, after having to wait for an hour at the general's headquarters, said: "This will be the last time General McClellan will give either myself or the President the waiting snub."

Stanton later ordered the transfer of the telegraph office from McClellan's headquarters to a room adjoining his office in the War Department, infuriating McClellan but delighting the President. Lincoln now spent many hours with his new war secretary in his favorite spot, the telegraph office, developing a warm and mutually beneficial friendship, reading war dispatches and discussing strategy. Stanton would run the War Department with incorruptible efficiency.

Stanton was not a military man. He was one of the best trial lawyers in the country. Lincoln and Stanton had met six years before when they were co-counsels for the defense in a famous case, a lawsuit brought for infringement of patent rights by Cyrus McCormick, the inventor of the reaping machine. Chicago was the original venue for the trial, thus necessitating a need for a local lawyer. Therefore, Lincoln was hired and given a fee. It was understood that Lincoln would present the legal arguments while his co-counsel, George Harding, would present the scientific one.

But then the case was transferred to Cincinnati, and there was no longer the need for a local Illinois lawyer, thus making Lincoln's presence moot. Unfortunately for Lincoln, he was not made aware of these new dynamics. He continued to prepare. Harding, meanwhile, teamed up with a new co-counsel, Edwin Stanton.

Lincoln arrived in Cincinnati. He stayed in the same hotel as Stanton and Harding, though Stanton and Harding never asked him to join them for a meal or go with them to and from the court. Stanton made it plain to Lincoln that he expected Lincoln to remove himself from the case. Lincoln complied but did not absent himself from the courtroom. He was "Honest Abe"; he had been paid to be there. He remained in Cincinnati to hear the arguments. Harding never opened Lincoln's brief.

This bullying went on for a week. Lincoln was humiliated by the snub but intrigued by the sophisticated courtroom arguments put forth by Stanton. In saying goodbye to a friend he had made in Cincinnati, he said he never expected to be there again as "things have so happened here as to make it undesirable for me ever to return…." And yet now Lincoln appointed the rude Stanton to one of the most powerful posts in the land.

———

Lincoln had misgivings about the wisdom of the professional soldiers running the war. So now, late into the night, he devoted himself to diligently studying a collection of manuals on military strategy to become an informed commander-in-chief. As a result of this research, Lincoln came to believe, and correctly so, that given the North's superior troop numbers, in order to beat the enemy, they had to attack several Confederate positions at the same time. This he told his generals. On January 27, 1862, he issued General War Order No. 1, marking February 22, Washington's birthday, as "the day for a general movement of the Land and Naval forces of the United States against the insurgents."

Spurred by Lincoln's order, on January 30, General Halleck telegraphed General Ulysses S. Grant to make preparations to take his fifteen thousand men to capture Fort Henry on the Tennessee River just south of the Kentucky border. Two days later, Grant started his expedition with his men on transports. On the fourth of February, Flag Officer Andrew H. Foote and his fleet of seven new ironclad river gunboats accompanied Grant's troops for convoy and attack. The plan was for the gunboats to bombard the fort from the river with a land assault by the troops. These divisions were joined by two others by land on February 5, the day Mary Lincoln invited five hundred people to the White House for a ball. The assault was to begin the next day.

CHAPTER 86

Lincoln Withstands a Hard Blow

lizabeth Keckley's relationship with First Lady Mary Lincoln had begun on a purely business basis. In the spring and summer of 1861, Keckley made fifteen or sixteen custom dresses for Mary. Keckley had a thriving business, dressing other Washington ladies of importance, including the wives of Secretaries Welles and Stanton and Adele Cutts Douglas, the widow of Stephen Douglas, who dressed in full mourning. Keckley had her dressmaking shop at 1017 Twelfth Street, where she also boarded.

In late fall 1861, however, Keckley found that she was at her Twelfth Street shop less and less and more and more at the White House, as Mary Lincoln expected Keckley to be at her beck and call.

In January 1862, the White House, under the direction of Mary Lincoln, issued five hundred invitations to an evening ball to be held at the White House on February 5. Mary enthusiastically prepared for her gala. The Marine Band would play in the vestibule. The most expensive caterer in the country, Maillard of New York, would cater the affair, and her guests would dine on an immense buffet featuring fat partridges, venison steaks, canvasback ducks, Virginia hams, terrapins, freshly shucked tidewater oysters, and tender pheasants, to be served from the fashionably late hours of midnight until three a.m. Towering bouquets of exotic flowers shipped from Philadelphia and New York would be arranged in blue-and-white porcelain vases on every table. A Japanese punch bowl would be the centerpiece, brimming with ten gallons of a champagne, arrack, and rum concoction.

Her staff would wear new mulberry-colored uniforms, the color complementing her new solferino-edged china set. For "Madame President," Keckley had designed a beautiful and terribly low-cut white silk dress with deep flounces of black lace looped with ribbons of black and white. There would be no dancing, insisted the President, and he opposed the idea of giving a private party with a restricted guest list, as it was not a state dinner. But he succumbed to his wife's wishes, the social and domestic sphere being hers. The President would pay all expenses, rumored to be over ten thousand dollars.

At the end of January, Willie Lincoln, 12, became ill. Mary Lincoln summoned Lizzie Keckley to his bedside. Keckley believed Willie had caught cold riding his new pony in the cold and wet weather that left the ground covered with a thick layer of foul-smelling mud. Willie's cold then graduated to chills and fever. There was cause for alarm: smallpox and typhoid fever had taken many lives in the city. Willie, Tad, and the Taft boys had also visited McClellan's home when the general was suffering from typhoid fever. Members of the Stanton, Seward, and Chase families had been struck with illness. The Lincolns consulted Dr. Robert Stone. Should they call off the ball? The doctor determined that Willie was improving. The Lincolns drew encouragement from the doctor's prognosis and did not cancel the ball.

***

Several days before the ball, the esteemed caterer, Maillard of New York, arrived at the White House with his team of waiters, cooks, and bakers. After much preparation, the great night, Wednesday, February 5, finally arrived. It was still cold but the day was clear and bright. "The moon in its first quarter shown on the freshly painted pillars of the White House." A little before nine o'clock, Lizzie Keckley, upstairs in the family's quarters, heard the clatter of carriages and noise as the first guests arrived. The doorkeeper had been given strict orders to admit only those bearing invitations.

Prior to this, Mary Lincoln sat before the mirror, frowning as Keckley brushed and pinned her hair, crowning her with a wreath of white and purple flowers. Keckley pinned a neckline corsage of crape myrtle at the First Lady's bosom. Mary Lincoln wore no jewelry but a string of pearls. Her dress had a long train. Mary's low-cut dress would spark a great deal of comment that night, her husband's being the first. Hearing the rustling of her crinolines as his wife entered the room, he looked up at her and jested:

Whew! Our cat has a long tail to-night. Mother, it is my opinion, if some of that tail was nearer the head.

Mary Lincoln (ca. 1861)

Keckley noted that the First Lady did not reply, took her husband's arm, and the two of them descended to meet their many guests. While the white people frolicked below, Keckley was obliged to nurse Willie Lincoln.

The President in his new black swallowtail coat and the First Lady with her long train hid their worry for their boy behind mechanical smiles, receiving their many distinguished guests in the center of the magnificently illuminated East Room. Streaming into the red, green, and blue parlors were European diplomats in their colorful sashes and medals, cabinet members, senators, representatives, Supreme Court justices, important people, and beautiful women from nearly every state in their most formal attire. The French and Prussian princes had come. General George and Ellen McClellan were there as were General John and Jessie Frémont. Kate Chase, 21, with her regal carriage, gorgeous in a "mauve-colored silk gown" that set off "her copper-colored hair," turned many heads. Guests gawked at the many White House renovations that had sparked such discussion in the capital.

As the guests mingled, gaped, and gossiped, Mr. and Mrs. Lincoln occasionally slipped upstairs to check on their boy. Willie "drew every breath with difficulty." The parents stroked his tiny and feverish hands. The joyful notes of the Marine Band wafted up into the gloom of the dim sickroom. Leaving Willie to the care of Lizzie Keckley, the parents returned to their guests, who, unaware of the scene unfolding upstairs, had a splendid time, promenading, feasting, and laughing in great merriment, safe as they were in the capital, guarded by a hundred thousand soldiers. The last guests lingered until almost dawn. In the basement, the servants worked all night to clean up. Some helped themselves to leftover claret and sauterne as they labored. Overworked, hot, and drunk, a fistfight broke out in the kitchen. When the sun came up, Willie was much worse. Lizzie Keckley was worn out from watching.

Willie had likely contracted typhoid fever, possibly from pollution in the White House water system drawn from the Potomac. Tens of thousands of Union troops were stationed along the river without proper latrines, thus contaminating the Washington water supply with fecal matter. House flies, feasting on human excrement and contaminated food, carried the disease to households. Typhoid fever works slowly, depriving its victim of digestive function over a period of weeks. It causes high fever, cramps, diarrhea, internal hemorrhage, vomiting, exhaustion, intestinal spasms, and delirium. It had been Mary's orders that the fetid water of the Potomac be piped into the White House just the year before at a cost of $4,420.

The newspapers reported the details of the White House ball in glorious detail, pronounced it an unqualified success while, at the same time, denouncing such festivity in wartime. Those who had not received invitations were much offended.

"Fort Henry is ours," General Grant wired General Halleck the next day, February 6. "I shall take and destroy Fort Donelson on the 8th." Grant's eastward march of twelve miles for the assault on Donelson was delayed by a severe rainstorm, but on February 16, Grant received the immediate surrender of Confederate commander Simon Buckner and fifteen thousand Confederate soldiers. It was a bloody fight. More than a thousand soldiers on both sides died, and three times that number were wounded and lying on the battlefield in the gathering cold.

These twin Union victories invigorated the North. Hundred-gun salutes were fired in jubilation across the land. Plans were made to illuminate the capital's public buildings in celebration of the twin victories and George Washington's birthday. President Lincoln promoted Ulysses Grant to major general.

The South was shaken. Mary Chesnut of South Carolina wrote:

> Confederate affairs are in a blue way. Roanoke taken, Fort Henry
> on the Tennessee open to them, and we fear for the Mississippi
> River too....Bad news is killing me.

Days passed, and Tad, too, fell ill. Willie's condition had greatly worsened. By mid-February, he slipped in and out of consciousness, tossing and turning in the night as his parents sat helplessly by his side, bathing his sweaty brow. Dr. Stone's therapies of Peruvian bark, calomel, and jalap given to Willie every half hour—when he was conscious—as well as home remedies of beef tea, blackberry cordial, and bland puddings could not arrest the progress of the terrible bacterial infection. With each passing hour, Willie grew more listless, dehydrated, and wasted. He called out for his friend, Bud Taft, who was sent for, to faithfully sit by Willie's side. On February 18, Willie Lincoln lapsed into a coma. The newspapers reported to a sad nation that the President's son was no longer expected to live.

At 5 p.m. on February 20, Lincoln's secretary, John Nicolay, was dozing on the couch in his office when the President burst in. "Well, Nicolay, my boy is gone—he is actually gone!" Lincoln then burst into tears and disappeared into his own office.

Lizzie Keckley was summoned. She recalled:

I assisted in washing [Willie] and dressing him, and then laid him on the bed, when Mr. Lincoln came in. I never saw a man so bowed down with grief....He came to the bed, lifted the cover from the face of his child, gazed at it long and earnestly, murmuring, 'My poor boy, he was too good for this earth. God has called him home.'

Great sobs choked his utterance....I did not dream that his rugged nature could be so moved.

Mary Lincoln lost all control and became completely disabled. Tad, who was still critically ill and in bed, could hear his mother screaming, thrashing, and sobbing in the adjoining room. Mary showed no desire to care for Tad. Willie, she declared, was her "perfect" child. She perceived his death as a personal abandonment and blamed God for taking him from her. She confined herself to her room. Friends, responding to the President's need for help, arrived at the White House to help with Mary and Tad and see to the funeral arrangements. Dorothea Dix, now the Superintendent of Women Nurses, recommended an experienced army nurse to care for Tad, who needed round-the-clock care. Mary Lincoln became essentially an invalid. The Lincolns' old friends, Senator Orville Browning and his wife, Eliza Caldwell Browning, were in constant attendance at the White House as was Lizzie Keckley. Doctors Robert Stone and Neal Hall were called upon to administer opiates and elixirs to sedate Mary. Lincoln sent a telegram to Mary's sister, Elizabeth Edwards, to come to Washington; she came for a spell but was soon chafing to return to her own family in Springfield, impatient with Mary's histrionics and demanding nature. She wrote her niece that "Aunt Mary is so constituted as to present a long indulgence of such gloom."

Grieving Bud and Holly Taft were expecting an invitation to the White House to see Tad. Instead, Mary Lincoln wrote their mother: "Please keep the boys home the day of the funeral. It makes me worse to see them."

Mary banned the Taft boys from the White House. Despite this, Lincoln sent for Bud to see Willie before he was placed in his casket. On February 24, many of the same guests who had attended the White House ball just nineteen days earlier made their way to the White House for Willie's funeral, which Mary Lincoln did not attend. The White House mirrors were draped in black crepe. Willie had been embalmed and seemed only to be sleeping in the coffin. His brown hair was parted as he had worn it in life. His eyes were closed. He held in one of his hands, crossed upon his breast, a sprig of mignonette, a flower with a heavier scent than honeysuckle.

A fearful storm had arisen in the city before the 2 p.m. service commenced, with pelting rain and high winds that uprooted trees, tore off roofs, and toppled church steeples. Lightning streaked across the dark sky and thunder shook the crockery. "People who tried to walk on the streets were blown along and had to grasp at railings and lamp posts to stop themselves." Violent gusts of wind blew out the skylights of the Library of Congress. Despite the strange tempest, a hundred mourners, drenched, made their way to the White House, sitting in a semicircle in the East Room under three enormous chandeliers as the Reverend Dr. Phineas Gurley delivered his half-hour eulogy of Willie Lincoln, calling him a "beloved youth…a child of bright intelligence and of peculiar promise." Seward, McClellan, Chase, senators, ambassadors, and soldiers listened to the preacher's words reverently, with hearts sorrowing for the President.

After the White House service, a procession of carriages followed the hearse to the Oak Hill Cemetery chapel in Georgetown. Following a short service there, the mourners departed, and Willie's casket was left alone by the altar. The next day, the President returned to see Willie's coffin temporarily placed in one of the crypts belonging to the family of William T. Carroll, until the time his son's body could be conveyed to Springfield.

Word soon got out that the President had been spotted in the cemetery two more times. He had returned to the tomb to have his son's coffin opened so that he could once more look upon Willie's sweet face. Lincoln could not bear to leave him alone in the cold tomb. Yet this he had to do, remembering his oath of office, and so, with a crushed heart, he returned to working eighteen-hour days to save the Union.

Part VIII

HOPE

(1862-1863)

In the summer of 1862, freedmen began to flock into Washington....They came with a great hope in their hearts....Many good friends reached forth kind hands, but the North is not warm and impulsive. For one kind word spoken, two harsh ones were uttered.

—*Elizabeth Keckley*

CHAPTER 87

Abolitionists Make Gains

Abolitionist sentiment was rising in the U.S. Congress and among Northerners. Anti-slavery bills met a warm reception in congressional committees, now freed of the Southern bloc. The President was pressured to do something about slavery. His critics accused him of folly, attempting to preserve slavery while fighting a slaveholding power. Lincoln did not think slavery would survive the war. He took small but significant steps toward emancipation in areas where he felt constitutionally empowered.

On March 6, with the support of Chase and Sumner, Lincoln proposed that Congress pass a resolution offering compensation to any state that adopted gradual abolishment of slavery. It was Lincoln's great hope that the four loyal slaveholding border states would accept this offer. To those who voiced objection to the cost of compensation, Lincoln pointed out that three months of war expenditures would buy all the slaves in the border states.

On March 13, a new article of war was passed that forbade army officers to return fugitive slaves to their masters. This settled the question raised by General Benjamin Butler and his contraband policy. As Union troops moved along the South Atlantic coast and in the lower Mississippi Valley, many slaves escaped and sought freedom and refuge in army camps. What to do with these "contrabands" remained a problem in need of a solution. Lincoln continued to think voluntary colonization was the answer. The Northern states did not want the "contrabands," nor did the colorphobic border states.

On April 16, President Lincoln signed the District of Columbia Compensated Emancipation Act into law, ending slavery in Washington. In the District of Columbia, slave owners were offered as much as $300 for liberating their slaves, and "about one thousand persons…presented claims. This measure was passed in opposition to many of the white residents of the capital, their hostility expressed by a statement issued by the Board of Aldermen who accused Congress of converting their city into "an asylum for free negroes, a population undesirable in every American community."

Lincoln was well aware of the social upheaval that would follow emancipation. A provision was inserted in this new D.C. emancipation law that provided appropriations for colonization outside the United States (where Lincoln hoped it might be possible for Blacks to escape legal and social discrimination and receive their full rights). However, only about sixty people in the district petitioned Congress for emigration to Central America. Most of the newly freed people were preoccupied with the pressing need for making a living and were not thinking about relocation. The largest employer of these former slaves and free Black people became the federal government. Washington and Alexandria, Virginia, were the main supply centers for the Eastern theater of the war. The Union Army and Navy employed thousands of Black men and women.

CHAPTER 88

McClellan Advances

Lincoln had long argued that if the war could be brought to a quick conclusion, the fragile Union coalition, made up of the Northern free states plus four slave states, could hold together without the controversial issue of slavery being injected. Lincoln needed George McClellan's Army of the Potomac to win a decisive victory in Virginia and capture the Confederate capital of Richmond, which was not only the capital of the Confederacy but "one of the few industrial cities in the South." Guns, steel, and even uniforms were made there. If Richmond fell, the Confederacy might collapse, ending the war.

By April 5, McClellan had finally moved his immense army out of Washington and advanced from Fort Monroe to the outskirts of Confederate-occupied Yorktown, Virginia, about fifty miles from Richmond. This advance would become known as the "Peninsula Campaign." Dug in behind earthworks at Yorktown were fewer than 13,000 rebels commanded by John B. Magruder. McClellan had about 55,000 men.

To convince McClellan that his force was enormous, the Confederate commander, Magruder, an amateur actor, marched a group of his men in and out of the woods in a continuous circle. He kept up an artillery barrage, scattered from various points, and ordered the band to play music loudly at night. The charade worked. McClellan telegraphed Washington that the Confederate force at Yorktown numbered "probably not less than 100,000 and probably more." He asked for reinforcements. Lincoln wrote McClellan to press forward and "break the enemy's line...at once. By delay, the enemy will relatively gain on you....you [must] strike a blow." McClellan ignored him and dug in, ordering the best-equipped army in history to keep building more and more impressive earthworks. The siege of Yorktown dragged on for a month, with occasional Confederate artillery shells lobbed at the Union observation balloon. It rained and hundreds of soldiers fell ill. Union soldiers awoke each morning to discover that, overnight, blood-sucking wood ticks that had wintered in the dry leaves of the Union camp had nestled into their flesh.

By the time McClellan put his hundred Federal guns in place and was ready to start bombarding Yorktown, the Confederates, on May 3, vanished so suddenly that their bread was left in the "kneading troughs, their pork over the fire, and biscuits half-baked." McClellan called it a victory. Now, both armies marched toward Richmond at a snail's pace on muddy roads in the pouring rain.

CHAPTER 89

Mary Lincoln Seeks Solace

B y May, Mary Lincoln had finally gotten out of her bed. Still medicated with laudanum, she had been spotted attending services at the New York Avenue Presbyterian Church in Washington. A fellow churchgoer wrote:

> This morning we went to Dr. Gurly's [*sic*] church and had the honor of sitting just behind Mr. And Mrs. President. He evidently got very tired—and she was so hid behind her immense black veil—and very deep black flounces—that one could scarcely tell she was there.

Abe Lincoln drew comfort from his conversations with the Presbyterian pastor, Rev. Phineas Gurley, discussing the state of the soul after death. Rev. Gurley said, "That is a subject of which Mr. Lincoln never tires." Mary, however, did not find solace in the belief that Willie was in a better place. How could she flee to God for solace when this same God had taken her son away from her?

Lizzie Keckley had sought out spiritualists after her son, George (passing as white to enlist), had been killed in Missouri at the beginning of the war, and she offered the same solution now to poor Mary Lincoln, hoping they could console her as well. From that spring on, Mary Lincoln's black barouche was often parked outside the Georgetown home of the mediums, Cranston and Margaret McCutcheon Laurie. Their daughter, Belle Miller, was an autokinetic medium whose special talent lay in levitating pianos. The Lauries' friend, Nettie Colburn, coordinated the séance, darkening the parlor and arranging her guests in a circle, with their hands placed on a table. Nettie would fall into a deep trance, bringing Mary messages from Willie and Eddie, and she was told they were happy.

While the President knew these mediums to be charlatans, he did not discourage Mary from attending their sessions, as she seemed to benefit from them, finding community in the dark circle touching hands. He was worried about his wife's sanity. Lizzie Keckley recalled:

> In one of her [Mary's] paroxysms of grief, the President kindly bent over his wife, took her by the arm, and gently led her to the window. With a stately, solemn gesture, he pointed to the lunatic asylum [Government Hospital for the Insane].
>
> 'Mother, do you see that large white building on the hill yonder? Try and control your grief, or it will drive you mad, and we may have to send you there.'

These days, Mary Lincoln looked less than the stylish Empress Eugénie and more like the widowed Queen Victoria, with her very public expression of grief. Mary's black crepe bonnet with veil made it impossible for her to turn her head. Like Victoria, Mary withdrew from performing the ceremonial functions of a First Lady, canceling the spring receptions at the White House and instructing John Hay to cancel the enormously popular spring and summer Saturday Marine Band concerts on the south lawn of the presidential grounds. Employing "the royal we," she wrote him on May 22, 1862: "When we are in sorrow, quiet is necessary."

Jealous Washington gossips said that God had punished Mary Lincoln for her frivolous behavior by taking Willie. They were wasting their time talking about Mary, as she no longer posed any social threat to them. The world of balls and gowns had lost its charm for Mary. After Willie's death, Mary had no thought of entertaining. Into this breach stepped Kate Chase, always acting to further her father's irrepressible goal to one day occupy the White House. Groomed from her teens to act as her thrice-widowed father's hostess, she took command, inviting critics of the Lincolns and the Lincoln administration into her father's sumptuously furnished mansion for candlelit dinners—with Chase occupying the head of the table—which were followed by music by a live band, dancing, and charades. In this relaxed atmosphere, conversation flowed freely, and Kate could practice "parlor politics," building up her father's base of support, creating a "rival court."

In May 1862, Chase's circle was jubilant when they learned that General David Hunter, a fiercely anti-slavery man who commanded the Department of the South, had issued an official order declaring "forever free" all slaves in South Carolina, Georgia, and Florida. In truth, the Union Army control did not extend much beyond the South Carolina Sea Islands. When Lincoln heard of this, he exclaimed: "No matter what I do—I am troubled every day with the rash and unexpected acts of my officers!"

Chase urged Lincoln not to revoke Hunter's decree. Nevertheless, Lincoln struck down Hunter's order, reserving for himself, as commander-in-chief, not a general in the field, the power to issue such a proclamation to free the slaves of a rebel state.

Lincoln used the Hunter decree to appeal to the border states again to embrace the government's offer of gradual, compensated emancipation. Lincoln reasoned that if the border states became free, the Confederacy would lose hope of winning their allegiance, which might shorten the war. The border states, who had stayed Union loyalists, did not understand why they should begin the process of emancipation while slavery was left intact in the Confederacy. They dismissed his offer.

Chase publicly disagreed with the President regarding Hunter's proclamation, denouncing Lincoln in talks with Sumner and others in the radical flank of the party, undermining his President's policy in correspondence with Horace Greeley, and accusing Lincoln of a lack of courage. Many Republicans sided with Chase, who had emerged as the leading anti-slavery influence among the President's councils. Although moderate Republicans supported Lincoln's actions, many radicals in the party were intensely disgruntled with his actions.

Lincoln drew heat from all sides. Influential Marylanders called the Hunter proclamation "an outrage" and demanded that Lincoln recall Hunter. Lincoln, battered from all sides, feared he was too radical for Democrats yet not radical enough for Republicans and would soon end up with no support. It seemed to many that Lincoln was shirking his duty as a leader and was acting merely as a moderator between contending factions. Despite such increasing pressure for a decisive action to end slavery, Lincoln delayed. The Northern public was not yet ready, he assessed. Many supported a war for the Union but not one for emancipation. There were hard public realities to deal with. Many, if not most, whites saw Black people as inferior and feared a massive influx of liberated slaves flooding the North and stealing white people's jobs and political rights. Lincoln was denounced in the press, in the Congress, and by other impatient longtime advocates of emancipation; Garrison called him "irresolute," and Henry Ward Beecher accused him of weakening the North by putting down "rebellion without touching its cause." While the criticism stung, Lincoln knew better than to force change upon the people. Lincoln said:

> Public sentiment is everything. With public sentiment, nothing can fail; without it nothing can succeed.

As for the South Carolina Sea Islands, where General Hunter had declared the slaves "forever free," Secretary Chase was quite familiar. In the early spring, he sent Edward L. Pierce there as the Treasury Department's agent. Pierce was tasked with recruiting Northern missionaries, teachers, and doctors and raising funds for educating, feeding, nursing, and clothing the ten thousand contrabands that were left behind there when the white population fled in advance of the Union troops. Also left behind were thousands of acres of unharvested cotton. It was a humanitarian crisis; the former slaves were starving, and many were naked or wearing rags from carpet shreds. The cotton crop needed to be brought in to provide needed revenue for the war and cotton for Northern textile factories and, therefore, labor superintendents were needed. The contrabands were to receive wages for their field labor in this endeavor.

After Hunter issued his emancipation decree, Pierce wrote Chase to inform him that in a second, not publicized decree, General David Hunter was requiring all able-bodied Black men in his district to serve in the army. An army draft was not in place for any Union men. Forcing unwilling men into service "should not be done with white men, least of all with blacks, who do not yet understand us," wrote Pierce, deploring Hunter's action. Though disapproving of Hunter's action, Chase could do nothing, as the War Department now had control of the Sea Islands.

One of the Sea Island volunteers from Philadelphia, Laura Towne, a homeopathic doctor, a teacher, and an abolitionist, wrote about the disturbing effect Hunter's order had on the contrabands on St. Helena's Island. On May 13, 1862, Towne wrote in her diary:

> The next day soon after breakfast Captain Stevens and two soldiers came up to the house and we sent for the men whose names he had got from Miss Walker, she being overseer of this plantation. There were twelve of them. Some stood on the porch, some below. Captain S. ordered them all below, and he said to them that

General Hunter had sent for them to go to him at Hilton Head, and they must go. The soldiers then began to load their guns. The negroes looked sad, one or two uneasy, and one or two sulky, but listened silently and unresisting....

All day yesterday and to-day one after another of the poor young superintendents have been coming in, saying it was the worst day of their lives....They had all got really attached to their hands, and were eager, too, to prove what crops free labor could raise....[T]hey thought it a shame to use force with these men who were beginning to trust to our law and justice.

Five hundred men were sent from this island to Beaufort yesterday and went to Hilton Head, to-day....

The day before Laura Towne made that diary entry, Robert Smalls, up the coast in Charleston, was thinking about his hometown of Beaufort. Smalls heard that General Hunter was enlisting contrabands at Beaufort. Smalls left Beaufort when he was twelve years old when his master sent him to be hired out. He had found work on the Charleston docks and, in time, met and married Hannah Jones, who was also enslaved. Smalls, 22, now worked as a "wheelman" on the side-wheel steamer *Planter*, which was contracted out to the Confederate Army as a transport ship operating in the Charleston Harbor and beyond. From the pilot-house of the *Planter*, far off in the water, Smalls could see the Union blockading vessels plying the water seven miles away.

On the evening of May 12, 1862, the *Planter* was docked at the wharf below General Ripley's headquarters. The ship's three white officers went ashore to spend the night, leaving Smalls and the crew on board. Smalls put on Relyea's uniform and a straw hat similar to the captain's and impersonated him as the pilot. Between 3 and 4 a.m. the next morning, he fired up the ship's engine. The crew of eight cast off quietly. After passing the Southern wharf, the ship stopped at another wharf to pick up the crewmen's families. Smalls guided the vessel past the five Confederate harbor forts safely, sailing past Fort Sumter at around 4:30 a.m. When Fort Sumter flashed the challenge signal, Smalls, in return, gave the correct hand signs. The fort gave the go-ahead signal, and Smalls sailed out into the open seas.

Smalls headed straight for the Union Navy fleet and hoisted a white bed sheet in place of the rebel flag. The *Planter* was seen by the *USS Onward*, which was about to fire its number 3 port gun on the approaching dark vessel until a crewman spotted the white flag. A war correspondent serving on the *Onward's* crew recalled the moment he saw the *Planter*:

> As she neared us, we looked in vain for the face of a white man. When they discovered that we would not fire on them, there was a rush of contrabands on her deck, some dancing, some singing, whistling, jumping; and others stood looking towards Fort Sumter, and muttering all sorts of maledictions against it…. One of the Colored men stepped forward, and taking off his hat, shouted, 'Good morning, sir! I've brought you some of the old United States guns, sir.'

This was Robert Smalls, and indeed, he had brought guns to the Union fleet; her armament included approximately 200 rounds of ammunition, a 32-pound pivot gun, a 24-pound howitzer and four other guns. Along with the boat, the artillery, and the ammunition, Smalls handed over a naval codebook and intelligence on the location of rebel troops. The codebook contained signals and a map of the mines and torpedoes in Charleston Harbor. This intelligence, plus more supplied by Smalls to the commander of the blockade squadron, Samuel Du Pont, at Port Royal, proved invaluable to the Union forces in the region.

Word of Small's daring deliverance of sixteen Black people from slavery to freedom—past Confederate harbor guns—spread quickly through the North, where Smalls was celebrated as a hero.

As the Union Army pushed into new parts of the Southern Confederacy in the spring and summer of 1862, slaves by the thousands fled to Union lines. Soldiers who had not previously expressed abolitionist sentiments often had a distinct change of heart once they witnessed the cruelties of slavery and the loyalty of the fugitives to the Union cause. James A. Garfield, commanding an Ohio unit in Tennessee, noted growing sympathy for the slave in the rank and file of his men. These soldiers engaged in political talks and wrote numerous letters home, describing the institution of slavery as they had seen it frank and up close, often expressing newfound emancipation sentiments, which, in turn, affected Northern politics. The Northern soldiers found the South a strange place. An enlisted man said that both the countryside and the people "all bore the impress of another life," finding it strange that Southerners would speak somewhat the same language as Northerners; they seemed so foreign. Many Union soldiers noted particularly the lack of Southern schools, and those were often in a tumble-down state.

Lincoln hoped that Northern armies would encounter pockets of loyal white Unionists in the South, but these seldom materialized. Edward Kittoe, Chief Surgeon of the 45th Illinois Volunteer Infantry, wrote of his impressions from Jackson, Tennessee, in a letter to Congressman Elihu. B. Washburne, on June 24, 1862:

> This is I think, the most beautiful town I have ever seen on this side of the Atlantic. There does not appear to have been much done in the way of trade. The lots are very large 3 & 4 acres together, the place seems to be made up of splendid residences and magnificent gardens.... [I]n fact the evidences of wealth, Luxury, and a sort of refinement meet you at every turn still there is a something also which keeps you constantly reminded of the curse of slavery, which hangs over this land.

The darkies seemed joyous at our presence, but the whites are sullen and looked spitefully and with an evident attempt to appear disdainfully indifferent to the women I cannot say ladies are peculiarly vindicative, one said the other day that if she was on the road to heaven and was obliged to pass under the old flag to get there she would turn and go the other way....

...I, in common with the majority here, am at a loss to understand how this very remarkable war is to be finished, if the government continues to pursue a course so well-calculated to foster the views of these rebels....

CHAPTER 90

McClellan's Army Advances to Within Nine Miles of Richmond

On June 26, the Confederate Army, under its new commander, Robert E. Lee, attacked the Army of the Potomac on the Virginia Peninsula. In a series of desperate skirmishes known as the Seven Days' Battles, Lee's army did not strike a decisive blow but succeeded in driving the Union Army back twenty miles and securing Richmond. McClellan was unnerved, his army demoralized. The morning after the vicious battle at Malvern Hill, a Union colonel remembered the sight that awaited him at dawn:

> Our ears had been filled [all night] with agonizing cries from thousands before the fog was lifted, but now our eyes saw [that] five thousand dead or wounded men were on the ground. A third of them were dead or dying, but enough of them were alive and moving to give the field a singular *crawling* effect.

By July 3, the Union Army was stalled at Harrison's Landing on the James River under the protection of naval guns. The fighting appeared to have ended despite calls from Union officers urging McClellan to stage a counteroffensive. McClellan had fired off accusatory telegrams to Washington, blaming the government in advance for any defeat he might incur. McClellan falsely maintained that he had not lost but failed to win as he was "overpowered by superior numbers." McClellan blamed Lincoln for withholding too many troops to defend Washington. On June 28, McClellan wrote War Secretary Stanton a letter that closed with this:

> I tell you plainly that I owe no thanks to you or any other persons in Washington—you have done your best to sacrifice this Army.

Although Lincoln could not sleep during the Seven Days' Battles, he would not allow himself to succumb to the gloom of defeat. In a June 28, 1862 letter to Secretary of State Seward, he reaffirmed his fixed purpose: "I expect to maintain this contest until successful, or till I die, or am conquered, or my term expires, or congress or the country forsakes me."

He called upon Seward to discreetly meet with Northern governors to arrange for the recruitment of three hundred thousand more troops. Two months earlier, War Secretary Stanton, overly confident at the time that victory was shortly at hand, had unfortunately shut down the recruiting offices.

CHAPTER 91

The Lincolns Retreat to the Soldiers' Home

Three miles northeast of the White House, up a winding path, was a beautifully wooded hill on which stood the Soldiers' Home. The three-hundred-acre establishment belonged to the government. The large, central building housed and fed disabled and retired veterans. Scattered on the grounds were several two-story stone cottages for the officers. In mid-June 1862, the Lincolns moved into a twelve-room cottage. The Home's breezy elevation, panoramic view of the city, the Potomac River, and the long line of forts in the hills offered the family a more private idyll away from the constant stream of job seekers at the White House. The shade tree canopies provided relief from the oppressive summer heat in the capital with its mosquitoes and the fetid stench from the Potomac Canal. Across the road was the new national cemetery, hastily established following the Battle of Bull Run and ever-expanding.

Mary still made occasional forays to town, often to visit the many makeshift hospitals in the city, taking fresh fruit, food, and flowers to the wounded soldiers, reading to them and talking to them, and writing their letters home. Hospital work demanded enormous fortitude, with its ghastly sights and smells and exposure to contagion. Soldiers dying of pneumonia, diphtheria, and typhoid lay on stretchers alongside legless, armless men in the same ward. Some physicians objected to women getting in their way in the hospitals;

others thought it unseemly for women to associate with partially clothed male patients.

The President kept up his busy schedule, commuting daily from the Soldier's Home to the War Department and the White House, sometimes on horseback or by carriage and, by summer's end, accompanied by a cavalry escort. At sunset, Tad would frequently meet his father and ride back with him to the cottage on his pony. When vacation time from Harvard rolled around, Robert came for visits. Close friends visited in the evening, sitting on the wide porch overlooking the abundant gardens or in a formal parlor lit by gas lamps. When alone, the President, relaxing in his slippers, read volumes of his favorite plays and poems by Shakespeare and Browning.

Before the war, the three-mile drive from the White House to the Soldiers' Home had been considered a fine, romantic one. On Independence Day 1862, however, the mood on that road was grim. Long lines of army ambulances were rolling into the city that day and almost every day, transporting sick, wounded, and dying Union soldiers from the bloody battlefields of Virginia to temporary Washington hospitals near Lincoln's summer residence. The *New-York Tribune* on July 8, 1862, reported that on July 4, possibly "the gloomiest since the birth of the Republic," the President:

...rode beside [the ambulances] for a considerable distance, conversing freely with the men, and seeming anxious to secure all the information possible with regard to the real condition of affairs on the Peninsula and the feeling among the troops from those who had borne the brunt of the fight.

Although the President's informants had already told him the disappointing results of the Seven Days' Battles, Lincoln hoped these soldiers could give him other news.

McClellan kept Lincoln optimistic, having just written him that "all things [were] looking bright." News correspondents published biased and inaccurate accounts, so it was hard to get a true account of the war in Virginia, so Lincoln can be forgiven for still placing trust in McClellan, with whom he was greatly dissatisfied but in whom he had invested a great deal of political capital. It was a confusing time. It was hard to know what to believe. That same night, for example, an exhausted Lincoln was literally pulled out of bed at his Soldiers' Home cottage by Union Quartermaster Meigs and former Minnesota Governor Henry Sibley, who, acting on a rumor, urged the President to "order the immediate flight of the Army" in Virginia, as the situation had become so grave. Lincoln did not budge.

To further muddle matters, Lincoln received a dispatch of McClellan's July 4 speech to his soldiers in which he declared that "...this army shall enter the capital of the so-called Confederacy."

Lincoln arranged to travel toward McClellan's headquarters at Harrison's Landing, Virginia, to put eyes on the situation. On July 8, accompanied by a small party, the President left Washington aboard the *Ariel* and took the twelve-hour journey in one-hundred-degree heat to McClellan's camp on the James River. The soldiers cheered when they glimpsed Lincoln sitting and smiling on the boat. McClellan boarded the vessel and, sitting alongside the President on the deck, handed him a letter outlining what the policy and goals of the war should be. McClellan warned that: "A declaration of radical views, especially upon slavery will rapidly disintegrate our present Armies."

McClellan concluded his letter by implying that he should be reinstated as general-in-chief. Lincoln stuffed the document in his pocket. (McClellan would send a similarly presumptuous memo to Stanton.) Lincoln made no comment; he had come to see the troops and to consult with McClellan's corps commanders, who were almost mutinous. Those interviews convinced Lincoln that to rely upon McClellan meant more stalemate. That evening, for three hours, the President reviewed one division after another, riding alongside General McClellan "holding in one hand the reins...and with the other a large-sized stove-pipe hat" that he tipped to the cheers of the soldiers, showing the soldiers that the nation sympathized with their struggle. In the Seven Days' Battles, the Union Army suffered 16,000 killed, wounded, and missing, while Lee's losses surpassed 20,000.

The next morning, Lincoln set sail for the capital:

> On the way up the Potomac, the boat was aground for several hours on the Kettle Shoals, and the whole party, including the President, availed themselves of the opportunity to take a bath and swim in the river.

The Union Army's devastating defeat on the Virginia Peninsula put the North in a black mood. Few recruits were joining the army. Governor Andrew of Massachusetts informed Lincoln that the recruits could not be increased so long as Lincoln continued to fight a war that left slavery intact.

Stanton, Chase and many Republicans, infuriated by McClellan's "noninterference with slavery memo," cried for Lincoln to remove him from command. Lincoln took issue; the army idolized their leader, and to remove him would further demoralize the troops. The Democrats, who were almost one hundred percent united against emancipation, would protest loudly; they were wooing McClellan to be the party's next presidential nominee.

Events moved quickly in mid-July. Lincoln returned to Washington on Thursday, July 10. Mary and Tad had gone to New York. On Friday, July 11, Lincoln named Henry W. Halleck as general-in-chief of all land forces. In a last-ditch effort, on Saturday, the 12th, Lincoln met with twenty-eight border state congressmen in the White House to get them to accept compensated emancipation coupled with colonization. He told the men that, regardless of the constitutional protection slavery enjoyed—the border states counted 420,000 slates and 2.6 million whites—slavery was eroding. "The pressure, in this direction, is still upon me, and is increasing," he told them. On Sunday, July 13, Lincoln attended the funeral of Secretary Stanton's infant son. On Monday, the 14th, the border state representatives rejected Lincoln's proposal.

The Confederacy was united in its common goal to destroy the Union. The rebel fighting force was formidable. This realization resulted in the 37th Congress passing two laws that indicated a harsher war policy, a broad shift in thinking how the war should be conducted. No longer was it to be solely a war between armies, not just a war to restore the Union, but a war to reconstruct it. This newer war would overturn the Southern social order. On July 17, the Congress passed the Militia Act that called for a draft of men to serve nine months and authorized African-American men to serve in the militias. Black men would earn $10 a month minus a $3 clothing ration, $6 less than white soldiers. The justification given for Black men's lower wages was that it was expected that Blacks would mostly work as laborers to free up white men for combat and not bear arms. The Navy already admitted Blacks.

In addition, the Congress passed a broader confiscation act, punishing traitors by confiscating their property, including slaves who "shall be deemed captives of war and shall be forever free." The bill was not enforceable; it was more a statement of policy. It was symbolic of what the war was becoming. No longer were Southern civilians shielded from the consequences of rebellion. Virtually every Republican supported this bill, but the President was troubled by many of its confusing aspects and wanted to veto it. He felt that power over slavery, if it existed anywhere in the federal government, was to be found in the executive branch's war powers, not the Congress, and only to be exercised by the President as commander-in-chief. He worried that Roger Taney's Supreme Court might object. In the end, he signed it on July 25, giving Confederates sixty days to abandon their rebellion or face the confiscation of their property.

The 37th Congress was extraordinarily productive. The Internal Revenue Bureau was established in the Treasury Department, and a three percent federal income tax was levied on incomes of more than $600 a year. In September 1862, Lincoln's monthly paycheck of $2,083.33 on his $25,000 annual salary would be reduced by $61. The Legal Tender Act laid the economic foundation for the Union war effort, creating a paper currency known as "greenbacks." The one-dollar bill featured the portrait of Secretary of the Treasury Salmon Chase, giving him a free campaign poster for the 1864 election in which he planned to challenge Lincoln for the Republican Party's presidential nomination.

CHAPTER 92

The Democrats Inflame the Nation with Hate Speech

1862 was a midterm election year. In the 1860 presidential election, the Democratic party had fractured. Now it worked to rebuild unity and win back some congressional seats with a heavy propaganda campaign. The towns along the Ohio River—where proslavery and anti-Black feeling was strongest—had been filling up with freed slaves since the spring. The states' Black codes were powerless to check this migration. White people saw their world turning upside-down. Using the power of the press, Democrats exploited this fear of displacement:

> [T]he policy of the Abolitionists…is to make the white people of the land merely the providers of board, clothing and education for the negroes of the South, free of cost….It is also the policy of filling the North, as well as the South, with four millions of idle uncontrollable [negroes]….—Washington *Star*, July 1862

> The Republican party…promised 'protection to laboring men;'… and they have protected labor by bringing contrabands to compete with and destroy it.—*Sunbury* Pennsylvania *Democrat*, July 1862

> We see it stated that already hundreds of runaway negroes are employed in Chester and Lancaster counties at the low rate of

ten cents a day!...[W]hite men have been discharged in this city and their places are supplied by cheap negro labor.—*Harrisburg* Pennsylvania *Patriot and Union*, ca. July 1862

The Democrats' propaganda campaign whipped up racial violence across the country.

In Toledo, Ohio:

On Tuesday last...[t]he Irish undertook to prevent the blacks from working, and for a time stones, clubs, knives, and pistols flourished in a frightful manner....

In Cincinnati, Ohio:

[Y]esterday, [a]bout noon, a gang of Irish stevedores, spying a solitary negro crossing the grade, pursued and peppered him with boulders....The only offense on the part of the negro...was his color....

In Brooklyn, New York:

[O]n Monday last in South Brooklyn, N.Y...a large mob of Irishmen, it appears, had determined to beat and burn to death if they could the colored women and children employed in two tobacco factories.

The Rev. Samuel May wrote that:

The worse and most degrading feature of slavery, exhibited by the people of the North, is the despicable *prejudice against color*,...I regard the war to be as needful for the discipline and instruction of the North, as for the overthrow of slavery. God's retributive hand is dealing with both sections of the land.

———

Where was a freed slave to go? As fugitive slaves pushed north-ward, many of them sought to cross the Ohio River to live in the river towns in the free states. Many of these states, however, Indiana, Illinois, and Ohio, for example, had laws on the books that restricted negro immigration into their states. While not strictly enforced before the Civil War, once the character of the war changed to that of slave liberation, Northern prejudices toward Black people were hardening rather than softening, as evidenced by the 1862 summer of violence in the free states. Republican Senator Lyman Trumbull of the free state of Illinois said:

> There is a very great aversion in the West—I know it to be so in my State—against having free negroes come among us. Our people want nothing to do with the negro.

Republican Congressman John Sherman of the free state of Ohio chimed in:

> In Ohio, we do not like negroes. We do not disguise our dislike.

Anti-Black bias existed both north and south of the Ohio River and infected both Republicans and Democrats.

———

In July 1862, a new contraband camp sprang up in the empty army barracks close to the Soldiers' Home in Washington. Lincoln passed it as he went to and from the White House. This new settlement called Camp Barker provided temporary relief—food, clothing, and shelter—and employment for former slaves uprooted by military oper-ations or fleeing from Maryland and Virginia, who became free upon entering the city. Once the freed men and women found employment and became self-supporting, they exited the camp as others arrived to take their places. Affordable housing in the area, however, was scarce. Many of these former slaves became squatters, building *ad hoc* shacks in alleys and empty lots in the capital city. In his life, Lincoln did not know many Black people. But he had eyes in his head. He lived by Camp Barker. The contrabands coming into the city were homeless and hungry, uprooted and displaced by war. He asked himself, everyone asked, once the four million slaves are emancipated, where would they all go? When they tried to settle in many of the free states, they were met with hostility and outright danger. And when they did coexist with white people, white people limited their rights and liberties and treated them like second-class citizens. Lincoln reasoned that if Black people, once freed, would voluntarily emigrate elsewhere to an American colony all their own, where they could enjoy full rights, free of the social ostracism they experienced from white people, then Lincoln might garner wider support to issue an emancipation proclamation. He believed that this plan would defuse the anti-emancipation feeling that was threatening Republicans in the upcoming election.

The Second Confiscation Act included a provision of $600,000 in support of voluntary colonization of African-Americans in another country, placed at the President's disposition. Radical Republicans thought the idea of removing an entire race to Central America, the plan the President was most enthusiastic about, was simply preposterous and inhumane, but many Congressmen went along with the President because colonization found wide support in the Midwest, border states, and Northwest.

On August 14, Lincoln met with a delegation of five Black leaders in the White House to pitch his plan on the benefits of colonization and to enlist their advocacy. Colonization was unpopular with Black people; the committee met with the President out of respect. A stenographer was present, and the President's remarks would be released in the papers.

Lincoln began speaking. "I think your race suffer very greatly, many of them by living among us, while ours suffer from your presence....It affords a reason why we should be separated." He asked if the men were freemen, to which one man replied, "Yes, sir."

> Your race are suffering...the greatest wrong inflicted on any people....I believe in its general evil effects on the white race. See our present condition—the country engaged in war!—our white men cutting one another's throats....[T]hen consider what we know to be the truth. But for your race among us there could not be war....

In broad strokes, Lincoln described a Central American country with great natural resources and a climate like that of "your native land—thus being suited to your physical condition." He concluded with an appeal for the committee to interest fifty men, women, and children to start on a colony.

The committee leader, Edward M. Thomas, the President of the Anglo-African Institute for the Encouragement of Industry and Art, sent the President a letter two days later, indicating that the committee was to confer with "leading colored men in Phila New York and Boston upon the movement of emigration to the point recommended in your address." Blacks received the proposal with widespread opposition.

Garrison was disgusted with the President's assertion that the native country of present-day Blacks was Africa:

> They are as much the natives of the country as any of their oppressors. Here they were born; here...they are entitled to live.

Frederick Douglass took particular affront to Lincoln's statement that, "But for your race among us there could not be war." Douglass emphasized that Blacks had not caused the war; slavery had. Douglass said that the President showed contempt for Black people. "He says to the colored people: I don't like you, you must clear out of the country."

The *Chicago Tribune* wrote that "all suggestions of deportation and colonization endorsed by the Government, will only...feed the fires that are already at work in our communities....The kindly heart of the President does not mean all this....It still will remain the great question what we shall do with [the freed slaves], but the solution will be aided and advanced by the early recognition of what we cannot do with them,—get rid of them."

———

At the request of the President, Senator Samuel C. Pomeroy of Kansas pressed forward with organizing Black emigration parties to Central America. By the end of August, he had received more than one hundred applications, including one from Frederick Douglass, writing that his two sons desired to apply.

CHAPTER 93

Lincoln's Critics Multiply

Six days after Lincoln met with the Black delegation at the White House, editor Horace Greeley published a strong letter in his *New-York Tribune* addressed to the President, titled "The Prayer of Twenty Millions," in which he proclaimed to speak for the majority in the North. Greeley pressed Lincoln to enforce the Second Confiscation Act and to immediately free the slaves as it was "preposterous" to put down the rebellion without eradicating slavery. With that Confiscation Act, Lincoln had already issued an ultimatum to the Confederacy. They had sixty days to cease the rebellion or face the confiscation of their slaves. Lincoln did not have to be reminded that the clock was ticking; a month was left to run. With recognition of Greeley's immense power, though, Lincoln replied quickly, using this as an opportunity to enunciate his platform in his own letter to Greeley, which he released to a rival newspaper, the Washington *National Intelligencer*:

> My paramount object in this struggle *is* to save the Union, and is *not* either to save or to destroy slavery. If I could save the Union without freeing *any* slave I would do it, and if I could save it by freeing *all* the slaves I would do that.
>
> What I do about slavery, and the colored race, I do because I believe it helps to save the Union….
>
> I have here stated my purpose according to my view of official duty; and I intend no modification of my oft-expressed personal wish that all men everywhere could be free.

Widely reprinted in Northern newspapers, Lincoln's letter received almost universal approval. In it, he offered assurance to Northerners who did not want the war to become an anti-slavery crusade. Yet he also signaled to anti-slavery advocates that he was open to taking action against slavery. Lincoln reminded citizens of his own moral clarity in regard to slavery—it was wrong—but that he would never let his personal beliefs interfere with his official duty.

Harriet Beecher Stowe was infuriated by Lincoln's response to Greeley. She was impatient with Lincoln's slowness in eradicating slavery. She had been expressing her opinions persistently in the *Independent*. Harriet decided to answer Lincoln's response to Greeley. She paraphrased Lincoln's words as if they might have been written by Christ himself, had he been in the White House. Published in the *Independent* on September 11, 1862, assuming the "voice" of Jesus, she wrote:

> My paramount object…is to set at liberty them that are bruised and *not* either to save or destroy the Union. What I do in favor of the Union, I do because it helps to free the oppressed…. I shall do less for the Union whenever it would hurt the cause of the slave, and more when I believe it would help the cause of the slave.

Stowe gave the impression that she was indifferent to the fate of the war-torn nation and did not understand the separation of church and state, that Lincoln was not a minister of the Word. Yet this was Mrs. Stowe's war; had not everyone told her that? *Uncle Tom's Cabin* had become the abolitionist manifesto, exposing slavery for the cruel and unjust institution it was. The book's emotional power had shifted Northern anti-slavery sentiment so profoundly that the Republican Party, founded on opposition to the extension of slavery into the territories, was founded. Senator Sumner said that if *Uncle Tom's Cabin* had not been written, "Lincoln could not have been elected President of the United States." Abolition had brought Harriet great wealth, international fame, success and honor, and abundant self-assurance. Harriet Beecher Stowe felt personal responsibility for the slaves. She felt God had given her power to use for good.

CHAPTER 94

The Two Armies Clash Again at Bull Run

Lincoln placed great hope for a victory from the newly created Army of Virginia, headed by Major General John Pope, now commanding all Federal troops north and west of Richmond. Pope was aggressive. Southerners hated him. He authorized—encouraged—his soldiers to seize food and supplies from Virginia farms and threatened to hang anyone, without a trial, who was suspected of collaborating with the Confederacy. Confederate General Robert E. Lee, a Virginian, called Pope a "miscreant" and was dead set on suppressing him. Once Lee received a report on August 5 that McClellan was leaving the Virginia Peninsula, confirming Lee's suspicions that McClellan and his Federals would soon head up the Chesapeake to reinforce Pope's army, Lee decided that Richmond was safe, and divided his army into two commands, sending Stonewall Jackson's wing to advance on Pope's forces around Culpeper, Virginia. By nightfall on August 9, the Federals were battered and had lost almost 2,400 men. They were forced to regroup. The two armies would meet up again at Manassas (Bull Run).

General Halleck found that his August 3 order to McClellan to move close to Washington to be available to Pope's army did not move McClellan even an inch. "I am almost broken down," complained Halleck, "I can't get General McClellan to do what I wish." For eleven days, McClellan, jealous of Halleck's promotion, procrastinated with protests and did not begin to move his troops until August 14, not reaching Aquia Creek until August 24. McClellan wanted to prevent Pope from being put in command of the combined Union armies.

On August 28, the Second Battle of Bull Run began. The Washington *Evening Star* reported that when the wind blew from the west, "the smell of the gunpowder was quite perceptible" in the city. Distant gunfire was heard. People huddled in the great hotels and on street corners, talking eagerly of the battle and trying to get news; rumors flew. During the first two days of the fighting, President Lincoln hunkered down for long hours in the crowded second-floor suite of the War Department telegraph office, awaiting dispatches from the front. McClellan had set up headquarters at Alexandria, and Lincoln wired him with requests for news from Manassas. McClellan was prompt to reply, but rather than giving information, he advised the President as to war strategy.

On Saturday, August 30, Lincoln's secretary, John Hay, rode out to see Lincoln at the Soldiers' Home. The President appeared, got on his horse, and the two men rode into town together, talking about the state of affairs. Hay wrote in his diary that:

> The President was very outspoken in regard to McClellan's present conduct. He said it really seemed to him that McC wanted Pope defeated. He mentioned to me a dispatch of McC in which he proposed, as one plan of action, to 'leave Pope to get out of his own scrape….' The President seemed to think him a little crazy.
>
> Later in the day…Stanton came in while we were waiting for him and carried us off to dinner…Stanton was loud about the McC business….He said that after these battles there should be one Court Martial…
>
> Everything seemed to be going well and hilarious on Saturday & we went to bed expecting glad tidings at sunrise. But about eight o'clock the President came to my room as I was dressing and calling me out, said, 'Well, John, we are whipped again, I am

afraid. The enemy reinforced on Pope and drove back his left wing and he has retired to Centreville.'

Pope's forces were crushed.

———

The next morning, Sunday, August 31, Clara Barton, in response to Secretary Stanton's urgent call for volunteer nurses to attend to the wounded, departed Washington by train in the rain. Later, she wrote to her cousin about what she found at Fairfax Railroad Station in Virginia:

I cannot tell you the scenes which awaited our eyes—the wounded were constantly coming, but no hospitals this time, only God's great one under the blue canopy.

The men were brought down from the field and laid on the ground beside the train and so back up the hill till they covered acres. The bales of hay and forage were broken open and the ground was littered like bedding for horses. They came till dark and then it was dark indeed. One lantern on the ground—made a requisition for candles—drew a few—the wind blew just enough to put them out every few minutes and the men lay so thick we could not take one step in the dark. By midnight there must have been three thousand helpless men lying in that hay.

We had two water buckets—five dippers—the store [supplies] which we carried to eat besides hard crackers—my one stew pan, which I remembered to take, and this made coffees for them. All night we made compresses and slings and bound up and wet wounds, [fed] what we could, traveled miles in the dark over those poor helpless wretches, in terror lest someone's candle fall in to the hay and consume them all....

At length, morning came, and we sent up the train with 1250, next 1000, next 1100, next 940, and so on.

On Monday the cavalry appeared in the wood opposite and a raid was hourly expected….[T]he danger became so imminent that Mrs. Fales thought it best to leave….I begged to be excused from accompanying her as the ambulances were up to the field for more and I knew I would never leave a wounded man there if I knew it, though I were taken prisoner forty times….

Sixteen of the Washingtonian volunteer nurses sent to Bull Run were captured by the Confederates.

———

Upon her return to Washington on Wednesday, Clara Barton had slept 1 ¼ hours since Saturday night. She found that McClellan's army was in the capital and, surprisingly, McClellan was in charge of it all. The citizens were bracing for an attack. Halleck had thought it wise to restore McClellan's command over both the Army of Virginia and the Army of the Potomac and Lincoln agreed.

Although he was still angry with McClellan over his delay in reinforcing Pope's army, Lincoln knew that McClellan was the most suitable general for reorganizing the badly demoralized (and many very ill) soldiers. Lincoln told Hay, "Unquestionably he has acted badly toward Pope! He wanted him to fail. That is unpardonable. But he is too useful just now to sacrifice." Lincoln did not consult his cabinet advisers; he knew they would object.

Meanwhile, unaware of the President's support of McClellan's restored command, Chase and Stanton organized a written protest to oust McClellan, which they planned to present to the President. Secretaries Stanton, Chase, Caleb Smith, and Edward Bates signed the document, but Gideon Welles disliked the idea of trying to control the President. Chase told Welles that "McClellan ought to be shot, and should, were he President, be brought to a summary punishment." The cabinet met with Lincoln on Tuesday, September 2, 1862. Seward was not present. He had been in Auburn. When he heard about the defeat at Bull Run, though, he hastened to the capital and was en route when the cabinet meeting convened.

The meeting had barely begun when the President stepped away momentarily, and Stanton, in his absence, stunned the cabinet with the update that McClellan had been ordered to take command of the forces in Washington. Upon his return to the room, Lincoln explained his decision, acknowledging that McClellan had the "slows" but was a good organizer. The cabinet discussed the matter; the feeling in the room was disturbed and despairing, more than at any other cabinet meeting, wrote Welles. The meeting ended with Stanton returning to his office "in the condition of a drooping leaf." Given the depressing war news, the relentless barrage of criticism Lincoln received for his conduct of the war, and now evidence that his cabinet opposed him in a great matter, he told the cabinet that at times, "he felt almost ready to hang himself."

When Secretary of State Seward finally arrived in the capital the following evening, he drove straightaway to the Soldiers' Home. As it were, Lincoln had visitors. Nevertheless, Lincoln begged his leave and proposed riding out with Seward, whom he called "Governor." The two friends enjoyed a conversational carriage ride. Despite his distress over the events at Bull Run, Seward's confidence that the North would prevail in the war worked like a tonic on the dispirited President.

Within days, Robert E. Lee led forty thousand rebel soldiers across the Potomac River and into Maryland, invading Union soil. Lee's marching troops were instructed to sing "Maryland, My Maryland" to inspire citizens to leave the Union and support his army. Instead, civilians shut their doors against the Southern invaders. Lee had hoped to find food for his troops and fodder for his horses in the fertile Maryland farmland. Rather, his troops were reduced to eating green corn and green apples. Although many of Lee's Confederate soldiers were elated from their victories through the summer, others were despondent, exhausted, tired of fighting barefoot and hungry, and uneasy about leaving the Confederacy; as a result, rebel soldiers and stragglers deserted by the thousands. Lee was on his way to Pennsylvania to find shoes and supplies for his army and cut crucial railroad lines in Harrisburg.

When McClellan's bluecoats marched through Maryland in pursuit of Lee's troops, the citizens gave them an enthusiastic welcome. On September 13, Corporal Barton W. Mitchell of the Twenty-seventh Indiana Infantry was walking in a field near Frederick, Maryland, when he found a copy of Robert E. Lee's Special Order Number 191, wrapped in an envelope around three cigars, dropped or left behind by a careless Confederate courier. The paper showed Lee's detailed battle plans for the four separate parts of his army. It was a fantastic bit of luck for McClellan, who boasted openly, "Here is a paper with which if I cannot whip Bobbie Lee, I will be willing to go home."

CHAPTER 95

Lee's Army Marches Toward Pennsylvania

I n each of the three theaters of war, the Confederates were poised for action. In Arkansas, General Thomas Hindman was planning to retake Missouri. Rebel forces in Mississippi were preparing a possible assault against General Grant's Army of the Tennessee. Lee had invaded the North. McClellan notified Lincoln that he had Lee's battle plans. Understandably, on September 14, 1862, Lincoln, Halleck, and Stanton were anxious for news of what McClellan was doing. The previous day, Lincoln had sprained his wrist checking his runaway horse during his morning ride from the Soldiers' Home to the White House. Lincoln's sore wrist was a minor inconvenience compared to poor Halleck's suffering. Halleck's hemorrhoids were so painful that he could not even stand. The treatment for this condition involved opium suppositories that made Halleck listless. Furthermore, Halleck was so stressed from the military crisis that his overall health was breaking down.

On the misty, grey morning of September 17, the rival armies faced one another from opposite sides of Antietam Creek, near the small Maryland town of Sharpsburg. McClellan had 70,000-80,000 men facing 50,000 rebels. The day began with an early morning Union assault through Miller's Cornfield. Over the course of three hours, these thirty acres would change hands six times with 10,000 casualties. There were no earthworks, so the blue and gray soldiers fought at close quarters with musket and cannon in the Cornfield and the West Woods for twelve bloody hours. At the end of the dramatic fighting, the number of killed, missing, and wounded men amounted to 23,000—a slaughter.

Firepower and sheer numbers allowed the Union Army to prevail, but the contest ended in more of a draw, McClellan having succeeded in stopping Lee from reaching Pennsylvania. The White House counted the Battle of Antietam as a Northern victory, but it was an incomplete one. McClellan had allowed the Confederate forces to get clean away, cross the Potomac River unmolested, and return to the safety of Virginia.

CHAPTER 96

The Time is Now

C learly, the confiscation of slaves by the Union armies aided the North's war effort by depriving the rebels of strength. While not all slaves in the Confederate Army served as soldiers, slaves built the rebels' fortifications, cooked their meals, washed their clothes, sewed uniforms, repaired railways, worked on farms and factories, in shipping yards and mines, served as hospital workers and tended the crops that supplied the food and fiber that fed and clothed them, freeing up the soldier to carry the musket. Now that he could proclaim a Union victory on the battlefield at Antietam, Lincoln was more assured of the North's support in liberating the slaves in the states and parts of States in rebellion. Consequently, he decided to issue an emancipation proclamation to liberate the slaves, claiming it was a military necessity, as such an action would greatly undermine the Confederates' ability to wage war, deprived of part of their economic engine of war—slaves.

On Monday, September 22, Lincoln convened his cabinet, telling them he had made a covenant with God that if the army drove the rebels from Maryland, he would issue his Emancipation Proclamation. Two months earlier, the President had met with his cabinet about issuing just such a proclamation, but at Seward's suggestion, he postponed it until he could proclaim a military victory.

With Chase and Stanton seated at his right and the others seated on his left, he opened the meeting by reading a funny story written by Artemus Ward. Then, he assumed a graver tone, saying:

I think the time has come now. I wish it were a better time. I wish that we were in a better condition. The action of the army against the rebels has not been quite what I should have best liked....

I have gotten you together to hear what I have written down. I do not wish your advice about the main matter—for that I have determined for myself. This I say without intending anything but respect for any one of you. But I already know the views of each on this question...and I have considered them as thoroughly and carefully as I can.

He welcomed any suggestions as to improvements to the expressions in his document. He continued:

One other observation I will make. I know very well that many others might, in this matter, as in others, do better than I can; and if I were satisfied that the public confidence was more fully possessed by any one of them than by me, and knew of any Constitutional way in which he could be put in my place. He should have it....

But though I believe that I have not so much of the confidence of the people as I had some time since, I do not know that, all things considered, any other person has more; and, however this may be there is no way in which I can have any other man put where I am. I am here. I must do the best I can, and bear the responsibility of taking the course which I feel I ought to take.

Then, he proceeded to read from the draft he had begun in the summer, which he kept concealed in a drawer, over which he had brooded and edited many days and nights since, both at the Soldiers' Home and at the White House, the document now encompassing four pages and, using scissors and paste to "insert the [confiscation] laws into his document," had "fixed it up a little" over the weekend to strengthen his rationale of military necessity. Lincoln's use of dry, legalistic language was deliberate, demonstrating his reliance on pragmatism rather than idealism to justify emancipation. So many times, he had already stated his moral clarity on the wrongness of slavery.

He began to read his Emancipation Proclamation, which announced at the end that, in one hundred days, on January 1, 1863, "all persons held as slaves" within any state or part of a state still in rebellion would be "then, thenceforward, and forever free." Lincoln cited as his authority for acting against slavery his war powers, although vaguely defined, to seize enemy resources. He had no constitutional power to act against slavery in the loyal border states. Lincoln's Emancipation Proclamation had more bearing than did the Second Confiscation Act (which was to take effect the next day), as that older document only freed slaves within Confederate areas that were already occupied by the Union Army. Additionally, as Lincoln's Proclamation was an executive decree, it had less chance of being overturned by a challenge from the proslavery Taney Supreme Court.

In the discussion that followed the reading of the decree, Stanton spoke emphatically in favor of the measure. Seward and Lincoln tinkered with the text. Only Postmaster General Montgomery Blair voiced dissent, not against emancipation, but out of fear that such an action might have a bad effect on the border states and the army and give the Democrats an edge in the election just weeks away. Lincoln felt he had done everything possible to bring the border states along. As for the election concern, Lincoln said that argument "had not much weight with him."

Chase had reservations, which he did not express in this meeting. Back in July, when Lincoln had first presented the Proclamation to the cabinet, Chase had astonished not just the secretaries but the President when he blurted out that he thought emancipation was "a great danger" and that it should be up to the generals to emancipate quietly and gradually. Lincoln exclaimed, "What! You Chase, the father of abolitionism, object!" Chase had shown his hand. Lincoln's slowness on the slavery issue was the reason Chase was the darling of the radicals; now that Lincoln was to get the credit for emancipating the slaves, on what platform was Chase to capture the 1864 Republican presidential nomination?

The next day, the Proclamation was released in the papers. Lincoln had altered the purpose of the war from restoring the old Union to one of creating a new one cleansed of bondage. The Civil War was now a revolution, a revolution in ideas. Serenaders came to the White House in celebration. Predictably, Northern anti-slavery advocates praised the measure. Black people rejoiced. Most of the radicals in Lincoln's own party were temporarily quieted. Rallies were held in every major city in the North—complete with bonfires, torchlit parades, and glorious speeches. Letters of commendation poured into the White House, addressed to President Lincoln, many from illustrious men of letters. Horace Greeley spelled out his appreciation in large letters in his *Tribune*: "God Bless Abraham Lincoln!"

The *Chicago Tribune* rhapsodized:

> President Lincoln has set his hand and affixed the great seal of the nation to the grandest proclamation ever issued by man....So splendid a vision has hardly shone upon the world since the day of the Messiah.

Lincoln could not help but be gratified; public praise had been in short supply, but flattery did not cloud his vision. Speaking with his Vice President Hannibal Hamlin, he mentioned that subscriptions to government securities and volunteering for the army had slowed to a trickle. He remarked: "The North responds to the proclamation sufficiently in breath, but breath alone kills no rebels."

In the South, the reaction to the Emancipation Proclamation was negative, although the President had no way of knowing how the African-Americans there were responding. Like many War Democrats,

General McClellan said he could not bear the thought of fighting for "such as accursed doctrine" as the Emancipation Proclamation. He drafted a protest letter to the President that he was persuaded not to send. Would the army mutiny? Or would the army fight for freedom? Many soldiers had expressed their ardent wish to destroy anything that helped to put down the rebellion.

Democrats accused Lincoln of presidential authoritarianism and drummed up racial prejudice to improve their chances at the polls. Lincoln's call for 600,000 more men for the military, the enforcement of the draft, and the suspension of the writ of *habeas corpus* reinforced the Democrats' portrayal of Lincoln as a dictator and alarmed journalists and voters alike. They denounced the (preliminary) Emancipation Proclamation as "a proposal for the butchery of women and children" that would unleash "scenes of lust…rapine… arson and murder."

Frances Seward wrote to son, Willy:

> The Proclamation, tho' far less than we hoped, & had a right to demand, after the expenditure of so much of the best blood of the nation, is still an advance, which we hail with joy, as the forerunner of proclamation of Liberty throughout *all* the land.

Lydia Maria Child worried about what might happen in the hundred-day grace period before emancipation went into effect, saying:

> It certainly is not much to wait three months longer, after waiting thirty years, but I divest myself of misgivings concerning contingencies that may intervene….It is giving time to rebels in the South and traitors in the North to mature their plans."

Frederick Douglass, who had whip marks on his back from his time as a slave, wrote, "We shout for joy that we live to record this righteous decree." Although he did not yet personally know Lincoln, he had the measure of the man. He assured his readers that, in the hundred-day grace period, they had no reason to doubt Lincoln's commitment. Lincoln would not take back his Proclamation. "If he has taught us to confide in nothing else, he has taught us to confide in his word."

While Harriet Beecher Stowe was jubilant to hear of Lincoln's Proclamation, she needed to be sure that Lincoln was serious in his intent about freeing the slaves on January 1. Harriet had completed about two-thirds of her address to the ladies of Great Britain and Ireland in which she was trying to influence public opinion there in support of the North. This written plea was actually a reply to an appeal the women of Britain had submitted to Harriet eight years earlier, pleading for the abolition of slavery in the States, containing the signatures of more than half a million British women. Regardless of the steps the North had now taken to fight for the slaves, England remained mum, as a strong party had arisen in England in favor of recognizing the South, as Southern cotton kept the English mills running.

Before she could comfortably cite the President's Proclamation, though, and submit the "Reply" to the *Atlantic Monthly* for January 1863 publication, she thought it wise to travel to Washington to speak to Lincoln herself. Also, her son Fred's regiment was at nearby Fort Runyon. She was anxious to see him. Fred, 22, had been treated for alcoholism in his teens. Ever since Harriet learned that Fred's army physician "was prescribing whiskey for his ague [malaria]," she wrote her daughter," I have had no rest."

CHAPTER 97

McClellan Disappoints Again

L incoln devoted himself to getting McClellan to move. He visited him in camp to inspire him to action, urging McClellan to move before the Confederates were reinforced and refitted. Lincoln reviewed the troops. He felt his trip was a success and that he had established a rapport with the army. Once back in Washington, he had Halleck send McClellan short but pointed messages, telling him to "cross the Potomac" out of Maryland and "give battle to the enemy or drive him south." Northern citizens, the President, the Republicans, and General Halleck had thrown up their hands in exasperation with McClellan.

U.S. President Lincoln meets with General George McClellan (6ᵗʰ from left) and his Union troops at Sharpsburg, following the battle of Antietam, Maryland (1862)

Weeks elapsed as McClellan excused his inaction due to a lack of supplies, shoes, and his tired horses. Lincoln responded, "Will you pardon me for asking what the horses of your army have done since the battle of Antietam that fatigue anything?" Conservative opposition to the Emancipation Proclamation, along with the army's idleness, did not help the Republicans in the fall elections. Consequently, the President's party suffered major reverses when the November election tallies were complete. The Republicans retained a slight majority in Congress but the state election results were more dismal.

Although McClellan had finally crossed the Potomac, he had moved so slowly—he took nine days to cross—that it gave Lee ample time to interpose Longstreet's corps between Richmond and the Union Army while Jackson remained in the Shenandoah Valley on McClellan's flank. The day after the November election, Lincoln asked Halleck to relieve McClellan of his command and replace him with General Ambrose Burnside, known as a fighting general. Lincoln told his secretary Hay, "I began to fear [McClellan] was playing false—that he did not want to hurt the enemy." Of McClellan's skills, Lincoln remarked, "He is an admirable engineer but he seems to have a special talent for a stationary engine."

CHAPTER 98

Harriet Goes to Washington

In later November, Harriet Beecher Stowe, accompanied by her oldest daughter, Hattie, and her younger sister, Isabella Beecher Hooker, arrived in Washington, D.C. The capital reporter for a Massachusetts paper covered the event: "Harriet Beecher Stowe is in Washington....I hear that Mrs. Stowe called on Mrs. Lincoln when she was in Boston (perhaps it was in New York)...."

Harriet called upon Mary Lincoln at the Metropolitan Hotel in New York. Traveling with the First Lady (along with Tad) was Mary's closest friend, Lizzie Keckley. Lizzie, as a founder of the Washington Contraband Relief Association, was circulating in both New York and Boston raising money for the society. The donors ranged from Black dining-room waiters to powerhouse journalist Frederick Douglass who contributed $200 and agreed to lecture for this cause. Mary wrote her husband that she had donated $200 to the project and asked him to send a check:

> [Lizzie] says the immense number of Contrabands in W- are suffering intensely, many without bed covering & having to use any bits of carpeting to cover themselves—Many dying of want.

Harriet's visit to Washington was altogether satisfying. She got the answers she had been seeking. She spent time with her son, now "Lieutenant" Fred—he had put on weight—and army life seemed to agree with him. She spoke with senators, department heads, and the President himself and attended the opening of Congress where, on December 1, she heard a clerk read from the President's second annual message these closing remarks:

> I can not make it better known than it already is that I strongly favor colonization; and yet I wish to say there is an objection urged against free colored persons remaining in the country which is largely imaginary, if not sometimes malicious.
>
> ...But it is dreaded that the freed people will swarm forth and cover the whole land. Are they not already in the land? Will liberation make them any more numerous? Equally distributed among the whites of the whole country, and there would be but one colored to seven whites. Could the one in any way greatly disturb the seven?
>
> ...And in any event, can not the North decide for itself whether to receive them?
>
> Fellow-citizens, we can not escape history. We of this Congress and this Administration will be remembered in spite of ourselves. No personal significance or insignificance can spare one or another of us. The fiery trial through which we pass will light us down in honor or dishonor to the latest generation. We say we are for the Union. The world will not forget that we say this. We know how to save the Union. The world knows we do know how to save it. We, even we here, hold the power and bear the responsibility. In giving freedom to the slave we assure freedom to the free—honorable alike in what we give and what we preserve. We shall nobly save or meanly lose the last best hope of earth. Other means may succeed; this could not fail. The way is plain, peaceful, generous, just--a way which if followed the world will forever applaud and God must forever bless.

While the President's words reassured Harriet of his intent to issue the Proclamation, Harriet had already decided to trust him the week before, on Thanksgiving Day. By invitation, she appeared on the speaker platform with Senator Pomeroy of Kansas for a great turkey feast for the people living in the contraband camp in the capital. Five hundred refugees were present. There was eating, singing of "Go Down, Moses," a rousing speech about freedom by the senator—with liberal amounts of clapping, laughing, and cries of "Amen," "That's so!", "Rise! Rise!" and "The Lord grant it!" from the audience. There were prayers by ministers "of all sorts of colors," reported an Indiana paper.

The Freedmen's Village in Arlington, Virginia

As Harriet could see for herself, the formerly enslaved people of the South were assembling without fear of a slave catcher snatching them up and sending them back to bondage. The Fugitive Slave Act that had propelled Harriet to write *Uncle Tom's Cabin* was a dead letter. After the event, Harriet hastened to her room to complete her "Reply" to the ladies of England to urge them to support the North in the war. She then mailed it right away to her editor, James Fields, for January publication. She concluded by writing:

> And now, sisters of England, think it not strange if we bring back the words of your letter…and lay them down at your door. We say to you, Sisters, you have spoken well: we have heard you; we have

heeded; we have striven in the cause, even unto death. Sister, what have you done, and what do you mean to do?...
In behalf of many thousands of American women,
Harriet Beecher Stowe.

CHAPTER 99

The Year Grinds to a Close

In the monthlong run-up to the President's New Year's Day signing of the Emancipation Proclamation, Lincoln's difficulties continued to mount. The previous month, Lincoln had been presented with a list of 303 Sioux men sentenced to death for their part in the Minnesota uprising of August and September. Lincoln demanded to see the trial proceedings and went through every one of the capital cases. The original trials had been a farce; the Indians were denied counsel and did not understand what was being said. After his review, Lincoln determined that thirty-nine of these condemned men were most clearly guilty and, on December 6, ordered their execution. So there would be no misunderstanding, he methodically wrote out in his own hand the phonetic spelling of each man's name: "Te-he-hdo-ne-cha," "Tazoo" alias "Plan-doo-ta," and so forth. At the end of the month, thirty-eight men were hanged.

On December 13, General Burnside's Virginia offensive resulted in a shocking Union defeat at the Battle of Fredericksburg. As news of the catastrophe and the report of 12,700 Union casualties spread, a wave of anger spread through the North and in the government, resulting in what the *Chicago Tribune* termed a "state of despondency and desperation." Although Burnside, Halleck, and Stanton received their share of abuse for the blame, it was the Lincoln administration that bore the brunt of criticism, the complaints becoming almost deafening. The President was pale and haggard, feeling the loss and deaths were his fault. He moaned and wrung his hands, saying, "If there is a worse place than hell, I am in it."

Due to a protracted whispering campaign by Secretary Chase, some radical Senate Republicans, thirsting for a victim for the military failure, had come to believe that Secretary of State Seward was the leader of "a malign influence which controlled the President, and overruled all the decisions of the cabinet." Believing Chase's account, Senate Republicans overwhelmingly voted to demand that the President oust Seward from his cabinet. Seward was informed and, over the President's objections, submitted his letter of resignation. Lincoln needed Seward.

In a meeting with nine senators, Lincoln defended Seward against the committee's charge that he had "improperly interfered" with decisions, pointing out particularly Seward's full support of the Emancipation Proclamation. Lincoln arranged for the nine Senators to meet with his cabinet, minus Seward, and hear what Lincoln's Cabinet secretaries had to say about his manner of conducting their affairs. Chase panicked at the thought of sharing the room with the senators, to whom he had told malicious tales of a dysfunctional cabinet.

The senators' resolutions included the charge that the President had not regularly consulted his full cabinet on important matters and that the cabinet was in disunity. Lincoln asked the cabinet to respond to that charge. Montgomery Blair, though he had sometimes differed with Seward, warned the committee not to meddle with the President's Cabinet. Most of the cabinet members agreed to having been consulted on important matters. What was Chase to do? If he repeated his frequent complaints, he would reveal his disloyalty to the President; if he sided with the President, he revealed his deception of the senators. He had no escape. He supported the President's statement that the cabinet had been consulted on matters of importance and that there was no lack of unity in the cabinet. The case against Seward collapsed and Chase was exposed.

The next morning, the President summoned Chase to the White House. Stanton and Welles were waiting in the executive office with

Chase when the President walked in. Lincoln turned to Chase, saying, "I sent for you, for this matter is giving me great trouble." Chase told Lincoln that he had prepared his resignation.

"Where is it?" asked Lincoln hurriedly, his eye lighting up. "Let me have it," he said, his fingers reaching out for the document of which Chase was reluctant to let go. Lincoln snatched the letter and opened it. "This…cuts the Gordian knot," he said, laughing, "I can dispose of this subject now."

Stanton offered his resignation, but Lincoln did not want it. He dismissed Chase and Stanton. Senator Ira Harris visited Lincoln shortly after Lincoln received Chase's resignation. Lincoln likened his feeling at that moment back to a time when he was a boy, and had worked out a way to carry pumpkins while riding horseback, saying, "I can ride on now. I've got a pumpkin in each end of my bag!" He wrote letters to both Seward and Chase, declining to accept their resignations and asking them to resume the duties of their departments.

Lincoln was proud he had been able to keep his cabinet together, one dominated by neither radicals nor conservatives. Additionally, Seward had been reassured of the President's allegiance and Chase, for a time, became less indiscreet in his remarks. Lincoln, in turn, became more businesslike and solicited more opinions from his cabinet colleagues. At a cabinet meeting on December 30, he presented the members with copies of his emancipation draft, asking for suggestions to the text. He added a concluding paragraph, proposed by Chase yet instigated by Senator Sumner:

> And upon this act, sincerely believed to be an act of justice, warranted by the Constitution, upon military necessity, I invoke the considerate judgment of mankind, and the gracious favor of Almighty God.

On New Year's Eve, 1862, writer Louisa May Alcott, 30, was in Washington, D.C. She was a voluntary nurse at the Union Hotel Hospital in Georgetown. When leaving Massachusetts to report for duty in the capital, Louisa felt "as if I was the son of the house going to war." She had just been awarded "the highest prize for the best short tale for *Frank Leslie's Illustrated Paper*." Among her responsibilities with the wounded soldiers, she assisted at amputations.

Now, on the eve of the signing of the Emancipation Proclamation, back in her rooms, she celebrated by "leaping from her bed at midnight and racing to the window" to shout and sing into the night air of the capital. She waved her handkerchief to a crowd of Black men gathered below. She fell into bed, listening to the crackle of firecrackers and choruses of hallelujah hymns sounding all night.

In contraband camps, homes, and churches across the country, Black and white Americans gathered for watch night parties to celebrate the coming of freedom for approximately three million people and, at midnight, celebrated with the reading of the Emancipation Proclamation as one hundred days had passed and not a single Confederate state had restored itself to the Union.

CHAPTER 100

Lincoln Issues the Emancipation Proclamation

New Year's Day, 1863, dawned sunny, crisp and cold in the nation's capital. After a fitful night's sleep, the President rose early, lit the fire and gaslights in his office, and made final revisions to his Emancipation Proclamation, this one deviating slightly from the preliminary version. He still proclaimed that "all persons held as slaves" within states and parts of states still in rebellion "shall be then, and thenceforward, and forever free," exempting the border states, Tennessee, and Union-controlled portions of Louisiana and Virginia. Lincoln made a significant addition, though, officially authorizing the recruitment of Blacks into the army. In liberating the slaves, the Emancipation Proclamation thus enlarged the scope and purpose of the war. Through his action, Lincoln set the republic on a course to become what it was meant to be from the beginning: a fair nation.

Lincoln sent his draft to the State Department for its official calligraphy. Shortly before 11 a.m., Seward returned with the Proclamation. Lincoln noticed a technical error in the format and returned the document to the State Department to be corrected. This delayed the signing until after the traditional New Year's Eve reception, scheduled from 11 a.m. until 2 p.m.

The first hour was set aside for Washington officials. Fanny Seward attended the White House reception dressed in blue silk with a white hat and an ivory fan. Having just passed her eigh-teenth birthday, this was her coming-out day, her debut into the social world. At noon, the cabinet members departed to prepare for their own house receptions. The gates of the White House then opened to the general public. Journalist Noah Brooks of California was there to record the shoving of the masses, the torn coats and bonnets. Brooks had first met Lincoln in Springfield seven years early. The President, vigorously shaking everyone's hand in the disorderly receiving line and awarding each person a kind remark and a smile, was much altered in appearance from those earlier days. A month earlier, Brooks had noted the change in the President's appearance:

> His hair is grizzled, his gait more stooping, his countenance sallow, and there is a sunken, deathly look about the large cavernous eyes.

Mary, wearing a "rich dress of black velvet," who had attended a séance the night before, looked sad and was unable to stay for the whole reception, this being the first one since Willie's death. After the guests departed, Lincoln went upstairs to his office for the signing of the document in the presence of a handful of friends. Seward and son, Fred, returned with the corrected draft. Fred recalled:

> The broad sheet was spread open before [the President] on the Cabinet table. Mr. Lincoln dipped his pen in the ink, and then holding it a moment above the sheet, seemed to hesitate. Looking around, he said:
>
> 'I never in my life felt more certain that I was doing right, than I do in signing this paper. But I have been receiving calls and shaking hands since nine o'clock this morning, till my arm is stiff and numb. Now this signature is one that will be closely examined, and if they find my hand trembled they will say 'he had some compunctions. But anyway, it is going to be done.'

So saying, he slowly and carefully wrote his name at the bottom of the proclamation. The signature proved to be unusually clear, bold, and firm, even for him, and a laugh followed at his apprehension.

Ordinarily, he signed "A. Lincoln." But today, he carefully wrote out his full name, saying, "If my name ever goes into history, it will be for this act, and my whole soul is in it." Seward then signed his name and carried it to the State Department where the great seal of the United States was affixed. Then, copies were sent out to the press.

———

At the suggestion of her friend, John Greenleaf Whittier, Charlotte Forten, a well-educated, refined, and beautiful school teacher from Massachusetts, had traveled to the Sea Islands to assist Laura Towne in teaching the contrabands at the Brick School on St. Helena Island. She had arrived in Beaufort the previous October and found that the word "'n----r' was plentifully used" by the Union soldiers. Laura Towne, was elated when Charlotte Forten arrived at Seaside Plantation and warmly welcomed her. The Black servants, though, snubbed her. Towne had to coax Aunt Becky to wait upon Forten and to clean her room. The contrabands did not know what to make of her, calling her "dat brown gal." Charlotte Forten was of mixed race, a mulatto. There were only a handful of mulattos among the ten thousand Black people of the Sea Islands. To the light-skinned Charlotte, this was a surprise. She wrote in her journal that, with few exceptions, in the school, "the children are all black," of completely African ancestry. One of her pupils was Elizabeth Smalls, Robert's daughter.

Charlotte Forten (1870s)

On January 1, 1963, Emancipation Day, Charlotte Forten wrote the following account:

[It] was a glorious one to us….We [went] to the celebration at Camp Saxton. There was an eager, wondering crowd of the freed people in their holiday-attire…and the happiest of faces. The band was playing, flags streaming, everybody talking merrily and feeling strangely happy….Some companies of the First Regiment were drawn up in line under the trees….

[From] the stand…[in] the crowd before us…were the black soldiers in their blue coats and scarlet pantaloons…men, women, and children, of every complexion, grouped in various attitudes under the moss-hung trees….The exercises commenced with a prayer….Colonel Higginson (of Secret Six fame) then introduced Dr. Brisbane, who read the President's Proclamation, which was enthusiastically cheered….Some of the colored people, of their own accord, commenced singing, 'My Country, 'tis of thee.'

The flags were delivered to the Black color bearers, Prince Rivers and Robert Sutton, who gave good speeches. Frances D. Gage, who had been the President at the Akron, Ohio woman's convention when Sojourner Truth was there, spoke as well. Gage had been urging Sea Island mothers to encourage their Black sons to enlist in the army.

On New Year's Day, the crowds in Boston grew anxious as the clock ticked away the hours and no confirmation came that Lincoln had signed the Proclamation. Since morning, an audience of three thousand had gathered at Tremont Temple, waiting for the "first flash of the electric wires." Frederick Douglass was there. At the Music Hall nearby, another group formed, including Henry Wadsworth Longfellow, Ralph Waldo Emerson, John Greenleaf Whittier, and Harriet Beecher Stowe. As the clock clicked past 9 p.m. and still no word was received at Tremont Temple, the crowd worried. Then, at 10 p.m., both groups received confirmation of the signing and shouts of "joy and gladness," tears and sobs filled the room. Meanwhile, over at the music hall, a man ran onto the stage shouting, "Lincoln has signed!" Amid the cheering, shouting, hugging, and weeping, a cry went up for "Harriet Beecher Stowe!" The crowd began to chant her name. To thunderous applause, Harriet appeared on the balcony, tears streaming from her eyes, and acknowledged the tribute.

In Washington, serenaders appeared on the White House lawn to applaud the President's action. Lincoln came to the window and bowed.

In the last months preceding the signing of the Proclamation, Lincoln's old friend, the Kentuckian slaveholder, Joshua Speed, paid him a visit. At first, Speed was opposed to the emancipation measure and told Lincoln so. Lincoln hoped Speed would see the wisdom of this act. Lincoln reminded Speed to think back to an event twenty years earlier in Springfield—when he and Mary called off their engagement—when Lincoln became so depressed he contemplated taking his own life. Lincoln reminded Speed of the thought that had pulled him back from the brink of death. Speed recalled that past moment:

> He said to me that he had done nothing to make any human being remember that he had lived—and that to connect his name with the events transpiring in his day & generation and so impress himself upon them as to link his name with something that would redound to the interest of his fellow man was what he desired to live for.
>
> He....said with earnest emphasis—I believe in this measure (the proclamation) my fondest hopes will be realized.

Afterword

Amerca's struggle to extend full rights to its Black citizens does not end with Lincoln's monumental Emancipation Proclamation. That story is far from over. But our story ends here. We can freeze, savor the moment, and send up a great big, Glory, Hallelujah!

Lincoln has sounded the death knell for slavery. Most of the nation's slaves are free and full of hope for a brighter future. Lincoln is still alive. He is still the president. England will not recognize the Confederacy, thanks in no small part to Harriet Beecher Stowe.

Although the bloody war still rages, now Black men will put on army uniforms and take up arms against the enemy, leading the Union to victory, and show the nation how brave, beautiful, and strong they are.

Acknowledgments

M
y first thanks go to the individuals who, long ago, gathered up personal letters, diaries, and miscellany and donated them to libraries. Then there are those wonderful editors who saw that these collections were printed up in books for us to read. Now we have librarians who have digitized these documents and made them available to us online. I have great gratitude to companies who, with a subscription, give us access to invaluable news articles from distant times. I truly appreciate the authors who have written the works upon which I depended to write this new study.

A special thanks goes to the archivists, Beth Burgess and Cat White, at the Harriet Beecher Stowe Center in Hartford, Connecticut, for providing me with letters from the E. Bruce Kirkham Collection. I appreciate the University of Rochester for allowing me access to Fanny Seward's personal diary. The Gilder Lehrman Institute of American History provided me with "receipt for sale of slave" photocopies. I would not have been able to read Goldfarb's thesis on Gamaliel Bailey without intervention from John Edmundson at UCLA. Alex at Penn State provided me with maritime info in relation to Gamaliel Bailey's trip to China. Ann Sindelar at Western Reserve Historical Society provided me with copies of letters in the Marius Racine Robinson Papers. Thanks go to the librarians at the University of Texas, who unshelved and reshelved many precious old books for me.

Thank you, David Provolo, for the dynamic cover design and Liliana Guia for her meticulous internal design and project management. I appreciate Celia Pool for her laborious copyediting and proofreading. Adrienne Bashista lent her outstanding library expertise to the copyright page. Teri Greenberg happily took on the thankless task of indexing. Author Ann Hagedorn imparted wisdom about the need for a history book to have structure, "bones," she says. Thank you, Brandon Janes at Jackson Walker, LLP for your legal support. Sara Kocek at Yellow Bird Editors has been infinitely helpful with directing me to trustworthy resources. David Sandoval at Postnet did beautiful marketing designs. I must not neglect to thank all the technical workers at Microsoft, Spectrum, and especially Sugganya at Clarivate, who tackle and remove the multitude of obstacles that daily threatened to derail my project.

Notes

The author has chosen to retain original spelling, punctuation, capitalization, and italics in quoted material except where changes are indicated by bracket.

FRONT MATTER

viii **"Instruction Includes"** "Florida Still Teaches 'Benefits' of Slavery," *Austin American Statesman* (Austin, Texas), June 4, 2024.

viii **"how government...capitalism"** "What Haley Didn't Say," *The New York Times* (New York), December 30, 2023.

ix **"its foundations"** Stephens, Alexander, "1861 Cornerstone Speech," *American Battlefield Trust*.

PART I: WORDS

1 **"But words"** Byron, George Gordon Byron Baron, *Don Juan*, A new Cantos I-VIII ed. (London: Printed by Thomas Davison, 1819).

CHAPTER 1: LYMAN FINDS HIS FAMILY

3 **"I am the son"** Beecher, Lyman, and Cross, Barbara M., *The Autobiography of Lyman Beecher* (Cambridge, Mass: The Belknap Press of Harvard University Press, 1961), I: 10-1.

4 **"Brimstone Beecher"** Applegate, Debby, *The Most Famous Man in America: The Biography of Henry Ward Beecher* (New York: Doubleday, 2006), 57.

5 **"I never saw"** Beecher, Lyman, and Beecher, Charles, *Autobiography, Correspondence, Etc., of Lyman Beecher*, D.D (New York: Harper, 1865), I: 178.

6 **"Would now write"** Hedrick, Joan D., *Harriet Beecher Stowe: A Life* (New York: Oxford University Press, 1994), 6 7.

6 **"I'm going to heaven"** Koester, Nancy, *Harriet Beecher Stowe: A Spiritual Life* (2014), 13-4.

CHAPTER 2: HARRIET WORRIES ABOUT LORD BYRON

8 **"My dear, Byron...Oh, I'm so sorry"** ibid., 21.

8 **"that great eternity"** ibid.

8 **"It was a fire"** ibid., 37-8.

CHAPTER 3: HARRIET PICKS UP HER PEN

9 **"Have not then"** Beecher, Catharine E., "Circular: Addressed to the Benevolent Ladies of the United States," *Teaching American History*.

10 **"Last night we"** Hedrick, J. D., 58-9.

10 **"You see my dear"** ibid., 64.

13 **"if we gain the"** ibid., 68.

13 **"the rising generation"** ibid.

CHAPTER 4: ABRAHAM GROWS UP IN A SLAVE STATE

16 **"he was stowing"** Coleman, J. Winston, *Slavery Times in Kentucky* (University of North Carolina Press, 1940), 173-4.

16 **"CASH FOR NEGROES"** "Cash for Negroes," *The Western Citizen*, July 24, 1816.

16 **"In the summer"** Rankin, John, Letters on *American Slavery: Addressed to Mr. Thomas Rankin, Merchant at Middlebrook, Augusta Co., Va.* (Boston: Isaac Knapp, 1838), 41-3.

18 **"that if we didn't"** Walters, Kerry S., *The Underground Railroad : A Reference Guide, Guides to Historic Events in America* (Santa Barbara, Calif) New York: Bloomsbury Publishing (US), 2012), 39.

CHAPTER 5: ABRAHAM TAKES TO THE RIVER

20 **"You would say"** Keneally, Thomas, *Abraham Lincoln: A Life* (New York: Penguin, 2003), 7.

23 **"the smartest man"** Donald, David Herbert, *Lincoln* (New York: Touchstone, 1995), 40.

24 **"My politics is short"** Freedman, Russell, *Lincoln : A Photobiography* (New York, N.Y.: Clarion Books, 1987), 133.

24 **"any live, fighting"** Donald, D. H., 45.

24 **"a piece of floating"** Herndon, William H., Weik, Jesse W., and Angle, Paul M., *Herndon's Life of Lincoln: The History and Personal Recollections of Abraham Lincoln* (Cleveland, Ohio: World Pub. Co, 1949), 66.

CHAPTER 6: WILLIE GARRISON IS ON FIRE

26 **"Garrison is a prophet"** May, Samuel J., *Some Recollections of Our Antislavery Conflict* (New York: Arno Press, 1968), 18-20.

27 **"My friend, do"** ibid., 36-7.

27 **"Brother May, I"** ibid.

CHAPTER 7: NATE STRIKES BACK

30 **"And I saw"** Parker, Nate, *The Birth of a Nation: Nat Turner and the Making of the Movement* (New York: 37 Ink/Atria, 2016), 3.

30 **"the great day"** Turner, Nat et al., *The Confessions of Nat Turner, the Leader of the Late Insurrection in Southampton, Va.* (Baltimore Md.: T.R. Gray, 1831), 11.

30 "Yet such was" ibid., 6-7.

32 "Here goes the" Johnson, F. Roy, *The Nat Turner Slave Insurrection* (Murfreesboro, N.C: Johnson Pub. Co, 1966), 93.

34 "You impudent scoundrel" Frederickson, George M., *William Lloyd Garrison* (New Jersey: Prentice-Hall, Inc., 1968), 103.

PART II: FREEDOM

37 "So the traveler" Tocqueville, Alexis de, *Democracy in America* (London: Saunders and Otley, 1835), 263.

CHAPTER 8: GAMALIEL GOES WEST

39 "delightful and fertile" "A Circular to the Citizens of the United States: To the Oregon Emigrants," *Sentinel and Democrat* (Burlington, Vermont), June 24, 1831.

39 "a scattering little" Goldfarb, Joel, "The Life of Gamaliel Bailey Prior to the Founding of the National Era; the Orientation of a Practical Abolitionist" (University of California, 1958).

41 "Our colored population" Drake, Daniel, "An Account of the Epidemic Cholera: As It Appeared in Cincinnati," *National Library of Medicine Digital Collections*, no., 19-20.

41 "wretched basin" Koester, N., 58.

42 "face quite shrunk" Smith, Matthew, "Pandemic Redux: Revisiting Cincinnati's 1849 Cholera in the Age of Covid-19," *Origins: Current Events in HIstorial Perspective*, 2020.

CHAPTER 9: HARRIET COMES OUT OF HER SHELL

43 "great Andover" Beecher, L., and Cross, B. M., 2: 183.

44 "corduroy roads" ibid., II: 210, Wilson, Robert Forrest, *Crusader in Crinoline, the Life of Harriet Beecher Stowe* (Philadelphia, London etc.: J.B. Lippincott Company, 1941), 94.

45 "The countries of Asia" Beecher, Harriet and Catharine, *Primary Geography for Children* (Cincinnati: Corey and Fairbank, 1833), 53, 8-61.

46 "Spencer de Cheyce" Goodwin, Doris Kearns, *Team of Rivals: The Political Genius of Abraham Lincoln* (New York: Simon & Schuster, 2005), 41.

46 "A New England Sketch" Beecher, Miss Harriet E., "The Prize Tale: A New England Sketch," *Western Monthly Magazine*.

46 "Harriet is a great" Hedrick, J. D., 29-30.

CHAPTER 10: LANE IS OPEN FOR BUSINESS

47 "I helped to load" Stanton, Henry Brewster, *Random Recollections*, 2d ed. (New York: Macgowan & Slipper, Printers, 1886), 43-4.

49 "took the lead" Beecher, L., and Beecher, C., II: 321.

49 "Over in the pew" ibid., II: 289.

65 **"literary woman"** ibid., 139-40.

65 **"whose mode of"** ibid., 93.

66 **"of a dark Syrian hue"** "American Anti-Slavery Society,"; "The Anti-Abolition Riots (1834)," BlackPast.

67 **"The next excitement"** Beecher, Lyman; Biggs, Thomas J.; Stowe, Calvin E., *The Annual Report of the Trustees of the Cincinnati Lane Seminary* (1834) (Cincinnati, Ohio: Corey & Fairbank, 1834).

CHAPTER 15: BIGGS GETS HIS REVENGE

68 **"He who would preach"** Lesick, L. T., 92.

69 **"to save the school"** Rugoff, Milton, *The Beechers: An American Family in the Nineteenth Century*, 1st ed. (New York: Harper & Row, 1981), 148.

70 **"a cauldron"** Applegate, D., 117.

70 **"The history of the world"** Rankin, John, "Essay on Lane Seminary Published in the *Cincinnati Journal*," *Ohio History Connection*.

71 **"set the fashion"** Sklar, Kathryn Kish, *Catharine Beecher; a Study in American Domesticity* (New Haven,: Yale University Press, 1973), 118, White, Barbara Anne, The Beecher Sisters (New Haven: Yale University Press, 2003), 20.

72 **"fabulous Beechers"** Campbell, Susan, *Tempest-Tossed: The Spirit of Isabella Beecher Hooker, Garnet Books* (Middletown, Connecticut: Wesleyan University Press, 2013), xiv.

CHAPTER 16: HARRIET GOES TO RIPLEY

73 **"we have all"** Hedrick, J. D., 96.

73 **"when the heartstrings"** ibid.

74 **"a big lighthouse"** Hagedorn, A., 56-7, 83.

75 **"Not even 'Uncle Johnny'"** ibid., 38.

CHAPTER 17: LOWRY RANKIN BOARDS THE *UNCLE SAM*

76 **"Every man knows"** ibid., 73.

76 **"Thy bondsmen"** Kipp, Laurie Maffly, "The Religious Roots of Abolition," *National Humanities Center/America in Class.*

76 **"On going aft"** Hagedorn, A., 76-80.

CHAPTER 18: THE BIRNEYS CROSS THE RIVER

81 **"a monstrous moral"** Birney, William, *James G. Birney and His Times* (New York,: D. Appleton and Company, 1890), 108.

82 **"dreary and cheerless"** Birney, James Gillespie, and Dumond, Dwight Lowell, *Letters of James Gillespie Birney, 1831-1857* (New York, London,: D. Appleton-Century Company, 1938), I: 296.

83 **"But I procrastinated"** Oller, John, *American Queen: The Rise and Fall of Kate Chase Sprague, Civil War "Belle of the North" and Gilded Age Woman of Scandal* (Boston: Da Capo Press, 2014), 23-4.

84 "The Dough-Faces* of the North," *The Liberator*, January 23, 1836.

85 "conduct has disarmed" Birney, W., 218-9.

CHAPTER 19: BIRNEY MISREADS THE TEA LEAVES

87 "we were dreadfully mobbed" Birney, J. G., and Dumond, D. L., 319-20.

CHAPTER 20: HARRIET BEGINS HER NEW LIFE

89 "cease to be Hatty" Stowe, Harriet Beecher, and Stowe, Charles Edward, *Life of Harriet Beecher Stowe* (Boston and New York: Houghton Mifflin and Company, 1889), 18.

89 "I feel as though" Hedrick, J. D., 97.

89 "Catharine Beecher" "Married," *Fall River Monitor* (Fall River, Massachusetts), March 19, 1836.

90 "I have half a" Hedrick, J. D., 100.

CHAPTER 21: THE SOUTH STOPS THE U.S. MAIL

3 "sentiments expressed" Applegate, D., 124, Wilson, R. F., 181-2, "From the Journal and Luminary," *The Philanthropist* (Cincinnati, Ohio), June 10, 1836.

93 "We of the South" *Charleston Courier* (Charleston, South Carolina), November 14, 1835.

94 "I have not ventured" Dillon, Merton Lynn, *The Abolitionists: The Growth of a Dissenting Minority* (New York: Norton, 1979), 91.

94 "Judge Lynch" Julius, Kevin C., *The Abolitionist Decade, 1829-1838: A Year-by-Year History of Early Events in the Antislavery Movement* (Jefferson, N.C.: McFarland & Co., 2004), 149.

CHAPTER 22: BIRNEY AND BAILEY STEP ON POWERFUL TOES

96 "Hitherto, when" "Southern Brethren," *The Philanthropist* (Cincinnati, Ohio), June 10, 1836.

97 "acquisition of Texas" Child, David Lee, "Texas," *The Philanthropist* (Cincinnati, Ohio), May 27, 1836.

97 "A citizen of Connecticut" "Another Reason," *The Philanthropist* (Cincinnati, Ohio), June 10, 1836.

98 "staggering more" "The Methodist Church," *The Philanthropist* (Cincinnati, Ohio), May 27, 1836.

CHAPTER 23: MATILDA ARRIVES IN CINCINNATI

99 "Lawrence had sold her" "Interesting Trial: John Lawrence Vs. Matilda, a Colored Girl," *The Daily Cincinnati Republican and Commercial Register* (Cincinnati, Ohio), March 16, 1837.

100 "cheerful, and good-hearted" "Birney Speaks of Matilda," *Cincinnati Daily Gazette*, March 21, 1837.

101 " laid out" Birney, J. G., and Dumond, D. L., I: 333.

CHAPTER 24: FLAME JETS BURST FORTH

102 **"elderly and gray-haired"** "Midnight Outrage on the Press," *The Liberator* (Boston, Massachusetts), July 30, 1836.

103 **"The citizens of Cincinnati"** "Midnight Outrage on the Press; Abolitionists Beware," *The Philanthropist*, July 15, 1836.

103 **"Sir, it is said"** Filler, Louis, *The Crusade against Slavery: 1830-1860* (Taylor & Francis, 2017), 1814, Wilson, R. F., 183.

104 **"abstain from further"** Aaron, Daniel, *Cincinnati, Queen City of the West, 1819-1838* (Columbus: Ohio State University Press, 1992), 306.

104 **"That any of our"** "Midnight Outrage on the Press; Abolitionists Beware."

104 **"A Fugitive from Justice"** "Narrative of the Late Riotous Proceedings against the Liberty of the Press," *Uncle Tom's Cabin & American Culture.*

CHAPTER 25: HARRIET'S BLOOD BOILS AND HER PEN FLOWS

105 **"MR. EDITOR"** Wilson, R. F., 184-5.

107 **"scribbling…I thought"** Koester, N., 77.

CHAPTER 26: JUDGE BURNET THROWS HIS WEIGHT AROUND

108 **"Morgan Neville, the man"** Lesick, L. T., 123, n. 41, Fladeland, Betty, *James Gillespie Birney: Slaveholder to Abolitionist* (New York: Greenwood Press, 1969), 138-9.

108 **"Publish no more"** "A Word of Advice to Abolitionists," *Cincinnati Republican* (Cincinnati, Ohio), July 21, 1836.

109 **"peaceably if it could"** Fladeland, B., 138-9.

109 **"For my part"** Wilson, R. F., 186.

109 **"two-thirds of the property"** Knuth, Haley Amanda, "Who Controls the Narrative? Newspapers and Cincinnati's Anti-Black Riots of 1829, 1836, and 1841" (Miami University, 2022), 3-4.

110 **"the little brown"** Nye, Russel B., "Marius Robinson: A Forgotten Abolitionist Leader," *Ohio History Journal.*

110 **"Birney! Birney!"** Fladeland, B., 141.

110 110 **"Who are you?"** Ibid.

111 **"That will teach them"** Taylor, Nikki Marie, *Frontiers of Freedom: Cincinnati's Black Community, 1802-1868* (Athens: Ohio University Press, 2005), locations 1628-34.

111 **"We have done enough"** Knuth, H. A., 4.

112 **"I stood in the doorway"** Hart, Albert Bushnell, *Salmon P. Chase* (New York: Chelsea House, 1980), 50.

113 **"Birney praised"** "The Cincinnati Journal Praised," *The Philanthropist*, August 5, 1836.

113 **"a man must perform"** Stahr, Walter, *Salmon P. Chase: Lincoln's Vital Rival* (New York: Simon & Schuster, 2021), 64.

CHAPTER 27: LYMAN AND HARRIET SURPRISE EVERYONE

114 **"his cravat tied"** Beecher, Catharine to Mary Cogwell, Mary Weld, May 29, 1837, Walnut Hills, Ohio.

114 **"Remember, if female"** Hedrick, J. D., 111-2.

115 **"such a trick"** ibid., 111.

CHAPTER 28: SALMON CHASE DOES HIS LEVEL BEST

117 **"She wanted to go"** "Interesting Trial: John Lawrence Vs. Matilda, a Colored Girl."

117 **"the source from whence"** ibid.

117 **"knew after she had"** ibid.

117 **"no black or mulatto"** Taylor, N. M., locations 2944-52.

118 **"a person held"** Stahr, W., 65-9.

118 **"have some of their front teeth"** Weld, T. D., 15.

118 **"a chastisement must be"** Stowe, Harriet Beecher, *A Key to Uncle Tom's Cabin; Presenting the Original Facts and Documents Upon Which the Story Is Founded* (London: T. Bosworth, 1853), Part II, Chapter 7.]

CHAPTER 29: MARIUS ROBINSON TAKES IT ON THE CHIN

119 **"curses, cries of drag"** Lerner, Gerda, *The Female Experience: An American Documentary* (New York: Oxford University Press, 1992), 59-65, Nye, R. B., 147n.

120 **"sat in their nests"** "Marius Robinson Speaks of His Mobbing," *The Liberator* (Boston, Massachusetts), July 21, 1837.

120 **"You have got to leave"** Galbreath, C.B., "Anti-Slavery Movement in Columbiana County," *Ohio History Connection*.

120 **"If you take him"** ibid.

121 **"frequently jerked me"** ibid., 366.

PART III: CONSCIENCE

123 **"Have English women"** Grimké, Angelina Emily, "Appeal to the Christian Women of the South," *Teaching American History*, 1836.

CHAPTER 30: THE GRIMKÉS BREAK OUT

125 **"What can I do?"** Lerner, Gerda, *The Grimke Sisters from South Carolina: Pioneers for Woman's Rights and Abolition* (New York: Schocken Books, 1971), 129.

125 **"But perhaps you will"** Grimké, A. E.,

127 **"A handsome mulatto"** Weld, T. D., 22-3.

128 **"His visit was"** Lerner, G., *The Grimke Sisters from South Carolina: Pioneers for Woman's Rights and Abolition*, 154.

128 **"How ridiculous"** ibid., 153-4.

128 **"immediate emancipation"** Barnes, Gilbert Hobbs, *The Antislavery Impulse, 1830-1844* (New York: Harcourt, 1964), 49, n24.

129 **"Congress shall make no"** ibid., 109-20.

120 **"devils and old maids"** ibid., 140-1.

130 **"We of the South"** ibid., 263, n3.

130 **"it is the duty"** "Proceedings of the Convention of American Women," *The Liberator* (Boston, Massachusetts), June 16, 1837.

131 **"clouds of petticoats"** "What Borough Do These Ladies Serve For?," *New York Spectator* (New York), May 18, 1837.

131 **"The white excluded"** "The Misses Grimke, from South-Carolina, Delivered Addresses before the Boston Female Anti-Slavery Society," *Pensacola Gazette* (Pensacola, Florida), July 29, 1837.

132 **"Devilina"** Lerner, G., *The Grimke Sisters from South Carolina: Pioneers for Woman's Rights and Abolition*, 8.

132 **"who so far forget"** "Timely Admonition," *Fall River Monitor* (Fall River, Massachusetts), August 12, 1837.

132 **"Heaven has appointed"** Grimké, Angelina Emily, *Letters to Catherine E. Beecher in Reply to an Essay on Slavery and Abolitionism* (Project Gutenberg, 1838), letter XI.

132 **"Miss B's cobwebs"** "Brief Remarks on Miss Catherine E. Beecher's Essay on Slavery and Abolitionism," *The Liberator* (Boston, Massachusetts), July 14, 1837.

132 **"Unfeminine course"** "Fair against Fair," *Mississippi Free Trader*, June 23, 1837.

133 **"proper behavior"** Perry, Mark, *Lift up Thy Voice: The Grimké Family's Journey from Slaveholders to Civil Rights Leaders* (New York: Viking, 2001), 153-5.

133 **"We cannot push"** Weld, T. D., Grimké, A. E., and Grimké, S., I: 427-32.

133 **"helpers"** ibid., I: 436-43.

CHAPTER 31: THE BEECHERS MAKE SOME CHANGES

134 **"It was hot"** Applegate, D., 134.

134 **"As he opened"** ibid.

134 **"Will you go"** Rugoff, M., 128-9.

135 **"their way from the wharf"** Applegate, D., 145.

136 **"At fifteen"** White, B. A., 21.

138 **"throw Lane Seminary"** Hedrick, J. D., 113.

141 **"Pray what is there"** Koester, N., 82.

CHAPTER 32: EDWARD BEECHER CONSIDERS LOVEJOY'S REQUEST

142 **"injustice and bad"** Foner, Eric, *The Fiery Trial: Abraham Lincoln and American Slavery* (New York: W. W. Norton & Co., 2010), 25.

143 **"to the friends of"** Ellingwood, Ken, *First to Fall: Elijah Lovejoy and the Fight for a Free Press in the Age of Slavery* (New York: Pegasus Books, 2021), 227.

143 "wise and the good" Beecher, Edward, *Narrative of Riots at Alton, in Connection with the Death of Rev. Elijah P. Lovejoy* (Alton Ill.: G. Holton, 1838), 27.

144 "[Celia] rushing past" Lovejoy, Joseph C., Lovejoy, Owen, and Adams, John Quincy, *Memoir of the Rev. Elijah P. Lovejoy; Who Was Murdered in Defence of the Liberty of the Press, at Alton, Illinois, Nov. 7, 1837* (New York: J.S. Taylor, 1838), 253.

144 "free inquiry" Beecher, E., 27.

145 "a very wicked" "Blood-Murder!," *Vermont Telegraph*, November 29, 1837.

145 "I am but one" Ellingwood, K., 265.

147 "a shock" ibid., 299.

147 "They desired to" Lovejoy, J. C., Lovejoy, O., and Adams, J. Q., 322.

147 "Here, before God" Brands, H. W., *The Zealot and the Emancipator: John Brown, Abraham Lincoln and the Struggle for American Freedom* (New York: Doubleday, 2020), 13.

147 "LOVEJOY, the first" Dillon, M. L., 95.

148 "Lovejoy dieth" May, S. J., 227.

148 "We have a menagerie" ibid.

149 "Do not be alarmed" Hedrick, J. D., 109.

149 "Instead, then" "Resist Not Evil," *The Liberator* (Boston, Massachusetts), December 22, 1837.

150 "now abroad in our land" Lincoln, Abraham, "Lyceum Address," *Abraham Lincoln Online.*

150 "famed for love" ibid.

150 "Turn then" ibid.

150 "Whenever this effect" ibid.

150 "How shall we fortify" ibid.

CHAPTER 33: CHARLES SUMNER BRUSHES UP HIS FRENCH

151 "a smacking breeze" Sumner, Charles; Pierce, Edward, *Memoir and Letters of Charles Sumner*, vol. 1 (1893), 211.

152 "He had quite a large" Pierce, Edward Lillie, *Memoir and Letters of Charles Sumner* (Boston: Roberts Brothers, 1877), January 20, 1838 journal entry.

153 "They appear to be" Donald, David Herbert, *Charles Sumner and the Coming of the Civil War* (New York: Knopf, 1960), Locations 775-87.

CHAPTER 34: ANGELINA MAKES A COMMAND DECISION

154 "A great excitement" "A Great Excitement," *New York Daily Herald* (New York), May 9, 1838.

156 "Are thy friends" Weld, T. D., Grimké, A. E., and Grimké, S., II: 653.

156 "two halves" ibid., II: 538.

156 "If you procure" ibid., II: 609-11.

157 **"[I]t is [hard] to find"** Thomas, Benjamin Platt, *Theodore Weld, Crusader for Freedom* (New Brunswick: Rutgers University Press, 1950), 159.

157 **"Dear Friend, Wilt thou"** "Wedding of Angelina Grimké and Theodore Weld (1838)," *Miami University/Empire and American Religion.*

158 **"Temple of Freedom"** Thomas, B. P., 165.

158 **"tabernacle of mischief"** Wickenden, Dorothy, *The Agitators: Three Friends Who Fought for Abolition and Women's Rights* (New York: Scribner, 2021), 11.

158 **"Men were seen"** ibid.

159 **"against the horrible"** Perry, M., 172-3, Lerner, G., *The Grimke Sisters from South Carolina: Pioneers for Woman's Rights and Abolition*, 241.

159 **"forcibly, if they must"** Perry, M., 173.

160 **"What is a mob?"** Birney, Catherine H., and Stone, Lucy, *The Grimké Sisters. Sarah and Angelina Grimké, the First American Women Advocates of Abolition and Woman's Rights* (Project Gutenberg, 1885), Chapter XV.

CHAPTER 35: GERRIT TALKS THE TALK AND WALKS THE WALK

165 **"I have a most important"** Stanton, Elizabeth Cady, *Eighty Years and More: Reminiscences (1815-1897)* (Boston: Northeastern University Press, 1993), 62.

165 **"Harriet, I have brought"** ibid.

166 **"I saw her pass"** Siebert, Wilbur Henry, and Hart, Albert Bushnell, *The Underground Railroad from Slavery to Freedom: A Comprehensive History* (Mineola, N.Y.: Dover Publications, 2006), Section 129.

166 **"he would no doubt rejoice"** Stanton, E. C., 64.

CHAPTER 36: ELIZABETH CADY GOES ROGUE

169 **"was severely destitute"** Lerner, G., *The Grimke Sisters from South Carolina: Pioneers for Woman's Rights and Abolition*, 295.

169 **"a hot beefsteak"** Stanton, Elizabeth Cady, Anthony, Susan B., and Gage, Matilda Joslyn, *History of Woman Suffrage* (Rochester, N.Y.: Susan B. Anthony, 1887), 392.

170 **"We are very much"** Weld, T. D., Grimké, A. E., and Grimké, S., II: 842.

170 **"Well, what have I said"** Stanton, E. C., 74.

170 **"I heard you call"** ibid.

171 **"anti-Slavery society"** Pickard, John B., "John Greenleaf Whittier and the Abolitionist Schism of 1840," *The New England Quarterly*, Vol. 37, no. 2), 253.

173 **"we shall be foiled…With a young woman"** Garrison, Wendell Phillips, and Garrison, Francis Jackson, *William Lloyd Garrison, 1805-1879: The Story of His Life* (New York: Century Co., 1885), II: 357.

173 **"Several men were sent"** Mott, Lucretia Coffin, and Tolles, Frederick Barnes, *Slavery and the "Woman Question": Lucretia Mott's Diary of Her Visit to Attend the World's Anti-Slavery Convention of 1840* (London: Friends' Historical Society, 1952), 29.

174 **"Goddess Delegates"** ibid., 30.

174 "out of order" ibid., 30, n1.

174 "Prove to me" Stanton, E. C., Anthony, S. B., and Gage, M. J., 62n.

CHAPTER 37: ANGELINA, SARAH, AND THEODORE COLLABORATE

176 "cooking potatoes" Birney, C. H., and Stone, L., 245.

177 "To her surprise" Stanton, E. C., 114.

177 "had a cheerless" Stanton, E. C., Anthony, S. B., and Gage, M. J., 392.

178 "It is just such a monument" Birney, C. H., and Stone, L., Chapter XVI.

178 178 "She thinks you have both" Weld, T. D., Grimké, A. E., and Grimké, S., II: 847.

178 178 "I began to think" Perry, M., 182.

178 178 "The Grimkés, I think" ibid.

179 179 "I do not think we ever" Birney, C. H., and Stone, L., Chapter XVI.

179 179 "We will prove" Weld, T. D., 9.

CHAPTER 38: LINCOLN ESCAPES TWICE

181 "The huzzas" Simon, Paul, *Lincoln's Preparation for Greatness: The Illinois Legislative Years* (Urbana: University of Illinois Press, 1971), 51.

184 "If such a resolution" ibid., 229.

184 "jumping scrape" "Summary of Legislative Debate on Resolution Commemorating the Battle of New Orleans, 8 January 1841," *The Papers of Abraham Lincoln Digital Library.*

184 "violent little Whig" Goodwin, D. K., 95.

186 "as a living and eternal" Donald, D. H., *Lincoln*, 87.

186 "Went to see 'Mary'" Wilson, Douglas L. et al., *Herndon's Informants: Letters, Interviews, and Statements About Abraham Lincoln* (Urbana: University of Illinois Press, 1998), 474-5.

186 "would hold the question" Donald, D. H., *Lincoln*, 87.

186 "I am now the most miserable" White, Ronald C., *A. Lincoln: A Biography* (New York: Random House, 2009), 112.

186 "Lincoln went crazy." Wilson, D. L. et al., 475.

187 "that intensity of thought" Shenk, Joshua Wolf, *Lincoln's Melancholy: How Depression Challenged a President and Fueled His Greatness* (Boston: Houghton Mifflin Co., 2005), 85.

187 "There is still one" ibid., 51.

187 "chief gem" Goodwin, D. K., 98.

CHAPTER 39: HARRIET KNOWS SOMETHING ABOUT SLAVERY

189 "became free when brought" Masur, Kate, *Until Justice Be Done: America's First Civil Rights Movement, from the Revolution to Reconstruction* (New York: W. W. Norton & Company, 2021), 189.

190 **"ferret them out"** Coffin, Levi, *Reminiscences of Levi Coffin* (Cincinnati, Ohio: Western Tract Society, 1876), 533.

191 **"He actually made me"** Stowe, Harriet Beecher, "Uncle Tom's Cabin, Chapter 45, Concluding Remarks," *Uncle Tom's Cabin and American Culture.*

CHAPTER 40: CHARLES DICKENS VISITS AMERICA

193 **"round the carriage"** Dickens, Charles, *American Notes for General Circulation* (London: Chapman and Hall, 1850), 79.

194 **"the headquarters"** ibid., 78.

194 **"the old one"** ibid., 85.

195 **"It is now little better"** ibid., 92.

195 **"In the negro car"** ibid., 92-3.

195 **"crazy, wretched cabins"** ibid., 94.

195 **"beautiful city"** ibid., 112.

196 **"Ran away, Negress Caroline…"** ibid., 162-4.

197 **"literary epidemic"** Koester, N., 88.

197 **"Henry, do you know"** Rugoff, M., 205.

197 **"The sudden death"** Koester, N., 95.

198 **"Dr. Drake gave me"** Hedrick, J. D., 174.

CHAPTER 41: MR. LINCOLN GOES TO WASHINGTON

199 **"all the facts"** Goodwin, D. K., 121.

200 **"unnecessarily and unconstitutionally"** ibid.

200 **"military glory"** Donald, D. H., *Lincoln*, 124.

200 **"miserable man of spots"** ibid., 125.

200 **"spotty Lincoln"** "Spotted Fever," *Illinois State Register* (Springfield, Illinois), February 25, 1848.

201 **"neither slavery nor involuntary servitude"** Goodwin, D. K., 123.

201 **"We should never knowingly"** "Abraham Lincoln to Williamson Durley, October 3, 1845," *The Papers of Abraham Lincoln Digital Library.*

201 **"I picked up one or two pieces"** Brands, H. W., *The Age of Gold: The California Gold Rush and the New American Dream* (New York: Doubleday, 2002), 16.

CHAPTER 42: HARRIET GOES TO A SPA

205 **"Time will fail me"** Belasco, Susan, *Stowe in Her Own Time: A Biographical Chronicle of Her Life* (Iowa City: University of Iowa Press, 2009), 67.

205 **"Kill the damned n----r"** Applegate, D., 188.

206 **"It grew on me"** ibid., 187.

206 **"If you were to step in"** ibid., 192.

207 **"sharply and strongly"** ibid., 205-6.

CHAPTER 43: ABSENCE OFTEN—BUT NOT ALWAYS—
MAKES THE HEART GROW FONDER

209 "a sort of negro-livery stable" Epstein, Daniel Mark, *The Lincolns: Portrait of a Marriage* (New York: Ballantine Books, 2009), 25.

210 "damned abolitionist" Harrold, Stanley, *Gamaliel Bailey and the Anti-Slavery Union* (Kent, Ohio: Kent State University Press, 1986), 125.

210 "a little engine" Herndon, W. H., Weik, J. W., and Angle, P. M., xxviii.

212 "Dear Mary, In this troublesome" Lincoln, Abraham to Lincoln, Mary, April 16, 1848, Washington, D.C.

216 "fancy girls" Ricks, Mary Kay, *Escape on the Pearl: The Heroic Bid for Freedom on the Underground Railroad* (New York: William Morrow, 2007), 183.

CHAPTER 44: THE WOMAN HOLD THEIR OWN CONVENTION

218 "females as well" Wellman, Judith, *The Road to Seneca Falls: Elizabeth Cady Stanton and the First Woman's Rights Convention* (Urbana: University of Illinois Press, 2004), 176.

218 "Why, Lizzie, thee" Baker, Jean H., *Sisters: The Lives of America's Suffragists* (New York: Farrar, Strauss and Giroux, 2006), 115.

CHAPTER 45: LINCOLN MEETS SEWARD

220 "sincere friends" Holland, William M., *The Life and Political Opinions of Martin Van Buren, Vice President of the United States* (Hartford: Belknap & Hamersley, 1836), 354.

220 "nauseous" Donald, D. H., *Lincoln*, 131.

200 "leaning himself" ibid.

222 "I reckon" Goodwin, D. K., 127.

222 "There goes a young man" Stowe, Harriet Beecher, *Uncle Tom's Cabin: Or, Life among the Lowly* (Boston, New York, Cambridge: Houghton Mifflin and Company, 1889), x.

223 "I believed it as good" Donald, D. H., *Lincoln*, 136.

CHAPTER 46: MILLY AND PAUL FIGHT FOR FAMILY

225 "There 'tis, now, Paul" Stowe, H. B., *A Key to Uncle Tom's Cabin; Presenting the Original Facts and Documents Upon Which the Story Is Founded*, Part 3, Chapter 6.

225 "the very best ways…sweet" ibid.

226 "Never a morsel" ibid.

228 "no room for the snuffles" Conkling, Winifred, *Passenger on the Pearl: The True Story of Emily Edmonson's Flight from Slavery* (Chapel Hill, North Carolina: Algonquin Young Readers, 2015), 72.

228 "There was the calaboose" ibid., 70.

230 "show dresses" Stowe, H. B., *A Key to Uncle Tom's Cabin; Presenting the Original Facts and Documents Upon Which the Story Is Founded*, Part 3, Chapter 6.

231 **"for the purpose of"** "The Edmondson Sisters," *The Evening Post* (New York), October 30, 1848.

231 **"How would you feel if"** Applegate, D., 227.

232 **"Gentlemen, they say"** ibid.

232 **"Take up another!"** Ibid.

232 **"that white man we have seen"** Ricks, M. K., 195.

233 **"Received of W.L. Chaplin"** ibid.

233 **"Thank God!"** Ibid., 196.

CHAPTER 47: WATER IS LIFE AND WATER IS DEATH

234 **"A person lately"** "The California Gold Mines; How to Reach California," *The Birmingham Journal* (Birmingham, West Midlands, England), January 27, 1849.

234 **"But the riches"** "California," *The Cincinnati Enquirer* (Cincinnati, Ohio), June 5, 1849.

235 **"obtained the necessary outfit"** Rosen, Fred, *Gold!: The Story of the 1848 Gold Rush and How It Shaped a Nation* (New York and London: Thunder's Mouth, 2005), 114-5.

236 **"That night, about 6 o'clock"** McNeil, Samuel, *Mc Neil's Travels in 1849, to, through and from the Gold Regions in California* (Columbus: Scott & Bascom, Printers, 1850), 14.

236 **"to go quietly"** Smith, Matthew D., "The Specter of Cholera in Nineteenth-Century Cincinnati," *Project Muse/Ohio History Connection*.

237 **"exaggerated reports"** ibid., 28.

238 **"suspended animation"** ibid., 35.

238 **"rendered sensitive"** Hedrick, J. D., 189.

238 **"Hearse drivers"** ibid.

238 **"many a poor creature"** ibid.

239 **"[T]he water smells"** Stowe, Harriet Beecher to Stowe, Calvin, August-September 1849, Walnut Hills, Ohio.

239 **"dropsy of the brain"** Stowe, H. B., and Stowe, C. E., 28.

239 **"Dear Sarah, The day after"** Stowe, H. B.,letter to Sarah Sturges Beecher, July 29, 1849, Cincinnati, Ohio.

CHAPTER 48: HARRIET TUBMAN CHOOSES LIBERTY

242 **"the use and hire"** Larson, Kate Clifford, *Bound for the Promised Land: Harriet Tubman, Portrait of an American Hero* (New York: Ballantine, 2004), 74.

242 **"Minty, [Harriet] aged about 27"** ibid., 78.

244 **"Miss Susan"** ibid., 38.

244 **"Now you know"** Clinton, Catherine, *Harriet Tubman: The Road to Freedom* (Boston, Mass.: Little, Brown, 2004), 19.

245 **"stood out like a bushel"** Larson, K. C., 42.

245 "broke my skull" ibid.

245 "I had no bed" ibid.

245 "and there I worked" ibid.

245 "didn't come across them" Humez, Jean McMahon, *Harriet Tubman: The Life and the Life Stories* (Madison, Wis.: University of Wisconsin Press, 2003), 165.

246 "On Saturday night" Larson, K. C., 85-6.

247 "Although the loss of property" McPherson, James M., *Battle Cry of Freedom: The Civil War Era* (New York: Oxford University Press, 1988), 79.

247 "I am for disunion" ibid., 68.

247 "higher law" ibid., 72-3.

247 "monstrous" ibid., 73.

247 "that most odious" "Complimentary—Senator Seward," *Portland Press Herald* (Portland, Maine), October 15, 1850.

247 "it is clear" McPherson, J. M., 68.

247 "We ask you to give" ibid.

247 "commenced with the agitation" Calhoun, John C., "Speech against Clay's Compromise Measures," *Teaching American History.*

247 "Satisfy them" "Slavery Diabolical," *The Liberator* (Boston, Mass.), April 25, 1851.

CHAPTER 49: HARRIET BEECHER STOWE IS INVIGORATED BY THE SEA AIR

252 "their constitutional duties" Webster, Daniel, "The Seventh of March Speech (1850)," *Bill of Rights Institute.*

253 "madness" Donald, D. H., *Charles Sumner and the Coming of the Civil War,* Location 3389.

253 "archanged ruined" ibid., 3397.

254 "saying he is sick a bed" Hedrick, J. D., 195.

254 "Since I began this note" ibid.

255 "Of late, there have seemed" Stowe, Harriet Beecher, "A Freeman's Dream: A Parable," *The National Era,* August 1, 1850.

256 "How far Dr. Stowe" Wilson, R. F., 244.

PART IV: COMPASSION

257 "I had two little" Belasco, S., 63-4.

CHAPTER 50: CITIZENS PROTEST THE BLOODHOUND LAW

259 "AFFLICTED AND BELOVED BROTHERS" "Abolition Convention-Cazenovia," *Southern Press* (Washington, D.C.), August 26, 1850.

CHAPTER 51: STEPHEN DOUGLAS FINDS THE VOTES

262 **"ten thousand cords"** Ceplair, Larry, Grimké, Angelina Emily, and Grimké, Sarah Moore, *The Public Years of Sarah and Angelina Grimké: Selected Writings, 1835-1839* (New York: Columbia University Press, 1989), 117-8.

262 **"Southern interest"** ibid.

263 **"unholy union"** Donald, D. H., *Charles Sumner and the Coming of the Civil War*, Location 3144.

263 **"a sheet of lightning"** Wickenden, D., 76.

264 **"extend a cordial"** ibid., 95.

CHAPTER 52: THE CRAFTS ENERGIZE BOSTON

266 **"jumped the broomstick"** Woo, Ilyon, *Master Slave Husband Wife: An Epic Journey from Slavery to Freedom* (2023), 62.

267 **"negro car"** ibid., 14.

268 **"You are very likely"** ibid., 67.

268 **"leave that cripple"** ibid., 113.

269 **"public negro whipper"** ibid., 215.

269 **"short, rowdyish-looking"** "Slave Hunters in Boston," *Boston Evening Transcript*, October 28, 1850.

269 **"unpleasant business"** Woo, I., 217.

270 **"Negroes and their friends…"** ibid., 226.

270 **"TO THE RESCUE"** ibid., 225-6.

271 **"SLAVE HUNTERS IN BOSTON!"** "Slave Hunters in Boston,"

271 **"That Macon Hews…"** ibid.

272 **"Slave Hunters!"** Woo, I., 235.

274 **"made some insinuations"** "Fatal Rencounter [*Sic*] in Macon," *The Daily Constitutionalist and Republic* (Augusta, Georgia), January 9, 1851.

CHAPTER 53: HARRIET HEARS THE KNOCK AND OPENS THE DOOR

275 **"[B]ut when I asked him"** Hedrick, J. D., 205-6.

276 **"who takes him"** Stowe, H. B.,letter to Catharine Esther Beecher, after September 18, 1850,

276 **"Now our beds are full"** ibid.

276 **"Just as I was beginning"** Jackson, John Andrew, *The Experience of a Slave in South Carolina* (Finsbury: Passmore & Alabaster, 1862), 32.

277 **"she might write as much"** Harrold, S., 142.

277 **"shocking cold"** Stowe, H. B.,letter to Calvin Stowe, December 7, 1850, Brunswick, Maine.

278 **"It snowed"** Stowe, Harriet (Hatty) to Stowe, Calvin, December 27, 1850, Brunswick, Maine.

278 **"the rattletrap house"** Hedrick, J. D., 200.

279 **"Now, Hattie, if I could"** ibid., 207.

279 **"I will"** ibid.

279 **"I wish Father"** Stowe, H. B.,letter to Calvin Ellis Stowe, December 27, 1850,

280 **"he who is to me"** Wagenknecht, Edward Charles, *Harriet Beecher Stowe: The Known and the Unknown* (New York: Oxford University Press, 1965), 38.

280 **"Must we forever"** Stowe, H. B.,letter to Henry Ward Beecher, February 1, 1851, Brunswick, Maine.

CHAPTER 54: HARRIET IS CALLED INTO GREATER BEING

281 **"a stout, copper-colored"** "1851: The Ordeal of Shadrach Minkins," *Long Road to Justice: The African American Experience in the Massachusetts Courts.*

282 **"the unrolling of a picture"** Koester, N., 113.

283 **"some brown paper"** Kirkham, E. Bruce, *The Building of Uncle Tom's Cabin* (Knoxville: University of Tennessee Press, 1977), 74.

283 **"Oh, mamma"** Koester, N., 113.

283 **"a colored woman…of various shades"** "United States District Court," *National Anti-Slavery Standard* (New York), March 20, 1851, "Our Philadelphia Correspondence," *New York Daily Herald* (New York), March 11, 1851.

284 **"Mr. Bailey"** Wilson, R. F., 260.

285 **"A New Story"** ibid., 262.

285 **"tired and worn"** Rourke, Constance, *Trumpets of Jubilee* (New York: Harcourt, Brace & World, 1963), 78.

CHAPTER 55: SOJOURNER GOES WEST

286 **"making myself a sort"** Nye, R. B., 149.

287 **"Goodness never had"** Stetson, Erlene, and David, Linda, *Glorying in Tribulation: The Lifework of Sojourner Truth* (East Lansing: Michigan State University Press, 1994), 137.

287 **"the most grossly wronged"** Washington, Margaret, *Sojourner Truth's America* (Urbana: University of Illinois Press, 2009), Location 4936.

287 **"so that those states"** Nye, R. B., 150-2.

289 **"stopped among colored"** Stetson, E., and David, L., 141-2.

289 **"the tall colored woman"** Washington, M., Location 5339.

289 **"black as the ace"** ibid., Location 4675, Mabee, Carleton, and Newhouse, Susan Mabee, *Sojourner Truth--Slave, Prophet, Legend* (New York: New York University Press, 1993), 65.

289 **"jumbled"** Mabee, C., and Newhouse, S. M., 63.

290 **"My brain is too stiff"** ibid., 62.

290 **"This I suppose"** Washington, M., Locations 5327-40.

290 **"give [Sojourner] as royal"** ibid.

291 **"thrown into a panic"** Stetson, E., and David, L., 145-6.

291 "An Abolition Affair!" Gage, F.D., "Sojourner Truth," *The Independent* (New York), April 23, 1863.

291 "It will ruin us" Stetson, E., and David, L., 142-3.

291 "Resolved that the inequalities" Stone, Lucy, and Anthony, Susan B., "The Proceedings of the Woman's Rights Convention, Held at Akron, Ohio, May 28 and 29, 1851 (Lccn 93838317)," *Library of Congress*.

291 "gross tyranny" "Proceedings of the Women's Rights Convention," *Anti-Slavery Bugle* (Salem, Ohio), June 7, 1851.

292 "Aren't I a woman" Gage, F. D.

292 "token of his will" Stetson, E., and David, L., 149-50.

292 "Go home" Washington, M., Location 5417.

293 "She said she was a woman" "The Rights of Woman," *New-York Tribune* (New York), June 6, 1851.

293 "She had heard the Bible" ibid., Gage, F. D.

294 "an old colored lady" "Women's Rights Convention," *Summit County Beacon* (Akron, Ohio), June 4, 1851.

294 "God, you drive" Stetson, E., and David, L., 165-6.

CHAPTER 56: WOMEN PUT ON THE PANTS

295 "its influences for good" Miller, Elizabeth Smith, *In the Kitchen* (Boston: Lee and Shepard, 1875), 17.

295 "A fern leaf" ibid., 18.

296 "ripened into" "Elizabeth Smith Miller," *New York History Net*.

296 "Soon after making"

296 "a captive set free" Stanton, E. C., 201.

297 "We...announce" "The New Costume for Ladies," *New-York Tribune*, June 12, 1851.

297 "short dresses" ibid.

297 "fast gaining ground" ibid.

297 "We may laugh" ibid.

297 "At Glen Haven" "Bloomerism," *Boston Evening Transcript*, June 25, 1851.

298 "the first American woman" "Glen-Haven Festival," *Frederick Douglass Paper* (Rochester, New York), June 26, 1851. *Library of Congress*.

298 "I am asked for a ditty" ibid.

300 "To tall, gaunt women" Stanton, E. C., 202.

300 "some good Democrats" Chrisman-Campbell, Kimberly, "When American Suffragists Tried to 'Wear the Pants'," *The Atlantic*.

301 "the old, swaddling" "Elizabeth Smith Miller."

301 "I do not wear" ibid.

CHAPTER 57: HARRIET BEECHER STOWE CHURNS
OUT THE CHAPTERS

303 "Question. Is it a part" Stowe, H. B., *A Key to Uncle Tom's Cabin; Presenting the Original Facts and Documents Upon Which the Story Is Founded*, Part 1, Chapter 2.

305 "immediate and electric" Stowe, Harriet Beecher, *The Writings of Harriet Beecher Stowe, with Biographical Introductions, Portraits, and Other Illustrations* (Cambridge: Houghton, Mifflin and Company, 1896), xxxii.

305 "always read it" Harrold, S., 143.

306 "I am trying" Sklar, K. K., 233.

307 "As soon as she" Koester, N., 117.

307 "her frizzy hair" ibid.

307 "Wherever I went" Greenwood, Grace, "Letter from Grace Greenwood," *National Era* (Washington, D.C.), October 2, 1851.

308 "Aunt Kate's head" Hedrick, J. D., 221.

308 "once in a while" ibid.

308 "with a very martyrized" ibid.

309 "Sundays only" Wilson, R. F., 281.

309 "The Story of the Age" "Uncle Tom's Cabin," *Burlington Weekly Sentinel* (Burlington, Vermont), April 1, 1852.

309 "Our readers will please" Wilson, R. F., 281.

310 "unprincipled man" Ricks, M. K., 251.

311 "would bring only" Wickenden, D., 103.

311 "Emily and I" Conkling, W., 146.

CHAPTER 58: HARRIET BEECHER STOWE GETS FEEDBACK

313 "Who would sing" Sumner, Charles, *Recent Speeches and Addresses* (Boston: Higgins and Bradley, 1856), 159.

313 "as a flash" Le Beau, Bryan, "She Told the Story, and the Whole World Wept," *American Quarterly*, Vol. 38, no. 4, (August 1986), 670.

313 "one of the greatest" White, B. A., 54.

313 "How she is shaking" Longfellow, Samuel, *Life of Henry Wadsworth Longfellow, with Extracts from His Journals and Correspondence* (Boston: Ticknor and company, 1886), 233.

313 "it is the most affecting" Belasco, S., xvii.

314 "I cannot read" Chase, Salmon P., and Niven, John, *The Salmon P. Chase Papers* (Kent, Ohio: Kent State University Press, 1993), 233.

314 "Mrs. Stowe's pen" Humez, J. M., 227-8.

314 "I've seen the real" ibid.

314 "Mrs. Harriet Beecher Stowe "Mrs. Harriet Beecher Stowe...Uncle Tom's Cabin... Mediocre Writer," *Camden Journal* (Camden, South Carolina), May 7, 1852.

315 "the best institutions" Wilson, R. F., 296.

315 **"most unwise thing"** Koester, N., 147.

316 **"On each side"** Hentz, Caroline Lee, *Marcus Warland; or, the Long Moss Spring. A Tale of the South* (Philadelphia: A. Hart, 1852), Chapter IV.

PART V: JUSTICE

317 **"Gentlemen…The only way"** Douglass, Frederick, Foner, Philip Sheldon, and Taylor, Yuval, *Frederick Douglass: Selected Speeches and Writings*, 1st ed. (Chicago: Lawrence Hill Books, 1999), 207-8.

CHAPTER 59: STEPHEN DOUGLAS EXPLODES A BOMB

319 **"extend the institutions"** McPherson, J. M., 122.

319 **"popular sovereignty"** ibid., 122-4, 8.

319 **"gross violation"** ibid., 123-4.

320 **"What kind of popular sovereignty"** Goodwin, D. K., 162.

320 **"Ah, you can't crawl…Douglas, no man"** ibid., 163.

320 **"This whole nation"** Beecher, Henry Ward, "The Crisis," *The Independent* (New York), March 2, 1854.

322 **"Come on, then, gentlemen"** Wickenden, D., 118.

323 **"We went to bed"** Sutton, Robert K., and Dole, Robert J., *Stark Mad Abolitionists: Lawrence, Kansas, and the Battle over Slavery in the Civil War Era* (New York: Skyhorse Publishing, 2017), 8.

324 **"by the sound of a fire-bell"** Sandburg, Carl, *Abraham Lincoln: The Prairie Years and the War Years-the Illustrated Edition*, ed. Goodman, Edward C. (New York: Sterling Publishing Co., Inc., 2007), 75.

324 **"sat on the edge"** Goodwin, D. K., 163-4.

324 **"I tell you, Dickey"** ibid., 164.

324 **"they would rush in"** Kunhardt, Philip B., Jr.; Kundhardt, Philip B. III, and Kunhardt, Peter, *Lincoln: An Illustrated Biography* (1992), 105.

324 **"Although volume upon volume"** Basler, Roy, Pratt, Marrion, and Dunlap, Lloyd, *The Collected Works of Abraham Lincoln* (New Brunswick: Rutgers University Press, 1953), II: 222.

324 **"I could not sleep"** Carpenter, F. B., *Six Months at the White House with Abraham Lincoln: The Story of a Picture* (New York: Hurd and Houghton, 1867), 512.

325 **"I am slow to learn"** Wilson, D. L. et al., 499.

326 **"the appearance"** Goodwin, D. K., 165.

326 **"I tell you the time"** Sandburg, C., 75.

326 **"with a tin, high-pitched"** White, R. C., 199.

328 **"had been canonized"** Basler, R., Pratt, M., and Dunlap, L., II: 236.

328 **"letting slavery into"** Lincoln, Abraham, "Peoria Speech," *National Park Service*.

328 **"real zeal for the spread"** ibid.

329 **"And you voted against"** Donald, D. H., *Lincoln*, 174.

329 "The doctrine of self-government" Lincoln, A., "Peoria Speech."

329 "having found the institution" ibid.

330 "return slavery" ibid.

CHAPTER 60: KANSAS OR BUST

334 "burlesque" McPherson, J. M., 147.

335 "every free white" "An Act to Organize the Territories of Nebraska and Kansas (Kansas-Nebraska Act (1854))," *National Archives:* Milestone Documents.

335 "The admission of Kansas" McPherson, J. M., 149.

336 "believed that the Sharps" Sutton, R. K., and Dole, R. J., 87.

336 "Beecher's Bibles" Applegate, D., 6.

337 "Cut his throat" Committee, United States House, *Report of the Special Committee Appointed to Investigate the Troubles in Kansas, with the Views of the Minority of Said Committee* (Washington: Cornelius Wendell, Printer, 1856), HathiTrust.

337 "I have been beaten" ibid., 381.

337 "Southerners to come" Nevins, Allan, *Ordeal of the Union 2: A House Dividing 1852-1857* (New York: Scribner, 1947), 433.

337 "Blood for Blood!" Ibid., II: 433.

CHAPTER 61: SUMNER VENTS HIS WRATH

340 "I shall make" Palmer, Beverly Wilson, "From Small Minority to Great Cause: Letters of Sumner to Salmon P. Chase," *Ohio History Connection.*

340 "cutting personal sarcasm" Wickenden, D., 124.

340 "the harlot slavery" Donald, D. H., *Charles Sumner and the Coming of the Civil War*, Location 5084.

340 "Mr. Sumner has added" "Exciting Scene in the Senate," *New-York Tribune* (New York), May 21, 1856.

341 "Black Republican" Donald, D. H., *Charles Sumner and the Coming of the Civil War*, Location 5179.

341 "Sumner may have friends" ibid., Location 5198.

342 "Mr. Sumner" ibid., Location 5231.

342 "I have read" ibid.

342 "I no longer saw" Sumner, Charles, and Hoar, George Frisbie, *Charles Sumner; His Complete Works: With Introduction by Hon. George Frisbie Hoar* (Boston: Lee & Shepard, 1900), 261.

343 "senseless as a corpse" Donald, D. H., *Charles Sumner and the Coming of the Civil War*, Location 5271.

343 "a thing like this" ibid., 5299.

CHAPTER 62: HELL HATH NO FURY LIKE JOHN BROWN SCORNED

345 "threatened by hundreds" Wickenden, D., 126.

345 "Brown's Station" Sanborn, F. B., *The Life and Letters of John Brown: Liberator of Kansas and Martyr of Virginia* (Boston: Roberts Brothers, 1885), 228.

345 "John's two letters" ibid., 193-4.

346 "radical, retaliatory" McPherson, J. M., 152-3.

347 "a tooth for a tooth" Villard, Oswald Garrison, *John Brown, 1800-1859: A Biography Fifty Years after, Etc.* (London: Constable, 1910), 160.

347 "His manner" Brands, H. W., *The Zealot and the Emancipator: John Brown, Abraham Lincoln and the Struggle for American Freedom*, 81.

347 "excited eagerness" ibid.

347 "They first took" Committee, U. S. H., 107.

348 "I found my father" ibid.

348 "The old man, who seemed" ibid., 106.

348 "Northern Army" ibid.

349 "They asked me" ibid., 1196.

349 "Old man Brown" ibid., 1196-7.

349 "denounced the deed" Utter, David N., "John Brown of Osawatomie," *The North American Review*, Vol. 137, no. 324, (November 1883), 443.

350 "the most blood-thirsty murderer" "From Kansas," *Daily Missouri Republican* (St. Louis, Missouri), November 10, 1856.

350 "A Kanzas Hero" "A Kanzas [*Sic*] Hero," *Boston Evening Transcript* (Boston, Massachusetts), January 6, 1857.

351 "And if I wanted a genuine" "Speech of Rev. T. W. Higginson," *The Liberator* (Boston, Massachusetts), January 16, 1857.

352 "putting a stop" Villard, O. G., 308.

353 "Here we found" Redpath, James, *The Public Life of Capt. John Brown: With an Auto-Biography of His Childhood and Youth* (Boston: Thayer and Eldridge, 1860), 198.

353 "God had created him" Villard, O. G., 310.

CHAPTER 63: THE REPUBLICAN PARTY RISES

354 "The vulgar Abolitionists" McPherson, J. M., 151.

354 "every Southern man" ibid.

355 "none are punished" Wickenden, D., 127-8.

355 "the outrage on Charles Sumner" Child, Lydia Maria, *Letters of Lydia Maria Child: With a Biographical Introduction by John G. Whittier* (Boston: Houghton, Mifflin and Co, 1883), 78-9.

356 "there's another great man" Goodwin, D. K., 187.

356 "Black Republicans" McPherson, J. M., 159.

356 "Fathers, save us" ibid.

357 "Bleeding Kansas" Wickenden, D., 127.

357 "Free Soil" McPherson, J. M., 161.

357 "a simple assault" Donald, D. H., *Charles Sumner and the Coming of the Civil War*, Location 5179, n29.

357 "He died a horrid" Sumner, Charles, *The Works of Charles Sumner* (Boston: Lee and Shepard, 1871), IV: 271.

358 "sailed in the Fulton" Seward, Frances Adeline Miller to Seward, Augustus H., March 9, 1857, Washington, D.C.

CHAPTER 64: TANEY RULES ON DRED SCOTT

359 "the weary tramp" "Local Intelligence: The Inauguration," *The Evening Star* (Washington, D.C.), March 4, 1857.

360 "difference of opinion" Goodwin, D. K., 189.

360 "A different opinion" "James Buchanan: Inaugural Address, March 4, 1857," *UVA/Miller Center*.

361 "are not included" Goodwin, D. K., 189.

361 "life, liberty, or property" McPherson, J. M., 176.

361 "the judges, without" Goodwin, D. K., 191.

362 "more repulsive abolitionist" ibid., 192.

363 "the most exquisite farce" White, R. C., 246.

364 "like boys" Basler, R., Pratt, M., and Dunlap, L., II: 448.

364 "the Administration and slave-power" Wickenden, D., 133.

364 "My dear Henry" Seward, F. A. M., letter to William Henry Seward, December 12, 1857, Auburn, New York.

365 "Douglas' abuse of us" Donald, D. H., *Lincoln*, 204-5.

CHAPTER 65: JOHN BROWN MEETS A GENUINE MOSES

366 "Nelson Hawkins" Villard, O. G., 290.

367 "[t]reason" Edelstein, Tilden G., and Higginson, Thomas Wentworth, *Strange Enthusiasm: A Life of Thomas Wentworth Higginson* (New Haven: Yale University, 1968), 209.

368 "The first I see" Humez, J. M., 24.

368 "I am succeeding" Clinton, C., 97.

369 "very bad man" Villard, O. G., 318.

370 "to get those arms" Harrold, S., 202-3.

370 "if they [the guns]" Villard, O. G., 339.

370 "I never was convinced" Sanborn, F. B., 458.

370 "Wilson a well as" ibid., 460.

371 "were not men" Villard, O. G., 340.

371 "a blush as of roses" "Le Marais Du Cygne," *The Civil War Muse*.

372 "gave out word" U.S. Senate, 36th Congress, "Report on the Investigation of the Harper's Ferry Events (the Mason Report)," *Digital Public Library of America*.

372 "Brown...was taken sick" ibid.

372 "Angels of mercy" Getz, L. M., 79.

CHAPTER 66: LINCOLN THROWS HIS HAT IN THE RING

374 "We hold these truths" Goodwin, D. K., 203.

375 "as thin as" Donald, D. H., *Lincoln*, 225.

375 "Mr. President...If we could first" "House Divided Speech," *Teaching American History*.

377 "Put that and that together" ibid.

378 "boldly and clearly" Donald, D. H., *Lincoln*, 210.

378 "poor, desperate creature" ibid., 210-1.

378 "I shall have my hands" ibid., 209.

379 "I was rather like the Hoosier" ibid., 225.

CHAPTER 67: LINCOLN EXPLAINS HIS VIEWS ON EQUALITY

380 "cover your prairies" Brands, H. W., *The Zealot and the Emancipator: John Brown, Abraham Lincoln and the Struggle for American Freedom*, 143.

380 "this government of ours" Donald, D. H., *Lincoln*, 210.

380 "I will say here" Basler, R., Pratt, M., and Dunlap, L., III: 16, "Great Debate between Lincoln and Douglas, at Ottawa, Illinois," *St. Paul Weekly Minnesotian* (St. Paul, Minnesota), August 28, 1858.

382 "I will say then" Basler, R., Pratt, M., and Dunlap, L., III: 145-6.

383 "legs dangling" Donald, D. H., *Lincoln*, 216.

384 "the boy who" Keneally, T., 73.

384 "a hearing on the great" Donald, D. H., *Lincoln*, 228-9.

384 "the most interesting" "Senator Douglas at Chicago," *The New York Times* (New York), July 13, 1858.

384 "I certainly am flattered" Goodwin, D. K., 212.

CHAPTER 68: FRANCES EXPANDS HER MISSION

386 "with the slightest possible" Wickenden, D., 120.

386 "Certainly, in conversing" ibid.

389 "irrepressible" Foner, E., 101-2.

CHAPTER 69: GAMALIEL BAILEY SAILS AWAY

390 "To my readers" Harrold, S., 211.

391 "When I tell you" ibid., 209.

392 "Not a movement" ibid., 212.

392 "The sad intelligence" "Death of Dr. Gamaliel Bailey," *The Liberator* (Boston, Massachusetts), June 24, 1959.

CHAPTER 70: JOHN BROWN SURFACES IN THE EAST

393 "lawfully-acquired earnings" Villard, O. G., 386.

394 "has been stealing" Lawrence, William, *The Life of Amos A. Lawrence: With Extracts from His Diary and Correspondence* (Houghton, Mifflin and Company, 1888), 130.

394 "Miles Standish" ibid., 125.

394 "a soldierly air" Brands, H. W., *The Zealot and the Emancipator: John Brown, Abraham Lincoln and the Struggle for American Freedom*, 181, Villard, O. G., 398.

395 "What good can they be" Villard, O. G., 401.

395 "perfect steel trap" ibid., 413.

CHAPTER 71: HARRIET TUBMAN TAKES CURTAIN CALLS

396 "It was curious to see" Humez, J. M., 25.

397 "Whereas, from the year 1817" "New England Colored Citizens' Convention," *The Liberator* (Boston, Massachusetts), August 26, 1859.

398 "Whereas, we are fully convinced" ibid.

398 "Miss Harriet Garrison" ibid.

CHAPTER 72: THE ALARM IS SOUNDED

399 "Express train bound east" Maryland. General Assembly, Senate, *Correspondence Relating to the Insurrection at Harper's Ferry, 17th October, 1859, Document Y* (Annapolis: B.H Richardson, 1860), 5.

399 "Your despatch" ibid., 5-6.

400 "a body of armed men" ibid., 7.

400 "Rioters have possession" ibid.

401 "As soon after daylight" Lee, Robert E., "Col. R. E. Lee's Report," *Virginia Humanities/Encyclopedia Virginia*, 1859.

404 "a time of stirring and exciting" Anderson, Osborne P., *A Voice from Harper's Ferry: A Narrative of Events at Harper's Ferry; with Incidents Prior and Subsequent to Its Capture by Captain Brown and His Men* (Boston: Anderson, Osborne P., 1861), Chapter XI, West Virginia Archives & History.Osborne P., 1861

405 "Capt. Brown was all activity" ibid.

405 "It was about twelve o'clock" ibid., Chapter XII.

CHAPTER 73: THE SECRET SIX REACT TO THE NEWS

407 "I and all my large circle" Child, Lydia Maria, Wise, Henry A., and Mason, Maria Jefferson Carr, *Correspondence between Lydia Maria Child and Gov. Wise and Mrs. Mason of Virginia* (Boston: The Anti-Slavery Society, 1860), 3.

407 "whetted knives" ibid., 5.

407 "would unman" Villard, O. G., 479-80n.

407 "Do you read your Bible" Child, L. M., Wise, H. A., and Mason, M. J. C., 16.

408 "Do you soften the pangs" ibid., 17.

408 "To all the personal" ibid., 26.

409 " thus beginning the irrepressible conflict" "The Outbreak at Harper's Ferry-Complicity of Leading Abolitionists and Black Republicans," *New York Daily Herald* (New York), October 20, 1859.

409 "In firing his gun" Garrison, W. P., and Garrison, F. J., 493.

PART VI: DEMOCRACY

411 "As I would not be" Basler, R., Pratt, M., and Dunlap, L., 532.

CHAPTER 74: LINCOLN DOES THE WORK

413 "About thirty miles" Villard, Henry, "Recollections of Lincoln," *The Atlantic*.

413 "irresistibly drawn" Richardson, Albert D., *The Secret Service: The Field, the Dungeon, and the Escape* (Hartford, Conn: American Pub. Co, 1866), 314.

414 "Old John Brown...So, if constitutionally" "Extracts from Mr. Lincoln's Speech in Leavenworth (Kansas)," *Chicago Tribune* (Chicago, Illinois), December 9, 1859.

414 "There is not much of it" White, R. C., 305.

415 "I am, in height" ibid., 307.

415 "good neutral ground" Goodwin, D. K., 229.

416 "a cheap excursion rate" ibid.

418 "Who were our fathers" Lincoln, Abraham, "Cooper Union Address," *Abraham Lincoln Online*, "National Politics: A Speech Delivered at the Cooper Institute Last Evening by Abraham Lincoln," *New-York Tribune* (New York), February 28, 1860.

418 "Does the proper division" Lincoln, A., "Cooper Union Address."

419 "But enough!" Ibid.

419 "John Brown's effort" ibid.

419 "Stand and deliver" ibid.

420 "Will they be satisfied" ibid.

420 "Neither let us be slandered" ibid.

421 "Let us have faith" ibid.

421 "the loud and uproarious" "Address by Hon. Abraham Lincoln," *New York Daily Herald*, February 28, 1860.

421 "my eloquent Western friend" ibid.

421 "He's the greatest man" Donald, D. H., *Lincoln*, 239.

421 "irrepressible conflict" Goodwin, D. K., 213-4.

422 "capital states..."ibid.

422 "the millions of fibers" ibid., 214.

422 "killed Seward with me" ibid.

422 "a masterly and triumphant" ibid., 215.

422 "go down to posterity" Stanton, H. B., *Random Recollections*, 213.

CHAPTER 75: THE PARTIES CHOOSE THEIR PRESIDENTIAL CANDIDATES

425 **"The Winning Man"** "The Winning Man-Abraham Lincoln," *Chicago Press & Tribune* (Chicago, Illinois), May 15, 1860.

427 **"I did not, the whole week"** Goodwin, D. K., 244.

427 **"Make no contracts"** ibid., 246.

428 **"all the hogs"** McPherson, J. M., 220.

428 **"I arise, Mr. Chairman"** Niven, John, *Salmon P. Chase: A Biography* (New York: Oxford University Press, 1995), 220, White, R. C., 328.

428 **"Abraham Lincoln, of Illinois, is selected"** "Proceedings of the National Republican Convention," *Chicago Press & Tribune* (Chicago, Illinois), May 19, 1860.

429 **"I shall be nominated"** Goodwin, D. K., 250.

429 **"as pale a ashes"** Stanton, H. B., *Random Recollections*, 216.

429 **"Father told Mother and I"** Krisher, Trudy, *Fanny Seward: A Life* (Syracuse, New York: Syracuse University Press, 2015), 50.

429 **"No truer or firmer"** Seward, Frederick William, *Seward at Washington as Senator and Secretary of State: A Memoir of His Life, with Selections from His Letters, 1846-1861* (New York: Derby and Miller, 1891), 452.

CHAPTER 76: LINCOLN GETS READY

432 **"The election of Abraham"** "Carrying out Their Principles," *Camden Journal* (Camden, South Carolina), September 25, 1860.

432 **"How do you do"** Goodwin, D. K., 255.

433 **"Mary, Mary"** ibid., 278.

433 **"Compromises based on the idea"** Wickenden, D., 170.

434 **"No state can"** Basler, R., Pratt, M., and Dunlap, L., IV: 154.

434 **"a great mausoleum"** Cooper, William J., Jr., *Jefferson Davis, American* (New York: Vintage Books, 2001), 346.

435 **"result of that ceremony"** Larson, Erik, *The Demon of Unrest: Saga of Hubris, Heartbreak, and Heroism at the Dawn of the Civil War*, First edition. ed. (New York: Crown, 2024), 168.

435 **"To this place"** Goodwin, D. K., 307.

436 **"The votes have been"** ibid., 308.

CHAPTER 77: THE LINCOLN TRAIN DRAWS NEARER TO WASHINGTON

438 **"dragged without hazard"** Larson, E., 264.

438 **"Abe, you can't play"** ibid.

440 **"there were squads"** Seward, F. W., 516.

441 **"We are not enemies"** Basler, R., Pratt, M., and Dunlap, L., IV: 271.

441 **"secession is the essence"** ibid., IV: 256.

441 "to hold, occupy" ibid., IV: 254.

443 "language of the fanatic" Goodwin, D. K., 336.

443 "I think there is a clank" White, R. C., 395.

CHAPTER 78: MARY GETS WHAT MARY WANTS

445 "was the most lovable…" Bayne, Julia Taft, *Tad Lincoln's Father* (Boston: Little, Brown, and Company, 1931), 8.

PART VII: PATIENCE

447 "Not by one word" Chesnut, Mary Boykin, and Williams, Ben Ames, *A Diary from Dixie* (Cambridge, Massachusetts: Harvard University Press, 1980), 38.

CHAPTER 79: THE SOUTH STRIKES

449 "An attempt will be made" McPherson, J. M., 272.

449 "There was a sound of stir" Chesnut, M. B., and Williams, B. A., 36.

450 "I knew my husband" ibid.

451 "very best soldier" Goodwin, D. K., 350.

452 "pollute" Kunhardt, P. B., Jr.; Kundhardt, Philip B. III, and Kunhardt, Peter, 149.

452 "Our men are not moles" ibid.

CHAPTER 80: WASHINGTON IS TRANSFORMED OVERNIGHT

454 "But little seems to be" Taft, Horatio Nelson, "The Diary of Horatio Nelson Taft, 1861-1865," *Library of Congress.*

455 "negroes gathered" Pierce, Edward L., "The Contrabands at Fortress Monroe," *The Atlantic.*

456 "I shall hold these negroes" Butler, Benjamin F., *Autobiography and Personal Reminiscences of Major-General Benj. F. Butler: Butler's Book: A Review of His Legal, Political, and Military Career* (Boston: A. M. Thayer, 1892), 257-8.

457 "Contraband Decision" "Freedom's Fortress: Escape to Freedom."

CHAPTER 81: THE CONFLICT DEEPENS

458 "Forward to Richmond" Goodwin, D. K., 370.

458 "You are green" Keneally, T., 109.

459 "The Union Army" Goodwin, D. K., 372.

459 "the Rebel Yell" National Geographic, Society et al., *Atlas of the Civil War: A Comprehensive Guide to the Tactics and Terrain of Battle* (Washington, D.C: National Geographic Society, 2009), 19.

459 "Mrs. Greenhow" Bayne, J. T., 140-1.

CHAPTER 82: LINCOLN SHAKES IT UP

462 "Do not allow us" McPherson, J. M., 353.

462 "Kentucky gone" Donald, D. H., *Lincoln*, 317.

462 "A. Lincoln. Now." Goodwin, D. K., 392.

463 "You are quite a female" ibid.

463 "taxed me so violently" ibid., "Notable Visitors: Jessie Benton Frémont (1824-1902)," *The Lehrman Institute: Mr. Lincoln's White House*.

463 "Were you not pleased" Goodwin, D. K., 393.

463 "was a measure" Wickenden, D., 188-9.

464 "settled according to laws" McPherson, J. M., 356.

CHAPTER 83: MARY PURSUES A SEPARATE AGENDA

465 "my beau monde friends" Keneally, T., 114.

466 "At Long Branch" "The Coming Excitement at Long Branch—Anticipated Arrival of Mrs. President Lincoln," *New York Daily Herald*, August 7, 1861.

467 "flub-a-dub" Goodwin, D. K., 402.

468 "Well, there we sat" Krisher, T., 68.

468 "Mrs. Lincoln begged" ibid.

468 "Mother, you are mistaken" Keckley, Elizabeth, *Behind the Scenes, or, Thirty Years a Slave and Four Years in the White House* (1868), Chapter VIII, Project Gutenberg.

469 "slave-catching order" Goodwin, D. K., 380.

469 "a slight demonstration" ibid.

470 "with bowed head" ibid., 381.

470 "Mr. Lincoln sat" ibid.

470 "There was no patriot" Keckley, E., Chapter VI.

CHAPTER 84: LINCOLN DEALS WITH MCCLELLAN

472 "Little Mac" "General M'clellan at New York," *The Manitowoc Pilot* (Manitowoc, Wisconsin), DEcember 5, 1862.

473 "unparalleled impudence" Keneally, T., 113.

473 "not to be making" Goodwin, D. K., 383.

474 "the making of false bills" Epstein, D. M., 339.

474 "It is said "It Is Said That..." *The Weekly News-Democrat* (Emporia, Kansas), December 21, 1861.

475 "The most brutal man" "The Most Brutal Man..." *Salem Weekly Advocate* (Salem, Illinois), November 7, 1861.

475 "the Hell-cat" Goodwin, D. K., 401-2.

CHAPTER 85: LINCOLN COMMANDS

476 "General, what shall I do" Donald, D. H., *Lincoln*, 330.

477 "he would like to borrow" ibid.

477 "can't keep a secret" Goodwin, D. K., 426.

477 "arm slaves" Donald, D. H., *Lincoln*, 326.

478 "a change of position" Goodwin, D. K., 411.

478 "were at least equally" Donald, D. H., *Lincoln*, 326.

478 "This will be the last" Nevins, Allan, *The War for the Union: War Becomes Revolution* (New York: Charles Scribner's Sons, 1960), 32.

480 "things have so happened" Goodwin, D. K., 175.

480 "the day for a general" ibid., 426.

CHAPTER 86: LINCOLN WITHSTANDS A HARD BLOW

482 "Madame President" "Another Rumor," *Detroit Free Press* (Detroit, Michigan), Dec. 28, 1861.

482 "the moon in its first" Epstein, D. M.

483 "Whew! Our cat has" Keckley, E., Chapter VI.

484 "mauve-colored silk...her copper-colored" Oller, J., 65, Epstein, D. M., 361.

484 "drew every breath" Kunhardt, Dorothy, and Kunhardt, Philip B., *Twenty Days; a Narrative in Text and Pictures of the Assassination of Abraham Lincoln and the Twenty Days and Nights That Followed--the Nation in Mourning, the Long Trip Home to Springfield* (New York: Harper & Row, 1965), 135.

485 "Fort Henry is ours" McPherson, J. M., 397.

485 "I shall take" ibid.

485 "Confederate affairs" Chesnut, M. B., and Williams, B. A., 187.

486 "Well, Nicolay" Goodwin, D. K., 419.

486 "I assisted I washing" Keckley, E., Chapter VI.

486 "perfect" Baker, Jean H., *Mary Todd Lincoln: A Biography* (New York: W.W. Norton & Co., 2008), 210.

487 "Aunt Mary" ibid., 212.

487 "Please keep the boys" ibid., 213.

487 "People who tried to walk" Kunhardt, D., and Kunhardt, P. B., 137.

488 "a beloved youth" Epstein, D. M., 369.

PART VIII: HOPE

489 "In the summer of 1862" Keckley, E., Chapter VII.

CHAPTER 87: ABOLITIONISTS MAKE GAINS

491 "about one thousand persons" Leech, Margaret, *Reveille in Washington: 1860-1865* (New York: Harper & Brothers, 1941), 299.

491 "an asylum" ibid., 298.

CHAPTER 88: MCCLELLAN ADVANCES

492 "one of the few industrial" Hakim, Joy, and Brooks, Diane L., *War, Terrible War, A History of Us* (New York: Oxford University Press, 2005), 89.

492 "Peninsula Campaign" Kunhardt, P. B., Jr.; Kundhardt, Philip B. III, and Kunhardt, Peter, 176.

492 "probably not less than 100,000" Ward, Geoffrey C., Burns, Ken, and Burns, Ric, *The Civil War: An Illustrated History* (New York: Knopf, 1990), 110.

493 "break the enemy's line" ibid.

493 "kneading troughs" ibid., 133.

CHAPTER 89: MARY LINCOLN SEEKS SOLACE

494 "This morning we went" Pratt, Harry E., *Concerning Mr. Lincoln: In Which Abraham Lincoln Is Pictured as He Appeared to Letter Writers of His Time* (Springfield, Illinois: The Abraham *Lincoln* Association, 1944), 94.

494 "That is a subject" Jones, Edgar Dewitt, *Lincoln and the Preachers* (New York: Harper and Bros., 1948), 37.

495 "In one of her [Mary's]" Keckley, E., Chapter VI.

495 "Mother, do you see" ibid.

495 "When we are in sorrow" Burlingame, Michael, *Abraham Lincoln: A Life* (Baltimore, Maryland: Johns Hopkins University Press, 2013), II: 260.

496 "parlor politics" Goodwin, D. K., 435.

496 "forever free" ibid.

496 "No matter what" Burlingame, M., II: 347.

497 "an outrage" ibid.

497 "rebellion without touching" ibid., II: 397.

497 "Public sentiment" Goodwin, D. K., 469.

498 "should not be done" Stahr, W., 392.

498 "The next day" Towne, Laura M., Holland, Rupert Sargent, and Alexander Street, Press, *Letters and Diary of Laura M. Towne: Written from the Sea Islands of South Carolina, 1862-1884* (Cambridge: Printed at the Riverside Press, 1912), 50-3.

499 "wheelman" "Stole a Whole Vessel," *Boston Globe* (Boston, Massachusetts), October 8, 1903.

500 "Good morning, sir!" McPherson, James M., *The Negro's Civil War: How American Negroes Felt and Acted during the War for the Union* (New York: Pantheon Books, 1965), Location 2601.

501 "all bore the impress" Catton, Bruce, and Lewis, Lloyd, *Grant Moves South* (Boston: Little, Brown, 1960), 293.

501 "This is I think, the most" ibid., 293-4.

CHAPTER 90: MCCLELLAN'S ARMY ADVANCES TO WITHIN NINE MILES OF RICHMOND

503 "Our ears had been filled" Ward, G. C., Burns, K., and Burns, R., 143.

503 "overpowered by superior" ibid., 144.

504 "I tell you plainly" Donald, D. H., *Lincoln*, 358.

504 "I expect to maintain" Seward, F. W., 101.

CHAPTER 91: THE LINCOLNS RETREAT TO THE SOLDIERS' HOME

506 "rode beside [the ambulances" Goodwin, D. K., 445. Pinsker, Matthew, *Lincoln's Sanctuary: Abraham Lincoln and the Soldiers' Home* (New York: Oxford University Press, 2003), 37.

506 "all things [were] looking" Pinsker, M., 39.

507 "order the immediate" ibid.

507 "this army shall enter" "Gen. M' Clellan's Address to His Soldiers," *New York Times* (New York), July 7, 1862.

507 "A declaration of radical" Goodwin, D. K., 451.

508 "On the way up" "By Telegraph: Morning & Afternoon Dispatches," *Buffalo Courier Express* (Buffalo, New York), July 12, 1862.

509 "The pressure, in this direction" Burlingame, M., II: 356.

509 "shall be deemed captives" McPherson, J. M., *Battle Cry of Freedom: The Civil War Era*, 500.

CHAPTER 92: THE DEMOCRATS INFLAME THE NATION WITH HATE

512 "On Tuesday last" "The Labor Question in the Free States-White Labor and Negro Labor," *The Jeffersonian* (West Chester, Pennsylvania), August 2, 1862.

512 "Yesterday, [a]bout noon" "The Anti-Negro Riots in Cincinnati," *Brooklyn Daily Eagle* (Brooklyn, New York), July 19, 1862.

512 "On Monday last" "Atrocious Outrage," *The Liberator* (Boston, Massachusetts), August 8, 1862.

512 "The worst and most degrading" "Letter from Mr. May," *The Liberator* (Boston, Massachusetts), August 29, 1862.

513 "There is a very great aversion" Woodward, C. Vann, "Seeds of Failure in Radical Race Policy," *Proceedings of the American Philosophical Society*, Vol. 110, no. No. 1, (2.

513 "In Ohio, we do not like" ibid.

515 "I think your race" "The Colonization of People of African Descent: An Interview with the President," *New-York Tribune* (New York), August 15, 1862.

515 "Yes, sir" ibid.

515 "Your race are suffering" ibid.

515 "your native land" ibid.

515 "leading colored men" Thomas, Edward M. to *Lincoln*, Abraham, August 16, 1862, Washington, D.C.

515 "They are as much the natives" "The President on African Colonization," *The Liberator* (Boston, Massachusetts), August 22, 1862.

516 "He says to the colored" "The President and His Speeches," *Douglass' Monthly* (Rochester, New York), September 1862.

516 "all suggestions of deportation" "What Shall We Do with the Blacks," *Chicago Tribune* (Chicago, Illinois), August 22, 1862.

CHAPTER 93: LINCOLN'S CRITICS MULTIPLY

517 "preposterous" Greeley, Horace, "The Prayer of Twenty Millions," *New-York Tribune* (New York), August 20, 1862.

517 "My paramount object" Basler, R., Pratt, M., and Dunlap, L., V: 388-9.

518 "My paramount object...is to set" Hedrick, J. D., 303.

518 "Lincoln could not have been" Wilson, R. F., 635.

CHAPTER 94: THE TWO ARMIES CLASH AGAIN AT BULL RUN

520 "miscreant" McPherson, J. M., *Battle Cry of Freedom: The Civil War Era*, 501.

520 "I can't get General" Donald, D. H., *Lincoln*, 370.

521 ""the smell of the gunpowder" Goodwin, D. K., 474.

521 "The President was very outspoken" Hay, John, Burlingame, Michael, and Ettlinger, John R. T., *Inside Lincoln's White House: The Complete Civil War Diary of John Hay* (Carbondale: Southern Illinois University Press, 1997), 37-8.

522 "I cannot tell you" Williams, Blanche, *Clara Barton: Daughter of Destiny* (New York: J.B. Lippincott Company, 1941), 74-5.

523 "Unquestionably he has acted" Hay, J., Burlingame, M., and Ettlinger, J. R. T., 39.

523 "McClellan ought to be shot" Goodwin, D. K., 478.

524 "slows" ibid., 479.

524 "in the condition of a drooping leaf" ibid.

524 "he felt almost ready to hang himself" ibid.

524 "Governor" ibid., 480.

525 "Here is a paper" McPherson, J. M., *Battle Cry of Freedom: The Civil War Era*, 537.

CHAPTER 96: THE TIME IS NOW

529 786 "I think the time has come" Chase, Salmon P., *Diary and Correspondence of Salmon P. Chase* (Washington, D. C: Government Printing Office, 1903), 87-8.

529 787 "One other observation" ibid., 88.

529 788 "insert the [confiscation] laws" White, R. C., 518, Donald, D. H., *Lincoln*, 374.

530 789 "all persons held as slaves" Foner, E., 218.

530 790 "had not much weight" Goodwin, D. K., 376.

530 791 "a great danger" Burlingame, M., 363.

530 792 "What! You Chase" ibid.

531 793 "God Bless Abraham Lincoln" "Comments of the Press Upon the President's Proclamation," *The Philadelphia Inquirer* (Philadelphia, Pennsylvania), September 24, 1862.

531 794 "President Lincoln has set his hand" "The President's Proclamation," *The Tribune* (Chicago, Illinois), September 28, 1862.

531 795 "The North responds" Donald, D. H., *Lincoln*, 378.

532 796 "such an accursed doctrine" Goodwin, D. K., 483.

532 797 "a proposal for the butchery" McPherson, J. M., *Battle Cry of Freedom: The Civil War Era*, 560.

532 798 "The Proclamation, tho'" Wickenden, D., 211.

532 799 "It certainly is not much" Karcher, Carolyn L., *The First Woman in the Republic: A Cultural Biography of Lydia Maria Child* (Durham: Duke University Press, 1994), 463-4.

532 800 "We shout for joy" "Emancipation Proclaimed," *Douglass' Monthly*, October 1862.

533 801 "If he has taught us" ibid.

533 802 "was prescribing whiskey" Hedrick, J. D., 304-5.

CHAPTER 97: MCCLELLAN DISAPPOINTS AGAIN

534 803 "give battle" Goodwin, D. K., 485.

535 804 "Will you pardon me" ibid., 389.

535 "I began to fear" McPherson, J. M., *Battle Cry of Freedom: The Civil War Era*, 570.

535 "He is an admirable" Kunhardt, P. B., Jr.; Kundhardt, Philip B. III, and Kunhardt, Peter, 192.

CHAPTER 98: HARRIET GOES TO WASHINGTON

536 "Harriet Beecher Stowe is in Washington" "From Washington," *Springfield Weekly Republican* (Springfield, Massachusetts), November 29, 1862.

536 "Lizzie says the immense number" Baker, J. H., *Mary Todd Lincoln: A Biography*, 231.

537 "I can not make it better" Basler, R., Pratt, M., and Dunlap, L., V: 534-7.

538 "Go Down, Moses" "Speech of Senator Pomeroy," *National Republican* (Washington, D.C.), November 29, 1862, "The Contraband Dinner," *National Republican* (Washington, D.C.), November 27, 1862.

538 "of all sorts of colors" "The Contrabands Enjoy Thanksgiving," *Journal and Courier* (Lafayette, Indiana), December 3, 1862.

538 "And now, sisters" Fields, Annie, and Stowe, Harriet Beecher, *Life and Letters of Harriet Beecher Stowe* (Boston: Houghton, 1897), 263-7.

CHAPTER 99: THE YEAR GRINDS TO A CLOSE

540 "Te-he-hdo-ne-cha" Donald, D. H., *Lincoln*, 394.

540 "a state of despondency" ibid., 399.

541 "If there is a worst place" Burlingame, M., II: 446.

541 "a malign influence" Stahr, W., 423.

541 "improperly interfered" ibid.

542 "I sent for you" Donald, D. H., *Lincoln*, 404.

542 "Where is it" ibid.

542 "Let me have it" ibid.

542   "This…cuts the Gordian" ibid., 405.

542   "I can ride on" ibid.

542   "And upon this act" ibid., 405-6.

543   "as if I was the son" Alcott, Louisa May et al., *The Journals of Louisa May Alcott*, 1st ed. (Boston: Little, Brown, 1989), 110.

543   "the highest prize" "Miss Louisa M. Alcott," *Boston Evening Transcript* (Boston, Massachusetts), December 24, 1862.

543   "leaping from her bed" Reisen, Harriet, *Louisa May Alcott: The Woman Behind Little Women* (New York: Henry Holt, 2009), 172-3.

CHAPTER 100: LINCOLN ISSUES THE EMANCIPATION PROCLAMATION

544   "all persons held as slaves" "Transcript of the Proclamation," *National Archives.*

545   "His hair is grizzled" Goodwin, D. K., 498.

545   "rich dress of black" ibid.

545   "The broad sheet" Seward, William H., and Seward, Frederick William, *Seward at Washington as Senator and Secretary of State: A Memoir of His Life, with Selections from His Letters, 1861-1872* (New York: Derby and Miller, 1891), 151.

546   "If my name ever goes" Goodwin, D. K., 499.

546   "'n----r' was plentifully used" Forten, Charlotte L., and Stevenson, Brenda E., *The Journals of Charlotte Forten Grimké* (New York: Oxford University Press, 1988), 389.

546   "dat brown gal" Rose, Willie Lee, *Rehearsal for Reconstruction: The Port Royal Experiment* (Indianapolis: Bobbs-Merrill, 1964), 161.

546   "the children are all black" Duran, Jane, "Charlotte Forten Grimké and the Construction of Blackness," *Philosophia African*, Vol. 13, no. 2, (Fall 2010/ Spring 2011)

547   "It was a glorious" Forten, C. L., and Stevenson, B. E., 428-35.

548   "first flash" Goodwin, D. K., 500.

548   "joy and gladness" ibid.

548   "Harriet Beecher Stowe!" Hedrick, J. D., 306.

549   "He said to me" Shenk, J. W., 189n.

Bibliography

Charleston Courier (Charleston, South Carolina). November 14, 1835.

"1851: The Ordeal of Shadrach Minkins." *Long Road to Justice: The African American Experience in the Massachusetts Court*s.

"Abolition Convention-Cazenovia." *Southern Press* (Washington, D.C.). August 26, 1850.

"Abraham Lincoln to Williamson Durley, October 3, 1845." *The Papers of Abraham Lincoln Digital Library.*

"An Act to Organize the Territories of Nebraska and Kansas (Kansas-Nebraska Act (1854))." *National Archives: Milestone Documents.*

"Address by Hon. Abraham Lincoln." *New York Daily Herald*. February 28, 1860.

"American Anti-Slavery Society." https://www.philanthropyroundtable.org/almanac/american-anti-slavery-society/.

"Another Reason." *The Philanthropist* (Cincinnati, Ohio). June 10, 1836.

"Another Rumor." *Detroit Free Press* (Detroit, Michigan). Dec. 28, 1861.

"The Anti-Abolition Riots (1834)." *BlackPast.*

"The Anti-Negro Riots in Cincinnati." *Brooklyn Daily Eagle* (Brooklyn, New York). July 19, 1862.

"Atrocious Outrage." *The Liberator* (Boston, Massachusetts). August 8, 1862.

"Birney Speaks of Matilda." *Cincinnati Daily Gazette*. March 21, 1837.

"Blood-Murder!" *Vermont Telegraph*. November 29, 1837.

"Bloomerism." *Boston Evening Transcript*. June 25, 1851.

"Brief Remarks on Miss Catherine E. Beecher's Essay on Slavery and Abolitionism." *The Liberator* (Boston, Massachusetts). July 14, 1837.

"By Telegraph: Morning & Afternoon Dispatches." *Buffalo Courier Express* (Buffalo, New York). July 12, 1862.

"California." *The Cincinnati Enquirer* (Cincinnati, Ohio). June 5, 1849.

"The California Gold Mines; How to Reach California." *The Birmingham Journal* (Birmingham, West Midlands, England). January 27, 1849.

"Carrying out Their Principles." *Camden Journal* (Camden, South Carolina). September 25, 1860.

"Cash for Negroes." *The Western Citizen*. July 24, 1816.

"The Cincinnati Journal Praised." *The Philanthropist*. August 5, 1836.

"A Circular to the Citizens of the United States: To the Oregon Emigrants." *Sentinel and Democrat* (Burlington, Vermont). June 24, 1831.

"The Colonization of People of African Descent: An Interview with the President." *New-York Tribune* (New York). August 15, 1862.

"The Coming Excitement at Long Branch—Anticipated Arrival of Mrs. President Lincoln." *New York Daily Herald.* August 7, 1861.

"Comments of the Press Upon the President's Proclamation." *The Philadelphia Inquirer* (Philadelphia, Pennsylvania). September 24, 1862.

"Complimentary—Senator Seward." *Portland Press Herald* (Portland, Maine). October 15, 1850.

"The Contraband Dinner." *National Republican* (Washington, D.C.). November 27, 1862.

"The Contrabands Enjoy Thanksgiving." *Journal and Courier* (Lafayette, Indiana). December 3, 1862.

"Death of Dr. Gamaliel Bailey." *The Liberator* (Boston, Massachusetts). June 24, 1959.

"The Dough-Faces* of the North." *The Liberator.* January 23, 1836.

"The Edmondson Sisters." *The Evening Post* (New York). October 30, 1848.

"Elizabeth Smith Miller." *New York History Net.*

"Emancipation Proclaimed." *Douglass' Monthly.* October 1862.

"Exciting Scene in the Senate." *New-York Tribune* (New York). May 21, 1856.

"Extracts from Mr. Lincoln's Speech in Leavenworth (Kansas)." *Chicago Tribune* (Chicago, Illinois). December 9, 1859.

"Fair against Fair." *Mississippi Free Trader.* June 23, 1837.

"Fatal Rencounter [Sic] in Macon." *The Daily Constitutionalist and Republic* (Augusta, Georgia). January 9, 1851.

"Florida Still Teaches 'Benefits' of Slavery." *Austin American Statesman* (Austin, Texas). June 4, 2024.

"Freedom's Fortress: Escape to Freedom."

"From Kansas." *Daily Missouri Republican* (St. Louis, Missouri). November 10, 1856.

"From the Journal and Luminary." *The Philanthropist* (Cincinnati, Ohio). June 10, 1836.

"From Washington." *Springfield Weekly Republican* (Springfield, Massachusetts). November 29, 1862.

"Gen. M' Clellan's Address to His Soldiers." *New York Times* (New York). July 7, 1862.

"General M'clellan at New York." *The Manitowoc Pilot* (Manitowoc, Wisconsin). DEcember 5, 1862.

"Glen-Haven Festival." *Frederick Douglass Paper* (Rochester, New York). June 26, 1851. *Library of Congress.*

"Great Debate between Lincoln and Douglas, at Ottawa, Illinois." *St. Paul Weekly Minnesotian* (St. Paul, Minnesota). August 28, 1858.

"A Great Excitement." *New York Daily Herald* (New York). May 9, 1838.

"House Divided Speech." *Teaching American History.*

"Interesting Trial: John Lawrence Vs. Matilda, a Colored Girl." *The Daily Cincinnati Republican and Commercial Register* (Cincinnati, Ohio). March 16, 1837.

"It Is Said That..." *The Weekly News-Democrat* (Emporia, Kansas). December 21, 1861.

"James Buchanan: Inaugural Address, March 4, 1857." *UVA/Miller Center*.

"A Kanzas [Sic] Hero." *Boston Evening Transcript* (Boston, Massachusetts). January 6, 1857.

"The Labor Question in the Free States-White Labor and Negro Labor." *The Jeffersonian* (West Chester, Pennsylvania). August 2, 1862.

"Le Marais Du Cygne." *The Civil War Muse*.

"Letter from Mr. May." *The Liberator* (Boston, Massachusetts). August 29, 1862.

"Local Intelligence: The Inauguration." *The Evening Star* (Washington, D.C.). March 4, 1857.

"Marius Robinson Speaks of His Mobbing." *The Liberator* (Boston, Massachusetts). July 21, 1837.

"Married." *Fall River Monitor* (Fall River, Massachusetts). March 19, 1836.

"The Methodist Church." *The Philanthropist* (Cincinnati, Ohio). May 27, 1836.

"Midnight Outrage on the Press." *The Liberator* (Boston, Massachusetts). July 30, 1836.

"Midnight Outrage on the Press; Abolitionists Beware." *The Philanthropist*. July 15, 1836.

"Miss Louisa M. Alcott." *Boston Evening Transcript* (Boston, Massachusetts). December 24, 1862.

"The Misses Grimke, from South-Carolina, Delivered Addresses before the Boston Female Anti-Slavery Society." *Pensacola Gazette* (Pensacola, Florida). July 29, 1837.

"The Most Brutal Man..." *Salem Weekly Advocate* (Salem, Illinois). November 7, 1861.

"Mrs. Harriet Beecher Stowe...Uncle Tom's Cabin...Mediocre Writer." *Camden Journal* (Camden, South Carolina). May 7, 1852.

"Narrative of the Late Riotous Proceedings against the Liberty of the Press." *Uncle Tom's Cabin & American Culture* (1836).

"National Politics: A Speech Delivered at the Cooper Institute Last Evening by Abraham Lincoln." *New-York Tribune* (New York). February 28, 1860.

"The New Costume for Ladies." *New-York Tribune*. June 12, 1851.

"New England Colored Citizens' Convention." *The Liberator* (Boston, Massachusetts). August 26, 1859.

"Notable Visitors: Jessie Benton Frémont (1824-1902)." *The Lehrman Institute: Mr. Lincoln's White House*.

"Our Philadelphia Correspondence." *New York Daily Herald* (New York). March 11, 1851.

"The Outbreak at Harper's Ferry-Complicity of Leading Abolitionists and Black Republicans." *New York Daily Herald* (New York). October 20, 1859.

"The President's Proclamation." *The Tribune* (Chicago, Illinois). September 28, 1862.

"The President and His Speeches." *Douglass' Monthly* (Rochester, New York). September 1862.

"The President on African Colonization." *The Liberator* (Boston, Massachusetts). August 22, 1862.

"Proceedings of the Convention of American Women." *The Liberator* (Boston, Massachusetts). June 16, 1837.

"Proceedings of the National Republican Convention." *Chicago Press & Tribune* (Chicago, Illinois). May 19, 1860.

"Proceedings of the Women's Rights Convention." *Anti-Slavery Bugle* (Salem, Ohio). June 7, 1851.

"Resist Not Evil." *The Liberator* (Boston, Massachusetts). December 22, 1837.

"The Rights of Woman." *New-York Tribune* (New York). June 6, 1851.

"Senator Douglas at Chicago." *The New York Times* (New York). July 13, 1858.

Sharp School: Pearson Longman, 2006.

"Slave Hunters in Boston." *Boston Evening Transcript*. October 28, 1850.

"Slavery Diabolical." *The Liberator* (Boston, Mass.). April 25, 1851.

"Southern Brethren." *The Philanthropist* (Cincinnati, Ohio). June 10, 1836.

"Speech of Rev. T. W. Higginson." *The Liberator* (Boston, Massachusetts). January 16, 1857.

"Speech of Senator Pomeroy." *National Republican* (Washington, D.C.). November 29, 1862.

"Spotted Fever." *Illinois State Register* (Springfield, Illinois). February 25, 1848.

"Stole a Whole Vessel." *Boston Globe* (Boston, Massachusetts). October 8, 1903.

"Summary of Legislative Debate on Resolution Commemorating the Battle of New Orleans, 8 January 1841." *The Papers of Abraham Lincoln Digital Library*.

"Timely Admonition." *Fall River Monitor* (Fall River, Massachusetts). August 12, 1837.

"Transcript of the Proclamation." *National Archives*.

"Uncle Tom's Cabin." *Burlington Weekly Sentinel* (Burlington, Vermont). April 1, 1852.

"United States District Court." *National Anti-Slavery Standard* (New York). March 20, 1851.

"Wedding of Angelina Grimké and Theodore Weld (1838)." *Miami University/Empire and American Religion*.

"What Borough Do These Ladies Serve For?" *New York Spectator* (New York). May 18, 1837.

"What Haley Didn't Say." *The New York Times* (New York). December 30, 2023.

"What Shall We Do with the Blacks." *Chicago Tribune* (Chicago, Illinois). August 22, 1862.

"The Winning Man-Abraham Lincoln." *Chicago Press & Tribune* (Chicago, Illinois). May 15, 1860.

"Women's Rights Convention." *Summit County Beacon* (Akron, Ohio). June 4, 1851.

"A Word of Advice to Abolitionists." *Cincinnati Republican* (Cincinnati, Ohio). July 21, 1836.

Aaron, Daniel. *Cincinnati, Queen City of the West, 1819-1838*. Columbus: Ohio State University Press, 1992.

Alcott, Louisa May, Joel Myerson, Daniel Shealy, and Madeleine B. Stern. *The Journals of Louisa May Alcott*. 1st ed. Boston: Little, Brown, 1989.

Anderson, Osborne P. *A Voice from Harper's Ferry: A Narrative of Events at Harper's Ferry; with Incidents Prior and Subsequent to Its Capture by Captain Brown and His Men*. Boston: Anderson, Osborne P., 1861. West Virginia Archives & History.

Applegate, Debby. *The Most Famous Man in America: The Biography of Henry Ward Beecher*. New York: Doubleday, 2006.

Baker, Jean H. *Mary Todd Lincoln: A Biography*. New York: W.W. Norton & Co., 2008.

Baker, Jean H. *Sisters: The Lives of America's Suffragists*. New York: Farrar, Strauss and Giroux, 2006.

Barnes, Gilbert Hobbs. *The Antislavery Impulse, 1830-1844*. New York: Harcourt, 1964.

Basler, Roy, Marrion Pratt, and Lloyd Dunlap. *The Collected Works of Abraham Lincoln*. New Brunswick: Rutgers University Press, 1953.

Bayne, Julia Taft. *Tad Lincoln's Father*. Boston: Little, Brown, and Company, 1931.

Beecher, Catharine to Mary Weld Mary Cogwell, May 29, 1837, Hollis Archives, Harvard, Schlesinger Library, Radcliffe Institute, Beecher-Stowe Family Papers, 1798-1957.

Beecher, Catharine E. "Circular: Addressed to the Benevolent Ladies of the United States." *Teaching American History*.

Beecher, Edward. *Narrative of Riots at Alton, in Connection with the Death of Rev. Elijah P. Lovejoy*. Alton Ill.: G. Holton, 1838.

Beecher, Harriet and Catharine. *Primary Geography for Children*. Cincinnati: Corey and Fairbank, 1833.

Beecher, Henry Ward. "The Crisis." *The Independent* (New York). March 2, 1854.

Beecher, Lyman, and Charles Beecher. *Autobiography, Correspondence, Etc., of Lyman Beecher, D.D.* New York: Harper, 1865.

Beecher, Lyman, and Barbara M. Cross. *The Autobiography of Lyman Beecher*. Cambridge, Mass: The Belknap Press of Harvard University Press, 1961.

Beecher, Lyman; Biggs, Thomas J.; Stowe, Calvin E. T*he Annual Report of the Trustees of the Cincinnati Lane Seminary (1834)*. Cincinnati, Ohio: Corey & Fairbank, 1834.

Beecher, Miss Harriet E. "The Prize Tale: A New England Sketch." *Western Monthly Magazine* (1834).

Belasco, Susan. *Stowe in Her Own Time: A Biographical Chronicle of Her Life*. Iowa City: University of Iowa Press, 2009.

Birney, Catherine H., and Lucy Stone. *The Grimké Sisters. Sarah and Angelina Grimké, the First American Women Advocates of Abolition and Woman's Rights*: Project Gutenberg, 1885.

Birney, James Gillespie, and Dwight Lowell Dumond. *Letters of James Gillespie Birney, 1831-1857*. New York, London,: D. Appleton-Century Company, 1938.

Birney, William. *James G. Birney and His Times*. New York,: D. Appleton and Company, 1890.

Bradley, James. "Brief Account of an Emancipated Slave Written by Himself, at the Request of the Oasis Editor." *Oberlin College and Conservatory*.

Brands, H. W. *The Age of Gold: The California Gold Rush and the New American Dream*. New York: Doubleday, 2002.

Brands, H. W. *The Zealot and the Emancipator: John Brown, Abraham Lincoln and the Struggle for American Freedom*. New York: Doubleday, 2020.

Burlingame, Michael. *Abraham Lincoln: A Life*. Baltimore, Maryland: Johns Hopkins University Press, 2013.

Butler, Benjamin F. *Autobiography and Personal Reminiscences of Major-General Benj. F. Butler: Butler's Book: A Review of His Legal, Political, and Military Career*. Boston: A. M. Thayer, 1892.

Byron, George Gordon Byron Baron. *Don Juan*. A new Cantos I-VIII ed. London: Printed by Thomas Davison, 1819.

Calhoun, John C. "Speech against Clay's Compromise Measures." *Teaching American History*.

Campbell, Susan. *Tempest-Tossed: The Spirit of Isabella Beecher Hooker*. Middletown, Connecticut: Wesleyan University Press, 2013.

Carpenter, F. B. *Six Months at the White House with Abraham Lincoln: The Story of a Picture*. New York: Hurd and Houghton, 1867.

Catton, Bruce, and Lloyd Lewis. *Grant Moves South*. Boston: Little, Brown, 1960.

Ceplair, Larry, Angelina Emily Grimké, and Sarah Moore Grimké. *The Public Years of Sarah and Angelina Grimké: Selected Writings, 1835-1839*. New York: Columbia University Press, 1989.

Chase, Salmon P. *Diary and Correspondence of Salmon P. Chase*. Washington, D. C: Government Printing Office, 1903.

Chase, Salmon P., and John Niven. *The Salmon P. Chase Papers*. Kent, Ohio: Kent State University Press, 1993.

Chesnut, Mary Boykin, and Ben Ames Williams. *A Diary from Dixie*. Cambridge, Massachusetts: Harvard University Press, 1980.

Child, David Lee. "Texas." *The Philanthropist* (Cincinnati, Ohio). May 27, 1836.

Child, Lydia Maria. *An Appeal in Favor of That Class of Americans Called Africans*. Boston: Allen and Ticknor, 1833.

Child, Lydia Maria. *Letters of Lydia Maria Child: With a Biographical Introduction by John G. Whittier*. Boston: Houghton, Mifflin and Co, 1883.

Child, Lydia Maria, Henry A. Wise, and Maria Jefferson Carr Mason. *Correspondence between Lydia Maria Child and Gov. Wise and Mrs. Mason of Virginia*. Boston: The Anti-Slavery Society, 1860.

Chrisman-Campbell, Kimberly. "When American Suffragists Tried to 'Wear the Pants'." *The Atlantic*.

Clinton, Catherine. *Harriet Tubman: The Road to Freedom*. Boston, Mass.: Little, Brown, 2004.

Coffin, Levi. *Reminiscences of Levi Coffin*. Cincinnati, Ohio: Western Tract Society, 1876.

Coleman, J. Winston. *Slavery Times in Kentucky*. University of North Carolina Press, 1940.

Committee, United States House. *Report of the Special Committee Appointed to Investigate the Troubles in Kansas, with the Views of the Minority of Said Committee*. Washington: Cornelius Wendell, Printer, 1856. HathiTrust.

Conkling, Winifred. *Passenger on the Pearl: The True Story of Emily Edmonson's Flight from Slavery*. Chapel Hill, North Carolina: Algonquin Young Readers, 2015.

Cooper, William J., Jr. *Jefferson Davis, American*. New York: Vintage Books, 2001.

Dickens, Charles. *American Notes for General Circulation*. London: Chapman and Hall, 1850.

Dillon, Merton Lynn. *The Abolitionists: The Growth of a Dissenting Minority*. New York: Norton, 1979.

Donald, David Herbert. *Charles Sumner and the Coming of the Civil War*. New York: Knopf, 1960.

Donald, David Herbert. *Lincoln*. New York: Touchstone, 1995.

Douglass, Frederick, Philip Sheldon Foner, and Yuval Taylor. *Frederick Douglass: Selected Speeches and Writings*. 1st ed. Chicago: Lawrence Hill Books, 1999.

Drake, Daniel. "An Account of the Epidemic Cholera: As It Appeared in Cincinnati." *National Library of Medicine Digital Collections*.

Duran, Jane. "Charlotte Forten Grimké and the Construction of Blackness." *Philosophia African* 13, 2, Fall 2010/Spring 2011: 89-98.

Edelstein, Tilden G., and Thomas Wentworth Higginson. *Strange Enthusiasm: A Life of Thomas Wentworth Higginson*. New Haven: Yale University, 1968.

Ellingwood, Ken. *First to Fall: Elijah Lovejoy and the Fight for a Free Press in the Age of Slavery*. New York: Pegasus Books, 2021.

Epstein, Daniel Mark. *The Lincolns: Portrait of a Marriage*. New York: Ballantine Books, 2009.

Fields, Annie, and Harriet Beecher Stowe. *Life and Letters of Harriet Beecher Stowe*. Boston: Houghton, 1897.

Filler, Louis. *The Crusade against Slavery: 1830-1860*: Taylor & Francis, 2017.

Fladeland, Betty. *James Gillespie Birney: Slaveholder to Abolitionist*. New York: Greenwood Press, 1969.

Foner, Eric. *The Fiery Trial: Abraham Lincoln and American Slavery*. New York: W. W. Norton & Co., 2010.

Forten, Charlotte L., and Brenda E. Stevenson. *The Journals of Charlotte Forten Grimké*. New York: Oxford University Press, 1988.

Frederickson, George M. *William Lloyd Garrison*. New Jersey: Prentice-Hall, Inc., 1968.

Freedman, Russell. *Lincoln: A Photobiography*. New York, N.Y.: Clarion Books, 1987.

Gage, F.D. . "Sojourner Truth." *The Independent* (New York). April 23, 1863.

Galbreath, C.B. "Anti-Slavery Movement in Columbiana County." *Ohio History Connection*.

Garrison, Wendell Phillips, and Francis Jackson Garrison. *William Lloyd Garrison, 1805-1879: The Story of His Life*. New York: Century Co., 1885.

Getz, Lynne Marie. *Abolitionists, Doctors, Ranchers & Writers: A Family Journey through American History*. Lawrence, Kansas: University Press of Kansas, 2017.

Goldfarb, Joel. "The Life of Gamaliel Bailey Prior to the Founding of the *National Era*; the Orientation of a Practical Abolitionist." University of California, 1958.

Goodwin, Doris Kearns. *Team of Rivals: The Political Genius of Abraham Lincoln*. New York: Simon & Schuster, 2005.

Greeley, Horace. "The Prayer of Twenty Millions." *New-York Tribune* (New York). August 20, 1862.

Greenwood, Grace. "Letter from Grace Greenwood." *National Era* (Washington, D.C.). October 2, 1851.

Grimké, Angelina Emily. "Appeal to the Christian Women of the South." *Teaching American History*, 1836.

Grimké, Angelina Emily. *Letters to Catherine E. Beecher in Reply to an Essay on Slavery and Abolitionism*: Project Gutenberg, 1838.

Grimké, Archibald Henry. *William Lloyd Garrison, the Abolitionist*. New York etc.: Funk & Wagnalls, 1891.

Hagedorn, Ann. *Beyond the River: The Untold Story of the Heroes of the Underground Railroad*. New York: Simon & Schuster, 2002.

Hakim, Joy, and Diane L. Brooks. *War, Terrible War*. New York: Oxford University Press, 2005.

Harrold, Stanley. *Gamaliel Bailey and the Anti-Slavery Union*. Kent, Ohio: Kent State University Press, 1986.

Hart, Albert Bushnell. *Salmon P. Chase*. New York: Chelsea House, 1980.

Hay, John, Michael Burlingame, and John R. T. Ettlinger. *Inside Lincoln's White House: The Complete Civil War Diary of John Hay*. Carbondale: Southern Illinois University Press, 1997.

Hedrick, Joan D. *Harriet Beecher Stowe: A Life*. New York: Oxford University Press, 1994.

Hentz, Caroline Lee. *Marcus Warland; or, the Long Moss Spring. A Tale of the South*. Philadelphia: A. Hart, 1852.

Herndon, William H., Jesse W. Weik, and Paul M. Angle. *Herndon's Life of Lincoln: The History and Personal Recollections of Abraham Lincoln*. Cleveland, Ohio: World Pub. Co, 1949.

Holland, William M. *The Life and Political Opinions of Martin Van Buren, Vice President of the United States*. Hartford: Belknap & Hamersley, 1836.

Humez, Jean McMahon. *Harriet Tubman: The Life and the Life Stories*. Madison, Wis.: University of Wisconsin Press, 2003.

Jackson, John Andrew. *The Experience of a Slave in South Carolina*. Finsbury: Passmore & Alabaster, 1862.

Johnson, F. Roy. *The Nat Turner Slave Insurrection*. Murfreesboro, N.C: Johnson Pub. Co, 1966.

Jones, Edgar Dewitt. *Lincoln and the Preachers*. New York: Harper and Bros., 1948.

Julius, Kevin C. *The Abolitionist Decade, 1829-1838: A Year-by-Year History of Early Events in the Antislavery Movement*. Jefferson, N.C.: McFarland & Co., 2004.

Karcher, Carolyn L. *The First Woman in the Republic: A Cultural Biography of Lydia Maria Child*. Durham: Duke University Press, 1994.

Keckley, Elizabeth. *Behind the Scenes, or, Thirty Years a Slave and Four Years in the White House*, 1868. Project Gutenberg.

Keneally, Thomas. *Abraham Lincoln: A Life*. New York: Penguin, 2003.

Kipp, Laurie Maffly. "The Religious Roots of Abolition." *National Humanities Center/America in Class*.

Kirkham, E. Bruce. *The Building of Uncle Tom's Cabin*. Knoxville: University of Tennessee Press, 1977.

Knuth, Haley Amanda. "Who Controls the Narrative? Newspapers and Cincinnati's Anti-Black Riots of 1829, 1836, and 1841." Miami University, 2022.

Koester, Nancy. *Harriet Beecher Stowe: A Spiritual Life*, 2014.

Krisher, Trudy. *Fanny Seward: A Life*. Syracuse, New York: Syracuse University Press, 2015.

Kunhardt, Dorothy, and Philip B. Kunhardt. *Twenty Days; a Narrative in Text and Pictures of the Assassination of Abraham Lincoln and the Twenty Days and Nights That Followed--the Nation in Mourning, the Long Trip Home to Springfield*. New York: Harper & Row, 1965.

Kunhardt, Philip B., Jr.; Kundhardt, Philip B. III, and Kunhardt, Peter. *Lincoln: An Illustrated Biography*, 1992.

Larson, Erik. *The Demon of Unrest: Saga of Hubris, Heartbreak, and Heroism at the Dawn of the Civil War*. First edition. ed. New York: Crown, 2024.

Larson, Kate Clifford. *Bound for the Promised Land: Harriet Tubman, Portrait of an American Hero*. New York: Ballantine, 2004.

Lawrence, William. *The Life of Amos A. Lawrence: With Extracts from His Diary and Correspondence*: Houghton, Mifflin and Company, 1888.

Le Beau, Bryan. "She Told the Story, and the Whole World Wept." *American Quarterly* 38, 4, August 1986: 668-74. https://doi.org/10.2307/2712701.

Lee, Robert E. "Col. R. E. Lee's Report." *Virginia Humanities/Encyclopedia Virginia*, 1859.

Leech, Margaret. *Reveille in Washington: 1860-1865*. New York: Harper & Brothers, 1941.

Lerner, Gerda. *The Female Experience: An American Documentary*. New York: Oxford University Press, 1992.

Lerner, Gerda. *The Grimke Sisters from South Carolina: Pioneers for Woman's Rights and Abolition*. New York: Schocken Books, 1971.

Lesick, Lawrence Thomas. *The Lane Rebels: Evangelicalism and Antislavery in Antebellum America*. Metuchen, N.J.: Scarecrow Press, 1980.

Lincoln, Abraham to Mary Lincoln, April 16, 1848, *The Papers of Abraham Lincoln Digital Library*.

Lincoln, Abraham. "Cooper Union Address." *Abraham Lincoln Online*.

Lincoln, Abraham. "Lyceum Address." *Abraham Lincoln Online*.

Lincoln, Abraham. "Peoria Speech." *National Park Service*.

Longfellow, Samuel. *Life of Henry Wadsworth Longfellow, with Extracts from His Journals and Correspondence*. Boston: Ticknor and company, 1886.

Lovejoy, Joseph C., Owen Lovejoy, and John Quincy Adams. *Memoir of the Rev. Elijah P. Lovejoy; Who Was Murdered in Defence of the Liberty of the Press, at Alton, Illinois, Nov. 7, 1837*. New York: J.S. Taylor, 1838.

Mabee, Carleton, and Susan Mabee Newhouse. *Sojourner Truth--Slave, Prophet, Legend*. New York: New York University Press, 1993.

Maryland. General Assembly, Senate. *Correspondence Relating to the Insurrection at Harper's Ferry, 17th October, 1859*. Annapolis: B.H Richardson, 1860.

Masur, Kate. *Until Justice Be Done: America's First Civil Rights Movement, from the Revolution to Reconstruction*. New York: W. W. Norton & Company, 2021.

May, Samuel J. *Some Recollections of Our Antislavery Conflict*. New York: Arno Press, 1968.

McNeil, Samuel. *Mc Neil's Travels in 1849, to, through and from the Gold Regions in California*. Columbus: Scott & Bascom, Printers, 1850.

McPherson, James M. *Battle Cry of Freedom: The Civil War Era*. New York: Oxford University Press, 1988.

McPherson, James M. *The Negro's Civil War: How American Negroes Felt and Acted during the War for the Union*. New York: Pantheon Books, 1965.

Miller, Elizabeth Smith. *In the Kitchen*. Boston: Lee and Shepard, 1875.

Mott, Lucretia Coffin, and Frederick Barnes Tolles. *Slavery and the "Woman Question": Lucretia Mott's Diary of Her Visit to Attend the World's Anti-Slavery Convention of 1840*. London: Friends' Historical Society, 1952.

National Geographic, Society, Neil Kagan, Stephen G. Hyslop, Harris J. Andrews, Harris J. Andrews, Stephen G. Hyslop, Neil Kagan, and Society National Geographic. *Atlas of the Civil War: A Comprehensive Guide to the Tactics and Terrain of Battle*. Washington, D.C: National Geographic Society, 2009.

Nevins, Allan. *Ordeal of the Union 2: A House Dividing 1852-1857*. New York: Scribner, 1947.

Nevins, Allan. *The War for the Union: War Becomes Revolution*. New York: Charles Scribner's Sons, 1960.

Niven, John. *Salmon P. Chase: A Biography.* New York: Oxford University Press, 1995.

Nye, Russel B. "Marius Robinson: A Forgotten Abolitionist Leader." *Ohio History Journal.*

Oller, John. *American Queen: The Rise and Fall of Kate Chase Sprague, Civil War "Belle of the North" and Gilded Age Woman of Scandal.* Boston: Da Capo Press, 2014.

Palmer, Beverly Wilson. "From Small Minority to Great Cause: Letters of Sumner to Salmon P. Chase." *Ohio History Connection.*

Parker, Nate. *The Birth of a Nation: Nat Turner and the Making of the Movement.* New York: 37 Ink/Atria, 2016.

Perry, Mark. *Lift up Thy Voice: The Grimké Family's Journey from Slaveholders to Civil Rights Leaders.* New York: Viking, 2001.

Pickard, John B. "John Greenleaf Whittier and the Abolitionist Schism of 1840." *The New England Quarterly* 37, 2: 250-4. https://doi.org/10.2307/364014.

Pierce, Edward L. "The Contrabands at Fortress Monroe." *The Atlantic,* November 1861.

Pierce, Edward Lillie. *Memoir and Letters of Charles Sumner.* Boston: Roberts Brothers, 1877.

Pinsker, Matthew. *Lincoln's Sanctuary: Abraham Lincoln and the Soldiers' Home.* New York: Oxford University Press, 2003.

Pratt, Harry E. *Concerning Mr. Lincoln: In Which Abraham Lincoln Is Pictured as He Appeared to Letter Writers of His Time.* Springfield, Illinois: The Abraham Lincoln Association, 1944.

Proud, Robin. "Lydia Maria Child." *Prairie UU Society.*

Rankin, John. "Essay on Lane Seminary Published in the Cincinnati Journal." *Ohio History Connection.*

Rankin, John. *Letters on American Slavery: Addressed to Mr. Thomas Rankin, Merchant at Middlebrook, Augusta Co.*, Va. Boston: Isaac Knapp, 1838.

Redpath, James. *The Public Life of Capt. John Brown: With an Auto-Biography of His Childhood and Youth.* Boston: Thayer and Eldridge, 1860.

Reisen, Harriet. *Louisa May Alcott: The Woman Behind Little Women.* New York: Henry Holt, 2009.

Richardson, Albert D. *The Secret Service: The Field, the Dungeon, and the Escape.* Hartford, Conn: American Pub. Co, 1866.

Ricks, Mary Kay. *Escape on the Pearl. The Heroic Bid for Freedom on the Underground Railroad.* New York: William Morrow, 2007.

Robinson, Marius to Emily Robinson, June 13, 1837, Marius Racine Robinson Papers, Western Reserve Historical Society.

Rose, Willie Lee. *Rehearsal for Reconstruction: The Port Royal Experiment.* Indianapolis: Bobbs-Merrill, 1964.

Rosen, Fred. *Gold!: The Story of the 1848 Gold Rush and How It Shaped a Nation.* New York and London: Thunder's Mouth, 2005.

Rourke, Constance. *Trumpets of Jubilee.* New York: Harcourt, Brace & World, 1963.

Rugoff, Milton. *The Beechers: An American Family in the Nineteenth Century.* 1st ed. New York: Harper & Row, 1981.

Sanborn, F. B. *The Life and Letters of John Brown: Liberator of Kansas and Martyr of Virginia.* Boston: Roberts Brothers, 1885.

Sandburg, Carl. *Abraham Lincoln: The Prairie Years and the War Years-the Illustrated Edition* edited by Edward C. Goodman. New York: Sterling Publishing Co., Inc., 2007.

Seward, Frances Adeline Miller to Augustus H. Seward, March 9, 1857, Seward Family Digital Archive, River Campus Libraries, University of Rochester.

Seward, Frances Adeline Miller to William Henry Seward, December 12, 1857, Seward Family Digital Archive, River Campus Libraries, University of Rochester.

Seward, Frederick William. *Seward at Washington as Senator and Secretary of State: A Memoir of His Life, with Selections from His Letters, 1846-1861.* New York: Derby and Miller, 1891.

Seward, William H., and Frederick William Seward. *Seward at Washington as Senator and Secretary of State: A Memoir of His Life, with Selections from His Letters, 1861-1872.* New York: Derby and Miller, 1891.

Shenk, Joshua Wolf. *Lincoln's Melancholy: How Depression Challenged a President and Fueled His Greatness.* Boston: Houghton Mifflin Co., 2005.

Siebert, Wilbur Henry, and Albert Bushnell Hart. *The Underground Railroad from Slavery to Freedom: A Comprehensive History.* Mineola, N.Y.: Dover Publications, 2006.

Simon, Paul. *Lincoln's Preparation for Greatness: The Illinois Legislative Years.* Urbana: University of Illinois Press, 1971.

Sklar, Kathryn Kish. *Catharine Beecher; a Study in American Domesticity.* New Haven,: Yale University Press, 1973.

Smith, Matthew. "Pandemic Redux: Revisiting Cincinnati's 1849 Cholera in the Age of Covid-19." *Origins: Current Events in Historial Perspective,* 2020.

Smith, Matthew D. "The Specter of Cholera in Nineteenth-Century Cincinnati." *Project Muse/Ohio History Connection* (2016).

Stahr, Walter. *Salmon P. Chase: Lincoln's Vital Rival.* New York: Simon & Schuster, 2021.

Stanton, Elizabeth Cady. *Eighty Years and More: Reminiscences (1815-1897).* Boston: Northeastern University Press, 1993.

Stanton, Elizabeth Cady, Susan B. Anthony, and Matilda Joslyn Gage. *History of Woman Suffrage.* Rochester, N.Y.: Susan B. Anthony, 1887.

Stanton, Henry Brewster. "Cheering Intelligence." *The Liberator* (Boston, Massachusetts). March 29, 1834.

Stanton, Henry Brewster. *Random Recollections.* 2d ed. New York: Macgowan & Slipper, Printers, 1886.

Stephens, Alexander. "1861 Cornerstone Speech." *American Battlefield Trust.*

Stetson, Erlene, and Linda David. *Glorying in Tribulation: The Lifework of Sojourner Truth.* East Lansing: Michigan State University Press, 1994.

Stone, Lucy, and Susan B. Anthony. "The Proceedings of the Woman's Rights Convention, Held at Akron, Ohio, May 28 and 29, 1851 (Lccn 93838317)." *Library of Congress.*

Stowe, Harriet (Hatty) to Calvin Stowe, December 27, 1850, Schlesinger Library, Harvard University, Hollis Archives, Beecher-Stowe Family Papers, 1798-1956.

Stowe, Harriet Beecher to Henry Ward Beecher, February 1, 1851, E. Bruce Kirkham Collection, H.B Stowe Center, Hartford, Connecticut.

Stowe, Harriet Beecher to Calvin Ellis Stowe, December 27, 1850, E. Bruce Kirkham Collection, H.B. Stowe Center, Hartford, Connecticut.

Stowe, Harriet Beecher to Calvin Stowe, December 7, 1850, E. Bruce Kirkham Collection, H.B. Stowe Center, Hartford, Connecticut.

Stowe, Harriet Beecher to Calvin Stowe, August-September 1849, Schlesinger Library, Harvard University, Hollis Archives, Beecher-Stowe Family Papers, 1798-1956.

Stowe, Harriet Beecher to Catharine Esther Beecher, after September 18, 1850, E. Bruce Kirkham Collection, H.B. Stowe Center, Hartford, Connecticut.

Stowe, Harriet Beecher to Sarah Sturges Beecher, July 29, 1849, E. Bruce Kirkham Collection, H.B. Stowe Center, Hartford, Connecticut.

Stowe, Harriet Beecher. "A Freeman's Dream: A Parable." The *National Era.* August 1, 1850.

Stowe, Harriet Beecher. *A Key to Uncle Tom's Cabin; Presenting the Original Facts and Documents Upon Which the Story Is Founded.* London: T. Bosworth, 1853.

Stowe, Harriet Beecher. "Uncle Tom's Cabin, Chapter 45, Concluding Remarks." *Uncle Tom's Cabin and American Culture.*

Stowe, Harriet Beecher. *Uncle Tom's Cabin: Or, Life among the Lowly.* Boston, New York, Cambridge: Houghton Mifflin and Company, 1889.

Stowe, Harriet Beecher. *The Writings of Harriet Beecher Stowe, with Biographical Introductions, Portraits, and Other Illustrations.* Cambridge: Houghton, Mifflin and Company, 1896.

Stowe, Harriet Beecher, and Charles Edward Stowe. *Life of Harriet Beecher Stowe.* Boston and New York: Houghton Mifflin and Company, 1889.

Sumner, Charles. *Recent Speeches and Addresses.* Boston: Higgins and Bradley, 1856.

Sumner, Charles. *The Works of Charles Sumner.* Boston: Lee and Shepard, 1871.

Sumner, Charles, and George Frisbie Hoar. *Charles Sumner; His Complete Works: With Introduction by Hon. George Frisbie Hoar.* Boston: Lee & Shepard, 1900.

Sumner, Charles; Pierce, Edward. *Memoir and Letters of Charles Sumner.* Vol. 1, 1893.

Sutton, Robert K., and Robert J. Dole. *Stark Mad Abolitionists: Lawrence, Kansas, and the Battle over Slavery in the Civil War Era.* New York: Skyhorse Publishing, 2017.

Taft, Horatio Nelson. "The Diary of Horatio Nelson Taft, 1861-1865." *Library of Congress.*

Taylor, Nikki Marie. *Frontiers of Freedom: Cincinnati's Black Community, 1802-1868.* Athens: Ohio University Press, 2005.

Thomas, Benjamin Platt. *Theodore Weld, Crusader for Freedom*. New Brunswick: Rutgers University Press, 1950.

Thomas, Edward M. to Abraham Lincoln, August 16, 1862, Library of Congress, Abraham Lincoln Papers: Series 1. General Correspondence. 1833-1916.

Tocqueville, Alexis de. *Democracy in America*. London: Saunders and Otley, 1835.

Towne, Laura M., Rupert Sargent Holland, and Press Alexander Street. *Letters and Diary of Laura M. Towne: Written from the Sea Islands of South Carolina, 1862-1884*. Cambridge: Printed at the Riverside Press, 1912.

Turner, Nat, Thomas R. Gray, Lucas, and Deaver. *The Confessions of Nat Turner, the Leader of the Late Insurrection in Southampton, Va.* Baltimore Md.: T.R. Gray, 1831.

U.S. Senate, 36th Congress. "Report on the Investigation of the Harper's Ferry Events (the Mason Report)." *Digital Public Library of America*.

Utter, David N. "John Brown of Osawatomie." *The North American Review* 137, 324, November 1883.

Villard, Henry. "Recollections of Lincoln." *The Atlantic*, February 1904.

Villard, Oswald Garrison. *John Brown, 1800-1859: A Biography Fifty Years after, Etc.* London: Constable, 1910.

Wagenknecht, Edward Charles. *Harriet Beecher Stowe: The Known and the Unknown*. New York: Oxford University Press, 1965.

Walters, Kerry S. *The Underground Railroad: A Reference Guide*. Santa Barbara, Calif New York: Bloomsbury Publishing (US), 2012.

Ward, Geoffrey C., Ken Burns, and Ric Burns. *The Civil War: An Illustrated History*. New York: Knopf, 1990.

Washington, Margaret. *Sojourner Truth's America*. Urbana: University of Illinois Press, 2009.

Webster, Daniel. "The Seventh of March Speech (1850)." *Bill of Rights Institute*.

Weld, Theodore Dwight. *American Slavery as It Is: Testimony of a Thousand Witnesses*. New York: American Anti-Slavery Society, 1839.

Weld, Theodore Dwight, Angelina Emily Grimké, and Sarah Grimké. *Letters of Theodore Dwight Weld, Angelina Grimké and Sarah Grimké, 1822-1844* edited by Gilbert Hobbs and Dumond Barnes, Dwight L. Gloucester, Massachusetts: P. Smith, 1965.

Wellman, Judith. *The Road to Seneca Falls: Elizabeth Cady Stanton and the First Woman's Rights Convention*. Urbana: University of Illinois Press, 2004.

White, Barbara Anne. *The Beecher Sisters*. New Haven: Yale University Press, 2003.

White, Ronald C. A. *Lincoln: A Biography*. New York: Random House, 2009.

Wickenden, Dorothy. *The Agitators: Three Friends Who Fought for Abolition and Women's Rights*. New York: Scribner, 2021.

Williams, Blanche. *Clara Barton: Daughter of Destiny*. New York: J.B. Lippincott Company, 1941.

Wilson, Douglas L., Rodney O. Davis, Terry Wilson, William Henry Herndon, and Jesse William Weik. *Herndon's Informants: Letters, Interviews, and Statements About Abraham Lincoln*. Urbana: University of Illinois Press, 1998.

Wilson, Robert Forrest. *Crusader in Crinoline, the Life of Harriet Beecher Stowe*. Philadelphia, London etc.: J.B. Lippincott Company, 1941.

Woo, Ilyon. *Master Slave Husband Wife: An Epic Journey from Slavery to Freedom*, 2023.

Woodward, C. Vann. "Seeds of Failure in Radical Race Policy." *Proceedings of the American Philosophical Society* 110, No. 1: 1-9. https://doi.org/10.2307/364014.

Illustration Credits

All internal images are in the public domain, courtesy of

Wikimedia
Library of Congress
New York Public Library
National Park Service
White House History

Index

Italicized page numbers followed by *p* indicate photos or illustrations.

saboteurs in, 453. *See also* Baltimore Riot; *Baltimore Sun*

Baltimore & Ohio Railroad, 399, 400, 404; Brown, John, stopping train, 399

Baltimore Riot, 453; Barton, Clara, and, 452; Massachusetts Sixth Regiment and, 452

Baltimore Sun: on Gamaliel Bailey career, 392

Barnett, Thomas: Tubman, Harriet, and, 245–46

Barton, Clara, 522–23; Baltimore Riot and, 452; comments on Fairfax Railroad Station, 522

Batavia, Ohio, 139

Bates, Edward, 431; as Attorney General in the Lincoln Administration, 433; as 1860 Republican presidential candidate, 415, 425; Greeley, Horace, as supporter of, 426; Lincoln, Abraham, and, 459; McClellan, George B., written protest to oust, 523

Battle of Antietam, 526–27, 535

Battle of Ball's Bluff, 469; Baker, Edward, killed in action at, 469; military blundering at, 473; POWs from in prison overseen by brother of Mary Todd Lincoln, 475; Stone, Charles P., and, 469

Battle of Bull Run, First, 458–59, 461, 465; Beauregard, P.G.T., and, 458; casualties, 459; Johnston, Joseph E., and, 458; Lincoln, Abraham, and, 459; POWs from in prison overseen by brother of Mary Todd, 475; Scott, Winfield, and, 459

Battle of Bull Run, Second, 520, 521; beginning, 521; Confederate capture of nurses, 523; Union defeat, 522, 524

Battle of Fort Donelson, 485

Battle of Fort Henry, 485

Battle of Fredericksburg, Union defeat at, 540

Beauregard, P.G.T.: Battle of Bull Run, and, 458; Chestnut, James, Jr., and, 450; Davis, Jefferson, Fort Sumter orders and, 449

Beecher, Catharine, 6, 44, 64, *136p*, 139, 252; on Beecher, Lyman, upon his third marriage, 114; boarding school in sister Harriet's Maine home, setting up, 306, 307; Cherokee Indian cause and, 9–10; Cincinnati, journey to, 43–44; Cincinnati, thoughts on moving to, 13; in Cincinnati during summer 1837, 139; as contradiction, 132–33; *Essay on Slavery and Abolitionism, with Reference to the Duty of American Females, An,* 132; female anti-slavery convention proceedings and, 140; fundraising trips, 67; Grimké, Angelina, and, 132, 133; Hall, James, campaign against, 71; in Hartford, 9; Lane Seminary slavery debates and, 55, 71; letter to sister Mary about running sister Harriet's Maine household, 306; living in sister Mary's house, 11; Misses Beechers' Western Female Institute, and, 88, 136, 138; as no-show at sister Harriet's wedding, 89; Semi-Colon Club and, 45; Stowe, Harriet Beecher, letter to about Thomas Upham's colonization opinion, 275. *See also* Hartford Female Seminary

Beecher, Charles, 6, 43, *136p*; Coffin, Sarah, marriage to, 189; father's disappointment in, 135; Lane Seminary and, 70, 90, 135; living in the West, 252; Wright, Mary, and, 135, 189

Beecher, Edward, *136p*; Alton anti-slavery convention and, 143, 144, 145; Fugitive Slave Act of 1850, denunciation of, 253; as Illinois College president, 13, 43, 139, 142; living in Jacksonville, IL, 139, 142; Lovejoy, Elijah P., and, 142, 143, 252; as minister, 135; *Narrative of Riots at*

Beecher, Isabella, *136p*; Cincinnati, journey to, 43–44; letter received from Mary Wright about Henry Beecher's graduation day, 134, 135, 136; Perkins, Mary Beecher, and, 136; Stowe, Harriet Beecher, and, 136, 137

Beecher, Isabella (wife of Edward Beecher): Fugitive Slave Act of 1850, denunciation of, 253; letter to Catharine Beecher, 149; letters to Harriet Beecher Stowe, 278, 279; Lovejoy, Elijah P., and, 252; Stowe, Harriet Beecher, visit to, 252

Beecher, James: Cincinnati, journey to 43–44

Beecher, Katherine (wife of William Beecher): home of, 140; letter to Harriet B. Stowe, 115; living in Putnam, OH, summer 1837, 139; Stowe, Harriet Beecher, visit to, 139

Beecher, Lydia Jackson, 114

Beecher, Lyman, *136p*; Beecher, Catharine, and, 13, 114; Beecher, Charles, and, 135; Beecher, George, and, 137, 197; Beecher, Harriet, and, 66, 197; Beecher, Henry Ward, and, 134, 197; in Boston, MA, 9; Brainerd, Thomas, and, 90; Byron, death of, and, 8; Catholics, sermon against in Boston, 68; Catholics, view on, 43; Cincinnati, journey to, 43–44; in Cincinnati, OH, 12, 13, 189; death of first child, 5; early life, 3–4; in East Hampton, NY, 4; fame of, 12; Foote, George, and, 46; fundraising trips, 67, 69; heresy charges against, 71; higher education, 4; Lane Seminary slavery debates and, 55; in Litchfield, CT, 5; living in the West, 252; Mahan, Asa, and, 69; Presbyterian Assembly in Pittsburgh, travel to, 90; Rankin, John, visit to, 73, 76; Second Presbyterian Church and, 82, 137; Stowe, Harriet Beecher, and, 306; Walnut Hills home, 44; wife, first, 4; wife, second, 6; wife, third,

114, 189. *See also* Lane Theological Seminary

Beecher, Mary, 9, *136p*; in Hartford, CT, 9; marriage of, 10. *See also* Perkins, Mary Beecher

Beecher, Roxana Foote, 4; Beecher, Lyman, and, 4; childhood, 4; children of, 4, 6; death of, 6; death of first child, 5; married life, 4–6; sister Mary, 5

Beecher, Sarah (wife of George Beecher): living in Batavia, OH, summer 1837, 139

Beecher, Sarah Coffin: Beecher, Charles, marriage to, 189; letter received from Harriet Beecher Stowe about having little time to write letters, 254

Beecher, Thomas, *136p*; Cincinnati, journey to, 43–44; letter received from Harriet Beecher Stowe about brother George's death, 197

Beecher, William, *136p*; home of, 140; living in Putnam, OH, summer 1837, 139; as minister, 135; visit from sister Harriet, 139; wife, 115

Beecher family: family portrait, *136p*; Lovejoy, Elijah P., murder and, 148–49. *See also names of specific Beecher family members*

"Beecher's Bibles," 336

Belknap, New Hampshire: Bloomers appear in, 296–97

Bell, John: as 1860 Constitutional Union Party presidential candidate, 430; 1860 election, votes received in, 433

Benton, Andrew: Lane Seminary slavery debates and, 56–57

Benton, Catherine: Beecher, Lyman, and, 3

Benton, Lot, 3; "New England Sketch, A" about, 46

Benton, Thomas Hart, 355; as Buchanan, James, supporter in 1856 presidential election, 356

Biggs, Thomas J.: *Cincinnati Journal* letter favoring colonization, 68; Lane Theological Seminary and, 49, 67

Birney, Agatha McDowell, 81, 82, 87, 88, 90; anti-abolitionists, return home after hiding from, 112; Birney, James, nonsupport of abolitionist views, 82; Cincinnati, move to, 81; death of, 164–65; Grimké-Weld wedding, offer to host, 157; Lawrence, Matilda, and, 100, 116; tuberculosis diagnosis, 86

Birney, David, 82

Birney, Dion, 82

Birney, Ellen: death of, 164

Birney, Florence, 81, 82, 103, 116; Smith family as guardian of, 165

Birney, George, 82, 103; Smith family as guardian of, 165

Birney, Georgiana, 87; death of, 101

Birney, James, Jr., Oberlin College and, 82

Birney, James G., 81, 84, 87, 96; abolitionism, religious view of, 97–98; American and Foreign Anti-Slavery Society and, 168, 171; as American Anti-Slavery Society agent, 113; American Colonization Society, denunciation of, 81; anti-abolitionist mobs, hiding from, 112; as anti-Garrison abolitionist, 164; as anti-women's rights, 164; Chase, Salmon, and, 82, 116; children, visiting at Gerrit Smith home, 165; Cincinnati, move to, 81; *Cincinnati Whig* attacks on, 84; *Essay on Slavery and Abolitionism, with Reference to the Duty of American Females, An,* view of, 132; Fitzhugh, Elizabeth, and, 165; Great Mob Meeting and, 85; Grimké-Weld wedding, offer to host, 157; handbill calling for body of, 104; immediate emancipation, advocacy for, 81, 82; Lane Seminary debates and, 81; Lawrence, Matilda, and, 100, 116, 118; Lawrence, Matilda, case, conviction and fine in, 118; Lawrence, Matilda, moving to safety, 103; "Letter on Colonization," 68; letters to Lewis Tappan, 87, 101, 112; as Liberty Party presidential nominee, 168; mob at home of, 110; on *Montreal* (ship), 168; moving family to safety, 103; press manipulation against, 108; pro-abolitionist pamphlet, 82; Pugh, Achilles, and, 86; Pugh, Achilles, printing office and, 110; Robinson, Marius, and, 286; Smith, Gerrit, and, 164; Stowe, Harriet Beecher, on, 109; threats to tar and feather, 109; warning to about possible mob attack on home, 83; Weld, Angelina Grimké, disagreement with about "woman question," 170; Weld, Theodore, and, 82; World's Anti-Slavery Convention and, 173, 174, 175. See also *Philanthropist, The*

Birney, William, 103; Graham, Joseph, and, 110–11; Oberlin College and, 82; as witness in Matilda Lawrence trial, 117

Bishop, Emeline: letter to Theodore Weld about student behavior, 63; as Ohio State Anti-Slavery Society convention delegate, 87

Black Codes and Laws: freed-slave migration and, 511, 513; Illinois, 380; Ohio, 61, 100, 117; Louisiana *Code Noir,* 303; post-Nat Turner's Rebellion, 33

Black Hawk War: Lincoln, Abraham, fighting in, 24, 415

"Black Republicans," 341, 350, 356, 387

Black schools, Cincinnati: in Baker Jones home, 61; proslavery mobs and, 61; Robinson, Marius R., and, 61; Wattles, Augustus, and, 61

"Black Signpost Road," 33

Blair, Charles: Brown, John, and, 395

of benefactors, 366–67, 393, 394; Smith, Gerrit, and, 351, 366, 367, 371; Stearns, George L., and, 352, 366, 367, 370; Sumner, Charles, and, 351; sword injury at Harper's Ferry raid, 402; Thoreau, Henry David, and, 351; Tubman, Harriet, and, 368, 394–95; Walker, George, and, 350; Wattles, Augustus, and, 372, 393, 394; Wattles, Sarah Grimké, and, 371; weapon purchases, 345; Yankee approval of, 409. *See also* Harper's Ferry, John Brown's raid on Federal Arsenal at

Brown, John, Jr., 344, 345; Pottawatomie Rifles and, 346

Brown, Mary Day, 344, 345; letter received from John Brown about malaria and Wattles family help, 373

Brown, Oliver, 345, 346

Brown, Owen, 344, 345, 346; arrival in Kansas, 346

Brown, Salmon, 344, 346

Browning, Eliza Caldwell: visits to Lincoln family after son Willie's death, 487

Browning, Orville: Lincoln, Abraham, and, 464; regarding Kentucky's value to Abraham Lincoln, 462; visits to Lincoln family after son Willie's death, 487

Browning, Robert, 506

Bruin, Joseph: Beecher, Henry Ward, and, 231; Chaplin, William, and, 230, 232–33; Edmonson sisters and, 226–27, 232, 233; *Pearl* slave escape incident and, 216

Bruin and Hill. *See* Bruin, Joseph

Brunswick, Maine: 1850 winter storm, 278; runaway slaves in, 275–76; Stowe, Harriet Beecher, living in, 251–56. *See also* Stowe, Harriet Beecher (1850–1852, Brunswick, ME)

Bryant, William Cullen: introduction of Abraham Lincoln at Cooper Union, 418. See also *New York Evening Post*

Buchanan, James: award offer for John Brown's capture, 394; as career politician, 385; as 1856 Democratic presidential candidate, 356; Grier, Robert C., and, 361; Lincoln, Abraham, and, 377; in Lincoln inaugural parade, 441; National Democrats aligned with, 383; notification of John Brown's raid at Harper's Ferry, 400; presidential inauguration, 359–60, 361; secession of Southern states and, 433; Seward, William H., banning from White House, 362; Seward, William H., on Dred Scott decision conspiracy involving, 361–62; Taney, Roger B., and, 360

Buck, Eliza: Stowe, Harriet Beecher, and, 204

Bucktown, Maryland, 241

Bullard, Eunice: Beecher, Henry Ward, and, 71, 135. *See also* Beecher, Eunice Bullard

Burnet, David G.: Burnet, Jacob and, 109; Republic of Texas and, 109

Burnet, Jacob: Birney, James, warnings to about continuing to publish *The Philanthropist*, 109

Burns, Anthony: attempted rescue of by abolitionists, 323; Boston arrest as fugitive slave, 322; Higginson, Thomas Wentworth, and, 351; return to slavery, 323; trial, 322

Burnside, Ambrose: Battle of Fredericksburg defeat and, 540; as replacement for George McClellan, 535

Butler, Andrew: Brooks, Preston S., and, 341, 342; death of, 357; Kansas slave state conspiracy, blamed by Charles Sumner for, 340

Butler, Benjamin: Cary, John Baytop, and, 456, 457; contraband policy,

456, 490; escaped slaves working as masons at Fort Monroe, and, 456; welcomed at Fort Monroe, 455

Byron, Lord: Beecher, Esther, and, 7, 8; Beecher, Lyman, and death of, 8; death of, 8; poetry of, 7–8; quote about words, 1; Stowe, Harriet Beecher, and, 7–8

Cady, Daniel: as anti-abolitionist, 169

Cady, Elizabeth: abolitionism, conversion to, 166; Powell, Harriet, and, 165–66; Smith, Gerrit, and, 165–66, 168, 169; Stanton, Henry B., engagement and marriage to, 168–69; wedding, 169. *See also* Stanton, Elizabeth Cady

Calhoun, John C., 327; Senate gag rule on anti-slavery petitions and, 130; warning about Union being in danger, 248

California: application for admission to the Union as free state, 247, 250; Coloma, 201; as free state, 219, 249, 250; Frémont, John C., and, 355; Gold Rush, 234–36; Marshall, James W., discovery of gold in, 201–2, 318; Mexican-American War and, 355; Sacramento, 442; San Francisco, 234, 236, 318; Treaty of Guadalupe Hidalgo and, 200; United States purchase of, 200, 201

Cameron, Simon: as 1860 Republican presidential candidate, 415, 425; Fort Sumter situation and, 449; government should "arm slaves" statement in message to Congress, 477; Lincoln, Abraham, nomination of as minister to Russia, 478; Lincoln, Abraham, removal of as Secretary of War, 477–78; Republican National Convention of 1860 and, 477; rumors about corruption and, 426

Camp Barker, 513–14

Capitol. *See* U.S. Capitol

Cartter, David K.: at 1860 Republican National Convention, 428

Cary, John Baytop: attempt to retrieve Charles Mallory's slaves from Fort Monroe, 456

"Case of the Edmonton Sisters, The," 231

Cass, Lewis: as 1848 Democratic presidential candidate, 219

Cato, Sterling: Brown, John, and 347

Channing, William Ellery: at Faneuil Hall December 1837 meeting, 148

Chaplin, William L., 260–61; abolition activism, abandonment of, 261; Bruin, Joseph, and, 230, 232–33; Edmonson, Paul, and, 232; Edmonson sisters and, 230, 232–33, 260; Gilbert, Theodosia, and, 260, 261; Glen Haven Water-Cure Institute and, 261; imprisonment, 261; *Pearl* slave escape and, 232, 260; release from Maryland prison, 261; slaves rescued by, 261; Stowe, Harriet Beecher, criticism of Edmonson sisters' treatment by, 310; Underground Railroad and, 261

Chapman, Maria: as Convention of Anti-Slavery Women speaker, 155, 160

Charleston, Illinois, 381

Charleston, South Carolina, 12, 93–4, 97, 433

Charlestown, Massachusetts: Ursuline convent, mob burning of, 68

Chase, Kate, 82, 453, *454p*; Anderson, Robert, and, 454; death of mother Kitty, 82; hosting dinners for Washington elites, 496; at White House Ball of 1862, 484

Chase, Kitty: death of, 82

Chase, Nettie, 453; Anderson, Robert, and, 454

Chase, Salmon, 421; appearance, physical, 46; Bailey, Gamaliel, and, 305, 390, 391; Birney, James, and, 116; Birney, James, on mob at Franklin

Charles Sumner, 355; Brown, John, attempts to visit in prison, 406–8; Brown, John, reactions to attempts to visit in prison, 407; Emancipation Proclamation, reaction to, 532; as Female Anti-Slavery Convention vice president, 130; Frémont, John C., 1856 support for, 355; Grimké sisters, letter to about need for a public life, 178; husband, 97; immediate emancipation, call for, 52; instruction manuals for mothers, 52; *Juvenile Miscellany, The,* 52; as *Liberator, The,* reader, 52; literary success, 53; *National Era,* published in, 211; on New York race riots, 94; *Oasis, The,* 86; Osgood, Lucy, and, 406; on Slave Power, 355

Chillicothe, Ohio, 197

cholera, 41–42; Beecher, Esther, ill with, 114; Blacks and immigrants, prevalence among versus whites, 41; cause per Dr. Daniel Drake, 237; Cincinnati summers and, 251; contaminated water and, 42; 1832 Cincinnati epidemic, 41, 44, 237; 1849 Cincinnati epidemic, 236–40; 1849 Monterrey, Mexico, epidemic, 236; Irish immigrants in Cincinnati blamed for, 237; Stowe, Samuel Charles "Charley," death from, 239; in Walnut Hills, Ohio, 238–40

Church Alley (Cincinnati): mob attack on Black residents of, 111

Cincinnati, Ohio: Bailey, Gamaliel, and, 39–42; Beecher children's thoughts on moving to, 13; Beecher family journey to, 43–44; Birney family move to, 81; Black schools, 61; Blacks barred from public schools in, 60; cholera epidemics, 41, 44, 236–40; Ohio State Anti-Slavery Society move to, 87; physicians, 40–41; public parks, lack of, 65; social problems, 251; Stowe family move from, 251; violence, white against Black in,

189. *See also names of specific Cincinnati newspapers*; Cincinnati Anti-Slavery Society; Cincinnati Board of Health; Cincinnati Sisters; Cincinnati Water Company, cholera and; Lane Theological Seminary; Misses Beechers' Western Female Institute; Stowe, Harriet Beecher (1832–1850, Cincinnati, OH)

Cincinnati Anti-Slavery Society, 83; Bailey, Gamaliel, and, 71; Robinson, Marius, and, 71

Cincinnati Board of Health, cholera and, 42

Cincinnati Commercial: Villard, Henry, and, 413

Cincinnati Gazette: Hammond, Charles, and, 83; publication of Lane Seminary Board rules against student anti-slavery activities, 69. See also *Daily Gazette* (Cincinnati)

Cincinnati Journal: Biggs, Thomas J., letter to favoring colonization, 68; publication of Lane Seminary Board rules against student anti-slavery activities, 69; separation of races, letter to regarding, 63

Cincinnati Journal & Luminary, The, 91; Beecher, Henry Ward, and, 92–93; Brainerd, Thomas, and, 90; "Franklin Letter" in, 105–7; Lusher, William D., refusal to accept at post office, 93

Cincinnati Republican: Birney, James, attacks on in, 108; Lawrence, Matilda, reporting on trial of, 116–17, 118; warnings to Ohio State Anti-Slavery Society, 108

Cincinnati Sisters, 62–63; Black community and, 62; marriage to American Anti-Slavery Society agents, 113; as Ohio State Anti-Slavery Society convention delegates, 87; treatment of by Cincinnati residents, 62. *See also* Bishop, Emeline; Lowe, Susan E.; Rakestraw, Emily

Cincinnati Water Company, cholera and, 237

Cincinnati Whig, 86; Birney, James, attacks on, 84

Civil War, 492–93, 503–4, 520–27; Battle of Antietam, 526–27, 535; Battle of Ball's Bluff, 469, 473; Battle of Ball's Bluff POWs, 473, 475; Battle of Bull Run, first, 458–59, 461, 465; Battle of Bull Run, first, POWs, 475; Battle of Bull Run, second, 520, 521, 522, 523, 524; Battle of Fort Donelson, 485; Battle of Fort Henry, 485; Battle of Fredericksburg, 540; beginning of, 450; Chase, Salmon P., inability to raise funds during, 476; Confiscation Act of 1861 and, 461, 462; contraband policy and, 490; General War Order No. 1, 480; invasion of Maryland by Robert E. Lee, 524–25; Peninsula Campaign, 492–93; Rebel yell and, 459; Seven Days' Battles, 503–4; siege of Yorktown, 493; Union objective to capture Richmond, Virginia, 476; Washington, D.C., appearing as military camp during, 454, 458. *See also names of Civil War military leaders and forts*; Baltimore Riot; Lincoln, Abraham (1861–1865, Civil War President)

Clay, Cassius: on Seward, William H., "State of the Country" speech, 422

Clay, Henry, 327; Missouri Compromise of 1820 and, 15, 250; Todd, Mary Ann, and, 184

Cleveland, Charles, 46

Cleveland, Ohio, 289, 415

Clinton, DeWitt: Erie Canal and, 181; Lincoln, Abraham, and, 181, 182

Clinton, Georgia, 266

Codding, Ichabod: new Republican Party and, 330

Code Noir, Louisiana: Stowe, Harriet Beecher, and, 303

Coffin, Sarah. *See* Beecher, Sarah Coffin

coffle, slave, *17p*, 55; description, 16–18; Edmonson sisters as witnesses to, 230

Colburn, Nettie, 495

Colby, Isaac: Birney, Agatha, diagnosis of, 86; mob ransacking office of, 111

Coleman, J. Winston, Jr.: on Edward Stone keeping slaves in cellar, 16

Collins, Eliza Smith: Collins, Robert, and, 266; Craft, Ellen, and, 266; Smith, James, and, 266

Collins, Robert: Collins, Eliza, and, 266; Fillmore, Millard, letter to, 273; Hughes, Willis H., and, 268; slaves, selling off, 266

Coloma, California: 1848 discovery of gold in, 201

colonization concept, voluntary: Lincoln, Abraham, and, 490; Lincoln, Abraham, meeting with Black leaders about, 514–15; Second Confiscation Act and, 514; unpopularity of among Black people, 514, 515; in Washington, D.C., emancipation proclamation, 491

colonization ideology: Biggs, Thomas J., letter favoring, 68; Birney, James G., letter opposing, 68; Lane Seminary slavery debates and, 58. *See also* colonization concept, voluntary; colonizationists

colonizationists, 50; Child, Lydia Maria, attack on in *An Appeal,* 52–53; Lane Seminary slavery debates and, 58. *See also* Biggs, Thomas J.; Finley, Robert

colorphobia, New England Colored Citizen Convention of 1859 and, 398

Columbus, Ohio, 69, 436

Colver, Nathaniel: World's Anti-Slavery Convention and, 173, 174

Dickey, James: Lane Seminary slavery debates and, 55; slave coffle description, 16–18, 55

Dickey, T. Lyle: Lincoln, Abraham, and 324

Diffey, Alexander, 400

Diggs, Judson: *Pearl* slave escape incident and, 215

District of Columbia Compensated Emancipated Law, 491; appropriations for colonization outside United States in, 492

Dix, Dorothea: alert about Lincoln assassination plot, 437; nurse recommendation for Tad Lincoln from, 487

Dodge, Francis, Jr.: missing slaves, 213; *Pearl* slave escape incident and, 215

Donaldson, Christian: potential mob attack on home of, 111

Donaldson, William: potential mob attack on home of, 111

Dorchester, Massachusetts: Grimké sisters speaking in, 131

Dorchester County, Maryland: Tubman, Harriet, birthplace of, 243

Douglas, Adèle Cutts: Douglas, Stephen A., widow of, 481; 1858 Senate campaign of husband and, 383

Douglas, Stephen A., 318, 376; appearance, physical, 326; Brooks, Preston S., cane beating of Charles Sumner and, 343; Committee on Territories, removal of as chairman of, 385; Compromise of 1850 and, 262; Douglas, Adèle Cutts, as widow of, 481; Dred Scott decision and, 361, 375, 385; 1854 Illinois State Fair speech, 326; 1854 lecture tour on providing a government to Nebraska Territory, 325; 1858 Senate campaign, number of miles traveled during, 383; 1858 Senate campaign speeches, 378; as 1858 Senate candidate, 374; 1858 Senate

reelection, 385; as 1860 Northern Democratic presidential candidate, 430; 1860 presidential election, favored Democratic candidate in, 385; 1860 presidential election, votes received in, 433; Fillmore, Millard, and, 262; Greeley, Horace, collaboration with to defeat Kansas admission as slave state, 364–65; Kansas-Nebraska Bill, Senate debate with Salmon Chase over, 320; Kansas slave state conspiracy, blamed by Charles Sumner for, 340; killing Missouri Compromise, 325; Lecompton Constitution, opposition to, 363–64, 375; Lecompton Constitution, Senate fight against, 364; Lincoln, Abraham, and, 375, 376, 377, 441; negrophobia, appeal to, 375; nickname, 326; popular sovereignty concept, 319, 320, 329, 331, 361, 363, 375; Reeder, Andrew Horatio, removal of as Kansas Territorial governor and, 334; September 1854 Chicago speech, 325; Seward, William Henry, and, 418; spelling change of name, 327; Todd, Mary Ann, and, 185, 374; transcontinental railroad Northern route scheme and, 319. *See also* Kansas-Nebraska Bill; Lincoln–Douglas 1858 debates

Douglass, Frederick, *259p*, 369, 396; autobiography, first, 303, 327; Brown, John, hiding, 366; Brown, John, planned Virginia raid and, 366, 395; Brown, John, raid on Harper's Ferry, and, 406; Emancipation Proclamation, and, 532–33, 548; Fugitive Slave Law, quote about, 317; Fugitive Slave Law Convention of August 1850 and, 259–60; Miner, Myrtilla, warning to about Normal School for Colored Girls, 311; National Woman's Rights Convention of 1850 and, 287; Radical Political Abolitionist Party convention and,

345; rebuttal to Stephen A. Douglas' speeches on Nebraska government, 326; requesting applications for Black emigration party to Central America for sons, 516; Seneca Falls Woman's Rights Convention of 1848 and, 218; on Seward, William H., "State of the Country" speech, 422; *Uncle Tom's Cabin,* and, 313, 315; Underground Railroad and, 386; on voluntary colonization plan of Abraham Lincoln, 515–16; Washington Contraband Relief Association donation, 536. See also *North Star*

Douglass, Grace Bustill, 124; as Female Anti-Slavery Convention vice president, 130; as Grimké-Weld wedding guest, 159

Douglass, Sarah Mapps, 124; as Grimké-Weld wedding guest, 159

Doyle, James: Pottawatomie killings, victim of, 347

Doyle, Mahala: Pottawatomie killings, witness to, 347–48

Doyle, William: Pottawatomie killings, victim of, 348

Drake, Daniel, 41; "blue pills" and, 198, 238; cholera, causes according to, 237; cholera reports, announcement of daily and, 237; Lincoln, Abraham, and, 186; railroads and, 97; Semi-Colon Club and, 46; Stowe, Harriet Beecher, and, 114, 198; Texas Aid Association and, 97

Drayton, Daniel: *Pearl* slave escape incident and, 214, 215, 216

Dred Scott decision, 360–62, 376–77; Seward, William H., on conspiracy between President Buchanan and Justice Taney in, 361–62

Dred Scott v. Sandford. See Dred Scott decision

Dresser, Amos: public flogging of, 94

Driscoll, Pete, 75

Du Pont, Samuel: Smalls, Robert, and, 500

Dunbar, The Reverend, 128

Dutton, Mary: Beecher, Harriet, maid of honor in wedding of, 89; Misses Beechers' Western Female Institute and, 44, 88; traveling back east from Cincinnati, 64, 65, 67, 190

Duvall, Bettie: Greenhow, Rose O'Neal, and, 460

Eagle (steamboat): Lawrence, Larkin, and, 99; Lawrence, Matilda, and, 99

East Hampton, New York, 4

Easton Star (Talbot Co., MD): runaway slave ads, 246–47

Eberle, John: Bailey, Gamaliel, and, 41; Jefferson Medical College and, 41

Edmonson, Amelia "Milly," 216, 224; children, 225, 226; Culver, Rebecca, and, 224, 226; Edmonson, Emily, reunion with, 310; Edmonson, Mary, reunion with, 310; Edmonson, Paul, marriage to, 225; Normal School for Colored Girls, living on campus of, 311

Edmonson, Emily, 213, *214p*, 216; Bruin, Joseph, and, 226–27; New Orleans, witnessing other slaves in, 229; Normal School for Colored Girls, working and living at, 310, 311; *Pearl* escape incident and, 213–15, 226; reunion with father Paul, 233; reunion with mother Milly, 310; Valdenar, Frances, and, 226; Wilson, Jonathan, and, 227–28. *See also* Edmonson sisters

Edmonson, Ephraim, 226, 229; *Pearl* escape incident and, 226

Edmonson, Hamilton, 225; Culver, Rebecca, and, 225; New Orleans, found by brother Richard in, 229; as runaway slave, 225

as slave state, 364–65; Emancipation Proclamation, reaction to in *New York Tribune,* 531; Lincoln, Abraham, and, 418; Mason-Child letters and, 408; Second Confiscation Act, imploring Abraham Lincoln to enforce, 517; Second Confiscation Act article, reply from Abraham Lincoln about, 517; Seward, William H., and, 418; Weed, Thurlow, and, 418

greenbacks, 510

Greenhow, Rose O'Neal, 459–60; as Confederate spy, 459; Duvall, Bettie, and, 460; Taft, Horatio, and, 459; Union map discovery in home of, 460; Wilson, Henry, and, 460

Greenwood, Grace: *National Era,* published in, 211; *Uncle Tom's Cabin,* letter about in *National Era,* 307

Grier, Robert C.: Buchanan, James, and, 361

Grimké, Angelina, 11, *11p,* 12; as American Anti-Slavery Society agent, 126; Charleston, S.C., Presbyterian Church, expulsion from, 12; as Convention of Anti-Slavery Women headline speaker, 155, 159, 160; female anti-slavery societies, quote about, 123; Garrison, William Lloyd, and, 124, 156; as "immediate emancipation, gradually accomplished" advocate, 128; letter to William Lloyd Garrison, 125; letter to Mary Beecher Perkins, 10–11; letters in *The Liberator* on abolitionist views, 133; Lovejoy, Elijah and Celia, rebuke of for self-defense use of force, 149; "Pastoral Letters" against, 132; as Quaker, 11, 12; Quakers, break from, 156; slavery study, 125; Society of Friends and, 124; Society of Friends, excommunication from after marriage, 156; Tappan, Julia, and, 128; Tappan, Lewis, and, 128; Weld, Theodore, and, 128; Weld,

Theodore, engagement to, 154–56. See also *Appeal to Christian Women of the South*; Grimké, Sarah; Grimké sisters; Grimké-Weld wedding; Weld, Angelina Grimké

Grimké, Sarah, 12, 124, 156; American Anti-Slavery Society and, 126; *American Slavery As It Is* research and publication, 179–80; anti-slavery work while at home, 179; as "immediate emancipation, gradually accomplished" advocate, 128; motivation for speaking truth about slavery, 127–28; on Northern Democrats cooperating with Southern slaveholders, 262; "Pastoral Letters" against, 132; as Quaker, 12; Society of Friends and, 124; Stanton, Henry B., visit and, 169; Tappan, Julia, and, 128; Tappan, Lewis, and, 128; Weld, Charles Stuart, and, 177. *See also* Grimké, Angelina; Grimké sisters; Wattles, Sarah Grimké; Weld, Angelina Grimké

Grimké sisters: American Anti-Slavery Society disavowal, 133; anti-slavery lectures, 128, 130–32, 134; Child, Lydia Maria, 1839 letter to about need for public life, 178; Mott, Lucretia, 1840 comments on returning to public sphere, 178; "Pastoral letters" against, 132; Tappans distancing selves from, 133; Weld, Theodore, view on feminist talk from, 133; Weston, Deborah, 1839 comments about, 178. *See also* Grimké, Angelina; Grimké, Sarah; Wattles, Sarah Grimké; Weld, Angelina Grimké

Grimké-Weld family, Graham diet and, 169

Grimké-Weld wedding, 157, 158–59

Guilford, Connecticut, 3

erick "Shadrach," trial for rescue of and, 303

Hazlett, Albert: Brown, John, raid on Harper's Ferry, and, 405

Helen/Hannah: Perdu, John, and, 283; trial of, 283

Hentz, Caroline Lee: *Lovell's Folly,* 46; *Marcus Warland; or, The Long Moss Spring,* 315–16; Semi-Colon Club and, 46, 315

Herald of Freedom (Lawrence, KS): indictment of for treasonous language, 338

Herndon, William "Billy": Greeley, Horace, and, 365; Lincoln, Abraham, and, 211, 324, 364; on Lincoln, Abraham, audience reception to 1858 Senate campaign speech, 378

Hertford County, North Carolina, 29

Hicks, Thomas Holliday: Lincoln, Abraham, and, 452; Union soldiers, refusal to let into Maryland, 452

Hindman, Thomas, 526

Higginson, Thomas Wentworth, 423; Brown, John, and, 351, 367, 371, 394, 406; Burns, Anthony, attempt to rescue, 323, 351; Emancipation Proclamation reading at Camp Saxton and, 547; letter received from Franklin Sanborn to stop John Brown's planned raid, 370; Sanborn, Franklin, and, 351; Secret Six, as one of John Brown's, 366, 367, 397; Tubman, Harriet, introduction of at Massachusetts Anti-Slavery Society meeting, 397

Hine, Lucius: Ohio Woman's Rights Convention of 1851 and, 290

Hooker, Isabella Beecher: accompanying sister Harriet to Washington, D.C., 536; *Uncle Tom's Cabin,* bitterness toward sister Harriet over, 314; visit from sister Harriet on her way to Maine, 252. *See also* Beecher, Isabella

hospitals, Washington, D.C., 505–6; Barton, Clara, on, 522; Government Hospital for the Insane, 495; Lincoln, Mary Todd, visits to, 505; temporary, 506; Union Hotel Hospital, Louisa May Alcott as nurse at, 543

Howe, Samuel: Brown, John, and, 367, 371, 406; hanging of John Brown, return to United States after, 423; letter to Henry Wilson to stop John Brown's Virginia plan, 370; Secret Six, as one of John Brown's, 366, 367; Wilson, Henry, letter to about stopping John Brown's Virginia plan, 370; as witness in Senate investigation into John Brown's raid at Harper's Ferry, 423

Hubbard, Mary Ward Foote, 5

Hudson, John D.: Underground Railroad and, 74

Hudson, Ohio, 147

Hughes, Mordecai B.: Robinson, Marius, and, 120–21

Hughes, Willis H., 269, 273; arrests of, 271, 272; attack on cab of, 272; Boston Vigilance Committee and, 269–70, 273; Collins, Robert, and, 269; Craft, Ellen, and, 268–69, 270; Craft, William, and, 268–69, 270, 271, 272; flight from Boston to New York, 273; Georgia, return to, 274; Knight, John, and, 269, 270; Knight, Thomas, murder of, 274; mob visit to, 273; poem about in *Evening Transcript* (Boston), 271–72

Hunter, David: decree requiring Black men to serve in the army, 498; emancipation order for South Carolina, Georgia, and Florida, 496, 498; Lincoln, Abraham, and, 496

Illinois, 39, 181; Alton, 142, 143, 144–45, 146; Beecher, Edward, and, 252; Black Laws, 380; Charleston, 381; election of 1860 results, 432; Jacksonville, 139, 142; Lincoln,

Abraham, and, 20, 22, 150, 181, 184, 324, 425, 428; Lincoln–Douglas debates in, 378, 380–83; McClelland, George B., in, 473; *New-York Tribune* readers in, 364; as political battleground in 1858, 384; Republican Party in, 330, 356; restrictions on Black settlement in, 513; Scott, Dred, and, 360; Springfield, 149, 374. *See also names of Chicago and Illinois newspapers*; Chicago, Illinois; Douglas, Stephen A.; Republican National Convention of 1860; Wigwam, the

Illinois Central Assembly: resolution disapproving formation of abolition societies, 142

Illinois College: Beecher, Edward, as president of, 13, 43, 139, 142

Illinois River, 22

Illinois State Fair, 1854: Douglas, Stephen A., speech at, 326; Douglas, Stephen A., rebuttal to Abraham Lincoln's speech, 330; Lincoln, Abraham, speech at, 327–30

Illinois State Register: on Illinois State Assembly meeting where Abraham Lincoln jumped out window, 183

"Immediate Emancipation" (story), 203

Independent: Beecher, Henry Ward, reaction to Kansas-Nebraska Bill in, 320–21; Stowe, Harriet Beecher, criticism of Abraham Lincoln in, 518

"Independent Gold Miner on His Way to California" cartoon, *235p*

Indian Removal Act, 10

Internal Revenue Service, establishment of, 510

Irwin, McDowell, 458

Ivanhoe (book), 7

Jackson, Andrew: Indian Removal Act and, 10

Jackson, "Aunt" Polly: Underground Railroad and, 74–75

Jackson, J. C.: Glen Haven Water-Cure Institute and, 297

Jackson, John Andrew: Stowe, Harriet Beecher, sheltering of, 276; Upham, Thomas C., and, 276

Jackson, Stonewall, 520, 535

Jackson, Tennessee: Kittoe, Edward, description of 501–2

Jackson Administration: as anti-abolitionist, 93

Jacksonville, Illinois, 139, 142

James River: Civil War and, 455, 503, 507. *See also* Fort Monroe

Jefferson Medical College (Philadelphia, PA): Bailey, Gamaliel, and, 41; Eberle, John, and, 41

Jerusalem, Virginia, 31

Jewett, John P.: as *Uncle Tom's Cabin* publisher, 308

Johnson, William, 18

Johnson, William: as Franklin House proprietor, 104

Johnston, John D., 22; Lincoln, Abraham, and, 21, 22

Johnston, Joseph E.: Battle of Bull Run, and, 458

Jones, Baker: Black Cincinnati school in home of, 61

Jones, Jonas: storage of weapons for John Brown, 352

Jones, Samuel J.: sack of Lawrence leader, 338, 339

Jones, Wharton, 222

Judd, Norman: Lincoln, Abraham, and, 437; Lincoln, Abraham, advisor to during 1860 campaign, 424; Lincoln, Abraham, as campaign manager for, 416; Republican National Committee and, 415

Juvenile Miscellany, The: Child, Lydia Maria, and, 52; subscription cancellations, 53

Lincoln, Abraham **(1847–1849, U.S. Congressman)**, *188p*, 199–200, 201, 327; appearance, physical, 220; Cass, Lewis, 1848 speeches deriding, 220; as 1848 campaign speaker at Whig rallies, 219, 220, 221; 1848 speeches, *Norfolk Democrat* comments on 220; Giddings, Joshua, and, 222, 223; Herndon, Billy, and, 211; jokes, telling, 208; Lincoln, Mary Todd, and, 212–13; mannerisms, 220; Polk, James K., blaming and criticizing for starting Mexican-American War, 199–200; Polk White House, visit to with wife Mary, 211; Seaton, William, and, 223; Seward, William Henry, and, 221–22; slavery, late 1848 changing view on, 222; Sprigg Boardinghouse stay in Washington, D.C., 208, 223; storytelling, 208; traitor, *Peoria Press* denunciation of as, 200; Van Buren, Martin, 1848 speeches deriding 220; Washington, D.C., abolition bill, discarding idea of, 223; as Whig, 199, 200; Wilmot Proviso and, 201, 212

Lincoln, Abraham **(1849–1859, lawyer, state legislator, political candidate)**: as ambitious, 385; Buchanan, James, and, 377; Chase, Salmon P., and, 384; Dickey, T. Lyle, and 324; Douglas, Stephen A., and, 365, 375, 376, 377; Douglas, Stephen A., view of as radical abolitionist, 380; as Eight Circuit lawyer, 324; 1854 Illinois State Fair speech, 327–30; 1856 vice presidential candidate, second place, 355–56; 1858 Senate campaign, miles traveled during, 382; 1858 Senate campaign, number of speeches made during, 382; 1858 Senate campaign speeches, 375–76, 377, 378; as 1858 Senate candidate, 374; 1860 presidential candidate, seen as potential, 384; Gillespie, Joseph, and, 330; Herndon, William,

and, 324, 375; in Illinois State Legislature, 330; law practice, return to post-1858 election, 384; Lecompton Constitution, thoughts on Stephen A. Douglas and, 364; National Democrats in 1858, and, 384; Pierce, Franklin, and, 377; reaction to Kansas-Nebraska Act, 324; Republican Party, leader of Illinois, 356; Republicans, 1858 alliances with prominent, 384; scrapbook, 1858 Senate debate speeches in, 385, 414; slavery, view on, 362, 374; Speed, Joshua, and, 325; Taney, Roger, and, 377; voice, Horace White description of in *Chicago Tribune,* 327; as Whig, 330. *See also* Lincoln-Douglas 1858 debates

Lincoln, Abraham **(1859–1860, presidential candidate)**, 430; advisors, 424; appearance, physical; 415; Bowen, Henry, and, 416; Brown, John, thoughts on, 413–14, 419; Bryant, William Cullen, introduction of at Cooper Union, 418; Chase, Salmon P., congratulatory letter to on winning the 1860 Republican presidential nomination, 429; Chicago newspaper editorials on, 425; Cooper Union Address (Feb. 27, 1860), 416, 418–20; Davis, David, and, 424, 426; 1859 Leavenworth, KS, speech, 414; 1859 speeches about Republican cause, 412; 1859 Troy, KS, speech, 413–14; 1860 election returns, waiting in the Capitol telegraph office for, 432; 1860 New England speaking tour, 421; 1860 Republican National Convention, during, 424; German-American voters and, 426; Greeley, Horace, and, 418; Herndon, William "Billy" and, 432; Judd, Norman, and, 414, 416; Know-Nothing Party, opposition to, 426; Nicolay, John, and, 431; photographic portrait by

to enforce Second Confiscation Act, 517–18; Gurley, Phineas, and, 494; Hamlin, Hannibal, and, 531; Harris, Ira, and, 542; Hay, John, and, 462, 463, 523, 535; Hicks, Thomas Holliday, and, 452; Hunter, David, and, 496; letter to William H. Seward on troop recruitment, 504; Lincoln, Tad, and, 506; McClellan, George B., and, 461, 466, 472, 473, 474, 507, 523, 526, 535; McClellan, George B., refusal to share war plans with, 477; McClellan, George B., visit to army camp of, 507, *534p*; McDowell, Irvin, and, 477; meeting with Black leaders about colonization concept, 514–15, 517; Meigs, Montgomery, and, 476, 507; Nicolay, John, anguished cry to about son's death, 486; reading, love for, 506; second annual message, 537; Seven Days' Battles, blamed by George B. McClellan for defeat in; 504; Seward, William H., and, 524; Seward, William H., defense of, 541; Sibley, Henry, and, 507; Speed, Joshua, and, 462, 548–49; Stanton, Edwin M., as co-counsel with in Cyrus McCormick patent rights case, 479; Stanton, Edwin M., as new Secretary of War under, 477, 478–80; Stowe, Harriet Beecher, criticism of in *Independent*, 518; viewing son Willie in his coffin after crypt placement, 488; voluntary colonization concept, and, 490–91, 514; volunteer soldiers enlistment bills, signing of, 461; Watt, John, and, 475. *See also* Emancipation Proclamation

Lincoln, Edward, 211

Lincoln, Mary Todd, *188p*, 199, 211, 414, 444–46, *444p*, 465–68, *483p*, 494–96; as ambitious, 385; Baker, Edward, funeral attire, 471; brother David Todd, and, 474–75; Browning, Eliza Caldwell, and, 487; Browning, Orville, and, 487; Confederate spy rumors about, 474; Douglas, Stephen A., and, 442; dressmaker, selecting, 439; Edwards, Elizabeth, and, 487; 1858 Lincoln–Douglas debates attendance, 383; 1860 Republican National Convention, during, 424; gentlemen callers at White House, 465; gossip about, 495; Hall, Neal, and, 487; Hay, John, and, 495; hospitals in Washington, D.C., visits to, 505; at inaugural ball, 442; inauguration, arrival in Washington, D.C., for, 439; Keckley, Elizabeth, and, 439–40, 474, 481, 487; Kentucky, return to, 212; letter received from Abraham after her departure from Washington, D.C., 213; Lincoln, Willie, reaction to death of, 486–87; money, attempts to raise, 467; *New York Herald*, planned trip reported in, 465–66; New York trip with Elizabeth Keckley, 536; New York trip with son Tad, 508, 536; Polk White House, visit to with Abraham, 211; President of the United States, hearing from Abraham that he was elected, 433; presidential inauguration of husband Abraham and, 442; presidential nomination, hearing from husband Abraham about his, 430; receipt of threatening painting, 435; remodel of White House, 466–67; séance participation, 495, 545; Seward, William H., and, 439; Seward, William H., dislike of, 465, 468; as shopaholic, 211–12; spiritualism and, 494–95; Stone, Robert, and, 487; Stowe, Harriet Beecher, meeting with, 536; Taft, Mary Cook, and, 444; Taft family, request to not visit White House after Willie's death, 487; visits with important Washington, D.C., women, 439; Washburne, Elihu, and, 439; Washington Contraband Relief Association donation, 536; Watt, John, and, 467; Watt, John, rumors of collusion with, 474–75; Watt, John, trip with, 475;

murder, 147; murder of, 146, 163, 191; as *Observer* editor, 142; Presbyterian General Assembly attendance, 142. See also *Observer*

Lovejoy, Owen: new Republican Party and, 330

Lovejoy family, anti-abolitionist stalking and harassment of, 143

Lovell's Folly: Hentz, Caroline Lee, and, 46

Lowe, Susan E., 62; letter to Theodore Weld on Black families' treatment of, 63; as Ohio State Anti-Slavery Society convention delegate, 87; Wattles, Augustus, marriage to, 113. *See also* Wattles, Susan Lowe

Lowell, Massachusetts: Grimké sisters speaking in, 131

Ludlow, Henry, 128

Lusher, William D.: refusal to accept *Cincinnati Journal & Luminary* at post office, 93

Lyman, Elizabeth: Harriet Beecher letter to about stagecoach travel, 65–66

Lynn, Massachusetts: Grimké sisters speaking in, 131

Lyons, Mary: Mount Holyoke Female Seminary and, 138

Macon, Georgia, 268, 269, 274

Magruder, John B., 492

Mahan, Asa: letter to Lyman Beecher about returning to Lane Seminary, 69

Maine: as free state, 15

Mallory, Charles K.: Cary, John Baytop, attempt to retrieve slaves of from Fort Monroe, 456; as slave master, 455

Mallory, Shepherd: Fort Monroe and, 455

Marais des Cygnes Massacre, 371–72, 375; poem by John Greenleaf Whittier about, 371–72

Marcus Warland; or, The Long Moss Spring, 315–16

Maria: Craft, Ellen, and, 266; owner James Smith rape of, 266

Marietta, Ohio, 138

Marshall, James W.: 1848 gold discovery at Sutter's Fort in California, 201–2, 234

Maryland: Anne Arundel County, 99; Baltimore, 25, 399, 452; Bucktown, 241; Chaplin, William L., jumped bail and fled from, 261; Confederate flags on homes in, 452; Dorchester County, 243; Eastern Shore, slaves running away from, 246–47; Frederick, 525; importance of to Washington, D.C., during Civil War, 451, 452; law about children born to slaves, 224; Monocacy, 399; Montgomery County, 213, 224; Perryville, 454; Poplar Neck, 242, 243; search for John Brown insurgents in after Harper's Ferry raid, 402, 404, 405; slaves fleeing from, 513; Sumner, Charles, and, 152–53; Talbot County, 246; Tubman, Harriet, escape from, 368. *See also* Baltimore, Maryland; Baltimore Riot; Battle of Antietam; Battle of Ball's Bluff; Civil War

Mason, James: on runaway slaves, 247; Senate committee to investigate John Brown's raid on Harper's Ferry and, 423

Mason, Maria J. C.: Child, Lydia Maria, condemnation of for desired John Brown prison visit, 407–8; Mason-Child letters, release of to Horace Greeley, 408

Mason-Dixon Line, 15

Massachusetts: Alcott, Louisa May, leaving to go to Washington, D.C., 543; Amherst College, 13, 64; Andover, 256, 312; Auburn, Massachusetts, 395; Brown, John, in, 345; Charleston, 68; Dickens, Charles, visit to, 193; Dorchester, 131; Forten, Charlotte, teacher in, 546, *547p*;

Medary, Samuel: Brown, John, award offer for capture of, 394; Wattles, Augustus, and, 394

Medford, Massachusetts, 406

Meigs, Montgomery: Lincoln, Abraham, and, 507; war council suggestion to Abraham Lincoln, 476

Memoirs of Phyllis Wheatley, The, 86

Methodist Church, 97–98

Mexican-American War, 199, 200; Frémont, John C., and, 355. *See also* Treaty of Guadalupe Hidalgo

Michigan: as free state, 96

Militia Act, 509

Miller, Belle, 494–95

Miller, Charles, Jr., 295

Miller, Charles Dudley: gift of house from in-laws, 295

Miller, Gerrit, 295

Miller, Libby (Elizabeth Smith): house as gift from parents, 295; Smith, Gerrit, on her wearing Bloomers, 300; wearing Bloomers, 296; wearing long skirts again after wearing Bloomers, 300–01; *Uncle Tom's Cabin,* letter received from Elizabeth Cady Stanton about, 313

Miller, William, 295

Mills, S. S.: Brown, John, raid on Harper's Ferry and, 402

Miner, Myrtilla, 310, 311; Beecher, Henry Ward, donation to for school furniture, 310; Douglass, Frederick, warning to about opening school, 311; Mott family support for school of, 311; Normal School for Colored Girls and, 310–11, 387; Seward family support for school of, 311; Stowe, Harriet Beecher, donation to buy land for school of, 311

Minkins, Frederick "Shadrach": arrest, 281; Hayden, Lewis, and, 281, 303; "rescue trial" and, 303–4

Misses Beechers' Western Female Institute: Beecher, Catharine, and, 44, 64, 65, 71; Beecher, Harriet, and, 44, 65; closing of, 136; Dutton, Mary, and, 44; Dutton, Mary, loss of money from closing of, 138; Stowe, Harriet Beecher, loss of money from closing of, 138; Tappan, Ann, and, 44

Mississippi: Davis, Varina, return to, 434; Pontotoc, 93; secession, 433

Mississippi River, 22, 39; Davis, Jefferson, plantation located along, 435–36; as natural North–South traffic highway, 318

Missouri: Brown, John, in, 393; Lincoln, Abraham, campaigning for William Henry Harrison in, 184; Pike County, 99; St. Joseph, 442; Scott, Dred, in, 360; as slave state, 15, 451. *See also* Civil War; Missouri Compromise of 1820

Missouri Compromise of 1820: Clay, Henry, and, 15, 250; Fillmore, Millard, and, 250; Lincoln, Abraham, interest in politics and, 415; Lincoln, Abraham, on origins of, 327–28; repeal of, 361; 36° 30' parallel and, 15, 318, 319, 328

Missouri Republican: disparagement of Elijah P. Lovejoy after his murder, 147

Missouri River, 345

Mitchell, Barton W.: discovery of Robert E. Lee's Special Order Number 191 in field, 525

Monocacy, Maryland, 399

Montgomery, Alabama: as first capital of the Confederacy, 436

Montgomery County, Maryland, 213, 224. *See also* Culver, Rebecca; Edmonson, Paul; Edmonson sisters

Montreal (ship), 168

Morgan, Edwin B.: Sumner, Charles, cane beating by Preston S. Brooks, and, 343

Morgan, John: Lane Board firing of, 69; as Lane Seminary Biblical scholar and professor, 49

Morris, Robert: "rescue trial" of, 303

Mott, Lucretia Coffin, *172p*, 386; American Anti-Slavery Society and, 54, 171; anti-slavery society credentials, 171; as Convention of Anti-Slavery Women speaker, 155, 160; as courtroom spectator for fugitive slave trial, 283; as Female Anti-Slavery Convention vice president, 130; on Grimké sisters returning to public sphere, 178; Grimké-Weld wedding, non-attendance at, 159; National Woman's Rights Convention of 1850 and, 286–87; Normal School for Colored Girls, support for Myrtilla Miner's, 311; opposition to Free Staters' armed retaliation over Kansas situation, 336; Orthodox Quakers view of as heretic, 174; Seneca Falls Woman's Rights Convention of 1848 and, 218; Stanton, Elizabeth Cady, and, 175; Tubman, Harriet, and, 243, 388; Underground Railroad and, 243; voyage to World's Anti-Slavery Convention, 172; World's Anti-Slavery Convention and, 171, 173, 175

Mount Holyoke Female Seminary: Lyons, Mary, and, 138

Mount Pleasant, Ohio, 120

mulattoes: Democratic banner in Charleston, SC, depicting, 381; Grimké, Sarah, on, 127; Lincoln, Abraham, and story of murder of, 150; Ohio Black Laws and, 100, 117; runaway slave advertisement for return of, 196; Sumner, Charles, on racial composition of French school and, 152. *See also* Edmonson, Milly; Edmonson, Paul; Forten, Charlotte; Lawrence, Matilda

Murfreesboro, North Carolina, 32

Narrative of Riots at Alton: In Connection with the Death of Rev. Elijah P. Lovejoy pamphlet, 149

Narrative of Sojourner Truth, 288, 289, 290

national cemetery, 505

National Era, 210, 369, 390, 391; circulation, 211, 305; Congressional news in, 211; mob violence against after *Pearl* escaped slave incident, 216–17; Stowe, Harriet Beecher, subscription to, 302; Stowe, Harriet Beecher, writing for, 253, 277; success of, 210; *Uncle Tom's Cabin* in, 303, 305, 392; *Uncle Tom's Cabin,* letter from Grace Greenwood about in, 307; *Uncle Tom's Cabin,* May 1851 notice about upcoming publication of, 285; writers published in, 211. *See also* Bailey, Gamaliel

National Intelligencer, 210; August 1831 blue-green sun article, 29; Lincoln, Abraham, reply to Horace Greeley about Second Confiscation Act enforcement in, 517

National Republican: publication of Willie Lincoln's poem "On the Death of Colonel Edward Baker," 470

National Woman's Rights Convention of 1850: Douglass, Frederick, and, 287; Mott, Lucretia, and, 286–87; Truth, Sojourner, and, 286, 287

Nebraska Territory, 318, 325

Nelson, Red: Francis, Lavinia, saving life of, 32

Neville, Morgan: Chase, Salmon, and, 109; Lane Seminary Exodus and, 108

New England Colored Citizen Convention of 1859, 397–98; resolutions, 397–98; Tubman, Harriet, at, 397

New England Emigrant Aid Company, 331, 334; Lawrence, Amos A., and, 352; purpose of, 323; Thayer, Eli, and, 323

New Garden, Ohio, 62

New Mexico: free-state constitution, 250; Texas claims to, 250; transcontinental railroad and, 318

New Orleans, Louisiana: Beecher, Charles, and, 189, 191; California Gold Rush, as stop on way to, 235–36; Civil War and, 477; Edmonson brothers and sisters as slaves in, 227–30; Johnston, John D., and, 22; Lincoln, Abraham, as flatboat pilot on journey to, 21–22, 181; Offutt, Denton, and, 22; Powell, Harriet, and, 166; slave market, 61, 79, 166, 216; slave ship to, 25–26; steamboat *Uncle Sam* and, 77; transcontinental railroad and, 318; Yellow fever epidemic in, 229–30

New Salem, Illinois: Lincoln, Abraham, and, 21–24

New Salem Debating Society: Lincoln, Abraham, and, 24

New York City: Union Square gathering on April 20, 1861, in support of the Union, 450. *See also names of specific New York City newspapers*; Beecher, Henry Ward; Birney, James G.; Brooklyn, New York; Plymouth Church; Tappan, Arthur; Tappan, Lewis

New York Daily Herald: Brown, John, accusations in of William H. Seward supplying guns to, 409; Grimké-Weld wedding announcement in, 154; Lincoln, Abraham, Cooper Union Address and, 421; White House leaks to, 475; Wikoff, Henry, and, 475

New-York Evangelist, 12; "Immediate Emancipation" story in, 203; Stowe, Harriet Beecher, pieces in, 191, 253, 277; Stowe, Harriet Beecher, 1843 essay criticizing Charles Dickens' literature in, 196–97; volunteer female teachers advertisement in, 61

New York Evening Post: Bryant, William Cullen, and, 418

New York Herald: Lincoln, Mary Todd, planned trip reported in, 465–66; Seward, William H., attack on in, 362; Wikoff, Henry, as White House social spy for, 465

New York Independent: Lincoln, Abraham, Cooper Union speech and, 416; Stowe, Calvin, announcement of Bowdoin induction in, 256

New York Married Women's Property Act of 1848: Seward, Frances, and inheritance of Miller House, 387; Stanton, Elizabeth Cady, and, 388

New York Spectator: commentary on Female Anti-Slavery Convention, 131

New York State: abolition of slavery in, 263. *See also* Brooklyn, New York; New York City

New York Times: Henry, Raymond, and, 391; on Illinois as political battleground, 1858, 384; on Lincoln, Abraham, inaugural address, 443

New-York Tribune: Child-Wise letters in, 407; circulation, 211; on Lincoln, Abraham, Cooper Union speech, 421; on Lincoln, Abraham, inaugural address, 443; Lincoln, Mary Todd, naming as White House leaker, 475; Second Confiscation Act, imploring Abraham Lincoln to enforce, 517; Seward, William H., "State of the Country" speech, 422; on Sumner, Charles, "The Crime Against Kansas" speech, 340; on Truth, Sojourner, Ohio Woman's Rights Convention of 1851 speech, 293; on Washington, D.C., during Civil War, 506

Newburyport, Massachusetts: Garrison, William Lloyd, birthplace of, 25; Grimké sisters speaking in, 131

Newburyport Free Press: Garrison, William Lloyd, and, 25

Oregon Country, Kelley's fraudulent 1832 expedition to, 38–39

Oregon Territory, British and American division of, 200

Osgood, Lucy: Child, Lydia Maria, and, 406

Otis, Harrison Gray: as Boston mayor, 34; Garrison, William Lloyd, and, 34

Panic of 1837, 137, 138, 143; bank closures and, 182; halting of Illinois internal improvement projects and, 182; Illinois State Bank and, 182, 183; Perkins family and, 137; Stowe, Calvin, and, 138

Parker, Theodore: Brown, John, sharing Virginia plan with, 367; Craft, Ellen, hiding of, 272; Secret Six, as one of John Brown's, 366, 367; tuberculosis, 394, 406, 423; as Craft wedding officiant, 273

Parsons, Luke: Brown, John, and, 353

Pearl slave escape incident, 213–15; Bailey, Gamaliel, anger directed at in wake of, 216, 217; Diggs, Judson, and, 215; Dodge, Francis, Jr., and, 215; Drayton, Daniel, and, 214, 215, 216; Edmonson, Emily, and, 226; Edmonson, Mary, and, 226; *National Era* office, mob violence against in wake of, 216–17; Sayres, Edward, and, 214, 216; Smith, Gerrit, funding of, 214; steamboat *Salem* and, 215; Underground Railroad and, 214, 216; Valdenar, Frances, and, 226. *See also* Edmonson, Emily; Edmonson, Mary; Edmonson sisters

Pennsylvania Anti-Slavery Society: Mott, Lucretia, and, 171; Pennsylvania Hall office, 155

Pennsylvania Freeman: Pennsylvania Hall and, 154; Whittier, John Greenleaf, and, 154

Pennsylvania Hall (Philadelphia), 154; abolitionists and, 155; auditorium in, 155; *Augusta Chronicle and Sentinel* letter denouncing, 158; dedication ceremony, 154, 158; destruction of by mob, 161, 163, 164; on fire, *162p*; Pennsylvania Anti-Slavery Society office in, 155; *Pennsylvania Freeman* office in, 154; Pennsylvania Hall Association and, 158; protesters outside of, 158. *See also* Convention of Anti-Slavery Women

Peoria Press, denunciation of Congressman Abraham Lincoln as traitor, 200

Perdu, John: Helen/Hannah, as owner of, 283

Perkins, Catherine: Beecher, Catharine, on behavior of at Harriet Beecher Stowe's Maine home, 308

Perkins, Mary Beecher, 10, 11, 43, *136p*, 139; Beecher, Isabella, living with, 136; letter received from Angelina Grimké, 10–11; letter received from sister Catharine about running Harriet's household, 306; Stowe, Harriet Beecher, visit to on way to Maine, 252. *See also* Beecher, Mary

Perkins, Thomas C., 10; financial failures, 137

Perryville, Maryland, 454

Philadelphia, Pennsylvania: Bailey, Gamaliel, and, 38; Jefferson Medical College, 41. *See also* Pennsylvania Anti-Slavery Society; Pennsylvania Hall (Philadelphia); Philadelphia Anti-Slavery Society; Philadelphia Female Anti-Slavery Society

Philadelphia, Wilmington, and Baltimore Railroad: Felton, Samuel, and, 437

Philadelphia Anti-Slavery Society: Mott, Lucretia, and, 171

Philadelphia Female Anti-Slavery Society, 124; seal, *287p*

645

Pottawatomie killings, 347–49, 350, 351; Brown, John, as perpetrator of, 347–49; Doyle, James, as victim, 347; Doyle, Mahala, as witness to, 347–48; Doyle, William, as victim, 348; Harris, James, as witness to, 348–49; Kansas guerilla warfare after, 349; news of reaching back East, 350; sacking of Lawrence, KS, as reprisal for, 349; Sherman, William, as victim, 348, 349; Wilkinson, Allen, as victim, 348; Wilkinson, Louisa, as witness, 348

Pottawatomie Rifles, 346

Powell, Harriet, 166; Cady, Elizabeth, and, 165–66; Canada, transport to, 166; Davenport, John, and, 166; Smith, Gerrit, and, 165–66

Powers, J. F.: Robinson, Marius, and, 120

Presbyterian Church: preacher shortage, 13; Roman Catholics, view on, 13

Presbyterian General Assembly: Beecher, Edward, and, 142; Lovejoy, Elijah P., and, 142

Primary Geography for Children: Beecher, Harriet, and, 13, 44–45

Pugh, Achilles: Birney, James, and, 86; Chase, Salmon, legal representation of by 113; Davies, Samuel W., appeal to for help, 103; mob destruction of printing business office and equipment, 102, 108, 109; as printer of *Philanthropist, The,* 86, 104; printing business office, 102

Purvis, Robert: Stowe, Harriet Beecher, misbelief of as colonizationist, 314

Putnam, Ohio, 115, 139, 140

Putnam County Female Anti-Slavery Society: petition forms for abolition of slavery in Washington, D.C., distribution of, 139–40

Quakers, 11, 124; American Anti-Slavery Society and, 54; anti-slavery work, 124; gradual emancipation of slaves

and, 33; Grimké, Angelina, break from, 156; as receptive to abolitionists, 119, 120; segregated seating in meetinghouses, 124; Virginia, removal of slaves from and, 33. *See also* Grimké, Angelina; Grimké, Sarah; Mott, Lucretia Coffin; Rakestraw, Emily; Society of Friends; Wattles, Sarah Grimké; Weld, Angelina Grimké; Whittier, John Greenleaf

race riots, Northern city, 94; Child, Lydia Marie, writing on, 94

racial violence, propaganda from Democrats and, 512–13

Radical Political Abolitionist Party convention: Brown, John, and, 345; Douglass, Frederick, and, 345; Smith, Gerrit, and, 345

railroads: Baltimore & Ohio, 399, 400, 404; Drake, Daniel, and, 97; Philadelphia, Wilmington, and Baltimore, 437. *See also* Felton Samuel; transcontinental railroad

Rakestraw, Emily, 62; marriage to Marius Robinson, 113. *See also* Robinson, Emily

Rankin, John: abolitionist family of, 73; as American Anti-Slavery Society agent, 113; anti-slavery activities, taking Lane Rebels' side concerning, 70–71; Beecher, Harriet, and, 73; Beecher, Lyman, and, 73; house, 74; Lane Seminary slavery debates and, 55; *Letters on American Slavery* and, 25, 52, 55, 56; Stowe, Calvin, and, 73, Underground Railroad and, 74, 75; Weld, Theodore, preaching at church of, 76. *See also* Rankin, Jean; Rankin, Lowry

Rankin, Jean, 73; house, 74; Underground Railroad and, 74. *See also* Rankin, John; Rankin, Lowry

Rankin, Lowry: apprenticeship, 77, 80; slaves in ship engine room, description of, 77–79; Weld, Theodore, and, 77, 80. *See also* Rankin, Jean; Rankin, John

Raymond, Henry: on Bailey, Gamaliel, 391

Realf, Richard: Brown, John, and, 353

Rebel yell, 459

Recorder (Fredericksburg): on Seward, William H., "Higher Power" speech, 248

Reeder, Andrew Horatio: arrest warrant issued for, 338; conversion to Free Soiler, 334; Kansas-Nebraska Bill supporter, 334; as Kansas Territorial Governor, 334; Pierce, Franklin, and, 334

Republic of Texas: Burnet, David G., and, 109

Republican National Committee: Judd, Norman, and, 415

Republican National Convention of 1860: Cameron, Simon, and, 477; Cartter, David K., and, 428; Chicago as location of, 416, 424; choosing location for, 415; first ballot vote breakdown, 427; Lincoln, Abraham, announcement of as Republican candidate for President, 428; Lincoln, Abraham, and Mary Todd Lincoln during, 424; possible locations for, 415–16; second ballot vote breakdown, 427; states switching votes to Lincoln at, 428; third ballot, 428; Wigwam, floor activity during, 427, 428; Wigwam, inside, 424, *425p*

Republican Party, new: abolitionist attacks on, 356–57; Codding, Ichabod, and, 330; 1856 campaign, distribution of "The Crime Against Kansas" during, 357; 1856 campaign slogans, 357; 1860 election, campaign to win, 431; 1860 election, final vote tally in, 433; 1860 presidential campaign, Southern press attacks on during, 431–32; Lovejoy, Owen, and, 330; Northerners as members, 376; opposition to extension of slavery, 355. *See also names of members of the new Republican Party*

Richardson, Albert D.: on Lincoln, Abraham, speech in Troy, KS, 413

Richmond, Virginia, 194; Confederate and Union troops on march to, 493; as second Confederate capital, 451, 458, 476, 492, 507; as Union target, 492. *See also* Seven Days' Battles

Richmond Enquirer: on Brooks, Preston, cane beating of Charles Sumner, 354; 1826 slave mutiny account in, 18; on Lincoln, Abraham, inaugural address, 443

Riley, John: Lawrence, Matilda, and, 116; Lawrence, Matilda, trial and, 118

Ripley, Ohio: Rankin, John, and, 25, 52, 55, 73; John Rankin, abolitionist visits to, 73, 76; Underground Railroad in, 74–75

Ripley College: Rankin, Lowry, and, 80

Rivers, Prince: at Emancipation Proclamation Camp Saxton reading, 548

Robinson, Charles: Brown, John, and, 350; imprisonment of, 338; Lawrence, KS, home burnt down in sack of, 399

Robinson, Emily, 119, 120; abolitionist activities, withdrawal from, 286; *Anti-Slavery Bugle* and, 287; as Ohio Anti-Slavery Society annual meeting delegate, 120; Putnam County, OH, move to, 120; Salem, OH, move to, 287; woman's rights movement and, 286. *See also* Rakestraw, Emily

Robinson, Marius, 60; as abolition lecturer, 119, 120; abolitionist activities, withdrawal from, 286; as American Anti-Slavery Society agent, 113, 121; *Anti-Slavery Bugle* and, 287; Birney, James J., and, 286; Cincinnati Anti-Slavery Society and, 71; Cincinnati black community

istration Assistant to Secretary of State, 436

Seward, Jenny, 467

Seward, William Henry, *221p,* 263, 421, 436, 438, 467, 523–24; Adams, Henry, and, 363; Black suffrage and, 426; Buchanan, James, at presidential inauguration of, 360; capital states, reference to slave states as 422; Charles II in exile, comparing self to, 412; on conspiracy between President Buchanan and Supreme Court justices in Dred Scott decision, 361–62, 376; Douglas, Stephen A., and, 418; Douglas, Stephen A., interrupting during Kansas-Nebraska Senate debate, 310; 1856 possible presidential candidate, 355; 1860 presidential election, Gamaliel Bailey support for in, 390; 1860 Republican National Convention and, 428–29; 1860 Republican National Convention, Thurlow Weed plan for, 427; as 1860 Republican presidential candidate, 415, 425; 1860 Republican presidential nominee, hopes of becoming, 386; Emancipation Proclamation and, 541, 545; Emancipation Proclamation, text changes to, 530; as Emancipation Proclamation signing witness, 545–46; Emmanuel, Victor (King of Italy), and, 389; entertaining both Northerners and Southerners in his home, 362–63; estimate on duration of Civil War, 451; European tour of 1859, 389, 390; European tour of 1859, return from, 421; extension of Black suffrage in New York and, 422; falling markets, concern about, 434; Forbes, Hugh, sharing John Brown's Virginia plan with, 369; Fort Sumter, reaction to Abraham Lincoln's decision to resupply, 449; Fort Sumter, sending word on evacuation decision, 448; Fugitive Slave Act of 1850 and, 422; Greeley, Horace, and, 418; Harp-

er's Ferry raid by John Brown, blamed for, 409, 426; "Higher Law" speech calling for no slavery in territories, 247–48; Kansas, Republican support for in, 414; Kansas-Nebraska Bill, Senate speech after passage of, 322; labor states, reference to free states as, 422; Lecompton Constitution, letter received from wife Frances on Stephen A. Douglas and, 364; Leopold I (King of Belgium) and, 389; letter of resignation from Lincoln cabinet, 541; letter received from Abraham Lincoln on troop recruitment, 504; Lincoln, Abraham, and, 221–22, 524; Lincoln, Abraham, as campaigner for, 431; Lincoln, Abraham, defense of, 541; Lincoln, Abraham, on inauguration security measures, 440–41; Lincoln, Abraham, thoughts on as 1860 Republican presidential candidate, 429; Lincoln, Mary Todd, attempted meeting with, 467–68; Lincoln, Mary Todd, and her dislike of, 465; Lincoln, Mary Todd, meeting at Washington, D.C., train station ahead of Lincoln inauguration, 439; Lincoln, Willie, at funeral of, 488; as Lincoln Administration Secretary of State, 433; magnetic personality, 363; McClellan, George B., attempted home visit to, 473; New Mexico, plan to admit as slave state, 433; newspaper attacks on, 362; *North Star,* monetary support for, 264; opposition to 1860 candidacy of, 418; pet bulldog, enemy poisoning of, 337; Pius IX (Pope) and, 389; *Recorder* comments on, 248; Scott, Winfield, Lincoln assassination plot alert and, 437; Seward, Fanny, idolization of, 389; Seward, Francis, control over, 387; Slave Power reaction to, 248; slavery, view on, 362; speech about slavery at 1848 Boston Whig rally, 221; "State of the Country" Senate speech, 422; Sumner, Charles, and, 389; Taylor, Zachary, as supporter of

Smalls, Elizabeth: Forten, Charlotte, and, 546

Smalls, Robert: daughter Elizabeth, 546; heroic actions on steamer *Planter* to help Union Army, 499–500; provision of artillery, ammunition, and intelligence documents to Union Army, 500; smuggling of slaves to freedom, 500

Smith, Ann "Nancy" Fitzhugh: Birney, Florence, and, 165; Birney, George, and, 165; Birney, James G., and, 164; Cady, Elizabeth, visit and, 168; as Female Anti-Slavery Convention vice president, 130; house gifted to daughter Libby, 295; letter received from Angelina Grimké Weld about Elizabeth and Henry Stanton visit, 169–70; Stanton, Henry B., visit and, 168

Smith, Anna, 251; Stowe, Harriet Beecher, and, 115, 192

Smith, Caleb: McClellan, George B., written protest to oust, 523

Smith, Gerrit, 423; as anti-Garrison abolitionist, 164; Birney, Florence, and, 165; Birney, George, and, 165; Birney, James G., and, 164; Bloomers, criticism of Elizabeth Cady Stanton for abandoning, 300; Bloomers, on daughter Libby wearing, 300; Brown, John, and, 351; Brown, John, belittling of, 371; Brown, John, sharing Virginia plan with, 367; Cady, Elizabeth, visit and, 168; Chaplin, William L., donation toward prison release, 261; Forbes, Hugh, and, 352; Fugitive Slave Law Convention of August 1850, and, 258; gifting house to daughter Libby, 295; as Grimké-Weld wedding guest, 159; home as abolitionist haven, 164; letter of introduction to Franklin Sanborn for Harriet Tubman, 369, 396; letter received from Angelina Grimké Weld about Elizabeth and Henry Stanton visit,

169–70; letter to Franklin Sanborn about stopping John Brown's Virginia plan, 370; Liberty Party convention, demand for female suffrage at, 218; New York State Lunatic Asylum, committed to by family after John Brown's raid, 406; North Elba colony and, 344, 352; Ohio Woman's Rights Convention of 1851, letter read at, 291; *Pearl* slave escape, funding, 214; Radical Political Abolitionist Party convention and, 345; Secret Six, as one of John Brown's, 366, 367, 368; Stanton, Henry B., visit and, 168; Tubman, Harriet, and, 368, 388; wealth of, 165; as women's rights supporter, 164

Smith, James: Collins, Eliza Smith, and, 266; Craft, Ellen, and, 266; rapist of his slave Maria, 266

Smith, John T.: Long, Henry, and, 279

Smith, Libby, 165. *See also* Miller, Libby Smith

Smith, W. Prescott, 399, 400

Society of Friends, 124; condemnation of slavery, 124; Grimké, Angelina, excommunication from after marriage to Theodore Weld, 156; Grimké, Sarah, and, 124. *See also* Quakers

Soldiers' Home, 524; Camp Barker contraband camp near, 513–14; Lincoln, Abraham, commute from to White House, 506; Lincoln family move to, 505

South Carolina: Charleston, 12, 93–94, 97, 433; secession, 433; secession convention and, 433

South Carolina Sea Islands: Hunter, David, effect of decree on contraband slaves living on, 498; Hunter, David, slaves declared "forever free" by, 498; Pierce, Edward L., and, 498

Southampton County, Virginia, 30

Southwestern Railroad Convention, 97

Speed, Joshua: Emancipation Proclamation and, 548–49; Frémont, John C., emancipation proclamation, Abraham Lincoln and, 462; Lincoln, Abraham, and, 325, 549; Lincoln, Abraham, discussion about Mary Todd with, 186, 187, 549

spies, Confederate: Greenhow, Rose O'Neal, 459–60; Lincoln, Mary Todd, rumors about John Watt relationship and, 474–75; in Washington, D.C., 434, 459–60; Watt, John, suspicion about, 474–75

Sprigg, Ann G. Thornton, 208. *See also* Sprigg Boardinghouse

Sprigg Boardinghouse, 208; Giddings, Joshua R., stay at, 208; Lincoln, Mary Todd, and, 208, 212; Lincoln family stay at, 208

Springfield, Illinois, 149, 374

Springfield, Massachusetts: Brown, John, wool merchant in, 350

Stanton, Edwin, 521, 524, 542; Battle of Fredericksburg, blamed for defeat at, 540; Emancipation Proclamation, reaction to, 530; funeral for infant son of, 509; Harding, George, and, 479; McClellan, George B., and, 526; McClelland, George B., call for Abraham Lincoln to remove, 508; McClellan, George B., written protest to oust, 523; McCormick, Cyrus, patent rights case, Abraham Lincoln as co-counsel with, 479; nurses, call for volunteer, 522; recruiting offices, premature shutdown of, 504; as replacement for Simon Cameron as Secretary of War, 477, 478–80; Seward, William H., "State of the Country" speech and, 422

Stanton, Elizabeth Cady: Bloomers, abandonment of for long skirts, 300; Bloomers, criticism from Gerrit Smith for abandoning, 300; Bloomers, father Daniel Cady forbidding wearing of in his home, 200; Bloomers, husband Henry's view of her wearing, 300; Bloomers, on negatives of wearing, 300; Bloomers, on positives of wearing, 296; Grimké-Weld house, visit to and thoughts on, 169; letter to Angelina Grimké Weld about returning to public sphere, 178; Mott, Lucretia, and, 175; New York Married Women's Property Act of 1848 and, 388; Ohio Woman's Rights Convention of 1851, letter read at, 291; Seneca Falls Declaration of Sentiments, assistance with from husband Henry, 218; Seneca Falls Woman's Rights Convention of 1848 and, 218; on ship *Montreal*, 168; *Uncle Tom's Cabin*, letter to Libby Smith Miller about, 313–14; World's Anti-Slavery Convention and, 174, 175. *See also* Cady, Elizabeth

Stanton, Ellen: Keckley, Elizabeth, and, 481

Stanton, Henry Brewster: American and Foreign Anti-Slavery Society and, 168, 171; American Anti-Slavery Society, salary owed from, 169; as American Anti-Slavery Society agent, 113; as anti-Garrison abolitionist, 164; as anti-women's rights, 164; Bloomers, on political implications of wife Elizabeth wearing, 300; Cady, Elizabeth, engagement and marriage to 168–69; Grimké-Weld home, visit to, 169; as Grimké-Weld wedding guest, 159; Lane Seminary slavery debates and, 55, 56; Lane Theological Seminary and, 47; Lovejoy, Elijah P., anger at William Lloyd Garrison for condemning, 148; Seneca Falls Declaration of Sentiments, assistance to wife Elizabeth with, 218; on ship *Montreal*, 168; Smith home, visit to,

168; wedding, 169; World's Anti-Slavery Convention and, 173, 174

Stearns, George L.: Brown, John, fundraising for, 352; Brown, John, providing weapons to, 352, 370; Brown, John, raid on Harper's Ferry, action in aftermath of, 406; Brown, John, return to United States after hanging of, 423; Brown, John, sharing Virginia plan with, 367; Secret Six, as one of John Brown's 366, 367, 406; Senate investigation of John Brown's raid on Harper's Ferry, as witness in, 423

Stearns, Mary Prescott, 406; Brown, John, and, 367

Stephens, Alexander: Taylor, Zachary, as supporter of for President, 219

Stone, Charles P.: Battle of Ball's Bluff and, 469

Stone, Edward: mansion of, 16; slave coffles of, 16–18, 55; as slave trader, 15–16; slaves wanted ad, 16

Stone, Robert: Lincoln, Mary Todd, doctor to after son Willie's death, 487; Lincoln, William "Willie," doctor to, 482, 486

Stowe, Calvin, 189, 190; abolitionism, letter to Harriet Beecher Stowe about, 141; Andover Theological Seminary professorship, 312; Beecher, Harriet, and, 73; Beecher, Harriet Porter, and, 73; Bowdoin College and, 251, 255, 256; cholera epidemic, letters to wife Harriet about, 238; Cincinnati, living in during summer 1837, 139; Cincinnati, living in while family was in Maine, 275; depression and weight gain, 203; Eliza, death of first wife, 73; "Franklin Letter," Harriet Beecher Stowe letter about, 107; Fugitive Slave Law of 1850, letter received from Harriet Beecher Stowe about wanting father Lyman to preach about, 279; inability or unwillingness to help wife

Harriet run the household, 306; as Lane Biblical literature professor, 44, 46, 49, 251, 255, 256; Lane Seminary, letter to wife Harriet about dissatisfaction with, 138; Lane Seminary, traveling for, 88; Lane Seminary Board, support of regarding rules against student anti-slavery activities, 69; letter to wife Harriet about his health and worries for family if he should die, 254; long trips away from home, 192; as multilingual, 90; Panic of 1837 and, 138; paranormal experiences of, 89–90; Rankin, John, visit to, 73, 76; salary, diminishing, 197; Semi-Colon Club and, 46, 73; Stowe, Charles Edward, birth of son and, 254; Stowe, Harriet Beecher, criticism of, 139; Stowe twins' birth and, 114; Stowe twins' names, instructions to wife Harriet regarding, 114–15; Theological Seminary of Andover, Massachusetts, and, 256; water-cure sanitarium stay, 203, 238; water-cure sanitarium stay, Lane Seminary paying during, 203–4

Stowe, Charles Edward, 254

Stowe, Eliza (daughter of H.B.S.), 115, 239; broken arm, 277–78; Brunswick, Maine, move and journey to from Cincinnati, 252; cholera illness in 1849, 239

Stowe, Eliza Tyler, 88, 90; death of, 73; Semi-Colon Club and, 46

Stowe, Frederick, 239; Civil War army service, 533; in Maine upon birth of brother Charles Edward, 254; teen alcoholism 533; visiting with mother Harriet in Washington, D.C., 536–37

Stowe, George: in Maine upon birth of brother Charles Edward, 254

Stowe, Georgiana, 197, 203

Stowe, Harriet Beecher. See Stowe, Harriet Beecher (1832–1850,

Charles, use of writing installment method of, 302; donation to Myrtilla Miner to buy land for school, 311; Edmonson sisters, financial support of while Oberlin College students, 310; "Freeman's Dream: A Parable, The," 254–55; Fugitive Slave Act of 1850, letter to brother Henry about preaching against, 280; Fugitive Slave Law of 1850, letter to husband Calvin about wanting Lyman to preach about, 279; Fugitive Slave Law of 1850 and, 275, 280; letter received from Calvin about his health and worries for the family if he should die, 254; letter to Sarah Beecher about having little time to write letters, 254; *National Era* pieces, 253, 277; *New-York Evangelist* pieces, 253, 277; quote empathizing with slave mothers who have their children taken from them, 257; setting up house, 253; sheltering fugitive slave John Andrew Jackson, 276; *Uncle Tom's Cabin,* research on slavery for, 302, 308; Upham, Phebe Lord, and, 255, 275, 277; Upham, Thomas C., and, 275; Upham, Thomas, letter about colonization opinion to sister Catharine, 275; winter storm of 1850 and, 278; writings, 253, 254–55, 277. See also *Uncle Tom's Cabin*

Stowe, Harriet Beecher (1852–1863, Andover, MA): Beecher, Edward, and fears about fame of, 314; Beecher, Henry Ward, jealousy toward, 314; Emancipation Proclamation, awaiting word of signing, 548; Emancipation Proclamation, Boston appearance upon signing of, 548; Emancipation Proclamation, reaction to, 533; England, non-recognition of Confederacy and, 550; fame of, 312; fan letters received, 312; Fields, James, and, 538; Hooker, Isabella Beecher, bitterness toward, 314; house, renovation of, 312;

letter to women of England urging support for the North in the Civil War, 538–39; Lincoln, Abraham, criticism of in *Independent,* 518; Lincoln, Abraham, second annual message and, 537; Lincoln, Mary Todd, meeting with, 536; Longfellow, Henry Wadsworth, and, 313; move to Andover, MA, 312; personal responsibility for slaves, feeling of, 519; Pomeroy, Samuel, and, 538; Sumner, Charles, anti-Kansas-Nebraska Bill signature campaign, and, 321; visiting with son Frederick in Washington, D.C., 536; Washington, D.C., trip, 536–38. See also *Key to Uncle Tom's Cabin: Presenting the Original Facts and Documents Upon Which the Story is Founded; Uncle Tom's Cabin*

Stowe, Harriet "Hattie" (daughter of H.B.S.), 115, 239; Brunswick, Maine, decorating Christmas tree in 1850, 278; Brunswick, Maine, move and journey to from Cincinnati, 252; trip to Washington, D.C., with mother Harriet in, 536

Stowe, Henry: Brunswick, Maine, move and journey to from Cincinnati, 252; cholera illness in 1849, 239

Stowe, Hepzibah, 139; criticism of daughter-in-law Harriet, 139

Stowe, Samuel Charles "Charley," 203; cholera, death from, 239; cholera illness, 239; Lane Cemetery as final resting place, 252

Strong, George Templeton: on Lincoln, Abraham, inaugural address, 443

Stroud, George: Stowe, Harriet Beecher, and legal pamphlet by, 303

Stuart, J.E.B.: Brown, John, raid on Federal Arsenal at Harper's Ferry, and, 400, 401, 402

Sumner, Charles, 304; anti-Kansas-Nebraska Bill signature campaign, Stowe,

250; Stuart, J.E.B., of, 400. *See also* Union Army

U.S. Capitol: Dickens, Charles, and, 193, 194; Sprigg's boardinghouse, proximity to, 208; under construction, 209

U.S. Congress, 30th, 222; recess of, 219

U.S. Congress, 31st: discord and violence in, 249

U.S. Congress, 36th: investigation into John Brown's raid on Harper's Ferry, 422–23

U.S. Congress, 37th: confiscation act, 509; income tax, levying of federal, 510; Internal Revenue Service, establishment of, 510; Legal Tender Act, 510; Militia Act, 509; productivity of, 510

U.S. Constitution: Article Four, 456; Atlantic slave trade ban and, 14; Dred Scott decision and, 360–61; First Amendment, 129; Fugitive Slave Clause, 118, 386; on slave population and congressional representation, 15; on slavery, protection of in slave states, 201, 326, 508; on slaves as property, 117–18

U.S. House of Representatives: Lincoln, Abraham, certification of votes for, 435, 436

U.S. Marines: Band, 208, 445, 481, 484, 495; Brown, John, raid on Federal Arsenal at Harper's Ferry, and, 401–3, *402p*

U.S. Navy. *See* Union Navy

U.S. Patent Office building, 209, 210; Rhode Island troops camped inside, 454

U.S. Post Office: anti-slavery literature backlash and, 93–94

U.S. Senate: gag rule against slavery-related petitions, 130; Missouri Compromise of 1820 and balance of power in, 15; Wilmot Proviso and, 200–1. *See also names of U.S. Senators*

U.S. Supreme Court, 377; Taney, Roger B., and, 270, 509, 530. *See also* Dred Scott decision

U.S. Treasury building, 209

Uncle Sam (steamboat): Rankin, Lowry, on slaves held in engine room of, 77–79

Uncle Tom's Cabin, 283–85, 518; as abolitionist manifesto, 518; Black dialect in, 305; book publisher and contract for, 308; Chase, Salmon, comments on, 305; coming soon publication notice for in *National Era,* 285; converting readers into abolitionists, 315; Douglass, Frederick, praise for, 313; first appearance in book form, 308; first installment in *National Era,* 303; Fugitive Slave Act of 1850 as catalyst for, 538; Lincoln, Abraham, election of and, 518; main characters, 304–5; Northern antislavery impulse and, 320; number of copies sold, 309; popularity of, 305, 307, 309; product spinoffs called "Tom-itudes" and, 313; Seward, Fanny, and, 313; Stowe, Harriet Beecher, criticisms of from Southern newspapers for, 314–15; Stowe, Harriet Beecher, distractions while writing, 306; Stowe, Harriet Beecher, first royalty check for, 310; Stowe, Harriet Beecher, letter to Gamaliel Bailey about upcoming, 284; Stowe, Harriet Beecher, slavery research and, 302; Stowe, Harriet Beecher, vision of Black man being beaten and, 282, 283; success of Harriet Beecher Stowe from publication of, 313; Sumner, Charles, and, 518; Sumner, Charles, on success of, 313; title page, *309p;* Tubman, Harriet, criticism of, 314; Tubman, Harriet, opposition to theatrical adaptations of, 314

marriage to, 113; Putnam County, move to, 120

Weed, Phebe Mathews: move to Putnam, 120. *See also* Mathews, Phebe

Weed, Thurlow: Greeley, Horace, and, 418; letter received from Abraham Lincoln about legality of states seceding, 434; Seward, William H., and, 355, 389, 412; Seward, William H., 1860 convention plan for, 427

Weld, Angelina Grimké: *American Slavery As It Is* research and publication, 179–80; anti-slavery cause work at home, 179; Birney, James G., disagreement with on "woman question," 170; Dawson, Betsy, and, 177; infant care, reading about, 177; letter to Gerrit and Nancy Smith about visit from Elizabeth and Henry Stanton, 169; life as wife and mother, 176, 177; petition rights, urging women to use, 163; Quaker asceticism and, 177; Stanton, Elizabeth Cady, letter to about returning to public sphere, 178; Stanton, Henry B., visit and, 169; Weld, Charles, caring for, 177; Weld, Theodore, marriage to, 176; *Young Housekeeper* book and, 176–77. *See also* Grimké, Angelina

Weld, Charles Stuart, 177

Weld, Theodore, 47, 176; as American Anti-Slavery Society agent, 70, 76; American Anti-Slavery Society agents, recruitment and training of, 113, 119; American Anti-Slavery Society thoughts on marriage of, 155; *American Slavery As It Is* research and publication, 179–80; anger at criticism of wife Angelina and sister-in-law Sarah, 178; *Appeal to Christian Women of the South and,* 126; Beecher, Harriet, thoughts on, 49; Beecher, Lyman, letter to imploring return to Lane, 69; Birney, James, and, 82; Birney, James, disseminating "Letter on Colo-

nization" of, 68; Bishop, Emeline, letter to regarding student behavior, 63; Bradley, James, and, 57; Grimké, Angelina, and, 128; Grimké, Angelina, during engagement to, 154–56; Grimké sisters, dissatisfaction with, 133; health of, 155; infant care, reading about, 177; Lane Seminary slavery debates and, 55, 56; Lane Theological Seminary and, 48, 49; Lowe, Susan, letter to about treatment from Black families, 63; Mathews, Phebe, letter to about abolitionists' prejudice, 63; Ohio State Anti-Slavery Society and, 71; Pennsylvania Hall, letter from read aloud at dedication ceremony for, 158; preaching at church of John Rankin, 76; Rankin, Lowry, and, 77, 80; Stanton, Henry B., visit and, 169; Tappan, Arthur, and, 61; Tappan, Lewis, admiration for marrying a feminist, 155; Tappan brothers and, 48. *See also* Grimké-Weld wedding

Welles, Gideon: McClellan, George, and, 523, 542

Welles, Mary Jane Hale: Keckley, Elizabeth, and, 481

West Sutton, Massachusetts: Bullard, Eunice, and, 134

West Virginia: formed as Union state, 461

Western Anti-Slavery Society: Robinson, Marius, and, 287

Western Medical Gazette: Bailey, Gamaliel, as writer for, 41

Western Monthly Magazine: Hall, James, and, 46, 71; Stowe, Harriet Beecher, stories in, 46, 88

Western Reserve College, Lane Rebels enrollment in, 70

Whig: attacks on James Birney, 108

Whig Party: disarray of in December 1848, 222; 1848 presidential candi-

www.ingramcontent.com/pod-product-compliance
Lightning Source LLC
Jackson TN
JSHW082110120925
90977JS00003B/10